AN INTRODUCTION TO THE LEGAL PROCESS

A Business

Law Text

with Integrated

Cases and

Problems

Richard S. Dalebout
Brigham Young University

SIMON & SCHUSTER
CUSTOM PUBLISHING

SIMON & SCHUSTER CUSTOM PUBLISHING
160 Gould Street/Needham Heights, MA 02494
Simon & Schuster Education Group

Contents

To Evie

Chapter Outline

CHAPTER OBJECTIVE is to identify and define commonly used legal terms and concepts

The objective of this chapter is to identify and define commonly used legal terms and concepts. This chapter is organized as follows:

- *Law Defined.* For practical purposes *law* may be defined as a rule or requirement made and enforced by government.

- *Criminal Law and Civil Law.* In the legal system of the United States, law may be classified as *criminal* law or *civil* law. Civil law may be further subdivided into *contract* law or *tort* law. Criminal law provides social control through a system of *punishment*. Civil laws provide a system of *compensation* for personal and economic injuries.

- *English Origins of Law.* The system of law (criminal and civil) used in the United States originated in *England.*

- *The U.S. System of Law.* In the United States, law is found in different forms: (1) *constitution*, (2) *statute*, (3) *regulation* and (4) *case law*, sometimes called *common law.*

- *Common Law.* The system of law used in the United States is generally referred to as a *common law* system. A common law legal system is one in which some of the law is created by judges. The person who initiates a lawsuit is called the *plaintiff* and the person who responds in that lawsuit is called the *defendant. Stare decisis* is a legal doctrine which requires that decisions of judges be consistent with previous decisions. Once an earlier decision *(precedent)* has been made, stare decisis requires that a subsequent decision based on similar facts be consistent with the earlier decision.

- *Conflicts in Laws.* There are more than 39,029 federal, state and local governments in the United States, and periodically there are conflicts in the laws they make. In the event of conflict between laws, federal law supersedes state and local law, and, state law supersedes local law.

- *Law Books.* Legislative law is usually found in books called a *code*. Case law is collected and published in books called *reporters.*

Law Defined

LAW is a rule or requirement made and enforced by government

For practical purposes, *law* may be defined as a rule or requirement made and enforced by government.[1] Suppose, for example, that the parents and teachers at the Lincoln Elementary School in Elm City approve a rule that it shall be unlawful to drive a motor vehicle at a speed more than 15 mph on the street in front of the Lincoln Elementary School. Is this rule a law? The answer is no, because the parents and teachers are not acting as members of government. But, if the City Council of Elm City (which is authorized by state law to adopt rules controlling the operation of motor vehicles) approves the 15 mph rule it will be law and the courts will enforce it.

Problem Solving. Please turn to Chapter Problems at the end of this chapter and solve Problem 1.1.

Criminal Law and Civil Law

Laws may be divided into two categories: *criminal* law and *civil* law. Criminal laws are designed to prevent social disruption through *punishment* such as fines or imprisonment. On the other hand, civil laws provide a system of *compensation* for personal and economic injuries. Civil laws may be further subdivided into contract law and tort law. Following are illustrations of criminal law, contract law and tort law:

CRIMINAL LAW prevents social disruption by punishment

- Criminal Law. Criminal laws are meant to deter social disruption (speeding, murder, theft) through a system of punishment. The· *duty* of each person (the description of what is prohibited) is imposed by government. For example, Jed steals Milly's car. A rule of law adopted by the state legislature (a statute) prohibits theft. This duty is enforced by punishment (jail or fine). Violation of this duty is the commission of a *crime*. Laws such as this are classified as *criminal* law.

CIVIL LAW is a system of compensation for personal and economic injuries

- Contract Law. Contract law is one form of civil law. Contracts describe voluntary economic relationships and they are enforced for the purpose of giving compensation to persons injured through violation of contracts. The legal *duty* (the description of what is required or prohibited) is voluntarily assumed, but enforced by government. For example, Milly is not required to sell her car to Jed, but if she agrees to do it, their arrangement may become a *contract*. Courts enforce the contract promises (duties) voluntarily entered into through a system of compensation. This classification of civil law is *contract* law.

- Tort Law. Tort law is another form of civil law. Tort law refers to harmful conduct which is not controlled by a contract. Tort violations are likewise enforced for the purpose of giving compensation for personal and economic injuries. The legal *duty* (the description of what is prohibited) is imposed by government. For example, Milly digs a hole in her front yard and neglectfully leaves it uncovered. In the dark Jed falls into the hole and is injured. Milly

---

[1] "Law" has been broadly defined as "the body of standards, principles and rules . . . *which the courts of that state apply* in the decision of controversies brought before them." RESTATEMENT (SECOND) CONFLICT OF LAWS § 4(1) (emphasis added). In more conventional terms, however, "law" refers to the *constitution* and *statutes* of a state. *See*, State v. Lacklen, 284 P.2d 998, 1004 (1955). "Law" also includes *case* law. *See*, Matter of Estate of Perlberg, 694 S.W.2d 304, 307 (1984).

has not committed a crime, and has not breached a contract; instead, she has violated the duty owed by each member of society to act reasonably and to avoid conduct which can be foreseen to cause harm. Milly must compensate (pay "damages" to) Jed for his injuries. This classification is *tort* law.

Law Classified			
Classification	**Examples**	**Duty**	**Enforcement**
Criminal Law (Crimes)	Speeding Murder Theft	Statute, Regulation or Ordinance	Fine or Imprisonment
Civil Law (Contracts)	Contracts for sale of cars, land, or employment	Perform promises described in contract	Compensation to injured party
Civil Law (Torts)	Negligence driving an automobile	Act reasonably and avoid "foreseeable" harm	Compensation to injured party

__Problem Solving__. Please turn to Chapter Problems at the end of this chapter and solve Problem 1.2.

English Origins of Law

The system of law (both criminal and civil) used in the United States comes from England. Most of the early settlements in North America were English colonies which were regulated by English law. When a royal grant established the government of a colony, it was not uncommon for the grant to provide that the colony would be regulated by English law and that the settlers would be entitled to the "privileges, franchises and immunities" of Englishmen. When the settlers received the rights of Englishmen they became part of a system where they had rights in property and personal liberty which were protected by law, and (in theory) even the king was bound to respect those rights. The English law was applicable to *all* the King's subjects, and so, in the language of the day, it was said to be a system of law which was "common" to all. Not surprisingly, this system of law became known as the "*common* law."

Although there was a revolution which divided Great Britain from its American colonies, the Americans retained the basic common law legal traditions of their English forefathers. Those traditions have been freely amended over more than two centuries, yet the flavor remains. This continuing acceptance of English common law legal traditions is sometimes openly expressed. For example, a Utah statute provides the following:

> **68-3-1. Common law adopted.**
> The *common law of England* so far as it is not repugnant to, or in conflict with, the constitution or laws of the United States, or the constitution or laws of this state, and so far only as it is consistent with and adapted to the natural and physical conditions of this state and the necessities of the

people hereof, is hereby adopted, and shall be the rule of decision in all courts of this state.[2]

American judges occasionally look back at English legal experience to solve a problem. For example, in a 1996 murder case known as *Loving v. U.S.*, the United States Supreme Court examined a rule adopted in the year 1190 by the English King Richard I. In *Loving*, a military court used procedural rules adopted by President Bill Clinton (acting as commander-in-chief of the armed forces) to sentence Loving, an Army private, to death for premeditated murder. Loving claimed that the procedures under which he was sentenced to die were unconstitutional because, as he claimed, the United States Constitution gave only Congress (and not the President) the power to adopt such procedures. The United States Supreme Court disagreed:

Loving v. U.S.
116 S.Ct. 1737 (1996)

Justice KENNEDY delivered the opinion of the Court.

The case before us concerns the authority of the President, in our system of separated powers, to prescribe aggravating factors that permit a court-martial to impose the death penalty upon a member of the armed forces convicted of murder.

I

On December 12, 1988, petitioner Dwight Loving, an Army private stationed at Fort Hood, Texas, murdered two taxicab drivers from the nearby town of Killeen. He attempted to murder a third, but the driver disarmed him and escaped. Civilian and Army authorities arrested Loving the next afternoon. He confessed.
* * *

Loving's first argument is that Congress lacks power to allow the President to prescribe aggravating factors in military capital cases because any delegation would be inconsistent with the Framers' decision to vest in Congress the power "To make rules for the Government and Regulation of the land and naval forces." U.S. Const., Art. I, § 8, cl. 14. * * *
* * *

We have undertaken before, in resolving other issues, the difficult task of interpreting Clause 14 by drawing upon English constitutional history. * * *

In England after the Norman Conquest, military justice was a matter of royal prerogative. The rudiments of law in English military justice can first be seen in the written orders issued by the King for various expeditions. [citation omitted.] For example, in 1190 Richard I issued an ordinance outlining six offenses to which the crusaders could be subject, including two punishable by death: "Whoever shall slay a man on ship-board, he shall be bound to the dead man and thrown into the sea. If he shall slay him on land he shall be bound to the dead man and buried in the earth." * * *
* * *

Separation-of-powers principles are vindicated, not disserved, by measured cooperation between the two political branches of the Government, each contributing to a lawful objective through its own processes. The delegation to the President as Commander in Chief of the authority to prescribe aggravating factors was in all respects * * * well within the delegated authority. Loving's sentence was lawful, and the judgment of the Court of Appeals for the Armed Forces is affirmed.

It is so ordered.

---

[2] UTAH CODE ANN. § 68-3-1.

The boundary lines of the *Loving* decision are illustrated by a sentence from the full opinion: "Under Clause 14, Congress, like Parliament, exercises a power of precedence over, not exclusion of, Executive authority." Thus, if Congress and the President adopted rules relating to capital punishment in the military which conflicted, the rule of the Congress would take precedence. But, that has not happened here. Instead, the President has adopted a rule and the Congress has not disagreed, and the President is not excluded from acting where the Congress has not.

Problem Solving. Please turn to Chapter Problems at the end of this chapter and solve Problem 1.3.

The U. S. System of Law

LAW IS FOUND in a constitution, statutes, regulations, or case law

Although they inherited their basic legal traditions from the English, Americans have gone their own way with respect to the details by which their system operates. At this point we leave the English and consider details of the legal system in the United States.

As in every legal system, some laws in the United States are more important than others. Thus, in the government of the United States, and in the government of each of the states (such as Florida or Iowa), there is a hierarchy of laws which starts with the most important and descends to the least important. In general—although there are some very important exceptions—that hierarchy is (1) constitution, (2) statute, (3) regulation and (4) case law. Each of these terms is discussed hereafter:

Constitution. Citizens of a country may adopt a document—called a constitution—which describes the powers and limitations of the government and the rights of the people in relation to the government. The powers, limitations and rights described in a constitution are law. The process of adopting a constitution normally includes the approving vote of the people and not just the approval of the legislative body. The United States of America has a formal, written constitution and each of the states in the United States has a formal, written constitution. Cities and counties usually do not have a constitution. A constitution is a superior form of law in the sense that it outranks any other law created within the government. For example, the Constitution of the United States is superior to laws enacted by the United States Congress and the Constitution of the State of Idaho is superior to laws enacted by the state legislature and to laws enacted by cities and counties. The Constitution of the United States is superior to the Constitution of the State of Idaho.

Statute. A statute is a written law adopted by the United States Congress or by the legislature of one of the states in the United States, which approves or disallows some form of conduct. Local governments, such as cities and counties, also have legislative powers, but the laws adopted by them are not called statutes. A law adopted by the legislative power of local government is often called an ordinance.

Regulation. A regulation is a written law adopted by a regulatory agency. Legislative bodies such as the United States Congress, or the legislature of a state in the United States, sometimes create agencies with power to regulate the specialized business of the government. For example, the United States Congress created the Environmental Protection Agency (EPA) and gave it power to adopt regulations controlling the disposal of toxic chemicals in the environment.

5

Case Law. A unique feature of the so-called "common law" legal system created by the English, and used in modified form by the Americans, is that a considerable amount of law in the system is created by *judges*. Judge-made decisions are called *case* law (or sometimes *common* law). Even though Americans have strayed from the English model in some ways, they have stayed faithful to the common law practice that allows judges to participate in the process of making law.

How do judges participate in the process of making law? In the U.S. legal system, constitutions, statutes and regulations are *not* comprehensive; that is, many laws which could be written in advance of problems are not. Why not write all law in advance? The answer is the belief that some of the most effective laws are those fashioned by judges on a case-by-case basis to solve real—and not imagined—problems. The manner in which judges solve legal problems on a case-by-case basis is discussed below.

Problem Solving. Please turn to Chapter Problems at the end of this chapter and solve Problem 1.4.

The Case Law Method

CASE LAW: iIn a common law legal system, much law is made by judges on a case-by-case basis

As discussed above, a common law legal system is a legal system in which some law is made by judges on a case-by-case basis. The manner in which judges make law, and the manner in which that judge-made law co-exists with legislative law (e.g. a statute) is the subject of the following discussion:

An Example. To understand how legislative and judge-made law can co-exist in a "common law" legal system, suppose that public disturbances are on the rise in the state of Utopia and the state legislature decides to adopt a statute which provides that "It shall be unlawful for a person to hit another." The legislators are undecided, however, about what *exceptions*, if any, to write into the statute they are preparing. For example, what if Milly *threatens* to hit Jed, can Jed hit back without violating the "no-hitting" statute? Or, what if Milly actually *hits* Jed, can Jed hit back without violating the "no-hitting" statute? Or, should it make a difference if one of the parties is bigger than the other, or if one is male and the other female. Should it make a difference if one of the parties has a weapon and the other does not? The legislature is so uncertain about how to provide for necessary exceptions that it adopts a statute which leaves that issue to be resolved by judges. The new statute provides:

> It shall be unlawful for a person to hit another without provocation, and a person in violation of this provision shall be liable in damages to the injured party.

Observe that this statute legislatively establishes a basic policy (that a person shall not hit another), but says nothing about what is, or is not, *provocation*. The issue of provocation is an exception which is left to the courts.

Applying the Statute. To understand how the "no-hitting" statute could be applied by a court, suppose that in a case known as *Able v. Baker* a judge is faced with a case in which Able, a drunk 225 lb. man, threatens to stab Baker, his 110 lb. girlfriend, with a knife. In self-defense, Baker hits and injures Able with a baseball bat. Able sues Baker. (Able, the injured party seeking compensation, is referred to as the *plaintiff*, and Baker, the alleged wrongdoer, is referred to as the *defendant*.) The judge searches in his law library and finds the "no hitting" statute described above. After hearing the evidence and reviewing the statute, the judge decides that the threat by the plaintiff was a sufficient *provocation* and therefore the defendant should *not* be liable to the plaintiff for damages.

Stare Decisis. The common law requires judges to be consistent in making decisions. The legal doctrine that requires consistency is called *stare decisis*. When a judge is in the process of making a decision, she should consider whether there are any earlier cases on the same subject. These earlier cases on the same subject are referred to as *precedent*. If a new "hitting" case arises, the doctrine of stare decisis requires that the new case be consistent with precedent, and precedent would be the decision in *Able v. Baker*. If the facts in two cases are the same, the rule of stare decisis requires that the result in the two cases be the same. The sophistication of this system is, of course, in deciding when the facts in two cases are sufficiently the same (requiring the same result) or when the facts in two cases are sufficiently different (allowing a different result). To learn how *stare decisis* operates, consider the next "hitting" case.

Another "Hitting" Case. A new "hitting" case (called *Carr v. Doxey*) arises in which two slightly intoxicated men in a tavern parking lot get into an argument over the ownership of an automobile hubcap. In the heat of the argument, Doxey (the defendant) hits Carr (the plaintiff) with a baseball bat and claims possession of the hubcap. Thereafter, Carr sues Doxey claiming compensation under the terms of the "no-hitting" statute.

Stare Decisis Applied. As she resolves the *Carr v. Doxey* case, the judge's thought process goes something like this: (1) the statute has a "no-hitting" policy and I must enforce it and grant compensation, except where provocation exists; (2) the issue of provocation is left to case law and there is *precedent* (an earlier case on the same subject) in a decision known as *Able v. Baker*; (3) *stare decisis* requires that my decision in *Carr v. Doxey* be consistent with the decision in *Able v. Baker*; that is, where the facts are the same, the decision should be the same; (4) in both *Able* and *Carr* the injured party was intoxicated, but the relevant fact in *Able* seems to be that the woman hit to defend herself, while in *Carr* the man hit to win an argument; (5) my decision in *Carr*, which is consistent with the decision in *Able*, is that hitting to win an argument is not adequate provocation and therefore Carr is entitled to compensation.

In an earlier paragraph, the comment was made that in the common law view "some of the most effective rules (laws) are those fashioned by judges on a case-by-case basis to solve real—and not imagined—problems." The Able and Carr cases are examples of how the common law can closely tailor decisions to meet real facts. This practicality is considered the genius of the common law.

Problem Solving. Please turn to Chapter Problems at the end of this chapter and solve Problem 1.5.

Conflicts in Laws.

CONFLICTS: federal law outranks state law, and state law outranks local law

In the *Able* and *Carr* decisions, the requirements of the statute were clear and the only problem was applying the statute and the related case law to the facts of the case. But, sometimes there are so many constitutions, statutes and regulations that they *conflict*. According to the 1992 United States Census of Governments there were *39,029*

7

governments in the United States. Specifically, there was one federal government, 50 state governments, 3,043 county governments, 19,279 cities and 16,656 towns. In addition, there are all of the regulatory agencies such as the Federal Trade Commission (FCC), the Internal Revenue Service (IRS) or the Environmental Protection Agency (EPA) which have been created by the United States Congress and the 50 state legislatures. The point is that all of the governments can make laws and most of the regulatory agencies can also, and some of those laws conflict.

Federal Law versus State Law. What happens when a law of the United States government (constitution, statute, regulation or case law) conflicts with the law of a state, or one of its political subdivisions (a city or a county)? The answer is found in the Supremacy Clause of the United States Constitution which is as follows:

> This Constitution, and the Laws of the United States which shall be made in Pursuance thereof; and all Treaties made, or which shall be made, under the Authority of the United States, *shall be the supreme Law of the land*; and the Judges in every State shall be bound thereby, any Thing in the constitution or Laws of any State to the Contrary notwithstanding.[3]

City of Burbank v. Lockheed Air Terminal Inc. is a United States Supreme Court decision that illustrates how the Supremacy Clause (quoted above) may be applied. The City of Burbank (a political subdivision of the State of California) adopted an ordinance that prohibited jet aircraft from taking off between the hours of 11 p.m. and 7 a.m. The City did this to make things quieter at night for people sleeping in nearby residences. This ordinance was challenged on the grounds that it was contrary to the provisions of the Federal Aviation Act and the Federal Noise Control Act. The Supreme Court held that federal supremacy included the power to completely take over an entire field of regulation—excluding any regulation by others. This power is called *preemption*:

City of Burbank v. Lockheed Air Terminal Inc.
411 U.S. 624 (1973)

MR. JUSTICE DOUGLAS delivered the opinion of the Court.

* * *

There is to be sure no express provision of pre-emption in the 1972 [Noise Control] Act. That, however, is not decisive. As we stated in *Rice v. Santa Fe Elevator Corp.*, 331 U.S. 218, 230, 67 S.Ct. 1146, 1152, 91 L.Ed. 1447:

> "Congress legislated here in a field which the States have traditionally occupied. * * * So we start with the assumption that the historic police powers of the States were not to be superseded by the Federal Act unless that was the clear and manifest purpose of Congress. * * * Such a purpose may be evidenced in several ways. The scheme of federal regulation may be so pervasive as to make reasonable the inference that Congress left no room for the states to supplement it. * * * Or the Act of Congress may touch a field in which the federal interest is so dominant that the federal system will be assumed to preclude enforcement of

---

[3] U.S. CONST. art. VI, para. 2 (emphasis added).

> state laws on the same subject. * * * Likewise, the object sought to be obtained by the federal law and the character of obligations imposed by it may reveal the same purpose. * * * Or the state policy may produce a result inconsistent with the objective of the federal statute."
>
> It is the pervasive nature of the scheme of federal regulation of aircraft noise that leads us to conclude that there is pre-emption. * * *
>
> Affirmed.

Admittedly, there was nothing in the two federal acts which directly conflicted with the Burbank ordinance. However, said the Court, the federal acts show a plan to assume control over the entire field of aircraft noise. Doing that, as discussed above, is preemption, which is part of the federal supremacy power. Thus, the Burbank ordinance was invalid on supremacy (preemption) grounds.

State law versus Local Law. In contrast to the conflict described above (federal law versus local law), suppose that a conflict exists between a state law and a local law, called an ordinance. In this context, state law normally supersedes local law. This conflict is illustrated in the following case, *City of Peggott v. Eblen*, where a city ordinance appeared to conflict with a state statute. Specifically, a local ordinance prohibited the use of pinball machines, while a state statute appeared to allow the use of pinball machines:

> **City of Piggott v. Eblen**
> **236 Ark. 390, 366 S.W.2d 192**
>
> HOLT, JUSTICE. The appellant, the City of Piggott, Arkansas, enacted Ordinance 209 declaring that: " * * * Pinball machines or other gaming devices are a public nuisance * * * " The ordinance further provides that it is unlawful for any business establishment or individual to possess pinball machines in any manner within the city. A violation of this ordinance is punishable by a fine of not less than \$5.00 nor more than \$25.00 per day.
>
> * * *
>
> Act 167 of 1931 [Ark.Stat. § 84-2601] provides that the business of owning, operating, or leasing such machines is a privilege for which licenses can be required and taxes imposed.
>
> Act 201 of 1939, [Ark.Stat. § 84-2602] as amended, specifically provides that amusement games played on pinball machines are lawful even though free games be given upon certain scores being made * * *
>
> Thus, it is readily apparent that a conflict exists between the questioned ordinance and the statutes * * *
>
> * * *. The statutes of our state, being paramount and supreme, have preempted the appellant in this field of legislation and, therefore, render the ordinance a nullity.
>
> * * * The trial court was correct in declaring the questioned ordinance invalid as being contrary to the Constitution and Statutes of this state. The decree is affirmed.

Problem Solving. Please turn to Chapter Problems at the end of this chapter and solve Problem 1.6.

Law Books

LAW BOOKS: statues are found in codes, and case law is found in reporters.

Before closing this chapter, it is important to discuss one last point. That point is: *where* (in what books) are all of the laws discussed above to be found? If a new problem involving "hitting" arose—like the hitting in the cases of *Able v. Baker* and *Carr v. Doxey* discussed above—where would the lawyers and the judge in the new case look to learn the "law" on that subject? The answer to the question is that the lawyers and judges in the new case would look in the state *code* for legislative law and in a *reporter* for the case law. That is what happened in *Carr v. Doxey*. In that case the judge used law from two different sources: first, he used legislative law (the no-hitting statute which he found in the state code) and second, he used earlier case law (the decision of a judge in *Able v. Baker* on the issue of provocation which he found in a reporter).

Codes and Reporters. Thus, for example, laws enacted by the United States Congress are collected in a set of books called the United States Code. The U.S. Constitution is printed in that code.

The decisions of the Arkansas Supreme Court, for example, are collected and published in *reporters*. The decisions of courts are public information and anyone can report those decisions. A review of the *City of Piggott* decision, which is discussed above, shows that it was published in at least two different reporters:

City of Piggott v. Eblen
236 Ark. 390, 366 S.W.2d 192

First, the decision is published in a reporter known as the Arkansas (Ark.) Reporter. The decision is found in volume number 236 of the reporter at page 390. In addition, the same decision is reported in a reporter series called the Southwest (S.W.) Reporter where it is found in volume 366 at page 192. Note that the *City of Piggott* decision is found in "S.W.*2d*." At some point there were, in the opinion of the publisher, too many volumes in the S.W. reporter series so a new series called S.W.2d was started. Some day the publisher of the Southwest Reporter may think that there are too many volumes in that series and a new series known as "S.W.*3d*" will be started.

As will be discussed later, there are many court systems in the United States and there is one or more reporter series for most of them. For example, decisions of federal appellate judges are currently reported in the third series of the Federal Reporter (F.3d), decisions of appellate courts in the Western United States are presently reported in the second series of the Pacific Reporter (P.2d) and reports from the South are presently reported in the second series of the Southern Reporter (S.2d).

Problem Solving. Please turn to Chapter Problems at the end of this chapter and solve Problem 1.7.

Chapter Problems

Problem 1.1

Milly fails to stop at a stop sign in the parking lot of the Elm City Shopping Mall. The stop sign was posted in the middle of the parking lot by the owners of the mall. Has she violated a law?

Problem 1.2

Which of the following is the most correct:
a. The objective of criminal law is to assist the victims of crimes.
b. The objective of civil law is to punish those who violate law.
c. None of the above is substantially correct.

Problem 1.3

In courts in the United States:
a. English law may be applied.
b. "Common law" applied to ordinary English people, but not to others.
c. English law must be applied.
d. None of the above is substantially correct.

Problem 1.4

The EPA adopts the following two regulations: First, a regulation prohibiting dumping nitric acid into rivers. Second, a regulation controlling the qualifications of airline pilots. Explain, why the first regulation is valid, but the second regulation is not.

Problem 1.5

Assume that the "no hitting" statute, the decisions in *Able v. Baker* and *Carr v. Doxey* and the doctrine of *stare decisis* all apply. Solve the following problem in a case known as *Echo v. Farr*. Ralph Echo and Martin Farr (and his wife) lived in different apartments in the same building and there was only one narrow road to the parking lot in the back. Ralph persisted in parking his car on the road, instead of in the parking lot and Martin was sometimes late for work because he couldn't exit the parking lot. The following testimony was given in a lawsuit by Ralph who claimed that Martin had hit him:

(Testimony of Martin Farr)

Q What happened that day.

A That evening he took it upon himself to park in the driveway again. He parked behind my wife so she couldn't get out and she needed to go to town. She tried to go ahead and back around his car which was impossible.

Q Were you present when that happened?

A No, I wasn't.

Q She told you what happened?

A Yes. Finally she had to go down and ask him to move his car, but he mumbled a few things to himself and acted pretty smart to her. When I got home his car was still parked in the driveway, so I went down and asked him to move his car.

Q What did he say to you?

A He refused to do it.

Q What did you tell him?

A That he better move it or I would move it for him.

Q What did he say to that?

A He said that he'd kick my b--- and I grabbed him and pushed him on his couch.

Explain whether Martin Farr is liable to Ralph Echo?

Problem 1.6

Solve the following hypothetical conflict of laws: Lisa, a resident of the state of Ohio and 15 years of age wishes to marry Pete, age 19 and a resident of the state of Kansas. They propose to marry in Ohio. A federal social security statute does not allow a woman to qualify for spouse's benefits before the age of 16; Kansas law does not allow women to marry before age 16, but Ohio law allows a woman to marry at age 15. Explain whether Lisa and Pete may be married according to plan.

Problem 1.7

Which of the following is true with respect to the *Loving* opinion in this chapter:

a) This opinion may be found in a code.

b) This opinion may be found in a reporter.

c) The volume in which the opinion is found is number 1737.

Chapter Outline

CHAPTER OBJECTIVE is to
describe state and federal
court systems and the
jurisdiction of these systems

The objective of this chapter is to (1) describe the organization of state court systems and the federal court system, and (2) to describe the nature and limits of the jurisdiction (power) of courts in these systems. This chapter is organized as follows:

- *State Trial Courts.* Each state has a court system with *trial courts* (often called "district" courts) at the base of the system. A trial court is the place where testimony is given and evidence received.

- *State Appellate Courts.* Most state court systems have two levels of appellate courts. The first level is often called "court of appeals." The second level is often called "supreme court." Appellate courts supervise the business of trial courts.

- *State Court Jurisdiction.* In general, a state court has *jurisdiction* (power) over persons, property and events within the state. A state court has jurisdiction over nonresidents to the extent it is fair to do so. In legal terms, fairness is referred to as *due process.*

- *State Court Venue.* *Venue* is the determination of the specific geographic location where a court will exercise its jurisdictional power.

- *Federal Courts.* The United States government operates a system of trial courts and appellate courts which is similar in structure to those of the states, with trial courts at the base and two levels of appellate courts supervising the business of the trial courts.

- *Federal Court Jurisdiction.* To have a case heard in federal court, the plaintiff must establish the existence of a *federal question* or jurisdiction based on *diversity of citizenship.*

State Trial Courts

Each of the 50 states in the U.S. has a system of *trial courts* and *appellate courts.* In general, the legislature of each of the 50 states is free to organize its court system as it chooses. The structure of all of these court systems has *trial courts* at the base; and, at the top, a structure of appellate courts to review the business of the trial courts.

STATE TRIAL COURTS are
commonly called a District
Court—a place where
testimony is given and
evidence received

General Jurisdiction Trial Courts. Most states call their trial court "district court," although they are free to use any name they choose. Utah, for example, calls it's trial courts "District Court," but California calls it's trial courts "Superior Court" and New

13

York calls them "Supreme Court." Whatever their name, these trial courts have "general" jurisdiction over all of the legal business in their particular court system.

Specialized or Limited Jurisdiction Trial Courts. In addition to trial courts of general jurisdiction, most states also create trial courts which have specialized or limited jurisdiction. For example, there are usually specialized trial courts known as juvenile courts which handle issues related to children under the age of eighteen years, and probate courts which distribute the estate of deceased persons. And, there are trial courts with limited jurisdiction known as city court, municipal court, traffic court or justice of the peace court, where traffic offenses, minor criminal cases and small civil claims are handled.

Trial Court Function. A trial court is the place where testimony is given and evidence received. This is the court room often seen on television and in the movies. This is where the famous Clarence Darrow and the fictitious Perry Mason examine and cross-examine witnesses and pace the floor, waving their arms and firing legal thunderbolts at the opposition. This is the place of Judge Ito and the infamous O.J. Simpson trial. Although usually much more orderly and even boring—particularly in business law cases—than the public perceives, this is where the basic decisions in a court system take place.

In either a civil or a criminal trial, a trial court is presided over by one judge. If neither of the parties requests a jury, the judge makes all decisions of fact and law himself.

If one of the parties requests a jury, the judge handles all questions of law, but the factual decision-making process is shared with the jury. Suppose, for example, that Jed is sued for driving his car too fast and colliding with a car driven by Milly, who is injured. In a trial with a jury, the judge, by ruling on questions of evidence, decides what evidence the jury will hear. In addition, the judge instructs the jury on the applicable law. Once the evidence and instructions on the law are received by them, (1) the jury decides the factual issues, such as how fast each party was traveling and the extent of injuries, and (2) the jury also decides issues of fact applied to law, such as whether the facts should be interpreted to mean that Jed was negligent.

Problem Solving. Please turn to Chapter Problems at the end of this chapter and solve Problem 2.1.

State Appellate Courts

STATE APPELLATE COURTS are courts where the work of trial courts is reviewed for error

If trial courts are the stuff of television and movies, appellate courts are the opposite as they toil in relative obscurity. Although the United States Supreme Court receives considerable media attention, most people do not understand it's role in relation to trial courts. That role is simple: appellate courts review the business conducted by trial courts to see if any mistakes have been made. No testimony is given and no evidence is received. There are no juries.

An appellate court consists of a number of judges, usually called "justices," who are often former trial court judges. There are an odd number of justices, such as five, seven or nine. An odd number is used to avoid deadlock in voting.

Briefs and Oral Argument. As part of the appellate process, each of the parties (acting through their lawyers) submit to the court a written *brief* in which they explain their position on the issues. Specifically, the brief attempts to persuade the court that there was—or was not—an error in the trial proceedings. In addition, the lawyers for the parties also appear in person, and in a hearing before the assembled justices of the court the lawyers take turns orally explaining their position and responding to questions from the justices. This process is called an *oral argument.*

Reversed or Affirmed. If the appellate court finds significant error in the trial proceedings, the trial court decision is said to be "reversed." A case may be reversed in whole or in part. If the case is reversed, it is normally returned ("remanded") to the trial court for the errors to be remedied. Because most trial court decisions do not include significant error, perhaps only 10% or less of appealed decisions are reversed and remanded. If appellate review does not uncover significant error in a decision, the case is "affirmed."

The table below shows a typical state court system with trial courts (named district court) at the bottom and two levels of appellate court above the trial courts:

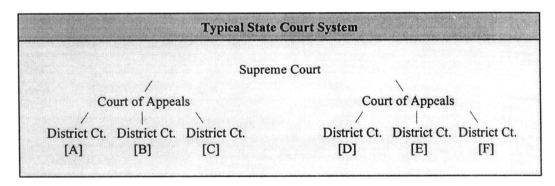

The business of appellate courts is time consuming and all states find it necessary to divide up that business among more than one appellate court. The most common method is illustrated above, where trial courts are divided up among two or more courts of appeal. In turn, the courts of appeal are supervised by a Supreme Court.

First Appeal. Appeals to courts of appeal are filed as a matter of "right;" that is, if the appeal is properly filed, the court *must* consider it, although the court is not required to agree with it. Accordingly, if a party in a trial in District Court [A] believes that the trial court judge has made an error, his remedy is to appeal to the Court of Appeals immediately above, and those justices must listen to his appeal.

Second Appeal. Inevitably, over the course of time, one Court of Appeals may make a decision inconsistent with a decision of the other Court of Appeals. This conflict explains the need for a second level appellate court. The most common name for such a court is Supreme Court, as shown in the table above. A major difference between the first appellate level (Court of Appeals) and the second appellate level (Supreme Court) is that all who wish may appeal to the first level, but appeals to the second appellate are usually done only with the permission of the court.

To understand the difference between the Court of Appeals and the Supreme Court in the table above, return to *Carr v. Doxey*, the hitting case discussed in Chapter 1. Suppose that *Carr* was decided by a trial court judge and then appealed to the Court of Appeals, on the left side of the table above, which affirmed that an argument over the ownership of a hubcap is *not* sufficient provocation to protect a person from liability for hitting another with a baseball bat. Thereafter, a similar case starts in a trial court on the right side and is then appealed to the Court of Appeals above it. But now a problem develops because the Court of Appeal on the right does the unexpected and decides—contrary to the decision in *Carr*—that a baseball bat *can* be used in an argument over a hubcap by the person who is the owner of the hubcap. Using a baseball bat, says the court, is a legitimate means of preserving possession of his personal property. Lawyers for the losing party in the new case desire to appeal to the state Supreme Court to resolve the conflict between the decisions of the two courts of appeal about whether a baseball bat can be used to resolve an argument over possession of a hubcap.

Writ of Certiorari. Appeals to the second appellate level are usually *by permission only* and a commonly used procedure to gain this permission is a *writ of certiorari*. Writ of certiorari is the old English term for a court order allowing a discretionary appeal. Lawyers asking the Supreme Court to hear the new baseball bat case submit a petition to the court explaining the conflict, and if the court agrees that a problem needs to be solved, it issues its writ of certiorari which commands the Court of Appeal on the right to send the record on appeal to the Supreme Court for further review.

Problem Solving. Please turn to Chapter Problems at the end of this chapter and solve Problem 2.2.

State Court Jurisdiction

STATE COURT
JURISDICTION means power
over resident persons,
property, and events, and
power over nonresidents to
the extent of due process

Resident Jurisdiction. In general, a state court has *jurisdiction* over residents of the state, property located in the state and events occurring in the state. Thus, the question of jurisdiction examines the extent of *power* a court has over persons, property and events. If the question is jurisdiction over a person, it may be referred to as *in personam* jurisdiction. If the question relates to the ownership or control of real property, it may be referred to as *in rem* jurisdiction.

Nonresident Jurisdiction. A more troubling question is the extent to which *nonresidents* can be compelled to travel to a state and participate in litigation. Can a resident of New York, for example, who purchases an automobile in New York but is then involved in an automobile accident in Oklahoma, bring suit against the automobile manufacturer in Oklahoma state courts? That is a question of *jurisdiction*.

If a layman was to examine the extent of state court control over *nonresidents*, he or she might say, "Well, whatever is fair." And although courts use different words, "whatever is fair" is precisely the standard they use. But, instead of using the word "fair," the courts use the phrase "due process," which means the same thing. The Fourteenth Amendment to the U.S. Constitution provides: "nor shall any State deprive any person of life, liberty, or property, *without due process* of law." In other words, the business of state courts is to sift through the rights of (resident and nonresident) persons to life, liberty and property, and they cannot do it without due process (fairness).

So, what is fair? In general, if nonresidents own property in a state, courts uniformly hold that it is fair to require them to come to the state and respond to litigation respecting it. If Milly lives in New Mexico but owns property in Idaho, she may be expected, for example, to come to Idaho and litigate if someone else claims the property or if someone else is injured on it.

In general, if a person "engages in business" or causes personal injuries in a state where he or she is not a resident, it is fair to require them to return and litigate issues related to that conduct. If Milly (a resident of New Mexico) sells mining machinery or is involved in an automobile accident in Idaho, it is fair that she be required to respond in Idaho state courts for her conduct. If a person has engaged in business to the point that it is fair to require them to respond in a state where they are not a resident the due process requirement is met. It is said that such persons have had the *minimum contacts* necessary to satisfy due process.

"Long Arm" Statute. If a person is sued, the litigation process begins when the defendant receives a summons and a copy of the complaint from a process server. This is called "*service of process*," and by this procedure a court gains jurisdiction over the person who is served. (This procedure is discussed more in Chapter 3.) If the defendant is a nonresident, state courts use what is popularly known as a "*long arm*" statute. Suppose that Milly, the New Mexico resident, is sued in the Idaho courts because some of the mining machinery she sold in Idaho is defective. Under the terms of the Idaho long arm statute, the process server is allowed to deliver the summons and complaint (service of process) to Milly in New Mexico, and by this procedure the "long arm" of the Idaho state court extends to New Mexico and requires Milly to respond in the Idaho lawsuit.

Earlier, the question was asked whether plaintiffs, residents of New York, could bring suit against an automobile manufacturer in Oklahoma state court after purchasing an automobile in New York and being involved in an automobile accident in Oklahoma? In the following case consider how the United States Supreme Court used jurisdictional concepts such as "due process" and "minimum contacts" to decide if it was fair ("due process") for the Oklahoma state courts to exercise jurisdiction over the automobile manufacturer:

World-Wide Volkswagen Corp v. Woodson
444 U.S. 286 (1980)

Mr. Justice White delivered the opinion of the Court.

The issue before us is whether, consistently with the Due Process Clause of the Fourteenth Amendment, an Oklahoma court may exercise *in personam* jurisdiction over a nonresident automobile retailer and its wholesale distributor in a products liability action, when the defendants' only connection with Oklahoma is the fact that an automobile sold in New York to New York residents became involved in an accident in Oklahoma.

* * *

The Due Process Clause of the Fourteenth Amendment limits the power of a state court to render a valid personal judgment against a nonresident defendant. * * * A judgment rendered in violation of due process is void in the rendering State and is not entitled to full faith and credit elsewhere. * * * Due process requires that the defendant be given adequate notice of the suit, * * * and be subject to the personal jurisdiction of the court * * *. In the present case, it is not contended that notice was inadequate; the only question is whether these particular petitioners were subject to the jurisdiction of the Oklahoma courts.

As has long been settled, and as we reaffirm today, a state court may exercise personal jurisdiction over a nonresident defendant only so long as there exist "minimum contacts" between the defendant and the forum State. * * * The concept of minimum contacts, in turn, can be seen to perform two related, but distinguishable, functions. It protects the defendant against the burdens of litigating in a distant or inconvenient forum. And it acts to ensure that the States, through their courts, do not reach out beyond the limits imposed on them by their status as coequal sovereigns in a federal system.

The protection against inconvenient litigation is typically described in terms of "reasonableness" or "fairness." We have said that the defendant's contacts with the forum State must be such that maintenance of the suit "does not offend 'traditional notions of fair play and substantial justice." The relationship between the defendant and the forum must be such that it is "reasonable * * * to require the corporation to defend the particular suit which is brought there." * * * Implicit in this emphasis on reasonableness is the understanding that the burden on the defendant, while always a primary concern, will in an appropriate case be considered in light of other relevant factors, including the forum State's interest in adjudicating the dispute * * *, the plaintiff's interest in obtaining convenient and effective relief, * * * at least when that interest is not adequately protected by the plaintiff's power to choose the forum; the interstate judicial system's interest in obtaining the most efficient resolution of controversies; and the shared interest of the several States in furthering fundamental substantive social policies.

* * *

Applying these principles to the case at hand, we find in the record before us a total absence of those affiliating circumstances that are a necessary predicate to any exercise of state court jurisdiction. Petitioners carry on no activity whatsoever in Oklahoma. They close no sales and perform no services there. They avail themselves of none of the privileges and benefits of Oklahoma law. The solicit no business there either through salespersons or through advertising reasonably calculated to reach the State. Nor does the record show that they regularly sell cars at wholesale or retail to Oklahoma customers or residents, or that they indirectly, through others, serve or seek to serve the Oklahoma market. In short, respondents seek to base jurisdiction on one, isolated occurrence and whatever inferences can be drawn therefrom: the fortuitous circumstance that a single Audi automobile, sold in New York to New York residents, happened to suffer an accident while passing through Oklahoma.

* * *

18

> Because we find that petitioners have no "contacts, ties or relations" with the State of Oklahoma, the judgment of the Supreme Court of Oklahoma is
> Reversed.

The fact that the plaintiffs lost on appeal does not mean they are completely "tossed out of court." Remember that the only issue on appeal was whether the trial could be held in Oklahoma. Having lost on that point, the plaintiff's still have the option to file suit in New York.

__Problem Solving__. Please turn to Chapter Problems at the end of this chapter and solve Problem 2.3.

State Court Venue

The issue of *venue* determines the specific geographic location where a court will exercise its jurisdictional power. In the paragraphs above it was said that Milly, a New Mexico resident, may be sued in the Idaho courts because some of the mining machinery she sold in Idaho was defective. But, where in Idaho will the litigation take place? Will it be, for example, in Boise on the west of the state, or in Rexburg on the east of the state? Normally, venue rules provide that contract litigation will be at the location the contract was formed and that tort litigation (for example automobile accidents) will be at the location where the accident took place. Thus, if Milly sold the mining machinery in Boise, venue rules provide that the litigation should be in Boise.

__Problem Solving__. Please turn to Chapter Problems at the end of this chapter and solve Problem 2.4.

Federal Courts

FEDERAL COURTS are a system of courts for federal and not state, legal business

The United States government operates a system of trial courts and appellate courts which is similar in structure to the court systems operated by the states. This court system exists to handle legal business related to federal law. The federal court system was not created as another place for people to take their divorces, real estate contracts and automobile accidents, which is the business of state courts. Rather, it is a court system which interprets federal law and handles criminal and civil cases where federal law is said to be violated.

The trial courts in the federal system are called District Court and there are District Courts located throughout the United States. The first level of appellate courts is called Court of Appeals and there are twelve of them scattered throughout the United States. The area (and District Courts within it) which is supervised by a Court of Appeals is called a circuit, and so the full name for one of the courts in the Western United States is the United States Court of Appeals for the Eleventh Circuit. There is a thirteenth circuit which has national jurisdiction to decide specialized cases such as customs and patent law. Finally, there is the United States Supreme Court which has power to review all decisions in the federal courts and power to review federal law decisions which may be made in the state courts. The table below shows the structure of the federal court system:

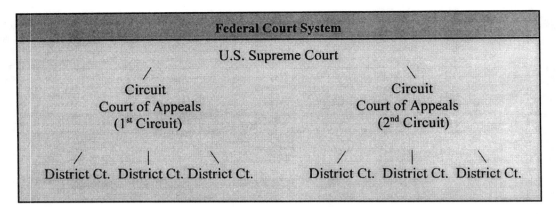

Federal Court System

U.S. Supreme Court

Circuit
Court of Appeals
(1st Circuit)

Circuit
Court of Appeals
(2nd Circuit)

District Ct.　District Ct.　District Ct.　　District Ct.　District Ct.　District Ct.

__Problem Solving.__ Please turn to Chapter Problems at the end of this chapter and solve Problem 2.5.

Federal Jurisdiction

To have a case heard in federal court, and not state court, the plaintiff must establish that the court has jurisdiction which means that there is a *federal question* or that there is *diversity of citizenship*.

__Federal Question.__ The U.S. Constitution provides that "[t]he judicial Power shall extend to all cases, in Law and Equity, arising under this Constitution, the Laws of the United States, and Treaties made, or which shall be made, under their Authority."[1] This provision means, of course, that a lawsuit may be heard in the federal courts if a federal law is at issue. For example, if John (a resident of Orlando, Florida) contracts to sell 1000 lbs of kumquats[2] to the ABC Fruit Company (a Florida corporation with principal offices in Miami, Florida), but fails to deliver, can ABC sue John in federal court? The answer is no because the law of contracts is generally a matter of state law, and the lawsuit must be filed in Florida state court. But, suppose that the reason John did not deliver the kumquats[2] is that a regulation of the United States Department of Agriculture (USDA) temporarily banned their transportation to prevent the spread of kumquat worms. If John thinks the regulation is improperly applied to him, can he sue the USDA in federal court to prevent its enforcement? The answer is yes because the USDA regulation is a law of the United States, and the question of its validity is a "federal question" over which the federal courts have jurisdiction.

__Diversity of Citizenship.__ Although, in general, the federal courts do not exercise jurisdiction over non-federal business, it is nevertheless true that the federal courts have jurisdiction over cases involving "diversity of citizenship." To understand this category of jurisdiction it must be remembered that in 18th Century America the thirteen colonies were

---

[1] U.S. CONST. art. III, § 2.

[2] Kumquat: any of several small yellow to orange citrus fruits.

not always cooperative with each other. The perception existed, for example, that a person from Virginia who was forced to litigate against a person from New York, in the state courts of New York, would not be treated fairly; that the New York Courts would naturally favor the person from New York. The consequence of this perception—whether it was accurate or not—was that the framers of the Constitution gave the federal courts jurisdiction over cases where the litigants were citizens of different ("diverse") states. Thus, the person from Virginia could have his lawsuit heard in the federal courts upon a showing (1) that the parties to the lawsuit were citizens of different states, and (2) that the amount in dispute exceeded $50 (today the amount is $50,000).

Problem Solving. Please turn to Chapter Problems at the end of this chapter and solve Problem 2.6.

Problem 2.1

What is the name of the trial courts of general jurisdiction in the State of Ohio?

Problem 2.2

With reference to the Typical State Court System table, which of the following courts issue a writ of certiorari:

a.   Trial court
b.   Court of Appeals
c.   Supreme Court
d.   None of the above.

Problem 2.3

Which of the following is fundamentally inconsistent with the others:

a.   Minimum contacts.
b.   Doing business.
c.   Due process.
d.   None of them is fundamentally inconsistent with the others.

Problem 2.4

Which of the following is most correct:

a)   The question of jurisdiction is irrelevant if venue cannot be established.
b)   the question of venue is irrelevant if jurisdiction cannot be established.
c)   Both are correct.

Problem 2.5

Which of the following is most correct:

a)   A writ of certiorari may be used to appeal a case from a federal district court located in the 9th Circuit to the 10th Circuit Court of Appeals.
b)   A writ of certiorari may be used to appeal a case from a federal district court located in the 9th Circuit to the 9th Circuit Court of Appeals.
c)   Both are correct.
d)   Neither is correct.

Problem 2.6

Which of the following are most closely related: (1) diversity of citizenship, (2) federal question, (3) amount in controversy over $50,000.

a)   1 and 2.
b)   1 and 3.
c)   2 and 3.

Chapter Outline

CHAPTER OBJECTIVE:
learn the principal events in a
civil trial

The objective of this chapter is to describe the events that take place in a civil trial. The chapter is organized as follows:

- *The Process of Litigation.* The process of litigation may be subdivided into five parts: pleading, discovery, motions, trial and appeal.

- *The Pleading Stage.* Pleadings are the documents in which each party states it's claims. They include: *complaint, answer, counterclaim* and *reply.*

- *The Discovery Stage.* In the discovery stage of a lawsuit each party is entitled to access to all of the available evidence to use for preparation and trial. The three most common discovery techniques are (1) *interrogatories*, (2) *depositions*, and (3) *demands for production of documents.*

- *The Motion Stage.* A motion is a formal request that a court do something. A motion for summary judgment is the most common motion. In it, a court is asked to grant judgment summarily, without further proceedings or a trial. This motion is granted when there is no dispute about the facts, or the facts as applied to the law.

- *The Trial Stage.* The trial of a civil action includes the following (1) pre-trial conference, (2) jury selection, (3) opening statements, (4) plaintiff's case, (5) direct examination, (6) cross-examination, (7) defendant's case, (8) direct examination, (9) cross-examination, (10) instructions, (11) plaintiff's summation, (12) defendant's summation, (13) deliberation, (14) verdict, and (15) post-trial motions and judgment.

- *The Appeal Stage.* A party dissatisfied with the trial process or result may appeal to the appellate courts. The appeal will be successful if the party appealing (the appellant) can identify an error in the trial proceedings.

The Process of Litigation

Chapter 1 discussed what is law, and what is not. Chapter 2 discussed state and federal court systems in which law is enforced. This chapter will take the next step and discuss the *process* of litigation by which law is enforced in the courts.

LITIGATION consists of
pleading stage, discovery
stage, motion stage, trial stage
and appeal stage

The process of litigation may be subdivided into five parts or stages: pleading, discovery, motions, trial and appeal:

1. In the *pleading* stage, each party states the legal claims he or she has against the other.

2. In the *discovery* stage, each party obtains evidence for use in the trial.

3. In the *motion* stage—having the benefit of evidence produced in the discovery stage—each party may file motions asking the court to do a variety of things suggested by the evidence. The most common motion is a motion for summary judgment in which the court is asked to summarily (without a trial) dismiss claims or grant judgment.

4. In the *trial* stage (if the case is not settled) each party puts evidence in front of a judge or jury, who makes a decision.

5. In the *appeal* stage (if there is one) the losing party asks an appellate court to remedy any errors which may have occurred in the trial.

The balance of this chapter explores the meaning of these five stages of litigation in the context of a lawsuit regarding a claim for payment for a motorcycle, and a claim for personal injuries:

The Pleading Stage

Historical Background. In early England, the courts were controlled by a king or queen and a person "pleaded" for justice, he did not demand it. Consequently, the documents by which a person asserted a claim against another became known as *pleadings*, which is a term that is still used today.

To put the concept of *pleadings* in context, assume that Jed Doe and Milly Roe have a legal dispute: Milly bought a motorcycle from Jed but won't pay for it because she claims the front brakes are defective. Moreover, claims Milly, the defective front brakes caused her to crash and she suffered cuts and bruises.

Jed (the *plaintiff*) commences a lawsuit to collect the purchase price of the motorcycle from Milly (the *defendant*). The lawsuit will start in state court because there is no federal jurisdiction (there is no federal question and there is not diversity of citizenship). The lawsuit will include the following pleadings[1]:

PLEADINGS consist of complaint, answer, counterclaim and reply

Complaint. The plaintiff, Jed, prepares a document called a Complaint (see Document 3.1 at end of this chapter) which states his legal claims against the defendant, Milly. Specifically, Jed claims that Milly purchased a motorcycle from him and agreed to pay him $15,000, which she has failed to do. The original of the Complaint is filed with the court and a copy is delivered to the person being sued, together with a *Summons* which

---

[1] **Rule 7(a) Pleadings.** There shall be a complaint and an answer; a reply to a counterclaim denominated as such; an answer to a cross-claim, if the answer contains a cross-claim; a third party complaint, if a person who was not an original party is summoned under the provisions of Rule 14; and a third party answer, if a third party complaint is served. UTAH R. CIV. P. 7(a).

requires the defendant to respond to the Complaint. Delivering the Summons and Complaint to the defendant is called *service of process*.

Answer. The defendant, Milly, responds by preparing an Answer (see Document 3.2 at end of this chapter) which states whether the allegations of the Complaint are true and any defenses she may have to the allegations of the Complaint. In this case, Milly admits purchasing the motorcycle and agreeing to pay $15,000 for it, but she alleges that the motorcycle is defective and the full purchase price should not be paid. The original Answer is filed with the court and a copy is sent to the plaintiff.

Counterclaim. In addition, if the defendant has a legal claim against the plaintiff, that claim is stated in a Counterclaim (see Document 3.2 at end of this chapter). In this case, Milly alleges that Jed sold her a defective motorcycle and the defects caused Milly personal injuries for which she should receive compensation. Again, the original is filed with the court and a copy is sent to the plaintiff.

Reply. The plaintiff, Jed, responds to the Counterclaim by preparing a Reply (see Document 3.3 at end of this chapter) which states whether the allegations of the Counterclaim are true, and any defenses he may have to the allegations of the Counterclaim. Specifically, Jed asserts that the motorcycle was not defective and that Milly should not receive any compensation from Jed for her personal injuries. The original of the Reply is filed with the court and a copy is sent to the defendant.

In the manner above, each party to a controversy may assert the claims he or she has against any other party to the same controversy. The objective is that all of the claims related to the "motorcycle" problem will be disposed of in the same lawsuit.

The Discovery Stage

Once the parties have asserted their claims against each other in the process of pleading, the next stage in the litigation process is the discovery stage. In the "discovery" stage of a lawsuit, each party is entitled to access to all of the available evidence. The idea behind discovery is that placing each party in possession of all of the evidence will promote settlements and shorten trials. Like a poker player who can see the other player's cards, a lawyer who can examine all of the evidence his opponent will use at trial is likely to settle a lawsuit or drop it if he does not have a winning hand.

DISCOVERY TECHNIQUES include interrogatories, depositions and requests for production of documents

Discovery is a self-help system in the sense that the opposition is not required to volunteer information, but information must be disclosed on demand. The three most common discovery techniques are (1) the use of interrogatories, (2) the use of depositions, and (3) the use of demands for production of documents.

Interrogatories.[2] A set of interrogatories is a list of written questions sent by one party to another. In the motorcycle case, Jed may send Milly a set of interrogatories (see Document 3.4 at end of this chapter) which ask questions such as "did you consume any

---

[2] **Rule 33(a) Interrogatories**. Any party may serve upon any other party written interrogatories to be answered by the party served . . . . UTAH R. CIV. P. 33(a).

25

alcoholic beverages during the five hours immediately prior to the occurrence of the accident." Milly must respond with written answers to interrogatories (see Document 3.5 at end of this chapter). In turn, Milly may send Jed a set of interrogatories and Jed must answer them. Each party may send more than one set of interrogatories.

Depositions.[3] Lawyers for the parties may personally question other parties or witnesses and have the questions and answers reported by a court reporter. For example, Jed's lawyer suspects that Milly is faking details of her accident to avoid paying the purchase price for the motorcycle. He may question her in front of a court reporter as part of his preparation for trial. (See Document 3.6 at end of this chapter.) This questioning process is called "taking a deposition," and the resulting record of questions and answers may be used at trial.

Request for Production of Documents.[4] This is a written demand which may be made by either party. The demand accomplishes what the title suggests: a demand that the other party produce documents in its possession. For example, if Milly does not have a copy of the motorcycle purchase contract she may request that Jed produce his copy so she can photocopy it and use it at trial.

The Motion Stage

Motion for Summary Judgment. At some point in trial preparation, the pleadings and information received through discovery may suggest to one of the parties that the significant facts in the case are not in dispute and that the case should therefore be resolved in their favor, without a trial. Under those circumstances a *motion for summary judgment* may be filed. Suppose, for example, that Milly learned that the motorcycle she bought from Jed was a stolen motorcycle. If that is true, there is no point in proceeding any further with the case because Jed cannot recover for the "sale" of a stolen motorcycle which must be returned to the lawful owner. In such a case, Milly would file a motion for summary judgment and include supporting documents which show that the motorcycle was stolen. The court will grant her motion unless Jed can submit evidence that the motorcycle was not stolen, or at least submit enough evidence that ownership is a debatable issue. If the question of ownership is debatable, the court must allow the issue to go to trial.

In fact, it is Jed who files a motion for summary judgment (See Document 3.7 at end of this chapter) asking the court to dismiss Milly's Counterclaim. His view, based on the deposition of Milly, is that Milly was racing the motorcycle, and that led to her injuries, not any defect in the brakes. In his view this fact (that Milly was racing, which was the cause of her injuries) is so clear that a jury could not reach any other conclusion. Thus,

---

[3] **Rule 30(a) Depositions.** After commencement of the action, any party may take the testimony of any person, including a party, by deposition upon oral examination. UTAH R. CIV. P. 30(a).

[4] **Rule 34(a) Production of Documents.** Any party may serve on any other party a request (1) to produce and permit the party making the request, or someone acting on his behalf, to inspect and copy, any designated documents . . . or (2) to permit entry upon designated land or other property in the possession or control of the party upon whom the request is served for the purpose of inspection and measuring, surveying, photographing, testing, or sampling the property . . . . UTAH R. CIV. P. 34(a).

argues Jed, her counterclaim for injuries should be summarily dismissed leaving only the contract issue for trial. (Note that it is possible for summary judgment to resolve some, but not all, of a lawsuit.)

SUMMARY JUDGEMENT is granted if there is no genuine issue as to any material fact

The Standard for Motions for Summary Judgment. The rules of civil procedure provide, in effect, that a trial court need not conduct a trial if the result is already known. In legal jargon, the rule on summary judgment provides that a trial need not be held on an issue if "there is no genuine issue as to any material fact"[5] related to that issue. Thus, if the judge knows (beyond any reasonable dispute) that Milly was racing the motorcycle, and that was the cause of her injuries, he can grant summary judgment in favor of Jed. But, if the racing issue is debatable (meaning the jury could decide either way) there is, indeed, an issue with respect to a material (important) fact and summary judgment cannot be granted.

The following two cases illustrate the standard for granting a motion for summary judgment. In the first case, *King v. Tanner*, the question was whether the trial court properly granted summary judgment in a claim for slander. The plaintiff, King, sued the defendant, Tanner, for slander because she said that he (King) was the father of her child. DNA tests submitted to the court showed with 99.993% certainty that, indeed, plaintiff was the father of the child. Because truth is a defense to a claim of slander, the defendant moved for summary judgment dismissing the plaintiff's claim. King resisted the motion.

King v. Tanner
539 N.Y.S.2d 617 (1989)

GERARD E. DELANEY, Justice.

* * *

The test to be applied on a motion for summary judgment is that the one opposing a motion for summary judgment must produce evidentiary proof in admissible form sufficient to require a trial of material questions of fact on which he rests his claim or must demonstrate acceptable excuse for his failure to meet the requirement of tender in admissible form; mere conclusions, expressions of hope or unsubstantiated allegations or assertions are insufficient.

* * *

Mr. King has, in opposition to this motion, submitted only an affirmation by his attorney, Mr. Ferrari, which while it raised some of the issues above, is insufficient as a matter of law to oppose defendant Tanner s motion for summary judgment dismissing the first cause of action for slander * * * *

The Court having found that the admission of the DNA probe test results is proper on such a motion and plaintiffs having failed as a matter of law to sufficiently raise any material question of fact on the issue of falsity (or truth) of the alleged slander, motion by defendant Tanner to dismiss the first cause of action for slander is granted with prejudice * * * *

[Affirmed]

---

[5] **Rule 56(c) Summary Judgment.** The [summary] judgment sought shall be rendered forthwith if the pleadings, depositions, answers to interrogatories, and admissions on file, together with the affidavits, if any, show that there is no genuine issue as to any material fact and that the moving party is entitled to a judgment as a matter of law. UTAH R. CIV. P. 56(c).

This one was easy. The defendant submitted *facts* demonstrating that King was the father of the child. King introduced no *facts*. Because—on the *facts*—a judge or a jury could only reach one result (that King was the father of the child), the trial court properly granted summary judgment.

In the second case, *Randolph v. Commodore Cruise Lines*, the trial court granted summary judgment, but that ruling was appealed and reversed. The appellate court held that summary judgment should not have been granted because the central issues in the case were *not* established before trial. That is, at least one important fact was unresolved and therefore the outcome was uncertain (or debatable). Therefore, summary judgment should not have been granted:

Randolph v. Commodore Cruise Lines
589 So.2d 1019 (1991)

PER CURIAM

Commodore Cruise Lines passenger Sarah Randolph claims she sustained bodily injuries when a dining room chair she had been sitting on collapsed and she fell to the deck. We reverse the summary judgment granted in the appellee cruise line s favor.

Randolph alleged her injury occurred on June 21, 1988. On October 24, 1990, she filed the instant suit. Commodore argued that Randolph s action was time-barred by the terms of her ticket, which set forth a one-year action limitation. Randolph claimed that she had never received a ticket; thus, her suit should not be time-barred.

The important and disputed issue of fact was whether Randolph ever received a ticket. In her response to Commodore s request for admissions, Randolph admitted to complying with boarding procedures. However, she also clearly stated in the same set of responses, that she had paid cash to a fellow church member and had, in return, received a boarding pass but no ticket.

The trial court, in granting summary judgment, considered Randolph s admission of compliance with boarding procedures along with the affidavit of a ship worker who stated that boarding required presentation of a ticket and the employee s statement that this procedure is strictly complied with.

We conclude that, an issue of fact remained as to whether Randolph had received a ticket and thus could be charged with notice of the suit time limitation. This disputed fact precludes the summary judgment ordered.

Accordingly, the judgment granted in the cruise line s favor is reversed and the case is remanded for further proceedings.

Compare the decisions in *King* and *Randolph*. In *King*, the defendant submitted the paternity test results with her motion for summary judgment and the plaintiff (the alleged father) had nothing to submit in opposition to it; he was not able to claim that he had any contrary evidence on paternity to produce at trial. He could not produce enough evidence to make the question of paternity at least debatable. That being so, a trial for slander (slander is a claim that a person's reputation has been damaged with false information) must necessarily be resolved in favor of the defendant mother, and the court granted summary judgment. But, in *Randolph*, there was an unresolved dispute about whether the injured plaintiff ever received a ticket; and, until that issue was resolved, the question whether she had filed her lawsuit in time could not be resolved. Accordingly, summary judgment should not have been granted.

Returning to Jed's motion, should the judge in *Doe v. Roe* grant summary judgment? Is the evidence that Milly was racing and that racing caused her injuries debatable? In the court's view it is debatable whether she was racing, and Jed's motion for summary judgment will be denied because it is possible for a jury to conclude either that Milly was or was not racing. The court can grant summary judgment only if the only conclusion on the evidence is that Milly was racing and that (and not a defect in the brakes) was the cause of her injuries.

It should be noted that the processes of pleading and discovery are not mutually exclusive. Thus, if the discovery process uncovers facts that had not been known before, it is possible that one or more of the parties may want to amend their pleadings, and that is normally allowed. At some point, however, the pleading and discovery processes come to a close by common agreement, or by order of the court. At that point it is time for trial.

Trial Stage

TRIAL STAGE includes pretrial conference and trial

Pre-Trial Conference. In civil cases, the trial stage of litigation normally starts with a pretrial conference involving the judge, the attorneys and sometimes the parties. This is where business related to the trial is handled. The conference may take place in the courtroom, but often it takes place in a conference room, or even in the judge's chambers. The atmosphere is more like a business meeting than a trial. One item of business is that Milly has filed a demand for a jury trial and has paid the required jury fee and the judge accordingly orders that a jury will be used. In addition, Milly received hospital treatment in the amount of $350 after her motorcycle accident. To the judge it seems obvious that she received this treatment, even though the *cause* of the injuries is in dispute. Thus, he orders that the hospital bill for $350 is admitted for purposes of trial, but reserves the question of what the *cause* of the injuries was.

Also at the pre-trial conference, both parties acknowledge that there was a contract of sale for the motorcycle. That is not disputed and the judge orders the contract admitted for purposes of trial. The unresolved facts concerning the contract are whether Milly has paid as the contract requires, and whether she has an obligation to make all of the payments because a defect in the motorcycle caused her injuries.

By going through this process, the judge forces the parties to admit to propositions that are really not disputed and to focus clearly on the propositions that are disputed. By doing this it is the estimate of the judge that the case can be tried in one long day. The parties and the judge consult their calendars and agree on the day for trial. A pre-trial order including all the decisions of the conference is signed by the judge and placed in the court file.

On the scheduled day, the trial in *Doe v. Roe* proceeds in the following order:

Jury Selection. A large number of prospective jurors are present and information about them is gathered by questioning. This questioning process is sometimes called *voir dire*. The questioning may be done by the judge or by the lawyers, and each state chooses the method it prefers. In the state where *Doe v. Roe* is tried, questioning of jurors is by the judge. The purpose of the questioning is to determine the qualifications of the prospective jurors. In the process of questioning, it becomes obvious that some prospective jurors are more qualified than others. Lawyers for the two sides are allowed to "challenge" prospective jurors and have them removed from consideration. Challenges are in two forms (1) challenges for cause, and (2) peremptory challenges.

A prospective juror may be dismissed "for cause" on the motion of the judge or on the motion of one of the parties. If one of the parties proposes the dismissal of a juror, that action is called a "challenge for cause." To be dismissed "for cause" means that the prospective juror does not have a necessary qualification. For example, a juror may be disqualified because he or she is a relative of one of the parties; or, a juror may be disqualified because he or she is recovering from surgery and cannot sit for long periods of time.

In addition to challenges to cause, the parties are also allowed peremptory challenges where they are allowed to excuse prospective jurors for non-legal reasons. For example, in *Doe v. Roe*, Jed may favor people who have experience in business because he thinks they might look favorably on his attempt to collect an unpaid bill. On the other hand, Milly may favor people who look like they have a low income because she thinks these people may have been harassed by a bill collector and would sympathize with her position. Generally, the number of peremptory challenges is fixed by law.

In *Doe v. Roe*, the judge dismisses one prospective juror for cause because she is not a U.S. citizen. Thereafter, the judge proposes to allow each party three peremptory challenges, so he excuses all but 14 of the remaining prospective jurors. (At the beginning of the jury selection process, the names of prospective jurors had been arbitrarily placed in numerical order; that is, the names of prospective jurors were "drawn out of a hat," and the judge simply excuses all but the first 14 names remaining on the list of prospective jurors.) Then, starting with the plaintiff, the judge allows the plaintiff to eliminate a prospective juror, and then allows the defendant to eliminate a prospective juror, and so on, until eight jurors are left. In each instance, the attorneys (peremptorily) challenge a prospective juror they guess might be unfavorable to their case.

Opening Statements. After the jury is selected and sworn in, the trial starts with the opening statements of the attorneys. In an opening statement, an attorney is permitted to outline his or her case. In the process of this statement, the attorney gives a general road map describing the major issues, the anticipated testimony of witness and the high points of their case. The objective is to educate the jury so it will understand the evidence as it unfolds. This is not the famous, impassioned closing argument to the jury because at this point no evidence has been received to argue about.

The plaintiff's lawyer, Jane North, gives an opening statement in which she says that evidence from Jed will show that Milly owed $15,000 to Jed and that there was no good reason for not paying it. She says that it will become obvious that any talk about a motorcycle accident is just a "smoke screen" to avoid payment.

The defendant's lawyer, Frank Able, also gives an opening statement, although he could have reserved his opening statement until the beginning of the defendant's case. He admits that the money was not paid, but says that Jed's bad behavior excused or delayed payment and that Milly has an offsetting claim because the motorcycle was defective.

Plaintiff's Case. Jed Doe, the plaintiff, is the first witness. Jed says that he sold a new motorcycle to Milly, the defendant, and that it was in "mint" condition. He says that he has asked several times for payment, but no payment has been made. Milly, he says, made no complaints about the condition of the motorcycle until he began to seriously press her for payment. On cross-examination, Jed admits that he might have been a bit pushy and rude in demanding payment, but that was the only thing that seemed to get Milly's attention. After cross-examination, North rests her case.

Direct Examination. Because Jed was her witness, North is limited to a style of questioning called "direct examination." In direct examination, the attorney must use genuine questions which do not "lead" the witness; that is, her questions should not include their answer. For example, a *proper* question would be:

Q   How much did Ms. Roe agree to pay for the motorcycle?

A   She agreed to pay $15,000 for it.

In contrast, an example of an *improper* question is:

Q   Ms. Roe agreed to pay $15,000 for the motorcycle, didn't she?

A   Yes.

Cross-examination. An attorney who does not call a witness is allowed to "cross examine" the witness. The assumption is that the witness may be hostile or not friendly to the opposing attorney, who should accordingly be allowed a more rigorous style of questioning. The following is an example of cross examination by Frank Able, Milly's attorney:

Q   Mr. Doe, isn't it a fact that you were rude to Milly?

A   No

Q   But, you called her on the telephone three times in one afternoon, didn't you?

A   Well, yes.

Q   And, the last time you called, you told her that you would sue her for everything she had, didn't you.

A   It wasn't as bad as you make it sound.

Defendant's Case. After the plaintiff "rests" his case, it is time for the defendant to present her evidence. In her testimony, Milly acknowledges she has not paid for the motorcycle, but she says that she has not paid for it because it was defective. She goes on to describe an accident she had on the motorcycle when the front brakes "grabbed" and she lost traction and fell to the ground, suffering a variety of cuts and bruises. A picture is introduced into evidence showing bruises on her left leg and a cut with nine stitches on her left elbow. She was treated at a hospital emergency ward at a cost of $325, but was not admitted into the hospital. (The bill for $325 was admitted without objection.)

On cross-examination, Milly admits that she had never complained about the condition of the motorcycle until Jed got rude trying to collect the purchase price because she "didn't think the accident was that big a deal." She also admitted accelerating rapidly to about 50 mph to show Morris Conlan "what it would do." She says that was as fast as she went, but when confronted with her deposition ("about 55 mph") she admits going 55 mph, but no more than that. After cross-examination, Frank Able rests his case.

Instructions. When all of the evidence is in, the judge instructs the jury on the law that applies to the case. When the judge is finished, each of the attorneys is allowed to "argue" their case to the jury.

Plaintiff's Summation. After a break, with all of the evidence in, the summations (often called "closing arguments") begin. This is the point at which—if the movies and television are to be believed—each attorney rises and gives a dramatic and impassioned plea to the jury in behalf of the client. Sadly, though, in civil cases dealing with economic issues, the arguments tend to be more matter-of-fact and business-like than the media versions. At this point each attorney will review the evidence and attempt to persuade the jury that the evidence favors their client.

Jane North, Jed's attorney, goes first. She reminds the jury that the defendant has admitted receiving the motorcycle and not paying for it. According to her, there is no defect in the motorcycle; the accident was caused by Milly showing off. In any event, Milly was not seriously hurt and the claim for injuries was just a "smoke screen" to avoid payment. Jane closes by telling the jurors that the evidence is "clearly" in favor of Jed: he should receive payment of the unpaid purchase price, and Milly should receive nothing.

Defendant's Summation. Frank Able, Milly's attorney, sums up his case by admitting, again, that Milly owes the money. Turning a blind eye to the contract law described in the judge's instructions, Frank appeals to the jury's sense of fairness and argues that contracts should be interpreted in a human context: Jed should expect a loss in payment when he is rude and threatening. As for the motorcycle, he says that front brakes on a new motorcycle should not "grab," and that is the evidence that the machine is defective. Milly's injuries, says Frank, speak for themselves and she deserves some compensation. Jane North, Doe's attorney, is allowed some time for rebuttal argument, but she doesn't add anything new.

Jury Deliberation.[6] When the "arguments" are finished, the jury is excused from the court room. A court official, the bailiff, leads them to a private room where he leaves the judge's instructions and the exhibits on the table and leaves, closing the door behind him. He remains outside to keep intruders away and to carry messages to the judge, if there are any.

The jury members have been instructed by the judge to choose one of their number to act as "foreman." Apart from that, they are relatively free to "deliberate," to discuss the evidence and arrive at a verdict in their own manner. In the present case, the jury select one of their number as foreman, and then quickly agree that the defendant has breached the contract and she owes money to the plaintiff. That is easy enough, but then the jury has trouble deciding how much money the plaintiff should receive.

One juror argues the plaintiff should get the full $15,000 he is asking for because the judge's instructions require the jury to give the plaintiff the contract amount. This proposal loses on a 1-7 vote because the other jurors believe the plaintiff should not receive so much money because he was too pushy and maybe that was the whole problem.

Someone suggests that Jed and Milly should each be given what they were asking for: Doe should get $15,000 and Roe should get $15,000, with the result that each of them would get nothing. This time the vote is 2-6 against. The dilemma is that most of the jurors believe that the defendant owes $15,000 to the plaintiff, but they don't want to give it to him.

One juror asks the others what they will agree to. At this point, it seems as if the jury instructions are set aside as the jurors began to apply their "seat of the pants" ideas of what seems right. The bargaining begin in earnest, but along tangents. One juror, for example, observes that the plaintiff is being greedy, that he probably could have settled the lawsuit by paying Milly's hospital bills. An older woman wonders why a girl would want to ride a motorcycle?

---

[6] Based on jury deliberations described in Curt E. Conklin & Richard S. Dalebout, *If an Accountant goes to Court: Reflections on How a Jury may Decide the Case*, NEW ACCOUNTANT, September, 1995.

Finally, as a compromise, a juror suggests that Milly should at least be reimbursed for her hospital bills of $325 and $1,000 for her bruising and scars. The vote on this is 7-1 in favor, but the holdout juror votes against because no defect had actually been proved in the motorcycle. And then it is suggested that the plaintiff might not actually get all he is entitled to because he will have to pay his attorney. Tired now, someone says, "how about $15,000 for Doe and $500 for the girl," and, surprisingly, all agree.

Verdict. The jury foreman writes down the decision of the jury on a piece of paper supplied by the court (this is the "verdict") and tells the bailiff that they have finished. That message is passed on to the judge who convenes the parties in the courtroom and has the bailiff bring the jury back into the court room. The verdict is read out loud and the jury is excused.

Post-Trial Motions and Judgment. Normally, a judge will enter a judgment in the same amount as the verdict. He can only vary from the verdict if the jury decision is outside the bounds of reason. If the verdict is outside the bounds of reason, he can enter a judgment "notwithstanding the verdict." This motion is technically called a motion for *judgment n.o.v.* (n.o.v. represents the Latin *non obstante verdicto*, or notwithstanding the verdict). Jed moves for entry of a judgment (n.o.v.) of $15,000 for him and no recovery for Milly. The theory of Jed's motion is that there was no credible evidence on which the jury could grant Milly $500.

If the judge had been handling the case without a jury he would not have awarded anything to Milly. However, the jury has decided to give her $500, and he cannot say that decision was completely outside of the boundaries of reason. Therefore, he denies Jed=s motion and enters a judgment according to the jury verdict.

Appeal

APPEAL is a review of trial court decisions

Following the trial, either party may appeal issues where they believe the trial court erred. The result is an opinion in which the court affirms or reverses the decision made at the trial court level. If there was an appeal, the appellate court would either *affirm* the decision as was done in the *King* decision (discussed earlier in the chapter) if there was no error; or, it would *reverse* the decision as was done in the *Randolph* decision (also discussed earlier in the chapter).

In this case, neither of the parties is entirely happy with the decision, but their dissatisfaction is not worth an appeal because it is likely that the judgment would be affirmed by the appellate court, and, the amount of money at issue does not make an appeal worthwhile.

Problem Solving. Please turn to Chapter Problems at the end of this chapter and solve Problem 3.1.

Document 3.1

Jane North
Attorney for Plaintiff
1533 Kearns Building
Elm City 84101
Telephone: (802) 989-6473

IN THE THIRD JUDICIAL DISTRICT COURT

Jed DOE,	
Plaintiff,	COMPLAINT
vs.	
Milly ROE	Civil No. 97-125
Defendant.	

Plaintiff, Jed Doe complains and alleges as follows:

1.   Plaintiff and defendant are both residents of Bloomfield County.

2.   On or about July 1, 1996, the defendant, Milly Roe purchased a motorcycle from the plaintiff and promised to pay the sum of $15,000 therefor.

3.   Defendant Milly Roe has failed to pay $15,000 after demand.

WHEREFORE, plaintiff prays judgment against defendants as follows:

1.   For damages in the amount of $15,000.

2.   For interest and the costs of this action.

DATED this 17th day of January, 1997.

Jane North
Jane North
Attorney for Plaintiff

Frank Able
Attorney for Defendant
45 Cragun Blvd
Elm City 84101
Telephone: (802) 989-1028

IN THE THIRD JUDICIAL DISTRICT COURT

Jed DOE,
 	
          Plaintiff,
 	
vs.
 	
Milly ROE
 	
          Defendant.
	ANSWER AND
	COUNTERCLAIM
	
	Civil No. 97-125

ANSWER

Defendant, Milly Roe, answers the complaint of plaintiff as follows:

1.   Admits the allegations of paragraphs one (1), two (2) and three (3).

Affirmative Defense

1.   The motorcycle for which the sum of $15,000 was promised, was and is defective, for which reason the agreed amount should not be paid.

COUNTERCLAIM

1.   On or about July 1, 1996, the defendant purchased a motorcycle from the plaintiff as alleged in the complaint.

2.   Said motorcycle was and is defective.

3.   The defects in the subject motorcycle were the proximate cause of personal injuries suffered by the defendant in a motorcycle accident.

4.   The injuries suffered by the defendant in the subject motorcycle accident are reasonably valued at $15,000.

WHEREFORE, the defendant prays judgment as follows:

1. Dismissing the Complaint of the plaintiff, with prejudice.

2. Granting defendant judgment on her counterclaim.

3. For interest and costs of court.

DATED this 25th day of January, 1997.

Frank Able
Frank Able
Attorney for Defendant

Document 3.3

Jane North
Attorney for Plaintiff
1533 Kearns Building
Elm City 84101
Telephone: (802) 989-6473

IN THE THIRD JUDICIAL DISTRICT COURT

Jed DOE,
 	
                    Plaintiff,
 	
vs.
 	
Milly ROE
 	
              Defendant.
	REPLY
	
	Civil No. 97-125

Plaintiff, Jed Doe reply to the counterclaim as follows:

1. Plaintiff denies paragraphs one (1), two (2), three (3) and four (4) of the Counterclaim

Affirmative Defense

Plaintiff affirmative alleges that misuse caused the injuries suffered by the Defendant.

WHEREFORE, Plaintiff prays that the Counterclaim of the Defendant be dismissed with prejudice.

DATED this 2nd day of February, 1997.

Jane North
Jane North
Attorney for Plaintiff

Document 3.4

Jane North
Attorney for Plaintiff
1533 Kearns Building
Elm City 84101
Telephone: (802) 989-6473

IN THE THIRD JUDICIAL DISTRICT COURT

Jed DOE,	
Plaintiff,	PLAINTIFF'S FIRST SET OF INTERROGATORIES TO DEFENDANT
vs.	
Milly ROE	Civil No. 97-125
Defendant.	

The Plaintiff, Jed Doe, submits the following interrogatories to the defendant to be answered in the time and manner required by the Rules of Civil Procedure:

INTERROGATORY NO. 1: Describe where the motorcycle accident described in paragraph 3 of the Counterclaim took place.

INTERROGATORY NO. 2: Did you consume any alcoholic beverages during the five hours immediately prior to the occurrence of the accident?

INTERROGATORY NO. 3: How fast were you traveling at the time of the accident?

Dated this 10th day of March, 1997.

Jane North
Jane North
Attorney for Plaintiff

Document 3.5

Frank Able
Attorney for Defendant
45 Cragun Blvd
Elm City 84101
Telephone: (802) 989-1028

IN THE THIRD JUDICIAL DISTRICT COURT

Jed DOE,
 	
            Plaintiff,
 	
vs.
 	
Milly ROE
 	
          Defendant.
	DEFENDANT'S ANSWERS TO PLAINTIFF'S FIRST SET OF INTERROGATORIES
	
	Civil No. 97-125

The defendant submits the following answers to the plaintiff's first set of interrogatories.

INTERROGATORY NO. 1: State where the motorcycle accident described in paragraph 3 of the Counterclaim took place.

ANSWER: On the Beach Road, West of Elm City.

INTERROGATORY NO. 2: Did you consume any alcoholic beverages during the five hours immediately prior to the occurrence of the accident?

ANSWER: No.

INTERROGATORY NO. 3: How fast were you traveling at the time of the collision?

ANSWER: 55 miles per hour.

Dated this 20th day of May, 1997.

Frank Able
Frank Able
Attorney for Defendant

Document 3.6

Jed DOE,	
Plaintiff,	DEPOSITION OF MILLY ROE
vs.	Civil No. 97-125
Milly ROE	
Defendant.	

BE IT REMEMBERED that on Thursday, the 15th day of April, 1997, commencing at the hour of 2:00 p.m., the deposition of Milly Roe, the defendant herein, produced as a witness at the instance of the plaintiff herein, in the above-entitled action now pending in the above-named court, was taken before Jackie Webster, a Certified Shorthand Reporter. Said deposition was taken pursuant to notice and stipulation and in accordance with the Rules of Civil Procedure.

PROCEEDINGS

Milly Roe

One of the defendants herein, called as a witness by and on behalf of the plaintiff in this matter, after having been first duly sworn, was examined and testified as follows:

EXAMINATION

BY MS. NORTH:

Q   Would you just state your full name?

A   Milly Roe.

Q   You are the defendant in this action?

A   Yes, I guess.

Q   Did you purchase a motorcycle from Jed Doe in July of last year?

A   Yes.

Q   Have you paid him for it?

A   No.

Q   Has it been in your possession since that time?

A   No, my cousin rode it once.

Q   Except for that, has the motorcycle always been in your possession.

A   Most of the time.

Q   When wasn't it in your possession?

A   For a while in November.

Q   Where was it in November?

A   In the police impound lot.

Q   How did it get there?

A   I was in an accident down on the Beach Road and they took me to the Emergency Room at the hospital.

Q   Was that the accident you refer to in your Counterclaim, the one where you suffered personal injuries?

A   That's right.

Q   How did that accident happen?

A   I was going North on Beach Road and put on my brakes to make the big turn, right about where the red barn is, and I put on the brakes to slow down and they just locked up and I came off the bike.

Q   When you say they locked up, do you mean the front brakes?

A   Yeah.

Q   Was anyone else close to you also on a motorcycle?

A   Yes, Morris Conlan was.

Q   Were you racing Conlan?

A   No, we were just messing around.

Q   How fast were you going when you crashed?

A   About 55 mph.

Q   Could you have been going a little faster.

A   Maybe, but I don't think so.

Q   Didn't you crash because you were racing Conlan and you came into the turn too fast.

A   That's not true, it may have looked like we were racing, but we really weren't.

Q   How much was your hospital bill?

A $350.

MS. NORTH: I don't have any further questions.

Document 3.7

Jane North
Attorney for Plaintiff
1533 Kearns Building
Elm City 84101
Telephone: (802) 989-6473

IN THE THIRD JUDICIAL DISTRICT COURT

Jed DOE,
 	
    Plaintiff,
 	
vs.
 	
Milly ROE
 	
    Defendant.
	MOTION FOR
	SUMMARY
	JUDGMENT
	
	Civil No. 97-125

The plaintiff Jed Doe hereby moves the court for its order of summary judgment, dismissing the counterclaim, with prejudice.

This motion is based on the deposition of Milly Roe White and applicable law.

DATED this 1st day of May, 1997.

        <u>Jane North</u>
        Jane North
        Attorney for Plaintiff
        Jed Doe

Problem 3.1

The following materials relate to a lawsuit known as *Brown v. White*:

Mr. Brown. On July 11, 1994, at 2:40 A.M., a 1992 Chevrolet automobile owned and driven by Robert Brown collided with a horse. At the time of the collision, the automobile was southbound in the outside lane of state road 89, near 1100 North in Farmington, Utah. The horse, which was killed, was owned by A. B. White of Farmington, Utah. The car was damaged beyond repair. Mr. Brown suffered neck injuries and ultimately had surgery where bones in his neck were fused. He now suffers from a 15 permanent partial disability. Formerly a roofer, he must now find a new occupation.

Brown cannot afford to hire a lawyer on an hourly basis. As an alternative he and his lawyer, Marilyn Albert, have entered into a *contingent fee* agreement: Albert will represent Brown, and if she was successful she will receive 40 percent of the amount recovered as her compensation. If Albert is not successful she will receive no compensation.

a) *As a matter of opinion, is it honest (ethical) for Brown's attorney to work on a "contingent fee" basis?*

Apart from the facts of the accident, the only facts known to Brown and his lawyer are that (1) the horse was owned by A. B. White, (2) the owner of the property where the horse was kept was Michael Black and (3) a man by the name of Jed Blue may have been doing construction work on the property. Marilyn Albert prepared a Complaint (similar to Document 3.1 at the end of the chapter) and a Summons which she had served on the defendants White, Black and Blue.

b) *As a matter of opinion, is it fair (ethical) to sue another person, when liability is not clear, that is, when you are not certain that the other person (e.g. Jed Blue) was at fault?*

Mr. White. A. B. White knew, of course, that his horse had been hit by an automobile and killed. He kept the horse in a rented field next to the road where the accident occurred. After the accident he discovered that approximately ten feet of the fence had been cut and removed. At that point he did not know who had removed the fence. After being served with the summons and complaint, he looked into the matter more seriously and learned that construction work had taken place on an irrigation ditch located next to the cut in the fence. White was told by neighbors that the construction work was done by Michael Black, the man who owned the field where White kept his horse. Other neighbors said that a man named Blue was actually doing the construction work.

White was not sure who was at fault in the matter, but he believed (a) that Brown, the plaintiff, may have been negligent (the police officer's report states that Mr. Brown's speed was 65 mph in an area posted 55 mph) or (b) that Black or Blue may have caused or permitted the fence to be cut, allowing the horse out onto the road. To protect White's interests, his attorney filed an Answer (similar to Document 3.2 at the end of the chapter) to the Complaint of

Brown, and a Counterclaim (similar to Document 3.2 at the end of the chapter) against Brown.

Mr. Black. Black was surprised to be served with the summons and complaint from Brown. He knew of the accident but thought it had nothing to do with him. The cross-claim from White was likewise a surprise. These pleadings made Black realize for the first time that the construction near the fence may have been related to the accident. The irrigation ditch near the fence was being constructed by Jed Blue, Black's neighbor. Blue had asked permission to move the fence, if necessary, to get his equipment into place to dig the ditch. Black had given his consent, with the understanding that the fence would be replaced in its original condition. Black concluded that Blue, or his workers, must have been the ones who cut the fence and failed to repair it. To protect his interests, Black's attorney filed an Answer (similar to Document 3.2 at the end of the chapter) to the Complaint.

Mr. Blue. After he was served with the summons and complaint, Mr. Blue investigated and concluded that one of his workers cut the fence and failed to replace it. Mr. Blue, however, had two concerns. First, even if his workers were negligent, Blue believed the real cause of the accident was the conduct of Brown. If, Mr. Blue reasoned, Brown had been driving more carefully, he would not have hit the horse. And second, even if Brown was not negligent, the amounts of money claimed by Brown for his personal injuries and the damage to his car, and by White for the loss of his horse, appeared to be excessive. To protect Blue's interests, Blue's attorney file an Answer to the Complaint.

c) *As a matter of opinion, is it honest (ethical) for Blue to deny liability under the circumstances above when he knew that his workers cut the fence which let the horse escape onto the highway?*

Mr. Brown. When Marilyn Albert received White's Counterclaim she filed a Reply (similar to Document 3.3 at the end of the chapter) in response.

Interrogatories. Defendant White wanted to learn what Brown was doing the night of the accident. He particularly wanted to know if Brown had been drinking. The investigating officer's report suggested that Brown had been speeding (65 mph in a 55 mph zone); did Brown admit he had been going 65 mph? In addition, he wanted to know if Brown was insured. There would be little point in pursuing the suit against Brown for loss of the horse if Brown had no insurance. Hoping to get the information he wanted without a great deal of trouble or expense, White decided to submit *Interrogatories* (similar to Document 3.4 at the end of the chapter) to Brown. Brown responded to the interrogatories with *Answers to Interrogatories* (similar to Document 3.5 at the end of the chapter).

Deposition. The facts related to control of the horse had now become pivotal to the development of Brown's case. Had Mr. White failed to keep the animal fenced in? Had Blue cut down (and failed to replace) the fence for his ditch repair work? The horse had belonged to White, so Brown and Albert decided that they should take White's *deposition* (similar to Document 3.6 at the end of the chapter). They thought that White would know more about what had happened to the horse than anyone else.

Albert had her secretary call each of the other attorneys in the case to find a mutually convenient time for the deposition. Albert prepared a *Notice of Taking Depositions*. On the date and time specified in the deposition notice, Mr. White and his attorney appeared at Ms. Albert's office, where Ms. Albert and the other attorneys who wished to attend questioned Mr. White about the accident.

d) *Explain how the processes and results of using interrogatories and a deposition different.*

Motion For Summary Judgment. White thought the deposition demonstrated that he had nothing to do with the accident. He thought that the judge should dismiss Brown's claim against him without a trial because there was no evidence to support Brown's claim. White filed a *motion for summary judgment*s (similar to Document 3.7 at the end of the chapter). The plaintiff had earlier taken his deposition and in support of his motion he submitted the following excerpts from that deposition:

* * *

Q   Were you [White] aware that Jed Blue was going to be putting in an irrigation ditch?

A   No.

Q   You had no idea that was going to take place?

A   I had no idea they were going to do it.

Q   Did you ever see them working on your property?

A   Not until the morning we went out there after the accident.

Q   Now, let me ask you this. You had mentioned that the fence is a mesh fence; is that correct?

* * *

Q   You were aware of an accident involving your horse at some point in time; is that correct?

A   That's correct.

Q   When did you first become aware of that?

A   About 3:00 o'clock in the morning, the phone rang and said this is the sheriff's office at Farmington, said we want to let you know your horse was killed. So, I went over to the field. As I got to the fence, I looked over and saw the construction. Well, I went and parked and walked over and they had pinned the fence back.

e) *Should the trial court grant or deny the motion for summary judgment?*

(Assume for the moment that the motion for summary judgment was not granted and that the case proceeded to trial.) The trial was conducted just like the trial in the "motorcycle" case between Jed and Milly.

The jury verdict was (1) that Brown had been 40% negligent, White 0% negligent, Black 25% negligent and Blue 35% negligent, and (2) that Brown had suffered injuries in the amount of $100,000 and Black had suffered injuries in the amount of $1000.

f)   *Explain under what circumstances a trial court judge may grant a motion for entry of judgment n.o.v.*

g)   *Explain why it is unlikely that an appellate court would reverse in Brown v. White.*

Chapter 4
Crimes

Chapter Outline

CHAPTER OBJECTIVE: to learn what is (and is not) a crime, and the process of criminal prosecution

The objective of this chapter is to describe what is (and what is not) a crime, and, the processes by which crime is prosecuted. The chapter is organized as follows:

- *Crimes.* A crime is a violation of law which is punishable by fine or imprisonment. Only legislative bodies and authorized regulatory bodies can decide what is and what is not a crime. Criminal actions and civil actions are not mutually exclusive. Misdemeanors are lesser offenses and felonies are more serious offenses.

- *Intent.* Successful criminal prosecution requires proof that the prohibited act was done intentionally. People are presumed to intend the natural consequences of their actions.

- *Criminal Offenses.* Examples of criminal offenses are: murder, manslaughter, aggravated assault, rape, theft, robbery, burglary, receiving stolen goods, theft by deception and obstruction of justice. Each part or "element" in the definition of a crime must be proved to obtain a conviction.

- *Pleas.* There are five kinds of "pleas" to a criminal charge: not guilty, guilty, no contest, not guilty by reason of insanity, and, guilty and mentally ill.

- *Defenses.* Defenses to a criminal charge include: infancy, intoxication and entrapment.

- *Burden of Proof.* The persuasiveness of the government's case must be proof convincing "beyond a reasonable doubt."

- *Constitutional Rights.* Constitutional rights of criminal defendants include: protection against unreasonable searches, protection from arbitrary arrest, protection against "double jeopardy," protection against self-incrimination, the right to due process, a guarantee of a fair trial, and the right to reasonable bail, fines and punishment.

- *Misdemeanor Criminal Proceedings.* Misdemeanor criminal cases (including arraignment, trial and sentencing) all take place in the same court.

- *Felony Criminal Proceedings.* A person charged with a felony is either indicted by a grand jury or receives a preliminary hearing in a court of limited jurisdiction. If the preliminary hearing shows there is probable cause to believe that a crime has been committed and that the defendant committed it, the defendant is "bound over" for trial in a court of general jurisdiction where arraignment, trial and sentencing take place.

- *XIV Amendment.* The "due process" clause of the XIV Amendment incorporates the protections of the Bill of Rights and applies them to criminal prosecutions conducted by states.

Crimes

CRIME is a violation of a statute, regulation or ordinance which is punishable by fine or imprisonment

A *crime* is the violation of a statute, regulation or ordinance (a local law) which is punishable by fine or imprisonment. For example, a state legislature may enact a statute like the following relating to theft:

76-6-406. Theft — Elements.[1]
A person commits theft if he obtains or exercises unauthorized control over the property of another with a purpose to deprive him thereof.

Legislative Act. Only legislative bodies and authorized regulatory bodies can decide what is and what is not a crime. A court in a *criminal* case may not, for example, invent the crime of theft and enforce it by case law as is done in *civil* cases. (Recall the cases in Chapter 1—*Able v. Baker* and *Carr v. Doxey*—where the trial court in a civil case made up the rule of law as part of the decision-making process.) In criminal cases, a trial court *cannot* make up the substantive rule of law (e.g. "A person commits theft if he obtains or exercises unauthorized control over the property of another with a purpose to deprive him thereof") as part of the decision-making process. That is a legislative function.

That does not mean, however, that there is no place in the criminal process for rules made by trial court judges. Judges are allowed, for example, to make decisions on procedural and interpretive issues. Suppose, for example, that a student sneaks into the office of another person and uses the telephone to talk to his friend in Johannesburg, South Africa. The theft statute described above provides that taking the property of another with intent to deprive him thereof is a crime. The statute does not, however, explain what is meant by *property*. That is, is telephone service "property" for purposes of a theft statute? Although the courts may not *create* the basic definition of theft—as the legislature did in the paragraph above—they may nevertheless *interpret* the statute and determine whether intangible telephone service is "property" within the meaning of theft as defined above.

Objective. Crimes are viewed as offenses against society in general, as well as offenses against individuals, and the objective of a criminal prosecution is to promote justice by deterring criminal violations, punishing the offender, and rehabilitating him or her, if possible. This objective is different than the law governing civil actions (torts or

---

[1] UTAH CODE ANN. § 76-6-404.

contracts) where the objective of lawsuits is to compensate the injured party rather than to punish the wrongdoer.

Criminal Actions and Civil Actions. Criminal actions and civil actions are not mutually exclusive and a wrongdoer may face both criminal and civil actions arising out of the same conduct. For example, Milly, who is drunk, speeds past a stop sign and into an intersection, injuring Jed, a pedestrian. The government may prosecute Milly for the crime of driving under the influence of alcohol, and Jed may bring a civil action (tort) against her for compensation for his injuries. This is not "double jeopardy" (which is prohibited by the Fifth Amendment to the Constitution) because double jeopardy applies only to criminal punishment, and in this case only one criminal action is brought against Milly.

Misdemeanors and Felonies. Generally, crimes are divided into two categories: misdemeanors are the *less* serious offenses and felonies are the *more* serious offenses. In general, misdemeanors are punished by a fine (perhaps $1.00-$2,500) and imprisonment in the county jail, and felonies are punished by a fine (perhaps $2,500-$10,000) and imprisonment in the state prison. A limited number of felonies—usually murder—are "capital" felonies where one of the punishments is death.

Prosecution by Government. Criminal actions are prosecuted *only* by government and not by private parties. That means that the title of a criminal case will always be something like *Elm City v. Milly Jones* or *State of Kentucky v. Jed Smith*.

Problem Solving. Please turn to Chapter Problems at the end of this chapter and solve Problem 4.1.

Intentional Conduct

INTENT: in general, criminal conduct is intentional conduct

In general, criminal conduct is *intentional* conduct. If Milly causes the death of Jed by dropping a paint bucket onto his head from an overhead scaffold, it is a crime if Milly *intended* to cause Jed's death. In contrast to injuries caused by neglect or omission, the emphasis on *intentional* conduct suggests that Milly made a choice. And, if Milly has a choice (to kill Jed or not), the idea is that the existence of punishment may persuade Milly to not do what is prohibited.[2]

Punishment is used in the law of crimes as a deterrent. From the perspective of deterrence, punishment makes no sense if an act is unintentional and no choice is being made; that is, if Milly unknowingly bumped the bucket off the scaffold as she was painting, the possibility of punishment will have no deterrent effect.

---

[2] Negligent homicide is an exception to the requirement that crimes are based on intentional conduct. A person causing the death of another by means of reckless disregard for the safety of another (sometimes called "criminal negligence") may be convicted of negligent homicide.

Intent. A crime is proved if the government proves that the accused intentionally did a prohibited act. For example, if Milly takes Jed's lawnmower from his garage intending to use it and return it, but forgets, she is not guilty of theft because she does *not* have the *intent* to deprive Jed of the machine. On the other hand, if Milly takes Jed's lawnmower, intending to use it and keep it, she has committed the crime of theft because she *does* have the *intent* to deprive him of it. In the law of crimes, the concept of "criminal intent" or "evil intent" or "wrongful mental state" is sometimes labeled with the Latin phrase *mens rea* (pronounced mehns *ray*-uh).

The issue of intent (*mens rea*) can be a difficult issue in a criminal trial. Suppose, for example, that Milly, a university student, goes into her campus bookstore and stops to browse through the adventure novels. She places her textbooks on the floor and picks up two novels; then, she puts one of the adventure novels down on top of her textbooks while she turns the pages of the other novel. After a while, she places the novel she is reading back on the shelf, picks up the stack of books on the floor, and leaves the bookstore. Has Milly committed theft? She has, if she *intended* to take the novel without paying for it, and the law *presumes* that whatever she did she *intended* to do.

In a successful criminal prosecution the government must prove (1) the doing of the prohibited act, and (2) that the doing of the prohibited act was done with *mens rea*. In this case, the prosecutor proves the act of taking the book and that is the prohibited act. Milly is presumed to intend the natural consequences of her acts; therefore, if she took the book she is presumed to have intended to take the book, and this establishes *mens rea*. The result is the government has proved its case.

Presumption. But, suppose that Milly was absent-mindedly thinking of her calculus examination and never intended to take the book. Is there anything she can do? The answer focuses on the *presumption* that because she took the book without paying for it, that is what she meant to do. Something presumed is not conclusively established, and Milly may attack the presumption by telling her story. She may tell the judge or jury how the book came to be mixed with her textbooks, and about her calculus examination; and, under oath, she may tell them that she really did not intend to take the book. If they believe her, the government has not proved a necessary element of its case (*mens rea*) and their case fails and she is acquitted. On the other hand, if they do not believe her, Milly is guilty.

Problem Solving. Please turn to Chapter Problems at the end of this chapter and solve Problem 4.2.

Criminal Offenses

CRIMINAL OFFENSES: each part or "element" in the definition of a crime must be proved to obtain a conviction

Some crimes, such as murder or robbery, are well-known to the public, while other crimes such as theft by deception or obstructing justice are more obscure. A sampling of criminal offenses is provided in the following table. In each case, a criminal conviction requires proof of each piece or element of the offense, plus the existence of criminal intent.

Crimes	
Crime:	**Elements of Proof:**
Murder	Intentionally or knowingly causing the death of another
Manslaughter	Recklessly causing the death of another
Aggravated Assault	Intentionally causing serious bodily injury to another
Rape	Sexual intercourse with another person without that person's consent
Theft	Exercising control over the property of another with intent to deprive him thereof
Robbery	Intentionally taking the personal property in the possession of another from his person, against his will by means of force or fear
Burglary	Entering or remaining in a building with intent to commit a felony or theft or commit an assault on any person
Receiving Stolen Goods	Retaining or disposing of the property of another knowing that it has been stolen, or believing that it probably has been stolen
Theft by Deception	Obtaining control over property of another by deception and with a purpose to deprive him thereof
Obstruction of Justice	With intent to hinder, prevent or delay the discovery, apprehension, prosecution, conviction, or punishment of another: conceals the commission of an offense from a magistrate . . . or conceals, destroys or alters physical evidence

Elements. As noted above, in a criminal prosecution each part or "element" in the definition of a crime must be proved to obtain a conviction. For example, if Milly, a professional thief, slips a wallet out of the back pocket of her victim, Jed, so smoothly that the victim does not realize it is gone until later, may she be successfully prosecuted for *robbery*? The answer, of course, is no. Although Milly intended to do wrong, it cannot be proved that she acted "through force or fear," because her victim was not aware the wallet was being taken. Can Milly be successfully prosecuted for *theft*? The answer is yes, because acting with intent (mens rea), Milly obtained control of the property of her victim "with a purpose to deprive him thereof."

Problem Solving. Please turn to Chapter Problems at the end of this chapter and solve Problem 4.3.

Pleas.

A is a statement by a ndant of: not guilty, guilty, contest" or mentally ill

In the movies, if Milly is arrested and taken before a judge, the judge might say: "So how do you plead, guilty or not guilty?" Knowing the answer to the "guilty or not guilty" question tells the judge whether the next major step in the proceedings is a sentencing (if the defendant pleads guilty) or a trial (if the defendant pleads not guilty). This way of doing things is inherited from the English. In early English legal experience a person "pleaded" with the king or his officers for various forms of justice or leniency, depending on the nature of the problem. Thus, a person caught "red-handed" might "plead" guilty, and then ask for mercy, but a person wrongfully accused might "plead" not guilty and ask for justice. The American criminal justice system continues this practice, and today a defendant is allowed a variety of "pleas." For example, Utah criminal procedure allows a defendant five kinds of pleas:

> 77-13-1.[3] **Kinds of Pleas.** There are five kinds of pleas to an indictment or information:
> (1) Not guilty;
> (2) Guilty;
> (3) No contest;
> (4) Not guilty by reason of insanity; and
> (5) Guilty and mentally ill.
> An alternative plea of not guilty or not guilty by reason of insanity may be entered.

Not Guilty. Depending on what crime has been charged, a defendant has a variety of defenses that can be used to attempt to avoid criminal liability. The most obvious defense, of course, is the straight-forward claim that the defendant is *not guilty* of the offense. The claim may be one of mistaken identity—as in "officer, you've got the wrong guy"—or like Milly, the pickpocket, it may be based on the assertion that although she committed theft, she didn't commit the burglary she is charged with.

Guilty. Contrary to the image created by the media, most (but surely not all) persons charged with a crime are, in fact, guilty of some criminal offense and the majority plead guilty. Why is this? The answer is that when police have evidence of criminal activity, they take that evidence to a government lawyer called a "prosecutor" who evaluates the evidence and decides whether the evidence is strong enough to win a conviction. If there is not sufficient evidence to win a conviction, the prosecutor usually refuses to file criminal charges. Thus, the government typically does not file charges unless it is convinced it can win. And because they only file charges when they are convinced they can win, they usually do.

There is another dimension to the relatively high number of guilty pleas. Unfortunately, there is sometimes a "bargaining" element to criminal law. Suppose, for example, that Jed and John get in a fight and John is killed. The evidence suggests that during the fight Jed became so angry he tried to kill John, and succeeded; but, the evidence is not clear. The prosecutor tentatively files a charge of murder, but if he is convinced (then or later) that a jury will not convict on the ambiguous evidence, he offers Jed a "plea bargain." That is, he agrees to amend the criminal charges to the less serious crime of aggravated assault, if Jed will plead guilty to that charge. Jed, who has argued all along that he had no intent to commit murder, knows that, indeed, he acted with intent to cause

---

[3] UTAH CODE ANN. § 77-13-1.

serious bodily harm to John and could easily be convicted of that. By pleading guilty to aggravated assault he will avoid the risk (no matter how slight) that he will be convicted of murder. Thus, he accepts the plea bargain and pleads guilty to the reduced charge.

No Contest. In legal effect, *this is the same as a plea of guilty*, but it serves a psychologically necessary function in criminal justice. Return to the story of Milly, the student charged with stealing a book from the university bookstore. Suppose that she submits to a polygraph ("lie detector") examination to prove her innocence. To her dismay, the results show that, indeed, she intended to steal the book. Incensed, Milly continues to claim she is innocent. But, after calming down she realizes that although the polygraph results are not admissible at trial, she nevertheless is likely to be convicted. Milly is allowed to plead "no contest," meaning she did the acts amounting to theft, and she will be punished for it, but she is not forced to say the word "guilty" because she keeps insisting—without any evidence to support it—that she isn't really "guilty."

Mentally Ill. A person who is truly "insane" (mentally ill) does not understand the difference between right and wrong and is not deterred by the possibility of punishment, in the conventional sense of things. For this person a criminal proceeding is pointless. Within the bounds of fairness ("due process"), the federal government and each of the 50 states are free to devise their own definition of the mental impairment commonly referred to as "insanity" or mental illness.

A person who was, or is, mentally ill is allowed a variety of pleas that take that situation into account. A person who can establish that he or she did not have criminal intent because of mental disease or defect cannot be held criminally liable, but such persons are commonly committed to a mental institution for treatment of the condition that avoids liability. On the other hand, a person who was sane when committing a crime, but is now mentally ill will be committed to a mental institution until the time he or she is able to participate meaningfully in a criminal trial.

__Problem Solving__. Please turn to Chapter Problems at the end of this chapter and solve Problem 4.4.

Defenses

DEFENSES are diminished or nonexistent criminal intent because of infancy, intoxication, or entrapment

If a criminally prohibited *act* has occurred, most defenses focus on *intent* (mens rea), or more precisely the lack of it. This is the claim of Milly, the university student in the bookstore. Examples of defenses which attempt to excuse conduct because of diminished or nonexistent criminal intent are infancy, intoxication or entrapment.

Infancy. Knowing that at some point a child is too young to understand the difference between right and wrong for purposes of forming criminal intent, most states establish a minimum age, such as fourteen years of age, at which a person may be held criminally responsible.

Many states give specialized courts ("juvenile courts") jurisdiction over criminal conduct by persons under the age of eighteen, and in these courts the issue of intent is blurred by substituting the vaguer notion of "juvenile delinquency" in the place of conventional criminal liability. In this context, for example, it may be possible for a fifteen-year-old shoplifter to be dealt with on the basis of being "delinquent," although not criminally liable.

Intoxication. In general, the criminal laws are not friendly to the proposition of voluntary intoxication as a defense to criminal liability. By definition, voluntary intoxication is a condition entered into voluntarily, and if intoxicated Jed bludgeons Sam with a piece of pipe (aggravated assault) in the local tavern, the general view is that he must be held to intend the natural consequences of his conduct. In this perspective, Jed's decision to drink became inseparable from his decision to commit a criminal act. Only in cases of extreme intoxication have the courts been inclined to consider that intoxication overrides or diminishes criminal intent.

Entrapment. Entrapment occurs when police officers or their agents induce a person to commit a criminal offense he or she is not otherwise inclined to commit. However, merely affording a person an opportunity to commit an offense is not entrapment. A successful defense of entrapment requires proof that the suggestion and the inducement to commit a crime came from the police or police agents, and, that the defendant was not predisposed to commit a crime.

For example, in the following case, *Jacobson v. United States*, federal officers enticed the defendant into purchasing pornographic literature by targeting him with "26 months of repeated mailings and communications from Government agents and fictitious organizations." Jacobson said that he finally became curious and wanted to know what "all the trouble and the hysteria over pornography [was about] and I wanted to see what the material was." He ordered two magazines containing nude photographs of teenage and preteen boys and was thereafter charged and convicted of violating the Child Protection Act of 1984. He appealed and the case was ultimately heard by the United States Supreme Court:

Jacobson v. United States
112 S.Ct. 1535 (1992)

Justice White delivered the opinion of the Court.
* * * *

* * * [T]here can be no dispute that the Government may use undercover agents to enforce the law.

In their zeal to enforce the law, however, Government agents may not originate a criminal design, implant in an innocent person's mind the disposition to commit a criminal act, and then induce commission of the crime so that the Government may prosecute. Where the Government has induced an individual to break the law and the defense of entrapment is at issue, as it was in this case, the prosecution must prove beyond reasonable doubt that the defendant was disposed to commit the criminal act prior to first being approached by Government agents.
* * * *

* * * By the time [Jacobson] finally placed his order, he had already been the target of 26

> months of repeated mailings and communications from Government agents and fictitious organizations. Therefore, although he had become predisposed to break the law by May 1987, it is our view that the Government did not prove that this predisposition was independent and not the product of the attention that the Government had directed at [him] since January 1985.
> [Reversed]

With respect to entrapment, suppose that undercover police officers open the Ahctog[4] Pawn Shop and "spread the word" in the world of the criminally inclined that they are willing to buy "hot" merchandise. Are the persons who sell stolen goods to the pawn shop (who may or may not be the thieves who stole the goods) "entrapped" in relation to the offense of selling stolen goods? Obviously not, because the police have merely provided an opportunity for the offense to take place.

__Problem Solving__. Please turn to Chapter Problems at the end of this chapter and solve Problem 4.5.

Burden of Proof

BURDEN OF PROOF in criminal cases require proof of guilt beyond a reasonable doubt

How persuasive must the evidence of the government be in a criminal case? Is it enough, for example, that the defendant is "probably" guilty? The answer is no, it is not enough that the defendant is "probably" guilty because mere probability leaves open a substantial possibility that the defendant is *not* guilty. The measure or standard of the evidence—called the "burden of proof"—is high in criminal cases and requires evidence sufficient to persuade a jury that the defendant is guilty *beyond a reasonable doubt*.

__Problem Solving__. Please turn to Chapter Problems at the end of this chapter and solve Problem 4.6.

Constitutional Rights

CONSTITUTIONAL RIGHTS are rights described in the Bill of Rights of the United States Constitution

The Bill of Rights of the United States Constitution provides a number of "rights" that work to the benefit of criminal defendants. The following table is a list of the more significant of those constitutional rights, and the place they are found in the Constitution:

---

[5] Ahctog reversed is "Gotcha."

Constitutional Rights		
Right	**Origin**	**Example of Function**
Protection against unreasonable searches	Amendment IV	Searches must be reasonable. In general, a search warrant (based on "probable cause") is required for police to conduct searches
Protection from arbitrary arrest	Amendment IV	Arrest must be reasonable and reasonableness requires "probable cause"
Protection against "double jeopardy"	Amendment V	Defendant may not be tried twice for the same alleged criminal offense
Protection against self-incrimination	Amendment V	Defendant is not required to "testify" against himself during investigation or at trial
Due Process	Amendment V and Amendment XIV	Substance and procedure of law must be fundamentally fair
Guarantee of fair trial	Amendment VI	Defendant is entitled to speedy and public trial and trial by jury, and has the right to confront witnesses and the right to an attorney
Reasonable bail, fines and punishment	Amendment VIII	Excessive bail and fines, and cruel and unusual punishment prohibited

Problem Solving. Please turn to Chapter Problems at the end of this chapter and solve Problem 4.7.

Misdemeanor Criminal Proceedings

MISDEMEANORS are crimes which are less serious

The procedural path leading to the trial of a criminal defendant differs according to the severity of the crime. As discussed above, crimes which are less serious are called misdemeanors. Suppose that Milly is caught using a stolen credit card to buy a pair of shoes and is charged with misdemeanor theft by deception. In a routine case, she might take the following procedural path:

A Misdemeanor Criminal Trial		
Step	**Court**	**Function**
Bail Hearing	A trial court of limited jurisdiction (such as city court, municipal court or justice of the peace)	Bail (money or property deposited with the court to guarantee the defendant will return) is fixed
Arraignment (the business of Bail Hearing and Arraignment may be done together or at separate times)	Trial Court of limited jurisdiction	Defendant given copy of complaint (which states the charges); plea of guilty or not guilty entered. If plea is guilty, the defendant is sentenced; if pleas is not guilty, trial date fixed.
Trial	Trial Court of limited jurisdiction	If defendant pled not guilty, judge or jury determines guilt or innocence of defendant; if guilty, defendant is sentenced
Appeal	Appellate Court designated by statute	Case reviewed and affirmed or reversed

In Milly's case, all proceedings (except an appeal) are before the same court. Thus, if Milly wants to plead guilty, it is possible for her to appear before the judge and plead guilty and be sentenced, all at the same initial court appearance. On the other hand, if Milly believes she is not guilty—like Milly, the university student, who was charged with stealing a book from a bookstore—there may be two or more appearances before the judge before final arrangements for trial are finished. But, with or without a trial, misdemeanor cases such as these tend to be disposed of without too much delay.

Problem Solving. Please turn to Chapter Problems at the end of this chapter and solve Problem 4.8.

FELONIES are crimes which are more serious

Felony Criminal Proceedings

Felonies are serious criminal offenses. For most people it is devastating to be charged with a felony and face legal costs, public embarrassment, and the possibility of a fine and lengthy imprisonment. Thus, an immediate difference between misdemeanor and felony proceedings is that in felony proceedings the trial is preceded by either a grand jury indictment or a preliminary hearing, which is used to reduce the possibility of government misconduct and to screen out frivolous criminal charges.

In an example at the beginning of this chapter, Milly is charged with felony theft and robbery in the case where she slips a wallet out of the back pocket of her victim so smoothly that the victim does not at first realize it is gone. After her arrest, Milly is brought before the court on a First Appearance where she is apprized of her constitutional rights and her right to a preliminary hearing.[5]

A *preliminary hearing* is held in a court of limited jurisdiction to determine if there is probable cause to believe that a crime has been committed and that the defendant is the person who committed it. At the preliminary hearing, the government shows film from a surveillance camera in which the defendant can be plainly seen standing in a group of people, taking a wallet from the victim who is completely unaware of what is happening. At the end of the hearing, and noting that robbery requires evidence that the property is taken by "force or fear," the lower court judge (1) dismisses the charge of robbery upon the grounds that there *is not* probable cause to believe that robbery has occurred, and (2) "binds over" the defendant for trial on the charge of theft upon the grounds that there *is* probable cause to believe that theft has occurred. ("Double jeopardy" does not apply because the defendant is not yet in jeopardy.) In a routine felony case, the path followed by Milly might be something like the following:

A Felony Criminal Trial		
Step	**Court**	**Function**
First Appearance	Trial Court of limited jurisdiction (such as city court, municipal court or justice of the peace)	Bail is fixed and the defendant is given a copy of the complaint
Preliminary Hearing	Trial Court of limited jurisdiction	Preliminary Hearing: is there probable cause to believe offense was committed by defendant. If probable cause exists, case is "bound over" for trial
Arraignment	Trial Court of general jurisdiction (for example, the District Court)	Bail is fixed; defendant is given a copy of the revised complaint; defendant enters plea of guilty or not guilty entered; defendant sentenced if plea is guilty
Trial	Trial Court of general jurisdiction	Judge or jury determines guilt or innocence of defendant; defendant is sentenced
Appeal	Appellate court designated by statute	Case reviewed and affirmed or reversed

In Milly's case, the preliminary hearing has benefitted both the government and the defendant. Milly is benefitted because the unfounded charge of robbery was dismissed and she was saved the stress and expense of responding to it. On the other hand, with the charge of robbery eliminated, Milly is more free to deal with the charge she cannot avoid and she pleads guilty to theft and is sentenced.

---

[6] This is the normal procedure in a state criminal proceeding. A grand jury is occasionally used in state proceedings and is used in federal criminal proceedings.

Problem Solving. Please turn to Chapter Problems at the end of this chapter and solve Problem 4.9.

The Role of the XIV Amendment

Turn back to the table which illustrates the Constitutional Rights of defendants. When discussing the Bill of Rights, a student of legal history will note two things: (1) the Bill of Rights is actually the first ten amendments to the United States Constitution, and (2) the original purpose of the Bill of Rights was to protect people from the power of the *national government*, not to protect people from the powers of the individual states. Thus, the question may be asked, what does the Bill of Rights have to do with a criminal case in which, for example, the *State of Virginia* (not the United States government) is prosecuting someone?

Bill of Rights. The beginning of the answer to the question above is that in the 18th Century a *state* (for example, the State of Virginia) could prosecute a person for theft and give no thought to the "constitutional rights" described in the Constitutional Rights table. Why? Because the "constitutional rights" contained in the Bill of Rights were originally designed to protect people from the conduct of the *federal* government, *not from the conduct of a state*. That is why, for example, the First Amendment begins: *"Congress* shall make no law respecting an establishment of religion . . ." "Congress" was the federal congress, and it was that Congress that was being restrained.

The point of this discussion is to discover how the "constitutional rights" described in the Bill of Rights—which originally had no application to the conduct of states—are *now* applied to criminal prosecutions *by states*. How can the Bill of Rights, which was adopted as a restraint on the activities of the national government, be used as a restraint on the activities of a state?

Due Process. The answer to how the restraints of the Bill of Rights are now applied against the states is found in the "due process" language of the XIV Amendment, which was adopted in 1868, after the civil war. The XIV Amendment provides in part: "nor shall any *State* deprive any person of life, liberty, or property, *without due process of law.*"[6] The language of this amendment was adopted at the end of the civil war as a means of preventing the former slave states of the South from limiting the freedom of former slaves. For many years this "due process" language was relatively dormant. Then, in the 20th Century, the United States Supreme Court became convinced that many states in the Union were depriving criminal defendants of their fundamental rights. Looking around for a way to make the *states* provide criminal defendants with the rights described in the Bill of Rights, the justices of the Supreme Court returned to the "due process" language of the XIV Amendment.

Doctrine of Incorporation. The strategy adopted by the Supreme Court was simple. The justices interpreted the "due process" language of the XIV Amendment to refer

---

[7] U.S. Const. amend. XIV, § 1.

to the protections of the Bill of Rights. Thus, for example, when faced with the question could a criminal defendant in a New York court be twice prosecuted for the same criminal conduct (so-called "double jeopardy"), the answer is simple. The answer is that the XIV Amendment says that no *state* can deprive a person of life, liberty, or property (be put in jail or be fined) without *due process*, and due process means the fundamental guarantees of the Bill of Rights; therefore, New York state can not violate the protection against double jeopardy. It is by this XIV Amendment "due process" line of reasoning that the various constitutional rights described in the table describing constitutional rights are applied to the criminal justice process in the individual states. The proposition that the "due process" requirement of the XIV Amendment includes or "incorporates" the guarantees of the Bill of Rights is sometimes called the "doctrine of incorporation."

Following are two cases in which the United States Supreme Court uses the XIV Amendment to apply protections from the Bill of Rights to the conduct of states as they prosecute individuals for criminal conduct:

The Right to Counsel. The first case, *Gideon v. Wainwright*, illustrates how the United States Supreme Court uses the XIV Amendment and the doctrine of incorporation to make the right to counsel guarantee of the VI Amendment applicable to the conduct of the State of Florida. Clarence Earl Gideon was charged with burglarizing a Florida poolroom in 1961. He pled not guilty and because he was indigent he asked that a lawyer be appointed to represent him, but the court refused:

> The COURT: Mr. Gideon, I am sorry, but I cannot appoint Counsel to represent you in this case. Under the laws of the State of Florida, the only time the Court can appoint Counsel to represent a Defendant is when that person is charged with a capital offense. I am sorry, but I will have to deny your request to appoint Counsel to defend you in this case.[7]

Mr. Gideon—who was convicted of burglary—knew that the VI Amendment provided that a criminal defendant had the right "to have the Assistance of Counsel for his defense" and he kept insisting that an attorney should be appointed to represent him, even though he was being prosecuted by the State of Florida and not the United States.

His case ended up before the United States Supreme Court. In the following case, notice how the court uses the XIV Amendment to apply the guarantees of the VI Amendment to a criminal prosecution conducted by a state:

---

[8] Gideon v. Wainwright, 372 U.S. 335, 337 (1963).

> ## Gideon v. Wainwright
> ### 372 U.S. 335 (1963)
>
> Mr. Justice BLACK delivered the opinion of the Court.
>
> * * *
>
> We think the Court in *Betts* had ample precedent for acknowledging that those guarantees of the Bill of Rights which are fundamental safeguards of liberty immune from federal abridgment are equally protected against state invasion by the Due Process Clause of the Fourteenth Amendment . . . . [T]his Court has looked to the fundamental nature of original Bill of Rights guarantees to decide whether the Fourteen Amendment makes them obligatory on the States. Explicitly recognized to be of this "fundamental nature" and therefore made immune from state invasion by the Fourteenth, or some part of it, are the First Amendment's freedoms of speech, press, religion, assembly, association, and petition for redress of grievances. For the same reason, though not always in precisely the same terminology, the Court has made obligatory on the States the Fifth Amendment's command that private property shall not be taken for public use without just compensation, the Fourth Amendment's prohibition of unreasonable searches and seizures, and the Eighth's ban on cruel and unusual punishment * * * *
>
> * * *
>
> Not only these precedents but also reason and reflection require us to recognize that in our adversary system of justice, any person haled into court, who is too poor to hire a lawyer, cannot be assured a fair trial unless counsel is provided for him. This seems to us to be an obvious truth.
>
> * * *
>
> The judgment is reversed and the cause is remanded to the Supreme Court of Florida for further action not inconsistent with this opinion.
>
> Reversed.

Mr. Gideon received a new trial and this time represented by counsel—he was acquitted. ("Double jeopardy" did not apply because the reversal of the conviction was at Mr. Gideon's request, not at the request of the government. That is, the *government* did not choose to put Mr. Gideon in jeopardy a second time.)

Miranda. The following is the famous "*Miranda*" opinion, which is well-known to those who watch police shows in the media ("you have the right to remain silent . . . ." etc.). This was a criminal action by the State of Arizona against Ernesto Miranda on a charge that he kidnaped and raped an eighteen-year-old woman. Police interrogated Miranda for about two hours and received a confession from him. However, they did not advise him that he had the right to remain silent or that he had the right to have a lawyer present during questioning. In *Miranda*, as in *Gideon*, constitutional guarantees from the Bill of Rights were applied to state conduct using the doctrine of incorporation. In the following opinion, the court discusses the V Amendment guarantee against self-incrimination:

Miranda v. Arizona
384 U.S. 436 (1966)

Mr. Chief Justice Warren delivered the opinion of the Court.

The cases before us raise questions which go to the roots of our concepts of American criminal jurisprudence; the restraints society must observe consistent with the Federal Constitution in prosecuting individuals for crime. * * *

* * * *

At the outset, if a person in custody is to be subjected to interrogation, he must first be informed in clear and unequivocal terms that he has the right to remain silent. * * *

* * * *

The warning of the right to remain silent must be accompanied by the explanation that anything said can and will be used against the individual in court. This warning is needed in order to make him aware not only of the privilege, but also of the consequences of forgoing it. * * *

The circumstances surrounding in-custody interrogation can operate very quickly to overbear the will of one merely made aware of his privilege by his interrogators. Therefore the right to have counsel present at the interrogation is indispensable to the protection of the Fifth Amendment privilege under the system we delineate today.

* * * *

In order fully to apprise a person interrogated of the extent of his rights under this system then, it is necessary to warn him not only that he has the right to consult with an attorney, but also that if he is indigent a lawyer will be appointed to represent him. * * * The warning of a right to counsel would be hollow if not couched in terms that would convey to the indigent—the person most often subjected to interrogation—the knowledge that he too has a right to have counsel present.

[The court held that Mr. Miranda's confession was inadmissable because he was not advised of his rights in the manner described above. For that reason his conviction was reversed.]

Note that *Miranda* applies to persons being interrogated by the police. Keep this point in mind in answering the following problem.

__Problem Solving__. Please turn to Chapter Problems at the end of the end of the chapter and solve Problem 4.10.

Chapter Problems

Problem 4.1

Which of the following is correct:

a) All criminal actions must be brought by authority of the government.
b) "Double jeopardy" prohibits the co-existence of a civil action and a criminal action based on the same incident.
c) "Misdemeanor" refers to crimes against a person and "felony" refers to crimes against property.

Problem 4.2

Albert picks up a candy bar in a store and leaves without paying for it. When he is arrested outside the store, he apologizes and says that he meant to pay for the candy bar, but "he forgot." Explain if a prosecutor has enough evidence to charge Albert with theft?

Problem 4.3

In which of the following offenses is the necessary "intent" the most difficult to prove:

a) Murder
b) Rape
c) Aggravated Assault
d) Robbery

Problem 4.4

Explain the proper plea for a criminal defendant who committed the crime of theft in Utah, but has subsequently become mentally ill.

Problem 4.5

The police operate the Achtog Pawn Shop for the purpose of catching thieves who attempt to pawn goods they have stolen elsewhere. The police hire unsuspecting Milly, who thinks she is working as a clerk in a routine business, to work in the pawn shop. The police deliberately leave cash out on the counter to tempt Milly into stealing it. If Milly does steal the money, has she been entrapped? Explain.

Problem 4.6

Explain which of the following "burdens of proof" is most appropriately used in a criminal case:

(a) preponderance of the evidence,
(b) beyond a reasonable doubt, or
(c) beyond a shadow of a doubt.

Problem 4.7

Suppose that it is claimed that police officers in Mesa, Arizona, have arrested Sam without "probable cause." Explain what amendment(s) to the United States Constitution prohibit this conduct.

Problem 4.8

Explain what an arraignment is in criminal procedure.

Problem 4.9

May a judge at a preliminary hearing accept a plea (of guilty or not guilty) from the defendant? Explain.

Problem 4.10

Nervous Nellie is arrested on suspicion of theft and placed in the back of a patrol car. While traveling to the police station, she voluntarily (she is not questioned) starts talking and confesses to the theft. She does this hoping to get a "lighter" prison sentence. Can her confession be used against her?

Chapter 5
Intentional Torts

Chapter Outline

OBJECTIVE is to learn basic principles of intentional torts

This chapter introduces basic tort principles and then focuses specifically on intentional torts. The chapter is organized as follows:

Tort Principles

- *Tort.* The word "*tort*" means "wrong." It is a term applied to legal claims that are not categorized as crime or contract. Torts may be divided into torts of negligence and intentional torts.

- *Crimes and Torts.* Prosecution for a crime does not bar a civil lawsuit based on a tort for the same event.

- *Burden of Proof.* The burden of proof in civil actions (claims based on intentional tort are civil actions) is proof by a *preponderance of the evidence.*

- *Intent.* Intent is inferred from conduct: the law assumes that people intend the natural consequences of their actions.

Intentional Torts

- *Assault*: threats creating apprehension for physical safety.

- *Battery*: harmful or offensive physical contact.

- *False Imprisonment*: unlawfully confining another.

- *Infliction of Emotional Distress*: extreme and outrageous behavior causing emotional distress.

- *Defamation*: false statements injuring the reputation of another.

- *Invasion of Privacy*: (1) The use of a person's name or picture for commercial purposes, (2) unreasonable and highly offensive intrusions upon the seclusion of another, (3) public disclosure of private facts about another, and (4) placing another in a false light in the public eye.

- *Fraud*: (1) Misstatement of a material fact, (2) intentionally done to induce reliance by the victim, (3) justifiable reliance by the victim, and (4) damages to the victim caused by reliance on the misrepresentation.

67

- *Trespass:* Entering onto the land of another without consent.

- *Conversion*: Exercise of unauthorized, permanent dominion or control over the property of another.

Tort

The word "*tort*" is French in origin and means "wrong." In law, the word "tort" is applied to civil claims where something legally wrong is done which is neither criminal nor contractual in nature. Torts may be torts of negligence or intentional torts. Negligently driving an automobile and causing injuries is an example of a tort of negligence. Battery (harmful or offensive physical contact) is an example of an intentional tort.

Sometimes, the same conduct will be both a crime and an intentional tort. For example, Milly steals a television set from Jed for which she is criminally prosecuted and convicted, serving 30 days in jail. In Jed's eyes, the criminal prosecution is commendable, but it does nothing to compensate him financially for the stolen television set (which was never recovered). The result is that Jed files a civil lawsuit against Milly to obtain compensation, not punishment. The lawsuit is based on the law of torts.

Jed's thought process is straight forward: (1) *criminal* prosecution is good, but it's objective is punishment, not the payment of compensation, (2) breach of contract lawsuits result in compensation, but in this case there was no contract between Milly and Jed, (3) to gain compensation, he must show that Milly violated a *tort* duty called "conversion." (Conversion means the exercise of unauthorized, permanent dominion or control over the property of another.)

As noted above, the law of torts is divided into two categories: *intentional* torts and torts of *negligence*. This chapter considers intentional torts, and chapter six considers torts of negligence, and a related topic called strict liability.

Torts and Crimes

Milly's conduct in stealing Jed's television set created the possibility for two separate legal actions. In behalf of the community, the government made the decision to prosecute Milly and punish her for theft. With respect to that action, Jed could neither force the government to prosecute Milly if it didn't want to, nor could he stop the government from prosecuting Milly if he disagreed with it. In contrast, Jed made the decision to sue Milly to recover damages for conversion, and the action of the government in prosecuting Milly does not bar the lawsuit.

Many observers of the infamous "O.J. Simpson" case were confused when there was a second trial. But, in legal terms, the O.J. Simpson case was the same as the Jed and Milly case. First, the government prosecuted Mr. Simpson for the purpose of punishing him for the death of his former wife and her boyfriend. But, the standard of guilt in a criminal case is higher than the standard of liability in a civil case and the jury acquitted Mr. Simpson because it was not convinced beyond a reasonable doubt of his guilt. On the other hand, the families of the deceased people sued Mr. Simpson to recover damages for the tort of "wrongful death," and using the lower standard of liability in civil cases they were able to convince a jury that Mr. Simpson was the responsible party.

Problem Solving. Please turn to Chapter Problems at the end of this chapter and solve Problem 5.1.

Burden of Proof

URDEN OF PROOF : in civil ses the winning party must ove his or her case by a eponderance of the evidence

The burden of proof in civil cases is different than in criminal cases. In criminal cases the government is required to establish guilt "beyond a reasonable doubt;" mere probability that the defendant is guilty is not sufficient. In civil cases, however, the standard is that the winning party must prove his or her case by a *preponderance of the evidence*. Under this lesser standard, probability is sufficient and a defendant may be found liable if the evidence demonstrates that it is more likely than not that the defendant performed the acts in question.

"Elements"

LEMENTS " are the legal ings that must be proved to tablish a case

Each tort includes a list of the various things or "elements" that must be proved to establish a complete claim. For example, if Jed is to be successful in establishing his conversion claim against Milly, he must establish the following "elements" by a preponderance of the evidence: (1) that the televison belonged to him, (2) that Milly took possession of it without his permission (and he never regained possession of it) and (3) the value of the television.

On the other hand, Milly may have "defenses" which she can raise in opposition to Jed's claim. If Milly decided to contest Jed's claim she might attempt to prove things like the following: (1) that the television did not belong to Jed, but to his mother, or (2) that she was his girlfriend and he gave it to her, or (3) that the television was promptly returned to Jed. If any of these is true, Jed has failed to prove all of the elements of his tort claim and he is not entitled to judgment against Milly.

Problem Solving. Please turn to Chapter Problems at the end of this chapter and solve Problem 5.2.

Intentional Torts

VTENTIONAL TORTS: the law ssumes that people intend the atural consequences of their ctions

Intent.   The law assumes that people *intend* the natural *consequences* of their actions. Thus, if battery is defined as "the intentional act of causing harmful or offensive contact with the person of another," and Milly swings her fist at Jed, the question is not whether Milly intended to swing her fist, but whether she intended to hit Jed. Suppose that Milly swings her fist at Jed, but misses and hits Maria who is standing next to him; has battery occurred? (The answer is that a battery has occurred if Maria being hit by the wild swing is a "substantially certain" consequence of the wild swing.[1])

There are many intentional torts, some protecting persons and some protecting property. Following are some of the more common intentional torts, together with the basic elements that must be proved to establish a claim:

Intentional Torts	
Tort	**Description**
Assault	Placing another person in immediate apprehension for their physical safety
Battery	Causing harmful or offensive physical contact with another
False Imprisonment	Confining another within fixed boundaries where the victim is aware of the confinement or is harmed by it
Intentional Infliction of Emotional Distress	Extreme and outrageous behavior causing severe emotional distress
Defamation	Falsely injuring the reputation of another in writing (called libel) or orally (called slander)
Invasion of Privacy	(1) The use of a persons name or picture for commercial purposes, (2) unreasonable and highly offensive intrusions upon the seclusion of another, (3) public disclosure of private facts about another, and (4) placing another in a false light in the public eye
Fraud	(1) Misstatement of a material fact, (2) intentionally done to induce reliance, (3) justifiable reliance, and (4) damages caused by reliance on the misrepresentation.
Trespass	Entering onto the land of another without consent.
Conversion	Exercise of unauthorized, permanent dominion or control over property of another

**Problem Solving.** Please turn to Chapter Problems at the end of this chapter and solve Problem 5.3.

Assault

ASSAULT: the intentional act of placing another person in immediate apprehension for their physical safety

In the law of torts, assault is the intentional act of placing another person in immediate apprehension for their physical safety. This use of the word "assault" as a _threat_ of harm is different from the use of the word "assault" in criminal law where it is sometimes applied to the actual _act_ of harming.

---

[1] RESTATEMENT (SECOND) OF TORTS, §8A.

Apprehension. The "apprehension" which must be proved in the tort of assault is different than fear. When faced with a threat, reasonable people may become apprehensive at about the same time, if apprehension is a rational calculation of the danger involved. In contrast, people may experience fear at significantly different times. If Jed threatens to hit Milly she will be apprehensive, but whether she is fearful is uncertain. Because "apprehension" is viewed as a more certain measure, it is used instead of fear.

Physical Safety. Suppose that Randy, Jed's friend, threatens to tell Milly's parents about her conviction for theft of a television, and this makes Milly apprehensive. Is this assault? The answer is no, because assault involves a threat to the victim's *physical safety*, and Randy has threatened Milly's reputation. This same point, that one of the elements of assault is a threat to the victim's physical safety, is made in the following case:

Novak v. Rubin
514 N.Y.S.2d (1987)

[The plaintiffs received permission from the trial court to amend their complaint by adding a claim for assault. On appeal, the question was whether the trial court was correct in allowing this amendment.]

MEMORANDUM BY THE COURT. . . .

The day after the parties were involved in an automobile accident, the defendant telephoned the plaintiff Ronald Novak and threatened to harm the career of his wife, the plaintiff Rose Novak, a writer of so-called "romantic fiction", if Ronald Novak pursued any claims against the defendant arising from the accident. The defendant claimed that he would do this through his contacts in the industry, specifically through his girlfriend Katherine Falk, a publisher of "Romantic Times", a romance novel trade newsletter. . . .

[T]he ninth cause of action asserted in the proposed amended complaint alleges that by the aforementioned phone call, "[the] defendant assaulted [the] plaintiff * * * by maliciously threatening him with physical harm if an insurance claim was brought." Since a transcript of a tape recording of the telephone call reveals that the defendant specifically disavowed any intention to physically harm the plaintiffs, there is no basis for this claim, and therefore it should be dismissed.

[Reversed]

The *Novak* decision makes clear that the tort of assault involves a threat to cause physical harm. However wrong Rubin's conduct was, it was not an assault.

Battery

BATTERY: the intentional act of making harmful or offensive physical contact with another

Battery is the intentional act of making harmful or offensive physical contact with another. A principal element of battery is *intent*. Earlier in this chapter the question was raised whether battery occurs if "Milly swings her fist at Jed, but misses and hits Maria who is standing next to him?" The answer was that a battery has occurred if Maria's being hit by the wild swing is a "substantially certain" consequence of the wild swing. The following case is an illustration of that principle:

Smith v. Moran
193 N.E.2d 466 (1963)

SMITH, Justice.

The facts are not complex. Plaintiff [Smith] was a waitress at McCormick's Tavern and Restaurant on the day in question and was performing her duties in waiting on the trade. Some fifty to sixty patrons were in the place with possibly one or two tables vacant. Plaintiff and the defendant [Moran] were not acquainted and no conversation passed between them. At about eight o'clock P.M. defendant came into the restaurant with her little boy. Plaintiff heard her ask another waitress, one Dolores Nelson, if she might speak with her. Mrs. Nelson stated that she was too busy. Defendant then said, "You had better talk to me now". Plaintiff was standing with her back to a linen closet watching the trade. Mrs. Nelson was directly in front of her. Plaintiff heard a shot and heard Mrs. Nelson say, "Oh, My G-d". She heard another shot and felt a terrible pain in her left leg. She walked over to a doorway and "saw Mrs. Moran with a gun shooting at Mrs. Nelson."

* * * Defendant first contends that proof of specific intent to harm the plaintiff is required to sustain the allegations in Count I of this complaint and that such evidence is wholly lacking. She argues that the only evidence indicates an intention to harm Mrs. Nelson and not the plaintiff. * * * Prosser in his Handbook of Torts at page 33 states it this way:

> "If the defendant intends to commit an assault or a battery upon a third person, but succeeds instead in causing unintended harmful or offensive contact with the person of the plaintiff, the latter may recover as though the act were intended to affect him. In the typical case, the defendant throws a stick at A or shoots at A and hits B instead. The intent is said to be 'transferred' to the victim—which is obviously only a fiction, or a legal conclusion, to accomplish the desired result of liability."

It seems abundantly clear to us that if the act of the defendant in the instant case was unlawful, Count I properly alleges, and the evidence establishes a cause of action in the plaintiff.

In common terms, the *Smith* decision is not hard to understand. If a person performs an intentional act—swing a fist, throw a stick, shoot a gun—the law of torts holds him or her accountable for the intended consequences, and also for the reasonably foreseeable (although not specifically intended) consequences. Thus, when Moran shoots at Nelson, with Smith in harms way, Moran is said to "intend" to harm Smith, because it was reasonably foreseeable that Smith could be harmed.

Context. The question whether a battery has occurred—whether the physical contact is harmful or offensive—is very much a matter of context. For example, in one setting, contact hard enough to break bones (playing football) is acceptable, but in another setting, contact as light as a kiss (a boss kissing his secretary against her will) is not acceptable. Likewise, if John and others crowd into an elevator and Roger is pushed against the elevator wall, a battery probably has not occurred; but, if John shoves Roger against a wall in an argument, a battery probably has occurred.

The scope of the tort of battery may be explained by examining the "defenses" that a defendant may raise if sued for "battery." The following are further examples of the proposition that the existence, or non-existence, of battery is a matter of context:

Consent. One of the most common defenses to a claim of battery is the defense that the activity was consented to. A football player consents to physical contact, but a secretary kissed against her will does not. When John angrily pushes Roger against a wall there is no consent and battery occurs; but, when the same thing incidentally happens in an elevator there is consent. (In the eyes of the law, when Roger enters into an elevator, he impliedly consents to the normal and reasonable activities that occur in an elevator, even if he did not say so in words.) If a surgeon performs an operation with the permission of the patient, no battery occurs; but, an operation performed without consent is battery.

Self-Defense. A person may use physical force to defend himself. Thus, when John attempts to push Roger against a wall, Roger is entitled to resist, and in so doing he does not commit battery. But Roger's response must be reasonable and he cannot, for example, use a knife to stab John when the only apparent danger is a push against a wall.

Defense of Others. A person may use physical force to defend others. Thus, when John commences to push Roger against a wall, Roger's brother, Sam, may come to his defense and use reasonable force to protect Roger. In so doing, Sam is not liable for battery.

Defense of Property. A person may use physical force to defend property. Thus, if John breaks into Roger's house to steal a television set, Roger may use physical force to prevent the burglary. Roger may not use a gun to injure or kill John if the only threat is theft of the television, because one may not cause great bodily injury to merely protect property. But, as discussed above, Roger may use a gun to injure or kill John if that is reasonably necessary to prevent harm to himself.

Problem Solving. Please turn to Chapter Problems at the end of this chapter and solve Problem 5.4.

False Imprisonment

FALSE IMPRISONMENT: the intentional act of confining another within fixed boundaries

False imprisonment occurs when a person confines another within fixed boundaries where the victim is aware of the confinement or is harmed by it. A common circumstance involving claims of false imprisonment is the detention of suspected shoplifters. Milly, a clerk in the ABC Men's Store, observes Josh putting a silk tie in his pocket and walking out of the store. She confronts Josh and forces him to return to the manager's office and remain there until the police come. If, indeed, Josh has stolen a tie, Milly is entitled to stop him without liability. But, if Josh has not stolen a tie, she is liable for false imprisonment because she has confined him within the boundaries of the manager's office for a significant period of time, and Josh is conscious of the confinement.

Problem Solving. Please turn to Chapter Problems at the end of this chapter and solve Problem 5.5.

Intentional Infliction of Emotional Distress

The tort of intentional infliction of emotional distress is caused by a person who employs extreme and outrageous behavior which intentionally or recklessly causes emotional distress.[2] In the following case, *Samms v. Eccles,* the plaintiff brought an action for intentional infliction of emotional distress, the trial court dismissed it and the plaintiff appealed:

Samms v. Eccles
358 P.2d 344 (1961)

CROCKETT, Justice. Plaintiff Marcia G. Samms sought to recover damages from David Eccles for injury resulting from severe emotional distress she claims to have suffered because he persistently annoyed her with indecent proposals. * * *

Plaintiff alleged that she is a respectable married woman; that she has never encouraged the defendant's attentions in any way but has repulsed them; that all during the time from May to December, 1957, the defendant repeatedly and persistently called her by phone at various hours including late at night, soliciting her to have illicit sexual relations with him; and that on one occasion came to her residence in connection with such a solicitation and made an indecent exposure of his person. She charges that she regarded his proposals as insulting, indecent and obscene; and that her feelings were deeply wounded; and that as a result thereof she suffered great anxiety and fear for her personal safety and severe emotional distress for which she asks $1,500 as actual, and a like amount as punitive, damages. * * *

Due to the highly subjective and volatile nature of emotional distress and the variability of its causations, the courts have historically been wary of dangers in opening the door to recovery therefor. This is partly because such claims may easily be fabricated: or as sometimes stated, are easy to assert and hard to defend against. They have, therefore, been reluctant to allow such a right of action unless the emotional distress was suffered as a result of some other overt tort. Nevertheless, recognizing the reality of such injuries and the injustice of permitting them to go unrequited, in many cases courts have strained to find the other tort as a peg upon which to hang the right of recovery.   * * *

[But] our study of the authorities, and of the arguments advanced, convinces us that conceding such a cause of action may not be based upon mere negligence, the best considered view recognizes an action for severe emotional distress, though not accompanied by bodily impact or physical injury, where the defendant intentionally engaged in some conduct toward the plaintiff, (a) with the purpose of inflicting emotional distress, or, (b) where any reasonable person would have known that such would result; and his actions are of such a nature as to be considered outrageous and intolerable in that they offend against the generally accepted standards of decency and morality. * * * *

Reversed.

Revisit the table describing Intentional Torts and review the definition of the tort of intentional infliction of emotional distress. Note that the conduct by the defendant must be *extreme and outrageous* and the result must be *severe* emotional distress.

---

[2] RESTATEMENT (SECOND) OF TORTS, §46 (Outrageous Conduct Causing Severe Emotional Distress).

Problem Solving. Please turn to Chapter Problems at the end of this chapter and solve Problem 5.6.

Defamation

The tort of defamation consists of making false statements which damage another person's reputation. Defamatory statements may be made orally or in writing and they hold the victim up to hatred, contempt or ridicule in the community. Defamatory statements which are made *orally* are called *slander* and defamatory statements which are made in *writing* are called *libel*. Libel is a flexible classification that has been held to include such things as statues, signs, pictures and films. By definition, a statement is defamatory only if it is false, and for that reason courts have generally held that the First Amendment to the United States Constitution ("Congress shall make no law . . . abridging the freedom of speech, or of the press") does not protect a person who makes defamatory statements.

Publication. A defamatory statement can only cause harm to the victim's reputation in the community if it is communicated to third persons. For example, Milly may falsely say—in a room where only she and Jed are present—that Jed is a murderer, but that does not damage his reputation in the community. However, if the false statement is communicated to a third person, meaning someone other than Milly and Jed, then defamation has occurred. This necessary communication is called *publication* whether it is done orally or in writing.

Negligence Standard. Courts often use negligence (the absence of reasonable care) as the standard to determine whether a person will be liable for defamatory statements. If Milly writes in a high school reunion newsletter that Jed Smith (Class of '85) is in jail for murder, only to later discover that the person in jail is not Jed Smith, but a man named Jed Smithers, Milly has obviously libeled Jed Smith. But, Molly says it was an "honest mistake" because the chief of police and the school principal both told her that Jed Smith was the man in jail. If Milly exercised reasonable care in preparing her story, she was not negligent and is not liable for defamation. But, if the information she received and the level of care she exercised would not satisfy a reasonable person, she was negligent and thus liable.

Public Figures. If Jed Smith was a "public figure" like President Bill Clinton or basketball player Michael Jordan, then the negligence standard will be replaced by a liability standard sometimes called "actual malice." First Amendment values ("freedom of speech") persuade the courts that the public should be allowed considerable latitude to comment about the lives and doings of "public figures." People in politics, athletics and entertainment who intentionally place themselves in the public eye are "public figures." Events may also place a person in the public eye, and the sole survivor of an airplane crash may involuntarily become a "public figure." A public figure may recover damages for defamation only where the defendant acted with *actual malice*, which means that the defendant made false statements about the victim with *knowledge* that the statements were false or with *reckless disregard* for the truth of the statements.

The following case, *Seegmiller v. KSL, Inc.*, illustrates that courts apply different standards of conduct depending on whether the injured party is a private individual or a so-called public figure. In this case, a television station broadcast an "action report" in which it stated that horses belonging to the plaintiff were "suffering from chronic malnutrition and lack of medical attention." Claiming that this report was not true, the plaintiff sued for defamation. Using the public figure/actual malice standard, the trial court entered judgment on a directed verdict against the plaintiff. The plaintiff, asserting that he was not a "public figure," appealed.

Seegmiller v. KSL, INC.
626 P.2d 968 (Utah, 1981)

STEWART, Justice:

In this case we are called upon to decide the degree of fault which a "private figure" must prove in a defamation action against a media defendant * * *

New York Times, Co. v. Sullivan commenced the revamping of defamation law by establishing a qualified privilege for media defendants in actions brought by public officials. The Court held that a public official had to prove "actual malice" in order to establish a claim for relief. The Court defined actual malice to mean a deliberate misrepresentation or a reckless disregard for the truth or falsity of a statement. * * *

It is plain that the plaintiff in this case is not a public official. Nor does he fit the definition of a public figure. Definition of the term "public figure" is not without some difficulty, but general criteria for defining that term were established in *Gertz v. Robert Welch, Inc.* The Court stated:

> Those who, by reason of the notoriety of their achievements or the vigor and success with which they seek the public's attention, are properly classified as public figures . . . * * * Hypothetically, it may be possible for someone to become a public figure through no purposeful action of his own, but the instances of truly involuntary public figures must be exceedingly rare. For the most part those who attain this status have assumed roles of especial prominence in the affairs of society. Some occupy positions of such persuasive power and influence that they are deemed public figures for all purposes. More commonly, those classed as public figures have thrust themselves to the forefront of particular public controversies in order to influence the resolution of the issues involved. In either event, they invite attention and comment.

We are persuaded that the necessary degree of fault which must be shown in a defamation action brought by a "private individual" against the media is negligence. The need to provide the media with a margin for error is most clear and compelling in cases involving public officials and public figures. * * * But an appropriate reduction of the motivation for self-censorship, and the promotion of full-blown discussion of public issues does not require the same "breathing space' when a private individual is the plaintiff . . .

[Remanded for a trial on the merits.]

In this action the court made a mistake by applying the public figure/actual malice standard. Here, the plaintiff was merely a private individual, which means the television station owes him a higher degree of care. At trial, the standard will be one of "negligence," where the issue will be whether the television station acted with the degree of care a reasonable and prudent person would use to learn the truth of the matter the television station published.

Defenses. There are two significant defenses to a claim of defamation. First, *truth* is an absolute defense, and if Milly publicly states that Jed is a murderer—and it is true—Milly is protected from liability for defamation. This is a reasonable rule because the accurate community reputation for Jed is that of a murderer, and Milly does not damage that reputation by repeating it.

The second defense is called *privilege*, and a person with a "privilege" may make defamatory statements without liability. Legislators engaged in their official duties are privileged to speak freely without the threat of liability for defamation. For example, the United States Constitution gives senators and representatives a privilege to speak freely in the following language: "for any Speech or Debate in either House, they shall not be questioned in any other Place." Thus, if Milly is a United States senator and falsely referred to Jed Smith as a murderer in a speech before the Senate, she has an *absolute privilege* from liability for defamation.[3] But that privilege would not extend beyond her public duties, and Molly would be liable for defamation if, at a wedding reception, she falsely accused Jed Smith of being a murderer. Judges acting in their official capacities likewise have an absolute privilege.

Sometimes a privilege is conditional and not absolute. Thus, many states have a "shoplifting" statute which gives shopkeepers a conditional privilege from claims of assault, battery, shoplifting and defamation, if they act reasonably in detaining a person on a claim of shoplifting. Jed stops Milly in the parking lot of his store and in a loud and angry voice yells "stop, you lousy thief." It was later established that Milly had not stolen anything from Jed's store. Does the "shoplifting" statute protect Jed from Milly's suit for defamation? The answer is no, because Jed's privilege is conditioned on his acting reasonably. Because he did not act reasonably (it was not necessary to yell "stop, you lousy thief" to stop Milly for questioning) he has lost his conditional privilege and may be successfully sued for defamation.

Problem Solving. Please turn to Chapter Problems at the end of this chapter and solve Problem 5.7.

Invasion of Privacy

INVASION OF PRIVACY means using name or picture of another for commercial purposes; intrusions into seclusion of another; public disclosure of private facts; and, placing another in false light

The tort known as "invasion of privacy" is actually an umbrella covering four different forms of conduct—involving unwarranted intrusions into the solitude and privacy of others—for which courts have allowed recovery. Those forms of conduct are as follows:

- Using the name or picture of another for commercial purposes.

- Unreasonable and offensive intrusions upon the seclusion of another.

---

[3] U.S. CONST. art. I, §6, para. [1].

- Making public disclosure of facts concerning the private life of another.

- Placing another in a false light in the public eye.

Commercial Activities. It is an invasion of privacy to use the name or picture of another for commercial purposes. Cases in this category grow out of facts where the picture or name of another is used in advertisements to sell products such as flour or life insurance. However, the First Amendment to the United States Constitution ("Congress shall make no law . . . abridging the freedom of speech, or of the press") leads to holdings that news accounts and incidental references in books are not actionable.

Seclusion. It is an invasion of privacy to make unreasonable and offensive intrusions upon the seclusion of another. Into this category fall such activities as window peeping, unlawful searches of customer's handbags and unlawful wiretaps. On the other hand, such activities as taking a photograph of another in a public place or fingerprints taken by police are not actionable.

Public Disclosure of Private Facts. It is an invasion of privacy to give publicity to facts from the private life of another when so doing would be highly offensive to a reasonable person and the information is not of legitimate concern to the public.

False Light. It is an invasion of privacy to place another in a false light in the public eye. An example of this is a published article describing cheating by taxi drivers, with the article illustrated by a picture of a taxi driver who was not dishonest.

The following, *Stein v. Marriott Ownership Resorts, Inc.*, is a case discussing an alleged invasion of privacy. Plaintiff's husband was a Marriott employee. For entertainment at a Christmas party, Marriott employees edited otherwise innocent video interviews of their co-employees to make it appear they were describing intimate details of their personal lives. The plaintiff was not identified by name, but she believed she was identified because her husband was pictured in the video. She took offense and filed suit on the theory that her rights of privacy had been invaded. Defendants moved for summary judgment dismissing the plaintiff's complaint.

Stein v. Marriott Ownership Resorts, Inc.
323 Utah Adv. Rep. 31 (1997)

ORME, Judge:
　　In the instant case, plaintiff seeks protection of her right to privacy by asking this court to hold that she is entitled to proceed to trial to have a jury decide whether the video presented at the company Christmas Party violated her right to privacy, in that it subjected her to "shame [and] humiliation." Because plaintiff raises claims invoking all four of the distinct privacy torts, we address each below.

FIRST BRANCH: INTRUSION UPON SECLUSION

> [W]e stated that, in order to establish a claim of intrusion upon seclusion, a plaintiff must prove two elements by a preponderance of the evidence: (1) that there was "an intentional substantial intrusion, physically or otherwise, upon the solitude or seclusion of the complaining party," and (2) that the intrusion "would be highly offensive to the reasonable person." [Acknowledging that the video "was in poor taste," the court also noted that it was obviously "intended to be a joke."] * * * Plaintiff was not involved in the actual filming of the video, nor did she appear in the video. Plaintiff must show conduct by the defendant that is more intrusive than what occurred here. * * * [T]he trial court was correct in concluding that defendants' attempt at humor, albeit fatuous, did not rise to the level of being *highly* offensive to a *reasonable* person.
>
> **SECOND BRANCH: APPROPRIATION OF NAME OR LIKENESS**
>
> The second invasion of privacy tort alleged by plaintiff is the tort of appropriation of name or likeness for the benefit of another. This privacy tort . . . requires the plaintiff to establish three elements: (1) appropriation, (2) of another's name or likeness that has some "intrinsic value," (3) for the use or benefit of another.
>
> It is axiomatic that "[t]hat the interest protected by the [appropriation tort] . . . is the interest of the individual in the exclusive use of his own identity, in so far as it is represented by his *name or likeness*, and in so far as the use may be of benefit to him or to others." In order to invoke this protection, plaintiff must be able to establish that her identity in the video was represented by her name or likeness. In this case, there is absolutely no reference in the video to plaintiff's name or likeness.
>
> **THIRD BRANCH: PUBLICITY GIVEN TO PRIVATE FACTS**
>
> Turning to the facts in this case, plaintiff's claim of public disclosure of private facts must fail because there was no disclosure of any factual information regarding plaintiff's affairs.
>
> **FOURTH BRANCH: FALSE LIGHT**
>
> In the instant case, the trial court correctly concluded that the videotape did not place plaintiff in a false light. No reasonable viewer would treat the production as a factual commentary on plaintiff's sex life or any other private matter.

Suppose that it was *Mr.* Stein, the Marriott employee who had sued claiming an invasion of *his* privacy. Would the outcome be any different, or would the court continue to view the matter as a joke which no one would take seriously?

Problem Solving. Please turn to Chapter Problems at the end of this chapter and solve Problem 5.8.

Fraud

FRAUD is a misrepresentation of a material fact, intentionally done to induce reliance, with justifiable reliance and damages

Fraud is a tort in which deception is used to separate people from their property or money. For example, Milly sells a ring to Jed for $1,000. To persuade him to buy the ring, she intentionally and falsely tells him that the cut glass set in the ring is a diamond. The elements of the tort of fraud—applied to the "diamond" ring transaction—are as follows:

- *Misrepresentation of a material fact.* Milly has misstated a factual point which is relevant ("material") to Jed's decision to purchase the ring. In contrast, claims that "this is the best ring in town," and the like, are simply "puffery" and not the basis for a fraud action.

- *Intentionally done to induce reliance.* If Milly believed (wrongly) that the ring was a diamond ring there would be no fraud. Milly must act intentionally and misstate material facts for the purpose of inducing Jed to contract with her.

- *Justifiable reliance.* Jed must believe (rely) on what Milly tells him. If he knows the truth, or knows enough to be suspicious, he is not justified in relying on her assertions.

- *Damages caused by reliance on the misrepresentation.* If Milly's description of the ring as a diamond ring was in a brochure she sent to Jed, and Jed made his decision to buy the ring without reading the brochure, then Jed's loss would not be caused by the misrepresentation.

The following opinion, *Maybee v. Jacobs Motor Co.*, is based on the purchase of a 1984 Chevrolet van from an automobile dealer who represented that the van was "in good condition." Maybee, the buyer, asked no specific questions about the condition of the engine but, unknown to her, the van had a rebuilt engine using a 1966 engine block. And, as Maybee later discovered, the engine "dieseled" and leaked oil. (At trial, an expert testified that because of the high compression ratio the engine required high octane aviation fuel to run properly.)

Obviously, if Maybee had asked about the engine and was knowingly and falsely told that the engine was the original engine, fraud would be clearly demonstrated because the dealer would have made an intentional misstatement of an important fact for the purpose of inducing the buyer to purchase the van. The more difficult question is whether the more modest statement that the van is "in good condition" will suffice as the misstatement. In other words, will a measure of silence suffice as a "misstatement" where the dealer knows of the truth, and of the buyer's reliance, but remains deliberately silent? In the following opinion, the court deals with this issue:

Maybee v. Jacobs Motor Co.
519 N.W.2d 341 (1994)

Henderson, Justice.

Deceit [fraud] requires proof that the misrepresentation was material to the formation of the contract and that the other party relied on the misrepresentation to her detriment. Such misrepresentations include true statements which the maker knows or believes to be materially misleading because of the failure to state additional or qualifying matter. *Restatement (Second) of Torts* section 551(2)(e) [provides]:

One party to a business transaction is under a duty to exercise reasonable care to disclose

---

> to the other before the transaction is consummated * * *
>
> (e) *facts basic to the transaction*, if he knows that the other is about to enter into it under a mistake as to them, and that the other, because of the relationship between them, the customs of the trade or other objective circumstances, would reasonably expect a disclosure of those facts.
>
> When a person purchases a 1984 vehicle, is the presence, within that vehicle, of an engine built for a 1966 model which requires a fuel typically not used by vehicles on the road today, a fact basic to the transaction? The jury so found and this court finds that the evidence can support such a finding.
>
> Nevertheless, a new trial on all issues is warranted due to our decision on the second issue. During closing argument, Maybee's counsel stated that $1,500 would compensate his client. Somehow, the jury calculated compensatory damages at $14,750 and additionally awarded $75,000 in punitive damages. The jury verdict indicates passion and prejudice as well as inconsistencies with the instructions and law. A trial solely on Maybee's damages would require essentially the same evidence as a trial on both the substantive merits of the fraud claim and damages. Because these issues are so interwoven, we find that they are not separable. A new trial on both damages and liability is warranted even though the evidence does support liability, which remains a jury question.
>
> [Reversed for new trial on liability and damages.]

The defendant was foolish to go to trial on facts like those above. A wise attorney would have told the client that a jury is likely to be very offended when it hears about the condition of the van. Having learned it's lesson once, it is likely that this case was settled out of court and never tried again.

Problem Solving. Please turn to Chapter Problems at the end of this chapter and solve Problem 5.9.

Trespass

TRESPASS is entering onto the land of another without consent

Trespass means entering onto the land of another without consent. Trespass is classified as an intentional tort, but the motivation of the person is not a concern as long as the trespasser intends to be on the land. For example, if Milly voluntarily goes onto the land of Sam, she is a trespasser. But, if Jed forcibly carries Milly onto the land of Sam, she is not a trespasser.[4] The difference is that in the first case Milly *intends* to be on Sam's land, but in the second case she did not.

Milly may trespass even though she does not go on the land of another, she may do it using other persons or things. She may, for example, keep riding horses in the country. If a stray horse comes onto her land and she drives it into the pasture of her neighbor, she has trespassed.[5]

The most significant defense to a claim of trespass is, of course, the defense of consent. If Jed operates a flower shop, he has implied consented that members of the public may enter his shop for the purpose of conducting business. But, he may revoke that consent, and a person who refuses to leave may become a trespasser.

---

[4] RESTATEMENT (SECOND) OF TORTS §158 cmt.
[5] *Id.*

Problem Solving*.* Please turn to Chapter Problems at the end of this chapter and solve Problem 5.10.

Conversion

CONVERSION is exercising unauthorized, permanent control over the property of another

Conversion is the intentional act of exercising unauthorized, permanent control over the property of another. At the beginning of this chapter is an example in which Milly steals the television set of Jed. This is conversion, and in a civil lawsuit Jed is entitled to recover damages equal to the value of the television. Suppose, however, that Milly is a coal miner who inadvertently extends a tunnel past the boundary line between her property and Jed's property. The result is that she extracts and sells coal that belongs to Jed. This is also conversion.

In the example above, Jed is not required to prove that Milly knew that the coal she was mining and selling belonged to him, nor is he required to prove that she intended to harm him. The objective with the tort of conversion is to provide a legal mechanism for Jed to recover property that belongs to him. Milly's conduct was intentional and in that sense purposeful: she intended to mine and sell the coal, and she did. Jed receives no gift or bonus from Milly because he simply receives back what belongs to him; and, Milly is not punished because she merely returns what did not belong to her.

Chapter Problems

Problem 5.1

The "double jeopardy" clause of Amendment V of the United States Constitution provides "nor shall any person be subject for the same offence to be twice put in jeopardy of life or limb." Explain why Milly (who was both prosecuted and sued for the theft of a television) could not use a claim of "double jeopardy" to block the second legal action.

Problem 5.2

State all of the "elements" that must be proved in a successful tort action for assault. (See Intentional Torts table.)

Problem 5.3

John is telling a fish story and he intentionally throws his arms open wide to illustrate how big the fish was that he caught. Unknown to John, Mack is standing slightly behind and to the right of John and he is hit in the nose by John's hand.

    a. This is battery because John did an intentional act.
    b. This is battery because John should have looked before he swung out his arms.
    c. This is not battery because John did not intend to hit Mack.

Problem 5.4

In a "pickup" basketball game at the University gymnasium, Jed proves very adept at guarding his opponent. Jed is able to steal the ball frequently and often blocks the shot of his opponent. In frustration, Jed's opponent hits Jed in the face with his fist. Has battery occurred?

Problem 5.5

Milly is an avid skier and she goes to the local sporting goods store to examine the new Q-2 skis. Not knowing she is there, the owner locks the door and goes to the local sandwich shop and buys a sandwich which he brings back to the store to eat. The doors are locked for 15 minutes and during that time, Milly cannot leave the store. Milly, however was so engrossed with the new technical features of the Q-2 skis that she did not know, until later, that she could not have left the store if she had wanted to. Can Milly successfully sue the shop owner for false imprisonment?

Problem 5.6

Jed is homely, obnoxious and smelly (he eats a lot of garlic). On the other hand, Milly is a beautiful and intelligent person with a wonderful personality. Jed asks Milly to go with him on a date, and she says no; he asks again, and she says no; he asks again, and she says no; he asks again, and she says no. And so on. At what point in this process—if at all—has Jed committed the tort of intentional infliction of emotional distress?

Problem 5.7

Milly is a candidate for election to the city council. Milly says that Jed, her opponent, says one thing to one group, and another thing to other groups. Jed responds that Milly does the same thing and thus she is a hypocrite. The local newspaper quotes Jed's "hypocrite" comment. Can Milly successfully sue Jed for defamation?

Problem 5.8

Jed was once a child math prodigy who grew weary of the constant national media publicity. Twenty years later, as an adult, he drives a city bus and lives as a recluse in a modest three-room apartment. Timely news magazine publishes a series of articles on the theme "where are they now?" and it does an article on Jed. Jed sues Timely magazine for invasion of his privacy. Will he be successful?

Problem 5.9

Milly, a jeweler, sells a diamond ring to Jed for $900, telling him that she is giving him "the best deal in town." Later, he finds that he could have bought the same ring at another store for $750. Has Milly committed the tort of fraud?

Problem 5.10

Jed builds a shed near his house. An exceptionally strong wind dislodges the shed and blows it onto the property of Milly. Has trespass occurred?

Chapter 6
Torts of Negligence and Strict Liability

Chapter Outline

OBJECTIVE: to learn the rules relating to torts of negligence and the rules relating to strict liability

This chapter, which deals with liability for injuries caused by torts of negligence and strict liability. The chapter is organized as follows:

Torts of Negligence:

- *Analysis* to determine possible liability for negligent conduct may be determined by asking and answering four questions: (1) did the defendant have a *duty* (the foreseeability standard), (2) did the defendant *violate the duty* (violation of duty is negligence), (3) did the violation of duty *proximately cause* a legal injury, and (4) was there a legal *injury*.

- *Negligence* means violation of a legal duty. Every person has a legal duty to act as a reasonable man would act. By legal definition, a reasonable man acts to avoid an unreasonable risk of foreseeable harm to others. *Liability* means legal responsibility for negligent conduct.

- *Proximate Cause* means that negligence must be the cause in fact of foreseeable legal injuries.

- *Legal Injury* refers to the fact that not all injuries are deemed legally significant. *Damages* is a term for the amount of money to be paid on account of a legal injury.

- *Contributory Negligence* is a defense to a negligence claim. It refers to the negligence of the person making the claim, which contributed to the claimant's own injury.

- *Assumption of the Risk* is a defense to a negligence claim. It refers to risks known and voluntarily assumed, which contribute to the claimant's own injury.

- *Res Ipsa Loquitur* is a rule of evidence by which it is presumed that a defendant is negligent, after which it the defendant must prove that he or she is not negligent.

- *Comparative Negligence* is the mechanism by which multiple claims of negligence arising out of a single incident are compared and resolved.

Strict Liability:

- *Strict Liability.* Strict Liability refers to liability without fault or regardless of fault. It is applied (1) in circumstances involving unusually hazardous activities and (2) in circumstances involving defective products.

Introduction

Some torts ("wrongs") occur through negligence. An example of negligence is an automobile accident which occurs in an intersection because a driver is inattentive and fails to yield the right-of-way. In other cases, liability is strictly imposed (without intent or neglect) because a person engages in abnormally dangerous activities. An example of this is an excavation company using dynamite to remove rocks. The following discussion focuses first on torts of negligence, and then on strict liability.

Tort Analysis

NEGLIGENCE: liability for negligence is based on: (1) duty, (2) violation of duty (3) proximate cause, and (4) legal injury

Torts in which a person is said to be liable because of negligent conduct may be analyzed with a simple four-part test. To understand this four-part test, suppose that Jed digs a hole in front of his house, knowing that there is a natural gas pipe line somewhere under the surface. He knows there is a risk that he may hit the pipe line, but he nevertheless continues digging and accidently breaks it, resulting in an explosion and fire. The fire causes extensive damage to the house of Mr. Smith, Jed's neighbor.

Duty, Violation, Causation and Injury. Can Jed, acting as a reasonable man would act, *foresee* that harm would be caused to others because of his conduct? The answer is obviously yes, he can foresee harm resulting from his conduct. Therefore, he has a *duty* to refrain from digging until the location of the pipe line has been determined. If he does not refrain from digging in the area of the pipe line, he has *violated* his duty, and in the language of the law, he is said to be *negligent*. If Jed's negligence is the direct or "proximate" cause of the explosion and legal injuries, he will be liable for the payment of damages to compensate for those injuries.

This four-part analytical process (involving consideration of a duty, violation of that duty, causation and injury) may be summarized as follows:

DUTY: a person's duty is to act as a "reasonable man," and a reasonable man acts to avoid foreseeable harm

- **Duty.** Thinking as a *reasonable man,* Jed can *foresee* that digging blindly in the vicinity of a natural gas pipe line can cause harm. He can foresee harm to his neighbors and their property and he thus owes a *duty* to them to refrain from his digging activities.

- **Violation of Duty.** When Jed digs the hole, he *violates* the duty he owes to his neighbors. Violation of a legal duty is called *negligence*.

- **Proximate Cause.** If Jed's negligence is the direct, "proximate" cause of the legal injuries to Mr. Jone's house, Jed will be liable for those legal injuries.

- **Legal Injury.** Mr. Jones, whose house burned down, has suffered a legally recognizable *injury*. The dollar amount of that legal injury is called *damages.*

Each of the terms and concepts above—duty, the reasonable man standard, foreseeability, violation of duty, proximate cause, legal injury and damages—is discussed in more detail below.

__Problem Solving__. Please turn to Chapter Problems at the end of this chapter and solve problem 6.1.

Duty and It's Violation

Negligence is failing to exercise the care that a reasonable and prudent person exercises under the same or similar circumstances. The same thing, said in the language of the law, is that each person has a legal *duty* to act as a "*reasonable man*" would act. How does a "reasonable man" act? The answer is that *a reasonable man acts to avoid foreseeable harm* to others and their property.

Duty. Duty is a function of "foreseeability," because a reasonable person will act to avoid an unreasonable risk of foreseeable harm. Thus, if Jed knows (or should know) that a natural gas pipe line is near where he is digging, he can reasonably foresee hitting that pipe line and causing damage to persons and property in the vicinity. Thus, his duty is to not dig. By the same line of reasoning, if Jed does *not* know that a natural gas line is near where he is digging, he has no duty to refrain from digging because a reasonable person would not refrain from digging. It is in this fashion that foreseeability creates duty.

Violation of Duty. Violation of duty occurs when a person such as Jed has a duty (created by the existence an unreasonable of foreseeable harm) which is ignored. In contrast, if Jed digs in the area of the pipe line, not knowing that it is there, he violates no duty; and, if there is no duty, there can be no violation of duty.

The duty to act as a "reasonable man" would act does not include an obligation to be a volunteer. Thus, if Jed observes Milly drowning in the middle of her swimming pool, he does not have a legal duty to rescue her. This is so because he did nothing to cause the problem. However, in the pipe line example, Jed is a participant in the events and thus he must act to avoid the harms that his participation makes possible.

Liability is a term which is closely related to negligence. If Jed violates his duty (based on an unreasonable risk of foreseeable harm), he is said to be negligent. If his negligence is the proximate cause of injuries to others, he will be *liable* for the injuries. In this setting, liability means an obligation to pay money damages as compensation. (As a side note, is Jed "*guilty*" of negligence? Technically, the answer is *no* because the terms "guilty" and "innocent" are used in criminal cases, not civil cases. Jed would be negligent or liable, but not "guilty.")

The following case raises the question whether the defendant railroad owed a duty to the plaintiff. The railroad raised the question because— in their view— there was nothing in the circumstances which would make them "foresee" the possibility of harm to the plaintiff:

Palsgraf v. Long Island Railroad Co.
162 N.E. 99 (New York, 1928)

[Palsgraf, the plaintiff, was standing on railroad station platform, near some railroad scales, waiting for a train. A distance away, a passenger was running to catch a departing train, and railroad guards reached out to help him jump aboard. In the process, a package under the man's arm fell onto the tracks and exploded. The package, with no identifying markings on it, contained fireworks. The explosion caused the scales at the other end of the platform to fall and injure the plaintiff. At trial, the jury granted judgment in favor of the plaintiff and the defendant railroad appealed.]

CARDOZO, C. J.
* * *
The conduct of the defendant's guard, if a wrong in its relation to the holder of the package, was not a wrong in its relation to the plaintiff, standing far away. Relatively to her it was not negligence at all. * * *
* * *
* * * What the plaintiff must show is "a wrong" to herself; i.e., a violation of her own right and not merely a wrong to someone else, nor conduct "wrongful" because unsocial, but not "a wrong" to any one. * * * The risk reasonably to be perceived defines the duty to be obeyed * * * Here, by concession, there was nothing in the situation to suggest to the most cautious mind that the parcel wrapped in newspaper would spread wreckage through the station. If the guard had thrown it down knowingly and willfully, he would not have threatened the plaintiff's safety, so far as appearances could warn him. His conduct would not have involved, even then, an unreasonable probability of invasion of her bodily security. Liability can be no greater where the act is inadvertent.
* * * One who seeks redress at law does not make out a cause of action by showing without more that there has been damage to his person. If the harm was not willful, he must show that the act as to him had possibilities of danger so many and apparent as to entitle him to be protected against the doing of it though the harm was intended. * * * The victim does not sue derivatively * * * to vindicate an interest invaded in the person of another. * * * He sues for breach of a duty owing to himself.
* * * [To conclude otherwise] would entail liability for any and all consequences, however novel or extraordinary.

[Reversed.]

Suppose that Mrs. Palsgraf, the plaintiff, sued the man running to catch the train (we will call him Jed) instead of the railroad. Would she be successful in this action? The answer is found in repeating the foreseeability analysis in relation to Jed, instead of the railroad. The factual difference is that *Jed knows* what is in the package, even though the railroad did not. Knowing what is in package (explosive fireworks) can Jed foresee harm to others? The answer is that he knows that explosives can cause harm to people quite a distance away, probably including Mrs. Palsgraf. Because he can foresee that his conduct may cause harm to a group of people (including Mrs. Palsgraf) he has a duty not to do what he did. Because he violated that duty he would be liable to a person in the foreseeable group who is injured.

__Problem Solving__. Please turn to Chapter Problems at the end of this chapter and solve problem 6.2.

Proximate Cause

PROXIMATE CAUSE
 requires proof of cause in fact and legal cause

     A person is liable for negligent conduct only if that negligence is the direct cause of legal injury. The legal term for the connection between negligence and injury is *proximate cause*. The objective of "proximate cause" analysis is to separate those causes of injury which are direct from those which are remote or indirect. The concept of "proximate cause" is made up of two underling propositions which are called (a) "cause in fact" and (b) "legal cause."

     When the natural gas pipe line broken by Jed explodes, suppose that the following are the consequences: (1) the house of his neighbor, Mr. Smith, burns down; (2) thick, toxic smoke from the fire damages flowers at the nearby Fancy Floral Company; (3) Fancy Floral Company cannot deliver flowers to the wedding of their customer, Milly, and (4) because there are no flowers at her wedding, Milly suffers emotional distress.

     __Cause in Fact__. Was the negligence a cause in fact of the various injuries? A test called the *"but for"* test is sometimes used to answer the *cause in fact* question. *But for* the negligent conduct of Jed, would these injuries have occurred? The answer is *but for* the negligent conduct of Jed, the injuries would not have occurred. Therefore, Jed's negligent conduct is a cause in fact of all the injuries.

     __Legal Cause__. If the first question is whether Jed's negligent conduct was a cause in fact of the injuries, the second question is whether that conduct was the *legal cause* of the injuries? This is a question of law (and policy) not fact. The question is where to draw a line across the almost endless string of consequences of Jed's negligent conduct.

     The concept of "foreseeability" that was discussed in relation to duty is also used in relation to proximate cause. A line is drawn across the string of consequences of Jed's negligent conduct at that point where it must be said that Jed could not foresee those consequences. Thus, if Jed negligently digs in the vicinity of a natural gas pipe line (he knew the pipe was there, but ignored the risk), could he—if he acted as a reasonable man—*foresee* injury to his neighbor or his neighbor's house? The answer is that he obviously could foresee this injury and thus his negligent conduct is a *proximate cause* (it was both the cause in fact and legal cause) of the injury.

     In the following case, the court discusses foreseeability as a part of proximate cause:

> **McCain v. Florida Power Corp.**
> **593 So.2d 500 (Florida, 1992)**
>
> KOGAN, Justice.
> * * *
>
> Thomas McCain was injured when the blade of a mechanical trencher he was operating struck an underground Florida Power Corporation electrical cable. An employee of Florida Power had come out earlier and marked those areas where it would be safe to use the trencher. Although the evidence at trial was conflicting, there was some evidence indicating that McCain was in an area marked "safe" when he struck the cable. Later, a jury awarded McCain a verdict of $175,000, including a thirty-percent reduction for McCain's own comparative negligence.
>
> On appeal, the Second District reversed and remanded for entry of a directed verdict for Florida Power, concluding that the injury was not foreseeable. * * *
> * * *
>
> In the past, we have said that harm is "proximate" in a legal sense if prudent human foresight would lead one to expect that similar harm is likely to be substantially caused by the specific act or omission in question. In other words, human experience teaches that the same harm can be expected to recur if the same act or omission is repeated in a similar context. * * * However, as the *Restatement (Second) of Torts* has noted, it is immaterial that the defendant could not foresee the *precise* manner in which the injury occurred or its *exact* extent. * * * In such instances, the true extent of the liability would remain questions for the jury to decide.
>
> On the other hand, an injury caused by a freakish and improbable chain of events would not be "proximate" precisely because it is unquestionably unforeseeable, even where the injury may have arisen from a zone of risk. The law does not impose liability for freak injuries that were utterly unpredictable in light of common human experience. * * *
> * * *
>
> There * * * is sufficient evidence in this record that would justify a reasonable juror in concluding that McCain's injury was proximately caused by a breach of a duty imposed by law. * * * The * * * jury's verdict is reinstated.
>
> It is so ordered.

Is it possible to repeat what the court said (above) in *McCain* in simpler language? Suppose that Jed hits a golf ball which hits a lawn sprinkler, and then a tree, and then the top of a golf cart, and then the head of a stray dog, and then Milly, injuring her. Factually, did Jed *cause* Milly's injury? The answer is yes. However, is it also true that Milly's injury was "caused by a freakish and improbable (and unforeseeable) chain of events"? The answer to this is also yes. In such a case, said the court in *McCain*, what Jed did was the factual cause of Milly's injuries, but not the *proximate* cause of Milly's injuries. And the reason that Jed's conduct was not the *proximate* cause of Milly's injuries is because what happened was freakish, improbable and thus unforeseeable.

Using the analysis used above in *McCain*, was Jed's negligent conduct a *proximate* cause of the injury to *Fancy Floral*? The answer is probably not, because he could not *foresee* that he was putting Fancy Floral at risk. Is Jed's negligent conduct a proximate cause of the injury to *Milly*? Here, the answer is clearly no, because it was not *foreseeable*, and because this consequence was not foreseeable there is no legal cause and thus no proximate cause.

Problem Solving. Please turn to Chapter Problems at the end of this chapter and solve problem 6.3.

Injury

There is liability for negligent conduct only if it proximately causes a legally recognizable *injury*. If Jed's negligent conduct is the proximate cause of damage to his neighbor's house (it burned down) that is a legal injury. If Mr. Smith has suffered a legal injury, the next question is what to do about it, and the answer to that question is that Jed must pay *damages*. If the cost of repairing Mr. Smith's house is $150,000, that is the amount of Mr. Smith's damages. The words "injury" and "damage" are often used interchangeably.

Suppose that another neighbor of Jed's, Mrs. Jones, *thinks* (mistakenly) that her house will also burn down, but at the last second, it is saved and not damaged. Mrs. Jones is frightened but otherwise not injured. Although her temporary fright may be viewed as a form of injury, most court's would say that it is not sufficient to be legally recognizable and it is therefore not a *legal* injury.

Many harmful things may result from a negligent act, but not all of them are legally recognizable injuries. The law struggles to clearly identify those injuries it will recognize for the purpose of granting damages. Consider the following examples: in one case a widow was allowed to recover for mental anguish "for the unlawful mutilation and dissection of the body of * * * [her] deceased husband."[1] In another case a son was not allowed to recover damages for mental anguish from his father who, because of an extra-marital relationship with his mother, caused him to be born illegitimate.[2] In yet another case the court allowed damages for mental distress or anguish suffered by a consumer who drank part of the contents of a bottle of "Squirt" only to find a decomposed mouse in the bottle.[3]

Sometimes the courts refuse a recovery for social policy reasons, which was the case with the son who sued his father. At other times, however, the courts are willing to allow a recovery, but hesitate because measurement of the injury is difficult. For example, how much anguish is suffered by the person who consumed part of a dead mouse; is the anguish real or faked; and, if the anguish is real, how much money fairly compensates for the anguish?

In the following case, *Hughes v. Moore*, the defendant negligently lost control of his car, which crossed the front lawn of the plaintiff's house and onto the front porch of

---

[1] Larson v. Chase, 50 N.W. 238 (1891).

[2] Zepeda v. Zepeda, 190 N.E.2d 849 (1963).

[3] Shone Coca-Cola v. Dolinski, 420 P.2d 855 (1966).

that house. The plaintiff was standing in the doorway between the kitchen and front room and watched as the headlights of the speeding car came up to the front room picture window. As a consequence, she became nervous, could not sleep and experienced pains in her chest and arms. She could not continue to breast-feed her three-month-old baby because of a lack of milk. A psychiatrist said that the plaintiff experienced "anxiety reaction, with phobia and hysteria." Consider, as the court wrestles with whether it will allow recovery for emotional damages alone, or whether there is safety in allowing recovery for emotional damages only if accompanied by physical injuries:

Hughes v. Moore
197 S.E.2d 214 (Virginia, 1973)

I'ANSOR, JUSTICE.
* * *
We adhere to the view that where conduct is merely negligent, not willful, wanton, or vindictive, and physical impact is lacking, there can be no recovery for emotional disturbance alone. We hold, however, that where the claim is for emotional disturbance *and* physical injury resulting therefrom, there may be recovery for negligent conduct, notwithstanding the lack of physical impact, provided the injured party properly pleads and proves by clear and convincing evidence that his physical injury was the natural result of fright or shock proximately caused by the defendant's negligence. In other words, there may be recovery in such a case if, but only if, there is shown a clear and unbroken chain of causal connection between the negligent act, the emotional disturbance, and the physical injury.
* * *
In the case at bar, there was evidence that Moore suffered physical injuries which were the natural result of the fright and shock proximately caused by Hughes's tortious conduct.
[Affirmed]

The assumption behind the *Hughes* decision is that the existence of a physical injury gives assurance that claims of an accompanying mental or emotion harm are genuine and not fabricated. Some states accept this assumption. Other states are willing to deal with claims of mental or emotional harm independent of any associated physical injury.

Problem Solving. Please turn to Chapter Problems at the end of this chapter and solve problem 6.4.

At this point we make a change of emphasis. In the discussions above, the emphasis has been on what a plaintiff must prove to win a tort case. Now the emphasis shifts to what a defendant may prove to block the plaintiff and prevent the plaintiff from winning.

The Defense of Contributory Negligence

CONTRIBUTING NEGLIGENCE is a defense to a claim of negligence

Contributory negligence is a defense to a claim of negligence. Return to the problem in which Jed digs a hole in front of his house and suppose that he was digging the hole to build a fence between his house and that of Mr. Smith, and that Mr. Smith was helping him. If Mr. Smith knows there is a natural gas pipe line in the vicinity, he will also be negligent for the same reasons that Jed is negligent. That is, knowing there is a natural gas pipe line in the vicinity, he can foresee harm as the result if he participates in digging. "Contributory negligence" is a term applied to the negligence of a person making a claim. Thus, if Mr. Smith makes a claim against Jed, it is correct to say that Jed is negligent and Mr. Smith is "contributorily" negligent. Mr. Smith is contributorily negligent because his negligence contributes to his injuries.

On the other hand, if Jed's house also burns down, he may turn the tables and make a claim against Mr. Smith. In this context (with Jed as the plaintiff), the terminology changes and Mr. Smith's conduct is referred to as negligence and Jed's conduct is referred to as contributory negligence. Contributory negligence is a defense because a person uses it to show that the claimant should not recover because the claimant's injuries were caused by the claimant.

<u>Contributory Negligence as a Bar to Recovery</u>. Historically, contributory negligence was a bar to recovery. Another way of saying the same thing is that in former years only a non-negligent plaintiff could recover from other parties. In the past, under this rule, Mr. Smith could not recover from Jed because Mr. Smith is contributorily negligent, and, Jed could not recover from Mr. Smith because Jed is contributorily negligent.

This historical rule, that contributory negligence is a bar to recovery, has been abandoned in most states. In most states,[4] it has been replaced by a system known as "comparative negligence" in which the negligence (and contributory negligence) of the parties are compared and parties are allowed to recover from each other in proportion to their degree of fault (negligence). (The details of comparative negligence are discussed later in this chapter.)

<u>Problem Solving</u>. Please turn to Chapter Problems at the end of this chapter and solve problem 6.5.

<u>The Defense of Assumption of the Risk</u>

ASSUMPTION OF THE RISK
is a defense to a claim of
negligence

Assumption of the risk is another defense to a negligence claim. Returning again to Jed's pipe line accident, suppose that a photographer from the local newspaper wants to climb down into the hole and take pictures while crews are repairing the broken pipe. In this instance, the temporary risk of further explosion and fire is a known factor; that is, the photographer knows there has been an explosion and there is a continuing risk of another explosion. Understanding that risk, the photographer assumes the risk and climbs down into the hole. If the photographer (1) knows the risk, and (2) voluntarily assumes the risk, that conduct is a defense to a claim of negligence if an injury occurs.

Thus, if a worker negligently turns on the natural gas too soon and a wrench creates a spark and another explosion, the photographer has assumed the risk involved and that assumption of the risk is a defense for Jed and the gas company, just as contributory

---

[4] *See,* footnotes 5-7.

negligence is a defense. Just like contributory negligence, assumption of the risk was historically a bar to recovery in a negligence action. And just as it is with contributory negligence, assumption of the risk as a bar to recovery has been included in a comparative negligence system in which the proportion of fault (be it contributory negligence or assumption of the risk) is handled on a proportional basis. (Again, the details of comparative negligence are discussed later in this chapter.)

Problem Solving. Please turn to Chapter Problems at the end of this chapter and solve problem 6.6.

At this point, we make another shift of emphasis. At the first of the chapter, the discussion was about the plaintiff's case; then, the discussion turned to the defendant's case. Now, the emphasis shifts to rules which affect the manner in which the evidence of *both parties* is presented and analyzed. First discussed is a doctrine known as *res ipsa loquitur* which deals with relatively unusual cases where the obligation to prove (or disprove) the existence of negligence makes an unexpected shift from the plaintiff to the defendant. Next discussed are the rules that deal with who wins where *both* parties (plaintiff *and* defendant) are negligent. These rules are called *comparative* negligence.

Res Ipsa Loquitur

RES IPSA LOQUITUR: a rule of evidence where negligence by the defendant is presumed, but may be rebutted

The doctrine known as *res ipsa loquitur* applies to the occasional negligence case where a judge must change the normal order of things. In the normal order of things, a case begins with the plaintiff presenting evidence that the defendant was negligent; then, the defendant presents evidence that he was not. *Res ipsa loquitur* deals with those relatively rare cases where a judge decides that it is better to reverse this order and to *presume* that the defendant was negligent and require that the defendant put on evidence that he was *not* negligent, if he can.

A Rule of Evidence. *Res ipsa loquitur* is thus different than contributory negligence and assumption of the risk because those two are defenses to a claim of negligence whereas *res ipsa loquitur* is a rule that deals with the burden of proof (on the question of negligence).

Res ipsa loquitur is a Latin phrase that means "the facts speak for themselves." Under what circumstances will "the facts speak for themselves" and persuade a judge to shift the burden of proof regarding negligence? There are two requirements: (1) that the events causing injury must be of a sort that "do not ordinarily occur in the absence of negligence," and (2) that the instrumentalities involved must have been within the "exclusive control" of the defendant. For example, a passenger injured in a falling elevator may find it difficult to obtain evidence of negligence, even though it seems reasonable that negligence would usually be the cause of such an event. In such a case, the passenger would start her case by trying to convince the judge that this kind of event does not ordinarily occur in the absence of negligence and that the elevator was in the exclusive control of the defendant elevator company. If the judge is persuaded, negligence is presumed and the elevator company has the burden to prove that it was not negligent.

Suppose that Jed suffers internal injuries in the natural gas pipe line explosion and those injuries are surgically repaired by Dr. Milly who accidently leaves a surgical sponge in Jed's abdominal cavity. In a malpractice action, if Jed can establish the two requirements, (1) that leaving a surgical sponge in an abdominal cavity does not normally occur in the absence of negligence, and (2) that the surgeon (and her assistants) had exclusive control of the instrumentalities, then the burden of proof will shift to Dr. Milly and she may prove—if she can—that she was not negligent.

In the following case, the trial court applied *res ipsa loquitur* to a situation in which a lady was injured when the automatic door at a supermarket closed prematurely and injured her.

Madden v. Carolina Door Controls, Inc.
449 S.E.2d 769 (North Carolina, 1994)

ORR, Judge.

The first issue presented is whether * * * the charge [jury instructions] on the doctrine of *res ipsa loquitur* was improper under the facts presented. * * *

* * *

"The doctrine of *res ipsa loquitur* is merely a mode of proof and when applicable it is sufficient to carry the case to the jury on the issue of negligence. However, the burden of proof on such issue remains upon the plaintiff." [Citations omitted.] "*Res ipsa loquitur* (the thing speaks for itself) simply means that the facts of the occurrence itself) *warrant an inference of defendant's negligence,* i.e. that they furnish circumstantial evidence of negligence where direct evidence of it may be lacking." [Citations omitted.]

* * *

Thus, all the evidence, viewed most favorably for the plaintiff, permitted the jury to infer negligence on the part of defendant Carolina. The automatic door caused plaintiff's injuries; the automatic doors do not ordinarily close and knock people down after they have been checked and serviced without some negligent action or omission; Defendant Carolina warranted that its servicing and safety checks were performed in such a manner so as to make the automatic doors safe for their ordinary use; Defendant Carolina had such control and management of the maintenance of the automatic door that it had superior means for determining the cause of the sudden closure on Mrs. Madden * * *

* * *

No error.

In this case, it was likely that the exact cause of the malfunction (assuming there was a malfunction) remained unknown. Thus, the effect of applying *res ipsa loquitor*—where the defendant was not able to rebut the presumption of negligence—was to resolve the case in favor of the plaintiff on the liability issue. Unresolved, of course, is proof of the amount of the plaintiff's injuries.

Problem Solving. Please turn to Chapter Problems at the end of this chapter and solve problem 6.7.

COMPARATIVE NEGLIGENCE: negligence of each party is expressed as a percentage of all negligence and the percentage of each party is compared

Comparative Negligence

Comparative negligence is the term that applies to the method by which multiple claims of negligence arising out of a single incident are compared and resolved. For example, two persons have possible claims that arise out of the original natural gas pipe line explosion: (1) Mr. Smith claims that Jed's negligence caused him personal injuries and caused his house to burn down, and (2) Jed claims that Mr. Smith's negligence caused him personal injuries. Mr. Smith claims $300,000 from Jed and Jed claims $100,000 from Mr. Smith.

As discussed above, the courts historically employed a rule that a party which was contributorily negligent could not recover damages from another party to those events. (Recall that under that old rule neither Mr. Smith nor Jed could recover because each of them appeared to be negligent or contributorily negligent to some degree.)

The rule that contributory negligence is a bar to recovery is generally viewed as too harsh and it has been abandoned in most states. Instead, most states have adopted a comparative negligence system. A typical *comparative* negligence system operates as follows:

- All of the legal wrong-doing in an event (negligence, contributory negligence, assumption of the risk, etc.) is lumped together and assigned a total of 100%.

- The 100% of fault is allocated among the participants according to the degree of their legal fault.

- The dollar amount of the damages of each party is reduced by the percentage of their fault.

- The method of comparing negligence is described in the law of each state. One method of comparison is referred to as the "pure" comparative negligence, and the other methods are referred to as "modified" comparative negligence.

"Pure" Comparative Negligence. In a so-called "pure" comparative negligence system[5] no party is automatically eliminated from the possibility of recovery, no matter how great their negligence. Thus, in the natural gas pipe line incident, it is *possible* that Jed, or Mr. Smith, can recover damages whether the percent of their negligence is as little as one percent or as great as 99%. The dominant feature of this system is that a party is not automatically barred from the possibility of recovery simply because the percent of his or her negligence is too great.

---

[5] States using a "pure" comparative negligence system include: Alaska, Arizona, California, Florida, Kentucky, Louisiana, Michigan, Mississippi, Missouri, New Mexico, New York, Rhode Island and Washington. 57B AM. JUR. 2D *Negligence* §1142.

Example. In all comparative negligence systems, the first task is to determine the percent of negligence attributable to each party *and* the amount of damage suffered by each party. Thus, Jed may be 60% at fault and suffer $100,000 in damages (personal injuries); and, Mr. Smith may be 40% at fault and suffer $300,000 in damages (personal injuries and damage to his house). Under these facts, using the "pure" comparative negligence system, the amount of damage Jed caused to himself is first subtracted from his damages ($100,000 less 60% leaves $40,000) and the same is done for Mr. Smith ($300,000 less 40% leaves $180,000). The result is that Jed is entitled to $40,000 from Smith, and Smith is entitled to $180,000 from Jed. Offsetting these two sums, the net result is that Smith will recover $140,000 from Jed.

Percentages of Negligence Switched. In contrast, consider the result if the percentages of negligence in the example above are switched and Jed is only 40% at fault while Mr. Smith is 60% at fault. Under these facts (with the amount of damages as described above), Jed's potential recovery, less reduction for his negligence, is $60,000. On the other hand, Mr. Smith's potential recovery, less reduction for his negligence is $120,000. Comparing these two sums ($120,000 and $60,000), the net result is that Mr. Smith is entitled to recover $60,000 from Jed.

The critical point in this last scenario (Jed at 40% and Mr. Smith at 60%) is that a party who is *more negligent* (but suffering greater damages) is allowed to recover from a party who is *less negligent* (but suffering less damages). This result, with a party who is *more* negligent recovering from a party who is *less* negligent, is not permitted in the modified comparative negligence systems.

"Modified" Comparative Negligence. The critical difference between a "pure" comparative negligence system and a "modified" comparative negligence system is that a modified system does not allow a party who is *more negligent* to recover from a party who is *less negligent*. This difference is accomplished by inserting language into the comparative negligence statute which provides that a party can recover from another only if the negligence of the recovering party is "*not as great*" as the negligence of the other person.[6] Another way of saying *almost* the same thing is a comparative negligence statute that provides that a party can recover from another only if the negligence of the recovering party is "*not greater*" than the negligence of the other person.[7] (The slight language difference in the two forms of modified comparative negligence systems is discussed below.)

Results Compared. Compare the results produced by the two systems (pure and modified) using the facts from the first version of the natural gas pipe line story. In the

---

[6] States using a "modified" ("not as great") comparative negligence system include: Arkansas, Colorado, Idaho, Kansas, Maine, North Dakota, Utah, West Virginia and Wyoming. 57B AM. JUR. 2D *Negligence* §1147.

[7] States using a "modified" ("not greater than") comparative negligence system include: Massachusetts, Minnesota, Montana, Nevada, new Hampshire, New Jersey, Ohio, Oklahoma, Oregon, Pennsylvania, Texas, Vermont and Wisconsin. 57B AM. JUR. 2D *Negligence* §1149.

pure system, with Jed 60% at fault and Smith 40% at fault, Smith recovered $140,000 from Jed. (Jed was entitled to $40,000 and Smith was entitled to $180,000, with Smith receiving $140,000 after the offset.) In the first version of the natural gas pipe line story, using a *modified* system, however, Jed can recover nothing because he is more negligent than Smith; but, Smith (after reducing his damages by the percent of his negligence) can recover $180,000 from Jed. Thus, the pure system results in $140,000 for Smith, but the modified system results in $180,000 for Smith.

Percentages of Negligence Switched. What if the proportions of fault are switched to those in the second natural gas pipe line story, where Jed is 40% at fault and Smith is 60% at fault? Under these facts, and using a pure system, Smith received $60,000 from Jed, even though Smith was more negligent than Jed. How is the result changed if a modified system is used? Using a modified system, Smith can recover nothing from Jed because he is more negligent than Jed. On the other hand, after reducing his damages by the amount of his negligence, Jed can recover $60,000 from Smith. Thus, under these facts, the *pure* system results in $60,000 for *Smith*, but the *modified* system results $60,000 for *Jed*.

50%/50%. As noted above, some modified comparative negligence systems allow recovery only if the negligence of the recovering party is "*not as great*" as the negligence of the other person. But, other modified systems allow recovery only if the negligence of the recovering party is "*not greater*" than the negligence of the other person. The language difference is significant if the jury assesses the negligence at an even 50% for each party. With negligence assessed at 50%/50%, the "*not as great*" language bars recovery by either party because a party cannot recover unless his or her negligence is "not as great" as the negligence of the other party. (At 50%/50% the negligence of each party is, in fact, *as great* as the negligence of the other party.) In contrast, the "*not greater*" language allows recovery if the jury finds negligence at 50%/50% because each party has shown that his or her negligence is not greater than the negligence of the other party. (In this last alternative, the party actually recovering damages would be the party with the greatest amount of damage, after offsets.)

"Defenses" in a Comparative Negligence System. When using a comparative negligence system, "negligence," "contributory negligence" and "assumption of the risk" are treated the same. All of them are lumped together for the purpose of assessing a percentage of "negligence."

In the following case, *Rigtrup v. Strawberry Water Users Ass'n*, plaintiffs, owners of a poultry business, sued their electricity supplier alleging that the supplier negligently caused a power outage which resulted in the suffocation of 40,000 chickens. Defendants asserted that the plaintiffs had assumed the risk of a power outage because their electrical system was not adequate, and, they had not installed an emergency generator. The plaintiff was found by the jury to have "assumed the risk" of loss from a power failure. Based on that finding, the jury then apportioned percentages of fault and found against the defendant power company.

> ### Rigtrup v. Strawberry Water Users Ass'n
> ### 563 P.2d 1247 (1977)
>
> CROCKETT, Justice:
>
> * * *
>
> The trial court submitted the issues as to defendant's negligence and plaintiffs' contributory negligence under appropriate instructions as to the duty of each party to exercise the degree of care which ordinary reasonable and prudent persons would exercise under the circumstances. It also explained to the jury that if they found the parties negligent, they should allocate the degree of negligence which each party contributed to the loss of the chickens. Pursuant thereto the jury answered * * * that the plaintiffs were negligent, which contributed 90 per cent to the loss; and that the defendant was negligent, which contributed ten per cent to the loss.
>
> The "Comparative Negligence Statute" * * * states:
>
>> Contributory negligence shall not bar recovery in [any] action . . . to recover damages for negligence . . ., if such negligence was not as great as the negligence . . . of the person against whom recovery is sought, but any damages allowed shall be diminished in the proportion to the amount of negligence attributable to the person recovering. As used in this act, "contributory negligence" includes "assumption of the risk."
>
> As is apparent from its language the purpose of that statute was to abolish contributory negligence as a complete defense and thus avoid the harshness which sometimes resulted when a party seeking redress was himself negligent, but only to a minor degree, in relation to the total causation of his injury or damage, but which nevertheless defeated his right to recovery. Injustices which sometimes resulted under that rule can now be minimized or avoided because, under the quoted statute, a party who has suffered injury through the negligence of another, may recover, even though negligent himself, if his contributory negligence is not as great as the negligence of the party who injured him. And conversely, if the negligence of the defendant wrongdoer is greater (presumably 51% or more of the total negligence) than that of the injured plaintiff (presumably 49% or less of the total negligence), the latter may recover any damages caused, diminished by the percentage of his own negligence.
>
> In conformity with the purpose and the express provisions of that statute, based on the findings of the jury that the negligence of the plaintiffs themselves was greater (90%) than the negligence of the defendant (10%), the trial court properly entered judgment for the defendant.
>
> [Judgment for the defendant affirmed.]

Just preceding the *Rigtrup* opinion is a discussion of the three ways "comparative negligence" can be used to resolve cases where both the plaintiff and the defendant have been negligent. Note the state statute quoted in the opinion and identify which of the three comparative negligence variations was used.

__Problem Solving__. Please turn to Chapter Problems at the end of this chapter and solve problem 6.8.

STRICT LIABILITY: liability without fault (without negligence)

At this point we leave the world of negligence as a basis for recovery and switch to consideration of another theory of recovery, which is called strict liability.

Strict Liability

Strict Liability refers to liability without fault or regardless of fault. Among other things, "fault" refers to conduct such as negligence, which is discussed above. (In the <u>Palsgraf</u> opinion at the beginning of this chapter, the railroad was not liable to Mrs. Palsgraf because it's employees were not negligent; that is, they were without "fault.") In contrast, the doctrine of strict liability imposes liability *without* proof of negligence or "fault."

In what circumstances are the courts willing to impose strict liability, meaning liability without proof of fault? The answer is (1) in circumstances involving unusually hazardous activities, and (2) in circumstances involving defective products.

Hazardous Activities. Strict liability is applied in cases where the court determines that the activity causing injury was unusually hazardous. Courts impose this doctrine as a matter of social policy to help ensure that people engaging in activities which are unusually hazardous to the public will be held responsible for the harms they cause. Courts have held that such things as using explosives, keeping wild animals or crop dusting (with toxic chemicals) are unusually hazardous activities.

If an injury is caused by an unusually hazardous activity, the plaintiff must prove (1) that the defendant, in fact, engaged in an unusually hazardous activity, (2) that the activity proximately caused injury to the plaintiff, and (3) the extent of the injury suffered by the plaintiff.

In the following case, *Klein v. Pyrodyne Corp.*, people injured by fireworks brought suit and asserted that the court should resolve the case using a theory of strict liability, and not other theories such as negligence:

Klein v. Pyrodyne Corp.
810 P.2d 917 (Washington, 1991)

GUY, Justice.

The plaintiffs in this case are persons injured when a rocket at a public fireworks exhibition went astray and exploded near them. The defendant is the pyrotechnic company hired to set up and discharge the fireworks. The issue before this court is whether pyrotechnicians are strictly liable for damages caused by fireworks displays. We hold that they are. * * *

* * *

The Kleins contend that strict liability is the appropriate standard to determine the culpability of Pyrodyne because Pyrodyne was participating in an abnormally dangerous activity.
* * *

* * *

Section 520 of the Restatement lists six factors that are to be considered in determining whether an activity is "abnormally dangerous". The factors are as follows:

(a) existence of a high degree of risk of some harm to the person, land or chattels of others;

(b) likelihood that the harm that results from it will be great;

> (c) inability to eliminate the risk by the exercise of reasonable care;
>
> (d) extent to which the activity is not a matter of common usage;
>
> (e) inappropriateness of the activity to the place where it is carried on; and
>
> (f) extent to which its value to the community is outweighed by its dangerous attributes. * * *
>
> * * *
>
> We find that the factors stated in clauses (a), (b), and (c) are all present in the case of fireworks displays. Any time a person ignites rockets with the intention of sending them aloft to explode in the presence of large crowds of people, a high risk of serious personal injury or property damage is created. That risk arises because of the possibility that a rocket will malfunction or be misdirected. Furthermore, no matter how much care pyrotechnicians exercise, they cannot entirely eliminate the high risk inherent in setting off powerful explosives such as fireworks near crowds.
>
> * * *
>
> CONCLUSION
>
> We hold that Pyrodyne Corporation is strictly liable for all damages suffered as a result of the July 1987 fireworks display. Detonating fireworks displays constitutes an abnormally dangerous activity warranting strict liability. * * *

Product Liability. A modified form of strict liability is also applied in *product liability* cases. A product liability case is one where a person is injured because the design or manufacture of a product poses an unreasonable risk of injury to the purchaser or user. Examples include defects in products like trampolines, ladders or recreational vehicles. Courts impose strict liability in this context based on the assumptions (1) that manufacturers of products profit from the products they sell and they can afford to compensate those injured through the use of their products, and (2) by including the cost of claims as part of their pricing structure they can spread the cost of claims among all product users.

The liability of manufacturers is not absolute, and the defenses of assumption of the risk or abusing the product may be used by a manufacturer to fend off claims by those who knowingly engage in misuse of the product which contributes to their own injury.

(The subject of product liability is discussed more fully in Chapter Nineteen.)

Problem Solving. Please turn to Chapter Problems at the end of this chapter and solve problem 6.9.

Problem 6.1

State the four-part test for tort actions based on a theory of negligence.

Problem 6.2

In the *Palsgraf* case in the chapter, suppose that the package carried by the passenger (the man that the guards helped onto the train) was bright orange in color with the words "AAA Fireworks" on the side. In what way—if any at all—would this change the outcome in the case?

Problem 6.3

The concept of "foreseeability" is used to establish duty and it is also used to determine whether proximate cause exists. There is a *difference* in how foreseeability is used in duty as opposed to proximate cause. It is a tough question, but can you identify the difference?

Problem 6.4

Which of the following is most correct:

a)   There is no liability for injuries which are not specifically foreseeable.

b) There is no liability if there is no duty.

c) There is no duty if there is no proximate cause.

Problem 6.5

Under the old "contributory negligence" system (the system that was used before the newer "comparative negligence" system), what was the maximum amount of money a contributorily negligent plaintiff could recover?

Problem 6.6

Explain the *difference* between the defenses of contributory negligence and assumption of the risk:

Problem 6.7

Explain if *res ipsa loquitur* is a "defense" to a claim of negligence:

Problem 6.8

Not long after "comparative negligence" was adopted in Utah, the Utah Supreme Court was faced with a case in which the jury verdict included percentages of negligence which were something like this: plaintiff (40%), defendant #1 (26%) and defendant #2 (34%). If the plaintiff's injuries were $100,000, how much, if anything, can the plaintiff recover from either or both defendants?

Problem 6.9

Explain, does "foreseeability" have any application in a strict liability case?

Chapter 7
Introduction to Contracts

Chapter Outline

OBJECTIVE: to learn basic terms and concepts related to contract law

This chapter introduces the law of contracts. The objective of this chapter is to learn introductory terms and concepts related to contract law. This chapter is followed by seven other chapters which describe various details of the contracting process. The chapter is organized as follows:

- *Importance of Contracts.* Contracts are the "building blocks" of business. They are the means by which businesses enter into the relationships where labor is obtained, money transferred and goods exchanged.

- *Contract Defined.* A contract may be defined as a promise or a set of promises for the breach of which the law gives a remedy, or the performance of which the law in some way recognizes as a duty.

- *Elements of a Contract.* A valid contract is made up of five elements: (1) offer, (2) acceptance, (3) consideration, (4) capacity and (5) lawful purpose.

- *Contract Classification.* Contracts may be classified as follows: (1) bilateral contract, (2) unilateral contract, (3) express contract, (4) implied in fact contract, (5) executory contract, (6) void contract, (6) voidable contract, and (7) unenforceable contract.

- *Two Sets of Rules.* There are two sets of contract rules: the older contract rules of the "common law," and the newer contract rules in the Sales article of the Uniform Commercial Code.

- *Sales Article.* The Sales article in the Uniform Commercial Code applies to transactions in "goods." In mixed transactions (a contract deal with both goods and services) the law applicable to the dominant part of the contract is applied. Sales rules are modified common law rules.

Importance of Contracts

CONTRACTS are the building blocks of business

Contracts are the "building blocks" of business. They are the means by which businesses enter into the relationships where labor is obtained, money transferred and goods exchanged. For example, consider how many contracts may have gone into the production of the sheet of paper on which this page of text is written:

Contracts
1. Corporation formed by use of **contracts**
2. Corporation **contracts** to buy forest
3. Corporation **contracts** with loggers to cut down trees
4. Corporation **contracts** with railroad to transport logs
5. Corporation **contracts** to sell logs to paper manufacturer
6. Manufacturer **contracts** to produce paper (lease building, buy chemicals, buy equipment, hire employees and advertise, etc.)
7. Wholesaler **contracts** to buy paper in bulk from manufacturer
8. Wholesaler **contracts** to sell paper to publisher
9. Publisher **contracts** with writer for writing and publication of book
10. Publisher **contracts** to sell finished book to bookstore
11. Bookstore **contracts** to sell book to student

Problem Solving. Please turn to Chapter Problems at the end of this chapter and solve problem 7.1.

Contract Defined

A *contract* may be defined as follows:

A contract is *a promise* or a *set of promises* for the breach of which the law gives a *remedy,* or the performance of which the law in some way recognizes as a *duty*.[1]

CONTRACT DEFINITION: a contract is a promise or a set of promises which the courts will enforce

A close reading of the definition above shows (1) that contracts are made of *promises*, but (2) not all promises are contracts—only the promises which the law will enforce with a legal *remedy* or recognize as a *duty* are contracts. For example, Milly may promise to pay Jed $1000 to beat up Sam, and Jed agrees. This arrangement is a *set of promises*, but the law obviously will not enforce it with a remedy (with money damages) or as a duty (with a court order) because it does not have a lawful purpose. By definition, this arrangement is not a contract. On the other hand, if Milly promises Jed $1000 if he will paint her house, and he agrees, an enforceable set of promises (a contract) has been entered into.

Problem Solving. Please turn to Chapter Problems at the end of this chapter and solve problem 7.2.

---

[1] RESTATEMENT (SECOND) CONTRACTS, §1.

Elements of a Contract

The arrangement above (Milly promises to pay Jed to beat up Sam) is obviously not a valid contract, but other arrangements are not so clear. For example, it is not uncommon for people to object to a "contract" on the grounds that one of the parties was too young, or one of the parties cheated, or the deal was not fair, or one of the parties did not perform his or her part of the deal. And so on. The essence of their argument is that the existence of these or other defects means that the courts should not enforce the promises with a remedy or as a duty. And they will be correct, some promises should not be recognized as contracts; yet, others should. For the student, the problem is to know *which* sets of promises will be enforced and which will not.

CONTRACT ELEMENTS are offer, acceptance, consideration, capacity and lawful purpose

Which promises will be enforced, and which will not? It is helpful to say that, in general, all valid contracts are made up of five elements:

1. Offer,
2. Acceptance,
3. Consideration,
4. Capacity, and
5. Lawful purpose.

If "a promise or a set of promises" satisfy all five of these requirements there is a valid contract:

- *Offer and Acceptance.* The promises which may become a contract are created in a process of offer and acceptance. In it's simplest form, Milly *offers* to sell her house to Jed for $200,000 and Jed *accepts* that offer; if the other contract elements are satisfied, a contract will exist. The existence of fraud, misrepresentation, duress and undue influence in the process of offer and acceptance may invalidate that process. (The process of offer and acceptance is discussed in Chapter 8 and the problems of fraud, misrepresentation, duress and undue influence are discussed in Chapter 9.)

- *Consideration.* Promises made in the process of contracting must be supported by consideration, which means that in return for promises made, the other party will incur a loss, detriment or change of legal position. In the example above, Milly promises to transfer her house to Jed. Is Milly's promise supported by consideration? The answer is yes, Jed's promise to transfer $200,000 to Milly is consideration. Similarly, is Jed's promise to transfer $200,000 to Milly supported by consideration? The answer is yes, Milly's promise to transfer her house to Jed is consideration. (The requirement of consideration is discussed in Chapter 10.)

- *Capacity.* Agreements will not be enforced if the parties do not have the capacity to understand the subject matter, nature and consequences of the contract promises they make. Minors under the age of 18 years or an elderly person suffering from Alzheimer's disease are examples of persons who do not have sufficient capacity to contract. (The requirement of capacity is discussed in Chapter 11.)

- *Lawful Purpose.* A contract must have a lawful purpose. Contracts related to gambling (where gambling is prohibited), to commit a crime, or to do an act prohibited by public policy are examples of "contracts" without a lawful purpose. (The requirement of a lawful purpose is discussed in Chapter 11.)

Satisfying the five elements above means that a contract has been formed. There are, however, other concerns and activities associated with contracts including: (1) must a contract be in writing (Chapter 12); (2) the creation of third party interests (Chapter 13); (3) the obligation of contract performance (Chapter 14); and, (4) the remedies available in the event of contract breach (Chapter 14).

Problem Solving. Please turn to Chapter Problems at the end of this chapter and solve problem 7.3.

Contract Classification

The discussion above focuses on the basic elements necessary to form and enforce all contracts. In addition, there are many descriptive labels placed on contracts which describe such things as the process of their formation, whether the promises of the parties come from words, actions or law, and whether the resulting contract is valid and enforceable. In a sense, this is no different than taking the subject of automobiles (cars) and subdividing it into how the cars were manufactured (by General Motors or Chrysler), what is their function (passenger cars and racing cars) and whether the cars may be operated (has the car been licensed, registered and insured). Following are seven basic contract classifications or terms:

BILATERAL CONTRACT has two promises

Bilateral Contract. In a bilateral contract, the offer and the acceptance are both in promise form: Milly promises to transfer her car to Jed who responds by promising to transfer $1000 to Milly. This transaction thus includes two promises ("*bi*" means two) and the contract is referred to as a "bilateral" contract.

UNILATERAL CONTRACT has one promise

Unilateral Contract. In a unilateral contract the offer is in promise form, but the acceptance is not. In a unilateral contract the offer contains a promise, and it is the expectation of the offeror (the person making the offer) that the offeree (person receiving the offer) will respond with performance, not with a promise. For example, Jed robs a bank and the bank offers a $5,000 reward for information leading to his capture. If Milly decides to claim the reward, it is not expected that she will call the bank and say, "I hereby accept your offer." Instead, it is expected that Milly (or anyone else) will accept the offer by performance, by producing information leading to Jed's capture. This transaction thus includes one promise ("*uni*" means one) and the contract is referred to as a "unilateral" contract.

In the following opinion, *Cook v. Johnson*, one of the issues concerning the appellate court was whether the agreement between the parties was bilateral or unilateral. The facts are not complicated: Cook sold a ranch to Johnson; and, thereafter, Cook and

Johnson apparently entered into a further agreement by which Cook would clean ditches on the ranch he had sold to Johnson. The trial court found in favor of Johnson, holding that there was no contract of any kind (neither bilateral nor unilateral). Cook appealed.

Cook v. Johnson
221 P.2d 525 (1950)

SCHWELLENBACH, Justice.
* * *

December 20, 1947, Johnson wrote Cook:

"Mr. Fulton Cook
St. Maries Idaho.
Dear Mr. Cook

I thot I wod drop you a line to day I ham hopen this finds you folks all O.K. with best wishes to you and famley. I am bout thee same as ever I am planen on goen way the first of thee year someplase.

Bout the ditchen you was to dow on my Farm goe a head an dow thee work what you think to bee needed and I will pay you later on when you send me thee bill I may not see you bee fore I goe away
　　　　　Your Truly
　　　　　[signed] L. D. Johnson"

Cook replied December 23d:

"If everything progresses satisfactorily and we do not have too much extreme weather conditions we will be at your ranch ready to extend the ditches for you by about January 20th. I have something like three weeks work with my machine on my ranch before I can get to your work but you can count on me doing the work as I promised you just as soon as I can get to it."
* * *

The law recognizes as a matter of classification, two kinds of contracts—bilateral and unilateral. A bilateral contract is one in which there are reciprocal promises. The promise by one party is consideration for the promise by the other. Each party is bound by his promise to the other. A unilateral contract is a promise by one party—an offer by him to do a certain thing in the event the other party performs a certain act. The performance by the other party constitutes an acceptance of the offer and the contract then becomes executed. Until acceptance by performance, the offer may be revoked either by communication to the offeree or by acts inconsistent with the offer, knowledge of which has been conveyed to the offeree. An example of this class of contract is the offer of a reward. * * *

The letters between the parties indicate that they had negotiated for some time with reference to appellant [Cook] cleaning out and extending the ditches. Those negotiations culminated in an offer by the respondent [Johnson] to pay upon performance by appellant and upon appellant's submission of a bill to him. Up to that point appellant was not obligated to perform. He could have accepted the offer by performance. But he went further than that and promised to do the work. The promises of the two men thereby became reciprocal and binding, each upon the other. The two letters constitute a binding reciprocal agreement between the parties. There was a definite proposal by respondent which was unconditionally accepted by appellant. The minds of the parties met. * * *

* * *

In the opinion above, Cook could have proceeded to do the ditching work on the basis of the December 20, letter from Johnson. This would, of course, have resulted in a unilateral contract because Johnson's letter contained a promise in offer form, and Cook was authorized to proceed with the work without any other response. However, Cook chose to respond, and his letter of December 23, in which he agreed to perform the work, converted the arrangement into a bilateral contract.

Problem Solving. Please turn to Chapter Problems at the end of this chapter and solve problem 7.4.

Express Contract. An express contract is one where the contract provisions are all expressed in oral or written words. An example is where Milly says to Jed, "I will give you $50 for your radio," and Jed says, "okay." In this example, all of the contract terms are expressed orally or in writing. (Compare express contracts with implied in fact contracts and implied in law contracts.)

Implied in Fact Contract. Some contracts, or parts of contracts, are "implied," which means that all or part of the agreement is based on communication that is neither written nor oral words. To imply something is to communicate it without stating it in words. In a non-contract example, suppose that Milly *says* to Jed: "All of the good students scored at least 85% on the statistics examination. If Jed received 80% on the examination, Milly's comment *implies* (without using words to directly state it) that Jed is not a good student.

As an example of a contract which is implied in fact, suppose that Jed walks into Milly's candy store where he is a regular customer, and seeing that Milly is busy he holds up a candy bar with a questioning look on his face. Milly sees him and nods her head in agreement; Jed nods his head in response. Neither Jed nor Milly has stated anything in words, but a reasonable interpretation of their conduct is that she agrees he may take the candy bar and he agrees he will pay for it. This contract is not "express" because no words have been expressed. Instead, the contract is implied-in-fact because the agreement is implied wholly from the facts.

Another example of an implied in fact contract occurs when Jed asks Milly, the plumber, to fix the broken pipe in his basement. He does not *say* he will pay her and she does not *ask* him if he will. The agreement to pay is implied by the facts. In this example, the contract is part express and part implied.

Contract Implied in Law. The implied in fact contracts described above are real contracts. They are discussed separately because all or part of the contract is formed in an unusual fashion—without words. In contrast, contracts which are *implied in law* are not real contracts, they are fictional contract obligations which are created by the law as a means enforcing payments where payments should be made.

As an example of an implied in law contract, suppose that Milly, a physician, provides emergency medical services to save the life of Jed, who is brought to her unconscious. In this circumstance, Jed did not nod his head, as he did with the candy bar, and he did not ask for the service to be performed, as he did with the plumber. Nevertheless, believing that it is only fair that Milly should be paid, the courts base the obligation to pay on a fictitious promise. This is not a real contract, but one created in legal fiction to provide a basis for requiring Jed to pay for the medical services. Contracts of this kind are sometimes referred to as *quasi* contracts, where the word "quasi" means "as if" or "approximately." Thus, Jed must pay Milly for the services he received based on a quasi contractual obligation.

In the following opinion, *Clark v. Peoples Savings & Loan Association*, the Department of Financial Institutions of the State of Indiana determined that Peoples Savings & Loan needed $9,000 more in assets if it was to stay in operation. To keep the business in operation the directors agreed to contribute the money and signed an affidavit that it had been done. The affidavit was false; the money was never paid. The government filed suit to collect the money. The problem for the court, of course, is that there was no "contract" between the State and the directors.

Clark v. Peoples Savings & Loan Association
46 N.E.2d 681 (1943)

FANSLER, Judge.
* * *

The action of the banking department in permitting the association to continue operating was procured not by a promise to pay the $9,000, but by false and fraudulent representation that the $9,000 had already been paid. There was no breach of a contract to pay. The complaint is denominated "complaint on contract." A quasi contract is a legal fiction invented by the common-law courts in order to permit a recovery by a contractual remedy of assumpsit in cases where, in fact, there is no contract, but where the circumstances are such that under the law of natural and immutable justice there should be a recovery as though there had been a promise. Under such circumstances, common-law courts have supplied the fiction of the promise in order to permit the remedy. Under our code, in which forms of action are abolished, no such fiction is necessary. In State v. Mutual Life Insurance Co. Of New York * * * the court quotes with approval from a New York case as follows: "'There is a class of cases where the law prescribes the rights and liabilities of persons who have not in reality entered into any contract at all with one another but between whom circumstances have arisen which make it just that one should have a right, and the other should be subject to a liability similar to the rights and liabilities in certain cases of express contract.'" In other words, where there is a wrong the court will find a remedy. At common law it was required that the remedy be found in one of the known causes of action, and the courts were driven to fictitious assumptions in order to find an appropriate remedy. Under the facts stated in the complaint before us, it cannot be doubted that justice and equity require that the defendants pay that which they falsely represented to have been paid by them. The complaint states a good cause of action, but it is not upon an oral contract or a written contract. So far as it is necessary to define it, it is an action upon a quasi contract implied from the situation of the parties. * * *
* * *

Judgment [for the State of Indiana] affirmed.

In the action above the court enforced a "contract," but, as the court openly admits, it is a contract that neither of the parties consented to in the conventional way. Instead, the contract was manufactured by operation of law to give a legal basis for granting a remedy that the court considered necessary.

Executory Contract. An executory contract is a contract where one or more of the promises are unperformed. For example, Jed pays Milly $30 to wash his car and his truck and Milly has washed the car, but not the truck. In this example, the promise to wash the truck is executory, meaning unperformed.

Void Contract. A void contract is not a contract at all. If Milly hires Jed to kill Sam, that relationship is in the form of a contract, but it is not a contract because the performance is unlawful. In legal jargon, a "contract" of this nature is said to be void *ab initio*, which means that the contract was void from its initiation or beginning. A contract may also be void if it violates public policy.

Voidable Contract. A voidable contract is a real contract which may become void. For example, Jed is a 15-year-old minor who buys a television set he does not need. As a minor, Jed has the choice to keep the television set and finish paying for it, or to return the television set and receive his money back. If Jed elects to keep the television set, the contract remains in force; but, if Jed elects to return the television set, the contract is made void. Thus, Jed's contract is void*able*, which means that it is capable of becoming void.

Unenforceable Contract. An unenforceable contract is a valid contract which may not be enforced. An example is an *oral* contract for teddy bears to be delivered to a toy store. Section 2-201(1) of the Uniform Commercial Code (discussed later) provides that "a contract for the sale of goods for the price of $500 or more is not *enforceable* . . . unless there is some *writing* sufficient to indicate that a contract for sale has been made." If the teddy bear contract is for $2000 and it is oral (not in writing) it may be perfectly valid, but not enforceable.

Problem Solving. Please turn to Chapter Problems at the end of this chapter and solve problem 7.5.

Two Sets of Rules

At this point, a confession must be made, which is that there are actually *two* sets of contract rules. In general, one set of rules applies to contracts for real estate and personal services, and the other set of rules applies to contracts for the sale of goods. The first set of rules, which applies to real estate and personal services, is called the common law of contracts, and the second set of rules, which applies to the sale of goods, is called the Uniform Commercial Code.

Common Law. The rules of the "common law" are the rules of contract law which Americans inherited from the English. These rules apply to transactions in *real estate*, and to transactions for *personal services*. An example of a real estate contract is a contract by which Milly sells her house to Jed. An example of a contract for personal services is a contract by which Milly, an attorney, contracts to write Jed's will.

Uniform Commercial Code. The second set of contracts rules is found in a much newer body of law known as the Uniform Commercial Code ("UCC"). That part of the of the UCC which specifically applies to buying and selling goods is referred to as "Sales." The Sales rules of the UCC are modified from the common law and apply to transactions in *goods* (for example, the contract by which Milly purchases a television set). (Other parts of the UCC deal with subjects like leases, negotiable instruments, bank deposits and collections, and so on.)

The following table illustrates the subject matter distinction between common law contract rules and Sales rules:

Type of Transaction	Common Law	UCC
Real Estate	X	
Goods		X
Personal Services	X	

Problem Solving. Please turn to Chapter Problems at the end of this chapter and solve problem 7.6.

"Sales" Contracts

As noted above, there are *two sets of contract rules*. The older set of contract rules are referred to as "common law" contract rules, and the newer rules are those found in the "Sales" article of the Uniform Commercial Code. In this text, Chapters 7 through 14 are a discussion of common law contract rules, and Chapters 15 through 19 are a discussion of Sales rules.

UNIFORM COMMERCIAL CODE is modified common law contract rules used for the sale of goods

Which Set of Rules? When analyzing a contract problem it is important to know which set of rules (common law or Sales) applies to the transaction. This is the equivalent of saying that if Jed proposes to play in a "ball" game, he should learn whether the game will be football or basketball so he can follow the correct set of rules. The rules of the contracting game—which are illustrated in the table above—are that the common law applies to transactions involving real estate and personal services, and Sales rules apply to transactions involving goods.

In general, as noted above, the system of classification described above is easy to follow because the common law is applied to contracts for real estate and personal services and Sales rules are applied to contracts for goods. On the other hand, some contract cases are confusing. It is like looking at a "ball" game and realizing that the players are wearing football helmets and bouncing a basketball. The problem is knowing what set of rules to apply: football rules or basketball rules. That is exactly the problem in some contract cases because the contracts involve, for example, personal services and goods. In such a case, it is difficult to know whether to use common law rules or Sales rules.

A common solution to the problem of what law to apply in cases where real property, personal services and goods are intermixed, is to determine which feature of the contract is *dominant* in dollar terms. Suppose, for example, that Milly agrees in the same contract to supply structural steel for bridge repair and install it. If the steel is valued at

$100,000 and the labor at $50,000, the courts will usually apply Sales rules because, in dollar terms, supplying goods is the *dominant* part of the contract. But, if the steel is valued at $50,000 and the labor at $100,000, the courts will usually apply common law rules because, in dollar terms, the labor is the *dominant* part of the contract.

An apparent intermixture of goods and services was the problem in the following case, *Advent Systems Ltd. v. Unisys Corp.*, where the plaintiff, Advent, sold computer software to the defendant, Unisys. On the one hand, computer software involves the personal services of computer programmers, which suggested that common law contract rules should apply. On the other hand, the work of the programmers was placed on a tangible computer disk, a "good," which suggested that the UCC should apply.

Advent Systems Ltd. v. Unisys Corp.
925 F.2d 670 (3rd Cir. 1991)

WEIS, Circuit Judge.
* * *

The district court ruled that as a matter of law the arrangement between the two parties was not within the Uniform Commercial Code * * * * As the district court appraised the transaction, provisions for services outweighed those for products and, consequently, the arrangement was not predominantly one for the sale of goods.
* * *

The Code "applies to transactions in goods." * * * Goods are defined as "all things (including specially manufactured goods) which are moveable at the time of the identification for sale." * * * The Pennsylvania courts have recognized that "'goods' has a very extensive meaning under the U.C.C. * * *
* * *

Computer programs are the product of an intellectual process, but once implanted in a medium are widely distributed to computer owners. An analogy can be drawn to a compact disc recording of an orchestral rendition. The music is produced by the artistry of musicians and in itself is not a "good," but when transferred to a laser-readable disc becomes a readily merchantable commodity. Similarly, when a professor delivers a lecture, it is not a good, but, when transcribed as a book, it becomes a good.

That a computer program may be copy-rightable as intellectual property does not alter the fact that once in the form of a floppy disc or other medium, the program is tangible, moveable and available in the marketplace. The fact that some programs may be tailored for specific purposes need not alter their status as "goods" because the Code definition includes "specially manufactured goods."

The topic has stimulated academic commentary with the majority espousing the view that software fits within the definition of a "good" in the U.C.C.

Applying the U.C.C. to computer software transactions offers substantial benefits to litigants and the courts. The Code offers a uniform body of law on a wide range of questions likely to arise in computer software disputes: implied warranties, consequential damages, disclaimers of liability, the statute of limitations, to name a few.

The importance of software to the commercial world and the advantages to be gained by the uniformity inherent in the U.C.C. are strong policy arguments favoring inclusion. The contrary arguments are not persuasive and we hold that software is a "good" within the definition in the Code.

In the case above, the appellate court solved the which-law-do-I-apply problem like a carnival huckster by simply making the personal services disappear. The court said that the personal services involved in preparing the software had merged into the tangible computer disk and disappeared. "Voila," all is now goods! And because only "goods" are being sold, the law of Sales obviously applied.

Problem Solving. Please turn to Chapter Problems at the end of this chapter and solve problem 7.7.

Problem 7.1

Article I, section 10 of the United States Constitution provides: "No State shall . . . pass any . . . Law impairing the Obligation of Contracts . . . ." Explain why this provision is important.

Problem 7.2

The text states that a contract may be defined as a promise or a set of promises for the breach of which the law gives a *remedy*, or the performance of which the law in some way recognizes as a *duty*. Why does this definition refer to both "remedy" and "duty."? Explain the difference between the two terms.

Problem 7.3

Jed says to Milly: "Here is my yacht, it is yours." Milly responds: "Thanks very much, I'll put it to good use." Is this a contract?

Problem 7.4

Except to explain *how* a contract was formed, is it important to know if a contract is unilateral or bilateral in origin?

Problem 7.5

Milly owns a piece of real estate which is next to a piece of real estate owned by Jed. Through a bureaucratic mixup Milly mistakenly pays some of the property taxes for Jed's property. Milly sues Jed to recover the money she paid. Should she claim a contract implied in law (a quasi-contract), or a contract implied in fact?

Problem 7.6

Jed provides accounting services to Milly, who is a merchant selling television sets. Explain whether the contract between them controlled by the common law or the Uniform Commercial Code?

Problem 7.7

A physician gives Milly a blood transfusion. The blood is tainted and Milly becomes ill with hepatitis. She decides to sue the physician. What contract law would apply: common law contract law or Uniform Commercial Code?

Chapter Outline

OBJECTIVE is to learn the
process of contract formation
(offer and acceptance)

This chapter focuses on the offer and acceptance process by which contracts are formed under the rules of the common law and the Uniform Commercial Code. The chapter is organized as follows:

- *Mutual Assent and Objective Theory.* The process of contract formation requires mutual assent, which means that the parties have the same intent, that they agree to the same thing. The objective theory of contracts means that the intent of a person is measured by what can be seen and heard and not by unexpressed thoughts.

- *Offer and Option.* An offer is a proposal to form a contract. An inquiry is not an offer. An offer remains in effect until it is terminated. An option is an offer which cannot be unilaterally terminated by the offeror.

- *Acceptance.* To form a contract, a valid offer must be accepted (agreed to) by the offeree, and the acceptance must be clear and unconditional.

- *Bilateral and Unilateral Contracts.* In a bilateral contract, the acceptance is made by giving a promise. In a unilateral contract, the acceptance is made by doing the requested performance.

- *Communication and Mailbox Rule.* Contracting actions (offer, rejection, counteroffer, termination, acceptance, etc.) must be communicated before they are effective. The so-called "mailbox" rule is an exception: an acceptance is effective when it is dispatched, not when it is received.

- *Completeness.* The process of offer and acceptance must result in a contract which is complete with respect to all material terms.

- *Promissory Estoppel.* A legal theory that stops people from denying the legal consequences of their promises. This theory is often used to provide a remedy in circumstances where regular contract theory cannot.

Mutual Assent

The objective of the offer and acceptance process is to assure that the parties to a "contract" agree to the same thing. This is called *mutual assent*, or in simpler terms, mutual agreement. For example, if Jed writes to Milly: "I will sell you my house for *$100,000,*" and Milly responds, " I agree, I will buy your house for *$95,000,*" there is not mutual assent because the parties have not agreed to the same bargain. On the other hand, if Jed says "I will sell you my house for $100,000," and Milly responds, "Okay," there is mutual assent because the parties have agreed to the same thing.

Another way of talking about "mutual assent" is to say that the law requires that the parties share the same *intentions*. Thus, in the first version of the example above it is clear that the parties have *not* reached a *mutual assent* because Jed's *intention* is to sell at $100,000, while Milly's *intention* is to buy at $95,000. In the second version of the example above it is equally clear that there *is* mutual assent because both parties intend that the sum of $100,000 will be the contract price.

__Problem Solving__. Please turn to Chapter Problems at the end of this chapter and solve Problem 8.1.

Objective Theory

OBJECTIVE THEORY: intent is measured by what is said and done

Suppose that in the second version of the transaction above Milly was not serious and did not really intend to buy at $100,000, even though she said she did. In this scenario, which will control, what Milly *said* or what she *thought*? The answer is that the law uses an *objective theory* to determine what the intentions of the parties are. The law measures the intent of a person by what can be seen and heard by the observation of reasonable people, and not by unexpressed thoughts. Intentions that can be seen and heard by others are considered more reliable and thus are referred to as *objective* intentions. In contrast are intentions which are not heard and thus cannot be proved. These intentions are referred to as *subjective* intentions. The answer to the problem above is that in the eyes of the law Milly *intends* to buy for $100,000 because that is what she *said* she wanted to do.

In the following opinion, *Barnes v. Treece*, the issue before the court was whether the defendant, Treece, *intended* to make an offer to contract, or whether he simply intended a joke. Treece was a promotor of "punchboards," which could be used at restaurants and other public places to win money. Appearing before the Washington State Gambling Commission, Treece stated: "I'll pay a hundred thousand dollars to anyone to find a crooked board. If they find it, I'll pay it." Barnes, who had two such "crooked" boards in his possession, called Treece on the telephone and told him of the boards and asked if the offer had been made seriously. Treece assured Barnes that the offer was serious; however, Treece subsequently refused to make good on his offer to pay $100,000 and Barnes sued. The trial court ruled in Barnes' favor and Treece appealed.

> **Barnes v. Treece**
> **549 P.2d 1152 (1976)**
>
> CALLOW, Judge.
> * * *
> The first issue is whether the statement of Treece was the manifestation of an offer which could be accepted to bind the offeror to performance of the promise. Treece contends that no contract was formed. He maintains that his statement was made in jest and lacks the necessary manifestation of a serious contractual intent.
> When expressions are intended as a joke and are understood or would be understood by a reasonable person as being so intended, they cannot be construed as an offer and accepted to form a contract. However, if the jest is not apparent and a reasonable hearer would believe that an offer was being made, then the speaker risks the formation of a contract which was not intended. It is the objective manifestations of the offeror that count and not secret, unexpressed intentions. * * *

> The trial court found that there was an objective manifestation of mutual assent to form a contract. This was a matter to be evaluated by the trier of fact.
>
> * * *
>
> The judgment is affirmed.

***Problem Solving**.* Please turn to Chapter Problems at the end of this chapter and solve Problem 8.2.

Offer

OFFER is a proposal to form a contract

Offer Defined. The process of forming a contract starts with an *offer*. An offer is a proposal to form a contract, and it includes a promise by the *offeror* (the person making an offer) to do or not do something if the proposal is accepted. The person receiving an offer is called an *offeree*. In the example above, Jed was the offeror and Milly was the offeree. When Jed (the offeror) said to Milly (the offeree) that he would sell his house to her for $100,000, he was proposing to form a contract with Milly, and his offer is understood to include a promise that he will transfer his house to her if she accepts his proposal.

Inquiries Distinguished. An inquiry is not an offer. In the example above, suppose that Jed says to Milly, "Will you give me $100,000 for my house," and Milly responds, "Yes, I agree to give you $100,000 for your house." In this version of the conversations between Jed and Milly, there is not a contract because Jed was asking a question, not making an offer. Jed's question does not demonstrate an intention to sell.

Termination of Offers. An offer remains in effect until it is terminated, and termination may occur in a variety of ways:

Rejection. An offer is terminated by rejection. Suppose that Jed writes a letter to Milly and offers to sell his house to her: "Milly, I'll sell you my house for $100,000, if you still want it." Milly responds with a letter which says: "Jed, thanks for offering to sell me your house, but I can't afford to buy it." Milly's response is a *rejection* of Jed's offer because a reasonable interpretation of her letter is that she will not buy the house. A rejection of an offer terminates that offer.

In the example above, suppose that a week after sending Jed the letter of rejection, Milly changes her mind. She writes Jed again, saying: "Jed, I've changed my mind about the house, I accept your offer to sell it to me for $100,000." This second letter is not an acceptance because there was not a valid offer for her to accept. There was no valid offer to accept because Milly's earlier rejection of Jed's offer terminated that offer. In legal terms, Milly's second letter was an attempt to breath life into a corpse.

Counteroffer. An offer is terminated by a counteroffer. In the example above, Jed's first letter was an offer to sell his house to Milly for $100,000. Suppose that Milly's first response to that offer was a letter which said: "Jed, with respect to your house, $100,000 is a bit steep, I'll give you $95,000 for it." Milly's response is a *counteroffer* and a counteroffer terminates the offer to which it responds. In legal terms, Jed's original offer is now dead.

Having received Milly's counteroffer letter, further suppose that Jed writes back to her and says: "Milly, $95,000 isn't enough for my house, but I will take $97,500 for it." The rule that a counteroffer terminates an offer also applies to terminate a counteroffer; thus, Jed's proposal to sell at $97,500 is a counteroffer which terminates Milly's counteroffer to buy at $95,000. This process can go on indefinitely, with each counteroffer terminating the counteroffer which preceded it. In this process Jed and Milly take turns being the offeror and the offeree.

Specified Time. An offer is terminated at the end of a specified time. If an offer states it will be open for a specified time, it automatically terminates at the end of that time. In the example above, suppose that Jed writes Milly: "Milly, I will sell you my house for $100,000, but I need your answer within 20 days." If Milly responds *30* days later with an acceptance of the offer, there is no contract because she was attempting to accept an offer that had terminated at the end of the 20-day period.

Reasonable Time. If an offer does not state when it terminates, it terminates at the end of a reasonable amount of time. It is sometimes difficult to know how much time is "reasonable," and it is thus difficult to know precisely when (or if) an offer has expired. The amount of time that is "reasonable" is often determined from the surrounding facts. For example, suppose that the house Jed keeps offering to sell to Milly is divided into apartments and rented to students at nearby Slippery Rock University. Jed writes to Milly on July 1: "Milly, I'm tired of dealing with messy students, I'll sell you the apartment house for $100,000." If Milly accepts on August 1, the offer is probably still valid and a contract is formed.

But, if Milly "accepts" Jed's offer on October 1, a month *after* the students have returned to school, there is not a contract because the offer from Jed has probably terminated. Why do we say that the offer has terminated? The answer is that Jed was motivated to sell by a desire to avoid dealing again with the university students—which Milly knew—which means that his intention was to sell the house before the students returned in the Fall. Thus, the date on which students return is (in view of the facts) a reasonable cut-off date for the offer.

Destruction of Subject Matter. An offer is terminated if the subject matter of the offer is destroyed. Destruction of the subject matter of a proposed contract automatically terminates the offer, with or without notice to the offeree. Thus, if Jed has offered to sell his house to Milly, but it burns down before she accepts, there is no contract because destruction of the subject matter (the house) automatically terminates the offer because Milly accepts it.

Problem Solving. Please turn to Chapter Problems at the end of this chapter and solve Problem 8.3.

Options.

OPTION is an offer that cannot be unilaterally terminated

An option is an offer which cannot be unilaterally terminated by the offeror. To learn what an option is, first consider what it is not. Suppose that Jed writes to Milly, "Milly, I'll sell you my house for $100,000 and I'll give you 30 days to accept." Milly considers the matter, talks to her bank and has an architect prepare some drawings showing how the house could be remodeled. Then, twenty days later, Milly is about to accept Jed's offer when she receives a letter from Jed: "Milly, I have changed my mind, I hereby withdraw my offer to sell the house." Can Jed unilaterally withdraw (terminate) his offer, even though the offer says it will be open for 30 days? The answer is yes (the offer can be unilaterally withdrawn) because Jed's offer is not in option form.[1]

How is Jed's offer converted into an option? An offer which cannot be unilaterally revoked—called an option—can be purchased, just like a loaf of bread can be purchased. Jed's offer becomes an option when Milly gives something of value to Jed, for example $50, in return for nonrevocability. This exchange of value for value creates a separate contract with respect to the offer. Suppose that Jed's offer to Milly is changed to be like this: "Milly, in return for your recent payment of $50 I offer to sell you my house for $100,000 and I give you 30 days to accept this offer." The payment of $50 creates an option contract and Jed cannot withdraw the offer during the 30-day period. In this context, Jed's letter to Milly (in which Jed says he has changed his mind and withdraws his offer) is *not* sufficient to terminate the offer.

__Problem Solving__. Please turn to Chapter Problems at the end of this chapter and solve Problem 8.4.

Acceptance

ACCEPTANCE is a clear and unconditional agreement to an offer

To form a contract, a valid offer must be accepted (agreed to) by the offeree, and the acceptance must be clear and unconditional. For example, assume that Jed has sent a letter to Milly in which he offers to sell her his house for $100,000. Which of the following responses by Milly is a valid acceptance: (1) "I accept, if you will let me pay the money at the rate of $10,000 per month, for ten months;" or, (2) I accept; can I pay the money at the rate of $10,000 per month, for ten months?"

Option (1) is not an acceptance. In option (1) the "acceptance" is conditional because Milly says "I accept *if,*" which means that there is no acceptance at all if Jed will not allow Milly to pay over a ten-month period. On the other hand, option (2) is an acceptance because it is unconditional. In option (2), Milly still wants to pay the money over a ten-month period, but the acceptance is not conditioned on Jed agreeing to let her do it.

---

[1] Beyond the scope of the present discussion is the possibility that a court may apply the doctrine of promissory estoppel and require Jed to reimburse Milly the cost of the architect's drawings. Promissory estoppel is discussed more at the end of this chapter.

Problem Solving. Please turn to Chapter Problems at the end of this chapter and solve Problem 8.5.

Bilateral Contracts

In legal jargon, the process of offer and acceptance results in either a bilateral contract or a unilateral contract:

BILATERAL CONTRACT is a contract formed by means of two premises

In a bilateral contract, the contract is formed through the exchange of promises. For example, in the Jed and Milly transactions, if Milly proposes to accept one of Jed's offers, she communicates with him and uses *words* such as "I agree." That is, she agrees (and thus promises) that if he will do what he has promised, she will pay him $100,000. This type of contract involves two promises: Jed's promise that he will transfer the house to Milly, and Milly's promise that she will transfer the money to Jed. Because it is based on *two* (or more) promises, this arrangement is called a **bilateral** ("*bi*"means two) contract.

Problem Solving. Please turn to Chapter Problems at the end of this chapter and solve Problem 8.6.

Unilateral Contracts

UNILATERAL CONTRACT is a contract formed by means of one promise

It is less common, but possible, to form a contract using only *one* promise, which is an arrangement called a **unilateral** ("*uni*" means one) contract. For example, Jed leaves a note at Milly's house: "Milly, I'll be back in about five days, and I'll pay you $1500 if you will paint my house while I'm gone." Reasonably interpreted, does Jed's offer show that he expects a letter or a telephone call in return, in which Milly says "I accept"? It appears that he does not expect a return promise; instead, he expects that if Milly agrees to his offer, she will proceed to paint his house. No other response is necessary. Because this is a contract based on a promise and performance, instead of a promise for a promise, it is called a unilateral contract.

Problem Solving. Please turn to Chapter Problems at the end of this chapter and solve Problem 8.7.

Communication

Although it seems obvious to say so, an offer must be communicated to the offeree, and an acceptance must be communicated to the offeror. In general—with the exception of the so-called "mailbox" rule (discussed below)—offers, terminations of offers, rejection of offers, counteroffers, and the like, are not effectively communicated until they are *received* by the person to whom they are sent. The process of communicating is relatively simple if the contracting parties are talking to each other in person, or on the telephone. But, if the contracting parties are contracting at a distance, and not by telephone, the method of communication and delays in communication can cause problems.

COMMUNICATION : contract communication must be done in a "reasonable" manner

Method of Communication. The first point of concern is *how*—by what method or means—can or must the communication be made? Although the question of "how" to communicate raises it's head in all phases of the contracting process, the problem is most acute in the process of acceptance of the offer. The vague general rule is that an offeree may accept an offer by using any method of communication that is *reasonable* in the circumstances. What is a reasonable method of communication? The following are some general rules:

Specified Method of Communication. If the offer *specifies* (requires) a method of communication to be used to accept an offer, that method *must* be used; it is the only method that is reasonable. Suppose that Jed writes to Milly: "I'll sell you my house for $100,000; please respond by Federal Express." Milly responds by letter which she sends through the US Mail. In this instance there is not a contract because the terms of the offer ("respond by Federal Express") have not been complied with. On the other hand, if Milly responds by Federal Express, her acceptance is effective when she deposits her letter with Federal Express—even if Federal Express fails to deliver the letter—because she has done what the offer requires.

Expressly Authorized Method of Communication. If the offer *authorizes* (but does not require) a method of communication to be used to accept, that method *may* be used. Suppose that Jed writes to Milly: "I'll sell you my house for $100,000; you may respond by Federal Express." In this instance, as before, Milly's acceptance is effective when she deposits it with Federal Express. Her acceptance is reasonable and effective because she has done what the offer authorizes; that is, "you *may* respond by Federal Express."

But, what if Milly—observing that the offer authorizes, but does not require, a response by Federal Express—chooses to respond by letter through the US Mail. Is there a valid acceptance? (It should be observed that Milly is obviously foolish to ignore the authorized means of communication because it eliminates risks; that is, even if the Federal Express letter is lost, she still has accepted because she used the *authorized* method of communicating her acceptance.).

The answer to the problem above is that her acceptance is valid only if the method she chooses to accept (US Mail) is reasonable. Thus, if she is accepting Jed's offer to sell his house, and there are no unusual factors in the transaction, a letter through the US Mail is probably reasonable and she has accepted. But, suppose that Jed is offering to sell Milly a truckload of perishable bananas; in this transaction the presumably slower US Mail system is probably too slow and thus unreasonable as a means of accepting.

Silence about Method. In many offers the text of the offer says nothing about the method of accepting. In such a circumstance the offeree is impliedly authorized to accept using the same method used to communicate the offer. Thus, if the offer is sent through the US Mail, the offeree is authorized to use that method to respond; and, if the offer is sent by Federal Express, the offeree is authorized to use that method to respond. In addition, the offeree may, of course, use any other method of acceptance that is reasonable under the circumstances.

Problem Solving. Please turn to Chapter Problems at the end of this chapter and solve Problem 8.8.

"Mailbox" Rule

The so-called "mailbox" rule is that an acceptance is effective when it is *dispatched*, not when it is *received*. This is, of course, an exception to the normal rule that communications in the process of contracting are effective when they are received, not when they are dispatched. To illustrate the need for the "mailbox" rule, consider the problem that can arise if there is not such a rule. On July 1, Jed (living in New York) writes to Milly (living in Los Angeles): "Milly, I'll sell you my house for $100,000." On July 10, Jed changes his mind and mails Milly a letter *terminating* the offer; and, at the same moment, Milly mails Jed a letter *accepting* the offer. Jed receives Milly's acceptance at about the same moment that Milly receives Jed's acceptance. If the rule is that all communications are effective only when received, the result in this case is uncertain.

The solution is simple: the rule is that an *acceptance* is effective when it is dispatched, not when it is received; that is, Milly's acceptance is effective when it is dropped into the "mailbox." In all other cases, the communication is effective when it is received.

How does the "mailbox" rule solve the problem above, where Jed receives Milly's acceptance at the same time that Milly receives Jed's termination? In this case, Milly's acceptance was effective at the moment she *dispatched* it; therefore, she accepted the offer before Jed terminated it, because Jed's termination was not effective until it was *received*.

In the example above, what if Milly's acceptance is never delivered (it is lost) although it was dispatched? The answer is that the mailbox rule places the risk that the acceptance may be lost on the offeror. If the acceptance was properly dispatched, the offer is accepted, and if the acceptance is thereafter lost, it is the offeror who is at risk.

Is it fair that the mailbox rule places the risk that the acceptance may be lost on the offeror? The answer is yes because a careful offeror can so easily turn the tables. Suppose that Jed's letter to Milly is as follows: "Milly, I'll sell you my house for $100,000; your acceptance will be effective when received." In this scenario, the offeror (Jed) has neatly shifted the risk of lost communications over to Milly (the offeree) by making *receipt* of the acceptance part of the requirements of proper acceptance.

(Although this turning of the tables solves the problem of lost communications in favor of the offeror, it renews the possibility and problem that an acceptance may be received by the offeror at about the same time that a termination is received by the offeree. This problem can only be solved by evidence as to the time of receipt, showing which document was received first and was thus effective first.)

The following opinion, *Soldau v. Organon Inc.*, involves the "mailbox" rule. Soldau was discharged from his employment with Organon and he sued claiming age discrimination. Then, he received a letter from Organon offering him *double* severance pay if he would sign an agreement dropping his lawsuit. He signed the agreement and dropped it in a mailbox and then went home and found he had received a check from Organon for the double severance pay. Realizing he could have the double severance pay and continue with his lawsuit, he returned to the post office and talked a postal employee into allowing him to retrieve his agreement from the mailbox. The issue was whether dropping the agreement into the mailbox constituted an acceptance.

Soldau v. Organon Inc.
860 F.2d 355 (1988)

PER CURIAM:

* * *

The district court granted summary judgment for Organon, stating "the release was deemed fully communicated to Organon, and a binding contract was formed, at the time plaintiff deposited the executed release in the mailbox. The fact that plaintiff retrieved the release from the mailbox is of no consequence under California statutory and decisional law."

The district court was clearly correct under California law. Soldau does not argue to the contrary. Instead he contends that the formation and validity of the release are governed by federal law, and would not have been effective unless and until it had been received by Organon. We need not decide which body of law controls. Under federal as well as California law, Soldau's acceptance was effective when it was mailed.

The so-called "mailbox" or "effective when mailed" rule * * * [is] adopted and followed as federal common law by the Supreme Court * * *.

We could not change the rule, and there is no reason to believe the Supreme Court would be inclined to do so. It is almost universally accepted in the common law world. It is enshrined in the Restatement (Second) of Contracts § 63(a) and endorsed by the major contract treatises.

Soldau rests his case upon decisions of the Court of Claims * * * rejecting mailing of the acceptance as the crucial event resulting in a contract, in favor of the receipt of the acceptance by the offeror. No other federal court has agreed. Commentators are also virtually unanimous in rejecting the Court of Claims' repudiation of the "effective when mailed" rule, pointing to the long history of the rule; its importance in creating certainty for contracting parties; its essential soundness, on balance, as a means of allocating the risk during the period between the making of the offer and the communication of the acceptance or rejection to the offeror; and the inadequacy of the rationale offered by the Court of Claims for the change.

Since Soldau's contractual obligation to release Organon in return for Organon's obligation to make the enhanced severance payment arose when Soldau deposited his acceptance in the post office mailbox, his subsequent withdrawal of the acceptance was ineffectual.

AFFIRMED.

What is unexplained in the *Soldau* opinion is why the company sent him a check before there was an agreement? The answer is that it was probably an office mistake.

Suppose that Jed sends a letter to Milly, an opera singer, offering her the lead part in the opera, *Carmen*, commencing July 1. Milly immediately drops a letter in the mailbox unconditionally accepting Jed's offer. The letter is lost in the mail. Not hearing from Milly, Jed hires Maria for the part. When Jed refuses to perform on the "contract," Milly sues Jed. Who wins? The answer is that Milly wins because a contract was formed when Milly's letter was placed in the mailbox.

Although this result may be a hardship on Jed, it is one he could easily have prevented by providing in his letter that an acceptance from Milly would only be effective when received by him. Thus, if Jed is careful, the risk of a lost letter is on Milly, but if he is careless, the risk of a lost letter is on him.

Problem Solving. Please turn to Chapter Problems at the end of this chapter and solve Problem 8.9.

Completeness

COMPLETENESS: at common law, a contract must be complete as to all material terms if it is to be enforced

The process of offer and acceptance must result in a contract which is complete with respect to all *material* (important) terms. If the express and implied terms of a "contract" leave material terms thereof incomplete, a court may refuse to enforce it. Suppose (again) that Jed writes to Milly: "Milly, I'll sell you my house," and Milly responds, "I'll take it." Although a court would probably enforce this agreement if the only thing missing was the date on which the house and money will be exchanged (the court would fix a reasonable time), many courts would refuse to enforce the agreement on the grounds that the price had been left out.

In the following opinion, *Action Ads, Inc. v. Judes*, the plaintiff, Judes, had medical expenses but no medical insurance. He claimed that his employer had agreed to provide him medical insurance and filed suit to enforce that agreement. The trial court decided in favor of Judes and the employer appealed. The issue for the court was whether the agreement between Judes and his employer was complete enough to enforce.

Action Ads, Inc. v. Judes
671 P.2d 309 (Wyo. 1983)

ROSE, Justice.
* * *

In the present case, the extent of the undertaking of Action Ads to furnish insurance is contained in the following term of the parties' employment contract:

"In addition, sixty days from your date of hire, Action Ads Inc. will provide a medical insurance program for you and your dependents."

The appellee [Judes] offered no evidence as to the risks insured against, the amount of coverage, or any other details of the "insurance program" that Action Ads, Inc. was obligated to provide. There was no proof of the insurance carrier contemplated by the parties. Most important, there was no showing that the injury actually sustained by Mr. Judes would have been covered by the insurance program had Action Ads fully complied with the employment contract.

It is apparent that the pertinent contract term is not sufficiently definite and certain to permit this court to determine the extent of the promised performance. Without that information, we are unable to measure the damages to which the promisee might reasonably be entitled in the event of a breach. The indefiniteness of the agreement is due to the absence of any evidence whatsoever concerning the elements of the insurance coverage that Action Ads was obligated to provide. Since the plaintiff failed to show to what extent, if any, the promised insurance program would have compensated him for his injury, we hold that the agreement to provide insurance was too uncertain and indefinite to be enforceable.

REVERSED.

Problem Solving. Please turn to Chapter Problems at the end of this chapter and solve Problem 8.10.

Promissory Estoppel

No system of rules is so perfect that it neatly solves all of the problems that human beings can generate, and contract law is no exception. The point is that an effective systems of rules must have a safety net that catches and resolves problems that do not fit into the system. In contract law, rules of *equity* are that safety net. *Promissory estoppel* is an example of the rules of equity that help courts solve unusual problems. Buried in this old-fashioned phrase are the words "promise" and "stop," and the idea related to them was that in some circumstances a person might make a "promise," that was not in contract form, which the courts would nevertheless enforce. That is, the courts would "stop" the promisor from avoiding responsibility for the "promise."

Promissory estoppel was employed to resolve a problem in *John Price Associates, Inc. V. Warner Electric, Inc.* In the world of construction contracting, the problem described in the *John Price* opinion is a common one: the John Price company prepared a bid to construct a government building and it used the estimates of "subcontractors" (those who would do roofing or concrete work, or, in this case, electrical work) as a basis for preparing its bid. Warner was the electrical subcontractor who gave an estimate to John Price. Price notified Warner that it was using the Warner bid and then signed the general contract.

Thereafter, Warner notified Price that it was raising its estimate. This action causes a difficult financial problem for Price because on the one hand it now has a fixed price contract to build the building; but, on the other hand, Warner wants to raise the price for the electrical work, thus raising the cost of fulfilling the contract. When Warner increased it's price, the John Price company filed suit to recover the difference between the original bid and the changed bid. The trial court found in Price's favor and Warner appealed.

John Price Associates, Inc. v. Warner Electric, Inc.
723 F.2d 755 (1983)

LOGAN, Circuit Judge.
* * *

We need not address the propriety of the trial court's finding that a contract existed between Price and Warner, since we agree that the doctrine of promissory estoppel barred Warner from withdrawing its bid. That doctrine provides that a promise that the promisor should reasonably expect to induce action by the promisee and that does induce such action by the promisee is binding if injustice can be avoided only by enforcement of the promise. * * * Warner submitted a bid * * * with the expectation that companies bidding on the general contract would rely on its bid in making their bids. Price relied on Warner's bid, and when Price found out that it would probably get the general contract, Price notified Warner of its reliance. Warner provided information to the government that permitted its approval as a subcontractor on the project. Price had entered into a binding contract before Warner notified it of any problems with the bid. In this situation promissory estoppel should apply to prevent Warner from withdrawing its bid. * * *

---

* * *
AFFIRMED.

__Problem Solving__. Please turn to Chapter Problems at the end of this chapter and solve Problem 8.11.

Chapter Problems

Problem 8.1

How can the concept of mutual assent apply to a unilateral contract where one of the parties makes no promise?

Problem 8.2

Jed and Millie are watching the "Miss World" contest on television and Jed, referring to one of the contestants, says: "I could get a date with her if I wanted." Millie responds: "I'd pay a hundred bucks to see *that*." Unknown to Millie, the contestant is a former high school classmate of Jed's and he gets a date with her. Must Millie pay the $100 to Jed?

Problem 8.3

Schiff is a self-styled tax rebel. He appeared live on CBS News Nightwatch, a nighttime television program with a viewer participation format. During the course of the Nightwatch program, Schiff repeated his long-standing position that, "there is nothing in the Internal Revenue code which I have here, which says anybody is legally required to pay the tax." Following a discussion of his rationale for that conclusion, Schiff stated: "If anybody calls this show—I have the Code—and cites any section of this Code that says an individual is required to file a tax return, I will pay them $100,000." A two-minute taped segment of the original Nightwatch interview was rebroadcast several hours later on the CBS Morning News. Newman saw the CBS Morning News and called the station and Schiff and provided the sections in question and demanded payment of the $100,000. When Schiff refused to pay, Newman filed suit. Was a contract formed between Schiff and Newman?

Problem 8.4

Jed writes to Milly: "I will sell you my house for $100,000 and you can have until July 1 to decide, if you send $50." Milly responds: "Okay, here is the $50." On June 15, Milly writes to Jed: "I'll give you $95,000 for your house." Jed responds: "No, $95,000 is not enough, I'll sell the house to someone else." Jed thereafter refuses to sell the house to Milly because he says her counteroffer has revoked his offer. Is Jed correct?

Problem 8.5

Milly writes to Jed: "I'll sell you my house for $100,000; if I don't hear from you within 30 days, I will assume we have a deal." Jed does not respond to Milly's letter. Is there a contract between Milly and Jed?

Problem 8.6

Jed enters Milly's candy shop where he has an account. Seeing that Milly is busy, he picks up a candy bar and holds it up so Milly can see it. Milly nods her approval and Jed leaves the store. Do these facts create a contract, and if there is a contract, is it bilateral or unilateral?

Problem 8.7

Jed leaves a note at Milly's house: "Milly, I'll be back in about five days, will you paint my house for $1500 while I'm gone? What is the proper way for Milly to accept?

Problem 8.8

Milly sends Jed a letter through the US Mail offering to sell her house to Jed for $100,000. In terms of method of communication, what is a safe way for Jed to respond?

Problem 8.9

On March 1, Jed, a Boston entertainment broker writes to Milly, an opera singer, and offers her a job singing the lead in *La Traviata*, starting July 1. The letter provides: "any acceptance must be received by me by April 1." Milly writes a letter accepting the offer, which she places in the mail on March 15. The letter is lost in the postal system and never delivered. Not hearing from Milly, Jed hires Maria to sing the lead. Milly shows up in Boston on July 1. Is there a contract between Jed and Milly?

Problem 8.10

In *Action Ads, Inc. v. Judes*, there were five appellate court judges. The majority (three judges) held that the contract for medical insurance was too incomplete to enforce. But, the other two judges dissented and said they thought that Judes should win; that is, that the "contract' should be enforced. How do you suppose that the dissenting judges would solve the "incompleteness" problem?

Problem 8.11

In *John Price Associates, Inc. v. Warner electric, Inc.*, what seems to be the most important factor persuading the court to rule in favor of John Price on a theory of promissory estoppel?

Chapter 9
Defects in Agreement

Chapter Outline

OBJECTIVE is to learn the defects that may occur in the contracting process.

The objective of this chapter is a focus on the various defects, such as dishonesty, mistake or compulsion, that may cause an apparent contract to unravel. The chapter is organized as follows:

- *Mutual Assent.* A contract requires *mutual assent*, or mutual agreement, which means that each party agrees to the same proposition. The remedy where there is not mutual assent is *recission*. The willingness to continue with a contract, despite a lack of mutual assent, is *ratification*. There are a variety of defects that may prevent achieving mutual assent, and among those defects are fraud, misrepresentation, mistake, duress and undue influence.

- *Fraud.* There is not mutual assent if one of the contracting parties has defrauded the other. The essence of *fraud* is dishonesty, meaning *intentional* wrongdoing. Fraud is based on (1) a false statement of a material fact, (2) the false statement was made with intent to deceive, and (3) the false statement was justifiably relied on by the injured party.

- *Misrepresentation.* There is not mutual assent if there is *misrepresentation.* Misrepresentation is much like fraud. The essential difference between them is that misrepresentation does not require proof of scienter (intentional concealment or misstatement of facts).

- *Mistake.* There is not mutual assent if there is a *mistake*. A court may refuse to enforce a contract if it was entered into on the basis of mutual mistake (a mistake by both parties). In contrast, mistakes which are unilateral (a mistake by one party only) are usually enforced.

- *Duress.* *Duress* refers to force or compulsion. If a party is compelled to enter into an agreement by force or compulsion, a meeting of the minds has not occurred and the agreement may be rescinded.

- *Undue Influence.* Contracts entered into because of *undue influence* may be rescinded. Undue influence requires evidence of (1) persuasion in an atmosphere of trust and confidence where one party has dominance over the other, and (2) the persuasion is unfair.

Mutual Assent

A contract requires **mutual assent**, or mutual agreement, which means that each party agrees to the same proposition. For example, if Milly sells a horse to Jed, but *hides* the fact that it has only three legs, there is not agreement on the same proposition because Millie is selling a horse with three legs and Jed is entitled to think he is buying a horse with four legs. In addition, if Milly and Jed are both "city slickers" and make a *mistake* and agree to the sale of a "horse," only to later learn that it was a mule, there is likewise not common agreement because neither of them agreed to sell or buy a mule. And, in the most extreme example of all, if Milly uses a gun to *force* Jed to sign a contract, there is likewise not common agreement. If, however, Millie and Jed agree to the sale of a horse, and it has four legs, and it is a horse, and the agreement is voluntary, then a valid agreement results.

The following case, *Whitaker v. Associated Credit Services*, illustrates an agreement which was *not* based on mutual assent. In *Whitaker*, the plaintiffs claimed violation of the Fair Credit Reporting Act. Hoping to dispose of the case by paying a small amount of money, the defendant prepared a settlement agreement in which there was an offer to pay $500 to the plaintiffs. The defendant's secretary, however, made a typographical error and typed in *$500,000* instead of $500. Obviously delighted, the plaintiffs quickly signed the agreement. The defendants asked the trial court to refuse to enforce the agreement for a number of reasons, one of which was that the obvious mistake meant that in contract terms there was not a "meeting of the minds" (because there was not *mutual assent*). The trial court judge decided not to enforce the agreement and the plaintiff appealed:

Whitaker v. Associated Credit Services
946 F.2d 1222 (1991)

MILBURN, Circuit Judge.
* * *

Finally, defendant argues that under general principles of contract law, the district court did not abuse its discretion in setting aside the judgment. Courts may apply general contract principles to determine what was intended in an offer of judgment and whether there has been a valid offer and acceptance. * * * A valid offer and acceptance requires a mutual manifestation of assent, a meeting of the minds as to the terms of the contract. * * * While plaintiffs contend that defendants manifested to them an offer of $500,000 to which they assented, there was in fact no meeting of the minds because plaintiffs were aware that such an offer was "outrageous." Furthermore, defendants never intended to make such an offer. The mistake was more than a wrongful assessment of the value of the case; it was a pure typographical error. Thus, there was no meeting of the minds and no valid offer and acceptance constituting an enforceable contract. Furthermore, as in this case, a district court may exercise its equitable powers to set aside a judgment under circumstances where it would be unconscionable to enforce it. * * *

* * *

AFFIRMED.

If a contract is entered into on the basis of a defect in the process of agreement, the most common remedy is *rescission*. To rescind a contract means to cancel it. The process of rescission requires that each party to return to their precontract position; and, in the transactions above, Jed will return the animal (the horse with three legs, the mule, or the horse purchased at gunpoint) to Milly and she will return the purchase price to Jed.

A party, like Jed, who is the victim of a defect in the process of agreement must act promptly to assert that claim, and demand rescission; otherwise, the view may be taken that the contract—defects and all—is acceptable. If Jed, the victim, accepts the flawed agreement and chooses not to take action on the defects, it is said that he has *ratified* the agreement. Thus, unknown to Millie, Jed may want the horse only for breeding purposes and a missing front leg may not significantly frustrate that objective. In such a case, if Jed is satisfied (but surprised) he may choose not to object and he has ratified his agreement with Millie.

Problem Solving. Please turn to the Chapter Problems at the end of this chapter and solve problem 9.1.

There are a variety of defects that may prevent achieving mutual assent, and among those defects are fraud, misrepresentation, mistake, duress and undue influence. Each of these is discussed hereafter.

Fraud

FRAUD means intentional misstatement of a material fact, justifiably relied on, causing detriment

In the context of contracts, *fraud* means to *intentionally* misrepresent facts for the purpose of inducing another person to enter into a contract. Like the horse with three legs, the result of fraud is usually a lack of mutual assent. By definition, conduct which is intentional excludes conduct which is based on accident or mistake. Specifically, fraud is based on the following parts or "elements":

- Element #1: A false representation of a material fact,

- Element #2: A false representation made with intent to deceive, and

- Element #3: A false representation justifiably relied on by the injured party.

Thus, for example, if Millie (in Idaho) writes to Jed (in Florida) and convinces him to buy "Speedy," the horse with three legs, by stating that Speedy is a normal horse and in good condition, she has (1) knowingly made a false statement about an important factual matter; (2) her intent is to deceive Jed; and, (3) he is justified in believing her. This is fraud, and Jed is entitled to rescind the contract if he acts promptly after learning the truth about Speedy.

Following is a more detailed discussion of each of the "elements" of fraud.

131

Element #1: False Representation of a Material Fact. Fraud commences with a false representation of a material *fact*, not a statement of *opinion*. A fact is something that exists or has occurred. Thus, "this is a bed that George Washington slept in," is a statement of fact, but "this is the best bed in the world," is an opinion. Similarly, "Speedy is a *nice* horse," is a matter of opinion, but "Speedy is a *normal* horse," is a statement of fact. In the context of fraud, or other defects in agreement, the courts generally distinguish between expressions of opinion and statements of fact, allowing the opinion, but taking action on statements of fact. They are likewise tolerant of routine salesman's "puffery;" such as "Madam, this is the finest sedan in Georgia," or predictions of the future, such as "you'll never be sorry you bought this car." The precise boundary line between statements of fact, and opinions, puffery and predictions, is not always clear and bright.

The following opinion, *Vokes v. Arthur Murray, Inc.*, started with Mrs. Audrey E. Vokes, whom the court describes as "a widow of 51 years and without family, [who] had a yen to be 'an accomplished dancer' with the hopes of finding 'new interest in life'." Taking advantage of Mrs. Vokes' hopes, the defendant sold her 2302 hours of dancing lessons for a cash total of $31,090.45. To sell these lessons to Mrs. Vokes, the defendants extravagantly praised her dancing abilities and potential as a dancer. The point of the opinion is whether the statements of the defendant were factual in nature, or in the realm of salesman's puffery:

Audrey E. Vokes v. Arthur Murray, Inc.
212 So.2d 906 (1968)

PIERCE, Judge.
* * *

[The] dance lesson contracts and the monetary consideration therefore of over $31,000 were procured from her by means and methods of Davenport and his associates [employees at Arthur Murray] which went beyond the unsavory, yet legally permissible, perimeter of "sales puffing" and intruded well into the forbidden area of undue influence, the suggestion of falsehood, the suppression of truth, and the free exercise of rational judgement, if what plaintiff alleged in her complaint was true. From the time of her first contact with the dancing school in February, 1961, she was influenced unwittingly by a constant and continuous barrage of flattery, false praise, excessive compliments, and panegyric encomiums, to such extent that it would be not only inequitable, but unconscionable, for a Court exercising inherent chancery power to allow such contracts to stand.

She was incessantly subjected to overreaching blandishment and cajolery. She was assured she had "grace and poise" that she was "rapidly improving and developing in her dancing skill"; that the additional lessons would make her a beautiful dancer, capable of dancing with the most accomplished dancers"; that she was "rapidly progressing in the development of her dancing skill and gracefulness", etc., etc. She was given "dance aptitude tests" for the ostensible purpose of "determining" the number of remaining hours instructions needed by her from time to time.

* * *

* * * The complaint alleged that such representations to her "were in fact false and known by the defendant to be false and contrary to the plaintiff's true ability, the truth of plaintiff's ability being fully known to the defendants, but withheld from the plaintiff for the

---

sole and specific intent to deceive and defraud the plaintiff and to induce her in the purchasing of additional hours of dance lessons." It was averred that the lessons were sold to her "in total disregard to the true physical, rhythm, and mental ability of the plaintiff." In other words, while she first exulted that she was entering the "spring of her life," she finally was awakened to the fact there was "spring" neither in her life nor in her feet.

* * *

The material allegations of the complaint must, of course, be accepted as true for the purpose of testing its legal sufficiency. Defendants contend that contracts can only be rescinded for fraud or misrepresentation when the alleged misrepresentation is as to a material fact, rather than an opinion, prediction or expectation, and that the statements and representations set forth at length in the complaint were in the category of "trade puffing," within its legal orbit.

It is true that "generally a misrepresentation, to be actionable, must be one of fact rather than of opinion." * * * But this rule has significant qualifications, applicable here. It does not apply where there is a fiduciary relationship between the parties, or where there has been some artifice or trick employed by the representor, or where the parties do not in general deal at "arm's length" as we understand the phrase, or where the representee does not have equal opportunity to become apprised of the truth or falsity of the fact represented. As stated by Judge Allen of this Court in *Ramel v. Chasebrook Construction Company*:

> "* * * A statement of a party having * * * superior knowledge may be regarded as statement of fact although it would be considered as opinion if the parties were dealing on equal terms."

It could be reasonably supposed here that defendants had "superior knowledge" as to whether plaintiff had "dance potential" and as to whether she was noticeably improving in the art of terpsichore. * * *

Even in contractual situations where a party to a transaction owes no duty to disclose facts when his knowledge or to answer inquiries respecting such facts, the law is if he undertakes to do so he must disclose the *whole truth*. * * * From the face of the complaint, it should have been reasonably apparent to defendants that her vast outlay of cash for the many hundreds of additional hours of instruction was not justified by her slow and awkward progress, which she would have been made well aware of if they had spoken the "whole truth."

* * *

It accordingly follows that the order dismissing the plaintiff's last amended complaint with prejudice should be and is reversed.

Reversed.

The *Vokes* case may be viewed from two perspectives: one is that the dance studio employees said things that were not true; the other is that they remained silent when a truthful statement was necessary. The court seemed to think that the defendants had failed on both counts.

The discussion changes now from the problem of *facts* to the problem of *nondisclosure*. Traditionally, a contracting party who kept silent about problems in a transaction did not commit fraud, because fraud required an affirmative *misrepresentation* of a material fact. (The meaning of "material" fact is discussed below.) The most extreme perspective of the attitude that silence is not fraud is described as *caveat emptor* ("let the buyer beware"). This extreme view saw no fraud in Millie selling Speedy, the three-legged horse, as long as she kept her mouth shut; but, called it fraud if she opened her mouth and lied about Speedy's good racing qualities.

There is, however, something deeply offensive about the proposition that a person can sell a three-legged horse and avoid responsibility simply because she remains silent about the defect. Thus, there is a growing trend for courts to impose an obligation to disclose; that is, silence about the fact that Speedy has only three legs is not always safe. (This problem of disclosure versus nondisclosure is discussed more in *Cousineau v. Walker*, below.) Examples of circumstances where silence is *not* sufficient include the following:

- *Fiduciary Relationship.* Silence is not safe, and a party has an obligation to disclose relevant information, if a fiduciary relationship (a relationship of confidence or trust) exists between the parties. Examples of this might include, attorneys, accountants, bankers or real estate agents and their clients.

- *Correcting Mistakes about Basic Assumptions.* Silence is not safe, and a party has an obligation to disclose information, if a contracting party is acting on the basis of a mistake which is central to the transaction and the mistake is known to the other party. An example is the sale of real estate with a water well; the well is known by the seller to be contaminated, but the buyer does not discover that fact during a reasonable investigation.

- *Supervening Events.* Silence is not safe, and a party has an obligation to disclose information, if supervening facts (new facts) arise. The parties negotiate the sale of a car, and the buyer examines the car; but, a day later, before the transaction is completed, the underside of the car is hit by a rock and the engine develops a serious oil leak. The seller knows of this condition.

Statements and opinions about applicable *law* are not representations of fact. Ordinarily, Millie does not have an obligation correct to Jed's plans to qualify for *tax* benefits from using Speedy for breeding purposes. But this obviously would not be true if Millie had expertise or training (or represented that she had expertise or training) that qualified her in tax law and she created a fiduciary relationship in relationship to taxation.

What is meant by a *material* fact? A material fact is an important fact; it is a fact which would be given serious consideration in making a decision. The fact that Speedy has only three legs would normally be material (important) in a transaction for his sale; but, the fact that he didn't like apples would not be material.

In the following case, *Cousineau v. Walker*, the court deals with whether a seller may remain silent and leave a buyer to investigate and learn the truth (*caveat emptor*: "let the buyer beware") in a real estate transaction. The property being sold was located along a highway, and two principal motivations for the buyer to buy were (1) highway frontage for commercial development and (2) the existence of gravel which would be removed and sold. At trial, it was obvious that there had been confusion about the extent of the frontage and the amount of gravel—much of the confusion being caused by the seller. The seller argued that the truth was obvious—if the buyer had only investigated—and the buyer had an obligation to make a reasonable investigation. The trial court found in favor of the seller, but the appellate court reversed. In their opinion the appellate court first concluded that facts about frontage and gravel are *material* (important) and then moved on to the issue of *disclosure*:

Cousineau v. Walker
613 P.2d 608 (1980)

BOOCHEVER, Justice
    * * *

    Materiality is a mixed question of law and fact. A material fact is one "to which a reasonable man might be expected to attach importance in making his choice of action." * * * It is a fact which could reasonably be expected to influence someone's judgment or conduct concerning a transaction. * * *

    We conclude as a matter of law that the statement regarding highway frontage and gravel content were material. A reasonable person would be likely to consider the existence of gravel deposits an important consideration in developing a piece of property. Even if not valuable for commercial extraction, a gravel base would save the cost of obtaining suitable fill from other sources. Walker's [seller's] real estate agent testified that the statements regarding gravel were placed in the listings because gravel would be among the property's "best points" and a "selling point." It seems obvious that the sellers themselves thought a buyer would consider gravel content important.

    The buyers received less than three-fourths of the highway frontage described in the listings. Certainly the amount of highway frontage on a commercial tract would be considered important. Numerous cases from other jurisdictions have held discrepancies to be a material which were similar in magnitude to those here.
    * * *

    The trial judge concluded as a matter of law that the plaintiffs "were not entitled to rely on the alleged misrepresentation."

    There is a split of authority regarding a buyer's duty to investigate a vendor's fraudulent statements, but the prevailing trend is toward placing a minimal duty on a buyer. Recently, a Florida appellate court reversed long-standing precedent which held that a buyer must use due diligence to protect his interest, regardless of fraud, if the means for acquiring knowledge concerning the transaction were open and available. In the context of a building sale the court concluded:

> A person guilty of fraudulent misrepresentation should not be permitted to hide behind the doctrine of *caveat emptor*. * * *

    The Supreme Court of Maine has also recently reversed a line of its prior cases, concluding that a defense based upon lack of due care should not be allowed in land sales contracts where a reckless or knowing misrepresentation has been made. * * * This is also the

---

135

prevailing view in California, Idaho, Kansas, Massachusetts, and Oregon. On the other hand, some jurisdictions have reaffirmed the doctrine of caveat emptor, but as noted in Williston on Contracts,

> [t]he growing trend and tendency of the courts will continue to move toward the doctrine that negligence in trusting in a misrepresentation will not excuse positive willful fraud or deprive the defrauded person of his remedy. * * *
>
> A buyer of land, relying on an innocent misrepresentation, is barred from recovery only if the buyer's acts in failing to discover defects were wholly irrational, preposterous, or in bad faith.
>
> Although Cousineau's [buyer's] actions may well have exhibited poor judgment for an experienced businessman, they were not so unreasonable or preposterous in view of Walker's [seller's] description of the property that recovery should be denied. Consequently, we reverse the judgment of the superior court.
>
> REVERSED and REMANDED.

In *Cousineau*, the court concluded that the facts at issue (frontage and gravel) were material facts and that the seller had an obligation to clarify misunderstandings concerning those facts. (The *Cousineau* opinion is placed in the chapter at this point to illustrate those two issues.) But, there is another question: did the sellers mislead the buyer's *intentionally*? If the seller acted intentionally, the seller committed fraud, but if the seller acted unintentionally, then only misrepresentation occurred. (The *Cousineau* court did not resolve the issue of *intent* because it was not necessary to resolve the case. The buyer merely wanted recission as a remedy, and recission is available in cases of fraud or misrepresentation.) At this point we move on to the question of *intent*.

Element #2: False Statement Made with Intent to Deceive. Fraud is *intentional* concealment or misrepresentation of material facts. This so-called "guilty knowledge" is referred to in legal jargon as *scienter*. Suppose that Jed sells Millie a ranch with a spring producing "pure, clear spring water," and later it is discovered that the spring is (and was) contaminated. Is this fraud? If there is no other evidence, the answer is no, because there is no evidence (only suspicion) that Jed *knew* the truth and *intentionally* concealed or misstated the facts. There is no evidence of scienter. Unless there is evidence that Jed *knew* the spring was contaminated, Millie cannot prove fraud and must rely on misrepresentation or mistake or another invalidating factor to obtain relief. This illustrates why, in the "real world," fraud is frequently claimed but only occasionally proved; that is, proving what a person (Jed) *knew*—as opposed to what they *did*— is usually difficult or impossible.

Element #3: False Statement Justifiably Relied On. To be actionable, a false statement must be *relied* on. If Millie tells Jed that Speedy is normal, but Jed's friend in Idaho tells him that Speedy has only three legs and Jed believes him, Jed has not *relied* on Millie's false statement and he cannot successfully claim she has defrauded him. The necessity to prove *reliance* was made in *Sharp v. Idaho Investment Corp.*, where Sharp purchased stock in a business which subsequently failed. Sharp filed suit to recover his investment and argued that literature distributed by the sellers was fraudulently misleading. In contrast, though, attorneys for the other side, Idaho Investment Corp., believed that the real reason Sharp invested was *not* because of the misleading literature. They believed that Sharp invested because he had had other business dealings with two of the principals in the new business (Neilson and Frazier) and believed that with their involvement the new business would be successful. Their point was that Sharp had relied on the business expertise of Neilson and Frazier and not on misleading literature, which he didn't read:

Sharp v. Idaho Investment Corp.
504 P.2d 386 (1972)

McFADDEN, JUSTICE.
* * *

Furthermore, Dr. Sharp did not read the prospectus or offering circular until after he had purchased the stock. Thus, any omission in the prospectus was not material to his decision to purchase.

Reliance is a fundamental element of fraud which must be proven by clear and convincing evidence. On direct examination Dr. Sharp was asked: "Doctor, would you tell me why you purchased stock in the Idaho Investment?" Dr. Sharp replied, "Because I believed Mr. Neilson. I was acquainted with Mr. Frazier and other officers of Sierra Life. I knew the officers and expected it to be a profitable venture." From Dr. Sharp's own testimony it is evident that rather than relying on the representations or misstatements by Idaho Investment and its agents he relied on expectations based on his experience with another corporation.

[Trial court decision in favor of Sharp, REVERSED.]

Reliance must be *justified.* Jed sells Milly a pill which, he says "will make you ten years younger." Milly believes it, however, any person of common sense knows that there is no pill known to medical science which makes a person younger. Thus Milly's reliance is not justified, and for lack of justifiable reliance, Milly cannot successfully assert fraud against Jed.

In the *Cousineau v. Walker* opinion (above) the court dealt with the question whether reliance was justified if the truth of a matter would be discovered through investigation. The *Cousineau* court said that courts in the United States are moving to the doctrine "that negligence in trusting in a misrepresentation will not excuse positive willful fraud or deprive the defrauded person of his remedy." In other words, willful fraud will not be excused simply because the victim negligently fails to discover the fraud. Applying that rule, if Milly, the seller of Speedy, the three-legged horse, intentionally hides Speedy's defect, Jed may claim justifiable reliance even though he neglects to inspect as thoroughly as he should.

Remedies. If Millie fraudulently sells Jed a three-legged horse, or if Jed fraudulently sells Millie a ranch with a contaminated spring, so what? In legal jargon, questions of result or outcome are referred to as "remedies," and the specific answer is that the injured party is entitled to remedies of *rescission* and *money damages.*

To understand the remedies of rescission and money damages, it is important to understand that fraud (sometimes known as "deceit") wears two hats. Wearing one hat, fraud is a *tort*, a form of wrong-doing like assault, false imprisonment or negligence, which is usually resolved by the payment of money damages. In the process of entering into a contract it is possible to commit the tort of fraud which means that the victim is entitled to money damages. Wearing another hat, fraud is a contract defense because contracts entered into on account of intentional false statements of material fact (justifiably relied on) are not really "contracts" at all, which means that the equitable remedy of rescission is appropriate.

The result of fraud wearing two hats is that when Millie fraudulently leads Jed into a "contract" for the purchase of Speedy, Jed is entitled to money damages for the tort of fraud, and to recission of the "contract." The same is true with respect to the ranch with a contaminated spring: Millie is entitled to tort damages and rescission of the contract. A few states require the injured party to make an election or choice: they may have tort damages or contract recission, but not both.

Problem Solving. Please turn to the Chapter Problems at the end of this chapter and solve problem 9.2.

Misrepresentation

MISREPRESENTATION: fraud without intent

Misrepresentation is the first-cousin of fraud. The difference between them is that misrepresentation does *not* require proof of scienter (*intentional* concealment or misrepresentation of facts). Return, again to Milly (in Idaho) who sells a three-legged horse to Jed (in Florida). Suppose that Milly's uncle in Montana died and left the horse to her, and she is simply selling a horse she has never seen and doesn't want. She has been erroneously told that the horse is normal and she repeats that error to Jed. The obvious difference in this example is Milly' state of mind. In the fraud examples (above) Milly *knew* that Speedy was abnormal and actively worked to conceal that fact from Jed; but, in this example, she is innocent but mistaken.

With the exception of scienter (intent to deceive), the elements of misrepresentation are the same as the elements of fraud. That is, misrepresentation requires proof of a false statement of a material fact; and, it also requires proof that the false statement was justifiably relied on by the injured party. In the "real world," misrepresentation will be used much more often than fraud simply because the difficult-to-prove element of intent to deceive is not required.

If misrepresentation is so much easier to prove than fraud, why would anyone bother with fraud? The answer is that fraud is a tort, but misrepresentation is not, and that difference is highlighted when the focus turns to remedies. If misrepresentation is proved, the injured party is entitled to the remedy of recission which, it will be recalled, means that the "contract" is invalidated and each party receives back what they have contributed to the relationship. But, the injured party is not entitled to damages beyond returning to *status quo*.

Problem Solving. Please turn to the Chapter Problems at the end of this chapter and solve problem 9.3.

Mistake

MISTAKE: mutual mistake allows rescission; but unilateral mistake does not

Mutual Mistake. In certain circumstances, a court will refuse to enforce a contract if it was entered into on the basis of *mutual* mistake (a mistake by both parties). The idea behind this is that a valid contract is theoretically based on mutual assent (mutual agreement) and, by definition, a contract based on mutual mistake is not based on mutual assent. In contrast, mistakes which are unilateral (a mistake by one party only) are usually enforced.

Mutual Mistake as to a Basic Assumption. A mistake which will make a contract voidable must be a mistake about a material fact which is assumed by both parties to be true. Suppose that Jed contracts to sell Millie a violin: (1) if they *both* believe the violin *is* a valuable Stradivarius violin, and then discover it is not, a *mutual* mistake has occurred; but, (2) if they both believe the violin *might* be a valuable Stradivarius violin, and then discover it is not, *no* mistake has occurred. In the first scenario, the violin as a valuable Stradivarius is a basic factual assumption on which the contract is based, and failure of that assumption upsets the reasonable expectations of both parties. On the other hand, in the second scenario, uncertainty and risk are basic assumptions and subsequently learning the truth does not upset the reasonable expectations of either party.

In general, assumptions about the existence, identity, quality or quantity of the subject matter qualify as basic factual assumptions. For example, in the old English case of *Raffles v. Wichelhaus,*[1] the contract was to transport cotton from Bombay on the ship "Peerless." The problem was that there were two ships by the name "Peerless," one leaving in October and the other leaving in December, which was too late for the buyer's purposes. The contract was voided because of mutual mistake: one party was contracting with respect to the Peerless leaving in October and the other with respect to the Peerless leaving in December. There was obviously a shared mistake about a basic factual assumption: the identity of the ship to be used.

The mutual mistake issue was raised in *Wilkin v. 1st Source Bank*. Wilkins purchased a house from a bank only to find it cluttered with "trash." The bank and the buyer agreed that the buyer would clean up the property and, in return, could keep any part of the "trash" it wanted. A previous owner had been a famous artist and, unknown to either party, valuable works of art were included in the "trash." The court applied the mutual mistake doctrine discussed above to solve the problem:

---

[1] 159 Eng.Rep. 375 (1864).

Wilkin v. 1st Source Bank
548 N.E.2d 170 (1990)

HOFFMAN, Judge.

* * *

Mutual assent is a prerequisite to the creation of a contract. * * * Where both parties share a common assumption about a vital fact upon which they based their bargain, and that assumption is false, the transaction may be avoided if because of the mistake a quite different exchange of values occurs from the exchange of values contemplated by the parties. * * * There is no contract, because the minds of the parties have in fact never met.

The necessity of mutual assent, or "meeting the minds," is illustrated in the classic case of *Sherwood v. Walker* (1887), 66 Mich. 568, 33 N.W. 919. The owners of a blooded cow indicated to the purchaser that the cow was barren. The purchaser also appeared to believe that the cow was barren. Consequently, a bargain was made to sell at a price per pound at which the cow would have brought approximately $80.00. Before delivery, it was discovered that the cow was with calf and that she was, therefore, worth from $750.00 to $1,000.00. The court ruled that the transaction was voidable:

> "[T]he mistake was not of the mere quality of the animal, but went to the very nature of the thing. A barren cow is substantially a different creature than a breeding one. There is as much difference between them...as there is between an ox and a cow...." * * *

Like the parties in *Sherwood*, the parties in the instant case shared a common presupposition as to the existence of certain facts which proved false. The Bank and the Wilkins considered the real estate which the Wilkins had purchased to be cluttered with items of personal property variously characterized as "junk," "stuff" or "trash." Neither party suspected that works of art created by Ivan Mestrovic remained on the premises.

As in *Sherwood*, one party experienced an unexpected, unbargained-for gain while the other party experienced an unexpected, unbargained-for loss. Because the Bank and the Wilkins did not know that the eight drawings and the plaster sculpture were included in the items of personality that cluttered the real property, the discovery of those works of art by the Wilkins was unexpected. The resultant gain to the Wilkins and loss to the bank were not contemplated by the parties when the Bank agreed that the Wilkins could clean the premises and keep such personal property as they wished.

The following commentary on *Sherwood* is equally applicable to the case at bar:

> "Here the buyer sought to retain a gain that was produced, not by a subsequent change in circumstances, nor by the favorable resolution of known uncertainties when the contract was made, but by the presence of facts quite different from those one which the parties based their bargain." * * *

The probate court properly concluded that there was no agreement for the purchase, sale or other disposition of the eight drawings and plaster sculpture, because there was no meeting of the minds.

[Affirmed.]

Unilateral Mistake. In the discussion above, the mistakes, or lack thereof, were mutual. But, what if the mistake is *unilateral*—by one party only. In general, a mistake which is unilateral is not a basis for invalidating a contract, because that would upset the reasonable expectations of the other contracting party. Consider, however, the opinion at the beginning of this chapter: *Whitaker v. Associated Credit Services*. In *Whitaker*, a typist made a mistake and wrote $500,000 in an agreement, instead of $500. This was a unilateral mistake, and normally such a contract would *not* be rescinded on the basis of mistake because, as noted above, rescission would upset the reasonable expectations of the other contracting party.

But, in *Whitaker*, there were no reasonable expectations to upset because the Whitaker's attorney knew when he received the $500,000 offer that something was wrong. As the court noted: "Plaintiffs' attorney himself characterized the offer of $500,000 as 'outrageous,' and admitted he was 'shocked' by the offer when he received it." In short, the Whitaker's knew when they received the offer that something was wrong. Thus, the rule with respect to unilateral mistake is that such mistakes will not be the subject of rescission *unless* the party not making the mistake knew or should have known of the existence of a mistake. In such cases, as in *Whitaker*, the remedy of rescission may be applied.

Suppose that Milly contracts to sell Jed a parcel of property which Jed buys believing that a new freeway will be constructed nearby. (Obviously, construction of a freeway near the land will increase the value of the land.) Later, Jed learns that he has made a mistake and a freeway will not be constructed near the land he has contracted to purchase. Milly knew nothing about a freeway; Jed's mistake was unilateral. In this case, a unilateral mistake will not suffice as a basis to rescind the contract.

__Problem Solving__. Please turn to the Chapter Problems at the end of this chapter and solve problem 9.4.

Duress

DURESS means compelling a person to contract by force or compulsion

Duress refers to force or compulsion. If a party is compelled to enter into an agreement by force or compulsion, a meeting of the minds has not occurred and the agreement may be rescinded. The simplest example of duress is where Millie uses a gun to force Jed to sign a contract. Obviously, this agreement may be rescinded at the request of Jed. To allow rescission because of duress, a court must find that (1) that the contract was induced by an improper threat, and (2) that the victim has no reasonable alternative but to enter into the contract.[2]

More difficult than the rather obvious example above is the problem of "economic" duress. In *Rich & Whillock, Inc. v. Ashton Development*, the plaintiffs were a new company which provided grading and excavating services for the defendant. After receiving some earlier payments from the defendant, the plaintiff submitted a final bill of $72, 286.45. Although there was no problem with the work, the defendants refused—apparently as a cost-saving device—to pay more than $50,000. Plaintiff's protested that they were a new company and loss of the unpaid difference might cause them to go broke. An officer of the defendant company then said: "I have a check for you, and just take it or leave it, this is all you get. If you don't want this,

---

[2] RESTATEMENT (SECOND) OF CONTRACTS, §175.

you have got to sue me." At that point, plaintiff's signed the compromise ($50,000) agreement while protesting that it was "blackmail" and that they were signing only to survive financially. Later, the plaintiffs sued to recover the unpaid balance. The trial court ruled in favor of the plaintiffs and the defendants appealed:

Rich & Whillock, Inc. v. Ashton Development, Inc.
204 Cal.Rptr. 86 (1984)

WIENER, Associate Justice.
* * *
California courts have recognized the economic duress doctrine in private cases for at least 50 years. * * * The doctrine is equitably based * * * and represents "but an expansion by courts of equity of the old common-law doctrine of duress." * * * As it has evolved to the present day, the economic doctrine is not limited by early statutory and judicial expressions requiring an unlawful act in the nature of a tort or a crime. * * * Instead, the doctrine now comes into play upon the doing of a wrongful act which is sufficiently coercive to cause a reasonably prudent person faced with no reasonable alternative to succumb to the perpetrator's pressure. * * * The assertion of a claim known to be false or a bad faith threat to breach a contract or to withhold a payment may constitute a wrongful act for purposes of the economic duress doctrine. * * * Further, a reasonably prudent person subject to such an act may have no reasonable alternative but to succumb when the only other alternative is bankruptcy or financial ruin. * * *

The underlying concern of the economic duress doctrine is the enforcement in the marketplace of certain minimal standards of business ethics. Hard bargaining, "efficient" breaches and reasonable settlements of good faith disputes are all acceptable, even desirable, in our economic system. That system can be viewed as a game in which everybody wins, to one degree or another, so long as everyone plays by the common rules. Those rules are not limited to precepts of rationality and self-interest. They include equitable notions of fairness and propriety which preclude the wrongful exploitation of business exigencies to obtain disproportionate exchanges of value. Such exchanges make a mockery of freedom of contract and undermine the proper functioning of our economic system. The economic duress doctrine serves as a last resort to correct these aberrations when conventional alternatives and remedies are unavailing.
* * *
Judgment affirmed.

In the *Whillock* case, the court obviously concluded that the defendant had gone beyond hard bargaining. In hard bargaining cases, the courts are not as concerned because a party that doesn't like the terms of the contract can simply refuse to contract. In *Whillock*, however, the leverage used by the defendant was the unlawful threat to breach a contract. That was the economic duress that made the subsequent contract unenforceable.

Problem Solving. Please turn to the Chapter Problems at the end of this chapter and solve problem 9.5.

Undue Influence

Contracts entered into because of undue influence may be rescinded. Undue influence requires evidence of (1) persuasion in an atmosphere of trust and confidence where one party has dominance over the other, and (2) the persuasion is unfair.[3] A simple example is one of Jed who is old and competent (but feeble) and stays with his niece, Millie, instead of living in a nursing home. Jed trusts Millie and relies on her to make important decisions. She tells him that if he will sell his ranch to her (at a greatly reduced price) he can stay with her; otherwise, it is the nursing home. If the reduction in the sales price is grossly disproportionate to the service he receives from staying with Millie, or, if she sends him to the nursing home after signing the sales contract, then the contract between them is unfair and subject to recission on the basis of undue influence.

A more difficult case is presented in *Odorizzi v. Bloomfield School District*, in which Odorizzi, an elementary school teacher, was arrested and charged with unlawful homosexual activity. The court stated the facts as follows: "Odorizzi declares he was under such severe mental and emotional strain at the time he signed his resignation, having just completed the process of arrest, questioning by the police, booking, and release on bail, and having gone for forty hours without sleep, that he was incapable of rational thought or action. While he was in this condition and unable to think clearly, the superintendent of the District and the principal of his school came to his apartment. They said they were trying to help him and had his best interests at heart, that he should take their advice and immediately resign his position with the District, that there was no time to consult an attorney, that if he did not resign immediately the District would suspend and dismiss him from his position and publicize the proceedings, his 'aforementioned arrest' and cause him 'to suffer extreme embarrassment and humiliation'; but that if he resigned at once the incident would not be publicized and would not jeopardize his chances of securing employment as a teacher elsewhere. Odorizzi pleads that because of his faith and confidence in their representations they were able to substitute their will and judgment in place of his own and thus obtain his signature to his purported resignation."

The trial court dismissed Odorizzi's complaint and he appealed. The issue before the court was, of course, whether the facts described in the complaint were enough to entitle Odorizzi to a trial on the issue of undue influence:

Donald W. Odorizzi v. Bloomfield School District
54 Cal.Rptr.533 (1966)

FLEMING, Justice.

* * *

However, the pleading does set out a claim that plaintiff's consent to the transaction had been obtained through the use of undue influence.

* * *

---

[3] RESTATEMENT (SECOND) OF CONTRACTS, §177.

143

The difficulty, of course, lies in determining when the forces of persuasion have overflowed their normal banks and become oppressive flood waters. There are second thoughts to every bargain, and hindsight is still better than foresight. Undue influence cannot be used as a pretext to avoid bad bargains or escape from bargains which refuse to come up to expectations. A woman who buys a dress on impulse, which on critical inspection by her best friend turns out to be less fashionable than she had thought, is not legally entitled to set aside the sale on the ground that the saleswoman used all her wiles to close the sale. A man who buys a tract of desert land in the expectation that it is in the immediate path of the city's growth and will become another Palm Springs, an expectation cultivated in glowing terms by the seller, cannot rescind his bargain when things turn out differently. If we are temporarily persuaded against our better judgment to do something about which we later have second thoughts, we must abide the consequences of the risks inherent in managing our own affairs.

However, overpersuasion is generally accompanied by certain characteristics which tend to create a pattern. The pattern usually involves several of the following elements: (1) discussion of the transaction at an unusual or inappropriate time, (2) consummation of the transaction in an unusual place, (3) insistent demand that the business be finished at once, (4) extreme emphasis on untoward consequences of delay, (5) the use of multiple persuaders by the dominant side against a single servient party, (6) absence of the third party advisers to the servient party, (7) statements that there is no time to consult financial advisers or attorneys. If a number of these elements are simultaneously present, the persuasion may be characterized as excessive. * * *

     * * *

We express no opinion on the merits of plaintiff's case, or the propriety of his continuing to teach school. * * * We do hold that his pleading, liberally construed, states a cause of action for rescission of a transaction to which his apparent consent had been obtained through the use of undue influence.

The judgment is reversed.

Problem Solving. Please turn to the Chapter Problems at the end of this chapter and solve problem 9.6.

Summary.

In summary, the existence of a valid, enforceable contract focuses on the formation process. Contracts are presumed to be valid and enforceable, but that ceases to be the case when formation of the contract is induced by fraud, misrepresentation, mistake, duress or undue influence. The existence of these improper influences destroys mutual assent and the disadvantaged party may ask for recission of the contract, and sometimes money damages.

Chapter Problems

Problem 9.1

In *Whitaker v. Associated Credit Services*, suppose that the typographical error was *$5,000* instead of $500,000. Would the result in the case have been the same?

Problem 9.2

In *Cousineau v. Walker*, was *caveat emptor* successfully applied?

Problem 9.3

You are an attorney handling a contract case for a plaintiff. You have evidence that the defendant made a number of *intentional* misstatements of fact for the purpose of inducing your client (the plaintiff) to enter into a contract for the sale of real estate. The remedy your client wants is recission of the contract. What theory (fraud or misrepresentation) will you pursue in favor of your client?

Problem 9.4

Return to *Wilkin v. 1ˢᵗ Source Bank* and suppose that the bank was selling off estate assets and offered to sell the Wilkins a safe belonging to the estate. In the safe is a locked compartment for which there is no key, and the bank—noting that there is no key—offered to sell the safe to the Wilkins for $100, and whatever they find in the compartment (if they can get it open) they can keep. If the Wilkin's buy the safe and manage to get the compartment open and find therein $20,000 in cash, can the bank rescind the agreement on the basis of

mistake, as they did in the original decision?

Problem 9.5

In *Austin Instrument, Inc. v. Loral Corporation* (272 N.E.2d 533), Loral complained that it had been forced to enter into a contract with Austin on the basis of economic duress. In 1965, Loral was awarded a contract to supply radar sets to the Navy, and Loral awarded a subcontract to Austin to supply some of the parts. In 1966, Loral received a second contract to supply radar sets to the Navy, and Loral solicited bids for some of the parts. Austin submitted a proposal for parts in the second contract. The following events followed: "Austin bid on all 40 gear components [for the second contract] but, on July 15, a representative from Loral informed Austin's president, Mr. Kraus, that his company would be awarded the subcontract only for those items on which it was low bidder. The Austin officer refused to accept an order for less than all 40 of the gear parts and on the next day he told Loral that *Austin would cease deliveries of the parts due under the existing subcontract* unless Loral consented to substantial increases in the prices provided for by that agreement—both retroactively for parts already delivered and prospectively on those not yet shipped—and placed with Austin the order for all 40 parts needed under Loral's second Navy contract. Shortly thereafter, Austin did, indeed, stop delivery. After contracting 10 manufacturers of precision gears and finding none who could produce the parts in time to meet its commitments to the Navy, Loral acceded to Austin's demands." Loral later sued to recover the extra money it had been forced to pay to Austin in relation to the first contract. Loral claimed it acted under duress. Will Loral be successful?

Problem 9.6

Based on the opinion in *Odorizzi v. Bloomfield School District*, did Donald Odorizzi *win* in his lawsuit?

Chapter 10
Consideration

Chapter Outline

OBJECTIVE is to learn the contract requirement known as consideration.

The objective of this chapter is to understand the contract requirement known as *consideration*. The chapter is organized as follows:

- *The Requirement of Consideration.* The feature which separates contracts from other relationships—such as giving a gift— is the requirement of consideration. One party makes a promise and "consideration" requires that the other party support that promise by giving (or giving up) something of legal value in return.

- *Bargained Exchange.* When considering whether a contract is supported by consideration, analysis focuses on the items of legal value that are bargained for.

- *Legal Sufficiency of Consideration.* Legal sufficiency of consideration (does it exist) is examined in terms of "detriment" and "benefit." Each party to a contract must confer a benefit or suffer a detriment.

- *Legal Adequacy of Consideration.* In contrast to the discussion of the legal *sufficiency* of consideration (does consideration exist) is the question whether consideration is legally adequate (is the consideration enough)? In general, courts will not invalidate a contract because the consideration is "inadequate" in relation to one of the parties.

- *Particular Problems Concerning Consideration.* The past consideration problem: things completed before the time of contracting are not sufficient consideration. The preexisting duty problem: promising to do something which is already a duty is not sufficient consideration. The illusory promise problem: promises which appear to create a duty or an obligation, but do not, are not sufficient consideration. Debt settlement problems: an agreement to pay an unliquidated debt provides sufficient consideration; but, an agreement to pay a liquidated debt does not provide sufficient consideration.

- *Promissory Estoppel.* Promises not supported by a contract may be enforced where a party has made a promise, knowing it will be relied upon, and the promise is justifiably relied upon and detriment caused.

An Overview of the Consideration Requirement

CONSIDERATION requires an exchange of something of legal value.

The feature which separates contracts from other relationships—such as giving a gift— is the requirement of *consideration*. In its simplest terms, the requirement of consideration means that the parties to a contract exchange something of legal value. Thus, the consideration requirement is met when Jed promises to give Millie an apple and, in return, Millie promises to give Jed an orange. This is a contract based on consideration because things of legal value are exchanged. The obvious contrast is a transaction where Jed promises to give Millie an apple and Millie promises nothing in return. This is a gift and not a contract because only Jed gives something of legal value; Jed's promise is not supported by consideration from Milly.

MUTUALITY requires that both parties give consideration.

In a contract, *both parties* must give consideration. Thus, in the transaction above, Jed's promise to give an apple is supported by Millie's promise to give an orange, and Millie's promise to give an orange is supported by Jed's promise to give an apple. The proposition that both parties must give consideration is sometimes referred to as *mutuality*.

It is not necessary that the consideration contributed to a contract be negative or unpleasant. In the apple and orange transaction above, Milly promises to give an orange to Jed. If Milly *loves* oranges, and hates to part with the one she has, then she may view her promise negatively. On the other hand, if Milly *dislikes* oranges, and will let them rot before she eats the one she has, then she may view her promise positively. Either way the courts don't care. The point is that the law relating to consideration does not care whether Milly *loves* or *dislikes* her orange, or *wants* or *does not* want to give it up. The orange is something of legal value, and promising to part with it (regardless of Milly's personal feelings about it) is sufficient consideration. The exchange of the orange for an apple is what the parties bargained for, and what is bargained for becomes the consideration. The feelings and motivations of the parties are not important.

To this point it has been said that consideration requires a "mutual" and "bargained for" exchange. In addition, it has been said that the mutual and bargained for exchange must be for something of legal value. What does "legal value" mean? Giving something of legal value may take a variety of forms, as the following examples illustrate. In each of the following examples, Jed promises to give $100 (which has legal value) and Millie promises to give something of legal value in return: (1) Jed promises to give Millie $100 if she will *repair his car*; (2) Jed promises to give Millie $100 if she will *repair his mother's car*; or (3) Jed promises to give Millie $100 if she will rest and *not repair anyone's car*.

In each of the examples above, Millie gave something of legal value because as part of a bargaining process she agreed to change her legal position and do (or not do) something which was otherwise not her previous obligation. In the first and second examples, Millie *gives* her labor, which is something of legal value. In the third example, Millie *gives up* the right to work, which is also something of legal value.

In the examples above, three things should not escape notice. First, sometimes the benefit of the legal value goes to a third party and not to the other contracting party. Thus, in the second example, Jed promises to give $100, and Millie promises to repair a car, but the car she will repair is not Jed's car, *it is his mother's car*. This is an example of a third party (and not the contracting party) receiving the benefit of the legal value.

The second thing that should not escape notice is that consideration may be *giving up* something. Thus, in the third example, Millie has the right to practice the trade of auto repair. The right to go places and do things is a valuable right, and if Millie is contractually deprived of that right she has given something of value, and that means that she has given adequate consideration.

The third thing that should not escape notice is that it is irrelevant that Millie may (or may not) enjoy that which she is contractually bound to do. In the third example, we don't care *why* Jed does not want Millie to work and—as discussed above— it is *not* required that Millie's performance be unpleasant or to her economic disadvantage, as long as she changes her legal position at Jed's request. When Millie gives up what is her legal right, she gives good consideration, just like a basketball player who loves to play basketball gives good consideration when he contracts to play professional basketball.

The following opinion, *Brads v. First Baptist Church*, discusses whether a lack of consideration invalidated a contract between a church and it's pastor. In this case, the pastor, Reverend Brads, was forced to retire for health reasons. Commencing in 1980, the Church congregation agreed to pay him a reduced salary, for life, and he agreed to help with Church affairs to the extent his health allowed. In 1990, the Church claimed that no consideration existed for their contract with Reverend Brads and stopped paying his salary. Reverend Brads brought suit and a jury found in his favor. On appeal, the court discussed the contention that the contract between Brads and the Church was not supported by consideration:

Brads v. first Baptist Church
624 N.E.2d 737 (1993)

GRADY, Presiding Judge.
* * *

Consideration is, of course, an element necessary for a binding contract, and a complete lack of any consideration is a valid defense to a breach of contract action. * * * Consideration may consist of either a detriment to the promisee or a benefit to the promisor. * * * A benefit may consist of some right, interest or profit accruing to the promisor, while a detriment may consist of some forbearance, loss or responsibility given, suffered or undertaken by the promisee. * * * Absent a showing of fraud, consideration is not deemed legally insufficient merely because it is inadequate. * * *

The evidence demonstrates that in 1980 Brads, while serving as pastor, told the deacons of the Church that his physician had recommended that Brads retire as active pastor because of health problems. Brads proposed a gradual reduction in the salary he was then being

---

paid, through a series of "step-downs," to a final amount representing approximately one-third of that salary. According to the evidence presented by Brads, all parties knew and understood this final step-down amount would be paid to Brads for life. The deacons accepted Brads' proposal.

The parties jointly prepared an agreement in writing, Plaintiff's Exhibit 1, which was presented to and adopted by the entire church congregation in 1980, and readopted by the congregation in 1985. By the terms of this document, the Church placed Brads on disability retirement status, conferred upon Brads the honorary title of Pastor Emeritus, allowed Brads to set up an office in the church, and allotted retirement benefits to Brads according to the step-down schedule agreed upon. Brads was obligated to aid, assist and advise whomever the church called as a new pastor, to the extent that Brads' health would allow. Over the course of the next ten years Brads preached occasionally at First Baptist Church, taught Sunday school classes there, served on the budget committee and helped with administrative matters.

The foregoing evidence, if believed, demonstrates that the Church received a benefit in the form of Brads' promise to assist a new pastor and that Brads received the benefit of payments, office space and title. Each party performed on these promises to confer an actual benefit on the other. Those benefits were a product of the agreement and subsequent to it.

While we recognize the conflicting nature of the testimony presented in this case, construing the evidence most strongly in favor of Brads and accepting such evidence as true * * * we conclude that there is some competent evidence to demonstrate the existence of consideration by Brads * * * *

[Affirmed]

Reconsider the *Brads* opinion as though it was an exchange for an orange. Reverend Brads sold a sick orange to the congregation: nobody knew just how sick the orange was, but that was part of the deal and the congregation agreed to take the orange "as is." Later, the congregation changed it's mind because it was not getting as much orange juice as it had hoped for. The response of the court—although hidden in legal jargon—is quite predictable: in exchange for the purchase price, Brads gave an orange which had some (although undetermined) legal value. Whether the value of the orange was great or little, there was *some* value and parting with that value was a detriment to him and a benefit to the congregation. Because Brad's promise included a detriment to him and a benefit to the congregation the consideration requirement is satisfied.

The adequacy of the consideration, whether each party got a "good deal" is not a question the courts, in the absence of some overreaching will normally address. The question is: was there some consideration?

Problem Solving. Please turn to Chapter Problems at the end of this chapter and solve problem 10.1.

The foregoing is, in summary form, the law on the requirement of consideration. What follows is essentially an elaboration or explanation of the principles described above.

Bargained Exchange

BARGAINED EXCHANGE: only that which is bargained for is consideration

When considering whether a contract is supported by consideration, analysis focuses on the items of legal value that are *bargained for*. For example, suppose that Millie sells her skis to Jed and feels a sense of relief at having done so. Is the "sense of relief" that Millie experiences part of the consideration supporting the sales contract? The answer is no, because the contract is a bargain for the exchange of money and skis, *not relief*. Millie did not sell or buy relief and neither did Jed.

On the same point (the requirement of a "bargained for" exchange), suppose that as a gesture of friendship, Millie offers to repair Jed's car for free, and he says "okay, and thanks." This is obviously a gift of her service, and not a contract, because Jed gives nothing of legal value in return for her service. Sometime later, and without the car repair in mind, Jed offers to repair the kitchen table of his friend Millie, and she says "thanks, that's great." This is also a gift of his service, and not a contract because Millie gives nothing of legal value in return for his service.

Neither party has bargained to give service in return for service given by the other. In short, Millie and Jed have each, independently, made a gift of service to the other. Each of them could change their mind and refuse to perform the service and there would be no contract liability.

How much would the facts above need to be changed to convert the relationship of Millie and Jed into a contract? Suppose that Millie says to Jed, "I'll fix your car *if* you will fix my kitchen table," and he says "okay." This is a contract, and the difference is that the *exchange* of services is *bargained for*; the *exchange* of services is part of the deal or bargain. In legal effect she has bargained: "in consideration of your promise to fix my table (if you will fix my table), I will fix your car;" and, in legal effect he has bargained: "in consideration of your promise to fix my car (if you will fix my car), I will fix your table." When they both agree to this mutual proposition, there is a contract.

Problem Solving. Please turn to Chapter Problems at the end of this chapter and solve problem 10.2.

Legal Sufficiency of Consideration

With respect to consideration, two questions are asked: (1) is the consideration legally sufficient (does it *exist*), and (2) is the consideration legally adequate (is it *enough*)?

LEGAL SUFFICIENCY: does consideration exist?

Legal *sufficiency* of consideration (does consideration exist) is examined in terms of "detriment" and "benefit." In general terms, consideration is a detriment to the party who gives it, and a benefit to the party who receives it. An example of this is the contract (described above) between Jed and Millie where Jed agrees to give Millie $100 if she will repair his car. Is there consideration for Jed's promise to pay $100? The answer is yes because Millie's work repairing the car is a *detriment* to her (she parts with her labor) and a *benefit* to Jed (he receives her labor). Thus, she gives legally sufficient consideration for Jed's promise. Is there consideration for Millie's work repairing Jed's car? The answer is yes because giving Milly $100 is a detriment to him (he parts with his money) and a benefit to Millie (she receives the money).

Frequently, though, the law recognizes the existence of consideration in circumstances where there is detriment on both sides, *but not a corresponding benefit.* An example of this is the contract between Jed and Millie where Jed pays Millie $100 and Millie agrees to repair the car of Jed's *mother.* When we ask if Milly gives consideration for Jed's promise to pay $100 it is observed that Millie suffers a detriment and gives a benefit, but the *benefit* conferred by Millie goes to Jed's *mother* (a non-contracting party), not to Jed. Because of examples like this the law acknowledges that there is legally sufficient consideration if a contracting party (in this case, Milly) suffers a *detriment*, without the requirement that the other party receive a benefit.

Repeating a point made above, a thoughtful reader may argue that, in the example above, Jed *did* receive a *benefit* because of the good feelings he experienced by providing a valuable service to his mother. The answer is that Millie did not *bargain* to provide good feelings and Jed did not *bargain* to purchase good feelings, they both *bargained* for the delivery of repair services. Only the detriments and benefits that are *bargained for* are considered in determining the existence of consideration.

In the third version of the Jed and Millie transaction above, Jed agrees to pay Millie $100 if she agrees not to repair anyone's car. Does Millie give legally sufficient consideration in this arrangement? The answer is yes because—as noted above—suffering a detriment is sufficient for consideration; conferring a benefit is not required. In this case, Millie has the legal right to repair cars and she gives up that right, to her detriment. Millie giving up the right to repair cars may, or may not, confer a benefit on Jed or someone else, but (again) the existence of a benefit is not *required.*

The next appellate opinion, *Hamer v. Sidway*, is an unusual old case where a young man was promised $5,000 by his uncle if he would "refrain from drinking, using tobacco, swearing, and playing cards or billiards for money until he became 21 years of age." (At the time, it would have been lawful for him to do these things.) The argument of the defendant was that the performance by the young man was neither a detriment to him nor a benefit to his uncle. The trial court thought that there was *not* sufficient consideration, but the appellate court disagreed:

152

HAMER v. SIDWAY [1]
27 N.E. 256 (1891)

PARKER, J.,

* * *

It appears that William E. Story, Sr., was the uncle of William E. Story, 2d; that at the celebration of the golden wedding of Samuel Story and wife, father and mother of William E. Story, Sr., on the 20th day of March, 1869, in the presence of the family and invited guests, he promised his nephew that if he would refrain from drinking, using tobacco, swearing, and playing cards or billiards for money until he became 21 years of age, he would pay him the sum of $5,000. The nephew assented thereto, and fully performed the conditions inducing the promise. When the nephew arrived at the age of 21 years, and on the 31st day of January, 1875, he wrote to his uncle, informing him that he had performed his part of the agreement, and had thereby become entitled to the sum of $5,000. The uncle received the letter, and a few days later, and on the 6th day of February, he wrote and mailed to his nephew the following letter: "Buffalo, Feb. 6, 1875. W. E. Story, Jr. — Dear Nephew: Your letter of the 31st ult. came to hand all right, saying that you had lived up to the promise made to me several years ago. I have no doubt but you have, for which you shall have five thousand dollars, as I promised you.

* * *

The defendant contends that the contract was without consideration to support it, and therefore invalid. He asserts that the promisee, by refraining from the use of liquor and tobacco, was not harmed, but benefitted; that that which he did was best for him to do, independently of his uncle's promise,— and insists that it follows that, unless the promisor was benefitted, the contract was without consideration, — a contention which, if well founded, would seem to leave open for controversy in many cases whether that which the promisee did or omitted to do was in fact of such benefit to him as to leave no consideration to support the enforcement of the promisor's agreement. Such a rule could not be tolerated, and is without foundation in the law. The exchequer chamber in 1875 defined "consideration" as follows: "A valuable consideration, in the sense of the law, may consist either in some right, interest, profit, or benefit accruing to the one party, or some forbearance, detriment, loss, or responsibility given, suffered, or undertaken by the other." Courts "will not ask whether the thing which forms the consideration does in fact benefit the promisee or a third party, or is of any substantial value to any one. It is enough that something is the something is promised, done, forborne, or suffered by the party to whom the promise is made as consideration for the promise made to him.

* * *

The order appealed from should be reversed * * * All concur.

The point here is that the young man had the legal right to drink, smoke, chew (and spit) and gamble. The theory of the defendant was incorrect: giving up those activities is giving up a legal right and that meant that he suffered a legal detriment,

---

[1] If this was a contract between William Story, 2d and his uncle, William E. Story, Sr., why are the parties to this action Hamer and Sidway? The answer is that the nephew sold his contract rights and they ended up in the hands of Hamer. Some years after the original contract was entered into, old Mr. Story died and Hamer—now the owner of the contract right—demanded that Sidway, the executor of the estate of the deceased Mr. Story, pay the contract. Sidway refused and Hamer sued Sidway.

even if he did not suffer a personal one. Thus, the appellate court was correct in reversing the trial court.

Problem Solving. Please turn to Chapter Problems at the end of this chapter and solve problem 10.3.

Legal Adequacy of Consideration

LEGAL ADEQUACY : is the consideration sufficient?

In contrast to the discussion of the legal *sufficiency* of consideration (does consideration exist) is the question whether consideration is legally adequate (is the consideration enough)? In general, courts will not invalidate a contract because the consideration is "inadequate" in relation to one of the parties. For example, suppose that Millie contracts to buy "Speedy," a young, untested, race horse for $20,000. Some may argue that Speedy is only worth $10,000 and others may argue that Speedy is worth $30,000, or more. If Speedy proves to be a winner, should the contract be reopened in favor of the seller; and, if Speedy proves to be slow as a sea slug, should the contract be reopened in favor of Millie?

In the eyes of the law, the contract for the sale of Speedy should not be reopened because a function of contracts is to resolve uncertainty about the present (what is Speedy worth now) and uncertainty about the future (what will Speedy be worth in the future)? An insurance company, for example, deals with the risk that some people will die early and some will die late, and, some people will have automobile accidents and some will not. Unless there has been dishonesty or unfairness which shocks the conscience of the court, the legal *adequacy* of consideration is irrelevant and the law will not rescue parties from the consequences of their judgment.

Problem Solving. Please turn to Chapter Problems at the end of this chapter and solve problem 10.4.

Particular Problems Concerning Consideration

The Past Consideration Problem. In the process of contracting, sufficient consideration must be given *at the time of contracting*, and that means that things done or given in the past do not count. In the process of contracting, the parties exchange promises which focus on things to be done (or not done) in the future. Thus, in the process of contracting, Millie promises that (in the future) she will fix Jed's car, and Jed promises that (in the future) he will pay Millie $100.

CONSIDERATION PROBLEMS: past consideration, preexisting duty and payment of a liquidated debt are not consideration.

Suppose that Jed rescues Millie's daughter from drowning in a swimming pool. In gratitude, Millie promises to pay Jed $100 for the next five years. Is there a contract between Jed and Millie? The answer is no. Millie has promised that (in the future) she will pay money to Jed. This is consideration on her part because paying the money is a detriment to her (and a benefit to him). At the time of contracting, what does Jed promise to do; does he give consideration? The answer is that he does not give consideration because he does not promise to do anything. All of Jed's participation is in the past and this is referred to as "past" consideration. Past consideration is not legally sufficient.

Problem Solving. Please turn to Chapter Problems at the end of this chapter and solve problem 10.5.

The Preexisting Duty Problem. A person does not give sufficient consideration in the process of contracting if the person merely agrees to do something he or she is already obligated to do. The classic illustration of this is Jed, a policeman, who refuses to perform his duty and investigate the theft of Millie's stereo. In frustration, Millie offers to pay Jed $100 if he will investigate the crime. Jed investigates the crime and claims the $100, which Millie refuses to pay. Is there a contract?

The answer to the question above is no because Jed does not give sufficient consideration for Millie's promise. At the time of contracting, Jed promised to investigate crime, which was something he was already under an obligation to do. He had a "preexisting" duty. In making his promise, Jed incurs no detriment because his legal duties are not changed: before the contract he was obligated to investigate the crime, and after the contract he was obligated to investigate the crime.

The following opinion, _Denney v. Reppert_, involves a bank robbery and a reward offered for capturing the robbers. The bank was willing to pay the reward money but could not determine which of a list of bank employees and police officers should have a share. The court decided that bank employees have a preexisting duty to aid their employer and thus could not participate in the reward. The court then turned it's attention to the police officers:

Denny v. Reppert
432 S.W.2d 647 (1968)

R.L. MYRE, Sr., Special Commissioner.

The sole question presented in this case is which of several claimants is entitled to an award for information leading to the apprehension and conviction of certain bank robbers.

    * * *

On June 12th or 13th, 1963, three armed men entered the First State Bank, Eubank, Kentucky, and with a display of arms and threats robbed the bank of over $30,000. Later in the day they were apprehended by State Policemen Garret Godby, Johnny Simms and Tilford Reppert, placed under arrest, and the entire loot was recovered. Later all of the prisoners were convicted and Garret Godby, Johnny Simms and Tilford Reppert appeared as witnesses at the trial.

The First State Bank of Eubank was a member of the Kentucky Bankers Association which provided and advertised a reward of $500.00 for the arrest and conviction of each bank robber. Hence the outstanding reward for the three bank robbers was $1,500. Many became claimants for the reward and the Kentucky State Bankers Association being unable to determine the merits of the claims for the reward asked the circuit court to determine the merits of the various claims and to adjudge who was entitled to receive the reward or share in it. All of the

---

claimants were made defendants in the action.

* * *

State Policemen Garret Godby, Johnny Simms and Tilford Reppert made the arrest of the bank robbers and captured the stolen money. All participated in the prosecution. At the time of the arrest, it was the duty of the state policemen to apprehend the criminals. Under the law they cannot claim or share in the reward and they are interposing no claim to it.

This leaves the defendant, Tilford Reppert the sole eligible claimant. The record shows that at the time of the arrest he was a deputy sheriff in Rockcastle County, but the arrest and recovery of the stolen money took place in Pulaski County. He was out of his jurisdiction, and was thus under no legal duty make the arrest, and is thus eligible to claim and receive the reward. In *Kentucky Bankers Ass'n et al. V. Cassaday*, 264 Ky. 351, 94 S.W.2d 622, 624, it was said:

"It is *** well established that a public officer with the authority of the law to make an arrest may accept an offer of reward or compensation for acts or services performed outside of his bailiwick or not within the scope of his official duties *** ."

The claimant Tilford Reppert was present with Garrett Godby and Johnny Simms at the time of the arrest and all cooperated in its consummation. The claimant Tilford Reppert personally recovered the stolen money. He recovered $2,000.00 more than the bank records show was stolen. This record does not reveal what became of the $2,000.00 excess.

It is manifest from the record that Tilford Reppert is the only claimant qualified and eligible to receive the reward. Therefore, it is the judgment of the circuit court that he is entitled to receive payment of the $1,500.00 reward now deposited with the Clerk of this Court.

The judgment is affirmed.

The outcome in *Denney* is easy to understand. A more difficult case to decide would be one in which the other police officers (Godby and Simms) were off-duty at the time of the robbery and as public-spirited citizens helped capture the crooks (doing all of this work while they were off-duty). In that case, the court would need to decide whether an *off-duty* police officer has a duty to act in apprehending criminals.

Problem Solving. Please turn to Chapter Problems at the end of this chapter and solve problem 10.6.

The Illusory Promise Problem. The word "illusion" refers to things which appear to exist, but do not. Some promises may appear to create a duty or obligation on the part of the promisor, but do not. Because the duty or obligation is merely an illusion they are "illusory" promises. A person making an illusory promise as part of the contracting process does not give sufficient consideration.

For example, Milly hires Jed to do yard work at her home: "for thirty days, at the rate of $30 per day, unless this agreement is earlier terminated by Milly." Although Jed's agreement includes sufficient consideration, Millie's does not. Millie's promise is not sufficient consideration because it is "illusory," and it is illusory because it is possible that it includes no detriment to Millie. There is no detriment to Millie because she may terminate the agreement and thus not pay anything to Jed.

Problem Solving. Please turn to Chapter Problems at the end of this chapter and solve problem 10.7.

Debt settlement Problems. The settlement of debts can provide challenging consideration problems. In general, (1) debtors may refuse to pay a debt because of a dispute concerning it (e.g., the car you "fixed" still doesn't run, so I won't pay for it); or, (2) debtors refuse to pay a debt for reasons unrelated to it (e.g., I won't pay because I want to buy a new house). Thus, some debtors have a legally good reason to refuse to pay debts, but others do not. In the first example, there is a legally good reason, but in the second example, there is not.

Two terms now come into play: they are *liquidated* debt and *unliquidated* debt. In the second of the examples above (I won't pay because I want to buy a new house) the debt is said to be *liquidated*, which means that the amount of the debt and the fact that it is owed is settled and not disputed. In contrast, in the first of the examples above (the car you "fixed" still doesn't run, so I won't pay for it) the debt is said to be *unliquidated* which means that the amount of the debt or the fact that it is owed is *not* settled and is disputed.

The point of this discussion is whether compromise agreements to pay liquidated debts or unliquidated debts are supported by consideration. In the first example above suppose that the amount claimed for car repair was $300, but to resolve the dispute Jed, the car owner, entered into a new contract with Milly, the mechanic, and agreed to pay her $200 instead of $300. In terms of consideration, is this contract reducing the amount payable down to $200 enforceable in either of the examples? (Can Milly later collect the remaining $100, or is the settlement agreement supported by consideration and thus an enforceable contract?)

The focus of the answer to the question above is that the debt in the first example is unliquidated—it is a debt that is not settled and is in dispute. By resolving the dispute in the first example, each of the parties suffer a detriment and there is consideration on both sides and the new contract is enforceable. With respect to Jed, the debtor: if the case had been litigated it is possible the court may have ruled that he would be required to pay nothing. By giving up the possibility that he would not be required to pay anything, Jed has suffered a detriment (and Millie has received a benefit). With respect to Millie, the creditor: if the case had been litigated it is possible the court may have ruled that she would collect the full $300. By giving up the possibility that she would collect the full $300, Millie has suffered a detriment (and Jed has received a benefit).

An arrangement like that above—to resolve a dispute over an unliquidated debt and pay it—is referred to in legal jargon as an *accord and satisfaction*. The *accord* is the agreement resolving the dispute and the *satisfaction* is the payment of the compromise amount.

In the second example (I won't pay because I want to buy a new house) the debt is liquidated. The debt is fixed and not disputed in any legal sense; Jed is simply refusing to pay for unrelated reasons. If the same deal is worked out between Milly and Jed where Jed pays Milly $200 in settlement, is there a valid contract? The answer is no. In this case only Millie, the creditor, has suffered a detriment. Jed has a preexisting duty to pay $300 (remember, the $300 amount is fixed and not disputed) and his new agreement to pay $200 is only an agreement to pay something he already owes. If Jed's new agreement is to pay what he already owes, he suffers no detriment, and if he suffers no detriment he does not give sufficient consideration for Millie's promise.

There can be no accord and satisfaction with respect to a *liquidated* debt because there is no consideration to support the compromise agreement: there can be no accord.

The following case, *E.S. Herrick v. Maine Wild Blueberry Co.*, involves an *unliquidated* debt; that is, the parties *disagreed* on the amount of money Maine Wild Blueberry Company owed to Herrick for blueberries. Maine had agreed to pay the going rate for blueberries (the "field rate"), but the parties disagreed on what that rate was. Maine paid 30¢ a pound, then an additional 2¢ a pound, and finally an additional 1¢ a pound. The letter with the final check (for 1¢ a pound) said that acceptance of the check was "final settlement." Herrick cashed the check and then demanded more money. Maine responded that the controversy had been settled by contract (an accord and satisfaction of an unliquidated debt).

E.S. HERRICK v. MAINE WILD BLUEBERRY CO.
670 A.2d 944 (1996)

DANA, Justice.

* * *

Maine Wild had initially paid Herrick for 1,240,755 pounds of blueberries based on a field price of 30¢. Early in 1991 Maine Wild advanced another 2¢ per pound and on May 1, 1991, Maine Wild sent a payment to Herrick with a cover letter stating: "[e]nclosed is a check for $12,407.55 representing final settlement for blueberries that Maine Wild purchased from you in 1990. Herrick cashed the check without first telling Maine Wild it was not accepting the check in final settlement. Herrick brought suit to recover the balance owed based on a 37¢ field price.

The [trial] court concluded there was no accord and satisfaction because it found that Maine Wild had agreed that it owed Herrick 33¢ per pound and it was simply paying that amount and because Herrick had previously made it clear to Maine Wild that it did not agree that 33¢ was the field price. The [trial] court found that 33¢ field price had been unilaterally determined rather than negotiated as the contract required and that if the field price had been negotiated it would have been 35¢ per pound. It entered a judgment that awarded Herrick damages in the amount of $24,815.00, plus interest and costs.

* * *

We have consistently concluded that a check bearing language that states " 'full and final payment' or 'in satisfaction of all claims' creates an accord and satisfaction when cashed or deposited by the payee."

* * *

> Maine Wild considered the check to be the final payment. Herrick's president admitted that he read the letter that included the language regarding the final settlement interpreted it as a statement made by Maine Wild not as a condition between them. He admits that he cashed the check, but that it did not occur to him that by cashing the check he was surrendering any claim under the contract. The creditor's intent is material to accord and satisfaction when the writing is ambiguous . * * * The language in the letter, however, was unambiguous. It represented "final settlement," and there is no exchange of correspondence of such a nature as to create doubt as to what Maine Wild intended or should reasonably have been understood by Herrick. * * * Furthermore, a creditor cannot generally avoid the consequences of his exercise of dominion by a declaration that he does not assent to the condition attached by the debtor. * * * "The law gave [Herrick] the choice of accepting the check on [Maine Wild's] terms or of returning it.' " *Graffam*, 304 A.2d at 80 (quoting *Farina*, 155 Me. At 248, 153 A.2d at 615).
>
> "The enforceability of an accord is governed by rules applicable to the enforceability of contracts in general." * * * Consideration is an essential element of a valid accord and satisfaction. * * * There was consideration for an accord and satisfaction in the instant case because the parties disputed the amount of the field price and the amount owed. * * * Thus, an accord and satisfaction barred any further recovery by Herrick under the 1990 contract as a matter of law and we need not reach the other issues raised by Maine Wild and Herrick.
>
> Judgment vacated. Remanded for entry of a judgment in favor of defendant.

Suppose, that in *Herrick* (above) both parties had agreed from the outset that Maine owed 37¢ a pound and that Maine's only reason for not paying was that they were short of cash. Then, Herrick sent the checks and letters just as described in the opinion above. Would there be an enforceable contract (an accord and satisfaction)? The answer, of course, is no. Under the revised facts, the debt would be *liquidated*, and promising to pay what is clearly owed is no detriment (it is a pre-existing duty), and if there is no detriment there is no consideration and no contract.

__Problem Solving__. Please turn to Chapter Problems at the end of this chapter and solve problem 10.8.

Promissory Estoppel.

PROMISSORY ESTOPPEL: a promise causing action or forbearance may be enforced to accomplish justice

Introduction. At this point we make a sharp change of direction and discuss how to resolve certain "contract" problems that "fall through the cracks." That is, how does the law solve certain "contract" problems where technically there is not a contract because all of the technical requirements of a contract have not been met?

For example, in *Feinberg v. Pfeiffer Co.*[2], a corporation bookkeeper, Mrs. Feinberg, was told "that she [would] be afforded the privilege of retiring from active duty in the corporation at any time she may elect to see fit so to do upon retirement pay of $200.00 per month, for the remainder of her life." A year and a half later, Mrs. Feinberg retired and began receiving the retirement pay of $200 per month. Some time after that, new management decided not to continue the retirement pay because, in their view, there was no contract requiring it.

---

[2] 322 S.W.2d 163 (1959).

Indeed, there was something to management's argument: Mrs. Feinberg's past service to the company was past consideration; and, looking to the future, the promise to pay her retirement required no balancing commitment from her (no consideration) to work or retire. If there is no consideration, there is no contract. And yet, *relying* on the promise of the company, Mrs. Feinberg retired early. It seems unfair that the company could avoid an obligation where they made the retirement promise to her *knowing* she would rely on it.

Promissory Estoppel. The problem of Mrs. Feinberg spotlights a recurring "contract" problem, which is whether it is possible to enforce promises *not* based on contract? The doctrine of promissory estoppel provides that in compelling cases such promises may be enforced. The doctrine of promissory estoppel is stated in § 90 of the Restatement of Contracts:

> "A promise which the promisor should reasonably expect to induce action or forbearance of a definite and substantial character on the part of the promisee and which does induce such action or forbearance is binding if injustice can be avoided only by enforcement of the promise."

Applying the rule above to Mrs. Feinberg, it is apparent that the company made a promise that they knew (or should have known) would induce action on her part. Indeed, acting in reliance on the company's proposal, Mrs. Feinberg retired, and justice requires enforcement of the company promise.

Another example where promissory estoppel was applied is *Hoffman v. Red Owl Stores, Inc.* Mr. Hoffman was an applicant to obtain a Red Owl shoe store franchise and, according to the court, Hoffman was told:

> that for the sum of $18,000 Red Owl would establish Hoffman in a store. After Hoffman had sold his grocery store and paid the $1,000 on the Chilton lot, the $18,000 figure was changed to $24,100. Then in November, 1961, Hoffman was assured that if the $24,100 figure was increased by $2,000 the deal would go through. Hoffman was induced to sell his grocery store fixtures and inventory in June, 1961, on the promise that he would be in his new store by fall. In November, plaintiffs sold their bakery building on the urging of defendants and on the assurance that this was the last step necessary to have the deal with Red Owl go through.

Despite their promises, the Red Owl company refused to finalize a contract with Mr. Hoffman, who then sued because of his losses. The obvious problem is that Hoffman had performed a number of acts which were to his detriment and would be consideration in a contract. On the other hand, Red Owl Stores had made a number of promises, but without a finalized contract they were not enforceable. In the following opinion, the Supreme Court of Wisconsin considers using the doctrine of promissory estoppel—a doctrine they had never used before—to solve Mr. Hoffman's problem:

160

Hoffman v. Red Owl Stores, Inc.
133 N.W.2d 267 (1965)

CURRIE, Chief Justice.

* * *

Recognition of a Cause of Action Grounded on Promissory Estoppel.

Sec. 90 of Restatement, 1 Contracts, provides (at p. 110):

"A promise which the promisor should reasonably expect to induce action or forbearance of a definite and substantial character on the part of the promisee and which does induce such action or forbearance is binding if injustice can be avoided only by enforcement of the promise."

* * *

Because we deem the doctrine of promissory estoppel, as stated in sec. 90 of Restatement, 1 Contracts, is one which supplies a needed tool which courts may employ in a proper case to prevent injustice, we endorse and adopt it.

Applicability of Doctrine to Facts of this Case.

The record here discloses a number of promises and assurances given to Hoffman by Lukowitz in behalf of Red Owl upon which plaintiffs relied and acted upon to their detriment.

Foremost were the promises that for the sum of $18,000 Red Owl would establish Hoffman in a store. After Hoffman had sold his grocery store and paid the $1,000 on the Chilton lot, the $18,000 figure was changed to $24,100. Then in November, 1961, Hoffman was assured that if the $24,100 figure were increased by $2,000 the deal would go through. Hoffman was induced to sell his grocery store fixtures and inventory in June, 1961, on the promise that he would be in his new store by fall. In November, the plaintiffs sold their bakery building on the urging of defendants and on the assurance that this was the last step necessary to have the deal with Red Owl go through.

We determine that there was ample evidence to sustain the answers of the jury to the questions of the verdict with respect to the promissory representations made by Red Owl, Hoffman's reliance thereon in the exercise of ordinary care, and his fulfillment of the conditions required of him by the terms of the negotiations had with Red Owl.

There remains for consideration the question of law raised by defendants that agreement was never reached on essential factors necessary to establish a contract between Hoffman and Red Owl. Among these were the size, cost, design, and layout of the store building; and the terms of the lease with respect to rent, maintenance, renewal, and purchase options. This poses the question of whether the promise necessary to sustain a cause of action for promissory estoppel must embrace all essential details of a proposed transaction between promisor and promisee so as to be the equivalent of an offer that would result in a binding contract between the parties if the promisee were to accept the same.

Originally the doctrine of promissory estoppel was invoked as a substitute for consideration rendering a gratuitous promise enforceable as a contract. * * * In other words, the acts of reliance by the promisee to his detriment provided a substitute for consideration. If promissory estoppel were to be limited to only those situations where the promise giving rise to the cause of action must be so definite with respect to all details that a contract would result were the promise supported by consideration, then the defendants' instant promises to Hoffman would not meet this test. However, sec. 90 of Restatement, 1 Contracts, does not impose the requirement that the promise giving rise to the cause of action must be so comprehensive in scope as to meet the requirements of an offer that would ripen into a contract if accepted by the promisee. Rather the conditions imposed are:

(1) Was the promise one which the promisor should reasonably expect to induce action or forbearance of a definite and substantial character on the part of the promisee?

(2) Did the promise induce such action or forbearance?

(3) Can injustice be avoided only by enforcement of the promise?

We deem it would be a mistake to regard an action grounded on promissory estoppel as the equivalent of a breach of contract action. As Dean Boyer points our, it is desirable that fluidity in the application of the concept be maintained. * * * While the first two of the above listed three requirements of promissory estoppel present issues of fact which ordinarily will be resolved by a jury, the third requirement, that the remedy can only be invoked where necessary to avoid injustice, is one that involves a policy decision by the court. Such a policy decision necessarily embraces an element of discretion.

We conclude that injustice would result here if plaintiffs were not granted some relief because of the failure of defendants to keep their promises which induced plaintiffs to act to their detriment.

Problem Solving. Please turn to Chapter Problems at the end of this chapter and solve problem 10.9.

Chapter Ten
Chapter problems

Problem 10.1.

The text discussion says that the consideration requirement is satisfied (and a contract exists) when Jed promises to give Millie $100 if she will rest and not repair anyone's car. Explain how it is that Millie satisfies the consideration requirement; it seems like Millie gets all benefit and suffers no detriment in this arrangement.

Problem 10.2.

Why does contract law require that consideration be "bargained for?"

Problem 10.3.

In *Hamer v. Sidway*, suppose that it was unlawful for the young man to drink, use tobacco, swear or play cards or billiards for money before the age of 21. Under these facts, would the young man's contract with his uncle be enforceable?

Problem 10.4.

Suppose in the *Brads v. First Baptist Church* case that the congregation had argued that although they received the promised services from Reverend Brads, they did not receive *enough*. Would this invalidate the contract between Brads and the Church?

Problem 10.5.

Jed, a morally unconscious person, observes Millie's daughter drowning in a swimming pool, but declines to take any action. In desperation, Millie says "I'll pay you $100 for five years if you will save her," and Jed says "okay" and dives into the swimming pool and saves the girl. In terms of consideration, is this an enforceable contract?

Problem 10.6.

What is the answer to the following question posed in the text in relation to the *Denney* opinion: "A more difficult case to decide would be one in which the other police officers (Godby and Simms) were off-duty at the time of the robbery and as public-spirited citizens helped capture the crooks (doing all of this work while they were off-duty)."

Problem 10.7.

Jed does not give sufficient consideration when he promises to do yard work at Milly's home "for thirty days, at the rate of $30 per day, unless this agreement is earlier terminated by Jed." Alter the language of Jed's promise so that he *does* give sufficient consideration.

Problem 10.8.

(The following is an admittedly difficult problem. If you can solve it, there is reason to believe you are beginning to understand the law relating to consideration.) The following are the facts: Millie loans $1000 to Jed, which is to be repaid on July 1. As the time for repayment approaches, suppose that Millie and

Jed enter into another contract to resolve differences about repayment. The new contract is arranged in three different ways. Which of the new contracts is supported by consideration and is thus enforceable:

Contract #1. On July 1, Jed refuses, without any explanation, to repay the $1000. To induce Jed to pay the money, Millie offers to sign a new contract in which she will receive only $500. Jed agrees and pays. Later, Millie decides that the new contract is not supported by consideration and she sues Jed to collect the remaining $500. Will she be successful?

Contract #2. On June 1, Millie offers to sign a new contract in which she will receive only $500 if Jed will pay the money on June 1, instead of July 1. Jed agrees and pays. Later, Millie decides that the new contract is not supported by consideration and she sues Jed to collect the remaining $500.

Will she be successful?

Contract #3. On July 1, Jed refuses to repay the $1000 claiming that the money was given to him as a gift and was not therefore repayable on July 1. In contrast, Millie thinks the transaction was a loan; however, Millie offers to sign a new contract in which she will receive only $500. Jed agrees and pays. Later, Millie decides that the new contract is not supported by consideration and she sues Jed to collect the remaining $500. Will she be successful?

Problem 10.9.

In the *Hoffman v. Red Owl Stores, Inc.* case, suppose that Hoffman's grocery store and bakery were failing financially and that he would have been forced to sell them, even if it had not been requested by Red Owl. How, if at all, would that change the outcome in the case?

Chapter 11
Legality and Capacity

Chapter Outline

OBJECTIVE: to learn that each contract must have a lawful purpose, and each party must have capacity.

The objective of this chapter is to learn that each contract must have a lawful purpose; and, that the parties to a contract must have legal capacity. The following is an outline of the chapter:

Lawful Purpose

- *Lawful Purpose.* A contract must not have an unlawful purpose.

- *Violation of Statute.* A contract to do something which is prohibited by a statute does not have a lawful purpose.

- *Violation of Public Policy.* A contract which violates public policy is illegal and unenforceable.

Capacity

- *Capacity.* A person must have capacity to enter into a valid contract.

- *Minority.* Most states provide by statute or case law that a person under the age of eighteen years does not have the capacity to contract.

- *Mental Impairment.* A person not able to understand the nature and consequences of a contract he or she enters into because of mental impairment may rescind that contract.

- *General Lack of Capacity.* A person lacking capacity to understand the nature and consequences of a contract for any other reason, such as age or intoxication, may rescind that contract.

Lawful Purpose

LAWFUL PURPOSE: each contract must have a lawful purpose.

A contract must not have an unlawful purpose. An obvious example of this principle is a "contract" in which Jed hires Milly to kill Sam. This is no contract at all because the arrangement between Jed and Milly is said to have been void from its beginning. The principle that a contract must have a lawful purpose has been summarized in the following language: "a bargain is illegal . . . if either its formation or its performance is criminal, tortious or otherwise opposed to public policy."[1]

---

[1] RESTATEMENT (SECOND) CONTRACTS, § 512.

The arrangement above, in which Jed hires Milly to kill Sam, never was a contract. If a contract is defined as a set of promises which the courts will enforce, there never was a time that the courts would enforce Jed and Milly's arrangement because performance of the arrangement would be the commission of a crime. That is why the arrangement between them is referred to above as a "bargain" and not a contract.

Although dealing with mislabeled cheese (which is not quite as spectacular as a murder) the case of *Blossom Farm Products v. Kasson Cheese Co.* shows how a court responds to a contract based on unlawful conduct. Milk products treated with the chemical Isokappacase produce more cheese. However, the resulting product is not viewed as "real cheese," and by Wisconsin statute it cannot be labeled or sold as real cheese. Kasson violated this law. Blossom Farm Products sold large amounts of Isokappacase to Kasson; they also knew that Kasson products were labeled as real cheese; thus, they knew of (and consciously profited from) Kasson's mislabeling. Blossom sued to collect $138, 306 for a delivery of Isokappacase and Kasson refused to pay on grounds that the contract was based on illegal conduct.

Blossom Farm Products V. Kasson Cheese Co.
395 N.W.2d 619 (1986)

SCOTT, Chief Justice.
* * *

The trial court held the contract "illegal and unenforceable." We restrict our holding to whether the contract is unenforceable. Our position is in keeping with the Restatement at §§ 178 and 182, which deals with the issue in terms of "unenforceability" rather than "illegality."
* * *

A promise may be unenforceable if it involves conduct offensive to public policy, even though the promise does not actually induce the conduct. * * * If the conduct to be engaged in by the promisor is deemed improper conduct because it is against public policy, the promisee's doing of specific acts to facilitate the improper use is a bar to recovery. * * *

State legislation which adopted federal standards of identity enforces the public policy of accurately distinguishing imitation or analog cheese from real cheese and labeling it accordingly. * * *. Even though Vande Yacht of Kasson testified that neither Podell nor Silverman [salesmen for Bloosom Farm Products] was directly told about the mislabeling, sufficient evidence reveals that Podell tacitly knew of Kasson's subsequent misbranding of its end product because of the economics of the situation. Furthermore, despite being aware of Kasson's improper conduct, Blossom chose to overlook it and continued to supply volume shipments to Kasson, thereby engaging in a course of dealing which facilitated Kasson in its improper conduct. This course of dealing benefited both Blossom and Kasson. Because mislabeling cheese involves conduct offensive to public policy, the trial court correctly concluded that the transaction which anticipated such improper conduct is unenforceable.
By the Court—Judgment affirmed.

The court in *Kasson Cheese* preferred to deal with the problem in terms of "unenforceability" instead of "illegality," but either way the result was the same. The result was that the court refused to enforce the contract between the two companies, which meant that Blossom Farm Products could not collect the money it was claiming.

Problem Solving. Please turn to Chapter Problems at the end of this chapter and solve Problem 11.1.

Violation of Statute. A "contract" to do something which is prohibited by a constitutional provision or a statute does not have a lawful purpose. The following are examples of bargains requiring conduct which is prohibited by a statute:

Bargains to Commit a Crime. The bargain described above (Jed hires Milly to kill Sam) is illegal because murder is a crime defined by statute. Likewise, if Jed, who is facing criminal charges of theft, hires Milly to pay $50,000 to Sam, a judge, to dismiss the theft charges, the bargain is illegal because bribery is a crime defined by statute.

Gambling Statutes. In many states, different forms of gambling are prohibited by constitutional provision or statute. This rule is easy to apply if the contract relates to casino-type gambling such as blackjack or slot machines. But, rules against gambling become more difficult to interpret when, for example, Safeway stores promote "bonus bingo" or Reader's Digest promotes a Reader's Digest Sweepstakes. This problem is illustrated in the Washington State case of *State v. Reader's Digest Association, Inc.*

In 1972, the Washington State constitution provided that "The legislature shall never authorize any lottery . . ." In general, a lottery (a form of gambling) exists if there is (1) a prize, (2) a chance, and (3) consideration. The defendant, Reader's Digest Association, mailed promotional literature to residents of Washington state which told them they had been "selected for a chance to win a valuable prize." The recipient could send in a "yes" form and buy merchandise and participate in the sweepstakes, or send in a "no" form and participate in the sweepstakes. Either form provided an equal chance of winning, and all prizes were awarded by chance.

In these cases there is usually a prize awarded by chance; the critical issue is whether the recipient contributes *consideration* for the opportunity to participate. The Supreme Court of Washington, in an earlier case, found that Safeway stores "bonus bingo" was prohibited gambling because studying promotional literature and traveling to the store was consideration. In the following case, the *trial court* concluded that the sweepstakes was *not* prohibited gambling, a conclusion which the Supreme Court reviewed:

State v. Reader's Digest Association, Inc.
Wash., 501 P.2d 290 (1972)

STAFFORD, Associate Justice.

The Washington State constitution, art.2, § 24 declares: "The legislature shall never authorize any lottery . . ." This provision is mandatory and self-executing. * * * It not only prohibits the state from conducting a lottery, but prohibits any form of lottery from being conducted within the state.

Necessary elements for a lottery are well settled: prize, chance and consideration. *

---

* * Respondent admits the elements of prize and chance. The only question is whether consideration exists.

While there are divergent views as to what constitutes consideration in the context of a lottery, * * * we have adhered to the view that consideration sufficient to support a contract is enough. * * *. In *Safeway Stores* we stated * * *: "Encompassed then within the term *consideration*, as the third element of lottery, *would be those acts of forbearances, promises, or conduct which in law are sufficient to support an agreement.*"

* * *

In holding that the "bonus bingo" game in Safeway Stores constituted a lottery, we found that the time, thought, attention and energy expended by members of the public in studying Safeway's advertising and journeying to a Safeway Store to procure a prize slip, as well as the actual increase in patronage that resulted from the contest amounted to consideration moving from player to promoter.

The Reader's Digest Sweepstakes is a mail order equivalent of Safeway's "bonus bingo." As with the Safeway promotion, the Sweepstakes requires no purchase to enter, and the entrant's chance of winning is not increased by making a purchase. In both cases these facts were conspicuously displayed on the promotion literature. The Sweepstakes is designed as an advertising attention getting device, as was "bonus bingo," and is, by respondents own admission, far superior to other forms of advertising. It has not only increased subscriptions to respondent's products, but has caused a corresponding increase in advertising revenues.

The only significant difference between "bonus bingo" and the Sweepstakes is that the latter does not require a trip to the store to secure an entry form. That difference, however, is not sufficient to distinguish the cases. The store visit, standing alone, was not the detriment to the participant that produced the benefit to Safeway. More critical was the participant's expenditure of time, thought, attention and energy in perusing Safeway's advertisements. The whole purpose of "bonus bingo" was to attract attention to its advertising. Similarly, the purpose of the Sweepstakes promotion is to attract attention to respondent's advertising. Respondent's own officer testified that the Sweepstakes is an "attention getting device" comparable to using "four colors in a brochure" or "tipping a penny into a mailing." Thus, in both "bonus bing" and the Sweepstakes the thing sought by the promoter from the participant was the latter's attention directed to the former's advertisements. This constitutes a detriment to the participant. The corresponding increase in sales that results from the success in attracting the attention of the participants constitutes the benefit to the promoter.

We said in *Safeway Stores* that "[c]onsideration for a lottery may be *both* gain and detriment *or one without the other.*" We have in the case before us, as in *Safeway Stores both* detriment to the participant and gain to the promoter. Thus, we hold as a matter of law that there is consideration sufficient to constituent a lottery.

* * *

The judgement is reversed and the case remanded to the trial court for entry of judgement consistent with the views expressed herein.

__Problem Solving.__ Please turn to Chapter Problems at the end of this chapter and solve Problem 11.2.

Usury Statutes. Usury is an old-fashioned word for the practice of charging interest, and particularly for the practice of charging a rate of interest which is greater than the rate allowed by statute. Thus, if a statute allows interest at a rate no greater than 30%, and Milly charges Jed 35% to borrow some money, Milly has committed usury and the agreement with Jed is unlawful. Traditionally, the penalty for usury was forfeiture of both principal and interest. More commonly, though, the penalty is forfeiture of all the interest, or the excess interest. Some states have repealed their usury statutes and allow the parties to an otherwise lawful contract to agree to any rate of interest.

Sunday Laws. Some older statutes and local laws—often enacted out of religious motivation—prohibit a wide variety of contracts and sales transactions done on Sundays. Although many cases uphold Sunday closing laws as a uniform day of rest—and not as a religious day—a poorly drafted statute of this type may easily violate constitutional rules against laws "prohibiting the free exercise" of religion.[2]

Sunday closing laws which are enforced are those which prohibit only specific forms of conduct such as selling alcoholic beverages at retail. A contract of this type may be enforceable because there are non-religious health and safety reasons to regulate the use of alcoholic beverages. If such a statute exists, and Milly contracts with Jed to work as a bar tender at her tavern on Sundays, the contract would be illegal and not enforceable.

Licensing Laws. Statutes, and regulations adopted pursuant to statute, and local laws, all regulate the activities of persons who deal with the public. Examples of such are barbers, lawyers, plumbers, landlords, stock brokers, public school teachers and real estate agents. In general, an unlicensed person who contracts to perform regulated activities has entered into an illegal and unenforceable bargain.

There are, however, exceptions to the proposition that contracts in violation of licensing laws will not be enforced. Licensing regulations are adopted for two reasons: the first is to *raise revenue* and the second is to *regulate conduct*, and courts will enforce the regulations to accomplish those objectives. Suppose, for example, that Urbana City has adopted a business licensing law requiring retail businesses to pay a monthly fee to the City "in an amount equal to .005% of the gross amount of all retail sales." If Jed, a florist, fails to pay his December licensing fee to the city, are all of his December contracts illegal and unenforceable? The obvious answer is no, the contracts are not all illegal and unenforceable. If the city brings suit, a court will probably recognize that the purpose of the licensing law is not to protect the public, but to raise *revenue*. Thus, the court will simply force Jed to make the payments, but leave his floral contracts untouched.

On the other hand, suppose that Millie, a plumber, decides to engage in dentistry because it is more profitable and has better working conditions. Contracts between Millie, who is not licensed, and her patients are illegal and Milly cannot enforce them. The licensing of dentists is to regulate their *conduct* and thereby protect the public. A court will enforce the licensing law to accomplish that regulatory purpose.

Housing regulations are usually enacted for the regulatory purpose of improving housing conditions, not to raise revenue. In the following opinion, *Noble*

---

[2] *See*, U.S. CONST., amend. I.

v. Alis, the issue is whether a rental contract will be enforced where the premises failed to meet specific housing codes. The renters, Noble and Odle, signed a rental contract for an apartment. Later, they decided not to move in and attempted to sublease the apartment, only to find that the apartment did not meet the housing code and could not be lawfully sublease. At that point, they declined to proceed further with their rental contract.

Noble v. Alis
474 N.E.2d 109 (1985)

NEAL, Judge.
* * *

Broadly speaking, the law is that a contract made in violation of a statute is void. * * * Only infrequently does a legislature, on grounds of public policy, provide that an agreement or term of agreement is unenforceable if it contravenes a statutory provision. * * * Courts too hesitate to brand an "illegal" bargain necessarily void and thus unenforceable; they engage in a balancing test and evaluate circumstances such as the nature of subject matter of the contract, the strength of the public policy underlying the statute, the likelihood that refusal to enforce the bargain or term will further the policy, and how serious or deserved would be the forfeiture suffered by the party attempting to enforce the bargain. * * * Judicial decisions emphasize a distinction between statutes for revenue and statutes for protection of the public health, safety, and welfare: in the case of an agreement made in contravention of a statute designed for the protection of the public, "it is more likely that the statute breaker will be denied the enforcement of his bargain." * * *

In our opinion, the lease in the instant case is unenforceable. We agree with appellants' contention that the policies of protection of public health, safety, and welfare and encouragement of compliance with the housing code are advanced by the registration and occupancy permit provisions of the Municipal Code. * * * The procedure to receive such a permit necessitates compliance with minimum housing standards: once the unit is registered residential, a temporary occupancy permit is issued. * * * The issuance of the temporary permit triggers an inspection by the Housing Department. * * * After the inspection, an occupancy permit is issued; or, if the unit did not "pass" inspection, additional time is granted to make the repairs necessary to bring the unit into compliance with the code. * * * Clearly, the policy of protecting the public from substandard housing is served by the registration-inspection-permit process: until the unit is registered, the Housing Code Enforcement Office is not aware of its existence and thus is unable to check its compliance with the housing standards set down in the code.
* * *

The decision of the trial court as to damages for rental payments is reversed, and Alis is ordered to return the $330.00 security deposit plus interest accrued at the statutory rate.

Problem Solving. Please turn to Chapter Problems at the end of this chapter and solve Problem 11.3.

Violation of Public Policy. A contract which violates *public policy* is illegal and unenforceable. Public policy is not a precisely defined legal concept, it is a reference to generally accepted values and procedures. An example of a generally accepted value is the American commitment to open and vigorous economic competition. In relation to that example, the American legal system favors a public policy of open and vigorous economic competition, and contracts which seriously infringe on that public policy are illegal.

An example of a contract provision which affects the public policy ideal of open and vigorous economic competition is a so-called "covenant not to compete":

Agreements not to Compete. An agreement not to compete—sometimes called a "covenant not to compete"— is exactly that, an agreement to not compete in business with another. Suppose, for example, that Jed sells his pharmacy business in Urbana to Milly. Milly pays for the building and furniture and stock on hand; and, she also pays for "goodwill," which is the financial value of Jed's reputation for good service and fair prices. It is this goodwill that is the real value of the business; it is the goodwill which will keep people coming into the pharmacy after Jed is gone.

The problem is how to effectively sell "goodwill." If Jed sells his pharmacy to Milly and then opens up another pharmacy next door, it is obvious that most of his former customers will come to his new business and not to the old one he sold to Milly. The consequence is that Milly will not buy the business unless she is assured that Jed will not compete with her. The problem is solved by placing a provision (a covenant) in the contract between Jed and Milly which prohibits Jed from competing with Milly in the pharmacy business.

This covenant not to compete between Jed and Milly can be seen from two different perspectives: on the one hand, it clearly limits economic competition, so it should be viewed as contrary to public policy. On the other hand, it stimulates the free exchange of business interests, because Jed's business could not be bought and sold at full value if the "goodwill" could not be protected. In this sense the covenant not to compete promotes public policy. On balance, the courts have chosen to enforce non-competition agreements so long as they (1) further a legitimate business purpose, (2) the limitation on competition is reasonable in scope of time and area, and (3) the limitation is not an undue hardship.

If there is a "covenant not to compete" in the sales agreement between Jed and Milly, and it prohibits Jed from engaging in the pharmacy business in Urbana, for one year, is it enforceable? The answer is that it is probably enforceable, for the following reasons: (1) the purpose of the covenant is legitimate because it makes possible the sale of a business; (2) in relation to the sale of a business, one year is a reasonable period of time, and the area of Urbana is a reasonable area because that is where the business operates; and (3) the limitation is not an undue hardship because Jed can go to any other location and engage in the pharmacy business.

Following is the opinion in *Superior Consulting Co., Inc. v. Walling* where the employer was attempting to enforce a covenant not to compete for six months, world wide:

Superior Consulting Co., Inc. v. Walling
851 F.Supp. 839 (1994)

COHN, District Judge.

* * *

It was undisputed that Walling violated his express agreement not to accept employment with any healthcare information systems consulting business for a period of six months following his termination. Under Michigan law, a noncompetition agreement is enforceable to the extent that it is "reasonable as to its duration, geographical area, and the type of employment or line of business." * * *

The six month time period of the noncompetition agreement is designed in part to protect proprietary information learned by the employee. * * *

Geographic limitations in non-competition agreements must be tailored so that the scope of the agreement is no greater than is reasonably necessary to protect the employer's legitimate business interests. Here, the non-competition agreement did not specify any geographic limitations. Such an agreement can be reasonable if the employer actually has legitimate business interests throughout the world. * * * SCC [Superior Consulting Co.] does business in forty-three states and a number of foreign nations. The unlimited geographic scope of the non-competition provision here was therefore not unreasonable.

The non-competition agreement here was also reasonable as to line of work, narrowly restricting its application to healthcare information systems consulting businesses. The agreement, through, did not restrict the type of work to which it applied. A limitation on working in any capacity for a competitor of a former employer is too broad to be enforceable. * * * The Court therefore restricted the noncompetition agreement so that it applies only to actual consulting and management work for competitors of SCC, and only in the competitors' healthcare information systems consulting businesses. So modified, the non-competition agreement is reasonable in scope.

The next factor considered was whether SCC would suffer irreparable harm if Walling was not enjoined from working for a competitor. Walling argued that SCC did not allege that it sought protection for the confidentiality of any particular information system developed by SCC which Walling might reveal to E & Y [Ernst & Young—Walling's new employer], and that Walling was not an employee whom SCC trained only to lose him at the point at which he was about to become useful. SCC said Walling could not prevent his knowledge of SCC's confidential methods from informing his work for a new employer in the field, and that Walling acquired detailed confidential information as to the specific needs and service provided to clients and specific clients of SCC.

Loss of customer goodwill and fair competition can support a finding of irreparable harm. Such losses often amount to irreparable injury because the resulting damages are difficult to calculate. *Basicomputer Corp. v. Scott*, 973 F.2d 507, 511-12 (6th Cir. 1992). Here, as in *Basicomputer*, it was undisputed that Walling had access to confidential client information while he worked at SCC. Use of this knowledge would enable Walling effectively to solicit SCC's clients, and to undercut SCC's rates while providing the same services provided by SCC.

[Injunction prohibiting Walling from competing granted.]

In *Walling*, the world-wide scope of the covenant is unusual. However, that scope was balanced by the facts that the six-month time period of the covenant is very reasonable, and, that Superior Consulting could show that they had genuine business interests in foreign nations.

Agreements to Commit a Tort. There are other contract arrangements which may violate public policy, one of which is an agreement to commit a tort. Thus, "a promise to commit a tort or to induce the commission of a tort is unenforceable on grounds of public policy."[3] An agreement between Jed and the Goodmonth Tire Company for Jed to make claims— which are known to be false—about Firerock tires in television advertisements is a contract to commit a tort and unenforceable.

Exculpatory Clauses. Another contract provision which may be contrary to public policy, and unenforceable, is a so-called exculpatory clause. A contract provision which purports to relieve persons from liability for wrongdoing is an exculpatory clause. Suppose that Milly buys an airline ticket, and in the contract fine print is a provision that "passenger releases airline for any claims or liability arising out of the negligence of the airline and it's agents and employees." This is an exculpatory clause.

Although exculpatory clauses are sometimes enforced, the courts are suspicious about them. The courts are suspicious for two reasons: the first reason is that an exculpatory clause may not be freely agreed to. Milly had no reasonable opportunity to negotiate with the airline about the exculpatory clause, which was pre-printed on her airline ticket. She probably didn't know the clause was part of her ticket contract, and if she did, there was nothing she could do about it. Contract provisions which a party can do nothing about are sometimes called "adhesion" contracts. The second reason for the courts to be suspicious is that a party using an exculpatory clause (for example, the airline) may thereafter relax its standards because it thinks it cannot be sued for negligence.

Based on concerns like those described above, the courts respond to exculpatory clauses in the following general ways:

- Exculpatory clauses are *not* enforced to avoid tort liability where the benefitting party owes a duty to the public. Thus, businesses such as common carriers (airlines, taxis, etc.) or utilities (deliverers of natural gas, electricity, etc.) which provide services which are important to the public interest may not use an exculpatory clause to avoid liability.

- Exculpatory clauses are *not* enforced to avoid tort liability arising out of residential property leases. Thus, if Milly leases an apartment from Jed, an exculpatory clause relieving Jed from liability for injuries is not enforceable.

- Exculpatory clauses are *not* enforced to avoid liability for wrongdoing which exceeds negligence. Thus, if Milly employs Jed as a butler at her home and the contract between them provides that Milly will not be liable to Jed for injuries resulting from intentional wrongdoing

---

[3] RESTATEMENT (SECOND) CONTRACTS, §192.

(Milly has a violent temper and throws things at servants), that provision will not be enforced.

- Exculpatory clauses will *not* be enforced if they operate contrary to an established public policy. Thus, a provision in the contract between Milly and Jed, the butler, waiving benefits under workers' compensation statutes will not be enforced.

- Exculpatory clauses *will* be enforced if they (1) are voluntarily entered into, (2) are specific, (3) do not purport to waive liability for wrongdoing, and (4) do not affect the public interest. In this context, exculpatory clauses have been enforced in favor of businesses such as skiing facilities, health clubs or amusement parks.

In the following case, *Milligan v. Big Valley Corp.*, the wife of a skier brought suit for damages on account of his death in a skiing accident. The decedent, Milligan, was participating in an Ironman Decathlon at Grand Targhee Ski Resort in Wyoming. "The decathlon consisted of several events, including swimming five pool laps, bowling one line, drinking a quart of beer, throwing darts, and both downhill and cross-country ski races."

As a condition of being allowed to participate in the downhill portion of the decathlon, Milligan was required to sign a "General Release of Claim" which provided, in part: "In consideration of my being allowed to participate in IRONMAN DECATHLON at Targhee Resort, Alta, Wyoming, I irrevocably and forever hereby release and discharge TargheeResort and the other sponsors of and any and all of the employees, agents or servants and owners of Targhee Resort and the other sponsors of IRONMAN DECATHLON officially connected with this event of and from any and all legal claims or legal liability of any kind, nature and description involving or relating to bodily injury or death suffered or sustained by me, or any property damage of mine, during my stay at Targhee Resort." Milligan was an experienced expert skier and a certified ski instructor. He apparently hit a tree while racing in the downhill ski race and was killed.

Milligan v. Big Valley Corporation
754 P.2d 1063 (1988)

CARDINE, Justice.
* * *

There is no dispute that the release in question was signed by the decedent. However, appellant argues that the exculpatory language contained in the release is invalid because it is contrary to Wyoming's public policy. Exculpatory agreements. releasing parties from negligence liability for damages or injury, are valid and enforceable in Wyoming if they do not violate public policy. * * ** "Generally, specific agreements absolving participants and proprietors from negligence liability during hazardous recreational activities are enforceable, subject to willful misconduct limitations." * * *

Exculpatory agreements, also referred to as releases, are contractual in nature. * * * Interpretation and construction of contractual agreements are questions of law for the court to

---

decide. * * *

This court recently addressed the issue of the validity and enforceability of a release in *Schutkowski v. Carey, supra.* In Schutkowski, a skydiving student brought a negligence action against her instructors after being injured during her first jump. This court held that a release signed by the student prior to her injuries excused her instructors from any liability for negligence. In reaching this holding, we adopted the four-part test found in *Jones v. Dressel,* 623 P.2d 370 (1981), to determine whether this type of release is valid and enforceable. This four-part test is applicable here. Thus, we consider:

> "(1) [Whether there exists] a duty to the public; (2) the nature of the service performed; (3) whether the contract was fairly entered into; and (4) whether the intention of the parties is expressed in clear and unambiguous language." *Id.* at 376.

A duty to the public exists if the nature of the business or service affects the public interest and the service performed is considered an essential service. Thus, our first inquiry is whether sponsoring, coordinating, and organizing a ski race is a business or service affecting the public interest and is considered an essential service demanding a public duty.

* * *

Types of services thought to be subject to public regulation, and therefore demanding a public duty or considered essential, have included common carriers, hospitals and doctors * * *, public utilities, innkeepers, public warehousemen, employers, and services involving extra-hazardous activities. * * * Generally, a private recreational business does not qualify as a service *demanding* a special duty to the public, nor are its services of a special, highly necessary nature. * * * Further, contracts relating to recreational activities do not fall within any of the categories above where the public interest is involved. * * *

* * *

Appellant argues that the release was entered into unfairly because it contained boiler plate language prepared solely by the resort and was an adhesive contract. The argument is without merit. The mere fact that a contract is on a printed form prepared by one party and offered on a "take it or leave it" basis does not automatically establish it as an adhesive contract. * * *

The final Schutkowski factor requires us to determine whether the release agreement evidences the parties' intent to release appellee from liability for negligent acts in clear and unambiguous language. * * *

* * *

The language could not be clearer. Examining the release in light of the purpose of the contract, it is clear that the parties intended to release the ski resort and all those involved in the Ironman Decathlon from liability. * * *

* * *

We conclude that the release is not void as a matter of public policy, that there is no genuine issue of material fact, and that appellee was entitled to judgment as a matter of law. The trial court was properly granted summary judgment. Accordingly, we affirm.

> *Problem Solving.* Please turn to Chapter Problems at the end of this chapter and solve Problem 11.4.

Capacity

CAPACITY: a person must have capacity to enter into a valid contract.

A person must have *capacity* to enter into a valid contract. In general, to have capacity a person must have the ability understand the nature and consequences of his or her contracts. For example, Jed is thirteen years old, Milly is 21 years old, but has Down's Syndrome, and Sam is 94 years old. Which of them has capacity to contact if each contracts to buy a Caribbean cruise?

The answer is that capacity (or the lack thereof) is handled differently depending on the nature of the claimed incapacity. That is, Jed's, Milly's and Sam's differing forms of incapacity are each handled differently. The following material discusses capacity (and the answer to the "Caribbean cruise" question) in relation to: (1) minority (being too young), (2) mental impairment, and (3) and general lack of mental capacity.

Minority. Most states provide by statute or case law that a person under the age of eighteen years does not have the capacity to contract. The language of one such statute is: "The period of minority extends in males and females to the age of eighteen years."[4] The provisions relating to minority then go on to provide: "A minor is bound not only for [the] reasonable value of necessaries but also by his contracts, unless he disaffirms them before or within a reasonable time after he attains his majority . . ."[5] (To "disaffirm" means to repudiate or annul.) These statutory provisions are typical, and their effect is to provide that a person under the age of eighteen years is a minor, and contracts entered into as a minor are not binding if they are disaffirmed during minority or within a reasonable period after reaching minority.

A minor is not required to prove lack of capacity. Jed, the thirteen-year-old, who purchased a Caribbean cruise, is not required to prove that he did not have the ability understand the nature and consequences of the contract. With minors, the lack of capacity is presumed; all Jed is required to do is to *disaffirm* the contract. Jed may disaffirm the Caribbean cruise contract with a letter like the following:

Dear Sir:

I hereby disaffirm the contract I entered into with your company for a Caribbean cruise. This action is taken because I was a minor (under the age of 18 years) at the time of contracting. I am returning the cruise tickets and hereby request the return of my partial payment of $300.

Sincerely,
s/ Jed

When can (or must) Jed disaffirm? The statute above provides—as the law in most states does—that Jed may disaffirm before age 18, or within a reasonable period thereafter. That means, of course, that if Jed is still age 13, he can disaffirm. Suppose, however, that Jed had entered into the contract a week before his 18th birthday. How long after age 18 does Jed have to disaffirm? In general, six months is a reasonable period of time after reaching age 18. Six months, however, is just a generalization.

---

[4] UTAH CODE ANN. § 15-2-1.
[5] UTAH CODE ANN. § 15-2-2.

176

Thus, if the contract is for perishable bananas, a disaffirmance must be within a matter of a few days to be reasonable; on the other hand, disaffirming a contract to buy real estate could be later.

Suppose that the cruise line did not at first realize that it was contracting with a minor; then, realizing it's mistake, it wishes to disaffirm the contract. Is this allowed? The answer is no; only the minor has the choice to disaffirm. A contract with a minor is viewed as being "void*able*," meaning that it remains valid unless the minor chooses to make it void by the process of disaffirmance.

As part of the process of disaffirming, must a minor return what he or she has received from the other contracting party? Traditionally, a minor is simply required to return what remains, but is not obligated to replace what is lost, damaged, destroyed or depreciated. In short, the other contracting party contracts with a minor at his or her peril. In some states, however, the older traditional rule is replaced by a rule that requires the minor to return all that he or she received as a condition of the right to disaffirm.

The following opinion, *Dodson v. Shrader* is a case where Dodson, age 16, bought a truck, drove it without proper care until the engine "blew up," and then parked it where it was hit by a "hit and run" driver. At that point, Dodson, still a minor, returned the truck to the dealer and disaffirmed the contract of purchase. The trial court did not require full restitution. On appeal, the Tennessee court struggles with the obligation of a disaffirming minor *to make restitution*. Notice that because Dodson is a minor the lawsuit had to be brought in his behalf by another person (apparently his father).

Joseph Eugene DODSON, a minor, by his next friend Gene DODSON, Plaintiff/Appellee v. Burns SHRADER, Jr., and Mary Shrader, individually and d/b/a Shrader's Auto Sales, Defendant/Appellant
824 S.W.2d 545 (1992)

O'BRIEN, Justice

This is an action to disaffirm the contract of a minor for the purchase of a pick-up truck and for a refund of the purchase price. The issue is whether the minor is entitled to a full refund of the money he paid or whether the seller is entitled to a setoff for the decrease in the value of the pick-up truck while it was in the possession of the minor.

* * *

We state the rule to be followed hereafter, in reference to a contract of a minor, to be where the minor has not been overreached in any way, and there has been no undue influence, and the contract is a fair and reasonable one, and the minor has actually paid money on the purchase price, and taken and used the article purchased, that he ought not to be permitted to recover the amount actually paid, without allowing the vender of the goods reasonable compensation for the use of, depreciation, and willful or negligent damage to the article purchased, while in his hands. If there has been any fraud or imposition on the part of the seller or if the contract is unfair, or any unfair advantage has been taken of the minor inducing him to make the purchase, then the rule does not apply. Whether there has been such an overreaching on the part of the seller, and the fair market value of the property returned, would

---

always, in any case, be a question for the trier of fact. This rule will fully and fairly protect the minor against injustice or imposition, and at the same time it will be fair to a business person who has dealt with such minor in good faith.

This rule is best adapted to modern conditions under which minors are permitted to, and do in fact, transact a great deal of business for themselves, long before they have reached the age of legal majority. Many young people work and earn money and collect it and spend it oftentimes without any oversight or restriction. The law does not question their right to buy if they have the money to pay for their purchases. It seems intolerable burdensome for everyone concerned if merchants and business people cannot deal with them safely, in a fair and reasonable way. Further, it does not appear consistent with practice of proper moral influence upon young people, tend to encourage honesty and integrity, or lead them to a good and useful business future, if they are taught that they can make purchases with their own money, for their own benefit, and after paying for them, and using them until they are worn out and destroyed, go back and compel the vendor to return to them what they have paid upon the purchase price. Such a doctrine can only lead to the corruption of principles and encourage young people in habits of trickery and dishonesty.

In view of the foregoing considerations, we conclude that the rule, as we have indicated, and which we have paraphrased from that adopted in the State of Oregon, will henceforth be the rule to be utilized in this State.

* * *

The case is remanded to the trial court for further proceedings in accordance with this judgment. The costs on appellate review are assessed equally between the parties.

The *Dodson* decision places Tennessee among those states which do not allow a minor to disaffirm with impugnity. As the *Dodson* decision makes clear, a Tennessee minor is responsible for loss of value in what he or she has purchased. Quite obviously, though, a minor would not be responsible to fully reimburse the adult if the adult had taken advantage of the minor.

What if a minor misrepresents his or her age for the purpose of contracting with an adult who would not otherwise contract with the minor? The older, traditional rule is that misrepresentation of age does not change the outcome; indeed, the act of misrepresentation may be viewed as further evidence that the minor lacks good judgment. In contrast, some states place limitations on the right to disaffirm when the minor has misrepresented his age. Those states which impose limitations do so in different ways. For example, some states allow the minor to disaffirm, but also allow the other party to bring suit against the minor on a theory of fraud (deceit) to recover damages for the harm caused by the fraud. Other states simply prohibit the minor from disaffirming a contract he has entered into because the minor misrepresented his age. The language of one statute which prohibits disaffirmance because of misrepresentation of age is as follows: "No contract can be thus disaffirmed in cases where, on account of the minor's own misrepresentations as to his majority or from his having engaged in business as [an] adult, the other party had good reason to believe the minor capable of contracting."[6]

---

[6] UTAH CODE ANN. § 15-2-3.

Necessaries. Suppose that Jed is an orphan, age 16, with no family or friends. He has skills as a carpenter, but cannot get work because he has no tools, and he cannot buy tools because he is a minor and cannot contract. Does the law contemplate that Jed must starve on the streets like character from a Dicken's novel? The response to this type of problem is that a minor is allowed to enter into enforceable obligations (not a *contract*) with respect to items which are viewed as necessary for survival. These necessary items are sometimes referred to as *necessaries*.

Necessaries are things such as clothing, food, shelter, medical care, tools of a trade, basic education and the like. The problem is that a minor, such as 16-year-old Jed, must have these necessary items, but if the theory that minors do not have capacity to contract is correct, a minor should not be held liable for contracts, even for necessaries. The response is to use a theory such as quasi-contract (contracts implied in law)[7] where the court has the option of forcing the minor to pay the *reasonable value* for the necessary items, but not a contract price. With reasonable value as the remedy (instead of a contract price) the court can protect the minor and still be fair to the other party.

With respect to necessaries, the interaction of legal theories works like this: (1) Jed is a minor who needs a hammer to earn a living. He contracts to buy a hammer (worth $35) from a sharp salesman who charges him $50; (2) Jed disaffirms the contract on the basis that he is a minor; (3) the salesman does not want the hammer back and claims that the hammer is a "necessary," which it is; (4) the court allows Jed to disaffirm, but on a quasi-contract theory forces Jed to pay $35 for the hammer because it was a necessary item. Through this interaction of theories it appears that contract theory—and common sense—have both been satisfied.

In the following opinion, *Webster Street Partnership, LTD v. Sheridan*, two minors, Sheridan and Wilwerding, entered into an apartment lease with adults who knew they were minors. When the minors asserted their minority to avoid the contract, the adults claimed that the apartment was a *necessary*.

Webster Street Partnership. LTD. v. Sheridan
368 N.W.2d 439 (1985)

KRIVOSHA, Chief Justice.

* * *

The evidence conclusively establishes that at the time the lease was executed both tenants were minors and, further, that Webster Street knew that fact. At the time the lease was entered into, Sheridan was 18 and did not become 19 until November 5, 1982. Wilwerding was 17 at the time the lease was executed and never gained his majority during any time relevant to this case.

* * *

As a general rule, an infant does not have the capacity to bind himself absolutely by

---

[7] Quasi contracts are discussed in Chapter 7.

contract. * * * The right of the infant to avoid his contract is one conferred by law for his protection against his own improvidence and designs of others. * * * The policy for the law is to discourage adults form contracting with an infant; they cannot complain if, as a consequence of violation that rule, they are unable to enforce their contracts. * * * "The result seems hardly just to the [adult], but persons dealing with infants do so at their peril. The law is plain as to their disability to contract, and safety lies in refusing to transact business with them."

However, the privilege of infancy will not enable an infant to escape liability in all cases and under all circumstances. For example, it is well established that an infant is liable for the value of necessaries furnished him. * * * An infant's liability for necessaries is based not upon his actual contract to pay for them but upon a contract implied by law, or, in other words, a quasi-contract. * * *

Just what are necessaries, however, has not exact definition. The term is flexible and varies according to the facts of each individual case. * * *

* * *

It would * * * appear that in the present case neither Sheridan nor Wilwerding was in need of shelter but, rather, had chosen to voluntarily leave home, with the understanding that they could return whenever they desired. One may at first blush believe that such a rule is unfair. Yet, on further consideration, the wisdom of the rule is apparent. If indeed, landlords may not contract with minors, except at their peril, they may refuse to do so. In that event, minors who voluntarily leave home but who are free to return will be compelled to return to their parents' home--a result which is desirable. We therefore find that both the municipal court and the district court erred in finding that the apartment, under the facts in this case, was a necessary.

* * *

REVERSED AND REMANDED WITH DIRECTIONS.

Ratification. Suppose that after turning age 19 and becoming adults in the eyes of Nebraska law, that Sheridan or Wilwerding in the *Webster Street* case continued to live in the apartment and pay rent. Would those facts change the outcome of the case? Ratification is action by a previous minor which evidences his or her consent (as an adult) to a previously avoidable contract. The answer to the question is that if the conduct of either of the young men was sufficient to demonstrate agreement as an adult, the contract is ratified and binding.

Mental Impairment. Actual lack of capacity because of mental impairment must be proved. This is in contrast to lack of capacity which is conclusively presumed because of minority. For example, Jed, the minor, was obligated to demonstrate his age, not his actual incompetence. In contrast, Milly, who has Down's Syndrome, must herself (or someone acting for her) demonstrate actual incompetence. If a court has found that she is not competent and has appointed a guardian to act in her behalf, Milly's Caribbean contract is considered void. On the other hand, some persons with Down's Syndrome—as with other forms of mental impairment—are remarkably capable. Depending on the nature and fairness of the transaction, Milly may not in all cases lack capacity, and her lack of capacity is a point she must *prove*. Where she has not been judicially declared incompetent, her cruise contract is described as void*able*.

Problem Solving. Please turn to Chapter Problems at the end of this chapter and solve Problem 11.5.

General Lack of Capacity. Parties to a contract are presumed to have capacity; and, thus, 94-year-old Sam is presumed to have capacity to contract. If Sam—or any other apparently normal person—does not understand the nature or consequences of a contract relationship, it is his obligation (or the obligation of someone acting in his behalf) to step forward and prove it. Otherwise, the contract will be enforced. Lack of capacity is viewed as an "affirmative defense" which is waived if not used. Taken out of legal jargon, this means: "use it or lose it."

Intoxication is sometimes asserted as evidence of lack of capacity. In general, voluntary intoxication is not viewed with favor unless it clearly deprived the contracting party of the ability to comprehend the nature and consequences of the contract.

The following opinion, *Lucy v. Zehmer*, is famous in legal circles. It reminds the reader of two elderly men arguing over who has caught the biggest fish. Zehmer had a farm which he had persistently refused to sell, despite the importuning of Lucy who wanted to buy it. While the two were sharing a bottle of whiskey, Zehmer said he decided to call Lucy's bluff and he (and his wife) agreed to sell, believing that Lucy didn't have enough money to buy. To his surprise, Lucy accepted his offer. Zehmer refused to deliver the property, claiming that the whole conversation was just a joke. He also claimed that he was too intoxicated to enter into a contract. The portions of the opinion reproduced below relates to the issue of intoxication.

Lucy v. Zehmer
84 S.E.2d 516 (1954)

BUCHANAN, Justice.

* * *

Lucy took a partly filled bottle of whiskey into the restaurant with him for the purpose of giving Zehmer a drink if he wanted it. Zehmer did, and he and Luch had one or two drinks together. Lucy said that while he felt the drinks he took he was not intoxicated, and from the way Zehmer handled the transaction he did not think he was either.

* * *

He [Zehmer] bought this farm more than ten years ago for $11,000. He had had twenty-five offers, more or less, to buy it, including several from Lucy, who had never offered any specific sum of money. He had given them all the same answer, that he was not interested in selling it. On this Saturday night before Christmas it looked like everybody and his brother came by there to have a drink. He took a good many drinks during the afternoon and had a pint of his own. When he entered the restaurant around eight-thirty Lucy was there and he could see that he was "pretty high." he said to Lucy, "Boy, you got some good liquor, drinking, ain't you?" Lucy then offered him a drink. "I was already high as a Georgia pine, and didn't have any more better sense than to pour another great big slug out and gulp it down, and he took one too."

* * *

The defendants insist that the evidence was ample to support their contention that the writing sought to be enforced was prepared as a bluff or dare to force Lucy to admit that he did not have $50,000; that the whole matter was a joke; that the writing was not delivered to Lucy and no binding contract was ever made between the parties.

It is an unusual, if not bizarre, defense. When made to the writing admittedly prepared by one of the defendants and signed by both, clear evidence is required to sustain it.

In his testimony Zehmer claimed that he "was high as a Georgia pine," and that the transaction "was just two doggoned drunks bluffing to see who could talk the biggest and say the most." That claim is inconsistent with his attempt to testify in great detail as to what was said and what done. It is contradicted by other evidence as to the condition of both parties, and rendered of no weight by the testimony of his wife that when Lucy left the restaurant she suggested that Zehmer drive him home. The record is convincing that Zehmer was not intoxicated to the extent of being unable to comprehend the nature and consequences of the instrument he executed, and hence that instrument is not to be invalidated on that ground. * * * It was in fact conceded by defendants' counsel in oral argument that under the evidence Zehmer was not too drunk to make a valid contract.

* * *

The complainants are entitled to have specific performance of the contract sued on. the decree appealed from is therefore reversed and the cause is remanded for the entry of a proper decree requiring the defendants to perform the contract in accordance with the prayer of the bill.

Reversed and remanded.

Problem Solving. Please turn to Chapter Problems at the end of this chapter and solve Problem 11.6.

Chapter Problems

Problem 11.1.

Suppose that Jed sells Milly a car, and Milly later uses the car as a "getaway" car for a bank robbery. Is the contract between Jed and Milly for the sale of the car invalid because it has an unlawful purpose?

Problem 11.2.

Sadri, a California resident, wrote out checks and signed two memoranda of indebtedness which allowed him to gamble at Caesar's Tahoe casino in Nevada. He incurred an indebtedness totaling $22,000 in two days of gambling. Suit was brought in California to collect the indebtedness after Sadri refused to pay. California permits some forms of gambling (for example, lotteries and horse racing), but has a public policy against the enforcement of gambling debts. Should the court decide in favor of Sadri or Caesar's Tahoe?

Problem 11.3.

In *Noble v. Alis*, Noble and Ellis never lived in the apartment. Assume, however, that they did live in the apartment for six months, and then used the housing code violations as a basis for refusing to pay their rent. Would these changes in the facts change the outcome?

Problem 11.4.

Suppose that the Urbana High School sponsored a "ski day" at the Sunpoint Ski Resort for it's senior class as a senior class party, and one element of the activities was a downhill ski race. Further suppose that students were asked to sign an exculpatory clause like that in *Milligan* which released the ski resort and the school district. Would it be enforceable?

Problem 11.5.

Suppose that Jed sells Milly a car and then realizes she is a minor. Can Jed (an adult) disaffirm the contract?

Problem 11.6.

Suppose that Milly is 17 years of age and also has Down's Syndrome. She buys a stereo, but later returns it and wishes to disaffirm. Which will be the most legally effective: her claim that she is a minor, or her claim that she has a mental impairment?

Chapter 12
Statute of Frauds and Parol Evidence

Chapter Outline

OBJECTIVE is to learn the requirements of the statute of frauds and the parol evidence rule.

The objective of this chapter is to learn the rules that require certain contracts to be in writing (the statute of frauds), and the rules that enforce that requirement (the parol evidence rule). This chapter is organized as follows:

Statute of Frauds

- *Introduction.* In general, contracts are not required to be in writing. Those contracts which must be in writing are identified in the statute of frauds.

- *Origins of the Statute of Frauds.* The original version of the statute of frauds was adopted in England in 1677, entitled A Statute for the Prevention of Frauds and Perjuries. The objective of the statute was to prevent perjured testimony in relation to oral contracts.

- *Statute of Frauds in the United States.* American colonists brought the English tradition of a statute of frauds to the American colonies. In varying forms, statutes of frauds have since been adopted by the states in the United States.

- *The Statute of Frauds.* The statute of frauds requires contracts concerning the following to be in writing: (1) an interest in real estate; (2) collateral contracts to pay a debt in the event of the failure or default of another; (3) long-term (more than one year) contracts; and, (4) promises by a personal representative to pay the debts of an estate.

- *An Interest in Real Estate.* Contracts for the sale of an interest in real estate will not be enforced unless they are in writing.

- *Collateral Contracts to Perform the Obligation of Another.* Collateral contracts in which one person promises to perform the obligation of another, in the event of failure or default, must be in writing to be enforced.

- *Long-Term Bilateral Contracts.* Bilateral contracts which by their terms cannot be performed within one year from the date of their formation must be in writing to be enforced.

- *Contracts to Personally Pay the Debts of an Estate.* Contracts in which the personal representative of an estate promises to personally pay a debt of the decedent must be in writing to be enforced.

Parole Evidence

- *The Parol Evidence Rule.* Parol evidence is evidence introduced at trial for the purpose of altering the terms of a written contract. The rule prohibits contract-altering evidence from the time a contract is signed, or before that time.

Introduction

In general, contracts are not *required* to be in writing, although a written contract is always a good practice. A contract which is not in writing is sometimes called an "oral" contract, and if there is a disagreement about the existence or terms of such a contract and a lawsuit is filed, witnesses provide the necessary evidence through their testimony.

But, some contracts *must* be in writing or they are not enforceable. The odd name for the rule that requires some contracts to be in writing is the *Statute of Frauds.* Once a contract is in writing, another rule, called the *Parol Evidence Rule*, comes into play. The parol evidence rule controls the evidence that may be used in court to attack the existence or terms of written agreements. These two rules (the statute of frauds and the parol evidence rule) are the subjects of this chapter.

Origins of the Statute of Frauds

STATUTE OF FRAUDS: prevents perjury caused by testifying falsely about oral contracts.

An Oral Contract. Suppose that Jed and Milly have a conversation in which Jed, an artist, agrees for $5000 to paint a portrait of Milly. Sam overhears the conversation. In this setting, Jed and Milly are the parties to the contract, and Sam is viewed as a "third party." If there is a breach of the contract because Jed refuses to paint, or Milly refuses to pay, *Jed, Milly and Sam* can testify about the formation and terms of the contract. This is how the problem would be handled today in the United States. In 17th Century England, however, the legal rules were different, and those different legal rules mark the beginning of the Statute of Frauds.

17th Century England. In 17th Century England, legal rules *prevented* Jed and Milly from testifying in their own lawsuit. That meant, of course, that evidence establishing the existence or terms of an oral contract had to come from third parties, such as Sam. In this setting, many dishonest practices related to perjury[1] developed. For instance, Milly might persuade a stranger, such as Jake, to falsely testify (to her advantage) because she could not testify herself. (It is said that one of the origins of the phrase "straw man" is the conduct of professional perjurers in the English courts of law in this period. These people could be found in the vicinity of the court with a few telltale pieces of straw tucked into the side of their shoe—hence the name "straw man"—as a signal that they would testify as instructed, for a price.)

Perjury by third parties was viewed as a form of fraud. The consequence of this

---

[1] A witness testifying falsely under oath in a court of law commits perjury.

scandalous behavior was the adoption by the English Parliament, in 1677, of a statute know as A Statute for the Prevention of Frauds and Perjuries. This English statute is now known by the shorter title of Statute of Frauds. The approach taken in the Statute of Frauds was to identify those types of contracts where fraud based on perjury was most common and to require those contracts to be in writing. Stated in other words, the Statute of Frauds required certain contracts to be in writing if they are to be enforced.

In the United States. As we have discussed before, American colonists brought English legal traditions to the North American colonies. Included in those legal traditions was the Statute of Frauds. Over the years, the legislatures of the various colonies (later states) adopted statutes of frauds. As with the original English Statute of Frauds, these American counterparts were designed to prevent false testimony regarding contracts by requiring certain contracts to be in writing.

Problem Solving. Please turn to Chapter Problems at the end of this chapter and solve Problem 12.1.

The Statute of Frauds

A statute of frauds requires certain contracts to be in writing; if they are not in writing they are not enforceable. Contracts which must be in writing are said to be "within" the statute of frauds. The contracts which are within the statute of frauds are the following:[2]

- Contracts for the sale of an interest in real estate.

- Collateral contracts in which one person promises, in the event of failure or default, to perform the obligation of another.

- Bilateral contracts which by their terms cannot be performed within one year from the date of their formation.

- Contracts in which the personal representative of an estate promises to pay a debt of the decedent.

Problem Solving. Please turn to Chapter Problems at the end of this chapter and solve Problem 12.2.

REAL ESTATE: a contract to sell and interest in real estate must be in writing.

An Interest in Real Estate. A contract for the sale of an interest in real estate is within the statute of frauds and must be in writing to be enforceable. Thus, if Jed contracts

---

[2] Contracts in which a promise of marriage is the consideration are traditionally part of the statute of frauds. However, there is a growing trend—based on public policy arguments—to refuse to enforce such contracts. Accordingly, the application of the statute of frauds to marriage contracts is not discussed.

to sell Blackacre[3] to Milly, that contract must be in writing or it will not be enforceable. But, suppose that Milly merely wants to buy the right to build a road across Blackacre to get to her ranch, must this contract also be in writing? The answer is yes, the statute of frauds applies to a contract for the sale of an *interest* in real property and is not limited to a sale of Jed's entire interest in Blackacre.

In like manner, contracts to remove gravel or to drill for oil are contracts for the sale of an *interest* in real estate. They are within the statute of frauds and must be in writing. In addition, suppose that Milly wants 30 days to decide whether to accept an offer from Jed to sell Blackacre; Jed agrees, and Milly gives him $100 to hold the offer open. Must this *option* be in writing? The answer is yes, because the effect of the option is to give Milly the right to purchase Blackacre, and that right is an *interest* in real property.

Full Performance. Full performance by the seller of an oral contract for the sale of real property provides an exception to the statute of frauds. Suppose that Jed orally contracts to sell Blackacre to Milly, and delivers a deed to her. Under these facts, where the seller has fully performed, most states treat the contract as enforceable.

Part Performance. Part performance by a buyer of an oral contract for the sale of real property is sometimes an exception to the statute of frauds. That is, the contract will be enforced—just as it was above—even though it is not in writing. Suppose that Jed orally contracts to sell Blackacre to Milly and she starts making payments to him and builds a house on it. Then, Jed claims any contract they may have between them is not enforceable because it is not in writing. Moreover, he claims that the money she paid was just rent and he files suit to have her removed from Blackacre.

The doctrine of part performance is based on equitable principles, not on legal principles. The objective is a focus on fairness, and to accomplish fairness the court will enforce the contract if the following two requirements are met:

1. The party seeking to enforce the contract has relied on the promises of the other party.

2. The party seeking to enforce the contract has changed his or her position to the extent that only enforcement will prevent injustice.[4]

Applying the part performance doctrine to Jed and Milly's transaction, it is clear that Milly has relied on Jed's promises by making payments to him and by building a house on Blackacre. The remedy associated with the doctrine of part performance is the equitable remedy of specific performance, not money damages. It would be unjust to refuse a remedy to Milly under these circumstances; therefore, the court will allow her the remedy of specific performance. The result of this ruling is that Milly will finish paying the contract price, and Jed will be compelled (specific performance) to deliver good title to

---

[3] "Blackacre" is as real as Jed and Milly. It is a make-believe, one-acre, parcel of real property that, for teaching purposes, changes it's characteristics to fit the moment.

[4] RESTATEMENT (SECOND) CONTRACTS, § 129.

Milly.

Part performance was claimed as an exception to the statute of frauds in the case of *Hickey v. Green*. Gladys Green orally agreed to sell a building lot to Mr. and Mrs. Hickey for $15,000 and accepted a check from them in the amount of $500. Relying on this contract, the Hickeys sold their home anticipating that they would build a new home on the lot. But, Mrs. Green got a better offer and refused to sell to the Hickeys claiming that her contract with them was not enforceable because it was not in writing. The Hickeys filed suit asking for specific performance of the sales contract.

HICKEY v. GREEN
442 N.E.2d 37 (1982)

CUTTER, Justice.

* * *

The present rule applicable in most jurisdictions in the United States is succinctly set forth in Restatement (Second) of Contracts, § 129 (1981). The section reads, "A contract for the transfer of an interest in land may be specifically enforced notwithstanding failure to comply with the Statute of Frauds if it is established that the party seeking enforcement, *in reasonable reliance on the contract* and on the continuing assent of the party against whom enforcement is sought, *has so changed his position that injustice can be avoided only by specific enforcement*" (emphasis supplied). * * *

* * *

The present facts reveal a simple case of a proposed purchase of a residential vacant lot, where the vendor, Mrs. Green, knew that the Hickeys were planning to sell their former home (possibly to obtain funds to pay her) and build on Lot S. The Hickeys, relying on Mrs. Green's oral promise, moved rapidly to make their sale without obtaining any adequate memorandum of the terms of what appears to have been intended to be a quick cash sale of Lot S. So rapid was action by the Hickeys that, by July 21, less than ten days after giving their deposit to Mrs. Green, they had accepted a deposit check for the sale of their house, endorsed the check, and placed it in their bank account. * * *

There is no denial by Mrs. Green of the oral contract between her and the Hickeys. This, under § 129 of the Restatement, is of some significance. There can be no doubt (a) that Mrs. Green made the promise on which the Hickeys so promptly relied, and also (b) she, nearly as promptly, but not promptly enough, repudiated it because she had a better opportunity. The stipulated facts require the conclusion that in equity Mrs. Green's conduct cannot be condoned. This is not a case where either party is shown to have contemplated the negotiation of a purchase and sale agreement. If a written agreement had been expected, even by only one party, or would have been natural (because of the participation of lawyers or otherwise), a different situation might have existed. It is a permissible inference from the agreed facts that the rapid sale of the Hickeys' house was both appropriate and expected. * * *

* * *

[The decision of the trial court was affirmed.]

Problem Solving. Please turn to Chapter Problems at the end of this chapter and solve Problem 12.3.

Collateral Contracts to Perform the Obligation of Another. Collateral

COLLATERAL CONTRACTS, are sometimes called "guarantees" and must be in writing.

contracts in which one person promises to perform the obligation of another, in the event of failure or default, must be in writing to be enforceable. An agreement of this kind is sometimes called a "guarantee". This is simpler than it sounds: Jed negotiates to have Sam, a CPA, perform an audit of his business, Jed's Landscaping. Sam is reluctant to do the work because of his concern that Jed may not have enough money to pay for it. To close the deal, Jed has his friend, Milly, promise to pay Sam, if he (Jed) does not.

Milly's promise is *collateral* to the contract between Jed and Sam. (Something which is "collateral" is something which is side by side or parallel to another.) Milly's promise runs side by side with the promise made by Jed: she promises to perform the contract *if* Jed does not. If this promise by Milly is not in writing, it cannot be enforced. Stated in other words, a promise to do a contract performance, *in the event of the failure of another person to do it*, must be in writing to be enforced.

A Conditional Promise. Suppose that the actual language of Milly's promise to Sam is: "I promise to pay for the audit of Jed's Landscaping." Must this promise be in writing? The answer is no, because this language is an *unconditional* promise to pay for the audit. But, if the language of Milly's promise to Sam is "I promise to pay for the audit of Jed's Landscaping, if Jed does not," must this be in writing? The answer is yes, because in this collateral promise, Milly promises to perform *in the event of Jed's failure or default.*

The Main Purpose Exception. Suppose that the real reason for the audit of Jed's Landscaping was that *Milly* wanted it done to help her decide whether to buy the business. The question to be asked is whether Milly's *main purpose* is to benefit Jed or to benefit her? If the main purpose of Milly's promise to pay (if Jed does not) is to benefit Jed, then her promise must be in writing to be enforceable. On the other hand, if the main purpose of Milly's promise to pay (if Jed does not) is to benefit her (not him), then the promise can be enforced without being in writing.

In the following opinion, *Wilson Floors Co. v. Sciota Park, Ltd.*, the Pittsburgh National Bank loaned $7,000,000 to Sciota Park to construct an apartment and office complex called The Cliffs. Sciota Park contracted with Wilson Floors to furnish and install flooring in the complex. Unfortunately, Sciota Park ran out of money when they were only two-thirds finished with The Cliffs. Nevertheless, the Bank requested Wilson Floors, and other subcontractors, to finish work on the project and assured them that if they returned to work, they would be paid. But, when the project was finished, the Bank refused to pay the $15,443.06 still owing to Wilson Floors, claiming that the obligation was barred by the statute of frauds. Wilson Floors said that their claim was not barred by the statute of frauds because the principal or leading objective of the bank in asking Wilson floors to continue work was to benefit the bank by finishing the project.

WILSON FLOORS CO. v. SCIOTA PARK, LTD.
377 N.E.2d 514 (1978)

SWEENEY, Justice

The central issue in this cause is whether the bank's oral promise to Wilson that

---

payments would be forthcoming upon a resumption of work at The Cliffs project constituted an enforceable oral contract.

R.C. 1334.05 provides:

"No action shall be brought whereby to charge the defendant, upon a special promise, to answer for the debt, default, or miscarriage of another person * * * unless the agreement upon which such action is brought, or some memorandum or note thereof, is in writing and signed by the party to be charged therewith or some other person thereunto by him or her lawfully authorized."

In paragraph one of the syllabus in *Crawford v. Edison* (1887), 45 Ohio St. 239, 13 N.E. 80, however, this court stated:

"When the leading object of the promisor is not to answer for another, but to subserve some pecuniary or business purpose of his own, involving a benefit to himself, or damage to the other contracting party, his promise is not within the statute of frauds, although it may be in form a promise to pay the debt of another, and its performance may incidentally have the effect of extinguishing that liability."

* * *

The facts in the instant cause reflect that the bank made its guarantee to Wilson to subserve its own business interest of reducing costs to complete the project. Clearly, the bank induced Wilson to remain on the job and rely on its credit for future payments. To apply the statute of frauds and hold that the bank had no contractual duty to Wilson despite its oral guarantees would not prevent the wrong which the statute's enactment was to prevent, but would in reality effectuate a wrong. * * *

Therefore, this court affirms the finding of the Court of Common Pleas that the verbal agreement made by the bank is enforceable by Wilson, and reverses the judgment of the Court of Appeals.

Judgment reversed.

Problem Solving. Please turn to Chapter Problems at the end of this chapter and solve Problem 12.4.

LONG TERM CONTRACTS (meaning more than one year) must be in writing.

Long-Term Bilateral Contracts. Bilateral contracts which by their terms cannot be performed within one year from the date of their formation must be in writing to be enforced. For example, on January 1, Milly hires Jed to work as her gardner for two years. That contract *cannot* be performed within one year, *measured from the date of contract formation*, and it must be in writing to be enforced.

Measured From Date of Formation. Suppose that on January 1, Milly hires Jed to work for her for one year, commencing July 1. Must this contract be in writing to be enforced? The answer is found by starting at the date of contract formation, which is January 1; then, measure forward until the time the contract will be fully performed. The resulting time period is eighteen months. Can this contract be performed within one year *measured from the date of contract formation*? The answer is obviously no. Thus, this contract in "within" the statute of frauds: it must be in writing or it cannot be enforced.

"Cannot" Be Performed. Change the facts slightly and suppose that on January 1, Milly hires Jed to work for her for the rest of his life. Must this contract be in writing to be enforced? The answer is found by applying the standard test: is it possible that this contract can be performed within one year from the date of it's formation? Here the

hypothetical answer to the hypothetical question is, yes it is *possible* because Jed may die next month; thus, the contract *may* be performed within the required one year. But, wait! In the example above (on January 1, Milly hires Jed to work for one year, commencing July 1) isn't it also possible that Jed will die in one month, just like it is possible in this example that Jed may die in one month? Yes, in both examples it is *possible* that Jed may die next month. Then why must the first contract be in writing, but not the second?

In the first example, the term of employment was a fixed term of two years. Thus, although Jed might die, that would be an incidental happening, and it certainly was not a planned event. Accordingly, because death was not a term of the contract, it is not included in the calculations, and the contract cannot by its terms be performed within the required one year. Thus, it must be in writing.

On the other hand, in the second example, death is an explicit term of the contract: Jed agrees to work for life. In this case, because death is an explicit term of the contract, the courts have held that it is possible that the contract may by its terms be performed within the required one year. Thus, it is not required to be in writing. Being candid, this exception does not make sense because a contract for life may be a very long-term contract. And, if we were writing the rules anew, we would surely eliminate this exception. But, for now, the best answer is that the courts allow this exception because that is the way they did things in England during the reign of Charles II.

In the following opinion, *Hodge v. Evans Financial Corp.*, Albert Hodge orally agreed to work at Evans Financial but was fired after less than a year. "According to Hodge's trial testimony, Tilley [president and chief operating officer of Evans Financial] asked Hodge at the second meeting what his conditions were for accepting employment with Evans. Hodge replied, 'No. 1, the job must be permanent. Because of my age, I have a great fear about going back into the marketplace again. I want to be here until I retire.'" When sued in a federal diversity action, Evans Financial responded that the oral contract was unenforceable under the statute of frauds.

HODGE v. EVANS FINANCIAL CORP.
823 F.2d 559 (1987)

WALD, Chief Judge:
* * *

A. Enforceability of the Agreement Under the District of Columbia Statute of Frauds.

Evans argues that the oral employment agreement between Evans and Hodge is unenforceable under the statute of frauds as enacted in the District of Columbia, which provides, in relevant part, that:

> An action may not be brought . . . upon an agreement that is not to be performed within one year from the making thereof, unless the agreement upon which the action is brought, or a memorandum or note thereof, is in writing . . . and signed by the party to be charged therewith or a person authorized by him.

D.C. Code § 28-3502. Because the agreement here contemplated long-term employment for a number of years, Evans argues that the statute requires it to have been in writing in order to be enforceable.

191

Despite its sweeping terms, the one-year provision of the statute has long been construed narrowly and literally. Under the prevailing interpretation, the enforceability of a contract under the statute does not depend on the actual course of subsequent events or on the expectations of the parties. Instead, the statute applies only to those contracts whose performance could not possibly or conceivably be completed within one year. The statute of frauds is thus inapplicable if, at the time the contract is formed, any contingent event could complete the terms of the contract within one year. * * *

This interpretation of the statute has been adopted by the District of Columbia courts. The District of Columbia Court of Appeals recently stated that if a contract is "by its terms capable, possible, or susceptible of performance within one year, the statute of frauds does not apply and an oral agreement may suffice." * * *

Hodge argues that, under this interpretation of the statute of frauds, a permanent or lifetime employment contract does not fall within the statute because it is capable of full performance within one year if the employee were to die within the period. Hodge's view of the statute's applicability to lifetime or permanent employment contracts has, in fact, been accepted by an overwhelming majority of courts and commentators. *See* Restatement (Second) of Contracts § 130 illustration 2 (1979) ("A orally promises to work for B, and B promises to employ A during A's life at a stated salary. The promises are not within the one-year provision of the Statute, since A's life may terminate within a year."); * * * 2 Corbin on Contracts § 446, at 549 & n. 35 (1950 and Supp.1984) ("A contract for 'permanent' employment is not within the one-year clause for the reason that such a contract will be fully performed, according to its terms, upon the death of the employee."); E. Farnsworth, contracts § 42 (1974 & Supp.1984) ("It is a well-settled general rule that a contract . . . to employ one for the duration of his life [or] a contract to give one 'permanent' employment . . . is not within [the statute] for the reason that contracts of this description are deemed possible of performance within one year from their formation, since, for example, the employee may die within that period.") (footnotes omitted).

* * *

* * * the oral contact between Evans and Hodge was not rendered unenforceable by the District of Columbia statute of frauds. * * *

[Affirmed]

Contracts Fully Performed. There is another exception to the rule against enforcing long-term, oral contracts. Recall the first example (above) where Milly hires Jed on January 1, to work for her for one year, commencing July 1. Full performance by one of the parties to a long-term, oral contract is an exception. Thus, if Jed fully performed under the contract, and then Milly refused to pay him, the contract would be enforced because Jed had already fully performed his part.

Problem Solving. Please turn to Chapter Problems at the end of this chapter and solve Problem 12.5.

Contracts to Personally Pay the Debts of an Estate. Contracts in which the personal representative[5] of an estate promises to personally pay a debt of the decedent must be in writing to be enforced. If Milly dies, Jed may be appointed the personal representative of her estate. That means that he will be charged with collecting all of her assets, paying all of her debts, and paying the remainder to her heirs. Creditors who claim that Milly owed them money must present their claims to Jed. Suppose that all of this is done, and a year later Sam demands that Jed pay him money that was owed by Milly. When Jed refuses, Sam says "Remember, you said not to bother filing a claim against the estate. You said you'd take care of it yourself." This claim to require the personal representative to pay a debt of the estate must be in writing to be enforced.

It is not unusual for claimants to appear on the legal horizon a long time after the death of someone they did business with. Having no other place to turn, they occasionally make claims like that by Sam, above. This provision of the statute of frauds makes great sense because it protects personal representatives, like Jed, from claims which may, or may not, be legitimate.

Problem Solving. Please turn to Chapter Problems at the end of this chapter and solve Problem 12.6.

The Parol Evidence Rule

Introduction. At this point, the focus changes to the courtroom. Whether they were required to (by the statute of frauds) or not, the parties to a contract put it into writing. Now, they are in court disputing the existence or meaning of their contract. Will the judge simply read the contract, or will she allow the parties to testify about it, and perhaps try and alter it's apparent meaning? This is the subject matter of the parol evidence rule.

Context. The so-called *parol evidence rule* regulates evidence that may be introduced in a trial concerning the existence or terms of a written contract. To understand the context in which the rule applies, suppose that Jed agrees in a written contract to sell Blackacre to Milly for $50,000. The written terms of the contract are that Milly will pay $10,000 per year for three years, and then pay $20,000 in the fourth year. Inconsistent with that agreement, however, Milly pays only $10,000 in the fourth year, and when Jed demands the remaining $10,000, Milly says: "Don't you remember, when we signed the contract you said the timing of the last payment wasn't important. You said I could have five years at $10,000 each year if I wanted." Jed responds: "Sure I said that, but it was only if you would let me keep my trucks at Blackacre, and you said you *wouldn't* let me keep my trucks at Blackacre. So, there was no deal."

When Jed and Milly can't agree on whether she is entitled to a fifth year to pay the last $10,000, Jed files suit, demanding damages or the return of the property. At trial, the written contract is received into evidence, and Jed testifies that the remaining amount of $10,000 has not been paid as described in the contract. When it is Milly's turn, she

---

[5] Other, older, terms for a personal representative are: executor, executrix, administrator and administratrix.

testifies that, indeed, she has not paid the last $10,000. Then, she starts to tell the court about the oral agreement giving her an additional fifth year. The effect of this testimony—as the judge fully understands—is to amend the terms of the written contract by giving Milly five years to pay instead of four years.

The Rule. Should the judge allow the "fifth year" testimony of Milly into evidence? "Parol" evidence means evidence *outside* of a written contract; thus, oral or written testimony which modifies the terms of a written contract is controlled by the *parol evidence rule*. This is the rule which resolves the admissibility of Milly's "fifth year" testimony. Specifically, the parol evidence rule *prohibits* the admission into evidence of contemporaneous oral or prior written evidence which is not part of a written contract and which alters or contradicts the terms of the written contract. The rule does not prohibit the introduction of evidence to resolve ambiguities, evidence establishing fraud, misrepresentation, mistake, duress, undue influence, and similar defenses, or evidence establishing subsequent modifications of a written contract.

Objective of the Rule. Before solving the judge's evidence problem, consider the larger policy issue involved with Milly's testimony. The issue is this: disputes about the terms of contracts are eliminated by putting contracts into writing, but if parties to a contract are allowed to later freely contradict those written terms, the problem remains. Stated in different terms, what is accomplished by choosing (or being required) to put a contract into writing if the parties may nevertheless contradict what is in writing? The response, in short, is that the value of written contracts is diminished to the extent the written terms are not enforced.

Ambiguity. The answer to the judge's problem with Milly's "fifth year" testimony is that parol evidence may not be received into evidence unless the terms of the written contract between Jed and Milly are ambiguous. In this case, the *written* terms are clear that a final payment of $20,000 will be made in the fourth year. Thus, because the written terms are clear (and not ambiguous), the judge should refuse to receive Milly's testimony into evidence.

What is meant by the proposition that the terms of a written contract may be *ambiguous*? Change the terms of the written contract between Jed and Milly to be: "Milly shall pay $10,000 per year for three years and the balance of $20,000 in the fourth year, unless the parties otherwise agree because of parking with respect to the fourth year." What does the phrase "unless the parties otherwise agree because of parking with respect to the fourth year" mean? The judge doesn't know what the phrase means; to him the phrase is ambiguous (unclear). Under this version of the facts, the judge will allow Milly to testify to the extent necessary to resolve the ambiguous part of the written agreement. That means that she will be allowed to testify to the conversation about an exchange of an additional fifth year in return for parking privileges at Blackacre.

"Integrated" Contract. Judges sometimes find it difficult to know what documents constitute a "contract." Suppose that Jed and Milly formed their written contract for Blackacre through a series of letters. In a first letter, Jed offers to sell to Blackacre to Milly with payment in full in the first year; in a second letter, Milly counteroffers, proposing to pay in full in ten years; in a third letter, Jed proposes payment in four years; and, in a fourth letter, Milly accepts (without reservation) Jed's proposal to pay in four years. At this point, when the four letters are combined ("integrated") together they appear to constitute a complete contract. Then, some time later, Milly sends a letter to Jed which says, among other things: "I think what we talked about on the telephone last night, about trading a fifth year for parking privileges, is a good idea."

In the story above, the judge must decide what the intent of the parties was; at what point did they consider the negotiations closed and the contract complete? The letters which the judge thinks constitute the contract are considered "integrated" together into one whole document. The implications of this decision by the judge are significant: on the one hand, if the judge decides that the integrated contract consists of the first four letters, then evidence (in the form of the fifth letter or in Milly's oral testimony about a telephone call) about the fifth year of payment are prohibited parol evidence. On the other hand, if the judge decides that the integrated contract consists of all five letters, then the language of the fifth letter is ambiguous, and to clarify that ambiguity the judge may receive oral testimony from Milly and Jed about the telephone conversation they had.

In the following opinion, *Slivinsky v. Watkins-Johnson Co.*, the plaintiff, Ms. Slivinsky, signed a written employment agreement in which she acknowledged that she was not being hired for any specific period of time and that she could be terminated at any time. Nevertheless, when she was later terminated, she claimed that she had been orally assured that her employment would be of indefinite duration if her work was satisfactory. She sued, claiming a violation of that oral understanding. At trial, the question was whether the written contract was the controlling document, or whether the oral understanding could be also considered.

SLIVINSKY v. WATKINS-JOHNSON CO.
270 Cal.Rptr. 585 (1990)

COTTLE, Associate Justice.

Slivinsky sent a formal letter of acceptance to the company on December 16, 1984, and reported for work, as agreed upon, on January 7, 1985. On that day, she signed the employee agreement which had been referred to in her application to Watkins-Johnson ("I understand that employment by Watkins-Johnson Company is conditional upon . . . execution of an Employee Agreement"). The last paragraph of the employee agreement, which was set apart from the body of the document and written in bold type, provided: "Employee acknowledges that there is no agreement, express or implied, between employee and the Company for any specific period of employment, nor for continuing or long-term employment. Employee and the Company each have a right to terminate employment, with or without cause."

As a result of the space shuttle Challenger disaster in January 1986, Watkins-Johnson experienced significant business losses and government contract cancellations. The management decided that a manpower cutback was essential to cope with the loss of business. Ultimately, 26 employees were selected for the Reduction in Force program, including Slivinsky, 14 members of her division, and 4 members of her department. Watkins-Johnson terminated her employment on June 20, 1986.

DISCUSSION

In her first and second causes of action, Slivinsky alleges that Watkins-Johnson breached its employment contract and breached its duty of good faith and fair dealing by terminating her employment "in an arbitrary, pretextual, and improper manner" "without cause and for reasons that have nothing to do with legitimate business justification" in violation of the parties' "express and implied in fact employment agreement" that she "would be able to continue her employment with defendants indefinitely so long as she carried out her duties in a proper and competent manner." She claims that during prehire interviews, she was assured that her employment would be "long-term," "indefinite," and "permanent," independent of business fluctuations, and subject only to termination for cause.

On appeal, Slivinsky claims that the evidence is disputed as to the parameters of the parties' employment agreement—Slivinsky arguing that it includes factors such as the duration of plaintiff's employment, promotions received, lack of criticism, oral assurances of job security and Watkins-Johnson's personnel policies and practices not to terminate employees except for good cause; Watkins-Johnson arguing that it is limited to the parties' express written contract defining the employment as at-will.

The dispositive issue, therefore, is whether we can look beyond the four corners of the parties' written agreements to ascertain the complete agreement of the parties. The answer to that question involves application of the parol evidence rule, a rule of substantive law precluding the introduction of evidence which varies or contradicts the terms of an integrated written instrument. If the parties intended that the Application and Employment Agreement constituted an integration, i.e., the "final expression of their agreement with respect" to grounds for termination, then those agreements "May not be contradicted by evidence of any prior agreement or of a contemporaneous oral agreement." * * *

Whether the agreement is an integration is a question of law for the judge. * * * "The court shall determine whether the writing is intended by the parties as a final expression of their agreement with respect to such terms as are included therein . . . ." * * * Additionally, "No particular form is required for an integrated agreement." Cite. "When only part of the agreement is integrated, the [parol evidence] rule applies to that part . . . ." * * * "If a writing is deemed integrated, extrinsic evidence is admissible only if it is relevant to prove a meaning to which the language of the instrument is reasonably susceptible. * * *

Applying these standards, we conclude that the contract was integrated with respect to the grounds for termination. Slivinsky's employment application specifically conditioned employment upon execution of an employee agreement. It further provided that if Slivinsky were to become employed by Watkins-Johnson, there "*will be no agreement expressed or implied*, between the Company and [Slivinsky] for any specific period of employment, nor *for continuing or long term employment*." When Slivinsky executed the Employee Agreement, she acknowledged "that there *is no agreement, express or implied*, between employee and the Company for any specific period of employment, nor *for continuing or long-term employment. Employee and the Company each have a right to terminate employment, with or without cause.*" (Emphasis added).

Reading these documents together, the only reasonable conclusion that can be drawn is that the parties intended that there *would be no other agreement* regarding termination *other than* that set forth in the Employee Agreement, i.e., that employment was terminable at the will of either party, with or without cause. * * *

* * *

We find as a matter of law that Slivinsky has failed to state any cause of action against her former employer, Watkins-Johnson.

The judgment is affirmed.

Fraud, Etc. Evidence establishing the existence of fraud, misrepresentation, mistake, duress, undue influence, and similar defenses to the enforcement of a contract are not prohibited by the parol evidence rule. For example, suppose that in the negotiations for the sale of Blackacre, Milly asks if the well on the property provides good water, and Jed responds that it does. In fact, Jed knows that the well is polluted by toxic chemicals and the water cannot be used for human consumption. This, of course, is fraud and fraud is a defense to the enforcement of a contract. Oral or written parol evidence may be introduced to prove fraud—without violating the parol evidence rule. Likewise, misrepresentation, mistake, duress, undue influence, and similar defenses may be established without violating the parol evidence rule.

An Example. To get a better understanding of how the parol evidence is used, consider the following testimony adapted from an actual case. In this case, "Jed" negotiated a contract in which he would sell a house to "Milly." The contract provided that Milly would pay for the house by getting a bank loan and paying all at once, or, she could make monthly payments to Jed; but, Jed decided not to sign it because he wanted all of the purchase price at once, not just monthly payments for the next 20 years. (This document was known at trial as Exhibit 4.) Instead, another contract was prepared which required Milly to borrow the purchase money from a bank, and this document was signed by Jed and Milly. (This document was known at trial as Exhibit 5.)

Because she had bad credit, Milly was never able to borrow the purchase price. And, she refused to move out of the house. She said that the understanding between her and Jed (referring to what later became known as Exhibit 4 and Exhibit 5) was that she would get bank financing, if she could. But, if she could not get bank financing, then she was entitled to make monthly payments. Jed disagreed and brought suit to have her evicted from the house and to recover rent for the nine months she had occupied it.

(As a side note, if the agreement between Jed and Milly had been oral, and not in writing, could it have been enforced? The answer is obviously no, because it is a contract for the sale of an interest in real estate, and that must be in writing to be enforced.)

At trial, the parties agreed that Exhibit 5 would be received into evidence. The dispute was with respect to Exhibit 4: Milly wanted it received to reinforce her shaky claim to make monthly payments, and Jed wanted it kept out. He claimed that (unsigned) Exhibit 4 violated the parol evidence rule because it purported to amend the terms of the (signed) Exhibit 5. Mr. Jones is attorney for Jed, and Mr. Smith is attorney for Milly. With Jed as the witness, this is the testimony:

BY MR. SMITH:

Q: I have what has now been marked as Exhibit 5 and ask if you can identify that please? (Indicating)

MR. JONES: I will stipulate Your Honor that is the contract that relates to the subject residence and I stipulate to its admission.

THE COURT: Alright, is that agreeable counsel?

MR. SMITH: That is agreeable.

THE COURT: No. 5 is received.

MR. SMITH: At this time we also offer No. 4.

THE COURT: Any objection to No. 4?

MR. JONES: Very much so, yes Your Honor. I think at this point we have come to one of the dividing lines in this case. Our objection is that it is totally irrelevant and we draw the Court's attention to the language at the bottom of No. 5. The language in No. 5 says, "This agreement supercedes earlier agreements [Exhibit 4] negotiated between the parties." Now it is my understanding of the law that the court is bound by the intentions of the parties as expressed in their written instruments and only if there is an ambiguity could the court go beyond that or permit extraneous matter whether written or otherwise and so we object on the ground that Exhibit 4 is totally irrelevant.

THE COURT: Well Exhibit 4 would appear to be irrelevant Mr. Smith. Do you have any comment?

MR. SMITH: Yes. In my opinion, we have a situation where we are talking about equity and possibly forfeiture and unjust enrichment and I think it would be helpful to the court to have all of the documents before the court.

THE COURT: Well I don't see ambiguity at this point. Maybe I will entertain a motion later in the proceedings to receive it. I am going to sustain the objection than at this time.

MR. SMITH: Very well.

Exhibit 5 had been received into evidence as a contract between the parties. The unsigned Exhibit 4, and the oral testimony which Milly would then offer in relation to it, was parol evidence in the sense that its terms would amended the terms of Exhibit 5. If Exhibit 5 is unambiguous—and it was—then the judge was correct that Exhibit 4 should not be received into evidence. When Milly could not get Exhibit 4 into evidence, her case was effectively lost because Exhibit 5 clearly provided that she could pay only through a bank loan.

__Problem Solving.__ Please turn to Chapter Problems at the end of this chapter and solve Problem 12.7.

Chapter Problems

Problem 12.1

Is the statute of frauds a rule dealing with the *tort* of fraud?

Problem 12.2

Suppose that a contract is said to be "without" or "outside of" the statute of frauds. What is meant by such a statement?

Problem 12.3

Jed agrees to give Milly an easement over Blackacre for the sum of $500. (An easement is the right to cross over the land of another, but not the right to possess the land.) Milly wants the agreement in writing, but Jed says that because he is selling no part of Blackacre to Milly, their agreement is outside of the statute of frauds. Is Jed correct?

Problem 12.4

The following is a quote from the full opinion in *Wilson Floors Co. v. Sciotia Park, LTD.*: "The bank representative . . . testified at trial that he had merely advised the subcontractors that adequate funds would be available to complete the job. However, two representatives of Wilson . . . testified that the bank representative had assured Wilson that if it returned to work, it would be paid." Based on this evidence, the court assumed that this transaction was "within" the statute of frauds, which meant that Wilson would win only if the "main purpose" exception applied. But—suppose that you are the lawyer for Wilson Floors—do the facts allow you to make a reasonable argument that the promise by the bank is *without* the statute of frauds, thus allowing Wilson Floors to win without reference to the main purpose rule?

Problem 12.5

In a telephone conversation on January 1, Milly hires Jed to work for ten months as a caretaker at her country estate in New Jersey starting when she returns from Europe on February 1. Milly is unexpectedly detained an does not return to New Jersey until July 1. Must this contract be in writing to be enforced?

Problem 12.6

In the text, Milly dies and Jed is made the personal representative. When Jed refuses to pay a claim made by Sam, Sam says that Jed made a promise. Suppose that this was Sam's testimony at trial: "Remember, you said not to bother filing a claim against the estate. You said, if the estate didn't pay it, you'd take care of it yourself." (Note: this statement is different than the statement in the text.) Does this change in the facts make a difference? Must this promise by Jed be in writing to be enforced?

Problem 12.7

Return to *Slivinsky v. Watkins-Johnson Co.*, and suppose that Slivinsky was claiming for fraud. Her claim is that she had a good job at another company and that representatives of Watkins-Johnson deliberately lied to her (falsely and intentionally telling her that her job with Watkins-Johnson would be long-term) to get her to come to work for them. Is this oral testimony admissible?

Chapter Outline

The objective of this chapter is to learn the law relating to third party beneficiary contracts and assignment contracts. The chapter is organized as follows:

Third Party Beneficiary Contracts

- *Privity of Contract.* Contracts are private relationships and non-parties—called "third parties"—normally do not have rights in those contracts. Third parties are normally said to not be in "privity."

- *Third Party Beneficiaries.* Third party beneficiaries are an exception to the privity rule. Third party beneficiaries are created by the intention of the original parties to benefit a third party.

Assignment Contracts.

- *Assignment.* An assignment is a transfer of a contract right. Assignments are usually in writing, but may be done orally and as a gift.

- *Delegation.* A delegation is not an assignment, it is a transfer of a contract *duty*.

- *Novation.* Novation is not an assignment, it is the *substitution* of one party to a contract for another person.

Introduction

This chapter focuses on what are called "third party" rights in contracts. *Third party* rights are an exception to the normal rule that contracts are *private* arrangements in which only the contract parties—and not third parties—have rights. For example, Jed contracts to sell Blackacre to Milly for $10,000. In this arrangement, all of the rights and duties belong to Jed and Milly. Only Jed has the duty to transfer Blackacre to Milly and the right to receive her payment; and, only Milly has the duty to pay the purchase price to Jed and the right to receive Blackacre. This contract between Jed and Milly is *private* in the sense that it excludes all others—all others meaning "third parties"—from rights and duties. The concept that a contract is a private relationship is described in contract law as "*privity*" of contract.

Third Parties. Who are "third parties" that normally do not have rights in the contracts of others? In the example above, all people who are not a part of Jed and Milly's contract are referred to as third parties. In the language of the law, third parties

200

are normally *not* "within privity." And, as noted above, a third party (not being within privity) normally has no rights or duties in relationship to the contracts of others.

The Exception. It is, however, possible for Jed and Milly to create rights (and sometimes, duties) in third parties where those rights otherwise would not exist. Third party rights are created in the form of *third party beneficiary contracts*, and *assignment contracts*, each of which is discussed hereafter.

Problem Solving. Please turn to Chapter Problems at the end of this chapter and solve Problem 13.1.

Third Party Beneficiary Contracts

Suppose that in the transaction between Jed and Milly (described above) Milly is buying Blackacre as a gift for her friend, Jane. Acknowledging this fact, Jed and Milly agree that the deed to the land will be delivered to Jane, and not to Milly. Jane is thus a *third party beneficiary* because it is *intended* that she will *benefit* from Jed and Milly's contract. The agreement between Jed and Milly, which makes Jane a third party beneficiary, might look like the following:

Agreement

For the sum of $10,000, the undersigned, Jed Finch, hereby agrees to sell Blackacre to Milly Jones. It is agreed that Blackacre shall become the property of Jane Sweeney and a warranty deed transferring said property shall be delivered to the said Jane Sweeney.

Dated this 21st day of July, 1998.

Jed Finch

Milly Jones

THIRD PARTY DONEE BENEFICIARY exists where the parties intend a gift to a third party.

Third Party Donee Beneficiary. In the example above, the *intent* of the parties is to facilitate a *gift* to Jane, Milly's friend. (Note that the agreement doesn't actually use the words "third party beneficiary;" it is sufficient that the meaning of the words of the agreement make Jane a third party beneficiary.) Another word for "gift" is "donation," and, thus, it may be said that Milly is making a donation to Jane. Placing all of the labels from this and the preceding paragraph together, Jane is a *third party donee beneficiary* of the contract between Jed and Milly.

THIRD PARTY CREDITOR BENEFICIARY exists where the parties intend performance in favor of a creditor of one of the parties.

Third Party Creditor Beneficiary. Another category of third party beneficiary is a third party *creditor* beneficiary. Changing the facts in the transaction above, suppose that Milly owes Jane $12,000. Milly doesn't have that much money, but she knows that Jane wants Blackacre, which she would accept in full satisfaction of the $12,000 debt. So, Milly contracts to buy Blackacre from Jed, with the understanding that title to Blackacre will be delivered to Jane. Thus, the intent of Jed and Milly is to transfer Blackacre to Jane. Jane is a *third party creditor beneficiary* in this version of the contract between Jed and Milly.

In the following case, *Snyder v. Freeman*, a corporation, General Aviation, owed the plaintiff, Phyllis Snyder, $5,402.50. Shareholders in the corporation, Mr. Freeman and Mr. Croom, agreed with new investors that if the new investors would invest $10,000 in the corporation, they (Freeman and Croom) would, among other things, cause the corporation to pay the debt to Ms. Snyder. The money was invested but the debt was not paid. Ms. Snyder sued, claiming she was a third party creditor beneficiary of the contract between the new investors and Freeman and Croom. The trial court was troubled by the fact that technically the $10,000 investment was paid to the corporation, not Freeman and Croom. Can Ms. Snyder prevail under these facts?

Snyder v. Freeman
266 S.E.2d 593

EXUM, Justice.

* * *

* * * The real test is said to be whether the contracting parties intended that a third person should receive a benefit which might be enforced in the courts. * * *

* * * [T]his Court [has] expressly adopted the analysis of the American Law Institute's Restatement of Contracts, §133, in determining whether a beneficiary of an agreement made by others has a right of action on the agreement. This section, Restatement 2d, Contracts §133 at 285 86 (1973), provides:

"§ 133. Intended and Incidental Beneficiaries

(1) Unless otherwise agreed between promisor and promisee, a beneficiary of a promisee, a beneficiary of a promise is an intended beneficiary if recognition of a right to performance in the beneficiary is appropriate to effectuate the intention of the parties and either

    (a) the performance of the promise will satisfy an obligation of the promisee to pay money to the beneficiary; or

    (b) the circumstances indicate that the promisee intends to give the beneficiary the benefit of the promised performance.

(2) An incidental beneficiary is a beneficiary who is not an intended beneficiary."

The commentary to § 133(a) reads, in part:

"b. *Promise to pay the promisee's debt.* The type of beneficiary covered by subsection (1)(a) is often referred to as a 'creditor beneficiary.' In such cases the promisee is surety for the promisor, the promise is an asset of the promisee, and a direct action by beneficiary against promisor is normally appropriate to carry out the intention of promisor and promisee, even though no intention is manifested to give the beneficiary the benefit of the promised performance."

Under this analysis, plaintiff's allegations are sufficient to permit her to prove that she is a creditor beneficiary of an implied contract between the signatories to the shareholders' agreement, as promisors, and the corporation, as promisee so that her right to enforce performance of this contract is "appropriate to effectuate the intention of the parties" under Section 133(1)(a) of the Restatement. Plaintiff alleges she is a creditor of General Aviation. The signatories to the agreement are alleged to be the beneficial owners of the corporation with full power to control it. Plaintiff must thus prove: The signatories promised each other and, by

> implication, the corporation itself, that if the corporation would issue 6,000 share of its stock, it would receive $10,000 capital. The agreement is tantamount to a promise by the signatories, *to cause the corporation* to issue the stock, to receive the capital, and to pay the plaintiff, among other creditors, out of the proceeds. The corporation was both plaintiff's debtor and, by implication, promisee of the agreements designed to retire the debt. The signatories caused the corporation to issue its stock and accept the capital; but they failed to cause it to pay plaintiff. For this breach, plaintiff may be entitled to recover as a direct, intended, creditor beneficiary of the implied promise of the signatories to the debtor corporation. The result is like the first illustration of an intended, creditor beneficiary given in Restatement 2d, Contracts at 287:
>
> > "A owes C a debt of $100. The debt is barred by the statute of limitations or by a discharge in bankruptcy, or is unenforceable because of the Statute of Frauds. B promises A to pay the barred or unenforceable debt. C is an intended beneficiary under Subsection (1)(a)."
>
> Although the signatories here do not *themselves* promise to pay the corporation's debt, plaintiff may prove that they have indeed promised to cause the corporation over which they have full control to pay plaintiff out of the proceeds raised pursuant to the agreement, for the breach of which she is entitled to recover against them individually. Agreements by shareholders to vote their shares so as to cause the corporation to take certain action are generally enforceable against the shareholders.
> [Reversed for trial.]

In the eyes of the Supreme Court of North Carolina, the investors contracted with the corporation for the payment of Ms. Snyder, thus making her a third party creditor beneficiary of that contract. In addition, Freeman and Croom, who controlled the corporation, impliedly agreed as part of the investment agreement that they would cause the corporation to pay Ms. Snyder. When Freeman and Croom did not perform as impliedly agreed, they became personally liable to Ms. Snyder.

THIRD PARTY BENEFICIARY: third party donee and creditor beneficiaries have standing but a third party incidental beneficiary does not.

Third Party Incidental Beneficiary. The last category of third party beneficiary is a third party *incidental* beneficiary. Suppose that Milly has a cabin in the mountains and she contracts to have Jed repair the road to make it easier for her to travel to her cabin. Incidentally, and quite by accident, these road repairs will make it easier for *Jane* to get to her (Jane's) cabin. There is no *intent* on the part of Jed and Milly to benefit Jane; thus, she is classified as a third party *incidental* beneficiary.

Careful examination of the three third party beneficiary contracts described above shows that in the first two (donee and creditor) contracts it was the *intent* of Jed and Milly to benefit Jane, the third party. In contrast, in the last contract (incidental) there was no *intent* on the part of Jed and Milly to benefit Jane. This intent (and corresponding lack of intent) is important because donee and creditor third party beneficiaries have *standing* to enforce the contracts which make beneficiaries; but, an incidental beneficiary does not have *standing* to enforce the contract which makes him or her a beneficiary.

STANDING: the right to participate in litigation—an acknowledgment that rights are at risk.

Standing. To have *standing* is to have the right to participate in litigation; it is an acknowledgment that the person has legal rights which are at risk. Suppose, for example, that Farmer Jones believes that his friend, Farmer Smith, is selling his cattle to the ABC Feedlot Company too cheaply, and that Smith will ultimately go out of business if he continues. To benefit his friend— as he believes—Jones files suit against Smith and ABC to block a cattle sale. ABC and Smith file a motion asking the court to dismiss Jones' suit upon the grounds that Jones lacks *standing*. In plain language, they say that the transaction between Smith and ABC is none of Jones' business. On the facts above, the motion to dismiss for lack of standing will be granted.

The courts say that donee and creditor beneficiaries have standing to enforce the contracts that make them beneficiaries because the parties who create these contracts (Jed and Milly) have expressed their intent that the third party beneficiaries may be a part of their private contract relationship. That is, donee and creditor beneficiaries have standing because they are within privity. By the same reasoning, incidental beneficiaries are not intended to be a part of the contract that made them a beneficiary, they are not within privity, and, they do not have standing.

Apply the concept of standing to the three contracts above. If title to Blackacre is not delivered to Jane, who is receiving it as a gift (a donee beneficiary), Jane has standing to file suit to enforce the contract. Likewise, if title to Blackacre is not delivered to Jane, who is receiving it in payment of a debt (a creditor beneficiary), Jane has standing to file suit to enforce the contract. But, in the last case, if the road repairs which incidentally benefit Jane (an incidental beneficiary) she does *not* have standing to file suit to enforce the contract.

In the case of *Burns, Jackson, Miller, Summit & Spitzer v. Lindner*, a Manhattan law firm claimed to be a third party beneficiary with standing to enforce a labor contract. The defendant, Lindner, was president of Local 100 of the Transport Workers Union of America, which "commenced * * * [a] strike which halted all mass transit in, and paralyzed the life and commerce of, the City of New York." The strike continued even in the face of a court order prohibiting it. In earlier years the union had signed an agreement in which they agreed to not to go on strike, and to provide "dependable transportation." The plaintiff law firm claimed to be an intended beneficiary of the union contract with standing to enforce it.

Burns Jackson Miller Summit & Spitzer v. Lindner
437 N.Y.S.2d 895 (1981)

KASSOFF, Justice.
* * *

Plaintiffs * * * seek recovery as a third party beneficiary of the collective bargaining agreement between defendant unions and the public employers. Plaintiffs particularly claim the benefit of the no-strike clauses contained in those agreements. Historically, New York has been in the vanguard of the development of the third-party beneficiary doctrine.

Extensive research by the court has failed to disclose any New York case where a public sector union breached an explicit no-strike clause of a contract which explicitly referred to protection of the interests of those who utilize that public service. In this regard, the facts before the court are highly unusual.

> The critical inquiry in third-party beneficiary claims is whether the contracting parties intended their contract to benefit third parties. The best evidence of such intent is language in the agreement to that effect. The TWU's agreement states one of its purposes is "[t]o assure to the people of the State of New York efficient, economic, sufficient and dependable transportation service * * * and to protect the interests of the public" * * * The TWU has also agreed "To cooperate with the authorities in a joint effort to place and keep the transit system on a safe, efficient, economical operation basis * * * .
>
> As a member of the public which depends on the public transit system and which employs dozens of personals who need the public transit system to get to and from work, plaintiffs argue that they are within the class of personas for whose benefit the TWU has promised to provide "dependable transportation service. * * *.
>
> A person not a party to a contract may sue for damages resulting from non-performance if the contract demonstrates that its primary intent was to benefit that person.
>
> Such cannot be said to be the case here. Where, as here, the government agency contracts for services which it bears no obligation to provide to the public, no duty can be found against the promissor on behalf of the member of the public unless the contract clearly makes the promissor answerable to that person for the breach. This, the court does not find.
>
> [Trial court decision dismissing the complaint, affirmed.]

Obviously, the court concluded that the plaintiffs were unintended (incidental) beneficiaries of the collective bargaining agreement. In fact, the third party claim discussed above was only one of several claims raised by the plaintiffs, and some of those claims survived and were not dismissed. The plaintiffs could not have been surprised that their third party beneficiary claim was dismissed because the law in most states holds—as the opinion above does—that members of the general public do not have standing to enforce (as third party beneficiaries) government contracts for public improvements and services.

Problem Solving. Please turn to chapter Problems at the end of this chapter and solve Problem 13.2.

Assignment Contracts

ASSIGNMENT is a transfer of contract rights.

A third party beneficiary is created at the time of contracting; but, in contrast, an *assignment* is a *later* transfer of a contract right to a third person.

Return to the contract where Jed sells Blackacre to Milly (above), and give the contract a slight twist. Suppose that Milly decides to purchase Blackacre from Jed simply as an investment; that is, she is buying the property for herself—there are no third party beneficiaries. The terms of the contract are that Milly will pay Jed $10,000 for the property, and two years later the property will become hers (and Jed will give her a deed). But, a year into the contract, circumstances change and Milly decides she needs some money and that Sam is willing to pay her $11,000 for Blackacre.

Milly is willing to give Sam the right to receive Blackacre. Can this be done by making Sam a third party beneficiary, even though it has been more than a year since the contract was formed? The answer, of course, is no because any third party beneficiaries would have been created *at the time* the contract was created.

205

The solution is that Milly will use the process of *assignment* to transfer her contract rights to Sam. Milly owns a contract *right*, which is the right to receive Blackacre in one a year. To transfer her contract right to Sam, Milly will simply sell it to him, just like she might sell him a pair of shoes. Transferring an earlier-created contract right to another person (a third person) is called an *assignment*.

An Assignment Contract. What is the process that Milly uses to assign her contract right to Sam? Usually, Milly will use a contract to make the assignment, and that contract might look something like this:

Assignment

For the sum of Eleven Thousand Dollars ($11,000) the
undersigned, Milly Jones, hereby assigns to Sam Smith all of her rights in
that certain contract by which Jed Finch sells Blackacre to Milly Jones.
Dated this 21st day of July, 1999.

Milly Jones

In the assignment contract above, Milly is referred to as the assignor and Sam Smith is referred to as the assignee.

Contracts Not Required. Although a written agreement of assignment will usually be used, that is not strictly required and an assignment can be done orally, unless the statute of frauds or some other statute requires a writing. Moreover, it is possible to make an assignment without a contract because an assignment can be a gift where no consideration is given.

Provisions Against Assignment. In general, all contract rights can be assigned, but there are some exceptions. The first exception is a contract where the terms forbid an assignment. Jed, for example, may lease his house to Milly for the period of two years, but not be willing to lease it to anyone else. Thus, he provides in the lease with Milly that "this lease may not be assigned," or "this lease may not be assigned without the prior written approval of the lessor." Contract provisions prohibiting assignment will be enforced, but they are strictly construed because there is a strong public policy which favors assignments.

Assignments That Change the Performance of the Obligor. The second exception to the general proposition that all contract rights can be assigned is where the assignment would alter the performance of the *obligor*. These are often contracts for the performance of personal services. Suppose, for example, that Jed has agreed to an employment contract which obligates him to be Milly's butler for a year. Then, unexpectedly, Milly decides to go to Europe for that year and assigns the employment contract to Sam, who is the president of the Dirty Dog Motorcycle Club.

The employment contract of Jed (the butler) gives him an obligation to perform and so he is referred to as an *obligor*. Is Jed's employment contract assignable? The rule is that a contract is not assignable if the assignment will materially alter the obligation of performance of the obligor. In this case, Jed's employment contract is not assignable because being Sam's butler is different work than being Milly's butler. Jed's obligation of performance is changed; therefore, the contract is not assignable.

On the other hand, if Jed is a professional hockey player, he may work for a corporation. In that case, playing hockey for corporation "A" may be viewed as no different an obligation than playing hockey for corporation "B," in which case Jed's employment contract would be assignable unless there is an agreement to the contrary.

In the following case, *Munchak Corporation v. Cunningham*, basketball star William John ("Billy") Cunningham claimed his contract to play basketball was not assignable. In this period, teams in a new basketball league, the American Basketball Association ("ABA") were in a bidding war for players with teams in the established National Basketball Association ("NBA"). Taking advantage of the situation, Cunningham left the Philadelphia 76ers and signed for more money with Southern Sports Corporation d/b/a ("doing business as") the Carolina Cougars. Then, Southern Sports Corporation sold it's basketball interests by assigning its franchise and player contracts to Munchak Corporation, which would operate the Carolina Cougars franchise. At this point, Cunningham claimed that his ABA contract was not enforceable because it had been improperly assigned. Like Jed, the Butler (above), Cunningham claimed that the assignment altered the nature of the personal services he was to provide. He then signed an even more lucrative contract with his former team, the 76ers. Munchak sued, asking for an injunction preventing Cunningham from playing for any team but the Cougars.

Munchak Corporation v. Cunningham
457 F.2d 721 (1972)

WINTER, Circuit Judge:
* * *

Cunningham's contention is that his contract was not assignable and that by reason of a purported assignment he is excused from performance arises from these facts. Cunningham's contracts with the Cougars were made at a time when Southern Sports Corporation, owned and operated primarily by James C. Gardner, was the owner of the Cougars's franchise. His contract with Southern Sports Corporation prohibited its assignment to another "club" without his consent, but it contained no prohibition against assignments to another owner of the same club. In 1971, Southern Sports Corporation assigned its franchise and Cunningham's contracts to the plaintiffs, who, as joint venturers, operate the franchise. Cunningham was not asked to consent, nor has he consented, to this assignment. While Cunningham's contracts require him to perform personal services, the services were to the club.

We recognize that under North Carolina law the right to performance of a personal relationship between the parties cannot be assigned without the consent of the party rendering those services. * * * But * * * some of such contracts may be assigned when the character of the performance and the obligation will not be changed. To us it is inconceivable that the rendition of services by a professional basketball player to a professional basketball club could be affected by the personalities of successive corporate owners. * * * Indeed, Cunningham had met only Gardner of Southern Sports Club, and had not met, nor did he know, the other stockholders. If Gardner had sold all or part of his stock to another person, Cunningham could not seriously contend that his consent would be required.

The policy against assignability of certain personal service contracts is to prohibit an assignment of a contract in which the obligor undertakes to serve only the original obligee. * * * This contract is not of that type, since Cunningham was not obligated to perform differently for plaintiffs than he was obligated to perform for Southern Sports Club. We, therefore, see no reason to hold that the contract was not assignable under the facts here.

For the reasons stated, we reverse the judgement of the district court and remand the case for entry of appropriate equitable relief.

Problem Solving. Please turn to Chapter Problems at the end of this chapter and solve Problem 13.3.

Assignment Problems

There are unique problems associated with assignments. The first problem is giving notice of the assignment to the obligor, and the second problem is that of multiple assignments of the same contract.

Notice. Suppose that Milly owes Jed $1,000 and Jed assigns the right to receive that money to Sam. However, Milly knows nothing of the assignment to Sam and innocently pays the money Jed. In a perfect world, Jed would promptly transfer the money to Sam, or, better still, inform Milly of the assignment and tell her to pay Sam directly. If that is done, there will be no problem.

But suppose that Jed takes the money and runs off to Acapulco with his girlfriend where he spends the money on hot tacos and sunshine. If Sam does not receive the money, is he entitled to payment from Milly (who will then have paid twice)? The answer is obviously no, Milly should not pay twice. The rule is that Milly is entitled to pay Jed until she receives notice of the assignment from Sam. If Milly is unsure whether the claim of assignment is genuine, she may require proof before she is obligated to pay Sam. This scenario makes it clear that it will usually be Sam, the assignee, who gives notice of the assignment.

In *General Factors, Inc. v. Beck*, the defendant, Beck, was faced with the possibility of being required to pay on a contract twice. A company called Tempe Sand and Gravel sold building material to Beck. Tempe was in trouble financially, and to speed up its cash flow, it assigned its accounts receivable (including the amounts to be paid by Beck) to General Factors who presumably gave immediate cash to Tempe. General Factors gave notice of the assignment to Beck (and demanded payment), but Beck's office workers mistakenly sent the payment to Tempe anyway. Tempe is now insolvent and cannot send the money on to General Factors, so General Factors has sued Beck for payment.

General Factors, Inc. v. Beck
409 P.2d 40 (1965)

UDALL, Justice.

* * *

* * * [T]he primary issue in this case concerns the question of notice of an assignment under the statutes and laws of the State of Arizona. The pertinent Arizona statute is A.R.S. § 44-805, subsec. A, which provides as follows:

> "If a debtor, *without actual notice* that an assignment of his account has been made, makes full or partial payment of his debt to the assignor, his debt shall thereby be extinguished or reduced." [Emphasis supplied]

The requirement of actual notice in the above statute would seem to import that the notice actually reach the debtor. Otherwise, where the debtor has paid his creditor prior to actual notice, his debt is extinguished or reduced according to the amount paid.

* * *

* * * [W]hether the statutory requirement of actual notice was fulfilled must be decided from the facts and attending circumstances of each case. The facts of this case tested by the above principles would seem to indicate the statutory requirement of actual notice was met. Appellant [General Factors] gave written notice addressed to appellee [Beck] personally that the account was being factored with them. The invoices were received at appellee's usual place of business by an employee who opened the letters, checked that amount due, and presented at a later date the invoices to appellee for payment.

There was testimony to indicate that appellee had made some payments to appellant in August, September, and October on prior accounts that were factored. There was also testimony that appellant Factors and appellee had negotiated to factor appellee's account receivables, and this method of business cannot be said to have been unknown to appellee.

The following excerpt from appellee's deposition illuminates the relationship between appellee and his employee:

> Q. Do you operate an office with secretaries and stenographers that handle your filing and your bookkeeping?
>
> A. I have one girl in there that answers that phone, works on the two-way radios, and does some office work, whatever she's told to do. And then I have an office manager."

At the trial, the office manager was referred to as a bookkeeper exclusively. Appellee admits the employee received the invoices but testified that he did not see any of the invoices with notices attached until he had made payments to Tempe Sand, and had been served with a notice of levy by the Internal Revenue Department.

There is support for the proposition that an agent or clerk ostensibly in charge of the place where the principal's business is carried on has apparent authority to accept notification in relation to the business. * * *

* * *

We therefore hold there was actual notice to the debtor under the facts of this case by the notification received by the employee within the meaning of A.R.S. § 44-805, subsec. A (1956) and appellee is liable for the invoices received by his employee prior to the date of payment to or on behalf of Tempe Sand.

* * *

In *Beck*, the defendant was made to pay twice because the first payment was made to the assignor, Tempe Gravel, after Beck had received actual notice that the account had been assigned to General Factors. Of course, Beck could sue Tempe Gravel to recover the money, but Tempe Gravel is now insolvent.

Multiple Assignments. The second problem associated with assignments is that of multiple assignments; that is, an assignor assigns the same contract right to more than one assignee. Suppose, for example, that Jed is a cheat who enters into three successive assignments of the same contract right (the right to receive $1,000 from Milly.) On July 1, he assigns the $1,000 contract right to John for $750, on July 2, he assigns the same $1,000 contract right to Judy for $750, and, on July 3, he assigns the same $1,000 to Jose for $750. Then, he quickly leaves for Acapulco (with his girlfriend), leaving John, Judy and Jose to fight over the assignment.

The American Rule. There are two different ways to solve this problem. The first solution is referred to as the "American rule," which is based on the reasoning that a person cannot sell what he or she does not have. Thus, having assigned the contract to John, Jed has nothing left to assign to Judy or Jose. Consequently, John is entitled to the contract assignment and Judy and Jose have nothing but a fraud claim (a tort) against Jed, if they can find him. This American rule result would be true, even if Judy or Jose were first to give notice of their assignments.

The English Rule. The other solution to the problem of multiple assignments of the same contract right is called the "English rule." This rule provides that the first assignee to give notice to Milly—without knowledge of another assignee's claim—has the better right. Thus, in the problem above, if Judy gave notice to Milly of the assignment from Jed to her, and did it without knowledge of the assignment to Milly of John or Jose, Judy would have the better right to the assignment.

Each state in the United States must decide which rule, American or English, will be the law for resolving the problem of multiple assignments of the same contract right.

Problem Solving. Please turn to Chapter Problems at the end of this chapter and solve Problem 13.4.

Delegation

DELEGATION is a transfer of contract duties.

A *delegation* is a transfer of a contract *duty*. It is not an assignment. The difference between a delegation and an assignment is that a delegation transfers a contract duty and an assignment transfers a contract right. It is common for a contract to accomplish a delegation and an assignment at the same time. Suppose, for example, that Milly has a contract that entitles her to $250 when she repairs Jed's garage door.

In a common arrangement she may enter into a contract with Sam in which she transfers the $250 to Sam (an assignment) on condition that he repair Jed's garage door (a delegation). Thus, an assignment and a delegation are often—but not necessarily—dealt with in the same contract.

A duty may not be delegated if its performance by a new party will alter the reasonable expectations of the person receiving the performance. In the following opinion, *Macke Company v. Pizza of Gaithersburg, Inc.,* the defendants argued that a contract for the installation and maintenance of cold drink vending machines in their pizza restaurants by Virginia coffee Service, Inc., could not be transferred to The Macke Company because there was a personal element to the service involved.

Macke Company v. Pizza of Gaithersburg, Inc.
270 A.2d 645 (1970)

SINGLEY, Judge.
* * *

In the absence of a contrary provision—and there was none here—rights and duties under an executory bilateral contract may be assigned and delegated, subject to the exception that duties under a contract to provide personal services may never be delegated, nor rights be assigned under a contract where *delectus personae* [choice of the person] was an ingredient of the bargain. * * * Crane Ice Cream Co. v. Terminal Freezing & Heating Co. 147 Md. 588, 128 A. 280 (1925) held that the right of an individual to purchase ice under a contract which by its terms reflected a knowledge of the individual's needs and reliance on his credit and responsibility could not be assigned to the corporation which purchased his business. In Eastern Advertising Co. v. McGaw & Co., 89 Md. 72, 42 A. 923 (1899), our predecessors held that an advertising agency could not delegate its duties under a contract which had been entered into by an advertiser who had relied on the agency's skill, judgment and taste.

* * *

[In the present case] we cannot regard the agreements as contracts for personal services. They were either a license or concession granted Virginia by the appellees, or a lease of a portion of the appellees' premises, with Virginia agreeing to pay a percentage of gross sales as a license or concession fee or as rent, * * * and were assignable by Virginia unless they imposed on Virginia duties of a personal or unique character which could not be delegated, * * *.

The appellees earnestly argue that they had dealt with Macke before and had chosen Virginia because they preferred the way it conducted its business. Specifically, they say that service was more personalized, since the president of Virginia kept the machines in working order, that commissions were paid in cash, and that Virginia permitted them to keep keys to the machines so that minor adjustments could be made when needed. Even if we assume all this to be true, the agreements with Virginia were silent as to the details of the working arrangements and contained only a provision requiring Virginia to "install * * * the above listed equipment and * * * maintain the equipment in good operation order and stocked with merchandise." We think the Supreme Court of California put the problem of personal service in proper focus a century ago when it upheld the assignment of a contract to grade a San Francisco street:

"All painters do not paint portraits like Sir Joshua Reynolds, nor landscapes like Claude Lorraine, nor do all writers write dramas like Shakespeare or fiction like Dickens. Rare genius and extraordinary skill are not transferable, and contracts for their employment are therefore personal, and cannot be

---

211

> assigned. But rare genius and extraordinary skill are not indispensable to the workmanlike digging down of a sand hill or the filling up of a depression to a given level, or the construction of brick sewers with manholes an covers, and contracts for such work are not personal, and may be assigned." * * *
>
> As we see it, the delegation of duty by Virginia to Macke was entirely permissible under the terms of the agreements.
>
> [Judgment in favor of defendants reversed.]

Problem Solving. Please turn to Chapter Problems at the end of this chapter and solve Problem 13.5.

Novation

NOVATION is a substitution of contract parties.

Another contract relationship often associated with assignments (or delegations) is that of **novation**. A novation looks something like an assignment or a delegation but is not. Return to the example of the garage door and suppose that Milly goes to Jed and tells him that she is simply too busy to do the work. She tells Jed that her friend Sam would be willing to take her place in the agreement, if that is acceptable to Jed. When Jed indicates his agreement, the old contract for the repair of the garage is amended to substitute Sam as the contracting party in the place of Milly—there is, in fact, a new contract and the former contract is cancelled. In short, a novation is a substitution of parties, not a transfer of rights or a delegation of duties.

Problem Solving. Please turn to Chapter Problems at the end of this chapter and solve Problem 13.6.

Chapter Problems

Problem 13.1

In the Introduction, Jed contracts to sell Blackacre to Milly. Is Jed within privity?

Problem 13.2

In *Snyder v. Freeman*, did the court conclude that Ms. Snyder had standing?

Problem 13.3

In *Munchak Corporation v. Cunningham*, Mr. Cunningham's contract requires him to perform *personal services*. Explain why the court held that his contract was assignable? (After all, it seems obvious that each basketball team is unique and playing for team A is different than playing for team B.)

Problem 13.4

Jed is a cheat who enters into three successive assignments of the same $1,000 contract right. (Milly is obligated to pay him $1,000.) On July 1, he assigns the $1,000 contract right to John for $750, on July 2, he assigns the same $1,000 contract right to Judy for $750, and, on July 3, he assigns the same $1,000 to Jose for $750. Then, he quickly leaves for Acapulco (with his girlfriend), leaving John, Judy and Jose to fight over the assignment. Judy was the first to give notice of the assignment to Milly; then John gave notice to Milly; and, last, Jose gave notice to Milly. (None of the assignees know of the other.) Using the American rule, who is entitled to the contract right? Using the English rule, who is entitled to the contract right?

Problem 13.5

Find the similarity: some contract rights cannot be assigned, and some contract duties cannot be delegated. Explain how these two rules are similar.

Problem 13.6

Find the difference. In an example in the text, Milly delegates to Sam her duty to repair Jed's garage door and simultaneously assigns to Sam the right to receive payment for the repairs. How is this simultaneous delegation and assignment different from a novation?

Chapter 14
Performance and Remedies

Chapter Outline

The objective of this chapter is to learn the rules related to the *performance* of contract obligations and the *remedies* an injured party is entitled to in the event a contract is breached. This chapter is organized as follows:

Performance

- *Conditions.* Some promises must be performed only if an event happens first. This is a *condition precedent*. Some promises are performed until an event terminates them. This is a *condition subsequent*. Some promises must be performed at the same time. These are *concurrent conditions*.

- *Performance.* In general, all contract conditions must be performed as the contract requires. This is *complete performance*. Contract performance which is substantial, but not complete, is called *substantial performance*. A contract performance which is deficient in one or more important ways results in a *material breach*. A clear refusal to perform as a contract requires, which is done before the date for performance, is called an *anticipatory breach*. A circumstance where contract performance cannot be done is the defense of *impossibility*. To be relieved of a contract duty, by performance or otherwise, is called *discharge*.

Remedies

- *Remedies.* If a contract is not performed as agreed, the injured party is entitled to compensation. *Compensatory damages* are paid to place the injured party in the condition he or she would be in if the contract was performed as promised. *Consequential damages* are paid to compensate for losses which result from some special circumstance. *Nominal damages* are an acknowledgment that technically a breach of contract has occurred, but no actual loss has been suffered. The rule of *mitigation* requires that an injured party make reasonable efforts to minimize losses.

- *Other Remedies.* *Liquidated damages* refers to a contract provision fixing, in advance, the amount of money damages to be awarded in the event of a contract breach. *Specific performance* is a remedy in which contract performance is specifically required by the court instead of the payment of damages. This remedy is allowed only where the payment of money damages will be inadequate.

Introduction

A contract is made up of promises to be performed in the future. Thus, Jed promises that on some date in the future he will deliver Blackacre to Milly; and, in return, Milly promises that on some date in the future she will give money to Jed. Each party owes complete *performance* of his or her contract promise to the other party. If each of them performs as agreed, they are *discharged* from further obligation. But, if one of them (or both of them), fails to perform as agreed, *breach* of contract has occurred and the injured party is entitled to a legal *remedy* against the nonperforming party.

Conditions

Conditions in General. Some promises are *conditional* and some are *absolute*. On that point, consider two different ways in which Jed's obligation to deliver Blackacre to Milly may be phrased: (1) "Jed shall deliver Blackacre to Milly on July 1," or (2) "Jed shall deliver Blackacre to Milly thirty days after she delivers $10,000 to him." The first statement is *absolute*, which means that Jed must perform on July 1, and there is no event which must happen first. In contrast, the second statement is conditional, which means that Jed must deliver Blackacre *only* if Milly first delivers money to him.

CONDITION PRECEDENT: performance commenced by the happening of an event.

Condition Precedent. Concurrent conditions are conditions which must be performed at the same time. The contract provision above—in which Jed must deliver Blackacre to Milly thirty days *after* she delivers $10,000 to him—is called a *condition precedent*. Conditions precedent often use language such as "if," "after," or "following." A condition precedent is an event which must happen to trigger a performance. In the example above, Jed must deliver Blackacre to Milly 30 days *after* Milly pays $10,000 to him. Conditions like this are relatively easy to analyze *if the performance in question is first identified*. In this case, the performance at issue is Jed's obligation to deliver Blackacre. When must he perform? Only after Milly delivers the money. Milly's delivery must occur first, therefore, it precedes and is called a condition precedent.

Problem Solving. Please turn to Chapter Problems at the end of this chapter and solve problem 14.1.

Concurrent Condition. If the parties to a contract must perform at the same time, their obligations are concurrent. If, for example, the contract between Jed and Milly provided that "the closing shall be on July 1, at which time Jed shall deliver Blackacre and Milly shall deliver $10,000, such a contract provision would be described as a **concurrent condition**.

CONDITION SUBSEQUENT: performance ended by the happening of an event.

Condition Subsequent. A *condition subsequent* focuses on a contract provision that may *cut off* contract performance. Changing the agreement between Jed and Milly, suppose that it provides: "Jed shall deliver Blackacre to Milly on July 1, but if she fails to deliver $10,000 to Jed by August 1, Blackacre shall be returned to Jed.

To understand why this version of the facts describes a condition *subsequent*, first identify the *performance* that is being analyzed. (This is important because in this version of the facts, there are several contract performances.) The contract performance we are concerned with is Jed's obligation to give Milly possession of Blackacre. It is unclear whether Milly's possession of Blackacre will be permanent or temporary, but Milly's decision about paying $10,000 will resolve that issue. Thus, Milly's payment (or non-payment) is the condition *subsequent*—it is the event which may cut off her possession of Blackacre. If Milly pays, her possession becomes permanent, but if she does not pay, her possession is cut off.

Express or Implied. In the examples above, the conditions have been clearly *expressed* in the terms of the contract. But, that is not always so; some conditions are *implied*. Suppose that Milly hires Jed to unload a cargo of wheat from her ship, the *Wheat Queen*, at the Houston (Texas) harbor on July 1. Jed fails to unload the ship and Milly sues. Jed defends by saying that the *Wheat Queen* did not come into harbor until July 15, so it was not possible for him to unload it on July 1. Milly, however, takes the unreasonable position that Jed's duty to unload the ship is absolute, and because the written (express) terms of the contract do not require the ship to be in harbor, it is not required.

But, the only reasonable solution to the *Wheat Queen* problem is to acknowledge that there is an *implied* condition precedent. That is, the contract between Milly and Jed must be interpreted to require the ship to come into the harbor before Jed has an obligation to unload it. This is an *implied* condition precedent.

Other conditions are also implied. For example, suppose that a contract provides that "Jed and Milly hereby agree that Milly shall purchase Blackacre from Jed for the sum of $10,000." This contract provision does not state whether Jed will deliver Blackacre first or Milly will deliver the $10,000 first. Because no order is stated, it is likely that a court would treat this contract provision as an implied concurrent condition where Jed delivers and Milly pays, both at the same time.

Problem Solving. Please turn to Chapter Problems at the end of this chapter and solve problem 14.2.

Performance

The discussion now changes to the extent and quality of contract *performance*. For example, a contract might provide that Milly's Custodial Service will clean the ABC Office Building for one month and be paid $3,000. Suppose, however, that Milly's cleaning crew cleans the offices but does a poor job. Must Jed accept the poor performance? Must he pay all or a part of the money? The problem of complete, partial, or failed performance is the subject of the present discussion.

COMPLETE PERFORMANCE: performance as the contract requires.

Complete Performance. In general, each party must perform as the contract requires. In that context, some things can be done perfectly, and where that is so, complete or strict performance of the contract obligation is required. Thus, if Milly

216

is required by contract to deliver $45,894.32, it is possible to deliver that amount, accurate to the penny. Likewise, if she is required to deliver a deed, it is possible to deliver it exactly as required. In these cases, anything less than complete or strict performance is a violation of the contract. A violation of the contract is called a "breach" of the contract.

Complete or strict performance is also required when a contract imposes an exact requirement or condition. For example, an accountant agrees to finish an audit by September 1. Where, as here, a precise finishing date is required, that requirement must be met.

Thus, in summary, complete performance is required where the nature of the act (paying money) makes complete performance possible. And, complete performance is required where a contract expressly requires it (finishing an audit by September 1).

Substantial Performance. Substantial performance is the term applied to contract performance which is less than complete. For example, Milly agrees (for $100,000) to construct a house for Jed with black shingles, but she forgets and installs brown shingles. In this case, the contract is substantially, but not completely, performed. The result is that Jed will be obligated to pay the contract price *minus* the cost of putting on new shingles. If black shingles cost $2,000, Milly is entitled to recover $98,000. There is an exception: if Milly *intentionally* installed brown shingles in violation of the contract, she may be viewed as being in material breach of the contract and not entitled to a recovery.

When and how to apply the substantial performance rule can sometimes be difficult. In the following opinion, *Jacob & Young v. Kent*, a contractor installed the wrong brand of pipe in the construction of a new home. Because "Reading" brand pipe was explicitly required and thus arguably a condition in the contract, the home owner demanded that the installed pipe be ripped out and Reading brand pipe installed. Among other things, the court struggled with whether the pipe requirement should be regarded as an absolute requirement (a condition) with replacement as the remedy, or whether the substantial performance rule should be applied, with damages for the loss of value.

JACOB & YOUNGS v. KENT
129 N.E. 889 (1921)

CARDOZO, J. The plaintiff built a country residence for the defendant at a cost of upwards of $77,000, and now sues to recover a balance of $3,483.46, remaining unpaid. The work of construction ceased in June, 1914, and the defendant then began to occupy the dwelling. There was no complaint of defective performance until March, 1915. One of the specifications for the plumbing work provides that—

"All wrought-iron pipe must be well galvanized, lap welded pipe of the grade known as 'standard pipe' of Reading manufacture."

The defendant learned in March, 1915, that some of the pipe, instead of being made

---

in Reading, was the product of other factories. The plaintiff was accordingly directed by the architect to do the work anew. The plumbing was then encased within the walls except in a few places where it had to be exposed. Obedience to the order meant more than the substitution of other pipe. It meant the demolition at great expense of substantial parts of the completed structure. The plaintiff left the work untouched, and asked for a certificate that the final payment was due. Refusal of the certificate was followed by this suit.

The evidence sustains a finding that the omission of the prescribed brand of pipe was neither fraudulent nor willful. It was the result of the oversight and inattention of the plaintiff's subcontractor. Reading pipe is distinguished from Cohoes pipe and other brands only by the name of the manufacturer stamped upon it at intervals of between six and seven feet. Even the defendant's architect, though he inspected the pipe upon arrival, failed to notice the discrepancy. The plaintiff tried to show that the brands installed, though made by other manufacturers, were the same in quality, in appearance, in market value, and in cost as the brand stated in the contract—that they were, indeed, the same thing, though manufactured in another place. The evidence was excluded, and a verdict directed for the defendant. The Appellate Division reversed, and granted a new trial.

We think the evidence, if admitted, would have supplied some basis for the inference that the defect was insignificant in its relation to the project. The courts never say that one who makes a contract fills the measure of his duty by less than full performance. They do say, however, that an omission, both trivial and innocent, will sometimes be atoned for by allowance of the resulting damage, and will not always be the breach of a condition to be followed by a forfeiture. * * *

* * *

Those who think more of symmetry and logic in the development of legal rules than of practical adaptation to the attainment of a just result will be troubled by a classification where the lines of division are so wavering and blurred. Something, doubtless, may be said on the score of consistency and certainty in favor of a stricter standard. The courts have balanced such considerations against those of equity and fairness, and found the latter to be the weightier.

* * *

In the circumstances of this case, we think the measure of the allowance is not the cost of replacement, which would be great, but the difference in value, which would be either nominal or nothing.

[Judgement in favor of the plaintiff affirmed.]

MCLAUGHLIN, J. I dissent. The plaintiff did not perform its contract. Its failure to do so was either intentional or due to gross neglect which, under the uncontradicted facts, amounted to the same thing, nor did it make any proof of the cost of compliance, where compliance was possible.

McLaughlin, the dissenting judge is technically correct: the requirement to install Reading pipe is an absolute requirement—a condition—that had to be met before the contractor is entitled to payment. The rule on this point is clear, an express condition which can be completely performed, must be completely performed. Cardozo, writing for the majority, admits they are twisting the rules a bit, but he argues that "equity and fairness" persuade them that tearing all the old pipe out to put in new pipe, that is no better, just doesn't make sense. For that reason, they apply the substantial performance rule.

Problem Solving. Please turn to Chapter Problems at the end of this chapter and solve problem 14.3.

Material Breach. A violation of a contract is a *breach* of a contract. And, if the breach is an important or significant one, it is called a *material* breach of the contract. Thus, if Jed is obligated to deliver Blackacre to Milly, and he does not, he has committed a material breach of the contract. If Milly is obligated clean the ABC Office Building and does a poor job, she has committed a material breach. If she has substantially performed, it is a simple matter to give Jed, the building owner, an offset for the amount of money necessary to do the job right.

Anticipatory Breach. Anticipatory breach refers to the situation where a contract party refuses to perform a contract obligation *before* (in anticipation of) the time the performance is due. Suppose, as described above, that Jed has promised to deliver Blackacre to Milly on July 1. If Jed writes Milly a letter on June 15, and tells her that he will not deliver the property on July 1, as agreed, he has committed an anticipatory breach of the contract.

Anticipatory breach must be clear. Suppose that Jed writes Milly: "Milly, as things stand right now, I have a better price for Blackacre and I will not be delivering a deed to you on July 1." Notice that Jed's statement is not clear. Jed's letter says, "as things stand right now," and that means that circumstances might change and there is a possibility that Jed may perform. In this case, Milly cannot file suit immediately but must wait to see it if, in fact, Jed performs.

Suppose, however, that the anticipatory breach by Jed is clear: "Milly, just a note to let you know that I am selling Blackacre to Sam and that I will not be delivering a deed to you on July 1." If the anticipatory breach is *clear*—as it is here—then Milly is excused from her performance requirement (delivering $10,000) and she can file suit against Jed before July 1.

Impossibility.

In some circumstances, performance of a contract obligation becomes impossible. Thus, if Milly has contracted to clean the ABC Office Building, she is freed from that obligation if the building burns down. But, suppose that Milly wants to leave and get married. In this circumstance, Milly can still perform, even though it is inconvenient; here she must perform, or pay to have someone else do the work for her. The test for impossibility is that the task is objectively unperformable. The fact that the task is *inconvenient* for Milly to perform does not demonstrate impossibility.

There are some limitations to the impossibility rule. The first is the death of a party, and if Milly dies without cleaning the office building, the obligation is discharged. The second is incapacitating illness, and if Milly is an accountant and is injured in an automobile accident and cannot perform, the obligation is discharged. The last is illegality, and if a new law makes operating a lottery illegal, a contract obligation requiring Milly to operate such a lottery is discharged.

In *Opera Co. Of Boston v. Wolf Trap Foundation*, a power failure during an electrical storm prevented an opera company from performing in an outdoor auditorium. Under the contract, Wolf Trap was required to provide lighting for the performance, but they argued that that performance was impossible because of the power failure. The Opera Company sued to collect their performance fee. They argued that a power failure was foreseeable and that Wolf Trap should have had standby power generation available.

OPERA CO. OF BOSTON v. WOLF TRAP FOUNDATION
817 F.2d 1094 (4th Cir. 1987)

DONALD RUSSELL, Circuit Judge:

* * *

As he [the trial court judge] read the contract Wolf Trap was obligated to provide sufficient lighting "for the performance to go on," and that power outages were "reasonably foreseeable," as there had been some outages in the past and while "none had affected a performance prior to this occasion," it was "readily foreseeable that a power outage could affect a performance." He, therefore, held Wolf Trap had not made out its defense of impossibility of performances and granted judgment for the plaintiff.

* * *

The modern doctrine of impossibility or impracticability * * * has been formulated in § 265, pp. 334-35 of the Restatement (Second) of Contracts in these words:

> Where, after a contract is made, a party's principal purpose is substantially frustrated without his fault by the occurrence of an event the non-occurrence of which was a basic assumption on which the contract was made, his remaining duties to render performances are discharged, unless the language or the circumstances indicate the contrary.

* * *

Applying the law as above stated to the facts of this case, we conclude, as did the district judge, that the existence of electric power was necessary for the satisfactory performance by the Opera Company on the night of June 15. While he seems to conclude that public safety was the main consideration on which the cancellation was based, he found that the power outage was the reason assigned for cancellation, and in that connection he found it to be questionable that "a generator could [have been] set up to provide additional light for the theater itself (when power from the utility company became unavailable) and still provide adequate light for the people who had to move backstage." Such findings meet the requirement of Restatement (Second) on Contracts § 263 for an event, the "non-occurrence of which was a basic assumption on which the contract was made" and accordingly satisfies the definition of an impracticability which will relieve the obligor of his duty to perform as declared in section 265 of such Restatement (which we have accepted as the proper present statement of doctrine of impossibility of performance as a defense to a breach of contract suit). The district judge, however, refused to sustain the defense because he held that if the contingency that occurred was one that could have been foreseen reliance on the doctrine of impossibility as a defense to a breach of contract suit is absolutely barred. As we have said, this is not the modern rule and he found that the power outage was foreseeable. In this the district judge erred. Foreseeability, as we have said, is at best but one fact to be considered in resolving first how likely the occurrence of the event in question was and, second whether its occurrence, based on past experience, was of such reasonable likelihood that the obligor should not merely foresee the risk but, because of the degree of its likelihood, the obligor should have guarded against it or

> provided for non-liability against the risk. This is a question to be resolved by the trial judge after a careful scrutiny of all the facts in the case. The trial judge in this case made no such findings. The cause must be remanded for such findings. In connection with that remand, the parties may be permitted to offer additional evidence on the matters in issue.
>
>   * * *
>
>   The judgment of the district court is reversed, and the action is remanded with instructions.

Loss of electrical power was a foreseeable problem, and without power it was impossible to provide the necessary lighting. But, how likely was such an occurrence, and how practical would it be to provide backup power sources? The appellate court said that the district court judge must answer the latter questions before ruling on the defense of impossibility. The case was returned to the district court for those findings to be made.

Problem Solving. Please turn to Chapter Problems at the end of this chapter and solve problem 14.4.

Discharge. Most contracts are performed to a degree acceptable to the parties. If a contract is performed as agreed, the parties are discharged from further obligation.

Remedies

Some contracts are not performed as agreed, and the resulting problem is how to compensate the injured party, or otherwise solve the problem. In the United States it is clear that the preferred solution for a breach of contract is the payment of money damages. Only if that form of remedy is *inadequate* are the courts inclined to use other remedies. The following discussion considers the various forms of money damages, and then other remedies.

COMPENSATORY DAMAGES: placing the injured party in the same condition as he would be with complete performance.

Compensatory Damages. The most obvious form of money damages is called *compensatory* damages. Suppose, again, that Milly contracts to clean the ABC Office Building. But, she fails to perform the job, and Jed must pay extra money to get the building cleaned on short notice. His contract with Milly was for $3,000, but he had to pay $4,000 to have the job done on short notice. In this case, Jed's loss or damage is $1,000. His reasonable expectation is to have the office building cleaned for $3,000. To get the job done, Jed must pay the $3,000, as agreed, and, he must pay an extra $1,000. Thus, the amount of his "damages" is $1,000.

Legal theorists sometimes say that Jed has an "expectation" interest in his contract with Milly. That is, the law should protect Jed's reasonable expectation in having the contract performed as agreed. Or, said in other terms, Jed is entitled to be placed in the position he would have been if the contract was performed as agreed.

CONSEQUENTIAL DAMAGES reimburse injured party for losses due to special circumstances.

Consequential Damages. Suppose, however, that one of the tenants in the ABC Office Building moves out because the building is dirty—and the building is dirty because Milly didn't clean it as agreed. It takes Jed three months to find a new tenant, and the loss of rental income is $1,500. This loss of $1,500 is consequential damage. Consequential damages refers to money paid for losses suffered as a *consequence* of a breach of contract.

Consequential damages are harder to establish than compensatory damages because of the requirement that losses must be proved with reasonable *certainty*. Thus, in the case above, Milly may object to the payment of consequential damages and attempt to show that the tenant moved because it was going out of business, or it got a lower rental rate somewhere else. In addition, consequential damages sometimes takes the form of claims for lost profits. In such a case, Jed may claim that his business lost money because the office was dirty and customers went elsewhere. Proving this claim with certainty, however, may be very difficult.

An additional requirement for the recovery of consequential damages is the requirement that the loss complained of was *foreseeable*. This requirement is illustrated in a famous old English case known as *Hadley v. Baxendale*. In this case, Hadley operated a flour mill, and a crankshaft in the mill machinery broke. Baxendale contracted to transfer the crankshaft for repairs and return it. He promised to return the crankshaft the next day, but did not do so for several days. The consequence was that Hadley lost several days profits and sued to recover those lost profits from Baxendale. If Baxendale had lost or damaged the crankshaft, the Hadley's would clearly have been entitled to *compensatory* damages. Here, however, the problem was lost profits and the court was concerned with whether Baxendale *knew* that absence of the crankshaft would have the effect of shutting down the mill. In other words, was this loss foreseeable? If so, reasoned the court, it would be fair to hold Baxendale liable for the lost profits; otherwise, it would not.

Hadley v. Baxendale
Court of Exchequer
156 Eng.Rep. 145 (1854)

ALDERSON, B.
* * * *
* * * Where two parties have made a contract which one of them has broken, the damages which the other party ought to receive in respect of such breach of contract should be such as may fairly and reasonably be considered either arising naturally, i.e., according to the usual course of things, from such breach of contract itself, or such as may reasonably be supposed to have been in the contemplation of both parties, at the time they made the contract, as the probable result of the breach of it. Now, if the special circumstances under which the contract was actually made were communicated by the plaintiffs to the defendants, and thus known to both parties, the damages resulting from the breach of such a contract, which they would reasonably contemplate, would be the amount of injury which would ordinarily follow from a breach of contract under these special circumstances so known and communicated. * * * Now, in the present case, if we are to apply the principles above laid down, we find that the only circumstances here communicated by the plaintiffs to the defendants at the time the contract was made, were, that the article to be carried was the broken shaft of a mill, and that the plaintiffs were the millers of that mill. But how do these circumstances show reasonably that the profits of the mill must be stopped by an unreasonable delay in the delivery of the shaft

---

by the carrier to the third person? Suppose the plaintiffs had another shaft in their possession put up or putting up at the time, and that they only wished to send back the broken shaft to the engineer who made it; it is clear that this would be quite consistent with the above circumstances, and yet the unreasonable delay in the delivery would have no effect upon the intermediate profits of the mill. Or, again, suppose that, at the time of the delivery to the carrier, the machinery of the mill had been in other respects defective, then, also, the same results would follow. Here it is true that the shaft was actually sent back to serve asa model for a new one, and that the want of a new one was the only cause of the stoppage of the mill, and that the loss of profits really arose from not sending down the new shaft in proper time, and that this arose from the delay in delivering the broken one to serve as a model. But it is obvious that, in the great multitude of cases of millers sending off broken shafts to third persons by a carrier under ordinary circumstances, such consequences would not, in all probability, have occurred; and these special circumstances were here never communicated by the plaintiffs to the defendants. It follows, therefore, that the loss of profits here cannot reasonably be considered such a consequence of the breach of contract as could have been fairly and reasonably contemplated by both the parties when they made this contract.

[Jury verdict for the plaintiff's reversed.]

Not fully explained in the opinion is the fact that in 1854, it was common for a mill to have spare shafts on hand, which the court and the parties knew. The opinion reflects that common understanding: thus, if Baxendale is to be held liable for losses occurring when there is no spare shaft on hand, Baxendale should be made aware of that circumstance. From this case grows the general requirement that consequential losses must have been foreseeable— within the contemplation (understanding) of the parties at the time they contracted.

Problem Solving. Please turn to Chapter Problems at the end of this chapter and solve problem 14.5.

Nominal Damages. An award of nominal damages is an acknowledgment that technically a breach of contract has occurred, but no actual loss has been suffered. Suppose, that Jed and Milly argue a lot and cannot get along. On one occasion, Jed observes that Milly was one hour late in cleaning carpets (the contract calls for carpet cleaning to be finished by 5:00 a.m, but on Thursday it was not finished until 6:00 a.m.). In a contrary mood, Jed sues Milly for breach of contract. If the court concluded that a breach occurred, it is likely that the judge would then award damages in the amount of $1.00 as *nominal* damages. The ideal of nominal damages suggests that loss, if any, was technical but not real.

Punitive Damages. Punitive damages are intended to *punish*, not to compensate. The general focus of contract damages is to compensate for losses; thus, granting punitive damages is done only in unusual cases. In the continuing soap opera of Jed and Milly and the contract to clean the ABC Office Building, suppose that Milly intentionally broke lights and clogged the toilets in the building. Indeed, the real reason Milly did not clean the building, as agreed—and caused the other damage—was that her brother had purchased a new office building called the XYZ Office Building and Milly was deliberately trying to drive tenants out of the ABC building and toward the XYZ building.

At some point, if Milly's behavior is sufficiently intentional, malicious and in bad faith, a court may award punitive damages. In breach of contract cases, punitive damages are not allowed unless the conduct causing the breach is also a tort.

MITIGATION: plaintiff must make reasonable efforts to minimize losses.

Mitigation. An injured plaintiff must make reasonable efforts to minimize losses. This requirement is referred to as **mitigation** of losses. For example, in the discussion about consequential damages, Milly fails to clean the ABC Office Building as agreed. Consequently, a tenant moves out of the ABC Office Building because it is not clean. If these facts are true, Jed is clearly entitled to consequential damages for lost rental income. The question is for what time period Jed is entitled to that compensation? Is he entitled to compensation for one month, three months, six months or a year of lost rental income? Clearly, Jed is not entitled to lost rental for a period beyond the lease term. Apart from that, Jed is required to make all reasonable efforts to get a substitute tenant, and he is entitled to compensation for whatever period the office is vacant. This requirement of mitigation applies to all types of damage claims.

In the following case, *Parker v. Twentieth Century Fox Film Corporation*, the film studio contracted to pay actress, Shirley MacLaine Parker, $750,000 for her services in a musical entitled "Bloomer Girl." The movie was to have been filmed in California. Then, the studio cancelled the Bloomer Girl project and, as a substitute, offered Parker a part in a dramatic western movie called "Big Country," which was to be produced in Australia. Parker refused the studio's offer and sued to enforce the contract. The studio defended by claiming that Parker had refused to mitigate her contract losses when she refused their Big Country offer. The trial court found for Parker.

PARKER v. TWENTIETH CENTURY-FOX FILM CORPORATION
474 P.2d 680 (1970)

BURKE, Justice.
* * *

In the present case defendant has raised no issue of *reasonableness of efforts* by plaintiff to obtain other employment; the sole issue is whether plaintiff's refusal of defendant's substitute offer of "Big Country" may be used in mitigation. Nor, if the "Big Country" offer was of employment different or inferior when compared with the original "Bloomer Girl" employment, is there an issue as to whether or not plaintiff acted reasonably in refusing the substitute offer. Despite defendant's arguments to the contrary, no case cited or which our research has discovered holds or suggests that reasonableness is an element of a wrongfully discharged employee's option to reject, or fail to seek, different or inferior employment lest the possible earnings therefrom be charges against him in mitigation of damages.

Applying the foregoing rules to the record in the present case, with all the intendments in favor of the party opposing the summary judgment motion—here, defendant—it is clear that the trial court correctly ruled that plaintiff's failure to accept defendant's tendered substitute employment could not be applied in mitigation of damages because the offer of the "Big

---

Country" lead was of employment both different and inferior, and that no factual dispute was presented on that issue. The mere circumstance that "Bloomer Girl" was to be a musical review calling upon plaintiff's talents as a dancer as well as an actress, and was to be produced in the City of Los Angeles, whereas "Big Country" was a straight dramatic role in a "Western Type" story taking place in an opal mine in Australia, demonstrates the difference in kind between the two employments; the female lead as a dramatic actress in a western style motion picture can by no stretch of imagination be considered the equivalent of or substantially similar to the lead in a song-and-dance production.

Additionally, the substitute "Big Country" offer proposed to eliminate or impair the director and screenplay approvals accorded to plaintiff under the original "Bloomer Girl" contract * * * and thus constituted an offer of inferior employment. No expertise or judicial notice is required in order to hold that the deprivation or infringement of an employee's rights held under an original employment contract converts the available "other employment" relied upon by the employer to mitigate damages, into inferior employment which the employee need not seek or accept. * * *

* * *

In view of the determination that defendant failed to represent any facts showing the existence of a factual issue with respect to its sole defense—plaintiff's rejection of its substitute employment offer in mitigation of damages—we need not consider plaintiff's further contention that for various reasons, including the provisions of the original contract set forth in the footnote 1, ante, plaintiff was excused from attempting to mitigate damages.

The judgment is affirmed.

Other Remedies

In addition to the recovery of damages (compensatory, consequential and nominal) in the normal fashion, there are other remedies such as liquidated damages and specific performance.

LIQUIDATED DAMAGES: a contract provision agreeing in advance to the amount of damages in the event of a contract breach.

Liquidated Damages. In the language of contracts, if a dollar amount is fixed and certain, it is said to be *liquidated*; thus, if a dollar amount for damages is *fixed and determined* in a contract, that predetermined dollar amount is referred to as "liquidated damages."

Often the harm caused by failure to perform a contract is difficult to assess. For example, how much loss (in dollars) is suffered if a sign advertising a McDougal's hamburger restaurant is installed late, or a freeway is not completed on time? In such cases, contract law allows parties to agree to liquidated damages.

There are two basic requirements for the use of a liquidated damages provision in a contract. First, the contract must involve a performance where the loss to be suffered, in the event of a breach of performance, would be difficult to calculate. Thus, if the Jed and Milly Road Construction Company is one month late in their contract to widen the I-15 freeway near Las Vegas, Nevada, how much has the State of Nevada lost in money damages? Who knows? Accordingly, this is a circumstance where damages on account of breach are difficult to calculate.

The second requirement for the use of a liquidated damages provision is that the amount agreed to must be reasonable. Said in other terms, the amount agreed to may not be a penalty. If the contract is for the payment of $35 million for the entire project, is the amount of $5 million per month reasonable? Probably not. Suppose, however, that $100,000 per month was agreed to as the amount of liquidated damages in the event of breach. Is this amount reasonable in light of the entire contract amount and the extent of inconvenience to travelers? The answer is probably yes.

As suggested above, a problem with liquidated damages provisions is that the amount of money described as liquidated is excessive, and thus unenforceable. In the following case, *AFLAC, v. Williams*, an attorney was fired with approximately three years left in his employment contract. The contract provided that if Williams was terminated, he was entitled to 50% of his salary for the balance of the employment term. Williams sued to collect the unpaid salary. AFLAC defended saying (1) as a matter of policy a client should be able to fire its attorney at any time, and (2) the amount of money described in the liquidated damages provision is unreasonable.

AFLAC, INC. v. WILLIAMS
44 S.E.2d 314 (Ga. 1994)

FLETCHER, Justice.
* * *

Our obligation to regulate the legal profession in the public's interest causes us to favor AFLAC's freedom in ending the attorney-client relationship without financial penalty over Williams' right to enforce the damages provision in his retainer contract. Requiring a client to pay damages for terminating its attorney's employment contract eviscerates the client should not be deterred from exercising his or her legal right because of economic coercion. Since the contract improperly imposes a penalty by requiring AFLAC to pay damages equal to half Williams' retainer, we conclude that the provision is unenforceable.

We reach the same conclusion even when evaluating the damages provision under contract law. The Georgia Code provides for liquidated damages when the parties agree what the damages for a breach shall be, "unless the agreement violates some principle of law." * * * In deciding whether a contract provision is enforceable as liquidated damages, three factors must exist. The injury must be difficult to estimate accurately, the parties must intend to provide damages instead of a penalty, and the sum must be a reasonable estimate of the probable loss. * * * "A term fixing unreasonable on grounds of public policy as a penalty." * * *

Contrary to the Court of Appeals, we conclude that the contract's damages provision improperly imposes a penalty by forcing AFLAC to pay damages for exercising its legal right to end the attorney-client relationship. The peculiar language of the provision demonstrates that the parties intended to deter AFLAC from discharging Williams and to punish the company if it did. The contract specifies AFLAC must pay 50 percent of the remaining sums due Williams under both the original seven-year term and the five-year renewal period. This provision requires AFLAC to pay an unreasonably high sum as damages, requires payment without considering Williams' duty to mitigate his damages, and obligates AFLAC to pay even if Williams is discharged for cause. Because the damages provision is not a reasonable estimate of Williams' damages and instead is a penalty imposed to punish AFLAC, we find it is unenforceable as a liquidated damages clause.

Judgment [in favor of Williams] reversed.

Problem Solving. Please turn to Chapter Problems at the end of this chapter and solve problem 14.6.

SPECIFIC PERFORMANCE: an alternative to money damages.

Specific Performance. Recall that at the beginning of the chapter it was noted that in the United States the preferred solution for breaches of contract is the payment of money damages. Only if that form of remedy is *inadequate* are the courts inclined to use other remedies. The equitable powers of the court allow it to use the remedy of specific performance if money damages are inadequate. Specific performance is a court order requiring a contract party to deliver a contract item as promised. Failure to deliver the item is punishable (fine or imprisonment) as contempt of court.

If Milly contracts to buy Blackacre to use it to expand the parking lot for her grocery store, the payment of money damages in the event of breach will not be completely adequate. What is needed is the land. In such cases, where the remedy at law is not adequate, the equitable remedy of specific performance may be used. In contrast, a contract for the delivery of 5,000 gallons of milk may be solved by the payment of money damages because one load of milk is not significantly different than another load of milk. On the other hand, if the contract is for the delivery of a Rembrandt painting, the item is unique (one painting will not replace another) and therefore specific performance may be allowed.

Problem Solving. Please turn to Chapter Problems at the end of this chapter and solve problem 14.7.

Chapter Problems

Problem 14.1

On June 1, Jed agreed by contract to buy Blackacre from Milly. He will pay Milly $30,000 at 8.5% interest over five years, "unless a bank agrees to loan the purchase price at a lower rate of interest, in which event the purchaser shall pay the full purchase price on July 1." In regard to Milly's obligation to receive payment of the purchase price over five years, is bank financing a condition precedent?

Problem 14.2

Milly agrees to buy Blackacre if Jed will reduce the purchase price from $40,000 to $35,000. Is this requirement a condition subsequent?

Problem 14.3

In *Jacob & Youngs v. Kent*, suppose that the contractor *intentionally* used the wrong brand of pipe. Would Justice Cardozo, and the rest of the majority, have reached the same result?

Problem 14.4

In *Opera Co. Of Boston v. Wolf Trap Foundation*, the appellate court said that a successful impossibility defense required proof that a power loss was sufficiently unlikely that Wolf Trap did not have an obligation to protect against it. ("This is a question to be resolved by the trial judge after a careful scrutiny of all the facts n the case.") How should the trial judge rule on this issue?

Problem 14.5

Suppose for the sake of argument that in *Opera Co. Of Boston v. Wolf Trap foundation*, that Wolf Trap was in breach of it's contract with the Opera Company. Further suppose that the Opera Company claimed the loss of $10,000 in profits because it could not sell it's t-shirts ("I Got Trapped at the Opera"). Would this claim for consequential damages be successful?

Problem 14.6

In *AFLAC, INC. v. Williams*, assume that Williams was an office manager and not a lawyer. How much in liquidated damages would the court enforce if Williams was terminated in violation of an employment contract?

Problem 14.7

In *Parker v. Twentieth Century-Fox Film Corporation*, assume that Parker was in breach of the contract for failing to agree to go to Australia and act in a dramatic western film. Parker's talents as an actress are clearly unique; could the studio get an order of specific performance compelling her to perform in the western film?

Chapter Outline

OBJECTIVE: to learn rules by which contracts are formed under the rules of Article 2 (sales) of the Uniform Commercial Code.

The objective of this chapter is to learn the rules by which contracts are formed under the rules of Article 2 (Sales) of the Uniform Commercial Code. This chapter is organized as follows:

- *Sales*. Sales law is found in Article 2 of the Uniform Commercial Code (UCC). Sales law consists of modified common law contract rules.

- *Goods*. Sales law applies to transactions in "goods." Goods are "all things . . . which are movable at the time of identification to the contract for sale."

- *Offer and Acceptance*. In general, the process of offer and acceptance is the same for Sales contracts as it is for common law contracts, but practicality is emphasized. Acceptance is by any reasonable means. A "Firm Offer" is an option to buy goods which is effective without consideration.

- *Statute of Frauds*. A contract for the sale of goods for the price of $500 or more is not enforceable unless there is some writing.

- *Parol Evidence*. A written document which the parties intend as a final expression of their agreement cannot be contradicted by evidence of any prior agreement or of a contemporaneous oral agreement.

- *Unconscionability*. If a contract or any clause of the contract is unconscionable at the time it was made, the court may refuse to enforce the contract or the clause.

Introduction

It has been observed earlier that there are two sets of contract rules: one is the rules of the common law and the other is the rules of the Uniform Commercial Code (UCC).[1] The contract rules of the common law have been discussed in Chapters 7 through 14. This Chapter 15 is the beginning of a discussion of the contract rules of the UCC.

In general, the rules of the common law apply to contracts involving real estate and personal services, while Article 2 of the UCC applies to contracts involving goods (sometimes called personal property). Following is a table

---

[1] The Uniform Commercial Code has been adopted in all of the states, except Louisiana, which has adopted part of it.

(reproduced from Chapter 7) which illustrates the subject matter of contracts under the common law and Article 2 of the UCC:

Contract Law		
Type of Transaction	Common Law	UCC (Article 2)
Real Estate	X	
Goods		X
Personal Services	X	

Article 2.

Article 2 in the UCC is the law which applies to the buying and selling of "*goods*." The buying and selling of goods is referred to in Article 2 as "Sales." From this point forward, the contract laws found in Article 2 of the UCC—the laws by which goods are bought and sold—will be referred to as *Sales* law.

ARTICLE 2 (Sales) consists of modified common law contract rules.

Modified Common Law. The older common law of contracts is the parent of Sales law in the sense that many basic concepts developed at common law are incorporated into Sales law. In general, it is fair to say that Sales law consists of modified common law contract rules. That means that knowledge of common law contract rules helps in understanding Sales law. Indeed, in those places where the authors of the Sales article were satisfied with common law contract rules, they made no changes at all and the old common law rules still apply. This is made clear in § 1-103 of the UCC which states: "Unless displaced [changed] by the particular provisions of this Act, the principles of [common] law and equity . . . shall supplement its provisions."

Problem Solving. Please turn to Chapter Problems at the end of this chapter and solve Problem 15.1.

Goods

GOODS: are all things which are movable at the time of identification to the contract for sale.

As shown in the table above, Sales law applies to "transactions in goods." [§ 2-102][2] What, technically, are *goods*? Goods are defined in § 2-105(1) as "all things . . . which are movable at the time of identification to the contract for sale." By this definition, automobiles are goods to which Sales law applies, but the services of the workers who assemble the automobiles are not. Athletic shoes are goods, but the services of the athlete who wears them are not, and neither is the house of the athlete.

---

[2] Relevant sections of the Uniform Commercial Code are in Appendix A. Please read §2-102 and other UCC sections as they are cited in the text.

Knowing whether common law rules or Sales rules apply to a particular contract is not always simple. Suppose, for example, that Milly contracts to have Jed repair *and* sell her television set. In this "mixed" transaction in which services are provided and goods sold, should a court apply common law or Sales law? In instances of "mixed" transactions (repairing the television is a personal service to which the common law normally applies, but selling the television is a Sales transaction to which Sales law normally applies) the courts often apply the law that applies to the *dominant* feature of the contract. Thus, if repairs to the television are reasonably valued at $100 and the sales price of the television is $300, a court may apply Sales law because the dollar value of the sale exceeds the dollar value of the repairs.

In the following case, *Advent Systems Ltd. v. Unisys Corp.*, the plaintiff, Advent, sold computer hardware and software to the defendant, Unisys. Advent claimed that Unisys had breached the contract and sued. One of the issues at trial was whether the contract between the parties was controlled by the common law of contracts or Sales law? Because software was a "major portion" of the contract (and arguably not "goods") the trial court ruled that the UCC did not apply. On appeal, the court of appeals disagreed:

Advent Systems Ltd. v. Unisys Corp.
925 F.2d 670 (1991)

WEIS, Circuit Judge.
* * *

The district court ruled that as a matter of law the arrangement between the two parties was not within the Uniform Commercial Code * * * * As the district court appraised the transaction, provisions for services outweighed those for products and, consequently, the arrangement was not predominantly one for the sale of goods.
* * *

The Code "applies to transactions in goods." * * * Goods are defined as "all things (including specially manufactured goods) which are moveable at the time of the identification for sale." * * * The Pennsylvania courts have recognized that "'goods' has a very extensive meaning under the U.C.C. * * *
* * *

Computer programs are the product of an intellectual process, but once implanted in a medium are widely distributed to computer owners. An analogy can be drawn to a compact disc recording of an orchestral rendition. The music is produced by the artistry of musicians and in itself is not a "good," but when transferred to a laser-readable disc becomes a readily merchantable commodity. Similarly, when a professor delivers a lecture, it is not a good, but, when transcribed as a book, it becomes a good.

That a computer program may be copy-rightable as intellectual property does not alter the fact that once in the form of a floppy disc or other medium, the program is tangible, moveable and available in the marketplace. The fact that some programs may be tailored for specific purposes need not alter their status as "goods" because the Code definition includes "specially manufactured goods."

The topic has stimulated academic commentary with the majority espousing the view that software fits within the definition of a "good" in the U.C.C.

> Applying the U.C.C. to computer software transactions offers substantial benefits to litigants and the courts. The Code offers a uniform body of law on a wide range of questions likely to arise in computer software disputes: implied warranties, consequential damages, disclaimers of liability, the statute of limitations, to name a few.
>
> The importance of software to the commercial world and the advantages to be gained by the uniformity inherent in the U.C.C. are strong policy arguments favoring inclusion. The contrary arguments are not persuasive and we hold that software is a "good" within the definition in the Code.

In *Advent Systems*, the court held that the services of computer programmer became a "good" when transferred into a tangible form, like the lecture of a professor becomes a good when placed in book form. It is clear that the court *wanted* to apply the Sales law if it could. This was apparent when the court said: "Applying the U.C.C. to computer software transactions offers substantial benefits to litigants and the courts," and the court went on to discuss those benefits. This is often true: parties often like using Sales law because it provides a clear statement of law on complicated contract issues.

Another Example. Suppose that Jed buys a mixed drink at a restaurant, and in the bottom of the glass there is an olive with a hole in it. Thinking that the hole in the olive indicates that the pit has been removed, Jed bites down on the olive. Contrary to his expectations, the pit is still in the olive and he breaks a tooth. Jed believes that selling this "misleading" product is a violation of his contract with the restaurant, and he sues for damages. The question is, what law applies to this mixed transaction: is the value of the service more than the value of the product, or is the value of the product more than the value of the service? In other words, should the court use Sales law or common law?

FOOD: serving food or drink for consumption is a sale.

Normally, a court will do as the court in *Advent systems Ltd. v. Unisys Corp.* (above) did and decide which part of the contract, services or product, is the dominant feature of the contract. In this case, however, there is a specific provision of the Sales law which is applied. The drafters of the Sales law anticipated that problems related to the sale of food would arise, so they wrote the following in § 2-314(1): "Under this section the serving for value of food or drink to be consumed either on the premises or elsewhere is a *sale*." This provision means, of course, that Jed's contract with the restaurant was formed under the Sales law, and not the common law.

Problem Solving. Please turn to Chapter Problems at the end of this chapter and solve Problem 15.2.

Good Faith

Before turning to the process of forming a Sales contract, it should be noted that "[e]very contract or duty within this Act [the UCC] imposes an obligation of *good faith* in its performance or enforcement." Good faith means "honesty in fact," and every party must act with good faith in the contracting process. [§ 1-203]

Forming a Contract

Once it is settled that a proposed contract is for the sale of goods—which means that Sales law applies—and acknowledging the general obligation of good faith, the balance of the chapter discussion turns to the formation of a Sales contract.

OFFER AND ACCEPTANCE: common law rules with an emphasis on practicality.

Offer and Acceptance. In general, the process of offer and acceptance is the same for Sales contracts as it is for common law contracts. The Sales article, however, emphasizes practicality. In the process of contracting, practicality means that whatever process of offer and acceptance is used, a contract results if the conduct of the parties recognizes the existence of a contract. [§ 2-204(1)] An illustration of this concern with practicality is § 2-206(1)(a) which provides that "an offer to make a contract shall be construed as inviting acceptance *in any manner* and *by any medium* reasonable in the circumstances.

The practicality and flexibility of the Sales article in contract formation is illustrated in *Gregory v. Scandinavian House*. In this case the defendant, Scandinavian House, solicited bids to replace the windows in a large apartment building. Plaintiff, J. Lee Gregory, Inc., responded with a bid of $453,067 (of which amount, approximately two-thirds was for materials and one-third was labor costs). Defendant responded: "Please consider this letter an indication of our intent to purchase the windows contained in your proposal dated February 8, 1990." Later, however, the parties disagreed on details of payment and the defendant canceled the project. The plaintiff sued. The first question was whether the Sales article applied, and the court held that it did because the dominant feature of the contract was the sale of goods. The next question was whether a contract was fully formed between the parties because many details in their arrangement were not settled.

J. Lee Gregory v. Scandinavian House
433 S.E.2d 687 (1993)

McMURRAY, Presiding Judge.
     * * *

Having determined that the UCC applies to this hybrid transaction, we look to the UCC to determine if plaintiff and Scandinavian House entered into a contract for the sale and installation of the windows. The UCC provides, in part: "A contract for sale of goods may be made in any manner sufficient to show agreement, including conduct by both parties which recognizes the existence of such a contract." [§ 2-204] It adds: "An agreement sufficient to constitute a contract for sale may be found even though the moment of its making is undetermined."

These (and other) provisions make it clear that the UCC "expands our conception of contract. It makes contracts easier to form, and it imposes a wider range of obligations than before. Contract formation is easier in several ways. Parties may form a contract through conduct rather than merely through the exchange of communications constituting

---

'offer and acceptance.' * * * Further, Article Two reduces the formalities required for contract formation. The statute of frauds (section 2-201) requires only a writing that 'indicate(s)' a contract was made, and 2-206 and 2-207 (1) abandons the requirement that an acceptance must coincide precisely with all the terms of the offer. Section 2-204(3) states: 'Even though one or more terms are left open a contract for sale does not fail for indefiniteness if the parties have intended to make a contract and there is a reasonably certain basis for giving an appropriate remedy.'" * * *

Given the UCC's broad concept of contract, we have no hesitation in concluding that plaintiff and Scandinavian House entered into a contract for the sale and installation of the windows. The letter of intent manifested a clear intention to contract. It stated, in part: "consider this letter an indication of our intent to purchase the windows contained in your proposal * * *" * * * In addition, the letter authorized plaintiff to begin work on the project. * * *

Assuming arguendo that the letter of intent was equivocal, we would find, nevertheless, that Scandinavian House intended to contract with plaintiff. Why? Because the conduct of the parties demonstrates an intention to contract. [§ 2-204(1) and § 2-207(3)] Lon Meyers gave a letter of intent to Gregory and informed him that Scandinavian House had awarded the windows contract to plaintiff. The letter of intent authorized plaintiff to take measurements and prepare shop drawings. Pursuant to the letter, plaintiff took measurements in the apartment house. That was no small undertaking and it could not have been done without the cooperation of Scandinavian House. Ultimately, plaintiff completed and delivered the shop drawings to Scandinavian House.

The conduct of the parties is inconsistent with the theory that they only agreed to agree. On the contrary, the conduct of the parties demonstrates that they intended to enter into a contract for the sale and installation of windows. See *Anderson, Uniform Commercial Code*, § 2-204:37, in which the author notes that (1) "conduct may be the commencement of performance under the contract" and (2) conduct "embraces not only acts but statements indicating the belief of the parties." The mere fact that plaintiff subsequently met with defendants to resolve the guarantee of payment issue does not negate the fact that the parties entered into a contract previously.

[Judgment in favor of Defendant, reversed.]

In this opinion it was clear that a letter from Scandinavian House authorized Gregory to proceed with the project and that Gregory did proceed with measurements and drawings. Thus, it was clear that the parties *intended* a contract. In addition, details of the transaction were clear enough to grant a remedy. [Review § 2-204(3)] The consequence was that the court enforced a contract between the parties.

Firm Offers. With respect to the process of offer and acceptance, § 2-205 ("Firm Offers") is unique. To illustrate how this section provides a result which is different from the result at common law, suppose that Milly writes Jed and offers (under common law rules) to sell him Blackacre for $100,000. The letter concludes: "you may have 30 days to decide and give me your acceptance, if that is your decision." Then, 15 days later, Milly writes Jed and says: "I've changed my mind and hereby withdraw my offer to sell you Blackacre. I hope this doesn't cause any inconvenience."

Can Milly break her promise and withdraw her offer? Because the subject of the transaction between Milly and Jed is real estate, the rules of the common law apply. At common law, an offer can be withdrawn any time before it is accepted, unless the offer has been converted into an option. An option is a contractual arrangement in which an offeror (Milly) agrees not to withdraw her offer for a specified period of time, and the offeree (Jed) gives valuable consideration in return. (For example, if Jed gave Milly $100 to keep her offer open, it would be an option.) In the Blackacre transaction, Jed has *not* given any consideration to Milly to hold her offer open; thus, Milly can withdraw her offer.

FIRM OFFER: a written offer by a merchant to buy or sell goods in a signed writing—giving assurance of irrevocability—is not revocable.

Now observe how § 2-205 ("Firm Offers") creates a different result in a Sales transaction. The first part of § 2-205 provides as follows: "An offer by a merchant[3] to buy or sell goods *in a signed writing* which by its terms gives assurance that it will be held open is *not revocable, for lack of consideration,* during the time stated" An offer that complies with the provisions of § 2-205 is referred to as a "firm offer." Suppose that Milly writes Jed and offers to sell him 1000 pounds of kumquats, with 30 days to accept. Can Milly—15 days later—withdraw her offer, as she did with Blackacre (above)? The answer is obviously no. If she is a *merchant*, Milly has made Jed an offer in a signed writing, and told him that he has 30 days to accept. Section 2-205 provides that an offer like Milly's is *not* revocable *for lack of consideration.*

In practical terms, the difference between the Blackacre transaction and the kumquat transaction is significant. With Blackacre, Milly can withdraw her offer, which means that Jed cannot accept her offer and form a contract. On the other hand, in the kumquat transaction, Milly has made what is called a *firm offer* under the provisions of § 2-205 and she cannot withdraw it. The consequence is that Jed can accept her firm offer and form a contract.

Problem Solving. Please turn to Chapter Problems at the end of this chapter and solve Problem 15.3.

Omissions. A perennial problem in contract formation is the problem of omissions; that is, the failure of parties to agree on all necessary terms. Milly, for example, contracts to sell 500 toasters to JedMart, but the contract between them does not state the *price* to be paid, nor does it state *where* the toasters will be delivered.

The older, and less flexible, rules of the common law required completeness and were not tolerant of omissions and conflicts. Faced with the omission problems in the "toaster" transaction, a judge enforcing older common law rules might say that there never was a contract between Milly and JedMart

---

[3] A "merchant" is defined in § 2-104(1) as "a person who deals in goods of the kind or otherwise by his occupation holds himself out as having knowledge or skill peculiar to the practices or goods involved in the transaction or to whom such knowledge or skill may be attributed by his employment of an agent or broker or other intermediary who by his occupation holds himself out as having such knowledge or skill."

because they never finished the process of agreeing on all of the important parts of their contract. The judge might say that "parties should make contracts and courts enforce them," the point being that the courts are not inclined to supply missing terms or resolve conflicts.

With respect to the formation of a contract, Sales law introduces a new philosophy, which is to enforce contracts wherever possible—even if they are incomplete with respect to important terms. The attitude of the Sales article is to enforce a contract wherever possible if the *intent* to contract is clear and there is enough information to calculate a remedy. In the peculiar language of the UCC: "even though one or more terms [e.g. price or place of delivery] are left open [forgotten] a contract for sale does not fail for indefiniteness," (1) so long as "the parties have intended to make a contract" and (2) "there is a reasonably certain basis for giving an appropriate remedy." [2-204(3)]

OMISSIONS: missing contract terms completed by Sales law provisions.

How does the philosophy of the Sales article work in practical terms? How, for example, can Milly contract to sell 500 toasters to JedMart—forget to provide for the price and place of delivery of the toasters —and still have an enforceable contract? The answer is that the Sales law has a number of contact provisions in reserve—in it's "back pocket," so to speak. The parties may supply their own contract provisions on each contracting point, but if one is missing, the Sales law simply takes an appropriate one from it's so-called back pocket and inserts it into the contract. What is the price for Milly's toasters? *If* the parties fail to agree on the *price* of the goods being sold, Sales law provides that the price will be "a reasonable [usually fair market] price." [§ 2-305(1)] Similarly, if Milly and JedMart had *forgotten* to provide for a place of delivery, that place—by default—would be "the seller's place of business or if he had none his residence." [§ 2-308(a)]

Just like the price and place of delivery are provided if the parties leave those terms out of their contract, the Sales Article also provides substitute rules relating to such things as time for delivery, warranties, title and risk of loss.

One place where supplying Sales law provisions for missing contract provisions does not work well is if the *quantity* of goods being purchased is missing from a contract. Thus, if Jed and Milly agree on the sale of toasters, but the quantity is missing, there is often no way to remedy the problem. In such a case there is not a "reasonably certain basis for giving an appropriate remedy" and thus there is not an enforceable contract.

Problem Solving. Please turn to Chapter Problems at the end of this chapter and solve Problem 15.4.

Conflicts. In contrast to the problem of omissions is the problem of conflicts. For example, Jed sends a purchase order to Milly ordering 1000 pounds of kumquats, and Milly responds with a preprinted confirming invoice, agreeing to the transaction. Printed on the back of Milly's invoice is a statement that interest at the rate of 1.5% per month will be added to any account more than 30 days in arrears. Is this interest statement part of the contract? This problem is sometimes referred to as a "battle of the forms," because each party may put self-serving fine print on the back of their preprinted forms, and sometimes the provisions conflict with each other.

CONFLICTS: a contract may be formed without agreement on all details.

Section 2-207 is designed to deal with the problem of conflicting contract terms. Subsection (1) makes clear that an "an expression of acceptance or a written confirmation," like Milly's, "*operates as an acceptance*." In other words, the existence or nonexistence of a contract does not depend on resolving minor contract terms. The only exception is a document which provides that the existence of an agreement is "made conditional" on agreement to the detail in question.

There is a contract between Jed and Milly because her confirmation was not conditional on Jed's agreement to the interest provision. [§ 2-207(1)] But, what about the 1.5% interest provision; is it part of the contract, or not? Subsection (2) provides that if Jed and Milly are *not* merchants, the interest provision is nothing more than a proposal. However, it is likely that Jed and Milly are merchants, because only a merchant would be interested in 1000 pounds of kumquats. Subsection (2) provides that "between merchants such terms [the interest term] become part of the contract unless . . . they materially alter it." On it's face, the 1.5% interest provision seems reasonable and not a material alteration of the contract and therefore that provision becomes part of the contract. [§ 2-207(2)]

In the following case, *Dale R. Horning Co. Inc. v. Falconer Glass Industries, Inc.*, the plaintiff purchased Spandral, a type of glass containing a ceramic backing. The glass was defective and Horning sued for damages. Defendant was a New York corporation and included the following on the back of it's preprinted forms:

> 15. GOVERNING LAW—All questions arising in connection with this order or the acceptance and acknowledgment thereof or the sale of goods covered thereby shall be resolved in accordance with the laws of the State of New York and any action or suit relating in any way thereto must be brought in the Supreme court of the State of New York, County of Chautauqua.

When plaintiff, an Indiana Company, brought suit, the defendant tried to enforce the provision above, which would compel the plaintiff to bring suit in New York:

Dale R. Horning Co. Inc. v. Falconer GLASS Industries, Inc.
9 UCC Rep Ser 2d 77 (1989)

McKINNEY, District Judge.
* * *

This case is another illustration that in today's business world, parties to a contract for the sale of goods rarely "agree" to many of the terms of their contract. Rather, as happened in this case, the parties often reach an oral agreement as to product, prices, and place of shipment, with their preprinted forms to follow in the days following the agreement. Fortunately in this case there is only one standard form involved, so we have a conflict only between an oral agreement and the terms of the form rather than an oral agreement and the parties' competing forms. The case calls for what is in theory a straightforward application of § 2-207 of the U.C.C.

Section 2-207 of the Code "has called a truce in the so-called battle of the forms and has effectively abolished the mirror image rule" under which the offer and acceptance had to match exactly. Greenberg, *Rights and Remedies Under U.C.C. Article 2*, 69 (1987). This section provides the following rules:

> "(1) A definite and seasonable expression of acceptance or a written confirmation which is sent within a reasonable time operates as an acceptance even though it states terms additional to or different from those offered or agreed upon, unless acceptance is expressly made conditional on assent to the additional or different terms.

> "(2) The additional terms are to be construed as proposals for addition to the contract. *Between merchants such terms become part of the contract unless:*

>> (b) they materially alter it...."

§2-207(1) & (2)(b) (emphasis added).

This section is intended to deal with two typical situations. The first is where an offer has been made and the acceptance comes by way of a standard form. The second is where the parties have already reached an agreement and the standard form is merely a "confirmation" of that agreement. * * *

In this case the court is presented with the latter scenario. The plaintiff's complaint and affidavit establish that an oral agreement was reached over the phone on August 4, 1986. The defendant does not dispute this. Indeed, the defendant's own standard form indicates that it "confirms verbal 8/4/86." Where an agreement already exists, the subsequent form is nothing more than a confirmation and the court's inquiry is not whether a contract exists. Rather, the focus is on the terms of the contract.

"The only real question when a confirmation is involved is whether the additional terms became part of the agreement under §2-207 (2)." * * * "If only one confirmation is sent and it contains an *additional* term, the general rules of §2-207 (2) apply." * * * "If both [parties] are merchants, it becomes part of the contract unless it materially alters the contract or is objected to." * * *

Thus, in this case, because an oral contract was created on August 4, 1986, the defendant's standard form of August 5, 1986, was a confirmation. Because both parties are merchants, each additional term of that confirmation became a part of the parties' agreement unless such term materially altered their preexisting contract.

* * *

Defendant argues that its forum selection clause purporting to require all suits to be brought in a New York court does not materially alter the contract. Thus, the defendant argues, because the existence of an enforceable forum selection clause will deprive a federal court of personal jurisdiction, * * * this court lacks personal jurisdiction and the action must be dismissed under Rule 12(b)(2).

The court, however, finds as a matter of law in this case that the forum selection clause materially alters the oral contract. At the time of contracting on August 4, 1986, the plaintiff had every reason to expect that it could sue Falconer for any future breach of

> contract in an Indiana state or federal court, as well as a New York state or federal court. The forum selection clause, though, would limit their choice of forum to a New York state court. This limitation is certainly the type that would surprise the plaintiff or work it hardship.
>
> [Defendant's motion to dismiss, denied.]

Problem Solving. Please turn to Chapter Problems at the end of this chapter and solve Problem 15.5.

Statute of Frauds

STATUTE OF FRAUDS: a contract for the sale of goods for the price of $500 or more must be in writing.

Some contracts for the sale of goods must be in writing if they are to be enforced. The statute of frauds provision in Sales law is in § 2-201. In general, "a contract for the sale of goods for the price of $500 or more is not enforceable . . . unless there is some writing." [§ 2-201(1)] There are, however, three major exceptions to this writing requirement and the following contracts may be enforced, even though they are *not* in writing: (1) "if the goods are to be specially manufactured for the buyer and are not suitable for sale to others in the ordinary course of the seller's business;" (2) "if the party against whom enforcement is sought admits in his pleading, testimony or otherwise in court that a contract for sale was made;" or (3) "with respect to goods for which payment has been made and accepted or which have been received and accepted." [§ 2-201(3)]

Suppose that Jed calls Milly on the telephone and orders 3,000 puffy, white bears at $3.00 each, which he hopes to sell on the streets of Salt Lake City during the 2002 Winter Olympics. On the front of each bear will be "SLC—2002." Later, Jed refuses to pay for the bears—which he has refused to receive. He refuses to admit the existence of a contract. Even if there is a contract, he says it is unenforceable because it violates the "statute of frauds." Who wins? The answer is that Milly will win because the bears are specially manufactured and, with "SLC—2002" on them, they cannot be sold "in the ordinary course" of Milly's business. [§ 2-201(3)(a)]

The result is the same with the other two exceptions to the UCC version of the statute of frauds. Even though it should be in writing, a contract is nevertheless enforceable if the opposite party admits "in his pleading, testimony or otherwise" that a contract was formed. Also, a contract which should be in writing is enforceable if the goods have been paid for, or at least received and accepted.

Parol Evidence

PAROL EVIDENCE: a written contract cannot be contradicted by evidence of a prior or contemporaneous agreement.

As discussed before, in relation to common law contracts, putting a contract in writing provides little benefit to the parties unless they are required to honor it. In that context, § 2-202 provides that a written document which the parties intend "as a final expression of their agreement" cannot be "*contradicted* by evidence of any prior agreement or of a contemporaneous oral agreement but

239

may be explained or supplemented." [§ 2-202] This rule is known generally as the parol evidence rule.

The following opinion in *Intershoe, Inc. v. Bankers Trust Co.* includes an attempt by the plaintiff, Intershoe, to introduce oral testimony contradicting a written document. A representative of plaintiff telephoned the defendant bank on March 13, 1985, and entered into a "futures" transaction. Specifically, the plaintiff sold Italian money (lira) at the current exchange rate in dollars. The actual exchange of money was to take place several months later in October of 1985. (In such a transaction, if the value of the lira rises in the intervening months, Intershoe will lose money; but, if the value of the lira declines, Intershoe will make money.) The bank sent plaintiff a confirmation slip stating: "WE [Bankers] HAVE BOUGHT FROM YOU [Interstate] ITL 537,750,000" and "WE HAVE SOLD TO YOU USD 250,000.00." This confirmation slip (stating an exchange rate of 2.151 lira per dollar) was sent to plaintiff and one of their representatives signed and returned it.

Some time later, the value of the lira apparently rose, meaning that Intershoe would lose more than $55,000 in the transaction. They refused to comply with the transaction claiming that it (Interstate) had *purchased*, not *sold* lira—that the bank confirmation slip had reversed the transaction. Plaintiff filed suit to rectify the situation and the defendant bank filed a motion to dismiss the suit. At issue was whether the plaintiff would be allowed to introduce oral evidence describing their view of the transaction.

INTERSHOE, INC. v. BANKERS TRUST CO.
571 N.E.2d 641 (N.Y. 1991)

HANCOCK, Judge.
* * *

Here, the essential terms of the transaction are plainly set forth in the confirmation slip: that plaintiff had sold lira to defendant, the amount of the lira it sold, the exchange rate, the amount of dollars to be paid by defendant for the lira, and the maturity date of the transaction. The signature of plaintiff's agent who signed and returned the confirmation slip five days later on March 18, 1985 signifies plaintiff's acceptance of these terms. Nothing in the confirmation slip suggests that it was to be a memorandum of some preliminary or tentative understanding with respect to these terms. On the contrary, it is difficult to imagine words which could more clearly demonstrate the final expression of the parties' agreement than "WE HAVE BOUGHT FROM YOU ITL 537,750,000" and "WE HAVE SOLD TO YOU USD 250,000.00."

The confirmation is not of some bargain to be made in the future but expresses the parties' meeting of the minds as to a completed bargain's essential terms—a sale of 537,750,000 lira at a rate of 2,151 for $250,000—made in a telephone conversation on March 13, 1985. The only evidence plaintiff has tendered does no more than contradict the stated terms of the confirmation slip—the very evidence which UCC 2-202 precludes. It does not address the critical question of whether the terms in the confirmation slip were intended to represent the parties' final agreement on those matters. We conclude that where, as here, the form and content of the confirmation slip suggest nothing other than that

---

it was intended to be the final expression of the parties' agreement as to the terms set forth and where there is no evidence indicating that this was not so, UC 2-202 bars parol evidence of contradictory terms * * *

We reject plaintiff's contentions that UCC 2-202 requires that there be some express indication in the writing itself or some other evidence that the parties intended it to be the final expression of their agreement. A holding that the writing must include express language that it represents the parties' final expression would introduce a technical, formal requirement not contemplated by the Code and one that would frustrate the Code's purpose of facilitating sales transactions by easing the process of contract formation * * *. To require that the record include specific extraneous evidence that the writing constitutes the parties' final agreement as to its stated terms would in many instances impose a virtually insurmountable obstacle for parties seeking to invoke UCC 2-202, particularly in cases involving large commercial banks and other financial institutions which typically close hundreds of transactions over the telephone during a business day. As a practical matter, a confirmation slip or similar writing is usually the only reliable evidence of such transactions, given the unlikely prospect that one who makes scores of similar deals each day will remember the details of any one particular agreement. Indeed, this case is illustrative inasmuch as neither of the participants had a specific recollection of the March 13, 1985 telephone conversation. As the dissent below aptly noted, a holding that plaintiff's proffered evidence is sufficient to thwart the application of UCC 2-202 would create a particularly troublesome precedent for commercial practice in currency futures transactions by providing a convenient "hedge' for one party or the other against currency fluctuations * * *. In sum, there is no triable issue of fact warranting denial of summary judgement to defendant * * *.

Plaintiff also argues that UCC 2-202 does not bar the parol evidence submitted in opposition to defendant's motion because it is offered to show that there was never a contract between the parties. This argument is unavailing. Plaintiff does not dispute that it entered into a foreign currency transaction with defendant; its only contentions is that the transaction called for it to purchase and not sell lira. Hence, the parol evidence is being used to contradict a term of the contract, not to show that there was no contract, and UCC 2-202 applies.

The order of the Appellate Division should be reversed, with costs, defendant's motion to dismiss the complaint and for summary judgement on its counterclaim should be granted * * *.

Problem Solving. Please turn to Chapter Problems at the end of this chapter and solve Problem 15.6.

Unconscionability

Section 2-302 gives a court the power to refuse to enforce a contract, or a clause in a contract, if it is *unconscionable*. Specifically, the section provides: "If the court as a matter of law finds the contract or any clause of the contract to have been unconscionable at the time it was made the court may refuse to enforce the contract, or it may enforce the remainder of the contract without the unconscionable clause."

UNCONSCIONABILITY: an unconscionable contract or clause may not be enforced.

In general, courts prefer a "hands-off" attitude, and if contracting parties freely bargain and reach a deal, the courts are very reluctant to interfere just because one of the parties suffers a loss. But, in extreme cases, § 2-302 gives a court the power to refuse to enforce contract provisions which shock it's conscience.

In *Jones v. Star Credit Corp.*, a court was asked to use § 2-302 as a basis for refusing to enforce a contract for the purchase of a home freezer. The purchasers were on welfare, and from the facts it may be inferred that they were not sophisticated in financial matters. A short version of the facts was stated by the court: "On August 31, 1965 the plaintiffs, who are welfare recipients, agreed to purchase a home freezer unit for $900 as the result of a visit from a salesman representing Your Shop At Home Service, Inc. With the addition of the time credit charges, credit life insurance, credit property insurance, and sales tax, the purchase price totaled $1,234.80. Thus far the plaintiffs have paid $619.88 toward their purchase." In fact, the freezer was worth about $300.

Jones v. Star Credit Corp.
298 N.Y.S.2d 264 (1969)

SOL M. WACHTLER, Justice.
* * *

There was a time when the shield of "caveat emptor" would protect the most unscrupulous in the marketplace— a time when the law, in granting parties unbridled latitude to make their own contracts, allowed exploitive and callous practices which shocked the conscience of both legislative bodies and the courts.
* * *

The law is beginning to fight back against those who once took advantage of the poor and illiterate without risk of either exposure or interference. From the common law doctrine of intrinsic fraud we have, over the years, developed common and statutory law which tells not only the buyer but also the seller to beware. This body of laws recognizes the importance of a free enterprise system but at the same time will provide the legal armor to protect and safeguard the prospective victim from the harshness of an unconscionable contract.

Section 2-302 of the Uniform Commercial Code enacts the moral sense of the community into the law of commercial transactions. It authorizes the court to find, as a matter of law, that a contract or a clause of a contract was "unconscionable at the time it was made", and upon so finding the court may refuse to enforce the contract, excise the objectionable clause or limit the application of the clause to avoid an unconscionable result. "The principle", states the Official Comment to this section, "is one of the prevention of oppression and unfair surprise". It permits a court to accomplish directly what heretofore was often accomplished by construction of language, manipulations of fluid rules of contract law and determinations based upon a presumed public policy.
* * *

Fraud, in the instant case, is not present; nor is it necessary under the statute. The question which presents itself is whether or not, under the circumstances of this case, the sale of a freezer unit having a retail value of $300 for $900 ($1,439.69[4] including credit

---

[4] $1,439.69 and $1,234.80 are both described in the opinion as the total amount..

charges and $18 sales tax) is unconscionable as a matter of law. The court believes it is.

Concededly, deciding the issue is substantially easier than explaining it. No doubt, the mathematical disparity between $300, which presumably includes a reasonable profit margin, and $900, which is exorbitant on its face, carries the greatest weight. Credit charges alone exceed by more than $100 the retail value of the freezer. These alone, may be sufficient to sustain the decision. Yet, a caveat is warranted lest we reduce the import of Section 2-302 solely to a mathematical ration formula. It may, at times, be that; yet it may also be much more. The very limited financial resources of the purchaser, known to the sellers at the time of the sale, is entitled to weight in the balance. Indeed, the value disparity itself leads inevitably to the felt conclusion that knowing advantage was taken of the plaintiffs. In addition, the meaningfulness of choice essential to the making of a contract, can be negated by a gross inequality of bargaining power. * * *

There is no question about the necessity and even the desirability of installment sales and the extension of credit. Indeed, there are many, including welfare recipients, who would be deprived of even the most basic conveniences without the use of these devices. Similarly, the retail merchant selling on instalment or extending credit is expected to establish a pricing factor which will afford a degree of protection commensurate with the risk of selling to those who might be default prone. However, neither of these accepted premises can clothe the sale of this freezer with respectability.

[The contract was "reformed" to require payment only for the amount already paid.]

Problem Solving. Please turn to Chapter Problems at the end of this chapter and solve Problem 15.7.

Problem 15.1

Based on the language of § 1-103, have the rules of consideration—learned in relation to common law contacts—been modified in the UCC?

Problem 15.2

A utility company provides electricity in a faulty manner. Specifically, electricity occasionally "surges" and the excess electricity causes damages to the machinery of the plaintiff. The plaintiff brings suit claiming a violation of the Sales law. Does the Sales law apply to the sale of electricity?

Problem 15.3

Milly, a merchant, calls Jed on the telephone and offers to sell him 1000 pounds of kumquats, with 30 days to accept. Can Milly—15 days later—withdraw her offer?

Problem 15.4

(The answer to this problem has not been covered in the text.) Milly contracts to sell 500 toasters to JedMart. Their contract has no provision about the *time* at which payment is due. In addition, there is an unresolved question about whether JedMart may pay by *check*.

What are the answers to these questions?

Problem 15.5

In the *Horning* decision, suppose that the confirmation from Falconer Glass contained the words: "This sales transaction is expressly conditioned upon the buyer's agreement to the following provisions:" After that language is printed the GOVERNING LAW provision discussed in the opinion. Based on these facts, refer to § 2-207 and explain how, if at all, the outcome in the *Horning* decision might be changed.

Problem 15.6

In the *Intershoe* decision, suppose that the confirmation slip from the bank included the following language: "This confirmation to be followed by a comprehensive agreement between the parties." How, if at all, would the results in the case change?

Problem 15.7

With reference to the *Jones* decision, suppose that the purchase price, and all associated charges totaled $700. How, if at all, would the outcome change?

Chapter 16
Title and Risk of Loss

Chapter Outline

OBJECTIVE: to learn rules of law related to title, third party claims to title and risk of loss.

The objective of this chapter is to learn the rules of law in the Sales article related to title, third party claims to title and risk of loss. The chapter is organized as follows:

Title

- *Title*. Title means legal ownership. Unless otherwise agreed, title passes to the buyer at the time and place the seller completes his performance with reference to the physical delivery of the goods.

- *Third Party Rights: Good Faith Purchasers*. A party with voidable title has the ability to give good title (to goods he has purchased from a seller) to a good faith purchaser (a third party). The party with voidable title has this power—even if the seller was defrauded or not paid—unless the goods were stolen from the seller.

- *Third Party Rights: Entrustment*. If the owner of goods entrusts them to a merchant with respect to goods of that kind, the merchant has the power to transfer all rights of the entruster to a buyer in the ordinary course of business.

Risk of Loss

- *Risk of Loss in Shipment Contracts*. Contracts for the transportation of goods from the seller to the buyer are presumed to be *shipment* contracts which means that the risk of loss in transit shifts to the buyer when the seller properly delivers the goods to the carrier.

- *Risk of Loss in Delivery Contracts*. If the seller has an obligation to deliver the goods to the buyer at a particular destination, the risk of loss in transit does not shift to the buyer until the seller tenders the goods to the buyer at the prescribed destination. This type of contract is a *delivery* contract.

Introduction

This chapter deals with three related topics. The first topic is *title*, sometimes referred to as ownership. In a Sales contract it is sometimes important to know when the buyer acquires title. It is also important to know what right the buyer has to demand title, if the seller does not provide clear title to the item the buyer has purchased.

The second topic is title claims by or against *third parties*. This topic is illustrated by supposing that Jed sells a horse to Milly, who gives him a check for the purchase price. Next, Milly sells the horse to Sam, an innocent third party, and then her check to Jed bounces. Does Sam, the third party, have good title to the horse, or can Jed reclaim it?

The third topic is referred to as *"risk of loss."* This topic is illustrated by Jed selling a horse located in Rigby, Idaho, to Milly, who is in Missoula, Montana. If the horse is killed while being transported to Montana, who bears the loss? And, specifically, is it important to know who owns (has "title" to) the horse to know who bears the loss?

Title

TITLE means ownership.

In practical terms, title means legal ownership, and the person who owns an item may be said to have title to it. "Title" is a legal concept and not a piece of paper. (For example, sometimes a certificate of title is issued naming the owner of an item such as an automobile, but the certificate is not the title, it is only evidence of the title.)

This part of the discussion deals with the point in time that a buyer acquires title (ownership) to the goods he or she is purchasing. This ownership usually occurs by contract and without the exchange of a formal "certificate" of title, unless the transaction involves items like automobiles, boats, motorcycles, etc.

TITLE: unless otherwise agreed, title passes to buyer at physical delivery of goods.

At Time and Place of Delivery. In general, title to goods passes to the buyer "at the time and place at which the seller completes his performance with reference to the physical *delivery* of the goods." [§ 2-401(2)] To illustrate this point, suppose that Jed, in Los Angeles, contracts to buy 20,000 pounds of apples from Milly, who is in Seattle, Washington. As will be discussed later in the chapter, some sales contracts are called *"shipment"* contracts which means that Milly's title ends when she puts the apples on a train in Seattle. Other sales contracts are called *"delivery"* contracts which means that Milly's title does not end until the apples are delivered in Los Angeles.

Application of the title-when-delivery-is-completed rule (above) to the agreement between Jed and Milly means (if the parties have not otherwise agreed) that in a *shipment* contract, Jed receives title when Milly successfully puts the apples on the train in Seattle. But, in a *delivery* contract, Jed receives title when the apples are delivered in Los Angeles.

Unless Otherwise Agreed. It is important to remember that title rules—like many others in the Sales article—are prefaced "unless otherwise explicitly agreed." This means, of course, that the contracting parties are at liberty to agree that title will pass "in any manner and on any conditions," including on an earlier or later date. [§

2-401(1)] There is one exception, which is that "title to goods cannot pass under a contract for sale prior to their *identification* to the contract."

For example, suppose that Jed finances the apple contract with Milly by borrowing money from First National Bank. Jed's contract with Milly provides that the *bank* will take title to the apples to ensure that its loan to Jed is repaid. This language providing that title will go to the bank, and not to Jed, takes advantage of the "unless otherwise agreed" language described above. The earliest time that the bank may receive title to the apples is when they are "identified" to the contract. (§ 2-401(1)) For the apples to be identified to the contract means that Milly has gone into her warehouse and separated out or otherwise "identified" the particular apples that will be transferred to Jed.

The following decision, *Synergistic Technologies v. IDB Mobile Communications*, involved complex contract and patent issues. The defendant, IDB, asked the court to grant summary judgment in it's favor. To decide that issue, it became necessary for the court to decide if and when the defendant, IDB was to become the owner of (have title to) the computer hardware and software it received from the plaintiff, Synergistic.

Synergistic Technologies v. IDB Mobile Communications
871 F.Supp. 24 (1994)

JOYCE HENS GREEN, District Judge.
* * *

In order to grant summary judgment on the ground suggested by defendant, the Court must also find that IDB is the "owner" of a copy of the program. The Statement of Work [the contract between the parties] is not clear on the issue of transfer of ownership of the software. Both parties point to the language of § 4.4 of the Statement of Work to support their position that the document does (or does not) provide for transfer of ownership for the software. If this matter turned solely on the Statement of Work, the Court would be unable to resolve the issue of ownership on summary judgment, given the dispute in interpretation of the Statement of Work between the parties.

However, this question is also governed by § 2-401 of the Uniform Commercial Code, D.C.Code Ann. § 28:2-401 (1991), which provides that "[u]nless otherwise explicitly agreed title passes to the buyer at the time and place at which the seller completes his performance with reference to the physical delivery of the goods." The parties not having explicitly agreed otherwise, title to the hardware and to a copy of the software passed to IDB at the time of delivery of the goods. Accordingly, IDB is the owner of a copy of the computer program and is entitled to copy and adapt the program in the limited manner described in § 117.
* * *

In sum, summary judgment is granted against plaintiff on the entirety of plaintiff's complaint.

A final point. In the transactions between Milly and Jed, it is understood that at some point Jed (or the bank) will become the owner of the apples—that they will receive title to them. But, suppose that does not happen; suppose that Jed (or the bank) does not receive title to the goods as agreed. What can they do? The answer to that question is one of the subjects of Chapter 17. In short, the answer to the question is in § 2-312, which provides that (unless otherwise agreed) each contract for sale includes "a warranty by the seller that . . . the title conveyed shall be good, and its transfer rightful." In other words, the contract between Jed and Milly includes a warranty (a promise) that Jed, the buyer (or the bank), will receive good title to the apples. And, if they do not receive good title to the apples, the contract is breached and Milly is liable in damages.

Problem Solving. Please turn to Chapter Problems at the end of this chapter and solve Problem 16.1

Third Party Rights

The discussion above dealt with Jed, or his bank, receiving title, and the questions of when that should occur and what could be done if it did not. The discussion now shifts from Jed to Milly; having delivered the apples, what can she do if she is not paid for them as agreed? Specifically, is she entitled to receive back the apples (or their value)?

GOOD FAITH PURCHASER: A sells to B who sells to C—C has good title unless B is a thief.

Good Faith Purchaser. Suppose that the apple transaction above is a shipment contract, which means that title to the apples passes to Jed when the apples are placed in the hands of the carrier in Seattle. [§ 2-509(1)(a)] In this version of the facts, Jed chooses to not use a bank loan but instead pays for the apples by check drawn on his account. When the apples are shipped, Jed immediately sells them to the ABC Apple Juice Co., who pays Jed in full. Jed then disappears. Meanwhile—and here is the problem—Jed's check to Milly is not paid because of insufficient funds.

When Jed's check "bounces" because of insufficient funds, Milly thinks the apples should still be *hers* because she has not been paid. On the other hand, ABC thinks the apples should be *its* because it paid for them in good faith and without any knowledge of Milly's claim. In this case, the law is on ABC's side. Section 2-403(1) provides that "a person with voidable title [Jed] has power to transfer good title to a good faith purchaser for value [ABC]." If we apply this rule to Jed's relationship with Milly, Jed's title to the apples is voidable because he did not pay as agreed; but, Jed, who is a person with voidable title, gives another person (ABC) good title if that person is a "good faith purchaser for value."

To qualify as a good faith purchaser for value, ABC must first show that it is a purchaser and did not receive the apples as a gift. That being so, ABC must next show that it acted in "good faith," which means "honesty in fact in the conduct or transaction concerned." [§ 1-201(19)] Satisfaction of the good faith standard means that ABC purchased the apples without knowledge of Milly's unsatisfied claim.

If ABC is *not* a good faith purchaser for value, Milly has a claim against ABC for the apples or their value. But, as noted above, if ABC *is* a good faith purchaser for value, Milly has no claim against ABC. Indeed, Milly may show that Jed was an imposter, that his check was dishonored, that the transaction was supposed to be a cash transaction or that Jed criminally defrauded her, but none of these claims will help her if ABC is a good faith purchaser for value. [2-403(1)] Milly, of course, has a clear claim against Jed for the amount of her loss [2-709(1)(a)]; but, that claim will do her no good if Jed has no money, or disappears.

The problem above is the same as the problem in a case known as *Lane v. Honeycutt*. Lane, the plaintiff, sold a new boat and motor to John W. Willis, for $6,285 and received a check for that amount from Willis. The check did not clear. Shortly thereafter, a man named Garrett sold the boat and motor to the defendant, Honeycutt. Garrett had apparently received the boat from "John W. Patterson," whose real name was John W. Willis. The chain of transactions was something like this:

Honeycutt didn't think he could afford the boat, but "he [Garrett] told me the price [$2500] and I was very pleasantly surprised." Honeycutt bought the boat and received no title, receiving only a temporary registration certificate. Thereafter, Lane attempted to get the boat and motor back from Honeycutt because he had not been paid. When § 2-403(1) was raised as a defense by Honeycutt, Lane countered that Honeycutt was not a good faith purchaser because the extremely low price and the lack of a certificate of title should have put him (Honeycutt) on notice that there were problems with the transaction.

Lane v. Honeycutt

188 S.E.2d 604 (1972)

VAUGHN, Judge.

* * *

We do not discuss the evidence and questions raised as to whether the check was a forgery, the transaction a cash sale or whether delivery was procured through fraud punishable as larcenous under the criminal law. Contrary to the law of this State as it may have been prior to the enactment of G.S. § 25-2-403, that statute now allows the vendee in such a transaction to transfer a good title to a "good faith purchaser for value."

The question, therefore, which we consider to be determinative of this appeal is whether there is any evidence to support the following findings of fact by the court. "(2) The Defendant, Jimmy Honeycutt, did not purchase the boat, motor and trailer in good faith."

* * *

Garrett told defendant he would let defendant have the boat for $2500. Defendant then paid Garrett a deposit of $100. Garrett had nothing to indicate that he was the owner of the boat, motor or trailer. Garrett told defendant he was selling the boat for someone else. "This guy comes down, you know, and does some fishing."

Two weeks later defendant returned to Garden City, South Carolina, with $2400, the balance due (on a boat, motor and trailer which had been sold new less than six months earlier for $6,285.00). On this occasion,

"Mr. Garrett had told me—well, he always called him, 'this guy' see, so I really didn't know of any name or anything, but he told me, 'this guy [Willis/Patterson] does a lot of fishing around here, but I can't seem to get ahold of him.' He said, 'I've called him, but I can't get ahold of him, so since you have the money and you're here after the boat' . . .; (s)ince you have the money and I can't seem to find him,' he said, 'I don't believe he would object, so I'll just go ahead and sign this title for you so you can go on and get everything made out to you.' He then signed the purported owner's name on the documents and he signed the title over to me then."

The so-called "document" and "title," introduced as defendant's exhibit No. 8, was nothing more than the "certificate of number" required by G.S. § 75A-5 and issued by the North Carolina Wildlife Resources Commission. This "certificate of number" is not a "certificate of title" to be compared with that required by G.S. § 20-50 for vehicles intended to be operated on the highways of this State. Upon the change of ownership of a motor boat, G.S. § 75A-5(c) authorizes the issuance of a new "certificate of number" to the transferee upon proper application. The application for transfer of the number, among other things, requires the seller's *signature*. A signature is "the name of a person written with his own hand." Webster's third New International dictionary (1968). Defendant observed Garret counterfeit the signature of the purported owner, John P. Patterson, on the exhibit. Following the falsified signature on defendant's exhibit No. 8, the "date sold" is set out as "June 12, 1970" and the buyer's "signature" is set out as George (illegible) Williams." There was no testimony as to who affixed the "signature" of the purported buyer, George Williams, and there is no further reference to him in the record.

Defendant's exhibit No. 9 is a temporary registration certificate from the North Carolina Department of Motor Vehicles. The temporary certificate was dated 19 February 1970 (two days prior to the sale by plaintiff to "Willis" alias "Patterson"). It describes the vehicle as "trailer, homemade, 1970" and was issued to "John Palmer Patterson." The vehicle registration license number which appears on the temporary certificate is 7567KH. Defendant received this certificate from Garrett. The trailer defendant received from Garrett was a 1970 Cox trailer. It bore the same registration plate number, 7567KH. Defendant did not receive a certificate of title to the Cox trailer that he obtained from Garrett which plaintiff now seeks to recover. Plaintiff retained possession of the manufacturer's certificate of origin for the Cox trailer and apparently no certificate of title has been issued for that vehicle.

[Judgment in favor of Lane affirmed.]

Of course, Honeycutt had to return the boat, motor and trailer to Lane because the totality of the circumstances would have alerted a reasonable person to the fact that there was something improper about the transaction. Knowing that there was something improper about the transaction, Honeycutt could not be a good faith purchaser and was not protected by the provisions of § 2-403(1) as ABC, the apple buyer was.

There is a major exception in relation to claims by a third party under § 2-403 and that is that a thief has *no* title, and certainly not *voidable* title. That means, of course, that a person buying stolen goods from a thief cannot receive good title, because they did not purchase from a person with good (or at least voidable) title.

Thus, if Jed stole the apples from Milly, Milly is entitled to recover the apples, or their value, from ABC.

(At this point, a perceptive student may wonder how Milly can protect herself? The answer goes beyond this chapter, but, in short, Milly can do things such as: (1) deferring delivery of the apples until the check has cleared and payment is assured, or (2) retaining a "security interest" in the apples. The law relating to security interests is in Article 9 of the UCC.)

Problem Solving. Please turn to Chapter Problems at the end of this chapter and solve Problem 16.2.

Entrustment. Another type of problem involving claims by or against third parties is referred to as "entrustment." In a transaction above, Milly *sold* apples to Jed, who then sold the apples to ABC. When Jed failed to pay for the apples, the question was whether Milly could recover the apples, or their value, from ABC. (And, as discussed above, § 2-403(1) did not allow Milly to recover the apples or their value from ABC—only from Jed.) The same was true in the *Lane v. Honeycutt* decision.

With entrustment the story is different because Milly merely *entrusts* goods to Jed, she does not *sell* goods to Jed. Thus, if Milly leaves her computer with Jed to be repaired, she has *entrusted* her computer to Jed, she has not *sold* it to him as she did with the apples. A significant problem arises if Jed thereafter (intentionally or unintentionally) sells the computer entrusted to him to Sam. If Jed has no money, or disappears, can Milly get her computer, or the value of the computer back from Sam? On this point § 2-403(2) provides: "[a]ny entrusting of possession of goods to a merchant who deals in goods of that kind gives him power to transfer all rights of the entruster to a buyer in ordinary course of business."

In the problem above, Sam wins. In this problem, if Jed is a merchant with respect to computers, and Sam is a buyer in ordinary course of business—which means that he buys in good faith and without knowledge of Milly's claims—Sam acquires Milly's title to the computer. [§ 2-403(2)] Milly would, of course, have a good claim against Jed for reimbursement of the value of the computer.

Section 2-403(2), dealing with entrustment, was at issue in the following decision, *Porter v. Wertz*. Porter, the plaintiff and the owner of a valuable oil painting entitled "Chateau de Lion-sur-Mur," by Utrillo, allowed a man by the name of Von Maker to take possession of the painting and place it in his (Von Maker's) home to decide if he wanted to purchase it. Von Maker allowed a man named Wertz to sell the painting to the Feigen Art Gallery. Von Maker and Wertz have disappeared or have no assets, and Porter demands the return of the painting (or it's value) from Feigen. Feigen says that his claim is protected by the entrustment provisions of § 2-403(2), but Porter says that is not so because neither Von Maker nor Wertz were art merchants.

251

PORTER v. WERTZ
416 N.Y.S.2d 254

BIRNS, Justice.

* * *

The provisions of statutory estoppel are found in section 2-403 of the Uniform Commercial Code. Subsection 2 thereof provides that "any entrusting of possession of goods to a merchant who deals in goods of that kind gives him power to transfer all rights of the entruster to a buyer in the ordinary course of business." Uniform Commercial Code, section 1-201, subdivision 9, defines a "buyer in [the] ordinary course of business" as "a person who in good faith and without knowledge that the sale to him is in violation of the ownership rights or security interest of a third party in the goods buys in ordinary course from a person in the business of selling goods of that kind . . . ."

In order to determine whether the defense of statutory estoppel is available to Feigen, we must begin by ascertaining whether Feigen fits the definition of "[a] buyer in [the] ordinary course of business." (UCC, § 1-201[9].) Feigen does not fit that definition, for two reasons. First, Wertz, from whom Feigen bought the Utrillo, was not an art dealer—he was not "a person in the business of selling goods of that kind." (UCC, § 1-201[9].) If anything, he was a delicatessen employee. Wertz never held himself out as a dealer. Although Feigen testified at trial that before he (Feigen) purchased the Utrillo from Wertz, Sloan, who introduced Wertz to Feigen told him (Feigen) that Wertz was an art dealer, this testimony was questionable. It conflicted with Feigen's testimony at his examination before trial where he stated he did not recall whether Sloan said that to him. Second, Feigen was not "a person . . . in good faith" (UCC, § 1-201[9]) in the transaction with Wertz. Uniform Commercial Code, section 2-103, subdivision (1)(b), defines "good faith" in the case of a merchant as "honesty in fact and the observance of reasonable commercial standards of fair dealing in the trade." Although this definition by its terms embraces the "reasonable commercial standards of fair dealing in the trade", it should not—and cannot—be interpreted to permit, countenance or condone commercial standards of sharp trade practice or indifference as to the "provenance," *i.e.*, history of ownership or the right to possess or sell an object d'art, such as is present in the case before us.

We note that neither Ms. Drew-Bear nor her employer Feigen made any investigation to determine the status of Wertz, *i.e.*, whether he was an art merchant, "a person in the business of selling goods of that kind." [UCC, § 1-201(9)] Had Ms. Drew-Bear done so much as call either of the telephone numbers Wertz had left, she would have learned that Wertz was employed by a delicatessen and was not an art dealer. Nor did Ms. Drew-Bear or Feigen make any effort to verify whether Wertz was the owner or authorized by the owner to sell the painting he was offering. Ms. Drew-Bear had available to her the Petrides volume on Utrillo which included "Chateau de Lion-sur-Mer" in its catalogue of the master's work. Although this knowledge alone might not have been enough to put Feigen on notice that Wertz was not the true owner at the time of the transaction, it could have raised a doubt as to Wertz's right of possession, calling for further verification before the purchase by Feigen was consummated. Thus, it appears that statutory estoppel provided by Uniform Commercial Code, section 2-403(2), was not, as Trial Term correctly concluded, available as a defense to Feigen.

[Judgment in favor of Porter, reversed.]

In the entrustment problem, and in the sales problem with respect to apples, the policy choice by the authors of the UCC is to protect the market place. Thus, the owner of property should take care not to place that property in the hands of others by way of sale or entrustment without adequate security. Once the choice to release the property has been made, and the owner sells or entrusts that property to another, the owner may thereafter lose his or her claim to the property if it gets in the hands of an innocent third party.

Problem Solving. Please turn to Chapter Problems at the end of this chapter and solve Problem 16.3

Risk of Loss

The discussion now shifts away from questions of title (ownership). The new point of discussion is the problem of "risk of loss" as goods are stored or moved from place to place. For example, if Milly is selling apples to Jed, and shipping them to him from Seattle to Los Angeles, and the train derails en route, who bears the loss? Under older law, the courts attempted to resolve risk of loss problems by asking who owns the apples? Under older law, whoever owned the apples bore the loss. That approach—the ownership approach—to solving risk of loss problems has been abandoned.

The point above needs to be repeated. Under Sales rules, the question of who bears the loss when goods are damaged or lost as they are stored or moved from place to place is *not* solved by reference to ownership (title). The reason ownership is not used to resolve loss problems is because title is sometimes moved from person to person for purposes of financing, which is a function that has nothing to do with managing the storage and movement of goods. The Sales rules recognize that loss problems should *not* be resolved by reference to title.

RISK OF LOSS IN A "SHIPMENT" CONTRACT: risk of loss shifts to Buyer when seller delivers goods to carrier.

FOB Place of *Shipment*: (§ 2-319(1)(a). Sales rules resolve loss problems by asking who has responsibility for storage and movement. To illustrate this point, return to the apple transaction where Milly, the seller, is in Seattle and Jed, the buyer, is in Los Angeles. The contract is FOB, Seattle, which means that Milly must "bear the *expense* and *risk* of putting them [the apples] into the possession of the carrier." [§ 2-319(1)(a)] In other words, Milly must pay to have the apples moved by truck to the train loading yard, and if the truck is in an accident on the way to the loading yard, Milly must bear the loss.

Risk of Loss in *Shipment* Contract: § 2-509(1)(a). At this point, with the apples delivered to the train loading yard, § 2-509 (1)(a) provides:

Where the contract [between Milly and Jed] requires or authorizes the seller [Milly] to ship the goods [the apples] by carrier . . . if it [the contract] does *not* require him [Milly] to deliver them [the apples] at a particular destination [the contract is FOB Seattle, which is not a destination requirement], the *risk of loss passes to the buyer* when the goods are duly delivered to the carrier [the railroad] . . .

In short, in a *shipment* contract—where the contract does not require the seller to deliver the goods to a particular destination— the risk of loss shifts to the buyer when the seller delivers the goods to the carrier. (Sales contracts are presumed to be *shipment* contracts unless the contract otherwise provides.) Specifically, the language quoted above provides that "the risk of loss passes to Jed, the buyer, when the goods are duly delivered by Milly to the carrier. Section 2-504 provides additional detail on this point by providing that Milly has completed the process of delivering the apples to the railroad company when she: (1) puts the apples in the possession of the railroad and makes a reasonable contract for their transportation, (2) sends to Jed the paperwork which will allow Jed to claim the apples in Los Angeles, and (3) notifies Jed that the apples have been shipped.

Problem Solving. Please turn to Chapter Problems at the end of this chapter and solve Problem 16.4.

In the following case, *NINTH STREET EAST, LTD. v. Harrison*, the plaintiff, NINTH STREET EAST, located in Los Angeles, sold men's clothing to Phillmore T. Harrison, the defendant, who operated a men's clothing store in Westport, Connecticut. When the goods reached the defendant, "[a] woman in charge of the store, identified as defendant's wife, requested the Old Colony truck driver to deliver the merchandise inside the door of defendant's store. The truck driver refused to do so. The dispute not having been resolved, Old Colony retained possession of the eight cartons comprising the shipment, and the truck thereupon departed from the store premises." Thereafter, the goods were lost and the plaintiff never recovered possession of them. The seller filed suit to obtain payment for the goods.

NINTH STREET EAST, LTD. v. Harrison
259 A.2d 772 (1968)

NORTON M. LEVINE, Judge.

＊ ＊ ＊

The basic problem is to determine the terms and conditions of the agreement of the parties as to transportation, and the risks and hazards incident thereto. The court finds that the parties had originally agreed that the merchandise would be shipped by common carrier F.O.B. Los Angeles, as the place of shipment, and that the defendant would pay the freight charges between the two points. The notations on the invoices, and the bill of lading, previously described, make this clear. The use of the phrase "F.O.B.," meaning free on board, made this portion of the agreement not only a price term covering defendant's obligation to pay freight charges between Los Angeles and Westport but also a controlling factor as to risk of loss of the merchandise upon delivery to Denver and subsequently to Old Colony as the carriers.

＊ ＊ ＊

The arrangements as to shipment were at the option of plaintiff as the seller, § 42a-2-311(1). Plaintiff duly placed the goods in possession of a carrier, to wit, Denver, and made a reasonable contract for their transportation, having in mind the nature of the merchandise and the remaining circumstances. Notice of the shipment, including the F.O.B. provisions, was properly given to defendant, as required by law, pursuant to the four invoices. § 42a-2-404; Uniform Commercial Code § 2-504, comment 5.

The law erects a presumption in favor of construing the agreement as a "shipment" contract, as opposed to a "destination" contract. § 42a-2-503; Uniform Commercial Code § 2-503, comment 5. Under the presumption of a "shipment" contract, plaintiff's liability for loss or damage terminated upon delivery to the carrier at the F.O.B. point, to wit, Los Angeles. The court finds that no persuasive evidence was offered to overcome the force of the statutory presumption in the instant case. * * * Thus, as § 42a-2-509(1) indicates, "[w]here the contract requires or authorizes the seller to ship the goods by carrier (a) if it does not require him to deliver them at a particular destination, the risk of loss passes to the buyer when the goods are duly delivered to the carrier." Accordingly, at the F.O.B. point, when the risk of loss shifted, Denver and Old Colony, as carriers, became the agents or bailees of defendant. * * * The risk of subsequent loss or delay rested on defendant, and not plaintiff. A disagreement arose between defendant's wife and the truck driver, resulting in nondelivery of the merchandise, retention thereof by the carrier, and, finally, disappearance of the shipment. The ensuing dispute was fundamentally a matter for resolution between defendant and the carriers, as his agents. Nothing in the outcome of that dispute could defeat or impair plaintiff's recovery against defendant.

       * * *

The court entertains substantial doubt about the credibility of the defense. Defendant initially professed an urgent need for the merchandise, for holiday sales. When, however, the delivery was tendered, on December 12, 1966, only some two weeks prior to Christmas, defendant, acting by his wife, saw fit to refuse the merchandise for the alleged reason that the truck driver was obligated to carry the cartons inside defendant's door. The defense arising out of the refusal is without merit. Defendant knew, or should have known, that his rejection exposed the shipment to time consuming delays and disputes. Hence, delivery in time for holiday business was actually frustrated, not by plaintiff, but rather by the action of defendant and his agent, based on a disagreement over a relatively minor item. Wholly apart from the conclusion, previously stated, that such refusal was the sole risk of defendant, the court finds that defendant's conduct was wrongful, arbitrary, and unreasonable, under all the circumstances.

In view of defendant's wrongful rejection, following the shifting of the risk of loss to him, he is liable to plaintiff for the entire purchase price of the merchandise.

Notice the comment in the next-to-the-last paragraph: "The court entertains substantial doubt about the credibility of the defense." In a civil case (as opposed to a criminal case), this is quite strong language. Judge Levine (a Connecticut judge) is making it clear that he thinks that Harrison is not telling the truth and that Harrison has concocted this refusal to accept the goods as an excuse because Harrison has changed his mind and does not want to receive and pay for the goods.

In any event, the judge does not really care what happened between the driver and the owner's wife in Connecticut. Why? Because the risk of loss is with the buyer in an "FOB, Los Angeles" contract. The buyer must pay for the goods, and if something happens to the goods in transit or at delivery, it is the buyer's problem, not the sellers.

Problem Solving. Please turn to Chapter Problems at the end of this chapter and solve Problem 16.5.

FOB Place of *Delivery*: (§ 2-319(1)(b). Contrary to what is discussed above, suppose that the apple contract between Milly and Jed provides that the sale will be "FOB Los Angeles." This is known as a "delivery" contract. (Recall, as noted above, that a *delivery* contract is unusual and that a *shipment* contract is presumed.) In this case, where the contract is FOB the place of destination, the rules change. In this context, § 2-319(b) provides that "the seller must at his own expense and risk transport the goods to that place [the destination] and there tender delivery of them . . ." This means, of course, that if the train derails en route to Los Angeles, Milly bears the loss.

RISK OF LOSS IN A "DELIVERY" CONTRACT: risk of loss shifts to buyer when seller tenders delivery at destination.

Risk of Loss in *Delivery* Contract: § 2-509(1)(b). In this case, with a destination contract, § 2-509(1)(b) provides the same result as just discussed. Here, § 2-509(1)(b) provides:

> Where the contract requires or authorizes the seller to ship the goods by carrier . . . if it *does* require him to deliver them at a particular destination and the goods are there duly tendered while in the possession of the carrier, *the risk of loss passes to the buyer* when the goods are there duly so tendered as to enable the buyer to take delivery.

In short, in a *delivery* contract—where the contract does require the seller to deliver the goods to a particular destination—the risk of loss shifts to the buyer when the goods are tendered to the buyer at the destination.

What does it mean to "tender" delivery? Section 2-503 answers this question by providing that the seller, Milly, must transport the apples to the delivery point and "put and hold conforming goods at the buyer's disposition and give the buyer any notification reasonably necessary to enable him to take delivery." Milly's tender of delivery must be at a "reasonable hour" and Jed must provide "facilities reasonably suited" to the delivery. [§ 2-503(1)(a) and (b)]

***Problem Solving*.** Please turn to Chapter Problems at the end of this chapter and solve Problem 16.6.

NonConforming Goods. In the risk of loss problems above it has been assumed that Milly has shipped *conforming* goods; that is, that Milly has shipped the goods that the contract calls for. Suppose, however, that the contract calls for Jonathan apples and Milly ships Delicious apples. In this case the goods are nonconforming. Section 2-510(1) provides that "where a tender or delivery of goods so fails to conform to the contract as to give a right of rejection the risk of their loss remains on the seller until cure or acceptance." That means, of course, that no matter whether the contract was a shipment or a delivery contract, the risk of loss remains on Milly until she has cured the problem or Jed has accepted the apples in their nonconforming condition.

Problem 16.1

This question focuses on the decision in *Synergistic Technologies v. IDB Mobile Communications*. Suppose that the contract between the parties (signed February 1) provided the following: (1) the hardware would be manufactured August 1; (2) the software programming would be finished September 1; (3) to facilitate financing of the transaction, title to the hardware and software would pass to the buyer when the contract was signed. Based on § 2-401, when did title to all of the goods pass to the buyer?

Problem 16.2

This question focuses on the decision in *Lane v. Honeycutt*. Suppose that Garrett had given Honeycutt the *title* to the boat, motor and trailer—all properly signed by John W. Willis. Would this change in the facts change the outcome in the case?

Problem 16.3

This question focuses on the decision in *Porter v. Wertz*. In that case, the Feigen Art Gallery lost because it did *not* buy from a *merchant* who had been *entrusted* with the painting. (Wertz was "a delicatessen employee.") Suppose, instead, that Wertz was a *merchant* who had stolen the painting from Porter. Under these facts, explain who would win, Porter or Feigen Art Gallery.

Problem 16.4

In the contract between Milly and Jed, assume that the contract is FOB Seattle and that Milly delivers the apples to the railroad and makes a reasonable contract for their transportation. Unintentionally, Milly forgets to notify Jed that the apples have been shipped. What effect, if any, does this omission have on the contract?

Problem 16.5

In the contract between Milly and Jed, assume that the contract is unclear about the transportation and delivery obligation. Who bears the risk of loss while the apples are in transit?

Problem 16.6

In *NINTH STREET EAST, LTD. v. Harrison*, suppose that the contract was a *delivery* contract, and not a *shipment* contract. Would that change in facts change the outcome?

Chapter 17
Warranties

Chapter Outline

OBJECTIVE : to learn about Sales warranties.

The objective of this chapter is to learn about warranties. The Sales article includes promises (called warranties) which are part of each sales contract, unless modified or excluded by the parties. The chapter is organized as follows:

- *Warranty of Title*. Unless otherwise agreed, each sales contract includes a warranty that the buyer will receive good title to the goods.

- *Express Warranty*. The goods tendered by the seller must match the statements, descriptions, samples or models which are part of the "basis of the bargain" between the parties. Sales "puffing" does not create an express warranty.

- *Implied Warranty of Merchantability*. Goods sold by a merchant must be merchantable. To be merchantable means that the goods must: meet trade standards; be of fair average quality; be fit for the ordinary purposes for which they are intended; not vary excessively in quality or quantity; be adequately contained, packaged and labeled; and, conform to any statements on the container or label. The serving for value of food or drink to be consumed either on the premises or elsewhere is included in the Sales article.

- *Implied Warranty of Fitness*. If the buyer relies on the seller's skill or judgment to select or furnish goods for a particular purpose, the goods must, in fact, be fit for that purpose.

- *Excluding or Modifying Warranties*. In general, all of the warranties described above may be modified by the agreement of the parties.

Introduction

WARRANTY is a contract promise.

A warranty is a promise. The Sales article includes several warranties (promises) which are automatically a part of each sales contract, although by common agreement they may be eliminated or modified. These warranties, and the process to eliminate or modify them, are as follows:

Warranties		
Warranty	*Section*	*Description*
Title	§ 2-312	Buyer is entitled to good title
Express	§ 2-313	Goods must match promises, descriptions and samples
Merchantability	§ 2-314	Goods sold by a merchant must be fit for ordinary purposes
Fitness	§ 2-315	Buyer may rely on the seller's skill and judgment
Exclusion or Modification	§ 2-316	Warranties may be excluded or modified

Warranty of Title

Section 2-312(1)(a) unambiguously provides that in a contract for sale, "the title [ownership] conveyed [to the buyer] shall be good , and its transfer rightful." This warranty applies unless the sales contract specifically provides otherwise. [§ 2-312(2)] Suppose that Jed, a private art collector, sells an oil painting to Milly for $10,000. (The painting is a picture of a pony entitled "Little Champion.") Jed had purchased the painting from Sam and it is later learned that Sam had stolen it from the real owner. Milly returns the painting to the owner and sues Jed, claiming that he has violated § 2-312(1). In this case, Milly will win because her title is not good and Jed has warranted that it would be.

Problem Solving. Please turn to Chapter Problems at the end of this chapter and solve Problem 17.1.

Suppose, in the problem above, that Jed (acting in good faith) told Milly during negotiations that he had been hearing rumors that some paintings sold by Sam may have been stolen. He tells Milly that because of the rumors he will sell her the "Little Champion" painting for $5,000, and not $10,000. Because of the rumors, he says that he cannot guarantee good title. Under these circumstances can Milly successfully sue Jed for violation of § 2-312(1)? The answer, of course, is no because § 2-312(2) is clear that good title is not required when specific language in the sales contract shows that Jed "is purporting to sell only such right or title as he or a third person may have."

Express Warranty

EXPRESS WARRANTY : is created from the seller's statements, descriptions and samples.

Statements, Descriptions and Samples. Express warranties are created when a seller makes statements and uses descriptions and samples to persuade a customer to buy. Thus, an olive oil salesman may tell a prospective customer: "the oil you will receive will be light in color, just like this sample;" a computer salesman may tell a prospective customer: "this computer will handle Prometheus 5.0 software;" and, a car salesman may tell a prospective customer that "this car will get 21 miles per gallon."

"Puffing." "You're gonna love this one; this Super Glide V-8 is the best car on the road; you can't go wrong." This is type of language is referred to as salesman's "puffing," and words of this nature do not create an express warranty. Nor, in general, do predictions about the future create an express warranty.

In the following case, *Martin Rispens & Son v. Hall Farms,* the court had to decide whether language on the side of a can of watermelon seeds ("top quality seeds with high vitality, vigor and germination") created an express warranty, or whether it was mere "puffing." The plaintiff, Hall Farms,[1] purchased watermelon seed from the defendant, Martin Rispens & Son, who was the seller. (Petoseed was the seed grower.) The resulting watermelon crop was infected with fruit blotch as a result of defective seeds. Hall Farms sued the seller and grower claiming, among other things, breach of express warranties. The express warranty claims were based on the statement "top quality seeds with high vitality, vigor and germination" which was printed on the label on the cans of seed. In the following opinion the Supreme Court of Indiana decides whether the express warranty claims of Hall Farms should be summarily dismissed. (Notice how *stare decisis*[2] plays a part as the court considers prior decisions in the process of making it's decision.)

Martin Rispens & Son v. Hall Farms, Inc.
621 N.E. 2d 1078 (1993)

KRAHULIK, Justice.
* * *

An express warranty requires some representation, term or statement as to how the product is warranted. *Candlelight Homes, Inc. v. Zornes* (1981), Ind. App., 414 N.E.2d 9980, 983. Stated another way, an express warranty may be created if the seller asserts a fact of which the buyer is ignorant, but not if the seller merely states an opinion on a matter on which the seller has no special knowledge and on which the buyer may be expected also to have an opinion and to exercise his judgment. *Royal Business Machines, Inc. v. Lorraine Corp.,* 633 F.2d 34, 41 (7th Cir. 1980). Thus, a seller's factual statement that a machine had a new engine constituted an express warranty. *Perfection Cut, Inc. v. Olsen* (1984), Ind.App., 470 N.E.2d 94, 95. Assurances by a seller that carpet would be replaced if any defects surfaced within one year of purchase was sufficient to create an express warranty. *Carpetland U.S.A. v. Payne* (1989), Ind.App., 536 N.E.2d 306, 308.

By contrast, statements of the seller's opinion, not made as a representation of fact, do not create an express warranty. *Thompson Farms, Inc. v. Corno Feed Products* (1977), 173 Ind.App. 682, 708, 366 N.E.2d 3, 18; *James J. White & Robert S. Summers, 1 Uniform*

---

[1] Originally, this case was probably known as *Hall Farms, Inc. v. Martin Rispens & Son*, but (confusingly) the case name was switched on appeal to *Martin Rispens & Son v. Hall Farms, Inc.* because Martin Rispens & Son are the appellants.

[2] *Stare decisis* is discussed in Chapter 1.

Commercial Code § 9-4, at 445 (3d ed. 1988) (hereafter *"White & Summers"*). The statement that a product "is the best" is simply puffing which does not create an express warranty. *Thompson Farms,* 173 Ind.App.at 708, 366 N.E.2d at 18.

Petoseed. The label on the Petoseed cans of Prince Charles watermelon seeds states that they are "top quality seeds with high vitality, vigor and germination." This printed label is the sole basis for Hall Farms' express warranty claims against Petoseed.

Hall Farms equates the phrase "top quality seeds" with the statement that the goods were "in good order, condition and repair," found to be an express warranty in *Continental Sand & Gravel, Inc. v. K & K Sand & Gravel, Inc.,* 755 F.2d 87, 90-91 (7ᵗʰ Cir. 1985), and with the statement that a truck was "road ready," held to be an express warranty in *Wiseman v. Wolfe's Terre Haute Auto Auction, Inc.* (1984), Ind.App., 459 N.E.2d 736, 737. We do not agree. The phrase contains no definitive statement as to how the product is warranted or any assertion of fact concerning the product, but is merely the opinion of Petoseed that the seeds are "top quality." The Court of Appeals correctly concluded that the statement "top quality seeds" is a "classic example of puffery." 601 N.E.2d at 435.

Hall Farms also argues that the Court of Appeals erred in holding that, although the phrase "with high vitality, vigor and germination" constituted an express warranty, Petoseed did not breach this warranty because the growth of the seeds conformed to the affirmation on the label. 601 N.E.2d at 435. This phrase is a promise that the seeds will perform in a certain manner; it is not simply the opinion of the seller. However, we are not able to determine as a matter of law whether this express warranty was breached. On the one hand, Petoseed asserts that the promise made was only that the seeds would germinate and grow, which according to Mark Hall, they did. On the other hand, Hall Farms asserts that the presence of the disease inhibited the vitality and vigor with which the plants grew. We agree with Hall Farms that the issue of whether the seeds which carried the watermelon fruit blotch had the capacity for natural growth and survival is one for the finder of fact. Thus, summary judgment is not appropriate on this express warranty claim.

Rispens.. Rispens' purchase order, the sole basis for Hall Farm's express warranty claim against Rispens, stated in pertinent part:

> [T]he seller agrees to deliver such seeds in good merchantable condition as hereinafter defined and of good germination for the crop of the current year. The phrase "in good merchantable condition" is defined as seeds properly fitted for seeding purposes, by thorough screening, and where necessary by hand picking; approximately free from foreign seeds distinguishable by their appearance.

The parties agree that the language "properly fitted for seeding purposes," created an express warranty, but they assign different meanings to it. Rispens asserts that the warranty is merely that the can contains Prince Charles watermelon seeds and not some other type of seed. Hall Farms asserts that the warranty contains a quality component promising that the seeds would be free of a latent bacteria such as the watermelon fruit blight. Although courts decide as a matter of law the existence of express warranties when the representations are in writing, if the writing is ambiguous, then its interpretation is one of fact. *First Fed. Sav. Bank v. Key Markets, Inc.* (1990), Ind., 559 N.E.2d 600, 603-4. Questions of fact exist as to the meaning of the express warranty and, thus, the Court of Appeals correctly held that Rispens is not entitled to summary judgment on whether this express warranty was breached. 601 N.E.2d at 437.

Hall Farms also argues that the phrase, "strictly high grade seeds," which appeared at the top of the purchase order, created an express warranty. The Court of Appeals held that this language may have constituted an express warranty, but Hall Farms failed to meet its burden of proof by presenting evidence about the meaning of this phrase, so Rispens was entitled to summary judgment. 601 N.E.2d at 435-6. Whether Rispens gave an express warranty which was breached encompasses a question of fact: in the seed industry, does "high grade" connote some promise that the seeds will be free from disease or is it merely puffing. However, it is Rispens' burden, as the movant, to show the absence of material fact. Having failed to do so, Rispens is not entitled to summary judgment on the express warranty claim.

      * * *

    In summary, we * * * remand this case to the trial court with directions to enter summary judgment against Hall Farms on all claims except those of breach of express warranties * * * and to proceed in a manner consistent with this opinion.

    Notice how carefully the court considered the language that was printed on the side of the seed can. For example, did the phrase "top quality seeds" create an express warranty? The answer is no; this is a statement of opinion and mere "puffery." How about the statement that the seeds would grow "with high vitality, vigor and germination"? Indeed, the seeds *grew*, but was that inhibited by the watermelon fruit blotch? Only an expert could answer that question; thus, summary judgment was not granted. It was necessary to have an expert describe the effect of watermelon fruit blotch on the growth of watermelons.

    What happens in the *Hall Farms* case at this point? The case returns to the trial court where experts will testify concerning the following points: (1) do seeds carrying the watermelon fruit blotch have the capacity for natural growth and survival, and (2) in the seed industry does "high grade" mean that the seeds will be free from disease, or is this language mere puffing? Based on the answers to these questions, the trial court will be entitled to make further rulings.

    Part of the Basis of the Bargain. The preceding discussion has focused on whether certain statements, descriptions or samples constitute an express warranty. If they do constitute an express warranty, the next question is whether the express warranty is part of the contract between the parties.

BASIS OF THE BARGAIN: to become part of a sales contract, a statement, description or sample must part of the bargain between the parties.

    Section 2-313 enforces the content of a seller's statements, descriptions or samples if they are "part of the basis of the bargain." In general terms, the phrase "part of the bargain," may be viewed as another way of saying that the seller's statements, descriptions or samples must be "part of the deal." The "part of the basis of the basis of the bargain" phrase refers to things the parties talk about, negotiate over, and rely upon.

    In the following case, *Harris v. Ford Motor Co., Inc.*, the plaintiff, William Harris, purchased a new 1989 Ford pickup truck. Some months later, one of the truck fenders began to discolor and, upon investigation, Harris learned that the fender had been scratched while the truck was being transported from the manufacturing plant to the dealer. The dealer had repaired and repainted the fender before selling the truck as "new" to Harris. Harris sued, claiming violation of an express warranty. Ford, and it's dealer, responded that the "New Car Warranty" book was in the truck when it was sold and that the warranty provisions therein allowed the seller to repair damage occurring while transporting the truck. Harris claimed, however, that the warranty book was *not* in the truck when he received it, but was delivered later. Because the warranty book was delivered *after* the bargain had been made, he said it was not "part of the bargain."

Harris v. Ford Motor Co., Inc.
845 F.Supp. 1511 (1994)

DeMENT, District Judge.
* * *

The plaintiff has also asserted that the disclaimer should not apply because the warranty booklet containing the disclaimer was delivered to the plaintiff "long after they had purchased the vehicle and thus was not a part of the 'basis of the bargain.'" * * * They argue that the disclaimer must have been delivered to them prior to the time they obligated themselves to purchase the vehicle. The evidence demonstrates that, at the time William Harris purchased the vehicle, the "New Car Warranty" was in the glove compartment of the truck, and that the plaintiff was aware of its presence. * * * Based upon this testimony, the court finds that the warranty was delivered to the plaintiff at the time of the sale and was part of the "basis of the bargain."

[Summary Judgment granted to Defendant.]

Notice that the decision above was on summary judgment, which means, of course, that the trial court judge viewed the case as being so clear-cut in favor of the defendant that there was no need for a trial. Because the truck warranties (and their limitations) were—to the buyer's knowledge—in the truck at the time of purchase, they were part of the basis of the bargain.

Problem Solving. Please turn to Chapter Problems at the end of this chapter and solve Problem 17.2.

Warranty of Merchantability

WARRANTY OF MERCHANTABILITY is only created by a merchant.

Sales by a Merchant. The warranty of merchantability created in § 2-314 is different than the other warranties because it applies only to sales by a *merchant*. A "merchant" is defined as "a person who deals in goods of the kind or otherwise by his occupation holds himself out as having knowledge or skill peculiar to the practices or goods involved in the transaction . . ." [§ 2-104(1)]

Merchantable. Goods sold by a merchant must be *"merchantable"* which means that they must meet the following standards:

§ 2-314(2) Merchantability Requirements	
Requirement	Explanation
(a) pass without objection in the trade under the contract description	For example, in the trade, is "fresh" orange juice the same as juice made from concentrate? If not, the latter cannot be substituted for the former "without objection."
(b) in the case of fungible goods, are of fair average quality within the description	(a) and (b) apply to agricultural bulk products and are to be read together.[3] If the contract is for "large" apples, are the delivered apples large on the basis of a fair average?
(c) are fit for the ordinary purposes for which such goods are used	A table knife, for example, must be suitable for eating, but need not be suitable when used as a screwdriver to repair a dishwasher.
(d) run, within the variations permitted by the agreement, of even kind, quality and quantity within each unit and among all units involved	How many cherries should be in a cherry pie? If the contract requires "one cup" in each pie, a precise cherry count is not required, but an "evenness" or reasonable balance is required, within the variations permitted by the agreement.
(e) are adequately contained, packaged, and labeled as the agreement may require	Unless otherwise agreed, frozen meat pies should, for example, should be in a container which allows cooking in a household oven.
(f) conform to the promises or affirmations of fact made on the container or label if any	If the label on frozen meat pies states "beef" pies, pork meat may not be substituted.

A virtue of the Sales article is that a buyer may contract with a merchant and have the advantage of all of the contract promises above, without the necessity of negotiating each of them separately. All of these warranties of merchantability apply, unless the contract between the parties negate or limit them.

FIT FOR ORDINARY PURPOSES: to be merchantable, goods must be fit for the ordinary purposes for which they are intended.

As shown in the table above, § 2-314(2) requires that to be merchantable, goods sold by a merchant must meet six different requirements. These requirements

---

[3] U.C.C. § 2-314 (1962) comment 7.

are widely used by purchasers who claim the existence of defects in products they have purchased.

For example, Milly sells 1,000 gallons of "fresh" orange juice to JedMart. When the juice arrives, it is found to be "from concentrate," and the plastic containers are very thin, and 50 gallons of juice have been lost because the containers ruptured. Even though there is no provision in the contract about these problems, the warranty of merchantability applies, and the juice must meet each of the six requirements of merchantability.

In this case, the JedMart will rely on the testimony of trade experts who will testify—if it is so—that orange juice labeled as "fresh" is not acceptable in the orange juice trade (it will not "pass without objection in the trade") if it is made from concentrate. Likewise, trade experts will describe the packaging that is normal in the orange juice trade for shipping orange juice. If the packaging used by Milly was less than that described by the experts, then the juice is not "adequately contained, packaged, and labeled."

Food or Drink to be Consumed. Special problems are caused where a buyer purchases food for purposes of consumption—not resale. Suppose that Milly buys a hamburger from Jed's Burger Emporium and, while eating the hamburger, cuts her mouth on a sliver of beef bone in the cooked meat. She claims that the sale of the hamburger violates § 2-314(2)(c) because Jed is a merchant and the hamburger is *not* "fit for the ordinary purposes for which such goods [the hamburger] are used."

In response to Milly's claim, Jed cleverly says that he has not violated the warranty of merchantability (§ 2-314) because the Sales article does not apply. It does not apply, he says, because there is more *service* involved in the transaction than product. In short, Jed argues that he and Milly are not involved in contract which is predominantly for the sale of goods. Jed's argument would be a very good one, except that the authors of the Sales article anticipated it with the following sentence in §2-314(1): "Under this section (§ 2-314) the serving for value of food or drink to be consumed either on the premises or elsewhere is a sale."

With respect to claims that food is not "fit for the ordinary purposes" for which it is intended, the difficulty is fashioning a *test* to separate those food products which are fit from those which are not. Most courts use a "reasonable expectations" test. Using this test, a court asks whether it is reasonable for a consumer to expect to find a sliver of beef bone in a hamburger patty. Because that is not a reasonable expectation, Milly would win her case.

In the following case, *Webster v. Blue Ship Tea Room, Inc.*, a customer in a sea food restaurant ordered fish chowder. The chowder included large chunks of fish, and in the process of eating some of that fish a piece of fish bone from the fish became caught in the throat of the plaintiff, Priscilla Webster. She sued, claiming a violation of the implied warranty of merchantability which requires food (which is sold for consumption) to be fit for the ordinary purposes for which it is intended.

Webster v. Blue Ship Tea Room, Inc.
198 N.E.2d 309 (1964)

REARDON, Justice.

* * *

We must decide whether a fish bone lurking in a fish chowder, about the ingredients of which there is no other complaint, constitutes a breach of implied warranty under applicable provisions of the Uniform Commercial Code, the annotations to which are not helpful on this point. As the judge put it in his charge, "Was the fish chowder fit to be eaten and wholesome?***[N]obody is claiming that the fish itself wasn't wholesome.**But the bone of contention here—I don't mean that for a pun—but was this fish bone a foreign substance that made the fish chowder unwholesome or not fit to be eaten?"

* * *

The defendant asserts that here was a native New Englander eating fish chowder in a "quaint" Boston dining place where she had been before; that "[f]ish chowder, as it is served and enjoyed by New Englanders, is a hearty dish, originally designed to satisfy the appetites of our seamen and fishermen"; that "[t]his court knows well that we are not talking of some insipid broth as is customarily served to convalescents." We are asked to rule in such fashion that no chef is forced "to reduce the pieces of fish in the chowder to minuscule size in an effort to ascertain if they contained any pieces of bone." "In so ruling," we are told (in the defendant's brief), "the court will not only uphold its reputation for legal knowledge and acumen, but will, as loyal sons of Massachusetts, save our world-renowned fish chowder from degenerating into an insipid broth containing the mere essence of its former stature as a culinary masterpiece." Notwithstanding these passionate entreaties we are bond to examine with detachment the nature of fish chowder and what might happen to it under varying interpretations of the Uniform Commercial Code.

* * * [The recipe for fish chowder is described here in delicious detail.]

Thus, we consider a dish which for many long years, if well made, has been made generally as outlined above. It is not too much to say that a person sitting down in New England to consume a good New England fish chowder embarks on a gustatory adventure which may entail the removal of some fish bones from his bowl as he proceeds. We are not inclined to tamper with age old recipes by any amendment reflecting the plaintiff's view of the effect of the Uniform Commercial Code upon them. We are aware of the heavy body of case law involving foreign substances in food, but we sense a strong distinction between them and those relative to unwholesomeness of the food itself, e.g., tainted mackerel * * * and a fish bone in a fish chowder. Certain Massachusetts cooks might cavil at the ingredients contained in the chowder in this case in that it lacked the heartening lift of salt pork. In any event, we consider that the joys of life in New England include the ready availability of fresh fish chowder. We should be prepared to cope with the hazards of fish bones, the occasional presence of which in chowders is, it seems to us, to be anticipated, and which, in the light of a hallowed tradition, do not impair their fitness or merchantability. While we are buoyed up in this conclusion by Shapiro v. Hotel Statler Corp., 132 F.Supp. 891 (S.D.Cal.), in which the bone which afflicted the plaintiff appeared in "Hot Barquette of Seafood Mornay," we know that the United States District Court of Southern California, situated as are we upon a coast, might be expected to share our views. We are most impressed, however by Allen v. Grafton, 170 Ohio St. 249, 164 N.E.2d 167, where in Ohio, the Midwest, in a case where the plaintiff was injured by a piece of oyster shell in an order of fried oysters, Mr. Justice Taft (now Chief Justice) in a majority opinion held that "the possible presence of a piece of oyster shell in or attached to an oyster is so well known to anyone who eats oysters that we can say as a matter of law that one who eats

> oysters can reasonably anticipate and guard against eating such a piece of shell * * *."
>
> Thus, while we sympathize with the plaintiff who has suffered a peculiarly New England injury, the order must be * * *. Judgment for the defendant.

Prior to the *Webster* opinion, the discussion focused on the point that most courts use a "reasonable expectations" test for purposes of deciding whether a food product is fit for the ordinary purposes for which it is intended. Did the *Webster* court use this test? Please answer this question in the following Chapter Problem.

Problem Solving. Please turn to Chapter Problems at the end of this chapter and solve Problem 17.3.

Warranty of Fitness

WARRANTY OF FITNESS arises when a buyer relies on a seller to select or furnish suitable goods.

The last of this group of warranties is the warranty of fitness. A warranty of fitness is created by the provisions of § 2-315 when a buyer relies on a seller to recommend goods which will fulfill the buyer's needs. Jed, for example, operates a summer camp and goes to Milly's Motors to buy outboard motors. He says that the motors must be powerful enough to pull a water skier. Knowing the purpose for which the motors will be used, and understanding that Jed is relying on her expertise to select suitable goods, Milly recommends the Viking 250 outboard motor. If, in fact, the motor is not powerful enough to pull a water skier, Milly has violated the warranty of fitness.

Later in this chapter is a case entitled *Trans-Aire Intern. v. Northern Adhesive Co.* in which the buyer claimed that defective adhesive violated a warranty of fitness. In that case, just like the one with Milly and the outboard motor, the question is whether the buyer, in fact, relied on the seller's expertise and judgment to select a product.

Problem Solving. Please turn to Chapter Problems at the end of this chapter and solve Problem 17.4.

Excluding or Modifying Warranties

EXCLUDING OR MODIFYING WARRANTIES: all warranties maybe excluded or modified.

Warranties may be excluded or modified by the terms of the contract between the parties. The requirements by which this is accomplished are described in § 2-316 and are different depending on which warranty is involved:

Express Warranty. An express warranty may be negated or limited by the words or conduct of the contracting parties, but the result cannot be unreasonable. [§ 2-316(1)] Suppose that Jed, a printer, enters into a contract to deliver 100 print copies of the famous painting "Alaskan Sunset," to Milly, the operator of a bookstore. In their contract negotiations, Jed sends a sample print, but includes the following notation: "I can't guarantee that the orange and red colors will reproduce exactly like the sample because the paper you have selected may absorb ink differently than that in the sample."

Normally, § 2-313(1)(c) creates an express warranty that the delivered goods will conform to samples that were part of the contract negotiations. But, in the example above, if the orange colors do not reproduce well—as Jed suggested might happen—Milly cannot successfully claim that the express warranty between them has been breached because the warranty was modified by the language of the negotiations. And, a limitation of this kind is allowed because it is obviously reasonable.

Implied Warranty of Merchantability. An implied warranty of merchantability may be excluded or modified. To accomplish this "the language must mention merchantability and in case of a writing must be conspicuous." [§ 2-316(2)] A warranty of merchantability may be "excluded by expressions like 'as is', 'with all faults' or other language which in common understanding calls the buyer's attention to the exclusion of warranties and makes plain that there is no implied warranty." [§ 2-316(3)(a)] In general, language excluding a warranty of merchantability "is sufficient if it states, for example, that 'There are no warranties which extend beyond the description on the face hereof."

Normally, § 2-314 creates an implied warranty that goods sold by a merchant will be "merchantable." Thus, in the apple transaction described above in this chapter, Jed, the buyer may expect that the apples he is purchasing will, among other things, be "of fair average quality." [§2-314(2)(b)] In fact, the apples Milly is selling are wormy and bruised and are fit only for applesauce or juice. In this case, she will be careful that the contract description refers only to "apples for sauce or juice." And, to avoid any claim that the apples she is selling must be fit for general purposes, she will also include language in the contract that provides: "There is no warranty of merchantability with respect to the subject goods, which are purchased with all faults." In this fashion, Milly has excluded the warranty of merchantability, and in the context of this contract, the exclusion is reasonable.

Implied Warranty of Fitness. An implied warranty of fitness may be excluded or modified. To accomplish this "the exclusion must be by a writing and conspicuous." As with the warranty of merchantability, a warranty of fitness may be "excluded by expressions like 'as is', 'with all faults' or other language which in common understanding calls the buyer's attention to the exclusion of warranties and makes plain that there is no implied warranty." [§ 2-316(3)(a)] And, language excluding a warranty of fitness "is sufficient if it states, for example, that 'There are no warranties which extend beyond the description on the face hereof."

An implied warranty of fitness is created when a seller understands "that the buyer is relying on the seller's skill or judgment to select or furnish suitable goods." (§ 2-315) For example, Jed goes to Milly's agricultural supply where he asks for a water pump which will pump water to the surface which is 20 feet below the ground. Milly says that she "recommends the Widget XJH." Although she is confident the pump will satisfy Jed, she is also aware that the information on box says "recommended for water down to 15 feet." To protect herself, Milly prints on the sales invoice: "There are no warranties which extend beyond the description on the face of the pump box." She draws Jed's attention to this limitation, and her reasons for adding this limitation. This language excludes the implied warranty of fitness. Under the facts it is reasonable and will be enforced.

The following case, *Trans-Aire Intern. v. Northern Adhesive Co.*, discusses issues related to both the creation and exclusion of an implied warranty of fitness. Plaintiff, Trans-Aire, converted automotive vans into recreational vehicles. Part of that conversion process included installing carpet and ceiling fabrics using an adhesive (Adhesive 7448) purchased from the defendant, Northern Adhesive Company. Stephen Fribley, a Trans-Aire engineer, tested the adhesive before it was purchased, but he did not test it under high temperatures which is the time an adhesive is most likely to fail. When the adhesive failed under high temperatures, Trans-Aire sued Northern claiming violation of an implied warranty of fitness. [§ 2-315] In response, Northern said that there was no such warranty because Trans-Aire had the opportunity to examine the adhesive as closely as it desired before purchasing it, and that a thorough examination would have revealed any defects. [§ 2-316(3)(b)]

Trans-Aire Intern. v. Northern Adhesive Co.
882 F.2d 1254 (7ᵗʰ Cir. 1989)

KANNE, Circuit Judge.
* * *

Initially, we hold that the district court correctly concluded that no warranty of fitness for a particular purpose existed. We agree with the district court that Trans-Aire cannot demonstrate that it relied upon Northern's skill or judgment in deciding to purchase Adhesive 7448, even assuming that Northern knew of the purpose for which Trans-Aire needed the adhesive.

Trans-Aire's chief engineer, Fribley, expressly stated in a deposition that he did not rely upon Northern's skill or judgment when Trans-Aire decided to purchase Adhesive 7448. Trans-Aire asserts that Fribley was not authorized to and did not negotiate the purchase of Adhesive 7448 and therefore his testimony is not dispositive of the issue whether Trans-Aire relied upon Northern's judgment. However, Trans-Aire's president, Higgins, clearly did make the final purchase decision and the record supports Northern's assertion that Higgins relied upon Fribley's recommendation. Furthermore, it is undisputed that Fribley's recommendation and Higgins' final decision were based upon the tests which Fribley conducted, not any express or implied representations made by Northern. We therefore must agree with the district court that Trans-Aire cannot demonstrate that an implied warranty of fitness for a particular purpose existed.

However, we need not dwell upon this issue because we agree with the district court that Trans-Aire excluded all implied warranties by its actions. Under section 2-316 of the Illinois Commercial Code, implied warranties are excluded when a party examines a product or sample "as fully as it desires" or "refuses to examine" the product or sample in a reasonable manner given the circumstances of the case. The undisputed facts and circumstances of this case preclude Trans-Aire's attempts to maintain an action based upon breaches of any existing implied warranties of fitness for a particular purpose or of merchantability.

As we indicated earlier, Northern offered the deposition testimony of Trans-Aire's former chief engineer, Fribley, to support its defense that Trans-Aire in fact tested samples of Adhesive 7448 "as fully as it desired." Fribley's undisputed testimony establishes that while he was Trans-Aire's chief engineer, Trans-Aire experienced problems with a 3M adhesive which it was using in its van conversion process and that he had contacted Northern to find a replacement. Northern sent a sample of Adhesive 7448 to Trans-Aire which Fribley tested in the usual laminating equipment. However, rather than testing the adhesive under summer-like conditions, the same conditions under which the 3M product had failed, Fribley stated that he performed the tests under "cool" conditions in the plant. He found the adhesive to be satisfactory under these conditions and reported the results to Trans-Aire's president, Higgins.

Fribley apparently realized that the cool conditions were inadequate to test the adhesive's performance characteristics during warmer weather. According to his undisputed testimony, he suggested to Higgins that the adhesive undergo heat testing because he knew that the inherent nature of contact adhesives is to soften with heat. Nevertheless, Trans-Aire's president believed that "the testing we had done proved the product satisfactory for our application."

Upon these facts, we must agree with the district court's finding that Trans-Aire clearly tested the samples as fully as it desired and refused to conduct further tests which would have confirmed a characteristic of contact adhesives which they already knew to be true, that they soften with heat. Trans-Aire attempts to argue that it did not have the means to discover the "latent defects" of the adhesive, because of the cool plant conditions at the time the tests were performed, and that section 2-316 does not exclude the implied warranties under these circumstances. *See* Ill.Ann.Stat. Ch. 26, para. 2-316 Comment 8 (Smith-Hurd 1963 & Supp. 1989) ("an examination under circumstances which do not permit chemical or other testing of the goods would not exclude defects which could be ascertained only by such testing"). We agree with the district court that this argument is without merit.

* * *

The district court's decision [granting summary judgment to Northern] is AFFIRMED.

No implied warranty of fitness was created because the buyer, Trans-Aire, had the opportunity inspect the adhesive in hot-weather conditions and chose not to. Before entering into the contract, if a buyer negligently examines the goods (or samples or models of the goods) or refuses to examine the goods—after demand by the seller that they be examined—"there is no implied warranty with regard to defects which an examination ought in the circumstances to have revealed to him." [§ 2-316(3)(b)]

__Problem Solving__. Please turn to Chapter Problems at the end of this chapter and solve Problem 17.5.

Chapter Problems

Problem 17.1

In *Porter v. Wertz,* in Chapter 16, Porter, the owner of a painting entrusted it to two crooks named Von Maker and Wertz who subsequently (and fraudulently) sold it to Feigen. When Porter sued to recover the painting (or it's value), Feigen had to pay Porter. However, in Chapter Seventeen, in the text just preceding this question, it is said that Mary, who likewise buys a stolen painting (as Feigen did) will "win." Solve this problem: why does Feigen "lose," and Mary "win?"

Problem 17.2

This question focuses on *Harris v. Ford Motor Co., Inc.* Suppose that the court found that the warranty booklet was *not* in the truck when it was purchased, just as Harris claimed. How, if at all, would this change in the facts change the outcome of the case?

Problem 17.3

There are two tests that a court may use to determine whether food is fit for the ordinary purposes for which such goods are used. One test is the so-called "foreign-natural" test. Using this test, the question is whether the "defect" is natural to the product, like a cherry pit in a cherry pie, or foreign to the product, like glass in a hamburger.. The other test is the so-called "reasonable expectations" test discussed in the chapter. In *Webster v. Blue Ship Tea room, Inc.*, which test did the court use to determine whether the chowder was "fit for the ordinary purposes for which such goods are used?" Did the court use the "foreign-natural" test or the "reasonable expectations" test?

Problem 17.4

Suppose that Jed goes to Milly's Motors and asks them to recommend a motor for his new 15 foot boat. Milly recommends a Viking 250 outboard motor. Thereafter, Jed attempts to pull his brother-in-law on waterskis and the motor is not powerful enough. He sues for violation of an implied warranty of fitness. [2-315] Will Jed win?

Problem 17.5

This question focuses on *Trans-Aire Intern. V. Northern Adhesive Co.* Suppose, that in the contracting process, Trans-Aire told Northern that it had had problems in the past with adhesive in hot-weather conditions and that it wished Northern to recommend an adhesive that would work well in hot-weather conditions. Thereafter, Northern recommended Adhesive 7448. Trans-Aire did not examine it; and, the adhesive failed. Is there an implied warranty of fitness, or has any such warranty been eliminated by the provisions of § 2-316(3)(b)?

Chapter 18
Performance and Remedies

Chapter Objective

OBJECTIVE is to learn performance and remedy rules.

The first objective of this chapter is to learn the rules by which a seller and buyer perform their contract obligations. The second objective of this chapter is to learn the "remedies" available to a seller, if the buyer does not perform as required; and, to learn the "remedies" available to a buyer, if the seller does not perform as required. The chapter is organized as follows:

Performance

- *Good Faith.* Each party to a contract must act in good faith, which means honesty in fact. In addition, merchants must observe reasonable commercial standards of fair dealing in their trade.

- *Performance by the Seller.* The goods delivered by the seller must strictly conform to the contract requirements. This is called the "perfect tender" rule. Special rules apply to performance by installments. The doctrine of commercial impracticability excuses a seller from contract performance.

- *Performance by the Buyer.* A buyer has the right to inspect goods before accepting them. If the goods conform to the contract, the buyer must accept them. Under limited circumstances, a buyer may revoke acceptance. The buyer must pay for conforming goods which have been accepted.

Remedies

- *Seller's Remedies.* In general, if a buyer repudiates the contract, the seller need not perform and may sue to recover damages calculated as the contract price minus fair market value of the goods. If the goods have been delivered, the seller may recover the contract price.

- *Buyer's Remedies.* In general, if a seller repudiates the contract, the buyer need not perform and may sue to recover damages calculated as the market price minus the contract price. The buyer may, if necessary "cover," which means the buyer may purchase replacement goods at the market price.

Introduction

This chapter deals with the duty of the seller and the buyer of a contract to *perform* as they have agreed, and the *remedies* that the seller or the buyer is entitled to in the event the contract is not performed as agreed.

Good Faith

Each party to a contract must act in *good faith*, which means honesty in fact. (§ 1-203) The obligation of good faith cannot be disclaimed by the parties. On the point of disclaimer, it will be recalled that, in general, the Sales article allows contracting parties to tailor a contract to suit their particular needs. (The ability to fit a contract to the needs of the parties is often signaled by the introductory phrase of many code sections which begins "unless the parties otherwise agree," and by the provisions of § 2-316 which allows the parties to negate or limit code warranties.) But, with respect to good faith, the parties are not allowed to "otherwise agree" or to disclaim.

With respect to good faith, merchants are held to a higher standard than other contracting parties. Section 2-103(1)(b) provides a special definition of good faith which applies to merchants only: "'Good faith' in the case of a merchant means honest in fact *and the observance of reasonable commercial standards of fair dealing in the trade.*"

Problem Solving. Please turn to Chapter Problems at the end of this chapter and solve Problem 18.1.

Performance by the Seller

Perfect Tender. The goods delivered by the seller in a sales transaction must strictly *conform* to the contract requirements. If *fish* chowder is the contract description, *clam* chowder will not do. If *brown* stockings are ordered by the buyer, *tan* stockings will not do. The requirement that the goods must strictly conform to the contract description is found in § 2-601 which provides that "unless otherwise agreed . . . if the goods or the tender of delivery *fail in any respect* to conform to the contract, the buyer may . . . reject the whole.

The common law doctrine of "substantial performance" does not apply to sales transactions. In discussions about common law contracts it was learned, for example, that performance of a contract calling for construction of a house with a black roof must be accepted even though the roof is brown. This is called substantial performance. (The problem is resolved by reducing the amount to be paid by the buyer by the amount necessary to alter the roof color.) But, as noted above, substantial performance is not accepted in a sales transaction, only complete compliance with the contract is allowed. This rule is called the "perfect tender" rule.

In the following case, *Moulton Cavity & Mold, Inc. v. Lyn-Flex Ind.*, the trial judge made the mistake of thinking that the doctrine of substantial performance could be applied to performance of a sales contract. Lyn-Flex manufactured and sold innersoles for shoes, and they contracted with Moulton to produce the molds that would be used to make the innersoles. The molds provided by Moulton were never quite right. The most serious problem "was 'flashing,' that is, a seepage of plastic along the seam where the two halves of the mold meet." Although the molds admittedly "could not produce a saleable innersole," Moulton nevertheless sued for payment, claiming substantial performance of the contract.

Moulton Cavity & Mold v. Lyn-Flex Industries
396 A.2d 1024 (1979)

DELAHANTY, Justice.
* * *

After the presiding Justice had charged the jury, counsel for plaintiff requested at side bar that the jury be instructed on the doctrine of substantial performance. Counsel for defendant entered a timely objection to the proposed charge which objection was overruled. The court then supplemented its charge as follows:

> The only point of clarification that I'll make, ladies and gentlemen, is that I've referred a couple of times to performance of a contract and you, obviously, have to determine no matter which way you view the contract to be, and there might even be a possible third way that I haven't even considered, whether the contract whatever it is has been performed and there is a doctrine that you should be aware of in considering that. That is the doctrine of substantial performance.

> It is not required that performance be in any case one hundred percent complete in order to entitle a party to enforcement of their contractual rights. That is not to say within the confines of this case that the existence of flashing would be excused or not be excused. It is just a recognition on the part of the law when we talk about performance, probably if we took any contract you could always find something of no substance that was not completed one hundred percent. It is for you to determine that whether it has been substantially performed or not and what in fact constitutes substantial performance.

> In your consideration, and as I say in this case, that's not to intimate that something like flashing is to be disregarded or to be considered. It's up to you based upon facts.

The jury returned a verdict in favor of plaintiff in the amount of $14,480.82.

* * *

[S]ection 2-601 states that, with certain exceptions not here applicable, the buyer has the right to reject "if the goods or the tender of delivery fail *in any respect* to conform to the contract . . ." (emphasis supplied). Those few courts that have considered the question agree that the perfect tender rule has survived the enactment of the Code. * * * We, too, are convinced of the soundness of this position.

In light of the foregoing discussion, it is clear that the presiding Justice's charge was erroneous and, under the circumstances, reversibly so. The jury was informed that "[i]t is not required that performance be in any case one hundred percent complete in order to entitle a

> party to enforcement of their contractual rights." Under this instruction, the jury was free to find that although plaintiff had not tendered perfectly conforming molds within the agreed period (assuming the jury found that the parties had in fact agreed on a specific time period for completion) it had nevertheless substantially performed the contract within the agreed time frame and was merely making minor adjustments when defendant backed out of the deal. Had the jury been instructed that plaintiff was required to tender perfectly conforming goods—not just substantially conforming goods—within the period allegedly agreed to and had they been instructed that, under Section 2-711, the buyer has the absolute right to cancel the contract if the seller "fails to make delivery," a different verdict might have resulted.
>
> [Reversed.]

The obvious mistake made by the trial court judge was allowing the case to go to the jury with instructions permitting a verdict based on substantial performance. Substantial performance is not an option under the Sales article. As discussed before, the seller's only option is "perfect" performance.

__Problem Solving__. Please turn to Chapter Problems at the end of this chapter and solve Problem 18.2.

INSTALLMENT CONTRACTS: does failure of one or more installments substantially impair the value of the whole contract?

Installment Contracts. Difficult problems are presented when a contract "requires or authorizes" the seller to send the contract goods in separate installments or shipments. If one—but not all—of the shipments is nonconforming, is the buyer permitted to reject the entire contract?

The answer is that "[w]henever non-conformity or default with respect to one or more installments *substantially impairs the value of the whole contract* there is a breach of the whole." But, on the other hand, if the non-conformity *does not* substantially impair the value of the whole contract, the buyer (1) must accept the nonconforming shipment if the seller gives reasonable assurance that the non-conformity will be cured; but, (2) may reject a nonconforming installment "if the non-conformity substantially impairs the value of that installment and cannot be cured." (§ 2-612)

Suppose that Milly is in the business of building picnic tables which are nine feet long. To build these tables, she orders nine-foot-long strips of redwood from Jed. They are to be delivered in three different shipments, in June, July and August. When the June shipment arrives, all of the strips are six-feet in length. The wood for the July and August shipments has already been cut and the redwood in those shipments will likewise be six feet in length. Because the non-conforming length of these strips impairs their value, and Jed cannot cure the problem in a timely fashion, Milly can obviously reject the *entire* contract, even though the July and August shipments have not been received.

But, suppose that when Jed learns of the problem in the June shipment, he is willing to promptly cure it in the July and August shipments. Milly may reject the June shipment because it is of no value to her and because the problem cannot be cured in a reasonable time. She must accept the July and August shipments *unless* doing so would "substantially impair the value of the whole contract." That means, if she can obtain a substitute shipment for June alone, she must do that and accept the July and August shipments. (Jed, of course, would be liable for Milly's losses in obtaining a substitute shipment.)

COMMERCIAL IMPRACTICABILITY occurs if unforeseen events make performance impracticable.

Commercial Impracticability. A seller must perform as the contract requires, unless events subsequently occur which make that performance impracticable. Section 2-615 provides that a seller is not in breach of contract for failure to perform "if performance as agreed has been made impracticable by the occurrence of a contingency the nonoccurrence of which was a basic assumption on which the contract was made."

Suppose that Jed has contracted to deliver 5,000 pounds of popping corn to Milly on August 1. Unknown to Milly, Jed intended to buy the corn from Elmer Johnson. However, Mr. Johnson's corn crop was damaged in a hail storm and Johnson had no corn to sell to Jed. Can Jed successfully claim commercial impracticability? The answer is no, because Jed's private intentions are not a basic assumption shared by the contracting parties. Jed's obligation is to acquire corn from another source and deliver it to Milly as agreed.

Suppose, however, that the contract between Jed and Milly called for Jed to deliver "Johnson Special" popping corn which he would acquire from Elmer Johnson. In this case, acquiring corn from Elmer Johnson is a basic assumption shared by the parties. If "Johnson Special" popping corn is not available because the Johnson corn crop is damaged by a hail storm, Jed will be excused from performance.

A common complaint by sellers is that they should be excused from performance because the costs of their performance have unexpectedly risen. In general, this excuse is not successful. On this point, a comment by the authors of the Sales article states: "Increased cost alone does not excuse performance unless the rise in cost is due to some unforeseen contingency which alters the essential nature of the performance."[1]

In the following case, *Maple Farms, Inc. v. City School District of Elmira*, the seller, Maple Farms, contracted in June of 1973 to provide milk to a school district. But, by December of 1973, the price of raw milk had risen by 23% and the seller would arguably lose $7,350 if forced to perform the contract. Maple Farms refused to perform, claiming commercial impracticability.

---

[1] U.C.C. (1962) § 2-615, cmt 4.

Maple Farms, Inc. v. City School Dist., Etc.
352 N.Y.S.2d 784 (1974)

CHARLES B. SWIRTWOOD, Justice.

* * *

The plaintiff goes to great lengths to spell out the cause of the substantial increase in the price of raw milk, which the plaintiff argues could not have been foreseen by the parties because it came about in large measure from the agreement of the United States to sell huge amounts of grain to Russia and to a lesser extent to unanticipated crop failures.

The legal basis of the plaintiff's request for being relieved of the obligation under the contract award is the doctrine known variously as "impossibility of performance" and "frustration of performance" at common law and as "Excuse by Failure of Presupposed Conditions" under the Uniform Commercial Code, § 2-615.

* * *

The doctrine enunciated by Uniform Commercial Code, § 2-615 was explained by the court [in Transatlantic Financing Corporation v. United States], 363 F.2d at page 315:

> "The doctrine ultimately represents the evershifting line, drawn by courts hopefully responsive to commercial practices and mores, at which the community's interest in having contracts enforced according to their terms is outweighed by the commercial senselessness of requiring performance. When the issue is raised, the court is asked to construct a condition of performance based on the changed circumstances, a process which involves at least three reasonably definable steps. First, a contingency—something unexpected—must have occurred. Second, the risk of the unexpected occurrence must not have been allocated either by agreement or by custom. Finally, occurrence of the contingency must have rendered performance commercially impracticable."

Applying these rules to the facts here we find that the contingency causing the increase of the price of raw milk was not totally unexpected. The price from the low point in the year 1972 to the price on the date of the award of the contract in June 1973 had risen nearly 10% and any businessman should have been aware of the general inflation in this country during the previous years and of the chance of crop failures.

However, should we grant that the first test had been met and thus the substantial increase in price was due to the sale of wheat to Russia, poor crops and general market conditions which were unexpected contingencies, then the question of allocation of risk must be met. Here the very purpose of the contract was to guard against fluctuation of price of half pints of milk as a basis for the school budget. Surely had the price of raw milk fallen substantially, the defendant could not be excused from performance. We can reasonably assume that the plaintiff had to be aware of escalating inflation. It is chargeable with knowledge of the substantial increase of the price of raw milk and that price varied. It nevertheless entered into this agreement with that knowledge. It did not provide in the contract any exculpatory clause to excuse it from performance in the event of a substantial rise in the price of raw milk. On these facts the risk of a substantial or abnormal increase in the price of raw milk can be allocated to the plaintiff.

[Motion for Summary Judgment in favor of school district granted.]

This decision makes clear that the rising and falling of prices is not the basis for a successful claim of commercial impracticability.

Problem Solving. Please turn to Chapter Problems at the end of this chapter and solve Problem 18.3.

Performance by the Buyer

The preceding discussion focused on the seller's obligation of performance. The focus now changes to the buyer and the buyer's performance obligations.

RIGHT OF INSPECTION.: a buyer has the right to inspect goods before paying for them.

Right of Inspection. A buyer has the obligation to accept and pay for goods which conform to the contract. The buyer can only know that the goods conform to the contract if he or she is allowed to *inspect* them. Thus § 2-513(1) provides that a "buyer has the right before payment or acceptance to inspect them [the goods] at any reasonable place and time and in any reasonable manner." (The buyer does not, however, have this right of inspection in C.O.D. deliveries.) Applying the right of inspection to the delivery of redwood planks, which is discussed above, it means that Milly has the right to take sample planks from the shipment and measure them to be sure they are the right length. And, as discussed above, when she finds that the planks do not conform to the contract specifications, Milly is not obligated to accept or pay for the planks.

But, it is not always that easy. Suppose, for example, that Jed's Chowder House buys clam chowder in commercial quantities from Milly, which Jed orders "lightly salted." The chowder arrives frozen in containers, as expected, and with labels which state: "Salt: Light." Jed has the right to inspect the goods, which he does diligently; but, salt content is hard to discern until clam chowder is thawed and cooked. Unfortunately, when the chowder is thawed and cooked it is obviously very salty and not usable by Jed. (After more discussion of "acceptance," the discussion will return to Jed and the salty chowder, and the question whether he can revoke his acceptance.)

ACCEPTANCE occurs when buyer (1) indicates acceptance, (2) fails to reject, or (3) does an act inconsistent with seller's ownership.

Acceptance. If, in fact, the chowder conformed to the contract, Jed must accept and pay for it. Acceptance occurs when the buyer, after inspection, (1) indicates his acceptance, (2) fails to make a rejection, or (3) does an act inconsistent with the seller's ownership. (§ 2-606) For the moment, Jed has accepted the goods because he has inspected them and indicated his acceptance. At this moment, Jed must pay for the chowder.

In the following decision, *Tai Wah Radio Manufactory Ltd. v. Ambassador Imports Ltd.*, the buyer, Ambassador, received some allegedly defective stereo cassette recorders from the plaintiff, Tai Wah. Ambassador complained about the defects, but apparently no action was taken. When a second shipment of recorders arrived, Ambassador took possession of them, not to accept them, but to "hold them hostage' to enforce a resolution of the problems with the first shipment. This is the exact language of the telex sent by Ambassador to Tai Wah:

"WE REFUSED THE DOCUMENTS [concerning the second shipment] 4 WE DID NOT WANT THE MRCHND. THE ONLY REASON WE PICKD UP THE GOODS IS FOR COLLATERAL AGST THE 1ST 2000 UNTS U HAD SENT. WE HAD RCVD SO MANY DAMGD PCS N COMPLAINTS FRM CSTMRS THT I FELT U HAD 2 COMPENSATE US 4 ALL THE REPAIR EXP AND PUNITIVE DAMAGES CAUSD 2 MY REPUTATION, BY HLDING THE GOODS IN A WAREHOUSE, I AM IN A BTTR POSITION 2 NEGOTIATE COMPENSATION 4 FOR THE 1ST SHPMNT. IF I JUST REFUSED THE GOOD N THEY WERE RETURND 2 U, I WLD NEVER RECEIVE ANY COMPENSATION FRM U 4 THE DAMAGES THE MRCHDS HAS CAUSED ME. ONC AGAIN, I DO NOT WNT THS GOODS, I JUST WANT 2 B COMPENSATD 4 ALL MY AGGRAVATION N MY EXPENSES. IN FACT, I HVE CSTMRS REFUSING 2 DEAL W ME ANYMORE BCZ OF THIS UNIT. BLV ME 100,000USD IS NOT ENOUGH 2 EVEN COMPENSATE THE LOSS OF GOOD CSTMRS. YR GOODS R NOT WHAT I WANT. ALL I WANT 2 DO IS COME 2 AN AGREEMENT WHERE I DO NOT LOSE ANY MONEY. I WLD JUST WANT 2 B COMPENSATD 4 MY LOSSES. NOTHING MORE THAN THAT."

Tai Wah Radio Manufactory Ltd. v. Ambassador Imports Ltd.
3 UCC Rep Serv 117 (1987)

MOTLEY, District Judge.

* * *

An additional problem exists in this case, however, which the court must consider. It is undisputed, based on the submissions in this case, that defendant accepted the second shipment for the sole purpose of negotiating a settlement with plaintiff concerning the money owing on the first shipment. Defendant obviously did not intend to pay for the second shipment of recorders and accepted the shipment with the knowledge that it would reject the recorders. In addition, it knew that the recorders were allegedly defective at the time of acceptance. The parties have not adequately addressed this issue in the papers submitted in connection with this motion for summary judgment.

Section 2-608 of the U.C.C. provides:

"(1)   The buyer may revoke his acceptance of a lot or commercial unit whose non-conformity substantially impairs its value to him if he has accepted it

    (a)   on the reasonable assumption that its non-conformity would be cured and it has not been seasonally cured; or

    (b)   without discovery of such non-conformity if his acceptance was reasonably induced either by the difficulty of discovery before acceptance or by the seller's assurances."

> Thus, a buyer with knowledge that goods are defective when he accepts them does not lose his right to revoke the acceptance if the acceptance was based on the reasonable assumption that the nonconformity would be seasonably cured but the cure was not effected. * * * In addition, acceptance may be revoked if the buyer, without discovering the nonconformity, was reasonably induced to accept the goods either by the difficulty of discovery before acceptance or by the seller's assurances. Neither of these exceptions is applicable to this case. When defendant accepted the second shipment of cassette recorders, it had knowledge of the recorder's allegedly defective nature. Defendant did not assume the plaintiff would cure this nonconformity. Thus, defendant did not have the right to revoke the contract for the second shipment.
>
> Although defendant may not have intended to keep the products when it took possession of the second shipment, this does not change the result. From the undisputed facts in this case, it is obvious that defendant was attempting to engage in a form of commercial "kidnapping" to compel plaintiff to resolve its differences with defendant. Defendant, instead of taking possession of the second shipment of recorders, should have rejected the second shipment. Plaintiff, in telexes, had advised defendant, prior to defendant's receipt of the second shipment, that the recorders had been shipped prior to plaintiff's receipt of defendant's first complaints about the first shipment and prior to plaintiff having the opportunity to make the needed corrections. Thus, defendant, with knowledge of the allegedly defective nature of the goods, should have rejected them. Accordingly, it is apparent that plaintiff is entitled to payment for the second shipment.
>
> [Partial summary judgment granted in favor of Tai Wah.]

Note that "partial" summary judgment was granted to Tai Wah. That means that Tai Wah won on the issue described above. There were, however, other issues between the parties. In the full opinion, the judge notes that Ambassador may have a good claim against Tai Wah for breach of warranty. Thus, the judge noted at the end of his full opinion:

> However, if it is established at trial that defendant complained in a timely manner about the defects in the goods, defendant may be entitled to damages for breach of warranty—the difference between the contract price of the recorders and their actual value. Since this amount would be an offset to the amount defendant allegedly owes plaintiff, entry of judgment is delayed until after the trial on this matter.

Problem Solving. Please turn to Chapter Problems at the end of this chapter and solve Problem 18.4.

REVOCATION OF ACCEPTANCE is allowed if defects are not cured or defects were not discoverable.

Revocation. Now—belatedly—understanding that the chowder is too salty, Jed has a decision to make: he may attempt to revoke his acceptance of the chowder, or he may choose to overlook the problem and keep the chowder and use it or resell it. Section 2-608 permits revocation of an acceptance in two circumstances. First, if the nonconforming, salty condition had been discovered during inspection, and Milly had said that the problem would be cured—but it was not—Jed could revoke the acceptance when the problem was not cured. This alternative does not apply, of course, because the nonconformity was not discovered during inspection.

The second, and more probable, alternative is that an acceptance may be revoked when failure to detect the nonconformity was "induced either by the difficulty of discovery before acceptance or by the seller's assurances." This alternative applies because the label ("Salt: Light") was a misleading assurance, and because the salt content was difficult to discover during a preliminary inspection. For this latter reason it would appear that Jed could revoke his acceptance of the chowder.

Payment. The most obvious obligation of a buyer is to pay for the goods he or she receives. With respect to payment, the two obvious questions are *when* the payment must be made, and in what *manner*—cash or check or some other method?

PAYMENT is due when buyer receives goods and may be in any reasonable manner.

On the question of *when* payment is made, § 2-310(a) provides that "payment is due at the time and place at which the buyer is to *receive* the goods." The word "receive" is used deliberately because—as discussed above—a buyer has the right to inspect the subject goods before accepting them. By providing for payment at the time the goods are received, payment is deferred to the time that the goods can be inspected. Then, if the goods conform to the contract, they are received and paid for; but, if the goods do not conform to the contract, they are rejected and not paid for.

The second question is the manner of payment: cash or check or some other method? In general, the buyer may pay using any reasonable method, unless the contract specifies a method of payment. The buyer may demand "legal tender" (cash) but must give the buyer an extension of time to procure it. Thus, § 2-511(2) provides that "[t]ender of payment is sufficient when made by any means or in any manner current in the ordinary course of business unless the seller demands payment in legal tender and gives any extension of time reasonably necessary to procure it.

Seller's Remedies

In some cases, a contract buyer fails to perform as the contract requires. In those cases, the sales article provides a variety of "remedies" that the seller may apply to resolve the problem. In general, the remedies available to a seller depend on the *location* of the goods, as shown in the table below:

Seller's Remedies	
Location of Goods	*Remedy*
Goods in Possession of Seller	• Cancel the contract [§ 2-703(f)] • Withhold delivery of the goods [§ 2-703(a)] • Resell the goods [§ 2-703(d) and § 2-706] • Recover damages for non-acceptance or repudiation [§ 2-708] • Recover the purchase price [§ 2-709]
Goods in Transit	• Stop delivery [§ 2-703(b) and § 2-705]
Goods in Possession of Buyer	• Recover the purchase price [§ 2-709] • Reclaim the goods [§ 2-702(2)]

In the following discussion, assume that Milly is a seller of custom manufactured light-weight aluminum wheels for off-road vehicles, and that Jed has ordered 3 dozen wheels to fit a *La Poubelle*,[2] a French, off-road vehicle.

Goods in Possession of Seller. If Jed *wrongfully* rejects the wheels when they are delivered, or accepts them when they are delivered, but thereafter *wrongfully* revokes his acceptance and sends the wheels back to Milly, or does other similar things [§ 2-703], the result is that Jed is in breach of the contract and Milly is in possession of the wheels. Likewise, if Jed contacts Milly before the wheels are ever shipped and repudiates the contract (anticipatory repudiation) so that the wheels are never shipped, the result is that Jed is in breach of the contract and Milly is in possession of the wheels.

Under these circumstances, with Jed in breach of the contract and Milly in possession of the wheels, Milly has a variety of remedies at her disposal: First, she may simply cancel the contract and forget about Jed. Her reasoning with such a decision may be that pursuing legal remedies against Jed would involve more expense and trouble than it is worth. Consistent with this decision, Milly is entitled to withhold delivery of the wheels, if they have not already been delivered. And, Milly is entitled to resell the wheels; that is, she is entitled to sell them to someone else.

If Milly wants to sue Jed for her losses, she must resell the wheels, if that is possible, and this she must do in a commercially reasonable manner, including notice to Jed, if the resale is a private sale and not a public sale (such as an auction). [§ 2-706] If Milly is lucky, she may actually make a *profit* on the resale, in which event she "is not accountable to the buyer [Jed] for any profit made on any resale." [§ 2-706]

SELLER'S REMEDY: in general, contract price minus market price.

In most cases, however, Milly will suffer a loss in the resale. In this circumstance, the amount of money damages she is entitled to receive is calculated by subtracting the resale price of the wheels from the contract price. [§ 2-706(1) and § 2-708(1)] Milly is also entitled to recover commercial charges, expenses and commissions—referred to as "incidental" damages—she has incurred in the process of reselling. [In some cases, the general policy of calculating damages by subtracting the resale price from the contract price may not "put the seller in as good a position as performance would have done." In such cases, § 2-708(2) provides that "the measure of damages is the profit (including reasonable overhead) which the seller would have made from full performance by the buyer."]

Returning to Milly's problem, it is a fact that in some cases "the seller is unable after reasonable effort to resell them [the goods] at a reasonable price or the circumstances reasonably indicate that such effort will be unavailing." Thus, if Milly is not able to resell the wheels, because they will fit only *La Poubelle* cars, and there is no commercially reasonable market for custom wheels for such cars, she may

---

[2] *La Poubelle*, translated, means the garbage can.

recover from Jed the full contract price, plus incidental damages. In such a case, Milly must allow Jed to take possession of the wheels, if he wishes to. [§ 2-709]

Goods in Transit. The discussion above, assumed that the buyer, Jed, was clearly in breach of the sales contract, and that Milly was in possession of the wheels. In some cases, however, the breach of contract occurs while the goods are in transit; that is, while the goods are in a truck and on the highway on the way to Jed. In such cases, § 2-705(1) provides that "[t]he seller [Milly] may stop delivery of goods in the possession of a carrier." Then, of course, she may pursue the remedies described above.

Goods in Possession of Buyer. Perhaps the most common example of breach of contract is the simple failure of the buyer to pay for the goods after receiving them. In this context, Jed receives and accepts the wheels and commences to sell them to customers, intending to pay for them, with his other payables, at the end of the month. But, for whatever reason, Jed fails to pay Milly. In this context, Milly's remedy is to recover the amount agreed to in the contract, together with incidental damages. [§ 2-709(1)] In some limited cases, Milly may recover the wheels from Jed, if they have not been sold, in which case, recovery of the goods is her exclusive remedy. [§ 2-702]

The following case, *Madsen v. Murrey & Sons Co., Inc.*, is a case in which the seller's remedy is at issue. Murrey is a seller of pool tables. Madsen, the buyer, had "an idea to develop a pool table which, through the use of electronic devices installed in the rails of the table, would produce lighting and sound effects in a fashion similar to a pinball machine." Madsen contracted to buy 100 tables, at $550 per table, for a total of $55,000, he paid $42,500 of the total, in advance. Madsen's ideas did not work out and he informed Murrey that he would not be able to take deliver of the 100 tables. Murrey's response was to dismantle the tables and use the parts it could; the balance of the parts were used as firewood.

Madsen filed suit to recover some of the money he had paid Murrey. Madsen claimed that Murrey had an obligation to mitigate (minimize) it's losses and to return that amount of money which was not necessary to cover it's losses.

> **Madsen v. Murrey & Sons Co., Inc.**
> **743 P.2d 1212 (1987)**
>
> HOWE, Justice:
> * * *
>
> Seller first contends that the trial court erred in concluding that it had failed to mitigate or minimize its damages in a commercially reasonable manner by not attempting to sell the 100 pool tables on the open market. It is a well-settled rule of the law of damages that "no party suffering a loss as the result of a breach of contract is entitled to any damages which could have been avoided if the aggrieved party had acted in a reasonably diligent manner in attempting to lessen
> his losses as a consequence of that breach. * * *
> * * *

The trial court found that seller's action in dismantling the tables and using the materials for salvage and firewood, rather than attempting to sell or market the tables at full or a discounted price, was not commercially reasonable. The court then concluded that seller had a duty to mitigate its damages and failed to do so. * * *

* * *

At trial, substantial evidence was presented concerning the value of the pool tables at the time of buyer's repudiation and refusal to accept delivery upon tender. This evidence varied from Mr. Murrey's testimony that the tables had no value because they were not marketable to Mr. Baker's testimony that the tables could have been sold for full value or a discounted value because the integrity and marketability of the tables were not impaired. Murrey partially disputed his own testimony by admitting that the tables could have been sold at a discount. The evidence presented a broad range from which the trial court could determine the value of the 100 pool tables. The trial court's finding that the tables had a value of at least $21, 250 was within the range of the evidence presented at trial. We will not overturn that finding.

* * *

The applicable statute to be used in determining seller's damages for nonacceptance or repudiation is Utah Code Ann. § 70A-2-708 (1980), which provides:

> (1) Subject to subsection (2) and to the provisions of this chapter with respect to proof of the market price (section 70A-2-723), the measure of damages for nonacceptance or repudiation by the buyer is the difference between the market price at the time and place for tender and the unpaid contract price together with any incidental damages provided in this chapter (section 70A-2-710), but less expenses saved in consequence of the buyer's breach.

Applying the trial court's finding that the pool tables if completed could have been sold for at least $21, 250, seller's damages are the difference between the market price ($21,250) and the contract price ($55,000), or $33,750. The trial court found that seller was not entitled to any incidental damages. Buyer is not entitled to any further credit for expenses saved by seller in consequence of buyer's breach. Since the $21,250 which the trial court charged seller with was for completed tables, no savings would have occurred. Under cite, buyer's right to restitution of advance payments on the contract ($42,500) is subject to offset to the extent that seller establishes damages ($33,750), for a total recovery of $8,750.

Buyer is entitled to recover from seller the sum of $8,750. The judgment is affirmed as modified.

Note that the court required the seller to mitigate it's damages in a Sales problem. This common law principle (mitigation) is not directly discussed in the Sales article, but the court nevertheless applied it in *Madsen*, which is a Sales case. This is a good example of the proposition that common law contract principles supplement the Uniform Commercial Code.

Problem Solving. Please turn to Chapter Problems at the end of this chapter and solve Problem 18.5.

Buyer's Remedies

In the discussion above, Milly, the properly performing seller of the custom wheels, has been the "good guy," and Jed the non-performing buyer of the wheels, has been the "bad guy." In the following discussion that orientation changes: Jed will now become the properly performing party who needs a contract remedy, and Milly will become the non-performing party who is in violation of the contract.

As with the remedies available to a seller, the remedies of a buyer vary according to the *location* of the goods, as shown in the table below:

Buyer's Remedies	
Location of Goods	*Remedy*
Goods in Possession of Seller	• Cancel the contract [§ 2-711(1)] • Recover damages for non-delivery or repudiation [§ 2-711(1)(b) and § 2-713(1)] • Cover and recover damages [§ 2-711(1)(a) and § 2-712] • Recover goods [§ 2-502] • Specific performance and replevin [§ 2-716(1) and § 2-716(3)]
Goods in Possession of Buyer	• Reject the goods [§ 2-601] • Revoke acceptance of the goods [§ 2-608] • Recover damages for non-delivery or repudiation [§ 2-713] • Recover damages for breach of warranty [§ 2-714]

Assume, again, that Milly is the seller of custom manufactured light-weight aluminum wheels for off-road vehicles, and that Jed has ordered 3 dozen wheels to fit a *La Poubelle*, French, off-road vehicle.

Goods in Possession of the Seller. If Milly fails or refuses to deliver the wheels as agreed, or if she delivers them but they do not conform to the contract and are thus rejected and sent back, she is in breach of the contract. In this context, Milly is in possession of the wheels, if they exist. (It is possible, of course, that the wheels do not exist because Milly failed to manufacture them.)

The first alternative available to Jed, when Milly fails to deliver conforming goods, is to simply cancel the contract because pursuing the matter is not worth the trouble and expense involved.

BUYER'S REMEDY: in general, market price minus contract price.

The second alternative available to Jed is that he may bring suit against Milly for his losses because he has not received the wheels. This alternative only makes sense if the market price of the wheels has risen since the contract was entered into. In this context we assume that Jed has given up the idea of selling *La Poubelle* wheels, but feels he is entitled to the profit he would have made in the transaction. In this alternative, § 2-713(1) provides that the amount of Jed's damages is calculated as "the difference between the market price at the time when the buyer learned of the breach and the contract price together with any incidental and consequential damages."

A third, and common, alternative focuses on the fact that Jed must have the wheels he has ordered from Milly. In this scenario, Jed has committed to provide wheels to the French Off-Road Exploration Club. Either he gets the wheels from Milly, or he must get them from someone else. The term applied to this alternative is "cover." To "cover" means that Jed goes to the market for custom wheels and buys 3 dozen wheels at the best price he can to substitute for the wheels he should have received from Milly. If the cost of the substitute wheels is more than the contract cost with Milly, Jed has been financially damaged. In this context, § 2-712(2) provides that "[t]he buyer [Jed] may recover from the seller as damages the difference between the cost of cover and the contract price together with any incidental or consequential damages."

A last, and far less common, alternative is the ability of Jed, the buyer, to force Milly to deliver the actual goods (the wheels) instead of forcing her to pay money damages. This may happen in three, slightly different ways. First, if Jed has paid some or all of the purchase price in advance, he may force Milly to deliver the wheels if she became insolvent within ten days after receiving the first advance payment. [§ 2-502(1)] Second, "if the goods are unique" and cannot be replace elsewhere, Milly may be compelled for that reason to deliver the wheels to Jed. This is called "specific performance." Last, even if the wheels are not unique, but the buyer, Jed, is not able to obtain cover, Milly may be compelled for that reason to deliver the wheels to Jed. This is called "replevin."

Goods in Possession of the Buyer. The buyer's remedies discussed above have assumed that the goods remain in the possession of the seller, if they exist. But, what are the remedies available to Jed, the buyer, if the goods are in *his* possession? Of course, if the goods conform to the contract, no remedy will be needed. Thus, the real focus of a discussion about buyer's remedies (where the goods are in the possession of the buyer) is what are the remedies available when the goods are non-conforming?

The first option available to a buyer who receives non-conforming goods is to reject them. The buyer has the right to inspect goods before accepting them and, in general, a buyer should always do that. Then, if the goods are non-conforming, they should be rejected. This is what the buyer should have done in the *Tai Wah* opinion, which is discussed earlier in this chapter.

In some cases, a seller, such as Milly, will acknowledge the defect in the goods and promise to correct it. If the time for performance has not expired, Milly has the right to cure a defect in the goods. [2-508(1)] Suppose, for example, that the contract required that the wheels be sprayed with a compound which will prevent stains on the aluminum parts. If the wheels were not sprayed, as the contract requires, Milly has the right to cure the defect, if the time for performance has not expired. On the other hand, the time for performance may have expired, but Jed is nevertheless willing to allow Milly to correct the problem. In that case, he should make a clear record that he is accepting only *on the assumption* that Milly will cure the defect. Then, if the defect is not cured, § 2-608(1)(a) allows Jed, the buyer, to revoke his acceptance.

As an alternative, Jed could choose to accept the defective wheels, but claim damages equal to the amount of the defects. If Jed promptly gives Milly notice of the defect, he is entitled to damages to the extent of the defect. [§ 2-607(3)] In these circumstances, "[t]he measure of damages for breach of warranty is the difference at the time and place of acceptance between the value of the goods accepted and the value they would have had if they had been as warranted." [§ 2-714(2)]

The last alternative may be that the non-conforming goods cannot be "fixed" and the buyer will choose to reject them and recover damages for breach of contract. Suppose that the *La Poubelle* uses a 15-inch wheel, but Milly mistakenly sends 14-inch wheels. In this circumstance, the wheels cannot be "fixed" and Jed rejects them. And, further suppose that the wheels were to be sold at a trade show and the trade show will be over before any replacement goods can be manufactured. Thus, Jed decides to simply sue for his financial loss. In these circumstances, "the measure of damages for non-delivery or repudiation by the seller is the difference between the market price at the time when the buyer learned of the breach and the contract price." [§ 2-713(1)]

Problem Solving. Please turn to Chapter Problems at the end of this chapter and solve Problem 18.6.

Chapter Problems

Problem 18.1

Jed is involved in a Sales transaction and he claims that the statutory obligation to act in good faith does *not* apply to him because he is not a merchant. Explain whether he is correct.

Problem 18.2

This question focuses on the "perfect tender" obligation discussed in the *Moulton Cavity & Mold v. Lyn-Flex Industries* opinion. Milly orders 100 *brown* widgets from Jed, but he only has *black* widgets in stock. Because Milly is a valued customer, Jed sends black widgets, with the following letter: "In reply to your recent order, I am sending black widgets because they are all I have in stock. If these are not acceptable, send them back." Is Jed in breach of contract by accepting Milly's contract order and then breaching the contract by sending nonconforming goods, which is a violation of the perfect tender rule?

Problem 18.3

This question focuses on the *Maple Farms, Inc. v. City School Dist.* opinion. Suppose that a bovine viral infection in the Maple Farms/City School District region affects all dairy cows and reduces milk production by 50%. What are Maple Farms contract obligations under these facts.

Problem 18.4

Review the facts in *Tai Wah Radio Manufactory Ltd. v. Ambassador Imports Ltd.* Obviously, what Ambassador intended to do was to force Tai Wah to make a financial adjustment concerning the first shipment of recorders. In hindsight, how could Ambassador have handled the matter better?

Problem 18.5

In *Madsen v. Murrey & Sons Co., Inc.*, the opinion quotes § 2-708 to describe the appropriate remedy. Among other things, the quoted language says that the seller is entitled to "any incidental damages." What are *incidental* damages?

Problem 18.6

This question focuses on the *Moulton Cavity & Mold* opinion at the beginning of this chapter. Assume that the contract price is $15,000. The innersole molds, as delivered, have a problem with plastic seepage. *Lyn-Flex*, the buyer, may, of course, refuse the molds because they do not conform to the contract. But, they are willing to accept the molds as they are; however, they do not want to pay the full price. What price must they pay, if they choose to accept the defective molds?

Chapter Outline

THE OBJECTIVE of this chapter is to learn negligence, sales warranties and strict liability as applied to product liability.

The objective of this chapter is to learn the legal doctrines of negligence, Sales warranty and strict liability as they apply to product liability. The chapter is organized as follows:

- *Product Liability.* Consumer products—things like trampolines, televisions, boats and food—which sometimes cause injuries to consumers or users cause special problems in relation to the application of the legal doctrines of negligence (and *res ipsa loquitor*), Sales warranties and strict liability.

- *Negligence.* A negligence theory may be used to recover for injuries caused by a negligently manufactured product. However, in products liability cases, a case based on negligence often fails because it is difficult to produce evidence that the defective product was *negligently* manufactured.

- *Sales Warranties.* Sales warranties may be effectively used in product liability cases. Section 2-314 is the principal warranty in relation to product liability. A limitation in relation to the use of Sales warranties is that such warranties may be excluded or modified in the Sales contract; and, the warranty usually extends only to a limited class of third persons.

- *Strict Liability.* The doctrine of strict liability applies to persons who are in the business of manufacturing or selling products. Strict liability is imposed if a product is defective (*unreasonably* dangerous), and the defective product proximately causes injuries to the consumer or user—not just purchasers. The manufacturer or seller may use the defenses of negligence, abuse of the product or assumption of the risk. Comparative responsibility is considered on a "percentage" basis as is done with comparative negligence.

Introduction

The subject of this chapter is *product liability.* In this chapter are discussed a variety of legal theories that may be used by a person injured in the use of a consumer product. For example, assume that too much carbonation is put into a two-liter bottle of root beer, with the result that when a consumer grasps it the lid pops off and injures the consumer's eye. What legal theory should the injured consumer use to gain compensation for the injury?

289

The objective of this chapter is to pull together the different legal theories that may be used by the injured consumer to recover damages for his or her injury. Those theories include the tort of negligence (including *res ipsa loquitor*), Sales warranties and strict liability. These legal theories have been discussed before, but not in the context of product liability.

Should the consumer (who was injured by the root beer bottle) use a tort theory and claim that the manufacturer and seller have been negligent? Should the consumer use a Sales warranty and claim that the bottle of root beer was not fit for the ordinary purposes for which it was intended? Or should the consumer use a strict liability theory and claim that the bottle of root beer was defectively manufactured? This is the subject matter of this chapter.

PRODUCT LIABILITY presents special problems in relation to negligence, sales warranties and strict liability.

Why is there a further discussion of the legal doctrines of negligence (and *res ipsa loquitor*), Sales warranties and strict liability? After all, these doctrines have been studied before in earlier chapters. The answer to that question is that the problem of *product liability* (defective products which cause injuries to consumers) presents unique problems associated with those doctrines. For example, the doctrine of negligence works well with such things as automobile accidents, bridges that collapse and explosions from natural gas leaks. But, when negligence is applied to consumer products—things like trampolines, televisions, boats and food—things which are sometimes anonymously manufactured (with difficult-to-trace defects) in one place and transported and sold in another place, special problems arise. The same is true with Sales warranties and strict liability; that is, special problems arise that are not seen in other contexts. Thus, product liability is studied as a separate subject to study the special application of legal doctrines to that problem.

In the material below, each theory (negligence, warranty and strict liability) will be discussed in turn, showing why each of them is effective (or not effective) in producing a financial recovery for an injured consumer of a consumer product.

Negligence

An injured consumer may sue the manufacturer and seller of defective goods using a theory of negligence. A successful negligence action requires proof of negligence (a duty and it's violation), proximate cause and damages.[1]

Assume that Milly was the consumer who was injured by the defective bottle of root beer discussed above. For purposes of a negligence action, it is not enough for Milly to prove that the bottle of root beer was defective; she must also prove that the defect was caused by someone's negligence. To prove negligence, Milly must become a detective and show that something was improperly done (or not done) which caused the defect. For example, suppose that she can prove that the pressure gauge on the carbonating device was defective. If Milly can prove that the production supervisor

---

[1] Negligence is discussed in Chapter 6.

knew the gauge was defective and allowed production to continue—over-pressurizing and under-pressurizing bottle contents—she has proved negligence.

But, in the "real" world, it is often difficult or impossible to prove the chain of events that make a product defective. Milly will be lucky if, like Hansel and Gretel, she can follow factual bread crumbs through the manufacturing process and identify the specific circumstances that caused a particular bottle of root beer to be over-pressurized. Often, it is the truth that no one knows what causes a problem like this; it just happens. And, looking at the problem with a more skeptical eye, it is also true that memories conveniently fade ("I don't remember") and records are conveniently lost. Either way, Milly may be able to prove a defect, but often she cannot prove that negligence caused the defect, and thus she cannot prove her case.

As an illustration of the simple problem of collecting evidence, consider the following quotation from the full opinion in *Embs v. Pepsi-Cola Bot. Co. of Lexington*,[2] a case which is discussed more at the end of this chapter. In *Embs*, the plaintiff was in a small grocery story store, standing near the produce counter, when there was an explosion. When Ms. Embs looked down, "she saw a gash in her leg, pop on her leg, green pieces of a bottle on the floor and . . . [a] Seven-Up carton in the midst of the debris." Ms. Embs was taken to a hospital, while a store employee was instructed to clean up the mess:

> She [Ms. Embs] was immediately taken to the hospital by Mrs. Stamper, a managing agent of the store. Mrs. Stamper told her that a Seven-Up bottle had exploded and that several bottles had exploded that week. Before leaving the store Mrs. Stamper instructed one of her children to clean up the mess. *Apparently, all of the physical evidence went out with the trash.*[3]

If Ms. Embs only option was to sue on a negligence theory, with an obligation to show a defective product and to demonstrate how negligence contributed to create the defective product, her task would be difficult, if not impossible, because much of the evidence "went out with the trash." (In fact, Ms. Embs did not use a theory of negligence, but used a theory of strict liability, which is discussed later.)

In summary, an injured consumer, like Milly, may use a negligence theory to recover for injuries caused by a negligently manufactured product. However, in products liability cases, a case based on negligence often fails because it is difficult to produce evidence that the defective product was *negligently* manufactured.

Res Ipsa Loquitor. The doctrine of *res ipsa loquitor* is sometimes used in connection with a negligence action.[4] In practical terms, *res ipsa loquitor* shifts the

---

[2] 528 S.W.2d 703 (1975).

[3] *Id.* at 504 (emphasis added).

[4] *Res Ipsa Loquitor* is discussed in Chapter 6.

burden of proof with respect to evidence from the plaintiff to the defendant. Thus, if a court is persuaded to use *res ipsa loquitor* in the root beer bottle case, it means that negligence on the part of the manufacturer is *presumed*, and the manufacturer may thereafter prove—if it can—that it was *not* negligent.

If the court is willing to apply *res ipsa loquitor*, it is a tremendous advantage to an injured plaintiff, like Milly, who is using a negligence theory. That raises the question of what circumstances will persuade a court to apply *res ipsa loquitor*? Recall from Chapter 6 that to persuade the court to apply *res ipsa loquitor*, Milly must prove two things: (1) that the event (over-pressurizing a bottle of root beer) "is of a kind [of event] which ordinarily does not occur in the absence of negligence,"[5] and (2) that the defendant had exclusive control of the manufacturing process. If Milly is successful on these two points, the court will presume that the manufacturer has been negligent, leaving the manufacturer (who has the best access to the witnesses and records) to prove it was not negligent—if it can.

Application of the doctrine of *res ipsa loquitor* obviously makes a negligence case easier to prove. But, even with the possibility of using *res ipsa loquitor*, winning a negligence-based case can be difficult. For example, consider how the court handled the use (or possible abuse) of *res ipsa loquitor* in *Jordan v. Coca Cola Bottling Co. of Utah*.

The plaintiff, Norman Jordan, worked in a smelter where he purchased a bottle of Coca Cola from a vending machine. While consuming the drink he discovered "three flies and other foreign matter" in it. According to his testimony, he became "sick and nauseated and remain[ed] sick intermittently for three days, and suffer[ed] from nausea and diarrhea." The trial court applied the doctrine of *res ipsa loquitor* which created a presumption that the bottling company had been negligent. The bottling company put on evidence by which it attempted to show that it had not been negligent, but the jury was not persuaded and found in favor of Jordan.

Again, it will be recalled from Chapter 6 that application of *res ipsa loquitor* requires proof (1) that the events causing injury must be of a type that do not normally occur in the absence of negligence, and (2) that the instrumentalities involved must have been within the exclusive control of the defendant. In *Jordan*, the bottling company appealed, claiming that exclusive control did *not* exist and therefore *res ipsa loquitor* should not have been applied by the court. From the full opinion, it is clear that the bottling company believed that Jordan's co-workers had played a prank on him. Their evidence at trial emphasized how many different people had had access to the bottled drink after it left the bottling plant.

---

[5] RESTATEMENT (SECOND) OF TORTS, § 328D.

> ## Jordan v. Coca Cola Bottling Co. of Utah
> ### 218 P.2d 660 (1950)
>
> PRATT, Chief Justice
> * * *
>
> The numerical weight undoubtedly favors the view that the doctrine of res ipsa loquitur does apply in cases generally of this type. Respondent has cited numerous cases to that effect. There are many others. * * *
>
> Appellant's argument is that the doctrine of res ipsa loquitur cannot be applied in this case because there has not been the exclusive control required and contemplated under that doctrine.
>
> * * *
>
> The evidence in the present case fails to establish lack of opportunity for tampering, but on the contrary establishes numerous opportunities for tampering by mischief minded persons or those bearing genuine ill will, as well as opportunities for substitution. We are informed of no less than fourteen persons having access to the vending machine, in addition to the fact that the key hanging in the guard closet presented an opportunity for others to gain access to the machine. There is nothing to indicate that there was not even more opportunity for tampering with the Coca Cola stored in the foreman's office. Factories and manufacturing plants where many men are thrown together, are noted for the horseplay and practical joking which there takes place, often with serious results. Another explanation is as consistent with the facts of this case as is the indication that defendant's negligence caused the injury. * * * We conclude that plaintiff has failed to make out a case rendering the maxim and doctrine of res ipsa loquitur applicable.
>
> The defendant produced evidence of a method of cleaning and washing the bottles, of refilling them and of inspecting them visually and electrically, all of which substantially rules out the likelihood of this bottle of Coca Cola having been bottled in its existing condition by this bottling plant. We conclude that there is not sufficient evidence on behalf of the plaintiff to sustain the burden of establishing a case for the jury.
> * * *
>
> The judgment is reversed and the case remanded for dismissal.

RES IPSA LOQUITOR: using this doctrine in product liability cases, it is difficult to prove "exclusive control."

In cases like *Jordan*, the plaintiff is, in practical terms, without a remedy. It is nearly impossible to prove negligence because it is nearly impossible to reconstruct the facts under which the product was manufactured. And because the product has passed through many hands on its way from the manufacturer to the consumer, courts may be reluctant to apply *res ipsa loquitor* because exclusive control cannot be clearly established.

Problem Solving. Please turn to Chapter Problems at the end of this chapter and solve Problem 19.1.

Having observed the difficulties associated with the use of negligence, and negligence combined with *res ipsa loquitor*, in product liability cases, we turn next to Sales warranties.

Sales Warranty

§2-314. This sales warranty requires that goods be fit for ordinary purposes, and properly packaged and labeled.

The Sales article of the Uniform Commercial Code includes promises, called "warranties" which apply to the sale of goods.[6] For purposes of product liability, the most important of these warranties is the implied warranty of merchantability found in § 2-314. The warranty of merchantability applies to sales by merchants and requires, among other things, that the goods must be "fit for the ordinary purposes for which such goods are used," that they "are adequately contained, packaged, and labeled," and that they "conform to the promises or affirmations of fact made on the container or label."

Keaton v. A.B.C. Drug Co.[7] illustrates the application of § 2-314 in cases where products are not adequately packaged. The plaintiff, Marilyn Keaton, was shopping in an A.B.C. Drug store when she reached up and grasped a bottle of bleach to pull it down from a high shelf. The cap was loose and her action in grasping the bottle caused the lid to come off and bleach splashed onto Keaton's face, causing eye injuries. Affirming a jury verdict in favor of Keaton, the court stated: "ABC, as a merchant of bleach, was required to adequately contain and package the bleach that it sold. Because bleach which spills via a loose cap is not adequately contained or packaged, a claim [warranty of merchantability] is supported."

Sales of Food. Product liability cases involving food present difficult questions about how to decide if the food is fit for ordinary purposes. [§ 2-314(2)(c)] How does one judge if food is "fit for the ordinary purpose for which such goods are used"? [§ 2-314(2)(c)] Most courts[8] ask whether the food meets the "reasonable expectations" of the consumer. A case dealing with this issue is *Webster v. Blue Ship Tea Room, Inc.*, which is discussed in Chapter 17. There, the court decided that pieces of fish bone were to be expected in chunks of fish in fish chowder because it was reasonable to expect bones which could not be removed from fish chunks.

In the following case, *Yong Cha Hong v. Marriott Corporation*, the plaintiff, Yong Cha Hong, ate a piece of chicken at a Roy Rogers Family Restaurant and claimed that there was a piece of worm in the chicken. Analysis demonstrated that, in fact, the item in question was not a piece of worm. The case was before the court on a motion for summary judgment. The court saw the problem in the following terms:

> [P]laintiff, in her deposition, steadfastly maintains that it was a worm, notwithstanding the expert analysis. If it was not in fact a worm, i.e.,

---

[6] Sales warranties are discussed in Chapter 17.

[7] 467 S.E.2d 558 (1996).

[8] A minority of courts resolve this question by asking whether the object or substance causing the alleged defect in the food is foreign or natural (the "foreign-natural" test) to the food. (This test works well if, for example, the defect in question is a sliver of glass in a hamburger, but it seems to miss the point if the problem with the hamburger is, for example, a sliver of beef bone, which would be disallowed.)

if the expert analysis is correct, it was either one of the chicken's major blood vessels (the aorta) or its trachea, both of which (the court can judicially notice) would appear worm-like (although not meaty like a worm, but hollow) to a person unschooled in chicken anatomy. The court must presume plaintiff to be inexpert as to chickens, even though she admits to some acquaintance with fresh-slaughtered chickens. * * * For the purposes of analyzing the plaintiff's warranty claim, the court will assume that the item was not a worm. Precisely how the aorta or trachea wound up in this hapless chicken's wing is a fascinating, but as yet unanswered (and presently immaterial), question.

If—as it appeared—the object eaten by the plaintiff was a chicken aorta or trachea, should the case dismissed? The defendant thought so and contended "that there can be no warranty recovery unless the offending item was a "foreign object," i.e., not a part of the chicken itself." That was the issue on which the court had to rule.

<table>
<tr><td>

REASONABLE EXPECTATION test is used to decide if goods are fit for ordinary purposes (§ 2-314).

</td><td>

Yong Cha Hong v. Marriott Corporation
3 UCC Rep.Ser.2d 83 (1987)

SMALKIN, District Judge.
* * *

The "reasonable expectation" test has largely displaced the natural/foreign test adverted to by defendants. In the circumstances of this case and many others, it is the only one that makes sense. In the absence of any Maryland decisional law, and in view of the expense and impracticality of certification of the question to the Court of Appeals of Maryland in this case, this court must decide the issue by applying the rule that that court would likely adopt some time in the future. * * * This court is confident that Maryland would apply the "reasonable expectation" rule to this warranty case, especially in view of the Court of Appeals' holding in *Bryer v. Rath Packing Co.*, * * * recognizing a negligence claim for the presence in a prepared food item of "something that should not be there" which renders the food unfit. * * *

Applying the reasonable expectation test to this case, the court cannot conclude that the presence of a trachea or an aorta in a fast food fried chicken wing is so reasonably to be expected as to render it merchantable, as a matter of law, within the bounds of U.C.C. § 2-314(2). This is not like the situation involving a 1 cm. bone in a piece of fried fish in Morrison's Cafeteria. Everyone but a fool knows that tiny bones may remain in even the best filets of fish. This case is more like Williams, where the court held that the issue was for the trier of fact, on a claim arising from a cherry pit in cherry ice cream. Thus, a question of fact is presented that precludes the grant of summary judgment. * * * The jury must determine whether a piece of fast food fried chicken is merchantable if it contains an inedible item of the chicken's anatomy. Of course, the jury will be instructed that the consumer's reasonable expectations form a part of the merchantability concept (under the theory of ordinary fitness, U.C.C. §2-314(2)(c)), as do trade quality standards (under U.C.C. § 2-314(2)(a)).

In short, summary judgment cannot be awarded defendants on plaintiff's warranty count, and their motion for partial summary judgment is, accordingly, denied.

</td></tr>
</table>

In the first paragraph of this opinion, there is some curious language in which Judge Smalkin asks what rule (foreign/natural or reasonable expectations) a *Maryland* court would adopt in this case. (As far as we can tell, this problem arose in Maryland, and Judge Smalkin's courtroom is located in Maryland.) So, why is Judge Smalkin asking what a Maryland court would do? Please answer this question in the following Chapter Problem.

__Problem Solving__. Please turn to Chapter Problems at the end of this chapter and solve Problem 19.2.

Third Parties. A disadvantage in pursuing a claim based on a Sales warranty is that some states place a limitation on third party claims. Suppose that Milly, the purchaser of the defective bottle of root beer, later handed the bottle to her friend, Jed, and then the lid popped off and injured Jed, not Milly, the purchaser. In relation to the seller, and Milly, the buyer, Jed is classified as a third party. There is disagreement in the legal community about whether non-purchaser third parties, such as Jed, should be permitted to sue the seller for breach of a Sales warranty. Section 2-318, which deals with that problem reflects that disagreement by allowing states to choose one of *three alternatives* as they adopt the Uniform Commercial Code.

THIRD PARTY CLAIMS: Sales warranty claims may have limits on third party claims.

Alternative A. In a state adopting Alternative A of § 2-318, Jed can recover for breach of a Sales warranty if he "is in the family or household of his buyer [Milly] or . . . is a guest in . . . [her] home if it is reasonable to expect that . . . [Jed] may use, consume or be affected by the goods." Suppose that Milly and Jed live in a state which has adopted Alternative A, and Milly is at Jed's house for a Super Bowl party, and it is there that she hands him the bottle and he is injured. Under Alternative A, Jed could not recover from the manufacturer on the basis of a Sales warranty because he is not a member of Milly's family or household, nor is he a guest in her home.

Alternatives B and C. But, suppose that Jed and Milly live in a state which has adopted Alternative B of § 2-318. This alternative "extends . . . [Sales warranties] to any natural person who may reasonably be expected to use, consume or be affected by the goods." Using this alternative, Jed could sue the manufacturer for his injuries because it is not unexpected that a purchaser will share food items with friends. (Alternative C is essentially the same as Alternative B, except that it extends coverage to "any person," instead of "any natural person." The difference, of course, is that Alternative C allows recovery by business associations instead of just natural persons.)

In summary, Sales warranties are an effective means of recovery for persons injured by the use of defective products. A Sales warranty is a more effective theory than a negligence theory in the sense that the plaintiff must only prove that the product does not meet warranty requirements, not how it got that way, or that it got that way through neglect. A potential flaw in the use of Sales warranties is that some states have limited recovery by third parties.

Strict Liability

Introduction. A doctrine known as **strict liability** is probably the most frequently used method by which courts handle the claims of persons injured in the use of defective products. One of the reasons for the relative popularity of the doctrine of strict liability is that its use does *not* include the problem of proving negligence or the limitations on third party claims, both of which are discussed above.

STRICT LIABILITY is described in Restatement (Second) of Torts § 402A.

Strict Liability. The doctrine of strict liability imposes liability on manufacturers and sellers of defective (unreasonably dangerous) products which proximately cause injuries to the user or consumer. The requirements of strict liability are as follows:

Strict Liability
Restatement (Second) of Torts § 402A.
(1) One who sells any product in a defective condition unreasonably dangerous to the user or consumer or to his property is subject to liability for physical harm thereby caused to the ultimate user or consumer or to his property, if (a) the seller is engaged in the business of selling such a product, and (b) it is expected to and does reach the user or consumer without substantial change in the condition in which it is sold. (2) The rule stated in Subsection (1) applies although (a) the seller has exercised all possible care in the preparation and sale of his product, and (b) the user or consumer has not bought the product from or entered into any contractual relation with the seller.

Applying the doctrine of strict liability (described in the table above) to Milly and the bottle of root beer, she must prove the following to recover against the manufacturer:

- That the seller is *in the business* of selling bottled root beer.

- That the bottle of root beer purchased by Milly was in a defective (*unreasonably dangerous*) condition when it left the hands of the manufacturer or seller (and that the condition of the bottled root beer was not thereafter substantially changed).

- That Milly suffered injuries which were *proximately caused* by the unreasonably dangerous condition of the bottle.

(Note, in the list above, that Milly is *not* required to prove that negligence was involved in designing or manufacturing the defective product. Nor is she required to prove that she *purchased* the product—only that she was a consumer or user.)

Following is a discussion of the strict liability requirements listed above:

In the Business. The doctrine of strict liability applies to those who are in business with respect to the products in question. Thus, Milly, a housewife who sells brownies once a year at the PTA bake sale is not, in general terms, *in the business* of selling bakery goods. On the other hand, if Milly operates a bakery and sells brownies on a regular basis, she is *in the business* of selling bakery goods. The doctrine of strict liability does *not* apply to Milly, the housewife, but it *does* apply to Milly, the commercial baker.

Unreasonably Dangerous. The doctrine of strict liability begins with a product which is defective because it is in an *unreasonably* dangerous condition to be used by the user or consumer. This point needs to be repeated: a manufacturer or seller becomes liable when a consumer or user is injured through the use of an *unreasonably* dangerous product, not through the use of a dangerous product. (In addition, the doctrine of strict liability requires that the product be in a defective condition when it leaves the seller. The seller is not responsible to alterations that others may thereafter make to the product.)

Suppose, for example, that Jed sells trampolines. The focus of his potential liability turns to the normal understanding of the consumer. As a reasonable person, Milly, the consumer, understands that a trampoline can put pressure on human joints because of its springing action. If she suffers a knee injury on one of Jed's trampolines, because of its springing action, she will not be able to demonstrate that the trampoline was *unreasonably* dangerous because she knew, or should have known, of the danger involved.

On the other hand, suppose that some of the trampolines sold by Jed are made with a light aluminum frame which is designed for use by children under the age of 12 years. He knows that it may collapse when a person over 175 lbs in weight jumps on it. If Milly, who weighs 200 lbs, uses the trampoline and is injured when it collapses, is Jed strictly liable? He is if there is no warning on the trampoline that clearly explains its weight limitations. The lack of a warning makes it *unreasonably* dangerous and therefore defective. In other words, its condition without the warning makes it dangerous for use by the consumer. A design limitation which the public would not normally anticipate must include a warning.

The question whether a *warning* is necessary to make a product not unreasonably dangerous was raised in the following case, *Travelers Ins. v. Federal Pacific Elec.* In this case a telephone switchboard was flooded at the RCA Global Communications offices in New York. Employees of the company dried out the equipment and started it up (by activating circuit breakers) without testing, as is usually done. "DeChiaro [an electrical technician] testified that he pressed the start button twice, and according to his and Castelli's [an electrical technician] trial testimony, there was a 'snap' and everyone ran from the room up the stairs and a 'big ball of fire' came right after them up the stairs." Traveler's insurance paid for the damage and then sued the manufacturer, Federal Pacific—which was its right under insurance law—to recover for any losses the manufacturer had wrongfully caused. Specifically, Traveler's said that Federal was strictly liable because the circuit breakers were defective or did not include adequate warnings about their operation.

Travelers Ins. v. Federal Pacific Elec.
625 N.Y.S.2d 121 (1995)

NARDELLI, Justice.

* * *

The jury found that the circuit breakers were not defectively or negligently designed. It found, however, that Federal was negligent in not giving adequate warnings and instructions and that this negligence was a proximate cause of the incident. It also found that damages were due to the misuse of the circuit breakers and switchboard by RCA's employees. It apportioned responsibility as follows: plaintiff 70%, defendant Federal 15%, and Uris Broad and Beaver Corporation (Uris), for whom the building was constructed, 15%.

Federal's contention that there was no duty to warn, since the circuit breaker was used in a way in which it as the manufacturer could not reasonably foresee, is without merit. "The question of foreseeability is one for the court when the facts are undisputed and but one inference can be drawn, it is for the jury when varying inferences may be drawn" * * * Since the evidence raised varying inferences, it was the province of the jury to decide whether the risk was foreseeable by defendant so as to impose a duty to warn * * *. Plaintiff's subrogor [RCA] was clearly a knowledgeable user of the circuit breakers, however; RCA did know of the danger with respect to which the warning was lacking.

Rosebrock v. General Electric Co., * * *, is cited by plaintiff as the seminal case that created the knowledgeable user exception. There, wooden blocks placed in a transformer for shipping purposes caused an explosion when the transformer was installed. The Court of Appeals noted, in that case: "If transformers, as known to the trade, were generally packed with wooden blocks in shipment, and the defendant had reason to believe that the power company knew this and would take them out, then the defendant would not be liable in selling its transformers without notice regarding the blocking because it would be guilty of no negligence" * * *.

In *Rosebrock*, there was conflicting evidence as to whether the power company knew of the wooden blocks, etc., and thus a factual issue was presented for jury determination. However,

> [t]here is "no necessity to warn a customer already aware—through common knowledge or learning—of a specific hazard" and, in the proper case, the court can decide as a matter of law that there is no duty to warn or that the duty has been discharged * * *. Plaintiff, an electronics technician, was a "knowledgeable user" of the connector plug, and thus there was no duty to warn.
>
> * * *

RCA's employees were the epitome of "knowledgeable users" of circuit breakers in a wet condition. Smith had a degree in electrical engineering with emphasis on power engineering. DeChiaro was a licensed electrician, and Castelli was an electrical technician at RCA for about 12 years.

* * *

Given the evidence as to the common knowledge of the minimal accepted practices in the field and the level of expertise, training and experience of the RCA electricians which

---

> encompassed the specific situation they faced, the * * * court should have found that there was no necessity on the part of Federal to warn RCA, which was already aware of the specific hazard, and the court should have granted Federal's motion entering judgement in its favor as a matter of law * * *.
>
> [Judgment as to Federal dismissed.]

DUTY TO WARN: a consumer/user is not entitled to a warning for dangers he already understands.

In short, there is no need to warn a consumer of a risk already known to the consumer. Although dangerous, the equipment was not *unreasonably* dangerous because "knowledgeable" consumers understood the risks involved in use of the equipment. Because the equipment was not unreasonably dangerous, it was not defective. Because the equipment was not defective, there was no strict liability.

The authors of the strict liability doctrine (quoted above) have stated: "A product is not in a defective condition [unreasonably dangerous] when it is safe for normal handling and consumption." [9] Thus, if Jed attempts to steal Milly's purse and she hits him over the head with an otherwise normal bottle of root beer, the manufacturer is not liable because the use is not within normal contemplation. Likewise, the manufacturer is not liable if Milly binges on root beer and becomes sick simply because she drinks too much.

Some products are *not* safe for normal use, but nevertheless are not defective (*unreasonably* dangerous). A baseball bat is an example of this. A baseball bat can cause serious injury or death, and may even be used as a weapon. But, it is not *unreasonably* dangerous because (1) it cannot be changed to make it safer, and (2) the consumer understands the dangers involved and needs no warning of them. Likewise, whiskey is dangerous, but it also is not *unreasonably* dangerous because "it cannot possibly be made entirely safe for all consumption"[10] and the consumer understands and needs no warning of the dangers involved in it's use.

Proximate Cause. Suppose that Milly buys and eats some worm-infested fruitcake, which she says makes her ill—just like Mr. Jordan claimed in *Jordan v. Coca Cola Bottling Co. of Utah* and Yong Cha Hong claimed in *Yong Cha Hong v. Marriott Corporation.* In addition to proving that the product was defective (because it was unreasonably dangerous) Milly must also prove that the defect *proximately caused* her illness.

Return to Milly, who is injured when a defective bottle of root beer explodes. Are the manufacturer and seller liable to her for her eye injury, caused by too much pressure in the bottle? The answer is yes. First, the beverage was sold to Milly by a manufacturer and seller who are in the business of selling bottled root beer. Second, with too much pressure in it, the bottle of root beer is defective because it is unreasonably dangerous. The product is unreasonably dangerous because the it is unsafe (unreasonably so) and because the consumer has no reason to know of that

---

[9] RESTATEMENT (SECOND) OF TORTS, § 402A, cmt. h.
[10] *Id.*

condition. Third, the defective condition of the bottled root beer proximately caused Milly personal injuries.

Problem Solving. Please turn to Chapter Problems at the end of this chapter and solve Problem 19.3.

Defenses. The next question is whether the manufacturer has any "defenses" in a strict liability claim? (That is, what conduct on the part of the consumer will bar recovery by the consumer?) If Sam was attempting to steal Milly's purse and she hit him over the head with a normal bottle of root beer, could she recover for her injuries if the blow to Sam's head caused the lid to pop off and hit her in the eye? (The obvious answer is that a manufacturer or seller is not liable for injuries caused by an unintended use or abuse of a product.)

The following paragraphs discuss the various "defenses" that may be used by a manufacturer or seller to prevent recovery by an injured consumer. These defenses include: (1) negligence by the consumer, (2) misuse or abuse of the product by the user or consumer, and (3) assumption of the risk by the consumer. In those cases where, for example, the product is defective and dangerous, and, the consumer misuses the product (or is negligent or assumes the risk), the proportion of responsibility is apportioned between the manufacturer/seller and the consumer on a comparative basis. Some states refer to this comparative system as comparative negligence, and others refer to it as comparative responsibility.

Negligence by the Consumer. Jed may purchase a SnowHopper snowmobile from Milly. While operating the snowmobile at high speed down a forest trail, he loses control and collides with a tree. The windscreen, which has become brittle from the cold, fragments into small pieces and one of those pieces causes Jed serious chest injuries. Jed sues, claiming that the windscreen should have been encased in a frame to keep it from fragmenting in a collision. He claims that collisions are reasonably foreseeable and this type of injury was foreseeable and easily preventable when the machine was designed and manufactured. Because of this design defect, Jed claims that the machine was unreasonably dangerous and therefore defective. In response, SnowHopper asserts that the principal cause of Jed's injuries was negligence in speeding down a forest trail.

Abuse of the Product. Suppose that Jed uses the tip of a table knife to tighten a screw on his wife's dish washer. The tip of the knife breaks off and Jed is thrown off balance and lurches forward with the result that his hand is injured by the knife. Jed sues, claiming that the knife is defective (unreasonably dangerous). He claims that use of the knife for routine tasks within a kitchen is foreseeable and that the knife should be strong enough for that use. On the other hand, Milly, the seller, claims that Jed has misused the product by applying it to uses for which it was never intended.

Assumption of the Risk. Assumption of the risk means that an injured consumer (1) knew of and appreciated a risk involved in a product use, and (2) voluntarily undertook that risk. For example, suppose that Milly, the 200 lb athlete, read the warning on her daughter's trampoline ("This device is not intended for use by any person over the age of 12 years or weighing more than 175 lbs.") but decided to use it anyway. Under these facts, the manufacturer or seller will assert that Milly understood the risk and voluntarily assumed that risk.

COMPARATIVE RESPONSIBILITY is a system which works like comparative negligence.

Comparative Negligence (Responsibility). In the discussion above (about defenses) it was asserted that a manufacturer or seller was strictly liable in relation to a defective product. In response, the manufacturer or seller has claimed that the consumer or user was negligent (the snowmobile), abused the product (the kitchen knife) or assumed the risks involved (the trampoline). There raise the question of how the responsibility of the parties will be compared. The answer is that most states use the comparative system they developed for use in relation to negligence cases.

It will be recalled from Chapter 6 that in cases where two parties are each negligent, 100% of negligence is apportioned between the parties (for example, A is 40% at fault and B is 60% at fault) and then damages are calculated. In most states, the same approach is taken with respect to strict liability: the responsibility of the manufacturer/seller is compared to the responsibility of the consumer/user. However, in the context of strict liability, the system is sometimes referred to as comparative responsibility instead of comparative negligence.

Thus, if a jury finds that Jed is negligent by operating the snowmobile too fast, and, that the SnowHopper company is responsible for making a defective machine, they must apportion the responsibility (100%) between Jed and SnowHopper. If the jury finds that Jed is 40% responsible and SnowHopper is 60% responsible, Jed will be able to recover 60% of the dollar value of his injuries. Thus, if his injuries are reasonably valued at $100,000, he will actually recover $60,000 from SnowHopper.[11] The same approach would be taken with respect to Jed's abuse of the kitchen knife and Milly's assumption of the risk involved in using a trampoline intended for children.

The following case, *Lutz v. National Crane Corp.*, is a case in which strict liability on the part of a crane manufacturer was compared against product misuse and assumption of the risk on the part of a deceased crane "groundman" by the name of Lutz.

A semi-trailer loaded with pipe overturned on a highway near Bozeman, Montana. Lutz was fastening chains to the pipe which were then moved by a crane to a waiting truck. Because some pipe were under power lines, the crane would drag the pipe sideways and—when clear of the power lines—lift the pipes up to the truck. Unfortunately, the tip of the crane touched a power line, and Lutz, the "groundman" who was holding the crane cable, was electrocuted. The plaintiff, Lori Lutz, suing on account of her husband's death, claimed the crane was defectively designed because the connection between the crane cable, and the chain at the end of it, was not

---

[11] Chapter 6 contains a more complete discussion of the operation of comparative negligence (comparative responsibility).

insulated. The defendant, National Crane, responded by claiming that dragging the pipe sideways was a misuse of the crane.

Lutz v. National Crane Corp.
884 P.2d 455 (1994)

HARRISON, Justice.

* * *

* * * Lori [Lutz] proceeded against National Crane on the theory of strict liability in tort, alleging that the crane—absent an insulated link—was defectively designed and unreasonably dangerous. National Crane raised the statutory affirmative defenses of assumption of risk and misuse.

The jury returned a $815,400 verdict in favor of Lori. That amount, however, was reduced by 20 percent, the percentage of responsibility allocated to Lutz. The $110,000 paid in settlement by other defendants was also deducted. Judgment was entered for $542,320, plus allowable costs. National Crane appealed from the verdict and judgment. Lori cross-appealed on the issues of assumption of risk and misuse, seeking to recover the jury's full determination of damages.

In 1987, the Montana Legislature enacted § 27-1-719, MCA, which established misuse as an affirmative defense in products liability cases. The statute provides that the defense may be asserted if "[t]he product was unreasonably misused by the user or consumer and such misuse caused or contributed to the injury." * * *

According to National Crane, two types of product misuse exist: 1) use for an improper purpose, such as using a glass bottle for a hammer; or 2) use in an improper manner, such as using a forklift on steep, rather than level, terrain. * * *

National Crane argues that Lutz used the crane in an improper manner by sideloading, or dragging the load, from beneath the power lines. * * *

* * *

According to National Crane, "a manufacturer is not responsible for injuries resulting from abnormal or unintended use of his product if such use was not reasonably foreseeable." * * *

* * *

In applying the misuse defense of § 27-1-719, MCA, to the facts of this case it is necessary to understand what the phrase "*un* reasonable misuse" means in the context of the statute. In using the term "unreasonable misuse," the plain language of the statute requires that if a misuse is "reasonable," then the defense is not available. Our statute clearly contemplates that manufacturers must expect, or, stated another way, must reasonably foresee, that their products will not always be used in precisely the manner for which they were designed or constructed—hence, the Legislature's use of the phrase "*un* reasonable misuse."

In the instant case, there is really no factual disagreement that cranes are often operated in close proximity to live electrical lines and that, as the evidence here indicates, side-loading is a not an uncommon, albeit improper, practice of crane operators and ground crews. Were that not the case, insulated links would not be as readily available and commonly used as they are and there would not be the high number of deaths and injuries from crane/power line contacts that there are.

Clearly, if, as here, the manufacturer expects or, stated another way, reasonably foresees, that its product is or will be subject to misuse in a certain fashion, then the fact that the user of the product actually does use—or, in the words of the statute, misuse—the product in that fashion can hardly be said to be "unreasonable." In short, reasonably foreseeable misuse is reasonable misuse. Furthermore, if the manufacturer reasonably foresees that its product can be misused in a certain fashion—i.e., that the offending misuse is "reasonable"—then the manufacturer does not have the benefit of a defense which exonerates or mitigates its breach of duty and its wrongful conduct in failing to design out or guard against the defect. To hold otherwise simply shifts the consequences of the manufacturer's breach of duty to the innocent, or perhaps, even negligent, user and, in violation of the statute, injects contributory negligence into the law of strict liability.

While "reasonableness" is generally a question of fact to be determined by the jury, cite, where, as in *Hart-Albin* and here, the party asserting the unreasonable misuse defense acknowledges the foreseeability of the misuse, then, as a matter of law, it is improper for the district court to submit that issue for determination to the trier of fact.

National Crane admits that the cranes which it manufactures can be misused through sideloading. National Crane also knows that if sideloading occurs in the vicinity of power lines, the possibility exists that its crane cables might contact power lines. It is undisputed that a crane/power line contact was foreseeable to National Crane. In fact, the record establishes that there are 2,300 crane/power line contacts in the United States each year and crane/power line electrocutions are the fifth leading cause of work-related deaths in the United States.

It is being admitted that the alleged misuse of the crane through sideloading was reasonably foreseeable to National Crane, we hold that, as a matter of law, the affirmative defense of unreasonable misuse is unavailable to National Crane. Therefore, we need not review whether the District Court correctly instructed the jury on misuse.

[The court also found against National Crane with respect to use of the defense of assumption of the risk.]

In light of our rulings on the affirmative defenses of misuse and assumption of risk, we remand and instruct the District Court to remove the 20 percent liability the jury apportioned to Lutz and instruct the District Court to reinstate the jury's full verdict of $815,400, minus the $110,000 paid by other defendants.

In *Lutz*, the court concluded that "sideloading" was so common, and thus so foreseeable, that it was not misuse of the crane. A crane must be fit for reasonably foreseeable uses, and if it is not, it is defective if it is unreasonably dangerous.

Problem Solving. Please turn to Chapter Problems at the end of this chapter and solve Problem 19.4.

Third Party Claims

A strict liability claim may be asserted by a consumer or user of a defective product; the claimant need not be a purchaser. In this context—looking from the perspective of a plaintiff—strict liability claims are easier to establish than Sales warranty claims, simply because the claimant is not required to prove that he or she purchased the product. Only status as a consumer or user is required to make a strict liability claim.

The point that consumers, users and *mere bystanders* may bring suit based on strict liability is highlighted in the following opinion of *Embs v. Pepsi-Cola Bot. Co. of Lexington*. As described earlier in this chapter, Embs was standing in a market when a bottle of Seven-Up exploded and caused her personal injuries. In this case, Embs was not a purchaser, consumer or user of the bottled drink, she was merely a bystander, who had no other relationship to the manufacturer or seller. May a person such as this bring suit based on strict liability? In the following opinion, the court considers comments by the authors of the *Restatement (Second) of Torts* § 402A (strict liability) and concludes that she is entitled to bring suit.

Embs v. Pepsi-Cola Bot. Co., of Lexington
528 S.W.2d 703 (1975)

LUKOWSKY, Justice.

* * *

The caveat to the section [Restatement of Torts (second) § 402A] provides that the Institute expresses no opinion as to whether the rule may not apply to harm to persons other than users or consumers. Comment on caveat o states the Institute expresses neither approval nor disapproval of expansion of the rule to permit recovery by casual bystanders and others who may come in contact with the product, and admits there may be no essential reason why such plaintiffs should not be brought within the scope of protection afforded, other than they do not have the same reasons for expecting such protection as the consumer who buys a marketed product, and that the social pressure which has been largely responsible for the development of the rule has been a consumer's pressure, and there is not the same demand for the protection of casual strangers.

The caveat articulates the essential point: Once strict liability is accepted, bystander recovery is *fait accompli*. * * *

* * *

The result which we reach does not give the bystander a "free ride." When products and consumers are considered in the aggregate, bystanders, as a class, purchase most of the same products to which they are exposed as bystanders. Thus, as a class, they indirectly subsidize the liability of the manufacturer, middleman and retailer and in this sense do pay for the insurance policy tied to the product.

* * *

For the sake of clarity we restate the extension of the rule. The protections of Section 402A of the Restatement of Torts 2d extend to bystanders whose injury from the defective product is reasonably foreseeable.

In the administration of the law we must be satisfied with proof which leads to a conclusion with reasonable probability where absolute logical certainty is not possible. We may be constrained to act upon indecisive evidence where complete proof is impossible. Then the logical, probative force of the evidence produced is measured in part by the test of whether it is the best evidence available. * * * The law does not require an injured plaintiff to go about picking up pieces of an exploded bottle while her leg bleeds profusely or the submission of these pieces, which are not obtainable because they have been discarded by the retailer, to an appropriate agency for the purpose of making a scientific inspection and determination as to defects.

It matters not that the evidence be circumstantial for as Thoreau put it "Some circumstantial evidence is very strong, as when you find a trout in the milk." There are some accidents, as where a beverage bottle explodes in the course of normal handling, as to which there is common experience that they do not ordinarily occur without a defect; and this permits the inference of a defect. * * * This is particularly true when there is evidence in the case of the antecedent explosion of other bottles of the same product. * * *

The conclusion, of course, is that Ms. Embs may bring suit based on strict liability, even though she was a bystander. She is not required to prove she is a consumer or user of the product. Or, if you will, this is an interpretation of the consumer/user language to the effect that bystanders are within the class of persons contemplated by the language consumer/user.

Multiple Claims

A last point. From the discussion above, it seems that in many cases a person injured by the use of a defective product will use the doctrine of strict liability as a means to gain a recovery. But there are instances where that may not be so. Thus, in instances where a product is inadequate, but not defective, a plaintiff may prefer to use a claim that an implied warranty of fitness for a particular purpose has been violated over a strict liability claim.

How does a plaintiff, commencing a lawsuit, decide which theory (negligence, warranty or strict liability) to pursue? This is a compelling question because sometimes it is only the process of discovery or trial that reveals a correct version of the facts. And without a reliable version of the facts, how can a plaintiff choose the best legal theory? (The same point is true for a defendant: how can a defendant know which defense is the best without the benefit of a correct version of the facts?)

The answer is that a plaintiff is not required to choose between theories (nor a defendant between defenses), but may pursue all of them. On this point, the rules of pleading state: "A party may . . . state as many separate claims or defenses as he has *regardless of consistency.*"[12] In other words, a party may assert multiple inconsistent claims and defenses. In fact, this is a common practice, and plaintiffs and defendants routinely assert all claims and defenses they have—or might have—and wait for the evidence to validate or eliminate these claims and defenses.

Allowing a plaintiff to assert multiple theories of recovery does not mean that a plaintiff is allowed multiple recoveries. If, for example, Milly is injured in a product liability case, and her injuries are fairly valued at $75,000, this is all she is entitled to recover, whether she is successful on one legal theory, or on many legal theories.

Problem Solving. Please turn to Chapter Problems at the end of this chapter and solve Problem 19.5.

---

[12] UTAH R. CIV. P. 8(e)(2) (emphasis added).

Chapter Problems

Problem 19.1

In *practical* terms, what is a significant problem (not discussed in the chapter) for a plaintiff's lawyer in *Jordan v. Coca Cola Bottling Co. of Utah* and *Yong Cha Hong v. Marriott Corporation* (a woman ate a piece of fried chicken that allegedly had a "worm" in it)?

Problem 19.2

Admittedly, a lot of the *Yong Cha Hong v. Marriott Corporation* case has been cut out, making this question more difficult. Nevertheless, why is Judge Smalkin asking what Maryland law is?

Problem 19.3

A drug company proposes to sell Baldban, a drug which restores the hair of bald men. However, a side effect is that it sometimes causes minor liver damage. Can this drug be sold without incurring strict liability losses?

Problem 19.4

In *Lutz v. National Crane Corp.*, assume —contrary to what was actually decided—that National Crane is 55% responsible because the crane is defective, and that Lutz is 45% responsible because of misuse and assumption of the risk. If the jury finds damages to be $900,000, how much will Lutz, the plaintiff, receive.

Problem 19.5

Jed, a baseball player wearing sunglasses, loses an eye when he is hit in the eye with a baseball. Contrary to what he was told by the seller, the "glasses" are made of glass and not plastic, and they shatter when hit by a baseball. In an actual case, a jury found the defendants *negligent*, in violation of *Sales warranties*, and, *strictly liable*. If Jed's injuries are valued at $100,000, how much will he receive?

Chapter Outline

The objective of this chapter is to define the term *negotiable instrument*; explain the uses of negotiable instruments; introduce Revised Article 3 of the Uniform Commercial Code; and, discuss the concept of negotiability. The chapter is organized as follows:

- *Negotiable Instrument.* A negotiable instrument is a specialized contract. It is specialized in three ways: (1) a negotiable instrument deals with the right to receive *money*; (2) a negotiable instrument is easily *transferred* from person to person; and, (3) a holder in due course of a negotiable instrument (discussed in a later chapter) has a *protected* right to receive payment.

- *Negotiable Instrument Uses.* A negotiable instrument may be used for at least two reasons: (1) a negotiable instrument is used as part of the process of extending *credit*; and, (2) a negotiable instrument is used as a *substitute for money*.

- *Revised Article 3.* The law relating to negotiable instruments is found in the *Uniform Commercial Code* (UCC). The UCC is divided into *Articles*, and the law of negotiable instruments is found in *Revised Article 3*.

- *Negotiability.* A contract is classified as negotiable if it meets the requirements found in § 3-104(a). To be negotiable, a contract must be *in writing* and *signed* and meet the following requirements: (1) it must contain an *unconditional promise or order*; (2) it must be for a *fixed amount of money*; (3) it must be *payable to order or bearer*; and (4) it must be *payable on demand or at a definite time*.

- *Contract Obligation.* A document which is not a negotiable instrument *may still be a contract* if it meets the requirements for contracts.

Introduction

Negotiable Instrument Defined. A negotiable instrument is a specialized contract which is used to transfer the right to receive money from person to person. If Milly borrows money to buy a new car, the bank does not give her a suitcase full of twenty dollar bills. Instead, it may give her a negotiable instrument called a cashier's check. This specialized contract gives Milly the right to receive money from the bank, and Milly easily transfers that right to the car dealer.

In addition—if the car dealer qualifies as a holder in due course—the law of negotiable instruments offers him great legal protection in his right to receive payment of the cashier's check.

Thus, a negotiable instrument is a contract which is specialized in three ways:

NEGOTIABLE INSTRUMENTS transfer money and protect the right of payment.

1.   *Money*: A negotiable instrument is a contract which deals with money.

2.   *Transfer*: A negotiable instrument is a contract which is easy to transfer from person to person, a process called negotiation.

3.   *Payment*: A holder in due course of a negotiable instrument is protected in his or her right to receive payment.

NEGOTIABLE INSTRUMENTS are used to extend credit and as a substitute for money.

Why Use Negotiable Instruments? Why use a negotiable instrument? There are two reasons, the first of which is the process of extending credit. When Milly borrowed money from her bank, she signed a promissory note in which she promised to repay the money she borrowed. Thus, use of the promissory note is part of the process in which the bank extended credit to Milly.

The second reason to use a negotiable instrument is as a substitute for money. Instead of giving her a suitcase full of cash, the bank used a cashier's check to give Milly the right to receive the money she had borrowed. Then, instead of giving a suitcase full of cash to the car dealer, she transferred the cashier's check to him. And, instead of carrying a suitcase full of cash to his bank, the car dealer simply transferred the cashier's check to his bank, which then collected the money from Milly's bank. Thus, the cashier's check is used as a substitute for money.

In summary, negotiable instruments may be used for two reasons:

1.   *Credit*: A negotiable instrument is used as part of the process of extending credit.

2.   *Substitute for Money*: A negotiable instrument is used as a substitute for money.

Problem Solving. Please turn to Chapter Problems at the end of this chapter and solve Problem 20.1.

THE LAW OF NEGOTIABLE INSTRUMENTS is in Revised Article 3 of the Uniform Commercial Code.

Revised Article 3. The law of negotiable instruments is found in the Uniform Commercial Code, which is often called the "UCC." The UCC is subdivided into "Articles," and the law of negotiable instruments is found in Article 3. Article 3 has been recently revised, and the most current version of negotiable instruments law is found in Revised Article 3 of the UCC. Selected provisions from Revised Article 3 are reproduced in Appendix A at the end of this chapter. The UCC, and periodic amendments thereto, are adopted independently by each state.

Types of Negotiable Instruments. There are several types of negotiable instruments. There are promissory notes, certificates of deposit, drafts, and a variety of checks. (Each of these types of negotiable instruments is discussed in Chapter 21.) Before discussing these various types of negotiable instruments, it is important to note that there is one thing they all have in common: they are negotiable. In this Chapter 20 there is a discussion of what it is that makes an instrument negotiable; then, in Chapter 21 there is a discussion of the various *types* of negotiable instruments.

Negotiability.

At this point there is a discussion of the rules which distinguish between documents which are negotiable and those which are not. This subject is called *negotiability*. The subject of negotiability is important because documents which *are* negotiable receive different treatment than documents which are *not* negotiable. (As will be learned later, the different treatment is that documents which are negotiable are more easily transferred, and the holder may receive preferential treatment in receiving payment.)

A Simple Illustration. Following are two documents, only one of which is a negotiable instrument. The rules which determine negotiability are found in § 3-104 (a) in Appendix A. Section 3-104 (a) is one of the most important sections in the law of negotiable instruments, so it is worth reading with some care. Please read Section 3-104 (a) and then decide which document is a negotiable instrument, and why.

Document 20.1

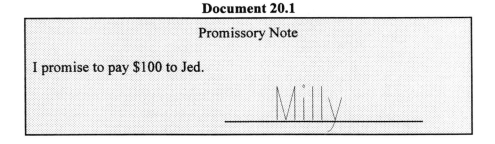

Promissory Note

I promise to pay $100 to Jed.

Document 20.2

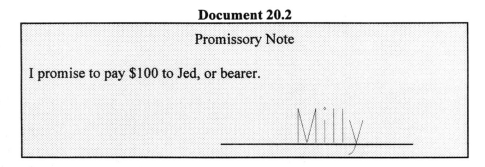

Promissory Note

I promise to pay $100 to Jed, or bearer.

Section 3-104 (a) (1) provides that a negotiable instrument must be "payable to bearer or to order." Thus, Document 20.2 is a negotiable instrument, but Document 20.1 is not. The point with respect to Document 20.1 and Document 20.2 is that the rules of negotiability are found in § 3-104 (a), and documents which conform to this subsection are negotiable instruments, and all others are not.

Negotiability Requirements

The balance of this chapter will be devoted to a discussion of the specific rules of negotiability, which will be done by studying § 3-104 (a) and related sections. To keep things simple, all of the documents in this chapter will be promissory notes. But, it is important to note—as will be learned in Chapter 21—there are a variety of negotiable instruments (for example, notes, drafts and checks) with a variety of different uses. All of them are subject to § 3-104 (a).

§ 3-104 (a). All negotiable instruments must be in writing and signed.[1] To qualify as a negotiable instrument, a document must meet the following requirements:

- Negotiable Instruments must include an *Unconditional Promise* or an *Unconditional Order*. [3-104 (a)]

- Negotiable Instruments must be for a *Fixed Amount of Money*. [§3-104 (a)]

- Negotiable Instruments must be Payable to *Order or to Bearer*. [§3-104(a)(1)]

- Negotiable Instruments must be Payable *on Demand or at a Definite Time*. (§3-104 (a) (2)]

In the following discussion, each of the four requirements described above is applied:

UNCONDITIONAL PROMISE OR ORDER: a negotiable instrument must contain an *unconditional* promise or order (to pay money).

Unconditional Promise or Order. The first requirement is that a negotiable instrument must contain an *unconditional* promise or order. Consider the next two documents and indicate which is negotiable and which is not:

---

[1] Section 3-103 (6) and (9) does not say *on what* the promise or order must be written. Negotiable instruments have been written on *paper* (the usual practice), on a *board* (in payment to a general contractor), on a *coconut* (from a friend in the South Pacific), and, on a *shirt* (to the IRS: "here is the shirt off my back"). Obviously, these instruments—if checks—would not pass through a checking system, but they are otherwise generally enforceable. Also, "*signed*" is liberally defined in § 1-201 (39) as "any symbol executed or adopted by a party with present intention to authenticate a writing."

Document 20.3

Promissory Note

I promise to pay $10,000 to the order of Jed if I get an inheritance from my grandfather.

_____

Document 20.4

Promissory Note

I promise to pay $10,000 to the order of Jed.

_____

Which of the two documents is negotiable? The answer is obvious: Document 20.3 is not negotiable, but Document 20.4 is. Document 20.3 is not negotiable because the promise is *conditional*—"I promise to pay, *if* I get an inheritance."

What is, and is not, *conditional* can sometimes be difficult to determine. Because this is a difficult problem, there is a separate section (§ 3-106) which deals exclusively with this issue. Please turn to Appendix A and read § 3-106 carefully and then decide which of the following paragraphs in Document 20.5 is acceptable:

Document 20.5

Promissory Note

I promise to pay $10,000 to the order of Jed.

[a] This instrument is subject to the provisions of a mortgage signed on the same day.

[b] This instrument is secured by a mortgage signed on the same day.

[c] This instrument is payable only from funds of ABC, Inc., a Michigan corporation.

_____

Option [a] is conditional, and thus not negotiable, because it is subject another writing, which is prohibited by § 3-106 (a) (ii). *Being subject to another writing* means that the other writing must be consulted to understand the rights of the parties to the instrument. On the other hand, option [b] is unconditional, and thus negotiable. As § 3-106 (a) provides: "*A reference to another writing* does not of itself make the promise or order conditional." In addition, option [c] is treated as unconditional, which means that it is negotiable. Section 3-106 (b) (ii) allows payment to be limited to a particular fund or source.[2]

In the following case, *Western Bank v. RaDEC Const. Co. Inc.*, the court had to decide whether the language "payee must prove clear title to material" in the corner of a check made it *conditional*, and thus not negotiable. RaDEC was a general contractor on a project, and Jerry Ball (dba Contractor's Carpet Center) was a subcontractor. Carpet Center was having financial problems and RaDEC agreed to advance it $8,743.52, provided the money was used to pay for carpet and supplies. To accomplish this purpose, RaDEC typed "payee must prove clear title to material" in the lower left-hand corner of the check.

Carpet Center did not honor the agreement with RaDEC (to use the money only for carpet and supplies) and RaDEC stopped payment on the check. Apparently, Carpet Center was no longer solvent, so a controversy developed between RaDEC and the bank. If the check is *conditional* it is not negotiable and RaDEC will win. On the other hand, if the check is *unconditional,* the bank will win because the check will be a negotiable instrument and the bank will be a holder in due course.[3] Thus, the court had to decide whether the language in question made the check unconditional.

Western Bank v. RaDEC Const. Co., Inc.
42 UCC Rep. Ser. (1986)

HERTZ, J.

* * *

The trial court directed a verdict for the Bank at the close of all the evidence, holding as a matter of law, that the phrase typed in at the lower left corner of the check, "payee must prove clear title to material," did not have the effect of making the check conditional, and that Bank was a bonafide holder in due course. This was a law question properly addressed by the trial court. * * *

SDCL 57A-3-104(1) sets forth four elements necessary to constitute a writing as a negotiable instrument. (a) It must be signed by the maker; (b) contain an unconditional promise or order to pay a sum certain in money and no other promise, order, obligation or power given by the maker or drawer except as authorized by this chapter; (c) be payable on demand or at a definite time; and (d) be payable to order or to bearer.

---

[2] The old version of Article 3 did not allow an author of a negotiable instrument to limit payment to a fund or source, but the Revised Article 3 does.

[3] Holder in due course status will be discussed in Chapter 23. A holder in due course has a protected right to receive payment.

In this case, there is no dispute that elements (a), (c) and (d) have been fulfilled. RaDEC claims, however, that element (b) has not been met because the check was a "conditional instrument" and therefore subject to his defenses.

RaDEC relies heavily on our decision in Bank of America v. Butterfield, 77 S.D. 170, 88 N.W.2d 909 (1958). In that case, the draft in question stated: "Subject to approval of title, pay to the order of Vernon H. Butterfield and Laura E. Butterfield." It is important to note that the phrase "subject to approval of title" immediately precedes the standard phrase, "Pay to the order of." The Bank of America, nevertheless, claimed it was a holder in due course and that the Butterfields should be held liable for the amount of the draft. In affirming the trial court we said:

> "In addition to other requirements, an instrument to be negotiable 'must contain an unconditional promise or order to pay a sum certain in money.'
> The promise or order to pay money contained in the draft in question is clearly not unconditional. The payment therein ordered is subject to approval of title. Consequently, it is not a negotiable instrument."

Negotiability is determined from the face, the four corners, of the instrument without reference to extrinsic facts. The conditional or unconditional character of the promise or order is to be determined by what is expressed in the instrument itself. * * *

RaDEC claims that the check was not a negotiable instrument because of the condition written on its face. Moreover, RaDEC argues that the location of the conditional language in the place usually reserved for "memo" is of little consequence, since the language itself was sufficient to give Bank notice that RaDEC's obligation to pay was conditioned upon Carpet Center's having proved clear title to the material.

The Bank, on the other hand, argues that the instant factual situation can be distinguished from that of Bank of America, supra., because in that case the conditional language, i.e., "subject to approval of title," preceded the words "Pay to the Order of" the Butterfields. Further, a witness for the Bank testified that RaDEC's "conditional" phrase was located at the place reserved for "memos" by the maker of drawer of the check, and as such were not calculated to draw the specific attention of the Bank's personnel in the ordinary day to day processing of checks.

We conclude that the phrase "payee must prove clear title to material" written where it was, did not make the check "conditional" thereby depriving the Bank of its status as a holder in due course. It appears that the notation in the "memo" area of the check is nothing more than a self-serving declaration by RaDEC for its own benefit and record keeping and for informational purposes only. An otherwise unconditional negotiable instrument cannot be rendered conditional by such a device.

[Judgment in favor of the Bank, affirmed.]

The bank won because the check in question was negotiable. The check was negotiable because the notation "payee must prove clear title to material" was typed in the "memo" corner of the check. The court concluded that the drawer, RaDEC, was simply making a notation to itself and did not intend to impose a condition on payment. If the notation had been placed in a manner that made payment conditional on an event happening—in this case, making sure that payment produced clear title to carpeting materials—then the check would have been conditional and nonnegotiable, and RaDEC would have won.

314

A FIXED AMOUNT OF MONEY: a negotiable instrument must require payment of a fixed amount of money (principal).

A Fixed Amount of Money. The second requirement of negotiability is that a negotiable instrument must require payment of a fixed amount of money. [§ 3-104(a)] Consider Document 20.6 and decide which options will destroy negotiability:

Document 20.6

Promissory Note

[a] I promise to pay 10,000 Mexican pesos to the order of Jed, one year from the date hereof.

[b] Interest on the principal amount shall run at 6%, but in no event shall the rate of interest be less than the lending rate of the Federal Reserve Board.

[c] In the event of default, the maker agrees to pay a reasonable attorney's fee and costs for enforcement.

All parts of Document 20.6 are acceptable; it is a negotiable instrument. Examine part [a] first. A negotiable instrument may be payable in the money of a foreign government, which includes Mexican pesos. This rule is described in § 1-201 (24).

But what about parts [b] and [c] of Document 20.6? Don't they violate the requirement that the amount of money must be "fixed"? The answer is found in the official comments that the authors of the UCC include with their work. The Official Comment to § 3-112 says that "the requirement of a 'fixed amount' *applies only to principal*." Understanding that the fixed amount requirement applies only to principal makes it easy to solve parts [b] and [c].

What about the interest rate in part [b]? It is obvious that in a time of inflation the lending rate of the Federal Reserve Board may rise, and if it rises above 6%, the interest rate will rise with it. This floating interest rate is acceptable for two reasons: first, section 3-112 (b) provides that the interest rate may be fixed or variable, and that the interest rate "may require reference to information not contained in the instrument." Second, as we learned above, the fixed amount requirement applies only to principal and not to interest or other charges.

The rule that the fixed amount requirement applies only to principal is also the answer to the provision for attorney's fees in part [c]. Attorney's fees and costs of enforcement are not part of the principal amount and they may therefore vary according to the facts of each case.

Problem Solving. Please turn to Chapter Problems at the end of this chapter and solve Problem 20.3.

Payable to Order or Bearer. The third requirement of negotiability is that a negotiable instrument must be payable *to order or bearer*. In the following document, Milly desires to properly prepare a negotiable instrument that will transfer $100 to Jed. One of the four options below is not acceptable. Decide which option is not acceptable, and why.

Document 20.7

Promissory Note
[a] I hereby promise to pay to Jed debt of $100 I owe to him.
[b] I promise to pay $100 to John, or to bearer.
[c] I promise to pay $100 to the order of Jed, or to bearer.
[d] I promise to pay $100 to the order of Jed.
_____ Milly

Examine Document 20.7 and observe in which of the options Milly is simply making promises or orders about payment, and in which she is agreeing to negotiability. In option [a] Milly promises to pay the money, but this option does not contain the language of negotiability; it is not payable to order or to bearer. Option [b] is negotiable; it is payable to bearer. Option [c] is negotiable; an instrument payable to order or to bearer is a bearer instrument. Option [d] is negotiable; it is payable to order. [§ 3-109(a)(1)]

It is important to understand the legal principle at issue. A document made out like option [a] is a *simple contract*. In contrast, a document made out like options [b], [c] or [d] is negotiable. Over many years, the understanding has developed that a person—like Milly—who uses the words *to order or to bearer* is agreeing that the document will be negotiable. The legal principle is that a negotiable instrument may be freely transferred and paid in ways that a simple contract is not.

Order. Another point needs to be made, and that is about the different ways the word *order* may be used in relation to negotiable instruments. One may laugh at the person who discusses automobiles and concludes that a *wheel* on which a car rides and a steering *wheel* must be the same thing because they are both called a "wheel."

But, there is a similar problem in the law of negotiable instruments because there the word *order* is used in two different ways.

Here are the two different ways the word *order* is used: First, the word *order* is used as part of the language by which the author of a document agrees that it will be negotiable. For example: "I promise to pay $400 *to the order* of John." Second, the word *order* is also used to distinguish between order instruments (drafts) and promises (notes). Specifically, in some instruments the author makes a *promise* to pay money: "I promise to pay $100 to the order of John." But, in other instruments, the author gives a command (an *order*) that another person, such as a bank, pay money: "To First Bank: *Pay* $100 to John, or bearer."

___**Problem Solving**___. Please turn to Chapter Problems at the end of this chapter and solve Problem 20.4.

Payable on Demand or at a Definite Time. The fourth requirement of negotiability is that a negotiable instrument must be payable on demand or at a definite time. In simple terms, the language of the instrument must make clear *when* the holder will be paid. A promissory note which provides for payment "on July 15, 2010," is negotiable, but a promissory note which provides for payment "on July 15, 2010, or thereafter," is not negotiable. As discussed above, an instrument which says nothing about when it is payable is called a "demand" instrument, which means that the holder is entitled to payment any time he or she presents it for payment.

Please read § 3-108, in Appendix A, which states rules about a definite time. Decide whether the promissory note in Document 20.8 is negotiable:

Document 20.8

Promissory Note
I hereby promise to pay $100 to the order of Jed on July 15, 2010, or thereafter at the option of the holder.
 Milly _____

Document 20.8 is negotiable. The person that the "definite time" rule protects is the holder, who is the person entitled to payment. In Document 20.8, the *holder* is entitled to payment on July 15, 2010, a definite time. If there is any extension of that time, it is at the option of the holder, which obviously does not place the holder at any disadvantage. Payment *at the will* of the holder, or *at the option* of the holder, is permitted by § 3-108 (a) and (b).

A definite time of payment was at issue in *Northern Bank v. Pefferoni Pizza Co.* Duane J. Dowd, acting as president of the Pefferoni Pizza Company, signed a promissory note in the face amount of $125,000, payable to W.E. Peffer Enterprises. The note made reference to other loan transactions and provided that the term (the period over which the money would be paid) and the interest rate of the Pefferoni note would change as the term and interest rate changed in the other loan transactions. That meant, of course, that it was impossible to know exactly when the Pefferoni note would be paid off. The court had to decide whether this lack of certainty as to time of payment made the note nonnegotiable.

Northern Bank v. Pefferoni Pizza Co.
555 N.W.2d 338 (1996)

SIEVERS, Judge.

* * *

The time of payment is definite if it can be determined from the face of the instrument. * * * If the extension is to be at the option of the maker, a definite time limit must be stated or the time of payment remains uncertain and the instrument is not negotiable. * * *

> When the maker or acceptor has the option to extend the time of payment or when the time is extended automatically upon a specified act or event, the holder has no power to determine when payment will be made. Thus, unless the option to extend is limited to an extension to a definite time, the holder will not know when he can expect payment. As a result, when the time for payment may be extended by the maker or acceptor or automatically upon the occurrence of a specified event, the instrument will be payable at a definite time only if this right is limited to extension to a further definite time.

4 William D. Hawkland & Lary Lawrence, Uniform Commercial Code Series § 3-109:05 at 141 (1994).

An instrument is payable at a definite time if by its terms it is payable (a) on or before a stated date or at a fixed period afer a stated date or (b) at a fixed period after sight. * * *

* * * We acknowledge that the collateral note [the Pefferoni note] will have to be paid off within 84 months following payment or reduction of the underlying notes [the other loan transactions]. The question is whether this is a further definite time.

> If the instrument is payable upon an event uncertain as to time of occurrence, it is also not payable at a definite time. It is irrelevant that the event is certain to occur or even that it has already occurred. Instruments which are payable "at death" or "upon the sale of the house" or "at earliest convenience" are not payable at a definite time. In none of these cases can a holder determine when payment is due by reference to the instrument alone.

4 Hawkland & Lawrence, supra, § 3-209:02 at 136. Furthermore, a note payable upon the acceptance of a loan commitment is not payable at a definite time. See, e.g., *Barton v. Scott Hudgens Realty*, 136 Ga.App. 565, 222 S.E.2d 126 (1975).

In *Cartwright v. MBank Corpus Christi*, N.A., 865 S.W.2d 546 (Tex.App.1993), the court found that a provision in a note allowing the maker the option to extend the note for up to 4 years constituted a definite time. However, *Cartwright* is distinguishable from the case before us. In *Cartwright*, the note was due September 24, 1985, subject to the maker's option to extend the note for up to 4 years. Thus, the note was payable at a fixed period, 4 years, after a stated date, September 24, 1985. In the instant case, the stated date, from which an extension of up to 84 months may be made, is the date of payment or reduction of the underlying notes, a date which, as discussed above, cannot be determined from the face of the collateral note.

The time of payment of the collateral note cannot be determined from the face of the

> note, nor was it reasonably ascertainable at the time the note was issued. Therefore, the collateral note is not payable at a definite time subject to extension to a further definite time at the option of Pefferoni. See § 3-109, comment 2 (Reissue 1980). The collateral note is not a negotiable instrument, and consequently, Northern is not a holder in due course. See Neb.U.C.C. § 3-302(1) (Reissue 1980). The collateral note may be enforceable as a contract and therefore subject to all claims and defenses arising out of that contract, see *P P Inc. v. McGuire*, 509 F.Supp. 1079 (D.N.J.1981), a matter which we need not decide on this appeal, but it is not enforceable as a negotiable instrument under article 3 of the U.C.C.
>
> CONCLUSION
>
> We conclude that the district court erred in granting summary judgment in favor of Northern, as the collateral note is not a negotiable instrument and Northern is not a holder in due course. Accordingly, we reverse the judgment of the district court.
>
> REVERSED.

The following is from the opinion above: "[the Pefferoni note] will have to be paid off within 84 months *following* payment or reduction of the underlying notes." The question, of course, is to know when— or if— the "underlying notes" will be paid off. That meant that there was no specific cut-off date by which the Pefferoni notes must be paid. Thus, the note was not payable at a definite time and was not negotiable.

Problem Solving. Please turn to Chapter Problems at the end of this chapter and solve Problem 20.5.

A Final Point

CONTRACT OBLIGATION: many instruments are enforceable as simple contracts, even though they are not negotiable.

Refer again to Document 20.1 and Document 20.2 at the beginning of this chapter. Having concluded that Document 20.1 is not a negotiable instrument, does that mean that Bill does not owe $100 to Amy? The answer is no, he still owes the money. A document which is not a negotiable instrument may still be a contract, and that contract may still be enforced. The difference is that Document 20.1 does not have the advantages of a negotiable instrument.

This point was made in the *Pefferoni Pizza* case which is discussed above. Having concluded that a certain document was not a negotiable instrument, the court observed: "The collateral note [the Pefferoni note] may [nevertheless] be enforceable as a contract." But, the court continued, the contract will be "subject to all claims and defenses arising out of that contract."

Problem Solving. Please turn to Chapter Problems at the end of this chapter and solve Problem 20.6.

Problem 20.1

Based on what you have learned so far, is the following a negotiable instrument? Please Explain.

> **Promissory Note**
>
> I promise to pay $500 to the order of Jed, or, at the maker's option, to deliver to the payee securities having an equal value.
>
> _Milly_

Problem 20.2

It is claimed that the following document is not negotiable because it is conditional in violation of § 3-104 (a). Specifically, it is claimed that the obligation to deliver a Cadillac constitutes a condition to the payment of the $10,000. Is the document negotiable? Please explain.

> **Promissory Note**
>
> I promise to pay $10,000 to the order of Jed, thirty days from the day hereof. This note is given in return for a 1990 Cadillac to be received by me.
>
> _Milly_

Problem 20.3

Is the following negotiable? Please explain.

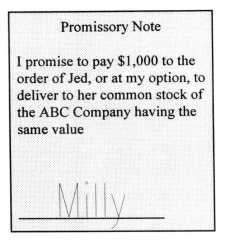

> **Promissory Note**
>
> I promise to pay $1,000 to the order of Jed, or at my option, to deliver to her common stock of the ABC Company having the same value
>
> _Milly_

Problem 20.4

Is the following negotiable? Please explain.

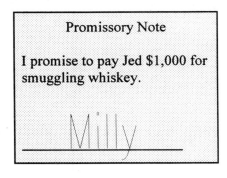

> **Promissory Note**
>
> I promise to pay Jed $1,000 for smuggling whiskey.
>
> _Milly_

Problem 20.5

Is the following a time instrument or a demand instrument? Please explain.

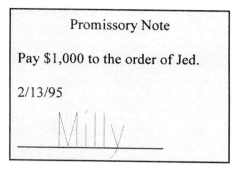

Promissory Note

Pay $1,000 to the order of Jed.

2/13/95

Milly

Problem 20.6

Which of the following—if found in the text of a "negotiable" instrument—would destroy its negotiability:

a] Non-Negotiable Draft

[b] You will recall that you owe me $1,000 as rent for the use of my mountain cabin last summer.

[c] Pay $1,000 to the order of my sister, Marsha Smith, 30 days after acceptance.

[d] This instrument is issued pursuant to the provisions of the cabin lease we signed last year.

[e] This instrument runs at 15% interest from the date of acceptance.

Chapter Outline

The objective of this chapter is to learn the different *types* of negotiable instruments and how some of them are used. The chapter is organized as follows:

- *Note.* A negotiable instrument containing a promise to pay money is called a note. (A mere *acknowledgment of debt*, such as an I.O.U., is not a note.) A note has two parties, a *maker* and a *payee*. Having several makers or several payees does not change the classification as "two-party." Notes may be payable on *demand* or after the expiration of a period of *time*. A negotiable instrument is payable on demand if it does not state when it is payable. (This rule applies to all negotiable instruments.)

- *Draft.* A negotiable instrument containing an order to pay money is called a draft. A draft has three parties, a *drawer*, a *drawee* and a *payee*. A drawee may be a person, a business or a bank. Sometimes the drawer and the drawee are the same person. (If the drawer is also the drawee, a draft is still classified as a "three-party" instrument.) When a drawee accepts, he or she is also called an *acceptor*. A draft may be payable on *demand* or after the expiration of a period of *time.*

- *Check.* If the drawee of a draft is a bank, and it is payable on demand, the instrument is called a check. A cashier's check is a check in which the drawer and the drawee are the same bank. A teller's check is a check in which the drawer is a bank and the drawee is another bank. A traveler's check is payable on demand, on or through a bank, and requires a countersignature; it is titled "traveler's check" or something similar.

Introduction

Negotiable instruments contain either a *promise* to pay money or an *order* to pay money. A promissory note is an example of a negotiable instrument which contains a *promise* to pay money. (To see an example of a promissory note, look at Document 21.1 below.) The two types of negotiable instrument which contain a promise to pay money are a *note* and a *certificate of deposit*. Each of these is discussed later in this chapter.

A check is an example of a negotiable instrument which contains an order pay money. (To see an example of a check, look at Document 21.5 below). Five types of negotiable instruments contain an *order* to pay money. These five types are the following: *draft, check, cashier's check, teller's check*, and *traveler's check.* Each of these types of negotiable instrument is discussed later in this chapter.

Promises

NOTE: a (promissory) note is a two-party promise to pay money, with a maker and a payee.

Note. A *note* is the simplest form of negotiable instrument. It has two parties, a *maker* who makes a *promise* to pay, and a *payee* who receives payment. [§§ 3-104(e), 3-103(9) and 3-103(5)] (An I.O.U. is not a note because it is merely an acknowledgment of a debt; it is not a promise to pay.) Document 21.1 is an example of a note in which Milly is the maker and Jed is the payee:

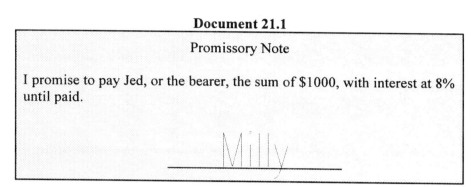

Document 21.1

Promissory Note

I promise to pay Jed, or the bearer, the sum of $1000, with interest at 8% until paid.

Milly
_____

When is Jed entitled to receive the money described in Document 21.1? On that point, a negotiable instrument is either a *demand* instrument or a *time* instrument. Document 21.1 is a demand instrument because Jed is entitled to receive the money any time he demands it. [§ 3-108(a)(ii)] On the other hand, if the language of Document 21.1 was "one year from the date of this instrument, I promise to pay . . ." it would be a *time* instrument because it would be payable after the passage of time (one year).

There are a variety of descriptive labels that can be attached to notes, depending on how they are used. Some of those descriptive labels are as follows:

Promissory Note: This is the most common name for a note because in a note the maker makes a promise to pay. Document 21.1 may be called a promissory note.

Demand Note: Document 21.1 is a promissory note, and it is sometimes called a demand note because the payee, Mike, is entitled to be paid any time he makes the demand.

Time Note: Document 21.1 is a promissory note, and if it contained the language "One year from the date of this instrument, I promise to pay . . ." it could be called a time note because time must pass before the note is paid.

Installment Note: Document 21.1 is a promissory note, and if it was payable at the rate of $100 per month it could be called an installment note because it would be payable in installments.

Mortgage Note: Document 21.1 is a promissory note, and if it contained language like "this note is secured by a mortgage on real property," it could be called a mortgage note.

Collateral Note: Document 21.1 is a promissory note, and if it contained language like "this note is secured by a security interest in personal property," it could be called a collateral note.

Problem Solving. Please turn to Chapter Problems at the end of this chapter and solve Problem 21.1.

Certificate of Deposit. A *certificate of deposit* is a note of a bank. [§ 3-104(j)] In a certificate of deposit, the bank promises to pay money to the payee named in the instrument. Document 21.2 is a certificate of deposit.

Document 21.2

Certificate of Deposit
First National Bank

This certifies that there has been deposited in the First National Bank the sum of $10,000.00.

Ten thousand and no/100~ Dollars which is payable to

the order of Jed on the 3rd day of July, 19 97 with interest to

maturity at the rate of 5.00 % per annum upon presentation and surrender of this certificate properly indorsed.

First National Bank

Date: January 3, 1997   by M. R. Owens

Cashier

Banks need money to loan to their customers and they will pay interest to use their customer's money. For example, First National Bank may be willing to pay a customer 5% to use a customer's money for six months and 6% to use the customer's money for one year. The customer deposits money with the bank for the period of time he or she chooses and in return the bank gives the customer a certificate of deposit which states the period of time and the agreed rate of interest. Document 21.2 is, of course, a six month certificate of deposit with interest at 5%.

Recall that a certificate of deposit is a note of a bank, and that a note is a two-party instrument with a maker and a payee. If a certificate of deposit has two payees: "pay to the order of Jed or Milly," does this make a certificate of deposit a three-party instrument; and, if there are three payees, Jed, Milly, or Sam, does that make a certificate of deposit a four-party instrument, and so on? The answer is that a certificate of deposit remains a two-party instrument, no matter how many payees or makers there are. There is one category of persons called maker, no matter how many persons are in that category, and there is one category of persons called payee, no matter how many persons are in that category. This rule applies to all of the other types of negotiable instruments.

Orders

DRAFT: a draft is a three-party order to pay money.

Draft. In contrast to the *promise* of the maker of a note, a *draft* contains an order by the author of the instrument that *someone else should pay*. [3-104(e)] A draft has three parties, a *drawer* who gives the order to pay, a *drawee* who is ordered to pay, and a *payee* who receives payment. [§ 3-103(a)(2) and (3)] In the following draft, Jed is the drawer, Milly is the drawee, and Sam is the payee:

Document 21.3

Milly Smith
123 Acorn St.
Kansas City, KS.

Pay $1,000 to the order of Sam Jones, thirty (30) days after sight. Interest at 15%.

Jed
_____

As with a note, a draft may be a demand instrument or a time instrument. Document 21.3 is a time draft because it is payable after the passage of time. It is payable thirty days after Sam shows it to Milly ("sight") and demands payment. If the words "thirty (30) days after sight" were deleted from Document 21.3, it would be a demand instrument, because Sam would be entitled to the money at the moment he made a demand for it. (Remember, an instrument which does not state when it is payable is payable on demand.)

Why would Jed order Milly to pay money? The answer is that Milly owes $1,000 to Jed or is willing to lend $1,000 to him. Being entitled to the money, Jed may then order it paid to someone else—in this case, Sam. For example, it may be that Milly bought a horse from Jed and consequently owes him $1,000. Or maybe Milly is a wealthy investor who is willing to loan money to Jed to earn interest. Whatever the reason, Jed has established an understanding with Milly; thus, Jed is entitled to sign a draft ordering Milly to pay the money to Sam.

Sam, the payee, takes Document 21.3 to Milly and shows it to her (this is called "sight"). If Milly acknowledges that she will pay the money, she writes "accepted" on the face of the instrument and signs it, and, in thirty days, she must pay the money to Sam. When Milly signs the draft, she is called an *acceptor* as well as a drawee. [§ 3-103(a)(1)]

Document 21.3 shows that a draft may be used to make a loan or repay a debt. If Milly is loaning money to Jed, the loan is completed when Milly pays the money as Jed directs. If Milly is repaying a debt, the debt is repaid when Milly pays the money as Jed directs.

An Example. Consider how a draft might be used in a more complicated commercial situation. Jed operates a shoe store in Phoenix and he proposes to buy 1,000 pairs of shoes from the ABC Shoe Company in San Diego. ABC will not extend credit to Jed, and so the following events take place:

- Jed goes to Second Bank in Phoenix and arranges to borrow $50,000 to buy the shoes.

- ABC delivers the crates of shoes to a trucking company in San Diego and receives a document called a "bill of lading."

- ABC prepares a draft and sends the draft and bill of lading to Second Bank in Phoenix, with instructions that the bank (or Jed, it's customer) may use the bill of lading to take possession of the shoes (when they are delivered in Phoenix) when the bank accepts and returns the draft to ABC.

The draft from the ABC Shoe Company looks like this:

Document 21.4

Draft

Second Bank
Phoenix, AZ

Pay $50,000 to the order of ABC Shoe Company, ten days after acceptance. Payment of this draft is consideration for a shipment of 1,000 pairs of shoes from ABC Shoe Company to Jed.

ABC Shoe Company

Date: __June 1, 1997__   by __Jane__

Treasurer

- When the shoes arrive in Phoenix, Jed examines them and finds them to be in good order. An officer of Second Bank writes accepted on the face of the note and signs it and sends it to ABC in San Diego. Jed uses the bill of lading to take possession of the shoes.

- Later, ABC Shoe Company negotiates the draft to its bank, the First Bank of San Diego. (They do this because they had earlier borrowed money from First Bank to manufacture the shoes it sold to Jed.) Some time after the passage of ten days, First Bank presents the draft to Second Bank for payment and Second Bank transfers the money to First Bank.

- Over an agreed period of months or years, Jed repays the $50,000 to Second Bank using proceeds from the sale of the shoes.

Problem Solving. Please turn to Chapter Problems at the end of this chapter and solve Problem 21.2.

CHECK: a check is a draft which is drawn on a bank and payable on demand.

Check. A *check* is a type of draft. A check is a draft which is (1) drawn on a bank, and (2) payable on demand. [§ 3-104(f)] The following is a check:

Document 21.5

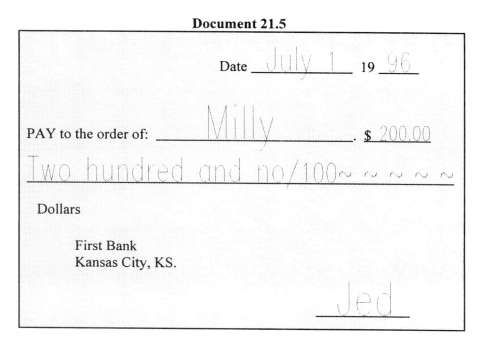

Document 21.5 is a draft and also a check, just like a Corvette is an automobile and also a sports car. A check is a specialized type of draft, just like a Corvette is a specialized type of automobile.

In what way is a check a specialized type of draft? It is specialized in the sense that (1) it must be drawn on a bank, and (2) it must be payable on demand. Examine how Document 21.4 (above) may be revised to make it a check:

```
┌─────────────────────────────────────────────────────┐
│ Second Bank                                         │
│ Phoenix, AZ                                         │
│                                                     │
│ Pay $50,000 to the order of ABC Shoe Company of San Diego, │
│ California, [~~ten days after acceptance~~].  Payment of this draft is │
│ consideration for a shipment of 1,000 pairs of shoes from ABC Shoe │
│ Company to Alvin.                                   │
│                                                     │
│                              ABC Shoe Company       │
│                                                     │
│                                     Jane            │
│ Date:  June 1, 1997              by _____       │
│                                      Treasurer      │
└─────────────────────────────────────────────────────┘
```

With the text in brackets removed, Document 21.6 is a check. Why? Because now it is a draft which is drawn on a bank and payable on demand.

The following opinion, *People v. Burke*, focuses squarely on whether a particular item is a *check* or a *draft*. Eugene Burke was in possession of some "checks" which had been stolen in a business burglary. He was caught by the police and charged with the criminal offenses of receiving stolen property and having possession of a blank *check* with an intent to defraud. Burke's clever response with respect to the second offense was that the items in his possession were *drafts*, but not *checks*.

People v. Burke
113 Cal. Rptr. 553 (1974)

CHRISTIAN, Associate Justice

Eugene Nealous Burke appeals from a judgment sentencing him to concurrent terms of imprisonment after a jury found him guilty of receiving stolen property (Pen.Code, § 496) and possession of a blank check with intent to defraud (Pen.Code, § 475).

* * *

Appellant contends that he should not have been convicted of violation Penal Code section 475: he was charged with possession of a blank check, but the evidence was that the forms which he possessed were not checks. The contention is expressed in terms of the court's *jurisdiction* to convict appellant under Penal Code section 475. But because Penal Code section 475 does not punish possession of all instruments for the transfer of money there are two real questions: does the statute reach the forms possessed by appellant and, if so, was the information fatally defective in that it charged possession of a check while the forms possessed by appellant were not checks?

A check is defined as "a draft drawn on a bank and payable on demand; . . ." Com.Code, § 3104, subd. (2)(b).) The instrument involved in this case is a draft. It states "Pay to the order of," followed by a blank where the name of the payee is to be written; it contains spaces where the sum of money and the signature of the drawer are to be written. But the instrument is not drawn on a bank. In banking practice, the name of the drawee bank frequently appears in the lower left corner of the instrument. Here, the name in the lower left corner is "Bank of America." The term "Payable through" is printed directly over the name of the bank. According to the Commercial Code, "An instrument which states that it is 'payable through' a bank or the like designates that bank as a collecting bank to make presentment but does not of itself authorize the bank to pay the instrument." (Com.Code, §3120.) The bank is not authorized to pay the instrument out of the drawer's account. (West's Com.Code Ann. (1964) § 3120, Uniform Com.Code Comment, p. 94.) In this case, the Bank of America was not a drawee because the instrument was "payable through" the bank. Therefore, the forms are not checks.

* * *

The judgment is affirmed as to count one (receiving stolen property) and reversed as to count two (possession of a blank check with intent to defraud).

It is occasionally the practice of some institutions to issue drafts that look very much like checks. The only difference is that the language of the instrument which describes the bank includes the phrase "payable through First National Bank," instead of "First National Bank." The point, of course, is that the instruments in question are payable *through* the bank, but not payable *by* the bank. These instruments are drafts, but not checks. In the case above, Burke was correct: he was in possession of a draft, but not a check.

<u>**Problem Solving**</u>. Please turn to Chapter Problems at the end of this chapter and solve Problem 21.3.

CASHIER'S CHECK: a cashier's check is a draft in which the drawer and the drawee are the same bank.

Cashier's Check. A *cashier's check* is a draft in which the drawer and the drawee are the same bank. [§ 3-104(g)] Document 21.7 is a cashier's check:

Document 21.7

Cashier's Check
PAY to the order of: Friendly Auto.   <u>$20,000.00</u>
<u>Twenty Thousand and no/100</u>   dollars.
First Bank   <u>M. R. Owens</u>
Atlanta, GA.   Cashier, First Bank.

Document 21.7 is a cashier's check because the drawer is First Bank which, through it's cashier, M. R. Owens, is ordering itself, First Bank (the drawee) to pay money to Friendly Auto (the payee).

The following opinion, *Kaufman v. Chase Manhattan Bank, Nat. Ass'n*, focuses on the difference between a *check* and a *cashier's check*. The latter, of course, is an instrument in which the drawer and the drawee are both the same bank. In *Kaufman*, a cashier's check in the amount of $17,000 was issued by the bank (with Kaufman as the payee) at the request of a person by the name of Ahmed Tigani, who was a bank customer. The bank issued the cashier's check thinking there was enough money in Tigani's account to cover it; but, when (in fact) there was not enough money, the bank stopped payment on the cashier's check. Ms. Kaufman, the plaintiff, brought suit to enforce the instrument. She filed a motion for summary judgment.

Kaufman v. Chase Manhattan Bank, Nat. Ass'n
370 F.Supp. 276 (1973)

EDELSTEIN, Chief Judge:

* * *

The issue presented to this court is whether or not a bank may stop payment on a cashier's check which has been properly issued by the bank and has been delivered to the payee. The issue must be resolved in favor of the payee.   * * *

A cashier's check * * * is a check drawn by the bank upon itself, payable to another person, and issued by an authorized officer of the bank. The bank, therefore, becomes both the drawer and drawee; and the check becomes a promise by the bank to draw the amount of the check from its own resources and to pay the check upon demand. Thus, the issuance of the cashier's check constitutes an acceptance by the issuing bank; and the cashier's check becomes the primary obligation of the bank. * * * Since a cashier's check is a bank's primary obligation, a cashier's check is presumed to have been issued for value. This presumption cannot be overcome by evidence that the bank did not receive consideration for the cashier's check from the payee. Such proof is irrelevant and provides no defense. * * * Hence, once the cashier's check has been issued and delivered to the payee, the transaction is complete so far as the payee is concerned. Any failure of the bank to charge such checks against the account of the depositor or to take other action to protect its own rights and interests will not affect the unconditional right of payment inuring to the payee. * * *

Furthermore, under N.Y.U.C.C. § 4-304, a stop-order comes too late if the order is received after the bank has accepted the item. Thus, because a cashier's check is accepted when issued, it is beyond the power of the bank to stop payment on it. * * *

Finally, because of the nature and usage of cashier's check in the commercial world, public policy favors a rule which prohibits the stopping of payment of these checks. As one court has aptly stated:

> A cashier's check circulates in the commercial world as the equivalent of cash... People accept a cashier's check as a substitute for cash because the bank stands behind it, rather than an individual. In effect, the bank becomes a guarantor of the value of the check and pledges its resources to the payment of the amount represented upon presentation. To allow the bank to stop payment on such an instrument would be inconsistent with the representations it makes in issuing the check. Such a rule would undermine the public confidence in the bank and its checks and thereby deprive the cashier's check of the essential incident which makes it useful. People would no longer be willing to accept it as a substitute for cash if they could not be sure that there would be no difficulty in converting it into cash.

* * *

Accordingly, plaintiff's motion is granted.

What is the difference between a check and a cashier's check? The answer is that a check is a draft drawn on a bank by one of it's customers and payable on demand. In contrast, a cashier's check is a draft drawn on a bank by that bank.

TELLER'S CHECK: a teller's check is a draft in which the drawer is a bank and the drawee is another bank.

Teller's Check. A teller's check is a draft in which the drawer is a bank and the drawee is another bank. [§ 3-1049(h)] Understanding that a cashier's check is a draft where the drawer and the drawee are the *same bank*, and a teller's check is a draft where the drawer and the drawee are *different banks*, what are the changes which must be made to Document 21.7 to convert it from a cashier's check to a teller's check? Document 21.8 is Document 21.7 converted it into a teller's check:

Document 21.8

[Cashier's] Teller's Check
PAY to the order of: Friendly Auto. $20,000.00
Twenty Thousand and no/100 dollars.
[First] Second Bank M. R. Owens
Atlanta, GA. Cashier, First Bank.

Obviously, the only change to convert the cashier's check into a teller's check is to provide that the drawee is a bank different than the drawer.

Problem Solving. Please turn to Chapter Problems at the end of this chapter and solve Problem 21.5.

TRAVELER'S CHECK: a traveler's check is payable on demand, on or through a bank, designated "traveler's check," and requires a counter signature.

Traveler's Check. A traveler's check is different than any of the other types of negotiable instruments described above. Following is an example of a traveler's check:

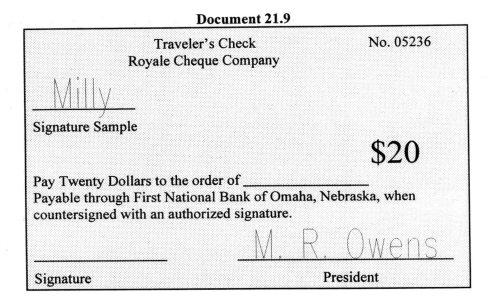

Examine the following language from § 3-104 (i)—which defines a traveler's check—and see if Document 21.9 meets all of the requirements. "'Traveler's check' means an instrument that:

(i) is payable on demand,

(ii) is drawn on or payable at or through a bank

(iii) is designated by the term 'traveler's check' or by a substantially similar term, and

(iv) requires, as a condition to payment, a countersignature by a person whose specimen signature appears on the instrument."

Is Document 21.9 a traveler's check? First, it is payable on demand. Second, it is drawn on or payable through a designated bank. Third, it is designated across the top by the term "traveler's check." Fourth, payment requires a countersignature matching the specimen signature. Thus, Document 21.9 is a traveler's check.

Here is how a traveler's check may be used. Milly plans a trip to Florida and she wants to take $2,000 with her, but she is afraid to carry that much in cash. So, she goes to First Bank and pays them $2,000, plus a fee of perhaps 1% ($20). In return, the bank givers her 20 traveler's checks like Document 21.9, which she signs on the top. When Milly buys a sweatshirt in Miami, she will write in the name of the Miami Sweatshirt Emporium as the payee, produce identification showing she is Milly, sign the bottom of the check with a signature that matches the one on the top, and give the traveler's check to the payee.

If Milly loses the traveler's checks, or they are stolen, the company that issued the checks will pay Milly the amount of the lost or stolen checks. The $20 fee compensates the bank for this risk.

Chapter Problems

Problem 21.1

Properly classify the following, explaining whether it is a draft, check, note, or none of these.

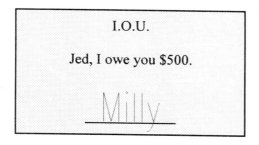

Problem 21.2

Explain which of the following is the most correct statement:

   a.   A draft is a three-party instrument, signed by a maker.
   b.   A draft is a three-party demand instrument.
   c.   A draft is a two-party instrument, signed by a drawer.
   d.   A draft is a three-party instrument, signed by a drawer.

Problem 21.3

Explain the meaning of the following statement: All checks are drafts, but all drafts are not checks.

Problem 21.4

Properly classify the following, explaining whether it is a draft, check, cashier's check or note, and whether it is a time instrument or a demand instrument.

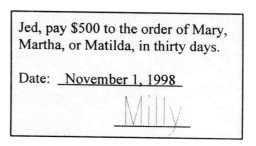

Problem 21.5

Explain the difference between a cashier's check and a teller's check.

Chapter 22
Negotiation

Chapter Outline

OBJECTIVE is to learn the rules of negotiation.

The objective of this chapter is to learn the rules of negotiation—the rules by which negotiable instruments are transferred from person to person. The chapter is organized as follows:

- *Negotiation.* Negotiation is a transfer of possession of a negotiable instrument by a person (other than the issuer) to a person who thereby becomes its holder.

- *Indorsement.* Negotiation may require an indorsement, and there are five types of indorsement: blank, special, qualified, restrictive and anomalous.

- *Blank Indorsement.* A blank indorsement consists of the signature of the holder of the instrument.

- *Special Indorsement.* A special indorsement identifies a person or persons to whom the instrument is payable.

- *Qualified Indorsement.* A qualified indorsement uses words such as "without recourse," and it's effect is to avoid liability on the part of the endorser to pay the instrument in the event of default.

- *Restrictive Indorsement.* A restrictive indorsement purports to place restrictions on the further negotiation of the instrument.

- *Anomalous Indorsement.* An anomalous indorsement is an indorsement by a person who is not a holder of the instrument.

Assignment versus Negotiation

NEGOTIATION is different than assignment.

Most contracts, including negotiable instruments, can be transferred from person to person. The point is that negotiating a *negotiable instrument* is usually *easier* than transferring other contracts. The following illustrates this difference:

Contract Assignment. If by contract—not using any negotiable instrument—Milly buys a set of encyclopedias (to be delivered at a later date) she owns a contract right, which is the right to receive the encyclopedias. It is possible for her to transfer that contract right (the right to receive the encyclopedias) to Jed. The transfer of a contract right is called an *assignment*. In the process of assignment, Milly and Jed will enter into a contract of assignment, after which Jed sends notice of the assignment to the encyclopedia company so it will deliver the books to him.

Negotiation. On the other hand, Document 22.1 (below) is a payroll check and a *negotiable instrument.* If Jed wants Milly to have Document 22.1, he may simply sign his name on the back of the check and hand it to Milly. This process is called *negotiation,* and it is usually much simpler than the process of assignment.

The Definition of Negotiation

This part of the chapter focuses on the definition of *negotiation.* Document 22.1 (Jed's paycheck) is a negotiable instrument, which will be the object of repeated attempts at negotiation throughout the balance of the chapter.

Document 22.1

	Date ___July 4___ 19 _96_
PAY to the order of: Jed Smith	
	$500.00
Five Hundred and no/100 _____	dollars.
First Bank Los Angeles, CA.	
	Richard
Wilson	

NEGOTIATION is the transfer of an instrument to a holder.

Negotiation is defined in § 3-20 (a) as follows:

- A *transfer of possession,* whether voluntary or involuntary

- of an *instrument*

- by a person *other than the issuer*

- to a person who thereby becomes its *holder*

Consider the meaning of each part of this definition:

Transfer of Possession. Negotiation requires a transfer of possession. If Jed signs his name on the back of Document 22.1, but does not hand it to Milly, there is not negotiation and the check is still his. Why? Because negotiation requires that an instrument be transferred, and Document 22.1 has not been transferred. On the other hand, if Jed signs his name on the back of his payroll check, and it is stolen from him, it has been transferred because transfer can be *voluntary* or *involuntary.*

335

Instrument. When the word "instrument" is used in Revised Article 3, it refers to a negotiable instrument. (Look again at Document 20.1 and Document 20.2 in Chapter 20.) If Jed signs the back of Document 20.1 and delivers it to Sam, a contract *assignment* has taken place, not a negotiation. Why? Because Document 20.1 is a contract and not a negotiable instrument and transfer of a contract is an assignment. But, if Jed signs the back of Document 20.2 and delivers it to Sam, negotiation has taken place. Why? Because Document 20.2 is a negotiable instrument.

Other than the Issuer. Section 3-201(a) (above) provides that negotiation is the transfer of an instrument by a person "other than the issuer." What is an issuer? Read § 3-105 (a) in Appendix A and then look at Document 22.1. Section 3-105(a) provides that the *issue* of an instrument "means the first delivery of an instrument by the maker or drawer, whether to a holder or a nonholder . . ." Thus, when Richard Wilson, the drawer in Document 22.1, delivers it to Jed, the payee, he is technically issuing the instrument. On the other hand, when Jed transfers the instrument to Sam (with any necessary indorsements) *negotiation* has taken place.

Holder. Negotiation is the transfer of an instrument to a person "who thereby becomes its holder." [§ 1-201 (20)] Section 1-201 (20) defines "holder' as "a person who is in possession of . . . an instrument . . . drawn, issued, or indorsed to him or his order or to bearer or in blank." If Jed simply transferred Document 22.1 to Milly—without signing it—Milly would not be a holder, and Document 22.1 would not have been negotiated. Why? Because the instrument is not drawn, issued, or indorsed to Milly.

Indorsement

INDORSEMENT means to sign (by signature or symbol) an instrument for the purpose of transferring it.

As noted above, Jed cannot negotiate Document 22.1 (to Milly) without signing the back. A signature placed on the back of an instrument for the purpose of negotiating it is called an *indorsement*. An indorsement is usually—but not always—required to negotiate an instrument.

Indorsement is defined in § 3-204(a) as a "signature." "Signed," according to § 1-201(39) "includes any symbol executed or adopted by a party with present intention to authenticate a writing." Thus, an indorsement is by a signature, but a signature may be in symbol form.

This chapter focuses generally on the process of negotiation and the indorsements used in that process. Specifically, this chapter focuses on when an indorsement is necessary, and what each type of indorsement accomplishes.

Types of Indorsement

TYPES OF INDORSEMENT are: blank, special, qualified, restrictive and anomalous.

There are five types of indorsement, as follows:

- Blank Indorsement

- Special Indorsement

- Qualified Indorsement

- Restrictive Indorsement

- Anomalous Indorsement

Following is an example of each of these five types of indorsement. Assume in the following discussions that Jed Smith is attempting to negotiate Document 22.1 to another party.

Blank Indorsement

The simplest type of indorsement is a blank indorsement, which consists of nothing more than Jed's signature on the back of the check. [§ 3-205(b)] Document 22.2 is the back of Document 22.1 and it shows a blank indorsement in which Jed, the payee, also becomes an indorser:

Document 22.2

Jed Smith

If Jed indorses, as shown in Document 22.2, and hands the check to Milly, negotiation is complete. Why? Because a negotiable instrument has been transferred to Milly, with an indorsement which makes her a holder.

Notice that Jed's blank indorsement does not name Milly as an indorsee. Because no indorsee is named, Jed could just as easily have handed the instrument to anyone else. At this point, the check is called a *bearer instrument*. [§ 3-109]

Milly is in possession of Document 22.1, which is now a bearer instrument because it is indorsed in blank by Jed. What is the simplest way for Milly to negotiate Document 22.1 to Sam Jones? The answer is that because it is a bearer instrument (no holder is specified), it can be handed from person to person, just like cash, and no further indorsement is required. Because no further indorsement is required, negotiation is complete as each transfer takes place.

Is it wise to use a blank indorsement? Usually, no. The reason is that a bearer instrument is just like cash. If the check is lost, the finder can cash it; and, if the check is stolen, the thief can cash it. This point is illustrated in the following case of *Walcott v. Manufacturer's Trust*.

In *Walcott*, the plaintiff, Kenneth Walcott, sent his paycheck ($359.05) and a money order ($251.54) to the Midatlantic Mortgage Company to pay his monthly house mortgage. On the back of the paycheck he *claims* that he placed a Midatlantic mailing sticker, signed his name and wrote the numbers "605032" (his mortgage number). The paycheck and the money order never reached Midatlantic. The paycheck—which is the item at issue here—was cashed at the Bilko Check Cashing Corporation. When cashed, there was not a Midatlantic sticker on the back of the paycheck. Bilko deposited the check in it's account at Manufacturer's Hanover.

According to Walcott, a thief must have stolen the check and cashed it. Moreover, in his view, the signature, sticker and mortgage number on the back of the paycheck created a special indorsement (see Document 22.3 for an example of a special indorsement), the terms of which were violated by Bilko and Manufacturer's Hanover. On the other hand, the bank observes that there was *not* a sticker on the back of the check when they dealt with it; thus, there was only a blank indorsement on the back. (See Document 22.2 for an example of a blank indorsement.)

Walcott v. Manufacturers Hanover Trust
507 N.Y.S.2d 961 (1986)

IRA B. HARKAVY, Judge
* * *

The issue presented to this Court is whether plaintiff's indorsement of his paycheck was such as to be a special or restrictive indorsement, thus limiting the negotiation of the instrument, or did it have the effect of creating a bearer instrument.

SPECIAL INDORSEMENT

Uniform Commercial Code § 3-204 subdivision (1) defines a special indorsement as being one that " . . . specifies the person to whom or to whose order it makes the instrument payable. Any instrument specially indorsed becomes payable to the order of the special indorsee and may be further negotiated only by his indorsement."

Examination of the back of the check, a photocopy of which, as previously stated, was introduced into evidence, reveals that Mr. Walcott did not specify any particular indorsee. In order for the alleged attached sticker to have served that purpose it must have also complied with UCC § 3-202 subdivision (2): "An indorsement must be written by or on behalf of the holder and on the instrument or a paper so firmly affixed thereto as to become a part thereof." The back of the check shows no sticker attached at all. Even if it had originally been affixed thereto, as plaintiff claims, it obviously became detached easily, thus failing to meet the indorsement requirements under the UCC to constitute a special indorsement.

RESTRICTIVE INDORSEMENT

As to the numbers written underneath plaintiff's signature, they did not have the effect of restricting plaintiff's indorsement. "An indorsement is restrictive which either (a) is conditional; or (b) purports to prohibit further transfer of the instrument; or (c) includes the words 'for conditional,' 'for deposit,' 'pay any bank,' or like terms signifying a purpose of deposit or collection; or (d) otherwise states that it is for the benefit or use of the indorser or of another person." UCC § 3-205.

This section of the Uniform Commercial Code is very specific. The series of numbers representing plaintiff's mortgage account was insufficient to restrict negotiation of plaintiff's check.

BLANK INDORSEMENT

> Plaintiff's indorsement had the effect of converting the check into a bearer instrument. The series of numbers having no restrictive effect, Mr. Walcott indorsed the check in blank, or otherwise stated, he simply signed his name. A blank indorsement under UCC § 3-204 subdivision (2) "... specifies no particular indorsee and may consist of a mere signature." Additionally, "An instrument payable to order and indorsed in blank becomes payable to bearer and may be negotiated by delivery alone..." Consequently, since plaintiff failed to limit his blank indorsement, the check was properly negotiated by delivery to third party defendant Bilko and properly cashed by them.
>
> Judgement * * * dismissing the complaint.

At first, one is inclined to sympathy for Walcott, who apparently lost his mortgage payment to a thief. On the other hand, evidence suggested that whoever cashed the check at Bilko had identification (including a driver's license) in the name of Kenneth Walcott. That led the court, in a footnote, to state: "This identification procedure creates doubt as to whether the check was actually stolen." If the judge's suspicions are correct, Walcott cashed the payroll check at Bilko and is now attempting to cheat Bilko and the bank by getting reimbursement for money he never lost.

Problem Solving. Please turn to chapter Problems at the end of this chapter and solve Problem 22.1.

Special Indorsement

SPECIAL INDORSEMENTS identify the person or persons to whom the instrument is payable.

A special indorsement specifies the person or persons to whom the instrument is payable. [§ 3-205 (a)] The principal difference between a blank indorsement and a special indorsement is, of course, that a special indorsement identifies the person or persons to whom the instrument is payable and a blank indorsement does not.

(For purposes of the following discussion of special indorsements, recall that Milly is the holder of the check which is Document 22.1, which Jed has indorsed to her by blank indorsement as shown is Document 22.2.)

At this point, if Milly wants to negotiate Document 22.1 to Sam Jones, and no one else, she can add a special indorsement like that pictured in Document 22.3, which is the back of Document 22.1:

Document 22.3

Jed Smith
Pay to Sam Jones
Milly Schwartz

When Milly hands Document 22.1 to Sam (with the indorsement shown in Document 22.3) negotiation is complete. At this point, Document 22.1 is called an *order instrument* because it is payable to a specified person or persons, instead of being a bearer instrument. Sam can cash the check, or, he can negotiate it to someone else. (To indorse the instrument to someone else, Sam can indorse Document 22.1 in blank, as was done in Document 22.2, or he may indorse it specially, as was done in Document 22.3. This shows that an instrument may change back and forth in it's character as a *bearer* instrument or an *order* instrument.)

Note that Milly wrote "Pay to Sam Jones" instead of writing "Pay *to the order* of Sam Jones." It will be recalled from Chapter 20 that words of negotiability (pay to order, or pay to bearer) must be used to make an instrument negotiable. This rule does *not* apply to indorsements. Thus, the language "Pay to Sam Jones" on the back of Document 22.3 is sufficient for negotiation, and the language of negotiability (pay to order, or, pay to bearer) is not required.

Observe, again, that Milly used a special indorsement (Document 22.3) to convert Jed's paycheck (Document 22.1) from a bearer instrument to an order instrument. Is there another way Milly could have accomplished the same thing? The answer is yes. (Please read § 3-205 (c) in Appendix A.) Section 3-205 allows Milly to do the following: "The holder [Milly] may convert a blank indorsement that consists only of a signature [Jed's indorsement shown in Document 22.2] into a special indorsement by writing, *above the signature of the indorser* [Jed's signature], words identifying the person to whom the instrument is made payable [Sam Jones]."

So, what can Milly do? She may write "Pay to Sam Jones" above Jed's signature, and the result is a special indorsement. Document 22.4 is an example of this method of converting a blank indorsement into a special indorsement:

Document 22.4

Pay to Sam Jones
Jed Smith

Document 22.3 and Document 22.4 are the two different methods Milly can use to convert a bearer instrument into an order instrument. Is there any practical difference between the two methods? The answer is yes, because in Document 22.3 Milly is required to sign her name, but in Document 22.4 Milly is *not* required to sign her name. This can be important if Document 22.1 is not paid by Richard Wilson.

Milly's use of the method illustrated in Document 22.4—in which she does not sign the instrument— may be important if Richard Wilson's check (Document 22.1) is not paid. It is important because one of the indorsers may have to pay it. On that point, § 3-415 (a) provides that "if an instrument [Document 22.1] is dishonored [not paid], an indorser is obligated to pay the amount due on the instrument." That means if Milly indorses, as shown in Document 22.3, she must pay the amount of the check to the holder if Richard Wilson, the drawer, does not. But § 3-401 (a) provides that a "person [Milly] is *not* liable on an instrument [Document 22.1] unless the person signed the instrument." Thus, if Milly negotiates Document 22.1 *without signing it*, as shown in Document 22.4, she is *not* obligated to pay the amount thereof to the holder, if Richard Wilson fails in his obligation to pay it.

Multiple Payees. At this point we make a temporary digression. In Document 22.3 and Document 22.4, the indorsements are to a single person: Sam Jones. But, what if an instrument is issued or specially indorsed to *two* (or more) persons? That scenario is the principle point of discussion in the following case, *GMAC v. Abington Cas. Ins. Co.*, where a check from an insurance company was made payable "to the order of Robert A. Azevedo and G.M.A.C."

Azevedo presented the check to the drawee bank and was paid. GMAC, which had rights in the check proceeds, received none of the money. Instead of going after Azevedo to recover the money, GMAC simply brought suit against the insurance company on the theory that the debt for which the check had been issued had not been paid. Abington, the insurance company, responded that the underlying debt had been paid because delivery of the check to one of the payees (who cashed it) was as good as delivering it to both payees.

GMAC v. Abington Cas. Ins. Co.
602 N.E.2d 1085 (1992)

NOLAN, Justice.
* * *

In this case, the drawee bank accepted the check, and payment was made to a payee. Ordinarily, an underlying debt is discharged when the check is "drawn on an account with sufficient funds to cover [it] at a solvent bank and is delivered to the payee." * * * Even delivery of a check to the payee's authorized agent who then cashes it, discharges the drawer's liability. * * * However, in this case, where there are copayees who are not in an agency relationship, a negotiable instrument cannot be discharged by the actions of only one payee. Section 3-116*(b)* expressly prohibits the discharge of an instrument except by *all* the payees. "[T]he rights of one [payee] are not discharged without his consent by the act of the other." * * * Without this rule, there would be no assurance that all the joint payees would receive payment and that the drawer's underlying obligation would be fully discharged.

Prior to the adoption of §3-116, the common law rule that any joint obligee has power to discharge the promisor by receipt of the promised performance, Restatement of Contracts §130(a) (1932), had created particular incongruities when applied to negotiable instruments. * * * The unpaid copayee could not collect from the *drawer* because the instrument was deemed discharged; on the other hand, the unpaid copayee could sue the *drawee* on a conversion of funds theory. * * * Section 3-116 settles the issue by requiring the endorsements of every joint payee before an instrument can be discharged. * * * The Restatement of Contracts (Second) expressly recognizes this exception to the common law rule.

Prohibiting the discharge of a check without all the necessary endorsements also accords with §3-603, which discharges a party's liability on an instrument only if payment or satisfaction is made to a holder. Lacking GMAC's endorsement, Azevedo could not have taken the check by negotiation and thereby become a holder. §3-202. Without payment to a holder, the liabilities of the parties to the check are not discharged. §3-603. This holding also comports with §3-419(1)(c), which provides that payment over a forged endorsement results in liability

341

for conversion rather than acceptance and discharge. Further, to hold that an instrument is discharged when payment is made to one copayee without the endorsement of the other would effectively convert a "payable to A *and* B" instrument into one "payable to A *or* B." Thus, to protect the rights of all joint payees as well as the integrity of the commercial paper itself, we hold that payment of a check to one copayee without the endorsement of the other copayee does not discharge the drawer of either his liability on the instrument or the underlying obligation. [An order dismissing the complaint of GMAC is reversed.]

In short, an instrument issued or specially indorsed to "Able, Baker *and* Carr" must be indorsed by all three— Able, Baker *and* Carr—for negotiation to take place. On the other hand, if the instrument is issued or specially indorsed to "Able, Baker *or* Carr," an indorsement by any one of those three is sufficient for negotiation.

Problem Solving. Please turn to chapter Problems at the end of this chapter and solve Problem 22.2.

Qualified Indorsements

QUALIFIED INDORSEMENTS avoid indorsers liability.

As described above, a person who *indorses* an instrument incurs liability. Thus, §3-415 (a) provides that a person, such as Milly, who endorses an instrument as she did in Document 22.3, is obligated to "pay the amount due on the instrument" if it is dishonored. Accordingly, when Milly endorses the check by signing her name (Document 22.3), she promises that if Richard Wilson and his bank refuse to pay the $500, Milly will pay the money.

Look again at Document 22.4. Suppose that Jed had signed his name so close to the top of the check that there was no room to insert Sam's name. There is another way for Milly to negotiate Document 22.1 *without* incurring indorser's liability. Section 3-415 (b) provides that "[i]f an indorsement states that it is made '*without recourse*' or otherwise disclaims liability of the indorser, the indorser is not liable . . . to pay the instrument." Thus, Milly may add the words "without recourse" to her indorsement, and she is not liable on her indorsement if Richard Wilson and his bank refuse to pay Sam. Document 22.5 is a special *qualified* indorsement:

Document 22.5

Jed Smith
Pay to Sam Jones
Milly Schwartz
Without Recourse

Problem Solving. Please turn to chapter Problems at the end of this chapter and solve Problem 22.3.

Restrictive Indorsement

In a restrictive indorsement, limitations or conditions are placed in the indorsement. [§ 3-206] The following are restrictive indorsements:

- An indorsement limiting payment to a particular person or otherwise prohibiting further transfer or negotiation of the instrument.

- An indorsement stating a condition to the right of the indorsee to receive payment.

To illustrate a restrictive indorsement, assume that Jed proposes to restrictively indorse Document 22.1. Following are some examples of the language he might use:

Document 22.6

Pay to Milly Schwartz only
(No Further Negotiation)
Jed Smith

Document 22.7

Pay to Milly Schwartz,
if she paints my house.
Jed Smith

Document 22.8

Pay to Second National Bank
For Deposit Only
Jed Smith

343

```
Pay to Milly Schwartz
In Trust, for the Centerville,
            AZ
Little League Baseball Ass'n
        Jed Smith
```

Legal Effect of the Examples. In Chapter 20, it was said that conditions or limitations may not be placed in a negotiable instrument. That rule, however, *does not apply to indorsements* where conditions or limitations are allowed to some degree. Following is a description of the legal effect of each of the restrictive indorsements above.

Document 22.6: Section 3-206 (a) provides that a restrictive indorsement such as this "is *not effective* to prevent further transfer or negotiation of the instrument." Thus, Milly, if she chooses, may disregard the restriction and negotiate the instrument to Sam Jones.

Document 22.7: The rules relating to this type of restrictive indorsement are in § 3-206 (b). Milly may present Document 22.1 to First Bank and receive payment, or she may negotiate the check to Sam Jones and Sam may present the check to the bank and receive payment. Neither the bank nor Sam is responsible to discover whether Jed's house has been painted. Section 3-206 (b) provides that a "person paying the instrument or taking it for value or collection *may disregard the condition,* and the rights and liabilities of that person are not affected by whether the condition has been fulfilled."[1]

However, if Milly had received the check in return for her agreement to paint Jed's house, *she* would still be liable to Jed in contract. This means, of course, that Jed could successfully sue Milly if she did not paint his house. In short, a restrictive indorsement is effective between the two parties to the indorsement, but it does not affect the rights of other parties.

Document 22.8: This restriction—"For Deposit Only"—is strictly enforced. The rules relating to this type of restrictive indorsement are found in § 3-206 (c). With

---

[1] This represents a change in the law. Under the former Article 3, all who received the instrument after Milly were responsible to learn if the condition had been met and the house painted. If the condition had not been met, Sam was not entitled to the money, and the bank was not entitled to pay the check.

this restriction, the amount of the check, $500, must be deposited to Jed's account at Second National Bank. If Second National Bank receives payment on the check from First Bank, the drawee, it must deposit the money to the account of Jed, or it will be liable to him for the amount of the check. Section 3-206 (c) (2) provides:

> [a] depositary bank [Second National Bank] that purchases the instrument [Document 22.1] or takes it for collection when so indorsed [the indorsement in Document 22.8] *converts* [taking money delaying to another] the instrument unless the amount paid by the bank with respect to he instrument is received by the indorser [Jed] or applied consistently with the indorsement [deposited to Jed's account]. (Emphasis added.)

Document 22.9: The rules relating to this type of restrictive indorsement are found in § 3-206 (d) . Milly may sell and negotiate the instrument to Sam Jones, who can pay her, and Sam will not be liable—and can collect on the check—unless he *knows* that Milly is violating her trust. Others are likewise free from liability unless they know that a violation of trust is involved.

It is stated above that the restrictive indorsement "For Deposit Only" is strictly enforced. In the following case, *AmSOUTH Bank v. Reliable Janitorial Serv.*, that proposition was put to the test. In that case, Reliable Janitorial Service (and Reliable Carpet Cleaning) used an office manager by the name of Rosa Pennington to make their bank deposits. She used a simply but effective method to steal from Reliable: (1) she opened a personal account at AmSOUTH for which she was given an account number; (2) she stamped "Reliable Janitorial Service, For Deposit Only" on company checks; and (3) she put her personal account number below the indorsement. The effect of this procedure was to misdirect checks belonging to Reliable into Ms. Pennington's account. In this manner she was able to gain control of approximately $71,641.58, which she promptly spent.

Reliable brought suit against AmSOUTH for conversion[2] of the money, because the bank had failed to obey the terms of the restrictive indorsements which required deposit to the account of Reliable. The trial court granted summary judgment in favor of Reliable, and AmSOUTH appealed.

AmSOUTH Bank v. Reliable Janitorial Serv.
548 So.2d 1365 (1989)

ALMON, Justice.
* * *

AmSouth's first issue is whether the trial court erred by granting summary judgment on Reliable's conversion claim. To examine this issue, we look to the statutes concerning restrictive indorsements and those concerning conversion. There is no dispute that Pennington stamped the checks whose funds she misdirected with the indorsement "For Deposit Only,

---

[2] *Conversion* is a civil action to recover money that another party has wrongfully "converted" to his or her use.

345

Reliable janitorial Service, inc.," or "For Deposit Only, Reliable Carpet Cleaning, Inc." Sections 7-3-205 and 7-3-206, Ala.Code 1975, address such indorsements. Section 7-3-205 provides:

> § 7-3-205. Restrictive indorsements.
>
> An indorsement is restrictive which either:
>
> (a) Is conditional; or
>
> (b) Purports to prohibit further transfer of the instrument; or
>
> (c) Includes the words 'for collection,' 'for deposit,' 'pay any bank,' or like terms signifying a purpose of deposit or collection; or
>
> (d) Otherwise states that it is for the benefit or use of the indorser or of another person.

Undeniably, the indorsements Pennington stamped on the checks were restrictive indorsements within the meaning of § 7-3-205(c).

Section 7-3-206 addresses the effect of such an indorsement, and, pertinently, that section provides:

> (3) Except for an intermediary bank, any transferee under an indorsement which is conditional or includes the words 'for collection,' 'for deposit,' 'pay any bank,' or like terms (subparagraphs (a) and (c) of section 7-3-205) *must* pay or apply any value given by him for or on the security of the instrument consistently with the indorsement . . . ." (Emphasis added.)

Thus, under the exact words of the statute, AmSouth *must* apply the value of Reliable's checks consistently with the indorsement, i.e., for deposit to Reliable's account.

Construing Ala.Code 1975, § 7-3-419, the trial court found AmSouth liable for conversion as a matter of law. The pertinent portions of § 7-3-419 provide:

> (1) An instrument is converted when:
>
> . . . .
>
> (b) Any person *to whom it is delivered for payment* refuses on demand either to pay or to return it . . . .
>
> . . . .
>
> (4) An intermediary bank or payor bank *which is not a depositary bank* is *not* liable in conversion solely by reason of the fact that proceeds of an item indorsed restrictively (sections 7-3-205 and 7-3-206) are not paid or applied consistently with the restrictive indorsement of an indorser other than its immediate transferor." (Emphasis added.)
>
> * * *
>
> [Section] 7-3-419(4) applies in this fact situation. That section provides that intermediary or payor banks that are *not* depositary banks are *not* liable in conversion "solely by reason of the fact that proceeds of an item indorsed restrictively (§§ 7-3-205 and 7-3-206) are not paid or applied consistently with the restrictive covenant." The inference from that section is that banks that *are* depositary banks *may* be liable in conversion "solely by reason of the fact that proceeds of an item indorsed restrictively (Section 7-3-205 and Section 7-3-206) are not paid or applied consistently with the restrictive indorsement." * * *
>
> [The action was affirmed on the point above, but reversed for other reasons.]

Thus, an indorsee under the terms of an indorsement "For Deposit Only" may be liable in conversion for misapplying the instrument.

Problem Solving. Please turn to chapter Problems at the end of this chapter and solve Problem 22.4.

Anomalous Indorsement

Please examine Document 22.10, which is the back of Document 22.1. Who is Michael Mitchell? He is a stranger to the instrument; he is not a holder and there is not need for him to indorse the check as it is transferred to Sam. Thus, his indorsement is called an anomalous indorsement. Section 3-205 (d) provides: "'Anomalous indorsement' means an indorsement made by a person who is not the holder of the instrument. *an anomalous indorsement does not affect the manner in which the instrument may be negotiated.*" But, refer to § 3-415 (a) which is discussed above. Suppose that Milly is negotiating Document 22.1 to Sam to pay off a debt, but Sam is suspicious about whether the check is any good. By adding his name—which he may do at Sam's or Milly's request—Michael Mitchell incurs indorser's liability and must pay Document 22.1 to Sam if the others do not.

Document 22.10

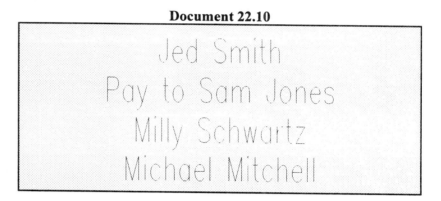

Problem Solving. Please turn to chapter Problems at the end of this chapter and solve Problem 22.5.

In the next five problems, please assume that the following negotiable instrument is being negotiated.

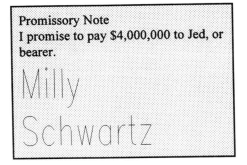

Promissory Note
I promise to pay $4,000,000 to Jed, or bearer.

Milly
Schwartz

Problem 22.1

Jed is in possession of the note above. What is the *simplest* way for him to negotiate it to Sam?

Problem 22.2

In the process of writing indorsements on the back of the note above, for purposes of negotiation, is it necessary to use the language of negotiability ("to the order of" or "to bearer")?

Problem 22.3

Jed is in possession of the note above. By what means does he negotiate to Sam so that (1) only Sam can further negotiate it, and (2) Jed is not liable to Sam if the note is not paid?

Problem 22.4

Jed is in possession of the note above. Jed writes the following on the back of the note: "Pay to Lucy, if she paints my house. Signed, Jed." Jed delivers the note to Lucy. Lucy does not paint Jed's house, but nevertheless writes the following on the back of the note: "Pay to Mary. Signed, Lucy." Lucy delivers the note to Mary. Can Mary successfully demand that Milly pay the note; or, must Mary wait until Lucy paints Jed's house?

Problem 22.5

The note above bears the following indorsement on the back: "pay to Scott. Signed, Jed." Following that indorsement, write one indorsement which is a special, restrictive, qualified, anomalous indorsement.

Chapter 23
Holder in Due Course

Chapter Objectives

OBJECTIVE is to learn the rules relating to the status of holder in due course.

The objective of this chapter is to learn the negotiable instruments rules related to the status of *holder in due course*. The chapter is organized as follows:

- *Holder in Due Course Requirements.* A holder in due course is a holder who meets the following requirements: (1) the holder has no knowledge of adverse claims to the instrument by others; (2) the holder gives value for the instrument; and, (3) the holder acts in good faith.

- *Contract Defenses.* In general, contract defenses cannot be successfully asserted against a holder in due course. Exceptions to that general rule are: infancy, lack of legal capacity, illegality, fraud in the execution and duress.

- *Shelter Rule.* A person who is a holder in due course transfers that status to his or her transferee, even if the transferee does not qualify as a holder in due course. A person involved in fraud or illegality with respect to the instrument cannot improve his or her position by transferring to, and receiving from, another person.

- *Consumer Transactions.* The status of holder in due course is not available in consumer credit transactions.

Introduction

This chapter focuses on the status of *holder in due course*. As the chapter discussion will illustrate, having the status of holder in due course is the crown jewel of the law of negotiable instruments.

HOLDER IN DUE COURSE: a person possessing this status is protected, but a contract assignee is not protected.

Holder in Due Course Illustrated. A holder in due course is a person who is a holder of a negotiable instrument and who meets three additional qualifications. Those three additional qualifications are that in the process of becoming a *holder*, the person receiving the instrument (1) receives the instrument *without knowledge* that there are any adverse claims or defenses associated with it, (2) gives *value* for it, and (3) acts in *good faith*.

Before giving a more detailed discussion of the three requirements to be a holder in due course (no knowledge, value, and good faith) it is important to understand why it is an advantage to be a holder in due course. The advantage to being a holder in due course is illustrated with a simple story in which Milly buys a car from Jed. The story of Milly and Jed is told twice. In the first version of the story, Milly uses a *simple contract*—not a negotiable instrument —to pay for the car. In the second version of the story, Milly uses a *negotiable promissory note* to pay for the car. The objective with the two versions of the story is to show that using a negotiable instrument produces a very different result than using a simple contract.

A Simple Contract. Jed sells Milly a car and commits fraud by telling her that it has gone only 50,000 miles, although it really has gone 150,000 miles. The following events transpire:

- On June 15, 1995, not knowing she has been cheated, Milly signs the following contract (not a negotiable instrument) in which she agrees to pay Jed for the car:

Document 23.1

Contract

This contract is entered into by and between Jed and Milly. By this contract, Jed sells a 1993 Volkswagen to Milly, which he represents to be in good working condition. The sales price is $12,000, which amount shall be paid by Milly to Jed at the rate of $300 per month, together with interest at the rate of 7.5% per annum until principal and interest are both satisfied. The first payment shall be on August 1, 1995. Jed represents that he is the owner of the automobile and entitled to sell it. Milly shall receive possession of the automobile on July 1, 1995, and the certificate of title shall be transferred to her on that date.

Signed June 15, 1995.

- Milly receives the car and commences making payments. Later, Milly learns she has been cheated and she notifies Jed that she will refuse to make any more payments.

- In the meantime, Jed assigns the contract to Martha. (The transfer of a contract right is called an *assignment*.) Martha has no knowledge that Jed had cheated Milly. Martha pays Jed $11,000 for the contract and she acts honestly.

- When Martha demands payments from Milly, Milly refuses and describes the fraud committed by Jed as her reason for refusing.

- Martha sues Milly to enforce payment of the contract.

350

In the transaction above, who wins, Milly or Martha? In contract law, people like Martha, who receive contract assignments, receive the rights of their predecessors, but no more. In these cases it is sometimes said that Martha "stands in the shoes" of her predecessor, Jed. This means that the legal defense (fraud) that Milly could use against Jed, she can also successfully use against Martha. That means, of course, that Milly wins. The recourse of Martha is to sue Jed to gain reimbursement.

A Negotiable Instrument. Now, consider the outcome in the story if all of the facts are the same, except that Milly promises to pay Jed using the following negotiable promissory note instead of a simple contract:

Document 23.2

Promissory Note

I promise to pay $12,000 to the order of Jed, with interest at the rate of 7.5%. Payments shall commence on August 1, 1995, and be at the rate of $300 per month until principal and interest are both satisfied. This instrument is given in return for a 1993 Volkswagen sold by the payee to the maker.

July 1, 1995

Milly
_____

As noted above, all of the facts remain the same, except that the transfer from Jed to Martha is by negotiation (not an assignment) because Document 23.2 is a negotiable instrument. (Jed's negotiation to Martha uses a special indorsement.)

When Martha sues Milly, who wins? The answer is that Martha is a *holder in due course* because she is a holder of a negotiable instrument who has received it (1) without knowledge of the legal problems between Milly and Jed, (2) for value—the payment of $11,000—and (3) she acts in good faith. Milly cannot successfully raise contract defenses (such as fraud) against a holder in due course. Thus, Martha wins and Milly must pay her. (The recourse of Milly is to sue Jed.)

The two versions of this story illustrate that the use of negotiable instruments gives *preferential treatment* to some of those who later possess the instrument. Those who receive the preferential treatment are those with the status of holder in due course. People involved in business often demand the use of negotiable instruments so that their successors will receive this preferential treatment.

Holder in Due Course Requirements

REQUIREMENTS: to be a holder in due course the protected person must (1) be a holder, (2) act without knowledge, (3) give value and (4) act in good faith.

If being a holder in due course is such a valuable status, how does one gain that status? The answer is that a holder in due course is first of all a *holder*. A holder is defined in § 1-201 (20) as "a person who is in possession of . . . an instrument . . . drawn, issued, or indorsed to him or his order or to bearer or in blank." Thus, if Milly issues a *negotiable* promissory note to Jed, who then negotiates it to Martha—Jed and Martha are each holders.

To be a holder *in due course* a holder must meet three requirements which are described in § 3-302 (a) in Appendix A. Read § 3-302 (a) and consider how Martha qualified as a holder in due course in relation to Document 23.2. The three requirements to be a holder in due course are the following:

A. The holder must acquire the instrument, *without knowledge* (sometimes called "notice") that any of the following exist: (1) that the instrument is forged, altered or incomplete, (2) that the maker or drawer has refused payment, (3) that someone else claims to be the true owner of the instrument, or (4) that some person obligated on the instrument has a defense to payment.

Martha: In the story above, Martha examined Document 23.2: all of the signatures seemed genuine; there was no evidence of alterations in the document and there were no blanks not filled in; and, Martha—who did not know Jed or Milly—had no reason to suspect that Milly might refuse payment. Martha has met this requirement.

B. The holder must acquire the instrument, *for value*, which means: (1) actually performing what has been promised, (2) canceling an old debt, (3) trading for another negotiable instrument, or (4) promising to do something which is irrevocable.

Martha: In the story above, Martha performed her obligation by giving Jed $11,000. But, if Martha had only promised to give the money to Jed, but before paying it she had learned of Milly's defense, she would not have given value and would not be a holder in due course. Martha has met this requirement.

C. The holder must acquire the instrument in *good faith*, which means "honesty in fact in the conduct or transaction concerned."

Martha: This is a routine transaction for Martha. She is truthful when she claims that she did not know that Jed had cheated Milly, or that Milly was refusing to pay the note. Martha has met this requirement.

Martha is a holder in course because: (1) she is a holder, because Jed indorsed the instrument specially to her and transferred it to her; (2) she had no knowledge of Milly's contract defenses against Jed; (3) she gave value, because she paid the agreed sum of $11,000 for the instrument; and, (4) she acted in good faith, which means she was honest in the transaction.

VALUE does not mean consideration; value must be preformed.

The Value Requirement. Before moving ahead, it must be noted that the "value" requirement sometimes causes problems. As discussed above, a holder must give value to qualify as a holder in due course. Section 3-303 (a) (1) is clear that "[a]n instrument is issued or transferred for value if . . . the instrument is issued or transferred for a promise of performance, *to the extent the promise has been performed*" (italics added).

In the story of Jed and Milly in relation to Document 23.2 (a negotiable instrument), Martha gave Jed $11,000 for a $12,000 note payable over time, and thus gave value for the instrument. But, what if Martha had promised to give $11,000, but had only delivered $6,000 when she learned of Milly's defense of fraud? Under these facts, is Martha a holder in due course? The answer is found in § 3-302 (d) in Appendix A, which is as follows:

> *If . . . the promise of performance that is the consideration for an instrument has been partially performed*, the holder may assert rights as a holder in due course of the instrument only to the fraction of the amount payable under the instrument equal to the value of the partial performance divided by the value of the promised performance. (Italics added.)

In their official comment to this provision, the authors of Revised Article 3 give the following example of how the formula described above should be applied:

> Payee negotiates a $1,000 note to Holder who agrees to pay $900 for it. After paying $500, Holder learns that Payee defrauded Maker in the transaction giving rise to the note. Under subsection (d) Holder may assert rights as a holder in due course to the extent of $555.55 ($500 divided by $900 = .555 X $1,000 = 555.55). This formula rewards Holder with a ratable portion of the bargained for profit.

Based on the provisions of § 3-302 (d) (quoted above) it is clear that by paying $6,000, Martha has given value and is a holder in due course to the extent of her $6,000 payment, plus "a ratable portion of the bargained for profit." (There was profit for her in the transaction, because she had promised to pay $11,000 for a note with a face value of $12,000.)

How much should Martha receive from Milly under these facts? The fraction is the amount Martha has paid, divided by the amount she promised to pay ($6,000 divided by $11,000 = .545). The amount Martha receives is the face amount of the note multiplied by the fraction ($12,000 X .545 =$6540). Martha is a holder in due course as to $6540.

Problem Solving. Please turn to Chapter Problems at the end of this chapter and solve Problem 23.2.

The sum of the discussion above is that a *holder in due course*, such as Martha, wins in litigation because she is able to defeat the claims (defenses) of the person (Milly) who—notwithstanding the claims—is obligated to pay the instrument in question. That is generally correct. However, there a few defenses that are good, even against a holder in due course. The list of such defenses is distressingly long; but, it should be noted that they are not defenses that are commonly seen in the "real world" of negotiable instruments.

Defenses

By way of review, in the original Jed and Milly transaction with a negotiable note (Document 23.2) Martha was a holder in due course of a negotiable note because (1) she had no knowledge of Milly's problems, (2) she had paid the full $11,000, and (3) she acted in good faith. Martha won her lawsuit against Milly because most claims or defenses of others cannot be successfully asserted against a holder in due course.

DEFENSES: the following defenses are effective against a holder in due course: infancy, duress, lack of capacity, illegality, fraud in the execution, and discharge.

Defenses Good Against a HDC. The discussion turns now to the *defenses* which may be successfully raised even against a holder in due course, such as Martha. The following list is taken from § 3-305 (a) (1) in Appendix A. For ease of understanding, the items on the list are applied to Martha's claim in relation to Document 23.2. Note that none of them will **prevent** Martha from forcing Milly to pay the note:

A.   "*Infancy* of the obligor to the extent it is a defense to a simple contract."

   Martha: If Milly had been a minor (less than 18 years of age), that defense could be successfully used against Martha, and Milly would not have to pay the note.

B.   "*Duress, lack of legal capacity, or illegality* of the transaction which, under other law, nullifies the obligation of the obligor."

   Martha: If, for example, Jed used a gun to compel Milly to sign the note, that would be an extreme example of duress and a defense that Milly could successfully use against Martha.

C.   "*Fraud* that induced the obligor to sign the instrument with neither knowledge nor reasonable opportunity to learn of its character or its essential terms."

   Martha: If Milly was from Finland and could not read the English language, and no one was available to interpret Document 23.2 for

354

her, and Jed lied to her and told her that the document she was signing was a delivery receipt for the car, that would be fraud in which Milly had neither knowledge nor reasonable opportunity to learn of the character of the document or its essential terms. This is sometimes called "fraud in the execution." (Later in the chapter there is an extended discussion of fraud in the execution.)

D.   *"Discharge* of the obligor in insolvency proceedings."

Martha: Filing a petition in bankruptcy is the most common example of a discharge in insolvency proceedings. If Milly filed in bankruptcy and received a discharge of her debts from the court, Martha could not force her to pay the note.

Infancy. The following case, *Kedzie and 103rd Currency Exchange v. Hodge,* illustrates the general ineffectiveness of contract defenses when used against a holder in due course.

This case involves a claim that a negotiable instrument—in the hands of a holder in due course—should not be enforced because illegality was involved in its issuance. Fred Fentress, an unlicenced plumber, agreed to install a flood control system at the home of Eric and Beulah Hodge, in return for which Mrs. Hodge wrote a check to him for $500. Fentress did not perform the work, but nevertheless cashed the check at the Kedzie & 103rd Street Currency Exchange. Meanwhile, Mrs. Hodge stopped payment on the check. The result was a suit by Kedzie—which claimed to be a holder in due course—against Hodge. The response of Mrs. Hodge was to assert a claim of "illegality" because Fentress was not licenced.

Kedzie and 103rd Currency Exchange v. Hodge
619 N.E.2d 732 (1993)

Justice FREEMAN delivered the opinion of the court:
* * *

No material fact remains to be resolved. The question is simply whether Hodge is entitled, as a matter of law, to a judgment of dismissal in view of the defense asserted under UCC section 3-305.

"Illegality" under Section 3-305.

Section 3-305 provides, in relevant part:
  "[A] holder in due course . . . takes the instrument free from

    (2) all defenses of any party to the instrument with whom the holder has not dealt except

---

(B) . . . illegality of the transaction, as renders the obligation of the party a nullity."

The concern is whether noncompliance by Fentress with the Illinois Plumbing License Law gives rise to "illegality of the transaction" with respect to the contract for plumbing services so as to bar the claim of the Currency Exchange, a holder in due course of the check initially given Fentress.

The issue of "illegality" arises "under a variety of statutes." * * * In view of the diverse constructions to which statutory enactments are given, "illegality" is, accordingly, a matter "left to the local law." * * * Even so, it is only when an obligation is made "entirely null and void" under "local law" that "illegality" exists as one of the "real defenses" under section 3-305 to defeat a claim of a holder in due course. * * * In effect, the obligation must be no obligation at all. If it is "merely voidable" at the election of the obligor, the defense is unavailable. * * *

* * *

A plaintiff is precluded from recovering on a suit involving an illegal contract because the plaintiff is a wrongdoer. * * * Enforcement of the illegal contract makes the court an indirect participant in the wrongful conduct. * * *

But a holder in due course is an innocent third party. * * * Such a holder is without knowledge of the circumstances of the contract upon which the instrument was initially exchanged. * * * The same rationale that precludes recovery by a wrongdoing plaintiff is inapplicable in determining such a holder's right to claim payment. * * * Enforcement of that claim does not sully the court. * * *

* * *

It is, therefore, not enough simply to conclude that the initial obligation to pay arising from a void contract or transaction is void. Negation of that obligation as between the contracting parties has little bearing on whether a holder in due course of an instrument should nevertheless be permitted to make a claim for payment.

The "local law" * * * of this state has been formulated upon this court's recognition, in cases predating the UCC, of legislative prerogative regarding negotiable instruments. In adopting the UCC and, in particular, section 3-305, our legislature chose to confer upon a holder in due course of a negotiable instrument considerable protection against claims by persons to it. Our legislature also continues to declare certain obligations void because of the circumstances of the agreements from which they arise and without regard to the status of who may claim ownership. * * * The selective negation of obligations reflects a legislative aim to declare what will and will not give rise to "illegality" in cases now governed by the UCC. As legislative direction indicates which obligations are always void, legislative silence indicates when the protection afforded a holder in due course must be honored.

We therefore reaffirm, today, the view this court has consistently recognized in cases predating the UCC. Unless the instrument arising from a contract or transaction is, itself, made void by statute, the "illegality" defense under section 3-305 is not available to bar the claim of a holder in due course.

According to the court, a contract with an unlicenced plumber is not always void. In other words, it was not inherently unlawful for Mr. and Mrs. Hodge to do business with an unlicenced contractor. Because the underlying transaction was not inherently unlawful, the court chose not to penalize a holder in due course by refusing to enforce the instrument.

Suppose, however, that Mrs. Hodge had given the check to Fentress in return for his agreement to murder her mother in law. This transaction is inherently unlawful. It is void, *ab inititio* (from the beginning). In this case, the court would undoubtedly refuse to enforce the instrument against a holder in due course.

This case, and the one which follows (*Federal Deposit Ins. Corp. v. Culver*), indirectly illustrate a practical point. That point is that holder in due course status is viewed as very important, and courts are not easily persuaded to avoid it through the use of one of the defenses described above. The evidence must be substantial to support such a defense if it is to be effective.

FRAUD IN THE EXECUTION is different than fraud in the inducement; fraud in the execution is relatively rare.

Fraud. Fraud is a defense often asserted against a holder in due course, but is rarely successful against a holder in due course. The reason for this focuses on the difference between fraud in the *inducement* and fraud in the *execution*. Fraud in the *execution* (which is difficult to prove) is successful against a holder in due course, but fraud in the *inducement* is not successful against a holder in due course. To understand the difference between these two types of fraud, consider the difference between two different events:

> *Example 1:* Jed sells Milly a car and commits fraud by telling her that it has gone only 50,000 miles, although it really has gone 150,000 miles. (Believing Jed, Milly signs the note.)

> *Example 2*: Milly was from Finland and could not read the English language, and no one was available to interpret the document for her, and Jed lied to her and told her that the document she was signing was a delivery receipt for the car. (Believing Jed, Milly signs the note.)

Note the difference between Example 1 and Example 2. In Example 1—sometimes called fraud in the inducement—Milly knows what she is signing, but she signs it because she is induced to sign it by Jed's dishonest sales pitch about the quality of the item she is buying. In contrast, in Example 2—sometimes called fraud in the execution—Milly does *not* know what she is signing, and has no reasonable opportunity to learn what it is.

The difference between fraud in the inducement and fraud in the execution is that *only the latter—fraud in the execution—may be successfully used against a holder in due course.* [§ 3-305(a)(1)(iii)] On the other hand, the more common fraud in the inducement, where Milly was cheated in the sales pitch, cannot be used successfully against a holder in due course.

The question of fraud as a defense against a holder in due course was raised in *Federal Deposit Ins. Corp. v. Culver*. The defendant, Gary Culver, was a farmer who hired Nasib Ed Kalliel to handle financial matters for his farm. After hiring Kalliel, Culver became aware that $30,000 had been transferred from the Rexford State Bank in Rexford, Kansas, to Culver's bank in Missouri, with the money apparently to be used to operate the farm. At that point, Kalliel asked Culver to sign a "receipt" (with a number of blanks) for the money from the Kansas bank. The "receipt" turned out to be a promissory note for $50,000, payable to the Kansas bank. Thereafter, Kalliel and the money disappeared.

The Rexford State Bank failed and the Federal Deposit Insurance Corporation (FDIC), standing in the shoes of the bank, sued to collect on the promissory note. The FDIC had the status of a holder in due course, so the only way for Culver to avoid liability was to assert the defense of fraud.

Federal Deposit Ins. Corp. v. Culver
640 F.Supp. 725 (1986)

Earl E. O'Connor, Chief Judge
* * *

Recognizing that "[t]here is no doubt that state and federal law provide the Federal Deposit Insurance Corporation with holder in due course status in the instant litigation, (Defendant's Brief of May 2, 1986, at 11) defendant concedes that the "personal" defenses of fraud in the inducement, estoppel, and failure of consideration would be ineffective against plaintiff's claim. * * * Accordingly, defendant seeks to assert the "real" defense of fraud in the factum [fraud in the execution]. Plaintiff denies that the facts as alleged by defendant constitute fraud in the factum. * * *

The "fraud in the factum" defense is codified at K.S.A. 84-3-305(2)(c), which provides as follows:

> *Rights of a holder in due course.* To the extent that a holder is a holder in due course he takes the instrument free from
>
> . . . .
>
> > (2) all defenses of any party to the instrument with whom the holder has not dealt *except*
> >
> > . . . .
> >
> > (c) such misrepresentation as has induced the party to sign the instrument with neither knowledge nor reasonable opportunity to obtain knowledge of its *character* or its *essential terms.*

(Emphasis added.) As suggested by our factual summary, defendant contends that he signed the note under the misapprehension that it was merely a receipt. He thus denies having knowledge of the document's "character" at the time he signed it. Moreover, because of the note's execution date, maturity date, principal mount and interest rate were all blank at the time he signed it, defendant contends that he had neither knowledge nor reasonable opportunity to obtain knowledge as to the note's "essential terms."
* * *

It is obvious from reading defendant's deposition that he is able to read and understand the English language. Thus, under the rule announced in [*Ort v. Fowler*, 31 K. 478, 2 P. 580 (1884)] defendant was negligent in relying on Gilbert's assurance that the note was only a receipt. Given the 1983 Kansas Comment referring to the *Ort* absence-of-negligence standard as "comparable to that required by [K.S.A. 84-3-305(2)(c)]," we must also conclude that defendant has failed to show the "excusable ignorance" necessary to establish fraud in the

---

358

> factum. In the words of the statute, we conclude as a matter of law that defendant had a "reasonable opportunity to obtain knowledge of [the document's] character" before he signed it.
>
> [Plaintiff's motion for summary judgment granted.]

What is the point of the *Culver* decision? It is that few fraud defenses are actually effective against a holder in due course. When people use a claim of fraud to avoid negotiable instruments, they usually mean fraud *in the inducement*: that they were cheated; that someone lied to them about what they were selling, buying or signing. This defense is not effective against a holder in due course.

Only fraud in the execution is effective against a holder in due course. This occurs only in the rare case that the defrauded party had "neither knowledge nor reasonable opportunity to obtain knowledge of its [the instruments] character or its essential terms." This circumstance is rare because it only applies when the signing party cannot understand what is being signed—no matter how badly he or she was otherwise cheated.

Problem Solving. Please turn to Chapter Problems at the end of this chapter and solve Problem 23.3.

The Shelter Rule

SHELTER RULE: a person who receives a negotiable instrument from a holder in due course has the status of a holder in due course.

One of the most important features of negotiable instrument law is the preferential treatment given to holders in due course. Without the protection of holder in due course status, negotiable instruments would not move freely in commerce. Thus, a great effort is made in negotiable instruments law to protect the holder in due course status, and the so-called *shelter rule* is part of that effort.

To understand the necessity for the shelter rule, consider the following problem. Recall Document 23.2 and assume that Martha is a holder in due course with respect to that instrument. Add a new fact and suppose that Martha wishes to negotiate Document 23.2 to Pete. But, before she can negotiate the note to Pete, the news media tells everyone the story of Jed cheating Milly. That means, of course, that in practical terms the note has apparently lost its negotiability because every person that Martha might negotiate it to has knowledge of the problem and thus cannot qualify as a holder in due course.

In the commercial world, the idea that Martha can be a holder in due course, and yet cannot negotiate the instrument to anyone else, is not acceptable. A way has to be found to let Martha transfer the document on to others. The solution to this problem is in § 3-203 (b), which provides as follows:

359

(b) Transfer of an instrument, whether or not the transfer is a negotiation, *vests in the transferee any right of the transferor to enforce the instrument, including any right as a holder in due course,* but the transferee cannot acquire rights of a holder in due course by a transfer, directly or indirectly, from a holder in due course *if the transferee engaged in fraud or illegality affecting the instrument.* (Italics added.)

The solution is simple: if Martha is a holder in due course, then Pete acquires that status with the note when he buys the note from Martha. This is because § 3-203 (b) (quoted above) provides that transfer of an instrument "vests in the transferee [Pete] any right of the transferor [Martha] to enforce the instrument." One right that Martha had in the note was her status as holder in due course, and that right vested in Pete when Martha transferred the note to him. That means that Pete can enforce the note as though he were a holder in due course.

Does the shelter rule mean that Pete can negotiate the note (Document 23.2) to Jed, and that Jed can now make Milly pay him because of the shelter rule, even though he defrauded her? The answer is no, because of the last part of § 3-203 (b) (quoted above). The shelter rule does not apply to a person, like Jed, who was part of the original fraud. Jed can never become a holder in due course, nor can he acquire that status from someone else.

Problem Solving. Please turn to Chapter Problems at the end of this chapter and solve Problem 23.4.

Consumer Transactions

CONSUMER CREDIT TRANSACTIONS: the holder in due course rule does not apply to consumer credit transactions.

There is a limitation to the holder in due course doctrine in relation to consumer transactions. To understand the limitation, it is first necessary to understand the problem that gives rise to the limitation: Jed sells Milly a SuperRoof for her house (it includes a life time guarantee) and she signs a promissory note for $10,000 to pay for it. Jed negotiates the note to First Bank for $9,000 and uses a small part of that money to pay some high school kids to put a cheap roof on Milly's house. Jed then moves away with most of the money and cannot be located. When she cannot get any satisfaction from Jed, Milly refuses to pay the bank. The bank sues Milly to enforce payment of the note. Milly's defense is breach of the contract to put a SuperRoof on her house. The bank, however, is a holder in due course and Milly's breach of contract defense is not good against a holder in due course. The result is that Milly must pay the bank, even though she was cheated.

To avoid problems like that above, the Federal Trade Commission (FTC) adopted Rule 433[1] which prevents use of the holder in due course doctrine in consumer credit transactions. In general, a consumer credit transaction is one where credit is

_____

[1] 16 C.F.R. § 433.2.

extended to a purchaser of a product intended for personal, family or household use. Rule 433 requires that the following be placed in the promissory note signed by consumer purchasers like Milly:

NOTICE

ANY HOLDER OF THIS CONSUMER CREDIT CONTRACT IS SUBJECT TO ALL CLAIMS AND DEFENSES WHICH THE DEBTOR COULD ASSERT AGAINST THE SELLER OF GOODS OR SERVICES OBTAINED PURSUANT HERETO OR WITH THE PROCEEDS HEREOF. RECOVERY HEREUNDER BY THE DEBTOR SHALL NOT EXCEED AMOUNTS PAID BY THE DEBTOR HEREUNDER.

The obvious result of placing the notice above in Milly's promissory note is that any defense Milly could use against Jed she can use against First Bank. In the lawsuit initiated by First Bank, the result would be changed and Milly would not be liable. Knowing that it will be subject to defenses like those made by Milly, First Bank will be much more careful in accepting negotiable instruments from questionable sellers like Jed.

The rule above came into question in the case of *De La Fuente v. Home Savings Assoc.* In that case, Aluminum Industries, Inc., represented by Roberto Gonzales, sold aluminum siding to Mr. and Mrs. de la Fuente who signed a promissory note to pay for it. The promissory note was negotiated to Home Savings and Aluminum Industries went out of business. Apparently the siding was over priced and the buyers refused to perform the contract. Home Savings sued to enforce the note and claimed that it was a holder in due course.

De La Fuente v. Home Savings Assoc.
38 UCC Rep. Ser. 196 (1984)

KENNEDY, J.

* * *

* * * [W]e disagree that appellee was entitled to the protection of a holder in due course of a negotiable instrument, because (1) the holder in due course doctrine has been abolished in consumer credit transactions by FTC regulations. * * * The note in question contained a notice in bold fact type which reads in part:

NOTICE

ANY HOLDER OF THIS CONSUMER CREDIT CONTRACT IS SUBJECT TO ALL CLAIMS AND DEFENSES WHICH THE DEBTOR COULD ASSERT AGAINST THE SELLER OF GOODS OR SERVICES OBTAINED PURSUANT HERETO OR WITH THE PROCEEDS HEREOF
. . . .

This FTC Rule, subjecting the holder of the notice to the claims and defenses of the debtor, is in direct conflict with the doctrine of the holder in due course. The Federal Courts have stated,

---

without so holding, that the effect of this FTC Rule is to abolish the holder in due course doctrine. * * *

The FTC, in its Statement of Basis and Purpose, specifically named the holder in due course doctrine as the evil addressed by 16 CFR § 433.2. "[A] consumer's duty to pay for goods and services must not be separated from a seller's duty to perform as promised . . ." * * * The FTC intended the Rule to compel creditors to either absorb the costs of the seller misconduct or return them to sellers. * * * The FTC "reach[ed] a determination that it constitutes an unfair and deceptive practice to use contractual boiler plate to separate a buyer's duty to pay from a seller's duty to perform." * * * The effect of this Rule is to "give the courts the authority to examine the equities in an underlying sale, and it will prevent seller from foreclosing judicial review of their conduct. Seller *and creditors* will be responsible for seller misconduct." * * * It was clearly the intention of the FTC Rule to have the holder of the paper bear the losses occasioned by the actions of the seller; therefore, the benefits of the holder in due course doctrine under Tex Bus & Com Code Ann § 3.302 are not available when the notice required by the FTC in 16 CFR § 433.2 is placed on a consumer credit contract.

We reverse the judgment of the trial court and render judgment that appellee [Home Savings] take nothing and that the contract, the subject of this suit, is null and void and that appellants recover against appellee, Home Savings, in the amount of $4,000 plus attorney's fees of $3,500 as found by the trial court. Costs are adjudged against appellee.

There is, however, a weakness in the system. That weakness is that Jed may violate the rule and not place the notice in the promissory note. In that case, Jed would be liable for violation of Rule 433, but the bank (if truly innocent) would be a holder in due course and could enforce the promissory note.

Problem 23.1

Jed owes Milly $500. Jed fraudulently induce Scott to write a check to Milly for $500, and in return Milly cancels the debt Jed owed her. When Scott realizes he has been defrauded, he stops payment on the check. Is Milly a holder in due course who can force Scott to pay her?

Problem 23.2

Jed, the payee of a negotiable promissory note payable in the amount of $1,000, indorsed it in blank and delivered it to Milly, who agreed to pay him $900 for the note. Thereafter, the following events occurred in the following order: (1) Milly learned that the maker had a defense to payment of the note, (2) Milly paid Jed $500, (3) Milly paid Jed $400. Explain Milly's rights in relation to the note.

Problem 23.3

Milly is an Italian immigrant with a third grade education who owns and operates a plumbing business. A salesman sells her aluminum siding for the front of her business for $5,000. She signs (but does not read) a contract for the siding, which is to be installed in three months. The siding is never installed. The document she signed was, in fact, a negotiable promissory note which has been negotiated to a holder in due course, ABC Finance, who demands payment. Must Milly pay the note?

Problem 23.4

On July 6, 1997, Milly signs and delivers the following to Jed:

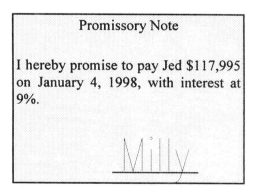

> Promissory Note
>
> I hereby promise to pay Jed $117,995 on January 4, 1998, with interest at 9%.
>
> Milly

The note was in payment for a piece of land which Milly bought from Jed. To induce Milly to buy the land, Jed told him it was in good condition; but, in fact, the land was contaminated with toxic chemicals. Jed negotiated the note to Sarah, a HDC. Sarah negotiated the note to Matthew, who knew that Milly had been cheated. Can Matthew enforce the note against Milly?

Chapter 24
When Things Go Wrong

Chapter Objective

OBJECTIVE is to learn the rules related to unpaid checks, negligence in preparing checks, and imposters or fictitious payees.

The objective of this lesson is to learn the rules related to: liability for payment of an unpaid check, negligence in preparing checks, and imposters or fictitious payees. The chapter is organized as follows:

- *Failure to Pay a Check: Insufficient Funds.* The drawer of a check must pay the check if it is dishonored by the bank upon which it is drawn. If a check is dishonored, an indorser is also liable, but only if prompt notice of dishonor is given. An indorser who indorses "without recourse" is not liable if a check is dishonored.

- *Negligence.* A person whose negligence contributes to the alteration of a check may not assert the alteration against a bank which pays it or a holder in due course.

- *Unauthorized Signatures (Forgeries).* An unauthorized signature (a forgery) is ineffective except as the signature of the unauthorized signer.

- *Imposters or Fictitious Payees.* A person in possession of an instrument is not a holder thereof if a preceding indorsement is forged. That rule does not apply where the forged indorsement is caused by the drawer (1) dealing with an imposter, (2) issuing a check to a payee who is not intended to have an interest in the check, or (3) issuing a check in favor of a fictitious payee.

Introduction

Sometimes thing go wrong with negotiable instruments. Sometimes those who should pay them—the makers and the drawees—will not or cannot. And sometimes things go wrong because of negligence or fraud. This chapter focuses on such things. To avoid confusion, all of the examples used in this chapter will involve only the use of checks.

Failure to Pay a Check

Insufficient Funds. This part illustrates what happens in a routine case if a check is not paid by the bank on which it is drawn. In the example below, Jed Smith is the owner of Smith Plumbing Company. He has a checking account at First Bank. He draws a check on First Bank, which is later dishonored because Jed does not have enough money in his account.

In the normal course of events, when Jed's check "bounces" because of insufficient funds, the following events occur:

1. Jed signs a check for $500, drawn on First Bank, which is issued to Milly, the payee.

2. Milly negotiates the check to Sam.

3. Sam negotiates the check to Mike.

4. Mike deposits the check at his bank, Second Bank.

5. Second Bank transmits the check to First Bank for payment.

6. First Bank refuses to pay the check because Jed does not have enough money in his account and returns it to the second bank.

7. Second Bank subtracts $500 from Mike's account and returns the check to him.

This sequence of events looks like this:

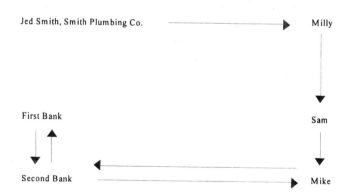

Liability. In the example above, the drawer and each indorser have the following obligations:

DRAWER must pay a dishonored check.

Drawer. As the drawer of the check, Jed must pay it if it is *dishonored.* [§ 3-414(b)] This means that the check must first be presented to his bank, First Bank, for payment. This requirement, which is called *presentment* [§ 3-501(a)] is satisfied when Mike, who is a *person entitled to enforce* the check [§ 3-301] demands that the drawee pay it. Then, if First Bank refuses to pay the check, Jed must pay it. *Dishonor* occurs when the bank refuses to pay the check. [§ 3-502(b)(1)] If Jed, the drawer, must pay

365

the dishonored check, he must pay it to a person entitled to enforce it (who is usually the holder) or an indorser who has paid it.

At this point it is not clear who Jed will end up paying. This is because Mike, who is the person entitled to enforce the check, has a choice: (1) he can take the check to Jed, the drawer, and demand payment, (2) he can give Sam, an indorser, notice of the dishonor of the check and demand that Sam pay it, or, (3) he can make demand on both Jed and Sam. (The motivation behind this choice may be purely economic: if Jed has money, but Sam does not, Mike will pursue his claim against Jed. On the other hand, if Sam has money, but Jed does not, Mike will pursue his claim against Sam. If Jed, Sam and Milly all have money, Mike may pursue his claim against all of them.)

INDORSER must pay a dishonored check if it has been presented and notice of dishonor has been given.

An Indorser. If Milly and Sam signed the back of the check in the process of negotiation, they are indorsers. The indorsers are each liable on the check, but the check must first be presented to the drawee, First Bank, for payment. [§ 3-502(b)(1)] Then, if the check is dishonored, Milly and Sam are liable in the order of their indorsements, unless they signed the check "without recourse."

If Milly or Sam qualified their indorsements by writing the words "without recourse" under their signatures, they are not liable to pay the instrument if it is dishonored. [§ 3-415(b)] (For an example of an indorsement "without recourse," see Document 22.5 in Chapter 22.) But, if their indorsements are not qualified ("without recourse") Sam or Milly must pay a dishonored check to a person entitled to enforce it, who is usually the holder, or a subsequent indorser who has paid it.

The liability of an *indorser* is like a piece of ice that will quickly melt and disappear if something is not done to preserve it. Milly and Sam must be given *notice* of the bank's dishonor if their liability is to be preserved. The notice rules that preserve the liability of an indorser are as follows:

- Liability on an indorsement expires if a check is not *presented for payment or deposited for collection* within thirty days after the indorsement is made. [§ 3-415(e)]

- In addition, liability to a subsequent party on an indorsement expires if *notice of dishonor* [§ 3-503(b)] is not given to the indorser within thirty days following the day on which the subsequent party receives notice of dishonor. [§ 3-503(c)(ii)]

The following case, *First American Bank v. Litchfield Co. Of S.C.* touches on a point made above: the obligation of a *drawer* to pay a check that he or she has issued has few limitations. In contrast, the liability of an indorser can easily slip away.

In *First American*, the drawer, Litchfield, issued a check for $13,711.11 to a company called Jensen Farley. Jensen Farley deposited the check at its bank, First American, and First American forwarded the check for payment to the drawee bank, Banker's Trust. Meanwhile, Litchfield decided that the money should not have been paid to Jensen Farley and stopped payment on the check. Accordingly, Banker's Trust refused to pay the check and returned it to First American. Through a variety of methods, First American then was able to gain reimbursement of $4,341.74 of the amount it had credited to the Jensen Farley account. However, Jensen Farley failed financially and approximately $9,369.37 remained unreimbursed.

Approximately three months after the stop payment, when Jensen Farley went into bankruptcy, First American made claim on Litchfield to be paid the unreimbursed amount. Litchfield claimed that it was not liable to First American because First American had failed to notify Litchfield of the dishonor.

First American Bank v. Litchfield Co. Of S.C.
353 S.E.2d 143 (1987)

BELL, Judge:
* * *

The drawer of a check engages that upon dishonor he will pay the amount of the draft to a holder in due course. * * * The drawer has the right to stop payment, but remains liable on the instrument to a holder in due course. * * * Since Litchfield has conceded First American was a holder in due course, Litchfield remains liable on the instrument unless it can establish a valid defense or set off.

Litchfield argues its liability was discharged by First American's failure to give timely notice the check had been dishonored. This defense is unavailing for two reasons.

First, failure to give notice of dishonor discharges a drawer only to the extent he is deprived of funds maintained with the drawee bank to cover the check because the drawee bank became insolvent during the delay. * * * A drawer is not otherwise discharged. In this case, Litchfield was not deprived of any funds in its account with Bankers Trust nor did Bankers Trust become insolvent during the delay. Thus Litchfield is not discharged.

Second, notice of dishonor is excused when the party to be charged has himself countermanded payment. * * * Since Litchfield ordered payment stopped, it was not entitled to notice of dishonor.

Litchfield argues Section 36-3-511(2)(b)[1] should apply only to notes, cashier's checks, or other instruments that would be presented directly to the maker. We see no basis for such a distinction. Article 3 of the Uniform Commercial Code governs checks except when its provisions conflict with Article 4. * * * Section 36-3-511(2)(b) refers to notice of dishonor of an "instrument," which means a negotiable instrument. * * * Litchfield's check was unquestionably a negotiable instrument. * * *

Litchfield argues strenuously that it is unfair to apply section 36-3-511(2)(b) to the drawer of a check who has no means of knowing whether the check has been negotiated to a holder. This reasoning misses the mark. The maker of an outstanding negotiable instrument is presumed to know the instrument is subject to transfer to a holder in due course. * * * The drawer is often without actual knowledge that his check has been negotiated, but that ignorance

---

[1] Former § 3-511(2)(b): "Presentment or notice or protest as the case may be is entirely excused when . . . such party has himself dishonored the instrument or has countermanded payment or otherwise has no reason to expect or right to require that the instrument be accepted or paid."

> in no way diminishes the rights of a holder in due course. To hold otherwise would, as a practical matter, destroy the negotiability of a check.
>
> For these reasons, we hold First American's delay in giving notice of dishonor does not discharge Litchfield's liability on the check. Other jurisdictions addressing this question have reached the same conclusion. * * *
>
> [Affirmed]

In short, as the drawer, Litchfield is unconditionally obligated to pay the instrument it issued. By using the words of negotiability (pay to the order of, or to bearer) Litchfield has consented that the instrument will be negotiable and may be negotiated from party to party. It also knows it must pay to a holder in due course, even if it has a claim or set-off against the original payee.

Problem Solving. Please turn to Chapter Problems at the end of this chapter and solve problem 24.1.

Failure to Pay a Check: A Lawsuit

In this part, we continue the story of the check issued by Jed Smith. Here, the question is whether Mike will sue Jed, Sam or Milly, and why.

If Mike Sues Jed. As noted above, Mike may choose to pursue Jed and ignore the indorsers. As a holder of the check, Mike is a person entitled to enforce it, and Jed must pay Mike. As illustrated in the *First American* opinion, notice of dishonor is not necessary to preserve Jed's (the drawer's) liability like it is with indorsers.

If Mike Sues Sam. Mike may choose to pursue Sam because he believes that Sam has money. As a holder of the check, Mike is a person entitled to enforce it against Sam. Sam must pay the check to a person entitled to enforce it, unless Sam indorsed it "without recourse," which he did not. Sam must pay Mike, *provided that the presentment and notice requirements were met.* The following dates apply:

Event	Date
Check issued	July 1
Milly indorsed	July 5
Sam indorsed	July 20
Mike indorsed and deposited	Aug. 15
Check returned to Mike	Aug. 25
Mike notifies Sam and Milly	Sept. 1

INDORSER LIABILITY requires presentment within 30 days of indorsement and notice of dishonor within 30 days.

Will Mike be successful in his suit against Sam? He will if the presentment and notice requirements were met. First, Sam will be liable to Mike if the check was presented for payment or deposited in a bank for collection within thirty days after the indorsement was made. [See § 3-415 (e)] Sam indorsed on July 20 and Mike deposited for collection on August 15, therefore, the presentment was in time. Second, Sam will be liable to Mike if Mike gave him notice of the dishonor within thirty days of the date

Mike received it. [See § 3-503 (c)] The check was returned to Mike August 25, which gave Mike notice of the dishonor. Mike gave Sam notice of the dishonor on September 1, therefore, notice of dishonor was in time, and Mike may proceed in his suit against Sam.

If Sam sues Milly. When Mike sued Sam, Sam responded by suing Milly in the same lawsuit. Sam's idea was that he would make Milly reimburse him for whatever he had to pay Mike, because Milly's indorsement warranty includes the promise that she will pay the check to a subsequent indorser who paid it. And, in fact, Sam is a subsequent indorser who paid the check. But, as we learned above, Sam will succeed against an indorser only if the presentment requirements are met. The notice of dishonor requirement is met because Mike gave notice to Milly within thirty days of the date he received it. (Milly does not need a separate notice from Sam because Mike's notice satisfied the requirement.)

But, there is a problem. Milly indorsed the check on July 1, but it was not deposited by Mike until August 15. The result is that the check was not presented for payment or collection within thirty days of Milly's indorsement, and Milly's indorser's liability expired. Sam cannot successfully sue Milly, although he can, of course, successfully sue Jed.

__Problem Solving__. Please turn to Chapter Problems at the end of this chapter and solve problem 24.2.

Failure to Pay a Check Revisited: Negotiation Without Indorsement

INDORSEMENT "without recourse" avoids indorser liability.

Negotiation Without Indorsement. In the problem above, we have assumed that Milly and Sam negotiated the check by signing their names on the back of the check. As long as they use one of the forms of indorsement which includes a signature, and do not sign "without recourse," they are liable as indorsers. But what if Milly's indorsement was in blank, and Sam did not sign the check, but negotiated it to Mike by handing it to him?

If Sam did not sign the check, but negotiated it to Mike by simply handing it to him, the warranty of indorsement does not apply. [See 3-415 (b)] Instead, only the *warranty of transfer* applies. A person who transfers a check, but does not sign it, makes the following promises:

- There are no missing indorsements, and the transferor is thus a person entitled to enforce the check.

- The signatures on the check are genuine and authorized.

- The check has not been altered.

- The check is not subject to defenses or claims that are good against the transferor.

- The transferor has no knowledge that the drawer filed in bankruptcy.

These are serious promises, but the most serious of all is *not* on the list: that is, the indorser's *promise to pay* the check if it is dishonored. The lawsuits of Mike against Sam, and Sam against Milly, are now revisited to learn how things change when one of the parties negotiates an instrument *without signing it*.

The Lawsuit Revisited: Mike sues Sam. When Mike sues Sam, the warranties of transfer, and not the indorser's warranty, apply. All necessary signatures on the back of the check were there, and all of them were genuine and authorized, and the check had not been altered. In addition, Jed, the drawer, had no defenses to payment, (even if he did, most of them would not be good against Sam if Sam was a holder in due course.) Moreover, Jed has not filed in bankruptcy. The result is that Sam has not violated the warranties of transfer. Most important, Sam in not *subject to the indorser's promise to pay the check in the event of dishonor*, so he is not liable to Mike.

The Lawsuit Revisited: Mike sues Milly? Milly signed the check and is thus liable on the indorser's promise to pay in the event of dishonor. The problem is—as learned above—that the check was *not* presented for payment or for collection within thirty days of Milly's indorsement. Thus Milly's promise has expired. The result is that Mike's only option is to bring suit against Jed, the drawer.

Negligence in Completing a Check

When things go wrong in the payment of a check, it is not always a failure to pay because of insufficient funds in the drawer's checking account. Lets change the facts and suppose that a problem arises because Jed, the drawer, was negligent—he did a sloppy job of filling out the check he gave to Milly—and Milly was dishonest and altered the check so that she would receive extra money.

Suppose that the check Jed gives to Milly is negligently completed in the following manner:

Document 24.1

	Date ___July 1___ 19 _96_
PAY to the order of: _____Milly_____	$ ___200.00___
_____Two hundred and no/100 ~ ~ ~ ~ ~ ~ ~ ~ ~ ~ ~ ~ ~ ~ ~ ~ ~ ~	Dollars
First Bank	
Kansas City, KS.	
	___Jed___
	Jed's Plumbing Company

When Milly receives the check, she realizes that she can change the principal amount of the check from $200 to $2200, and that the change will not be obvious. Milly adds the word "Twenty" (Twenty Two Hundred and no/100) and a numeral "2" ($2200) and negotiates the check to Sam. If Sam acts in good faith, how much is he entitled to receive from Jed?

A Lawsuit. When the altered version of Document 24.1 is presented for payment, it is paid. But, when Jed receives his bank statement at the end of the month, he realizes that the check he issued to Milly has been altered and he demands that the bank return $2,000 to his account. (Normally—if he has not been negligent— Jed will win in his claim against the bank because a bank can pay an altered check only according to its "original terms.")

NEGLIGENCE in preparing an instrument blocks recovery.

Negligence. However, Jed's duty as a drawer in the preparation of checks is to exercise ordinary care. In other words, Jed cannot act negligently in the preparation of checks. This duty is stated in § 3-406(a) as follows:

> A person whose failure to exercise ordinary care [negligence] substantially contributes to an alteration of an instrument is precluded from asserting the alteration or the forgery against a person who, in good faith, pays the instrument or takes it for value or for collection.

The bank responds by reminding Jed of his duty not to be negligent. The bank reminds Jed that if his failure to exercise ordinary care substantially contributed to the alteration of the check, he cannot assert the alteration against the bank which, in good faith paid the instrument. Because, in fact, Jed's negligence directly contributed to the alteration by Milly, Jed will lose in his lawsuit against the bank. (Jed would obviously win in a lawsuit to be reimbursed by Milly.)

The following case, *J. Gordon Neely, Etc. v. American Nat. Bank*, deals with a claim of negligence in completing a check. The plaintiff, J. Gordon Neely and his wife (doing business as Midas Muffler) employed Louise Bradshaw as a bookkeeper. From time to time, Bradshaw prepared routine checks with a large amount of space to the left of the designated amounts, which the Neely's signed. Unknown to the Neelys, "Bradshaw [later] altered the checks either by adding a digit or two to the left of the original amount, or by raising the first digit after using liquid erasure." Bradshaw then employed a scheme to divert the additional amount of the checks to her own use. When the scheme was uncovered, the Neelys sued the bank to recover the misappropriated money. One of the issues in the case was whether the Neelys had been negligent in signing checks with a large amount of space to the left of the designated amounts.

J. Gordon Neely, Etc. v. American Nat. Bank
403 So.2d 887 (1981)

ADAMS, Justice.

* * *

[W]e must next determine whether Neely, by its negligence, substantially contributed to the facilitation of the alterations. The Uniform Commercial Code does not define the negligence which will support the defense of § 7-3-406, and instructs that it is an issue strictly left to the fact-finder on a case by case approach. Code 1975, § 7-3-406, Comment 3. The official comment does advise, however, that "[n]egligence usually has been found where spaces are left in the body of the instrument in which words or figures may be inserted." * * * It is undisputed that Mrs. Neely signed the checks fully aware of the large gaps in front of the amount.

Similarly, two other examples of negligence are supported by the record: no inquiry was made into Bradshaw's veracity, although it was rumored that previously she had been in trouble with embezzlement in Tennessee, * * * and Neely failed to maintain internal controls so that the employee writing the checks was not also the principal person reconciling the bank statements * * *.

Although each state defines it separately, Alabama construes the phrase "substantially contributes," Code 1975 § 7-3-406, to mean that the drawer's negligence must proximately cause the making of the alteration. * * * Particularly pertinent to this case is the following description of proximate cause:

> When a person by his negligence produces a dangerous condition of things, which does not become active for mischief until another person has operated upon it by the commission of another negligent act, which might not unreasonably be anticipated to occur, the original act of negligence is then regarded as the proximate cause of the injury which finally results.

* * * Based upon a thorough and sifting review of the record, we conclude that the accumulation of Mrs. Neely's negligent conduct set in motion an unfortunate chain of events which proximately culminated in the alterations, thus establishing Neely's substantial contribution.

We will not disturb these findings that Neely's negligence substantially contributed to Bradshaw's alterations, because they are not clearly and patently erroneous. Therefore, because American National acted in a commercially reasonable manner and Neely's negligence substantially contributed to the material alteration resulting in the bank's payment to Bradshaw, Neely cannot recover from American National.

Based upon the foregoing analysis and conclusions, the judgment of the trial court is due to be, and is hereby, affirmed.

There is nothing new in the case above. It reinforces the standard legal proposition that a party cannot recover from another for losses proximately caused by his own negligence.

Unauthorized Signatures (Forgeries)

In the original story at the beginning of this chapter, suppose that Sam stole the check from Milly and forged her signature ("Milly") on the back and then transferred it to Mike. Can Mike successfully sue Milly or Jed when First Bank refuses to pay the check? No, because Milly and Jed each promised that, in the event of dishonor, they would pay the check to a person who is entitled to enforce the check, and that person is usually a holder. However, in this case, Mike is *not* a holder because the check was not negotiated to him. It was not negotiated to him because Milly's signature was forged, and negotiation requires a genuine indorsement.

FORGED SIGNATURE is not an effective signature.

Section 3-403(a) provides that "*an unauthorized signature is ineffective* except as the signature of the unauthorized signer in favor of a person who in good faith pays the instrument or takes it for value." Because the signature is ineffective, the negotiation is ineffective. The only person that Mike can successfully sue is Sam, because the signature "Milly" is effective as Sam's signature.

Problem Solving. Please turn to Chapter Problems at the end of this chapter and solve problem 24.3.

A Summary

Before moving on to the next point, it is important to summarize:

1. If a check is dishonored, the drawer (Jed) promises to pay it to the holder (Mike), or to an indorser who has paid it (Sam or Milly).

2. An indorser (for example, Milly) makes a similar promise: if a check is dishonored, she will pay it to the holder (Mike), or to a subsequent indorser who has paid it (Sam).

3. The liability of an indorser expires if there are time delays in relation to presentment and notice of dishonor.

4. The promises of a person who negotiates a check without indorsing it do not include a promise to pay the check if it is dishonored.

5. If a check is altered, the drawer is liable only according to the original terms of the check.

6. A person whose negligence substantially contributes to an alteration of an instrument is precluded from asserting the alteration.

7. A person who has received a check through a forged indorsement is not a holder and cannot enforce payment of the instrument from the drawer or prior indorsers.

Impostors or Fictitious Payees

From the foregoing, it is clear that the *holder* of a dishonored check may demand that the drawer or prior indorsers pay the instrument. But, there is, of course, an exception: a person in possession of a check which is dishonored because of a forged indorsement *cannot* demand that the drawer or prior indorsers pay the instrument. The reason for this is simple: if any of the indorsements preceding the "holder" are forgeries, the person in possession is, in fact, not a *holder*. The person in possession is not a holder because all necessary indorsements are not included. [§ 3-201(b)]

Thus, in the original story, if Sam forged the indorsement of Milly and "negotiated" the instrument to Mike, Mike is not a holder and has no standing to enforce the instrument against Jed or Milly. In this situation, Mike's only recourse is to sue Sam, who sold him the instrument. This point needs to be repeated: if Mike's chain of ownership includes a forged indorsement, he cannot successfully sue any of the persons before the forgery in the chain of ownership. This is fair because Jed and Milly do not control Sam's relationship with Mike. Mike is in a better position to control that relationship, and if he allows Sam to cheat him, he (Mike) should suffer the loss.

The logic of the foregoing is that Mike suffers the loss because *he* best controls the problem of the forged indorsement by Sam. But, suppose that *Jed*, the drawer, is the source of the problem. Suppose that it is *Jed's* conduct that puts Sam in a position to forge Milly's indorsement and cheat Mike. In that case, logic says that *Jed*, the drawer—and not Mike—should suffer the loss because Jed is the person who caused the problem.

IMPOSTERS OR FICTITIOUS EMPLOYEES. Dealing with these changes the liability of the drawer.

Examples. Following are three examples in which Jed, the *drawer*, is the person whose conduct makes a subsequent forged indorsement possible. These examples illustrate circumstances where Mike receives a check from Sam (or someone like him), who has forged Milly's indorsement, but it is *Jed* who has helped created the circumstances where that can happen.

1. *An Impostor*: Jed owes money to Milly, but he does not know her. Lucy appears at Jed's office and says that she is Milly. Jed believes her and gives Lucy a check payable to Milly. Lucy forges the indorsement "Milly" and negotiates the instrument to Mike.

2. *Payee Not Intended to Have an Interest*: Jed wants to improperly receive money from his company. He writes a check to ABC Supplies (a real customer) but does not deliver the check to them. Instead, he forges the name ABC Supplies on the back of the check and negotiates the check to Mike. (Jed uses the money he received from Mike for personal expenses.)

3. *Fictitious Payee*: Jed has a dishonest bookkeeper named Sam, who tells Jed that money is owed to a consultant named Milly. In fact, there is no person named Milly to whom Jed owes money. Relying on Sam, Jed writes a check to Milly. Sam signs the indorsement "Milly" and negotiates the check to Mike.

In each of these examples, the law of negotiable instruments views *Jed* as being the person who could have prevented the false indorsements. When the checks are in Mike's possession, why should Mike bear the loss when Jed should have prevented it?

At this point—if one of the three events described above occurs—the problem is how to allow Mike to enforce the instrument in his possession even though there is a forged indorsement in his chain of possession. The solution is bluntly simple: if one of the three events described above occurs, the resulting (forged) indorsement is treated as being "effective." Thus, if the indorsement of the name "Milly" or the indorsement of the name "ABC Supplies" is caused by one of the three circumstances above, Mike can force Jed to pay the check because he is a holder. He is a holder because all endorsements are now in place—the forged document now being considered effective. [§§ 3-404 and 3-405]

The following case, *Golden Years Nursing Home v. Gabbard*, illustrates what has been described above. Gabbard worked in the office of the Golden Years Nursing Home. The company sometimes gave short-term loans to employees. Knowing this, Gabbard would occasionally prepare checks in the names of existing employees of the company, and the unsuspecting nursing home administrator would sign them. In fact, the employees were not expecting the checks and Gabbard would forge their indorsement on the check and divert the money to her own use. When the scheme was uncovered, the nursing home sued the bank for reimbursement on the theory that the bank—like Mike in the examples above—was not a holder of the instrument because of the forged indorsements.

Golden years Nursing Home v. Gabbard
640 N.E.2d 1186 (1994)

Walsh, Presiding Judge
* * *

Articles 3 and 4 of the Uniform Commercial Code ("UCC"), R.C. Chapters 1303 and 1304, govern transactions involving negotiable instruments such as the checks in the present case. In the case of order instruments, payable to the order of a named payee, title is passed on the instrument and transferees of the instrument subsequent to the payee become "holders" of the instrument when it is negotiated and validly indorsed by the payee. * * * A holder has certain rights as against prior transferees of the instrument but is also subject to certain claims and defenses on the instrument and may be liable to subsequent transferees. * * * If certain requirements are met, a holder can attain the preferred status of a "holder in due course" ("HIDC"), which affords the most protection against claims or defenses of other parties or holders of the instrument. * * *

As a general rule, the forgery of a payee's indorsement on order paper, such as the employee loan * * * checks, breaks the chain of title and no subsequent transferee of the instrument can qualify as a holder. See R.C. 1303.40(A), which provides that "[a]ny unauthorized signature [defined in R.C. 1303.01(QQ) to include a forged indorsement] is wholly inoperative as that of the person whose name is signed * * *." * * * Therefore, because qualifying as a holder is a prerequisite to attaining HIDC status, generally no one who takes an order instrument with a forged indorsement can become an HIDC, and anyone who pays on an instrument containing a forged indorsement is liable thereon. * * *

However, there are two exceptions to the general rule, found in R.C. 1303.41 and R.C. 1303.42, whereby a forged indorsement is deemed to be validated and good title passes to a subsequent transferee who then becomes a holder and can attain HIDC status and protection against liability on the instrument. * * * The trial court found that Star Bank was not liable as a matter of law for paying on he employee loan checks presented by Gabbard due to the operation of the "padded payroll" or "fictitious payee" defense of R.C. 1303.41(A). We agree.

The padded-payroll or fictitious-payee defense, also known as the imposter rule, validates a forged payee's indorsement whenever the drawer or his employee has designated as payee someone who is not really intended to have an interest in the instrument. In such a case, good title passes to a subsequent transferee and the instrument will be properly payable out of the drawer/employer's bank account, despite a forged payee indorsement. * * *

The theory behind R.C. 1303.41(A) is that the risk of loss caused by a dishonest employee should be placed on the employer rather than the subsequent holder bank because the employer is normally in a better position to prevent such forgeries by reasonable care in the selection or supervision of employees, or, if not, is at least in a better position to cover the loss by fidelity insurance. * * * Furthermore, under R.C. 1303.41(A), the negligence of a bank in accepting an instrument with a forged payee indorsement is immaterial, as the statue is silent on the issue of the bank's lack of care. * * *

Because Gabbard, as a Golden Years employee, provided her employer with names of employees who had not really requested loans for the specific purpose of embezzling money without ever intending that the employees have an interest in the checks, we find that the trial court was correct in concluding that the padded-payroll defense of R.C. 1303.41(A) precluded Golden Years, the drawer of the checks, from asserting the forged payee indorsements against Star Bank. Contrary to Golden Years' contention, we also agree with the trial court that the defense is available to depositary banks such as Star Bank, as well as drawee banks who pay on instruments containing forged indorsements. Ohio App.3d at 169, 532 N.E.2d at 779 ("[W]e believe that the depositary/collecting bank should be permitted to raise the same Code defenses

available to a drawee/payer bank, including the imposter rule."). Therefore, we find that the trial court was correct in sustaining Star Bank's motion for summary judgment relative to the employee loan checks.

In sum, a person obtaining possession of an instrument through a forged indorsement is not a holder and cannot enforce the instrument. An exception, illustrated above, is that the person in possession of the instrument may enforce it if the first cause of the forged indorsement is conduct in the office of the drawer. In such a case, the forged indorsement is considered "effective" for the limited purpose of transferring ownership of the instrument to a subsequent holder.

Problem Solving. Please turn to Chapter Problems at the end of this chapter and solve problem 24.4.

Chapter Problems

Problem 24.1

A negotiable instrument is negotiated from Milly to Sam. Sam wishes to negotiate the instrument to Mike, but Sam also wishes to avoid indorser's liability if the check is dishonored. Can it be done? Explain.

Problem 24.2

Mike is the holder of a check negotiated to him by Sam. It was negotiated to Sam by Milly. The check was dishonored and returned to Mike on August 1. On August 20, Mike gave notice of the dishonor to Sam. On September 10, Sam gives dishonor to Milly. Mike now seeks to hold Sam and Milly liable on their indorser's liability. Will he be successful?

Problem 24.3

In the story diagramed at the beginning of this chapter, a negotiable instrument is negotiated from Milly to Sam. However, Milly's indorsement is forged. First Bank is made aware of the forgery and dishonors the check and it is returned to Mike. Who is liable on the check?

Problem 24.4

Douglas works as an accountant at the ABC Banana Co. He prepares a false invoice payable to the Yellow Heart Banana Co. in the amount of $1,500 and Jed (the office manager) signs an ABC check to pay the invoice. Douglas then forges the signature of the Yellow Heart Banana Co. and delivers the check to Sam. Sam negotiates the check to Mike. When First Bank dishonors the check because of the forgery, which is subsequently discovered, who is liable on the check?

Appendix A

Selected Articles from
The Uniform Commercial Code

APPENDIX A

The Uniform Commercial Code

ARTICLE 1 / General Provisions

Part 1 Short Title, Construction, Application and Subject Matter of the Act

§ 1-101. Short Title. This Act shall be known and may be cited as Uniform Commercial Code.

§ 1-102. Purposes; Rules of Construction; Variation by Agreement.

(1) This Act shall be liberally construed and applied to promote its underlying purposes and policies.
(2) Underlying purposes and policies of this Act are

(a) to simplify, clarify and modernize the law governing commercial transactions;
(b) to permit the continued expansion of commercial practices through custom, usage and agreement of the parties;
(c) to make uniform the law among the various jurisdictions.

(3) The effect of provisions of this Act may be varied by agreement, except as otherwise provided in this Act and except that the obligations of good faith, diligence, reasonableness and care prescribed by this Act may not be disclaimed by agreement but the parties may by agreement determine the standards by which the performance of such obligations is to be measured if such standards are not manifestly unreasonable.
(4) The presence in certain provisions of this Act of the words "unless otherwise agreed" or words of similar import does not imply that the effect of other provisions may not be varied by agreement under subsection (3).
(5) In this Act unless the context otherwise requires

(a) words in the singular number include the plural, and in the plural include the singular;
(b) words of the masculine gender include the feminine and the neuter, and when the sense so indicates words of the neuter gender may refer to any gender.

§ 1-103. Supplementary General Principles of Law Applicable. Unless displaced by the particular provisions of this Act, the principles of law and equity, including the law merchant and the law relative to capacity to contract, principal and agent, estoppel, fraud, misrepresentation, duress, coercion, mistake, bankruptcy, or other validating or invalidating cause shall supplement its provisions.

§ 1-104. Construction Against Implicit Repeal. This Act being a general act intended as a unified coverage of its subject matter, no part of it shall be deemed to be impliedly repealed by subsequent legislation if such construction can reasonably be avoided.

§ 1-105. Territorial Application of the Act; Parties' Power to Choose Applicable Law.

(1) Except as provided hereafter in this section, when a transaction bears a reasonable relation to this state and also to another state or nation the parties may agree that the law either of this state or of such other state or nation shall govern their rights and duties. Failing such agreement this Act applies to transactions bearing an appropriate relation to this state.
(2) Where one of the following provisions of this Act specifies the applicable law, that provision governs and a contrary agreement is effective only to the extent permitted by the law (including the conflict of laws rules) so specified:

Rights of creditors against sold goods. Section 2-402.
Applicability of the Article on Leases. Sections 2A-105 and 2A-106.
Applicability of the Article on Bank Deposits and Collections. Section 4-102.
Governing law in the Article on Funds Transfers. Section 4A-507.
Bulk sales subject to the Article on Bulk Sales. Section 6-103.
Applicability of the Article on Investment Securities. Section 8-106.
Perfection provisions of the Article on Secured Transactions. Section 9-103.

As amended in 1972, 1987, 1988 and 1989.

§ 1-106. Remedies to Be Liberally Administered.

(1) The remedies provided by this Act shall be liberally administered to the end that the aggrieved party may be put in as good a position as if the other party had fully performed but neither consequential or special nor penal damages may be had except as specifically provided in this Act or by other rule of law.
(2) Any right or obligation declared by this Act is enforceable by action unless the provision declaring it specifies a different and limited effect.

§ 1-107. Waiver or Renunciation of Claim or Right After Breach. Any claim or right arising out of an alleged breach can be discharged in whole or in part without consideration by a written waiver or renunciation signed and delivered by the aggrieved party.

§ 1-108. Severability. If any provision or clause of this Act or application thereof to any person or circumstances is held invalid, such invalidity shall not affect other provisions or applications of the Act which can be given effect without the invalid provision or application, and to this end the provisions of this Act are declared to be severable.

§ 1-109. **Section Captions.** Section captions are parts of this Act.

Part 2   General Definitions and Principles of Interpretation

§ 1-201. **General Definitions.** Subject to additional definitions contained in the subsequent Articles of this Act which are applicable to specific Articles or Parts thereof, and unless the context otherwise requires, in this Act:

(1) "Action" in the sense of a judicial proceeding includes recoupment, counterclaim, set-off, suit in equity and any other proceedings in which rights are determined.

(2) "Aggrieved party" means a party entitled to resort to a remedy.

(3) "Agreement" means the bargain of the parties in fact as found in their language or by implication from other circumstances including course of dealing or usage of trade or course of performance as provided in this Act (Sections 1-205 and 2-208). Whether an agreement has legal consequences is determined by the provisions of this Act, if applicable; otherwise by the law of contracts (Section 1-103). (Compare "Contract".)

(4) "Bank" means any person engaged in the business of banking.

(5) "Bearer" means the person in possession of an instrument, document of title, or certificated security payable to bearer or indorsed in blank.

(6) "Bill of lading" means a document evidencing the receipt of goods for shipment issued by a person engaged in the business of transporting or forwarding goods, and includes an airbill. "Airbill" means a document serving for air transportation as a bill of lading does for marine or rail transportation, and includes an air consignment note or air waybill.

(7) "Branch" includes a separately incorporated foreign branch of a bank.

(8) "Burden of establishing" a fact means the burden of persuading the triers of fact that the existence of the fact is more probable than its non-existence.

(9) "Buyer in ordinary course of business" means a person who in good faith and without knowledge that the sale to him is in violation of the ownership rights or security interest of a third party in the goods buys in ordinary course from a person in the business of selling goods of that kind but does not include a pawnbroker. All persons who sell minerals or the like (including oil and gas) at wellhead or minehead shall be deemed to be persons in the business of selling goods of that kind. "Buying" may be for cash or by exchange of other property or on secured or unsecured credit and includes receiving goods or documents of title under a pre-existing contract for sale but does not include a transfer in bulk or as security for or in total or partial satisfaction of a money debt.

(10) "Conspicuous": A term of clause is conspicuous when it is so written that a reasonable person against whom it is to operate ought to have noticed it. A printed heading in capitals (as: NON-NEGOTIABLE BILL OF LADING) is conspicuous. Language in the body of a form is "conspicuous" if it is in larger or other contrasting type or color. But in a telegram any stated term is "conspicuous". Whether a term or clause is "conspicuous" or not is for decision by the court.

(11) "Contract" means the total legal obligation which results from the parties' agreement as affected by this Act and any other applicable rules of law. (Compare "Agreement".)

(12) "Creditor" includes a general creditor, a secured creditor, a lien creditor and any representative of creditors, including an assignee for the benefit of creditors, a trustee in bankruptcy, a receiver in equity and an executor or administrator of an insolvent debtor's or assignor's estate.

(13) "Defendant" includes a person in the position of defendant in a cross-action or counterclaim.

(14) "Delivery" with respect to instruments, documents of title, chattel paper, or certificated securities means voluntary transfer of possession.

(15) "Document of title" includes bill of lading, dock warrant, dock receipt, warehouse receipt or order for the delivery of goods, and also any other document which in the regular course of business or financing is treated as adequately evidencing that the person in possession of it is entitled to receive, hold and dispose of the document and the goods it covers. To be a document of title a document must purport to be issued by or addressed to a bailee and purport to cover goods in the bailee's possession which are either identified or are fungible portions of an identified mass.

(16) "Fault" means wrongful act, omission or breach.

(17) "Fungible" with respect to goods or securities means goods or securities of which any unit is, by nature or usage of trade, the equivalent of any other like unit. Goods which are not fungible shall be deemed fungible for the purposes of this Act to the extent that under a particular agreement or document unlike units are treated as equivalents.

(18) "Genuine" means free of forgery or counterfeiting.

(19) "Good faith" means honesty in fact in the conduct or transaction concerned.

(20) "Holder," with respect to a negotiable instrument, means the person in possession if the instrument is payable to bearer or, in the case of an instrument payable to an identified person, if the identified person is in possession. "Holder" with respect to a document of title means the person in possession if the goods are deliverable to bearer or to the order of the person in possession.

(21) To "honor" is to pay or to accept and pay, or where a credit so engages to purchase or discount a draft complying with the terms of the credit.

(22) "Insolvency proceedings" includes any assignment for the benefit of creditors or other proceedings intended to liquidate or rehabilitate the estate of the person involved.

(23) A person is "insolvent" who either has ceased to pay his debts in the ordinary course of business or cannot pay his debts as they become due or is insolvent within the meaning of the federal bankruptcy law.

(24) "Money" means a medium of exchange authorized or adopted by a domestic or foreign government and includes a monetary unit of account established by an intergovernmental organization or by agreement between two or more nations.

(25) A person has "notice" of a fact when

  (a) he has actual knowledge of it; or
  (b) he has received a notice or notification of it; or
  (c) from all the facts and circumstances known to him at the time in question he has reason to know that it exists.

A person "knows" or has "knowledge" of a fact when he has actual knowledge of it. "Discover" or "learn" or a word or phrase of similar import refers to knowledge rather than to reason to know. The time and circumstances under which a notice or notification may cease to be effective are not determined by this Act.

(26) A person "notifies" or "gives" a notice or notification to another by taking such steps as may be reasonably required to inform the other in ordinary course whether or not such other actually comes to know of it. A person "receives" a notice or notification when

(a) it comes to his attention; or
(b) it is duly delivered at the place of business through which the contract was made or at any other place held out by him as the place for receipt of such communications.

(27) Notice, knowledge or a notice or notification received by an organization is effective for a particular transaction from the time when it is brought to the attention of the individual conducting that transaction, and in any event from the time when it would have been brought to his attention if the organization had exercised due diligence. An organization exercises due diligence if it maintains reasonable routines for communicating significant information to the person conducting the transaction and there is reasonable compliance with the routines. Due diligence does not require an individual acting for the organization to communicate information unless such communication is part of his regular duties or unless he has reason to know of the transaction and that the transaction would be materially affected by the information.

(28) "Organization" includes a corporation, government or governmental subdivision or agency, business trust, estate, trust, partnership or association, two or more persons having a joint or common interest, or any other legal or commercial entity.

(29) "Party", as distinct from "third party", means a person who has engaged in a transaction or made an agreement within this Act.

(30) "Person" includes an individual or an organization (See Section 1-102).

(31) "Presumption" or "presumed" means that the trier of fact must find the existence of the fact presumed unless and until evidence is introduced which would support a finding of its non-existence.

(32) "Purchase" includes taking by sale, discount, negotiation, mortgage, pledge, lien, issue or re-issue, gift or any other voluntary transaction creating an interest in property.

(33) "Purchaser" means a person who takes by purchase.

(34) "Remedy" means any remedial right to which an aggrieved party is entitled with or without resort to a tribunal.

(35) "Representative" includes an agent, an officer of a corporation or association, and a trustee, executor or administrator of an estate, or any other person empowered to act for another.

(36) "Rights" includes remedies.

(37) "Security interest" means an interest in personal property or fixtures which secures payment or performance of an obligation. The retention or reservation of title by a seller of goods notwithstanding shipment or delivery to the buyer (Section 2-401) is limited in effect to a reservation of a "security interest". The term also includes any interest of a buyer of accounts or chattel paper which is subject to Article 9. The special property interest of a buyer of goods on identification of those goods to a contract for sale under Section 2-401 is not a "security interest", but a buyer may also acquire a "security interest" by complying with Article 9. Unless a consignment is intended as security, reservation of title thereunder is not a "security interest", but a consignment in any event is subject to the provisions on consignment sales (Section 2-326).

Whether a transaction creates a lease or security interest is determined by the facts of each case; however, a transaction creates a security interest if the consideration the lessee is to pay the lessor for the right to possession and use of the goods is an obligation for the term of the lease not subject to termination by the lessee, and

(a) the original term of the lease is equal to or greater than the remaining economic life of the goods.
(b) the lessee is bound to renew the lease for the remaining economic life of the goods or is bound to become the owner of the goods,
(c) the lessee has an option to renew the lease for the remaining economic life of the goods for no additional consideration or nominal additional consideration upon compliance with the lease agreement, or
(d) the lessee has an option to become the owner of the goods for no additional consideration or nominal additional consideration upon compliance with the lease agreement.

A transaction does not create a security interest merely because it provides that

(a) the present value of the consideration the lessee is obligated to pay the lessor for the right to possession and use of the goods is substantially equal to or is greater than the fair market value of the goods at the time the lease is entered into,
(b) the lessee assumes risk of loss of the goods, or agrees to pay taxes, insurance, filing, recording, or registration fees, or service or maintenance costs with respect to the goods,
(c) the lessee has an option to renew the lease or to become the owner of the goods,
(d) the lessee has an option to renew the lease for a fixed rent that is equal to or greater than the reasonably predictable fair market rent for the use of the goods for the term of the renewal at the time the option is to be performed, or
(e) the lessee has an option to become the owner of the goods for a fixed price that is equal to or greater than the reasonably predictable fair market value of the goods at the time the option is to be performed.

For purposes of this subsection (37):

(x) Additional consideration is not nominal if (i) when the option to renew the lease is granted to the lessee the rent is stated to be the fair market rent for the use of the goods for the term of the renewal determined at the time the option is to be performed, or (ii) when the option to become the owner of the goods is granted to the lessee the price is stated to be the fair market value of the goods determined at the time the option is to be performed. Additional consideration is nominal if it is less than the lessee's reasonably predictable cost of performing under the lease agreement if the option is not exercised;
(y) "Reasonably predictable" and "remaining economic life of the goods" are to be determined with reference to the facts and circumstances at the time the transaction is entered into; and
(z) "Present value" means the amount as of a date certain of one or more sums payable in the future, discounted to the date certain. The discount is determined by the interest rate specified by the parties if the rate is not manifestly unreasonable at the time the transaction is entered into; otherwise, the discount is determined by a commercially reasonable rate that takes into account the facts and circumstances of each case at the time the transaction was entered into.

(38) "Send" in connection with any writing or notice means to deposit in the mail or deliver for transmission by any other

usual means of communication with postage or cost of transmission provided for and properly addressed and in the case of an instrument to an address specified thereon or otherwise agreed, or if there be none to any address reasonable under the circumstances. The receipt of any writing or notice within the time at which it would have arrived if properly sent has the effect of a proper sending.

(39) "Signed" includes any symbol executed or adopted by a party with present intention to authenticate a writing.

(40) "Surety" includes guarantor.

(41) "Telegram" includes a message transmitted by radio, teletype, cable, any mechanical method of transmission, or the like.

(42) "Term" means that portion of an agreement which relates to a particular matter.

(43) "Unauthorized" signature means one made without actual, implied, or apparent authority and includes a forgery.

(44) "Value". Except as otherwise provided with respect to negotiable instruments and bank collections (Sections 3-303, 4-208 and 4-209) a person gives "value" for rights if he acquires them

> (a) in return for a binding commitment to extend credit or for the extension of immediately available credit whether or not drawn upon and whether or not a charge-back is provided for in the event of difficulties in collection; or
>
> (b) as security for or in total or partial satisfaction of a pre-existing claim; or
>
> (c) by accepting delivery pursuant to a pre-existing contract for purchase; or
>
> (d) generally, in return for any consideration sufficient to support a simple contract.

(45) "Warehouse receipt" means a receipt issued by a person engaged in the business of storing goods for hire.

(46) "Written" or "writing" includes printing, typewriting or any other intentional reduction to tangible form.

As amended in 1962, 1972, 1977, 1987 and 1990.

§ 1-202. Prima Facie Evidence by Third Party Documents. A document in due form purporting to be a bill of lading, policy or certificate of insurance, official weigher's or inspector's certificate, consular invoice, or any other document authorized or required by the contract to be issued by a third party shall be prima facie evidence of its own authenticity and genuineness and of the facts stated in the document by the third party.

§ 1-203. Obligation of Good Faith. Every contract or duty within this Act imposes an obligation of good faith in its performance or enforcement.

§ 1-204. Time; Reasonable Time; "Seasonably".

(1) Whenever this Act requires any action to be taken within a reasonable time, any time which is not manifestly unreasonable may be fixed by agreement.

(2) What is a reasonable time for taking any action depends on the nature, purpose and circumstances of such action.

(3) An action is taken "seasonably" when it is taken at or within the time agreed or if no time is agreed at or within a reasonable time.

§ 1-205. Course of Dealing and Usage of Trade.

(1) A course of dealing is a sequence of previous conduct between the parties to a particular transaction which is fairly to be regarded as establishing a common basis of understanding for interpreting their expressions and other conduct.

(2) A usage of trade is any practice or method of dealing having such regularity of observance in a place, vocation or trade as to justify an expectation that it will be observed with respect to the transaction in question. The existence and scope of such a usage are to be proved as facts. If it is established that such a usage is embodied in a written trade code or similar writing the interpretation of the writing is for the court.

(3) A course of dealing between parties and any usage of trade in the vocation or trade in which they are engaged or of which they are or should be aware give particular meaning to and supplement or qualify terms of an agreement.

(4) The express terms of an agreement and an applicable course of dealing or usage of trade shall be construed wherever reasonable as consistent with each other; but when such construction is unreasonable express terms control both course of dealing and usage of trade and course of dealing controls usage of trade.

(5) An applicable usage of trade in the place where any part of performance is to occur shall be used in interpreting the agreement as to that part of the performance.

(6) Evidence of a relevant usage of trade offered by one party is not admissible unless and until he has given the other party such notice as the court finds sufficient to prevent unfair surprise to the latter.

§ 1-206. Statute of Frauds for Kinds of Personal Property Not Otherwise Covered.

(1) Except in the cases described in subsection (2) of this section a contract for the sale of personal property is not enforceable by way of action or defense beyond five thousand dollars in amount or value of remedy unless there is some writing which indicates that a contract for sale has been made between the parties at a defined or stated price, reasonably identifies the subject matter, and is signed by the party against whom enforcement is sought or by his authorized agent.

(2) Subsection (1) of this section does not apply to contracts for the sale of goods (Section 2-201) nor of securities (Section 8-319) nor to security agreements (Section 9-203).

§ 1-207. Performance or Acceptance Under Reservation of Rights.

(1) A party who, with explicit reservation of rights performs or promises performance or assents to performance in a manner demanded or offered by the other party does not thereby prejudice the rights reserved. Such words as "without prejudice", "under protest" or the like are sufficient.

(2) Subsection (1) does not apply to an accord and satisfaction.

As amended in 1990.

§ 1-208. Option to Accelerate at Will. A term providing that one party or his successor in interest may accelerate payment or performance or require collateral or additional collateral "at will" or "when he deems himself insecure" or in words of similar import shall be construed to mean that he shall have power to do so only if he in good faith believes that the prospect of payment or performance is impaired. The burden of establishing lack of good faith is on the party against whom the power has been exercised.

§ 1-209. Subordinated Obligations. An obligation may be issued as subordinated to payment of another obligation of the person obligated, or a creditor may subordinate his right to payment of an obligation by agreement with either the person obligated or another creditor of the person obligated. Such a subordination does not create a security interest as against either the common debtor or a subordinated creditor. This section shall be construed as declaring the law as it existed prior to the enactment of this section and not as modifying it. Added 1966.

Note: This new section is proposed as an optional provision to make it clear that a subordination agreement does not create a security interest unless so intended.

ARTICLE 2 / Sales

Part 1   Short Title, General Construction and Subject Matter

§ 2-101.   Short Title.   This Article shall be known and may be cited as Uniform Commercial Code-Sales.

§ 2-102.   Scope; Certain Security and Other Transactions Excluded From This Article.   Unless the context otherwise requires, this Article applies to transactions in goods; it does not apply to any transaction which although in the form of an unconditional contract to sell or present sale is intended to operate only as a security transaction nor does this Article impair or repeal any statute regulating sales to consumers, farmers or other specified classes of buyers.

§ 2-103.   Definitions and Index of Definitions.

(1) In this Article unless the context otherwise requires

(a) "Buyer" means a person who buys or contracts to buy goods.
(b) "Good faith" in the case of a merchant means honesty in fact and the observance of reasonable commercial standards of fair dealing in the trade.
(c) "Receipt" of goods means taking physical possession of them.
(d) "Seller" means a person who sells or contracts to sell goods.

(2) Other definitions applying to this Article or to specified Parts thereof, and the sections in which they appear are:

"Acceptance"   Section 2-606.
"Banker's credit"   Section 2-325.
"Between merchants"   Section 2-104.
"Cancellation"   Section 2-106(4).
"Commercial unit"   Section 2-105.
"Confirmed credit"   Section 2-325.
"Conforming to contract"   Section 2-106.
"Contract for sale"   Section 2-106.
"Cover"   Section 2-712.
"Entrusting"   Section 2-403.
"Financing agency"   Section 2-104.
"Future goods"   Section 2-105.
"Goods"   Section 2-105.
"Identification"   Section 2-501.
"Installment contract"   Section 2-612.
"Letter of Credit"   Section 2-325.
"Lot"   Section 2-105.
"Merchant"   Section 2-104.
"Overseas"   Section 2-323.
"Person in position of seller"   Section 2-707.
"Present sale"   Section 2-106.
"Sale"   Section 2-106.
"Sale on approval"   Section 2-326.
"Sale or return"   Section 2-326.
"Termination"   Section 2-106.

(3) The following definitions in other Articles apply to this Article:

"Check"   Section 3-104.
"Consignee"   Section 7-102.
"Consignor"   Section 7-102.
"Consumer goods"   Section 9-109.
"Dishonor"   Section 3-507.
"Draft"   Section 3-104.

(4) In addition Article 1 contains general definitions and principles of construction and interpretation applicable throughout this Article.

§ 2-104.   Definitions: "Merchant"; "Between Merchants"; "Financing Agency".

(1) "Merchant" means a person who deals in goods of the kind or otherwise by his occupation holds himself out as having knowledge or skill peculiar to the practices or goods involved in the transaction or to whom such knowledge or skill may be attributed by his employment of an agent or broker or other intermediary who by his occupation holds himself out as having such knowledge or skill.
(2) "Financing agency" means a bank, finance company or other person who in the ordinary course of business makes advances against goods or documents of title or who by arrangement with either the seller or the buyer intervenes in ordinary course to make or collect payment due or claimed under the contract for sale, as by purchasing or paying the seller's draft or making advances against it or by merely taking it for collection whether or not documents of title accompany the draft. "Financing agency" includes also a bank or other person who similarly intervenes between persons who are in the position of seller and buyer in respect to the goods (Section 2-707).
(3) "Between merchants" means in any transaction with respect to which both parties are chargeable with the knowledge or skill of merchants.

§ 2-105.   Definitions: Transferability; "Goods"; "Future" Goods; "Lot"; "Commercial Unit".

(1) "Goods" means all things (including specially manufactured goods) which are movable at the time of identification to the contract for sale other than the money in which the price is to be paid, investment securities (Article 8) and things in action. "Goods" also includes the unborn young of animals and growing crops and other identified things attached to realty as described in the section on goods to be severed from realty (Section 2-107).
(2) Goods must be both existing and identified before any interest in them can pass. Goods which are not both existing and identified are "future" goods. A purported present sale of future goods or of any interest therein operates as a contract to sell.
(3) There may be a sale of a part interest in existing identified goods.
(4) An undivided share in an identified bulk of fungible goods is sufficiently identified to be sold although the quantity of the bulk is not determined. Any agreed proportion of such a bulk or any quantity thereof agreed upon by number, weight or other measure may to the extent of the seller's interest in the bulk be sold to the buyer who then becomes an owner in common.
(5) "Lot" means a parcel or a single article which is the subject matter of a separate sale or delivery, whether or not it is sufficient to perform the contract.
(6) "Commercial unit" means such a unit of goods as by commercial usage is a single whole for purposes of sale and divi-

sion of which materially impairs its character or value on the market or in use. A commercial unit may be a single article (as a machine) or a set of articles (as a suite of furniture or an assortment of sizes) or a quantity (as a bale, gross, or carload) or any other unit treated in use or in the relevant market as a single whole.

§ 2-106. **Definitions: "Contract"; "Agreement"; "Contract for Sale"; "Sale"; "Present Sale"; "Conforming" to Contract; "Termination"; "Cancellation".**

(1) In this Article unless the context otherwise requires "contract" and "agreement" are limited to those relating to the present or future sale of goods. "Contract for sale" includes both a present sale of goods and a contract to sell goods at a future time. A "sale" consists in the passing of title from the seller to the buyer for a price (Section 2-401). A "present sale" means a sale which is accomplished by the making of the contract.

(2) Goods or conduct including any part of a performance are "conforming" or conform to the contract when they are in accordance with the obligations under the contract.

(3) "Termination" occurs when either party pursuant to a power created by agreement or law puts an end to the contract otherwise than for its breach. On "termination" all obligations which are still executory on both sides are discharged but any right based on prior breach or performance survives.

(4) "Cancellation" occurs when either party puts an end to the contract for breach by the other and its effect is the same as that of "termination" except that the cancelling party also retains any remedy for breach of the whole contract or any unperformed balance.

§ 2-107. **Goods to Be Severed From Realty: Recording.**

(1) A contract for the sale of minerals or the like (including oil and gas) or a structure or its materials to be removed from realty is a contract for the sale of goods within this Article if they are to be severed by the seller but until severance a purported present sale thereof which is not effective as a transfer of an interest in land is effective only as a contract to sell.

(2) A contract for the sale apart from the land of growing crops or other things attached to realty and capable of severance without material harm thereto but not described in subsection (1) or of timber to be cut is a contract for the sale of goods within this Article whether the subject matter is to be severed by the buyer or by the seller even though it forms part of the realty at the time of contracting, and the parties can by identification effect a present sale before severance.

(3) The provisions of this section are subject to any third party rights provided by the law relating to realty records, and the contract for sale may be executed and recorded as a document transferring an interest in land and shall then constitute notice to third parties of the buyer's rights under the contract for sale.

As amended in 1972.

Part 2   Form, Formation and Readjustment of Contract

§ 2-201. **Formal Requirements; Statute of Frauds.**

(1) Except as otherwise provided in this section a contract for the sale of goods for the price of $500 or more is not enforceable by way of action or defense unless there is some writing sufficient to indicate that a contract for sale has been between the parties and signed by the party against whom enforcement is sought or by his authorized agent or broker. A writing is not insufficient because it omits or incorrectly states

a term agreed upon but the contract is not enforceable under this paragraph beyond the quantity of goods shown in such writing.

(2) Between merchants if within a reasonable time a writing in confirmation of the contract and sufficient against the sender is received and the party receiving it has reason to know its contents, it satisfies the requirements of subsection (1) against such party unless written notice of objection to its contents is given within 10 days after it is received.

(3) A contract which does not satisfy the requirements of subsection (1) but which is valid in other respects is enforceable

(a) if the goods are to be specially manufactured for the buyer and are not suitable for sale to others in the ordinary course of the seller's business and the seller, before notice of repudiation is received and under circumstances which reasonably indicate that the goods are for the buyer, has made either a substantial beginning of their manufacture or commitments for their procurement; or

(b) if the party against whom enforcement is sought admits in his pleading, testimony or otherwise in court that a contract for sale was made, but the contract is not enforceable under this provision beyond the quantity of goods admitted; or

(c) with respect to goods for which payment has been made and accepted or which have been received and accepted (Sec. 2-606).

§ 2-202. **Final Written Expression: Parol or Extrinsic Evidence.** Terms with respect to which the confirmatory memoranda of the parties agree or which are otherwise set forth in a writing intended by the parties as a final expression of their agreement with respect to such terms as are included therein may not be contradicted by evidence of any prior agreement or of a contemporaneous oral agreement but may be explained or supplemented

(a) by course of dealing or usage of trade (Section 1-205) or by course of performance (Section 2-208); and

(b) by evidence of consistent additional terms unless the court finds the writing to have been intended also as a complete and exclusive statement of the terms of the agreement.

§ 2-203. **Seals Inoperative.** The affixing of a seal to a writing evidencing a contract for sale or an offer to buy or sell goods does not constitute the writing a sealed instrument and the law with respect to sealed instruments does not apply to such a contract or offer.

§ 2-204. **Formation in General.**

(1) A contract for sale of goods may be made in any manner sufficient to show agreement, including conduct by both parties which recognizes the existence of such a contract.

(2) An agreement sufficient to constitute a contract for sale may be found even though the moment of its making is undetermined.

(3) Even though one or more terms are left open a contract for sale does not fail for indefiniteness if the parties have intended to make a contract and there is a reasonably certain basis for giving an appropriate remedy.

§ 2-205. **Firm Offers.** An offer by a merchant to buy or sell goods in a signed writing which by its terms gives assurance that it will be held open is not revocable, for lack of consideration, during the time stated or if no time is stated for a reasonable time, but in no event may such period of irrevocability exceed three months; but any such term of assurance on a form supplied by the offeree must be separately signed by the offeror.

§ 2-206. Offer and Acceptance in Formation of Contract.

(1) Unless otherwise unambiguously indicated by the language or circumstances

(a) an offer to make a contract shall be construed as inviting acceptance in any manner and by any medium reasonable in the circumstances;

(b) an order or other offer to buy goods for prompt or current shipment shall be construed as inviting acceptance either by a prompt promise to ship or by the prompt or current shipment of conforming or non-conforming goods, but such a shipment of non-conforming goods does not constitute an acceptance if the seller seasonably notifies the buyer that the shipment is offered only as an accommodation to the buyer.

(2) Where the beginning of a requested performance is a reasonable mode of acceptance an offeror who is not notified of acceptance within a reasonable time may treat the offer as having lapsed before acceptance.

§ 2-207. Additional Terms in Acceptance or Confirmation.

(1) A definite and seasonable expression of acceptance or a written confirmation which is sent within a reasonable time operates as an acceptance even though it states terms additional to or different from those offered or agreed upon, unless acceptance is expressly made conditional on assent to the additional or different terms.

(2) The additional terms are to be construed as proposals for addition to the contract. Between merchants such terms become part of the contract unless:

(a) the offer expressly limits acceptance to the terms of the offer;

(b) they materially alter it; or

(c) notification of objection to them has already been given or is given within a reasonable time after notice of them is received.

(3) Conduct by both parties which recognizes the existence of a contract is sufficient to establish a contract for sale although the writings of the parties do not otherwise establish a contract. In such case the terms of the particular contract consist of those terms on which the writings of the parties agree, together with any supplementary terms incorporated under any other provisions of this Act.

§ 2-208. Course of Performance or Practical Construction.

(1) Where the contract for sale involves repeated occasions for performance by either party with knowledge of the nature of the performance and opportunity for objection to it by the other, any course of performance accepted or acquiesced in without objection shall be relevant to determine the meaning of the agreement.

(2) The express terms of the agreement and any such course of performance, as well as any course of dealing and usage of trade, shall be construed whenever reasonable as consistent with each other; but when such construction is unreasonable, express terms shall control course of performance and course of performance shall control both course of dealing and usage of trade (Section 1-205).

(3) Subject to the provisions of the next section on modification and waiver, such course of performance shall be relevant to show a waiver or modification of any term inconsistent with such course of performance.

§ 2-209. Modification, Rescission and Waiver.

(1) An agreement modifying a contract within this Article needs no consideration to be binding.

(2) A signed agreement which excludes modification or rescission except by a signed writing cannot be otherwise modified or rescinded, but except as between merchants such a requirement on a form supplied by the merchant must be separately signed by the other party.

(3) The requirements of the statute of frauds section of this Article (Section 2-201) must be satisfied if the contract as modified is within its provisions.

(4) Although an attempt at modification or rescission does not satisfy the requirements of subsection (2) or (3) it can operate as a waiver.

(5) A party who has made a waiver affecting an executory portion of the contract may retract the waiver by reasonable notification received by the other party that strict performance will be required of any term waived, unless the retraction would be unjust in view of a material change of position in reliance on the waiver.

§ 2-210. Delegation of Performance; Assignment of Rights.

(1) A party may perform his duty through a delegate unless otherwise agreed or unless the other party has a substantial interest in having his original promisor perform or control the acts required by the contract. No delegation of performance relieves the party delegating of any duty to perform or any liability for breach.

(2) Unless otherwise agreed all rights of either seller or buyer can be assigned except where the assignment would materially change the duty of the other party, or increase materially the burden or risk imposed on him by his contract, or impair materially his chance of obtaining return performance. A right to damages for breach of the whole contract or a right arising out of the assignor's due performance of his entire obligation can be assigned despite agreement otherwise.

(3) Unless the circumstances indicate the contrary a prohibition of assignment of "the contract" is to be construed as barring only the delegation to the assignee of the assignor's performance.

(4) An assignment of "the contract" or of "all my rights under the contract" or an assignment in similar general terms is an assignment of rights and unless the language or the circumstances (as in an assignment for security) indicate the contrary, it is a delegation of performance of the duties of the assignor and its acceptance by the assignee constitutes a promise by him to perform those duties. This promise is enforceable by either the assignor or the other party to the original contract.

(5) The other party may treat any assignment which delegates performance as creating reasonable grounds for insecurity and may without prejudice to his rights against the assignor demand assurances from the assignee (Section 2-609).

Part 3 General Obligation and Construction of Contract

§ 2-301. General Obligations of Parties. The obligation of the seller is to transfer and deliver and that of the buyer is to accept and pay in accordance with the contract.

§ 2-302. Unconscionable Contract or Clause.

(1) If the court as a matter of law finds the contract or any clause of the contract to have been unconscionable at the time it was made the court may refuse to enforce the contract, or it

may enforce the remainder of the contract without the unconscionable clause, or it may so limit the application of any unconscionable clause as to avoid any unconscionable result.

(2) When it is claimed or appears to the court that the contract or any clause thereof may be unconscionable the parties shall be afforded a reasonable opportunity to present evidence as to its commercial setting, purpose and effect to aid the court in making the determination.

§ 2-303. Allocation or Division of Risks.

Where this Article allocates a risk or a burden as between the parties "unless otherwise agreed", the agreement may not only shift the allocation but may also divide the risk or burden.

§ 2-304. Price Payable in Money, Goods, Realty, or Otherwise.

(1) The price can be made payable in money or otherwise. If it is payable in whole or in part in goods each party is a seller of the goods which he is to transfer.

(2) Even though all or part of the price is payable in an interest in realty the transfer of the goods and the seller's obligations with reference to them are subject to this Article, but not the transfer of the interest in realty or the transferor's obligations in connection therewith.

§ 2-305. Open Price Term.

(1) The parties if they so intend can conclude a contract for sale even though the price is not settled. In such a case the price is a reasonable price at the time for delivery if

(a) nothing is said as to price; or
(b) the price is left to be agreed by the parties and they fail to agree; or
(c) the price is to be fixed in terms of some agreed market or other standard as set or recorded by a third person or agency and it is not so set or recorded.

(2) A price to be fixed by the seller or by the buyer means a price for him to fix in good faith.

(3) When a price left to be fixed otherwise than by agreement of the parties fails to be fixed through fault of one party the other may at his option treat the contract as cancelled or himself fix a reasonable price.

(4) Where, however, the parties intend not to be bound unless the price be fixed or agreed and it is not fixed or agreed there is no contract. In such a case the buyer must return any goods already received or if unable so to do must pay their reasonable value at the time of delivery and the seller must return any portion of the price paid on account.

§ 2-306. Output, Requirements and Exclusive Dealings.

(1) A term which measures the quantity by the output of the seller or the requirements of the buyer means such actual output or requirements as may occur in good faith, except that no quantity unreasonably disproportionate to any stated estimate or in the absence of a stated estimate to any normal or otherwise comparable prior output or requirements may be tendered or demanded.

(2) A lawful agreement by either the seller or the buyer for exclusive dealing in the kind of goods concerned imposes unless otherwise agreed an obligation by the seller to use best efforts to supply the goods and by the buyer to use best efforts to promote their sale.

§ 2-307. Delivery in Single Lot or Several Lots.

Unless otherwise agreed all goods called for by a contract for sale must be tendered in a single delivery and payment is due only on such tender but where the circumstances give either party the right to make or demand delivery in lots the price if it can be apportioned may be demanded for each lot.

§ 2-308. Absence of Specified Place for Delivery.

Unless otherwise agreed

(a) the place for delivery of goods is the seller's place of business or if he has none his residence; but
(b) in a contract for sale of identified goods which to the knowledge of the parties at the time of contracting are in some other place, that place is place for their delivery; and
(c) documents of the title may be delivered through customary banking channels.

§ 2-309. Absence of Specific Time Provisions; Notice of Termination.

(1) The time for shipment or delivery or any other action under a contract if not provided in this Article or agreed upon shall be a reasonable time.

(2) Where the contract provides for successive performances but is indefinite in duration it is valid for a reasonable time but unless otherwise agreed may be terminated at any time by either party.

(3) Termination of a contract by one party except on the happening of an agreed event requires that reasonable notification be received by the other party and an agreement dispensing with notification is invalid if its operation would be unconscionable.

§ 2-310. Open Time for Payment or Running of Credit; Authority to Ship Under Reservation.

Unless otherwise agreed

(a) payment is due at the time and place at which the buyer is to receive the goods even though the place of shipment is the place of delivery; and
(b) if the seller is authorized to send the goods he may ship them under reservation, and may tender the documents of title, but the buyer may inspect the goods after their arrival before payment is due unless such inspection is inconsistent with the terms of the contract (Section 2-513); and
(c) if delivery is authorized and made by way of documents of title otherwise than by subsection (b) then payment is due at the time and place at which the buyer is to receive the documents regardless of where the goods are to be received; and
(d) where the seller is required or authorized to ship the goods on credit the credit period runs from the time of shipment but post-dating the invoice or delaying its dispatch will correspondingly delay the starting of the credit period.

§ 2-311. Options and Cooperation Respecting Performance.

(1) An agreement for sale which is otherwise sufficiently definite (subsection (3) of Section 2-204) to be a contract is not made invalid by the fact that it leaves particulars of performance to be specified by one of the parties. Any such specification must be made in good faith and within limits set by commercial reasonableness.

(2) Unless otherwise agreed specifications relating to assortment of the goods are at the buyer's option and except as otherwise provided in subsections (1)(c) and (3) of Section 2-319 specifications or arrangements relating to shipment are at the seller's option.

(3) Where such specification would materially affect the other party's performance but is not seasonably made or where one

party's cooperation is necessary to the agreed performance of the other but is not seasonably forthcoming, the other party in addition to all other remedies

(a) is excused for any resulting delay in his own performance; and

(b) may also either proceed to perform in any reasonable manner or after the time for a material part of his own performance treat the failure to specify or to cooperate as a breach by failure to deliver or accept the goods.

§ 2-312. Warranty of Title and Against Infringement; Buyer's Obligation Against Infringement.

(1) Subject to subsection (2) there is in a contract for sale a warranty by the seller that

(a) the title conveyed shall be good, and its transfer rightful; and

(b) the goods shall be delivered free from any security interest or other lien or encumbrance of which the buyer at the time of contracting has no knowledge.

(2) A warranty under subsection (1) will be excluded or modified only by specific language or by circumstances which give the buyer reason to know that the person selling does not claim title in himself or that he is purporting to sell only such right or title as he or a third person may have.

(3) Unless otherwise agreed a seller who is a merchant regularly dealing in goods of the kind warrants that the goods shall be delivered free of the rightful claim of any third person by way of infringement or the like but a buyer who furnishes specifications to the seller must hold the seller harmless against any such claim which arises out of compliance with the specifications.

§ 2-313. Express Warranties by Affirmation, Promise, Description, Sample.

(1) Express warranties by the seller are created as follows:

(a) Any affirmation of fact or promise made by the seller to the buyer which relates to the goods and becomes part of the basis of the bargain creates an express warranty that the goods shall conform to the affirmation or promise.

(b) Any description of the goods which is made part of the basis of the bargain creates an express warranty that the goods shall conform to the description.

(c) Any sample or model which is made part of the basis of the bargain creates an express warranty that the whole of the goods shall conform to the sample or model.

(2) It is not necessary to the creation of an express warranty that the seller use formal words such as "warrant" or "guarantee" or that he have a specific intention to make a warranty, but an affirmation merely of the value of the goods or a statement purporting to be merely the seller's opinion or commendation of the goods does not create a warranty.

§ 2-314. Implied Warranty: Merchantability; Usage of Trade.

(1) Unless excluded or modified (Section 2-316), a warranty that the goods shall be merchantable is implied in a contract for their sale if the seller is a merchant with respect to goods of that kind. Under this section the serving for value of food or drink to be consumed either on the premises or elsewhere is a sale.

(2) Goods to be merchantable must be at least such as

(a) pass without objection in the trade under the contract description; and

(b) in the case of fungible goods, are of fair average quality within the description; and

(c) are fit for the ordinary purposes for which such goods are used; and

(d) run, within the variations permitted by the agreement, of even kind, quality and quantity within each unit and among all units involved; and

(e) are adequately contained, packaged, and labeled as the agreement may require; and

(f) conform to the promise or affirmations of fact made on the container or label if any.

(3) Unless excluded or modified (Section 2-316) other implied warranties may arise from course of dealing or usage of trade.

§ 2-315. Implied Warranty: Fitness for Particular Purpose.
Where the seller at the time of contracting has reason to know any particular purpose for which the goods are required and that the buyer is relying on the seller's skill or judgment to select or furnish suitable goods, there is unless excluded or modified under the next section an implied warranty that the goods shall be fit for such purpose.

§ 2-316. Exclusion or Modification of Warranties.

(1) Words or conduct relevant to the creation of an express warranty and words or conduct tending to negate or limit warranty shall be construed wherever reasonable as consistent with each other; but subject to the provisions of this Article on parol or extrinsic evidence (Section 2-202) negation or limitation is inoperative to the extent that such construction is unreasonable.

(2) Subject to subsection (3), to exclude or modify the implied warranty of merchantability or any part of it the language must mention merchantability and in case of a writing must be conspicuous, and to exclude or modify any implied warranty of fitness the exclusion must be by a writing and conspicuous. Language to exclude all implied warranties of fitness is sufficient if it states, for example, that "There are no warranties which extend beyond the description on the face hereof."

(3) Not withstanding subsection (2)

(a) unless the circumstances indicate otherwise, all implied warranties are excluded by expressions like "as is", "with all faults" or other language which in common understanding calls the buyer's attention to the exclusion of warranties and makes plain that there is no implied warranty; and

(b) when the buyer before entering into the contract has examined the goods or the sample or model as fully as he desired or has refused to examine the goods there is no implied warranty with regard to defects which an examination ought in the circumstances to have revealed to him; and

(c) an implied warranty can also be excluded or modified by course of dealing or course of performance or usage of trade.

(4) Remedies for breach of warranty can be limited in accordance with the provisions of this Article on liquidation or limitation of damages and on contractual modification of remedy (Sections 2-718 and 2-719).

§ 2-317. Cumulation and Conflict of Warranties Express or Implied.
Warranties whether express or implied shall be construed as consistent with each other and as cumulative, but if such construction is unreasonable the intention of the par-

ties shall determine which warranty is dominant. In ascertaining that intention the following rules apply:

(a) Exact or technical specifications displace an inconsistent sample or model or general language of description.

(b) A sample from an existing bulk displaces inconsistent general language of description.

(c) Express warranties displace inconsistent implied warranties other than an implied warranty of fitness for a particular purpose.

§ 2-318. Third Party Beneficiaries of Warranties Express or Implied.

Note: If this Act is introduced in the Congress of the United States this section should be omitted. (States to select one alternative.)

Alternative A   A seller's warranty whether express or implied extends to any natural person who is in the family or household of his buyer or who is a guest in his home if it is reasonable to expect that such person may use, consume or be affected by the goods and who is injured in person by breach of the warranty. A seller may not exclude or limit the operation of this section.

Alternative B   A seller's warranty whether express or implied extends to any natural person who may reasonably be expected to use, consume or be affected by the goods and who is injured in person by breach of the warranty. A seller may not exclude or limit the operation of this section.

Alternative C   A seller's warranty whether express or implied extends to any person who may reasonably be expected to use, consume or be affected by the goods and who is injured by breach of the warranty. A seller may not exclude or limit the operation of this section with respect to injury to the person of an individual to whom the warranty extends.

As amended in 1966.

§ 2-319. F.O.B. and F.A.S. Terms.

(1) Unless otherwise agreed the term F.O.B. (which means "free on board") at a named place, even though used only in connection with the stated price, is a delivery term under which

(a) when the term is F.O.B. the place of shipment, the seller must at that place ship the goods in the manner provided in this Article (Section 2-504) and bear the expense and risk of putting them into the possession of the carrier; or

(b) when the term is F.O.B. the place of destination, the seller must at his own expense and risk transport the goods to that place and there tender delivery of them in the manner provided in this Article (Section 2-503);

(c) when under either (a) or (b) the term is also F.O.B. vessel, car or other vehicle, the seller must in addition at his own expense and risk load the goods on board. If the term is F.O.B. vessel the buyer must name the vessel and in an appropriate case the seller must comply with the provisions of this Article on the form of bill of lading (Section 2-323).

(2) Unless otherwise agreed the term F.A.S. vessel (which means "free alongside") at a named port, even though used only in connection with the stated price, is a delivery term under which the seller must

(a) at his own expense and risk deliver the goods alongside the vessel in the manner usual in that port or on a dock designated and provided by the buyer; and

(b) obtain and tender a receipt for the goods in exchange for which the carrier is under a duty to issue a bill of lading.

(3) Unless otherwise agreed in any case falling within subsection (1)(a) or (c) or subsection (2) the buyer must seasonably give any needed instructions for making delivery, including when the term is F.A.S. or F.O.B. the loading berth of the vessel and in an appropriate case its name and sailing date. The seller may treat the failure of needed instructions as a failure of cooperation under this Article (Section 2-311). He may also at his option move the goods in any reasonable manner preparatory to delivery or shipment.

(4) Under the term F.O.B. vessel or F.A.S. unless otherwise agreed the buyer must make payment against tender of the required documents and the seller may not tender nor the buyer demand delivery of the goods in substitution for the documents.

§ 2-320. C.I.F. and C. & F. Terms.

(1) The term C.I.F. means that the price includes in a lump sum the cost of the goods and the insurance and freight to the named destination. The term C. & F. or C.F. means that the price so includes cost and freight to the named destination.

(2) Unless otherwise agreed and even though used only in connection with the stated price and destination, the term C.I.F. destination or its equivalent requires the seller at his own expense and risk to

(a) put the goods into the possession of a carrier at the port for shipment and obtain a negotiable bill or bills of lading covering the entire transportation to the named destination; and

(b) load the goods and obtain a receipt from the carrier (which may be contained in the bill of lading) showing that the freight has been paid or provided for; and

(c) obtain a policy or certificate of insurance, including any war risk insurance, of a kind and on terms then current at the port of shipment in the usual amount, in the currency of the contract, shown to cover the same goods covered by the bill of lading and providing for payment of loss to the order of the buyer or for the account of whom it may concern; but the seller may add to the price the amount of the premium for any such war risk insurance; and

(d) prepare an invoice of the goods and procure any other documents required to effect shipment or to comply with the contract; and

(e) forward and tender with commercial promptness all the documents in due form and with any indorsement necessary to perfect the buyer's rights.

(3) Unless otherwise agreed the term C. & F. or its equivalent has the same effect and imposes upon the seller the same obligations and risks as a C.I.F. term except the obligation as to insurance.

(4) Under the term C.I.F. or C. & F. unless otherwise agreed the buyer must make payment against tender of the required documents and the seller may not tender nor the buyer demand delivery of the goods in substitution for the documents.

§ 2-321. C.I.F. or C. & F.: "Net Landed Weights"; "Payment on Arrival"; Warranty of Condition on Arrival.
Under a contract containing a term C.I.F. or C. & F.

(1) Where the price is based on or is to be adjusted according to "net landed weights", "delivered weights", "out turn" quantity or quality or the like, unless otherwise agreed the seller must reasonably estimate the price. The payment due on ten-

der of the documents called for by the contract is the amount so estimated, but after final adjustment of the price a settlement must be made with commercial promptness.

(2) An agreement described in subsection (1) or any warranty of quality or condition of the goods on arrival places upon the seller the risk of ordinary deterioration, shrinkage and the like in transportation but has no effect on the place or time of identification to the contract for sale or delivery or on the passing of the risk of loss.

(3) Unless otherwise agreed where the contract provides for payment on or after arrival of the goods the seller must before payment allow such preliminary inspection as is feasible; but if the goods are lost delivery of the documents and payment are due when the goods should have arrived.

§ 2-322. **Delivery "Ex-Ship".**

(1) Unless otherwise agreed a term for delivery of goods "ex-ship" (which means from the carrying vessel) or in equivalent language is not restricted to a particular ship and requires delivery from a ship which has reached a place at the named port of destination where goods of the kind are usually discharged.

(2) Under such a term unless otherwise agreed

(a) the seller must discharge all liens arising out of the carriage and furnish the buyer with a direction which puts the carrier under a duty to deliver the goods; and

(b) the risk of loss does not pass to the buyer until the goods leave the ship's tackle or are otherwise properly unloaded.

§ 2-323. **Form of Bill of Lading Required in Overseas Shipment; "Overseas".**

(1) Where the contract contemplates overseas shipment and contains a term C.I.F. or C.& F. or F.O.B. vessel, the seller unless otherwise agreed must obtain a negotiable bill of lading stating that the goods have been loaded in board or, in the case of a term C.I.F. or C. & F., received for shipment.

(2) Where in a case within subsection (1) a bill of lading has been issued in a set of parts, unless otherwise agreed if the documents are not to be sent from abroad the buyer may demand tender of the full set; otherwise only one part of the bill of lading need be tendered. Even if the agreement expressly requires a full set

(a) due tender of a single part is acceptable within the provisions of this Article on cure of improper delivery (subsection (1) of Section 2-508); and

(b) even though the full set is demanded, if the documents are sent from abroad the person tendering an incomplete set may nevertheless require payment upon furnishing an indemnity which the buyer in good faith deems adequate.

(3) A shipment by water or by air or a contract contemplating such shipment is "overseas" insofar as by usage of trade or agreement it is subject to the commercial, financing or shipping practices characteristic of international deep water commerce.

§ 2-324. **"No Arrival, No Sale" Term.** Under a term "no arrival, no sale" or terms of like meaning, unless otherwise agreed,

(a) the seller must properly ship conforming goods and if they arrive by any means he must tender them on arrival but he assumes no obligation that the goods will arrive unless he has caused the non-arrival; and

(b) where without fault of the seller the goods are in part lost or have so deteriorated as no longer to conform to the contract

or arrive after the contract time, the buyer may proceed as if there had been casualty to identified goods (Section 2-613).

§ 2-325. **"Letter of Credit" Term; "Confirmed Credit".**

(1) Failure of the buyer seasonably to furnish an agreed letter of credit is a breach of the contract for sale.

(2) The delivery to seller of a proper letter of credit suspends the buyer's obligation to pay. If the letter of credit is dishonored, the seller may on seasonable notification to the buyer require payment directly from him.

(3) Unless otherwise agreed the term "letter of credit" or "banker's credit" in a contract for sale means an irrevocable credit issued by a financing agency of good repute and, where the shipment is overseas, of good international repute. The term "confirmed credit" means that the credit must also carry the direct obligation of such an agency which does business in the seller's financial market.

§ 2-326. **Sale on Approval and Sale or Return; Consignment Sales and Rights of Creditors.**

(1) Unless otherwise agreed, if delivered goods may be returned by the buyer even though they conform to the contract, the transaction is

(a) a "sale on approval" if the goods are delivered primarily for use, and

(b) a "sale or return" if the goods are delivered primarily for resale.

(2) Except as provided in subsection (3), goods held on approval are not subject to the claims of the buyer's creditors until acceptance; goods held on sale or return are subject to such claims while in the buyer's possession.

(3) Where goods are delivered to a person for sale and such person maintains a place of business at which he deals in goods of the kind involved, under a name other than the name of the person making delivery, then with respect to claims of creditors of the person conducting the business the goods are deemed to be on sale or return. The provisions of this subsection are applicable even though an agreement purports to reserve title to the person making delivery until payment or resale or uses such words as "on consignment" or "on memorandum". However, this subsection is not applicable if the person making delivery

(a) complies with an applicable law providing for a consignor's interest or the like to be evidenced by a sign, or

(b) establishes that the person conducting the business is generally known by his creditors to be substantially engaged in selling the goods of others, or

(c) complies with the filing provisions of the Article on Secured Transactions (Article 9).

(4) Any "or return" term of a contract for sale is to be treated as a separate contract for sale within the statute of frauds section of this Article (Section 2-201) and as contradicting the sale aspect of the contract within the provisions of this Article on parol or extrinsic evidence (Section 2-202).

§ 2-327. **Special Incidents of Sale on Approval and Sale or Return.**

(1) Under a sale on approval unless otherwise agreed

(a) although the goods are identified to the contract the risk of loss and the title do not pass to the buyer until acceptance; and

(b) use of the goods consistent with the purpose of trial is not acceptance but failure seasonably to notify the seller of election to return the goods is acceptance, and if the goods conform to the contract acceptance of any part is acceptance of the whole; and

(c) after due notification of election to return, the return is at the seller's risk and expense but a merchant buyer must follow any reasonable instructions.

(2) Under a sale or return unless otherwise agreed

(a) the option to return extends to the whole or any commercial unit of the goods while in substantially their original condition, but must be exercised seasonably; and

(b) the return is at the buyer's risk and expense.

§ 2-328. Sale by Auction.

(1) In a sale by auction if goods are put up in lots each lot is the subject of a separate sale.

(2) A sale by auction is complete when the auctioneer so announces by the fall of the hammer or in other customary manner. Where a bid is made while the hammer is falling in acceptance of a prior bid the auctioneer may in his discretion reopen the bidding or declare the goods sold under the bid on which the hammer was falling.

(3) Such a sale is with reserve unless the goods are in explicit terms put up without reserve. In an auction with reserve the auctioneer may withdraw the goods at any time until he announces completion of the sale. In an auction without reserve, after the auctioneer calls for bids on an article or lot, that article or lot cannot be withdrawn unless no bid is made within a reasonable time. In either case a bidder may retract his bid until the auctioneer's announcement of completion of the sale, but a bidder's retraction does not revive any previous bid.

(4) If the auctioneer knowingly receives a bid on the seller's behalf or the seller makes or procures such a bid, and notice has not been given that liberty for such bidding is reserved, the buyer may at his option avoid the sale or take the goods at the price of the last good faith bid prior to the completion of the sale. This subsection shall not apply to any bid at a forced sale.

Part 4   Title, Creditors and Good Faith Purchasers

§ 2-401.   Passing of Title; Reservation for Security; Limited Application of This Section.
Each provision of this Article with regard to the rights, obligations and remedies of the seller, the buyer, purchasers or other third parties applies irrespective of title to the goods except where the provision refers to such title. Insofar as situations are not covered by the other provisions of this Article and matters concerning title become material the following rules apply:

(1) Title to goods cannot pass under a contract for sale prior to their identification to the contract (Section 2-501), and unless otherwise explicitly agreed the buyer acquires by their identification a special property as limited by this Act. Any retention or reservation by the seller of the title (property) in goods shipped or delivered to the buyer is limited in effect to a reservation of a security interest. Subject to these provisions and to the provisions of the Article on Secured Transactions (Article 9), title to goods passes from the seller to the buyer in any manner and on any conditions explicitly agreed on by the parties.

(2) Unless otherwise explicitly agreed title passes to the buyer at the time and place at which the seller completes his performance with reference to the physical delivery of the goods, despite any reservation of a security interest and even though a document of title is to be delivered at a different time or place; and in particular and despite any reservation of a security interest by the bill of lading

(a) if the contract requires or authorizes the seller to send the goods to the buyer but does not require him to deliver them at destination, title passes to the buyer at the time and place of shipment; but

(b) if the contract requires delivery at destination, title passes on tender there.

(3) Unless otherwise explicitly agreed where delivery is to be made without moving the goods,

(a) if the seller is to deliver a document of title, title passes at the time when and the place where he delivers such documents; or

(b) if the goods are at the time of contracting already identified and no documents are to be delivered, title passes at the time and place of contracting.

(4) A rejection or other refusal by the buyer to receive or retain the goods, whether or not justified, or a justified revocation of acceptance revests title to the goods in the seller. Such revesting occurs by operation of law and is not a "sale".

§ 2-402.   Rights of Seller's Creditors Against Sold Goods.

(1) Except as provided in subsections (2) and (3), rights of unsecured creditors of the seller with respect to goods which have been identified to a contract for sale are subject to the buyer's rights to recover the goods under this Article (Sections 2-502 and 2-716).

(2) A creditor of the seller may treat a sale or an identification of goods to a contract for sale as void if as against him a retention of possession by the seller is fraudulent under any rule of law of the state where the goods are situated, except that retention of possession in good faith and current course of trade by a merchant-seller for a commercially reasonable time after a sale or identification is not fraudulent.

(3) Nothing in this Article shall be deemed to impair the rights of creditors of the seller

(a) under the provisions of the Article on Secured Transactions (Article 9); or

(b) where identification to the contract or delivery is made not in current course of trade but in satisfaction of or as security for a pre-existing claim for money, security or the like and is made under circumstances which under any rule of law of the state where the goods are situated would apart from this Article constitute the transaction a fraudulent transfer or voidable preference.

§ 2-403.   Power to Transfer; Good Faith Purchase of Goods; "Entrusting".

(1) A purchaser of goods acquires all title which his transferor had or had power to transfer except that a purchaser of a limited interest acquires rights only to the extent of the interest purchased. A person with voidable title has power to transfer a good title to a good faith purchaser for value. When goods have been delivered under a transaction of purchase the purchaser has such power even though

(a) the transferor was deceived as to the identity of the purchaser, or

(b) the delivery was in exchange for a check which is later dishonored, or

(c) it was agreed that the transaction was to be a "cash sale", or

(d) the delivery was procured through fraud punishable as larcenous under the criminal law.

(2) Any entrusting of possession of goods to a merchant who deals in goods of that kind gives him power to transfer all rights of the entruster to a buyer in ordinary course of business.

(3) "Entrusting" includes any delivery and any acquiescence in retention of possession regardless of any condition expressed between the parties to the delivery or acquiescence and regardless of whether the procurement of the entrusting or the possessor's disposition of the goods have been such as to be larcenous under the criminal law.

Note: If a state adopts the repealer of Article 6-Bulk Transfers (Alternative A), subsection (4) should read as follows:

(4) The rights of other purchasers of goods and of lien creditors are governed by the Articles on Secured Transactions (Article 9) and Documents of Title (Article 7).

Note: If a state adopts Revised Article 6-Bulk Sales (Alternative B), subsection (4) should read as follows:

(4) The rights of other purchasers of goods and of lien creditors are governed by the Articles on Secured Transactions (Article 9), Bulk Sales (Article 6) and Documents of Title (Article 7).

As amended in 1988.

Part 5   Performance

§ 2-501.   Insurable Interest in Goods; Manner of Identification of Goods.

(1) The buyer obtains a special property and an insurable interest in goods by identification of existing goods as goods to which the contract refers even though the goods so identified are non-conforming and he has an option to return or reject them. Such identification can be made at any time and in any manner explicitly agreed to by the parties. In the absence of explicit agreement identification occurs

   (a) when the contract is made if it is for the sale of goods already existing and identified;
   (b) if the contract is for the sale of future goods other than those described in paragraph (c), when goods are shipped, marked or otherwise designated by the seller as goods to which the contract refers;
   (c) when the crops are planted or otherwise become growing crops or the young are conceived if the contract is for the sale of unborn young to be born within twelve months after contracting or for the sale of crops to be harvested within twelve months or the next normal harvest season after contracting whichever is longer.

(2) The seller retains an insurable interest in goods so long as title to or any security interest in the goods remains in him and where the identification is by the seller alone he may until default or insolvency or notification to the buyer that the identification is final substitute other goods for those identified.

(3) Nothing in this section impairs any insurable interest recognized under any other statute or rule of law.

§ 2-502.   Buyer's Right to Goods on Seller's Insolvency.

(1) Subject to subsection (2) and even though the goods have not been shipped a buyer who has paid a part or all of the price of goods in which he has a special property under the provisions of the immediately preceding section may on making and keeping good a tender of any unpaid portion of their price recover them from the seller if the seller becomes insolvent within ten days after receipt of the first installment on their price.

(2) If the identification creating his special property has been made by the buyer he acquires the right to recover the goods only if they conform to the contract for sale.

§ 2-503.   Manner of Seller's Tender of Delivery.

(1) Tender of delivery requires that the seller put and hold conforming goods at the buyer's disposition and give the buyer any notification reasonably necessary to enable him to take delivery. The manner, time and place for tender are determined by the agreement and this Article, and in particular

   (a) tender must be at a reasonable hour, and if it is of goods they must be kept available for the period reasonably necessary to enable the buyer to take possession; but
   (b) unless otherwise agreed the buyer must furnish facilities reasonably suited to the receipt of the goods.

(2) Where the case is within the next section respecting shipment tender requires that the seller comply with its provisions.

(3) Where the seller is required to deliver at a particular destination tender requires that he comply with subsection (1) and also in any appropriate case tender documents as described in subsections (4) and (5) of this section.

(4) Where goods are in the possession of a bailee and are to be delivered without being moved

   (a) tender requires that the seller either tender a negotiable document of title covering such goods or procure acknowledgement by the bailee of the buyer's right to possession of the goods; but
   (b) tender to the buyer of a non-negotiable document of title or of a written direction to the bailee to deliver is sufficient tender unless the buyer seasonably objects, and receipt by the bailee of notification of the buyer's rights fixes those rights as against the bailee and all third persons; but risk of loss of the goods and of any failure by the bailee to honor the non-negotiable document of title or to obey the direction remains on the seller until the buyer has had a reasonable time to present the document or direction, and a refusal by the bailee to honor the document or to obey the direction defeats the tender.

(5) Where the contract requires the seller to deliver documents

   (a) he must tender all such documents in correct form, except as provided in this Article with respect to bills of lading in a set (subsection (2) of Section 2-323); and
   (b) tender through customary banking channels is sufficient and dishonor of a draft accompanying the documents constitutes non-acceptance or rejection.

§ 2-504.   Shipment by Seller.   Where the seller is required or authorized to send the goods to the buyer and the contract does not require him to deliver them at a particular destination, then unless otherwise agreed he must

(a) put the goods in the possession of such a carrier and make such a contract for their transportation as may be reasonable having regard to the nature of the goods and other circumstances of the case; and

(b) obtain and promptly deliver or tender in due form any document necessary to enable the buyer to obtain possession of the goods or otherwise required by the agreement or by usage of trade; and

(c) promptly notify the buyer of the shipment.

Failure to notify the buyer under paragraph (c) or to make a proper contract under paragraph (a) is a ground for rejection only if material delay or loss ensues.

§ 2-505. Seller's Shipment Under Reservation.

(1) Where the seller has identified goods to the contract by or before shipment:

(a) his procurement of a negotiable bill of lading to his own order or otherwise reserves in him a security interest in the goods. His procurement of the bill to the order of a financing agency or of the buyer indicates in addition only the seller's expectation of transferring that interest to the person named.

(b) a non-negotiable bill of lading to himself or his nominee reserves possession of the goods as security but except in a case of conditional delivery (subsection (2) of Section 2-507) a non-negotiable bill of lading naming the buyer as consignee reserves no security interest even though the seller retains possession of the bill of lading.

(2) When shipment by the seller with reservation of a security interest is in violation of the contract for sale it constitutes an improper contract for transportation within the preceding section but impairs neither the rights given to the buyer by shipment and identification of the goods to the contract nor the seller's powers as a holder of a negotiable document.

§ 2-506. Rights of Financing Agency.

(1) A financing agency by paying or purchasing for value a draft which relates to a shipment of goods acquires to the extent of the payment or purchase and in addition to its own rights under the draft and any document of title securing it any rights of the shipper in the goods including the right to stop delivery and the shipper's right to have the draft honored by the buyer.

(2) The right to reimbursement of a financing agency which has in good faith honored or purchased the draft under commitment to or authority from the buyer is not impaired by subsequent discovery of defects with reference to any relevant document which was apparently regular on its face.

§ 2-507. Effect of Seller's Tender; Delivery on Condition.

(1) Tender of delivery is a condition to the buyer's duty to accept the goods and, unless otherwise agreed, to his duty to pay for them. Tender entitles the seller to acceptance of the goods and to payment according to the contract.

(2) Where payment is due and demanded on the delivery to the buyer of goods or documents of title, his right as against the seller to retain or dispose of them is conditional upon his making the payment due.

§ 2-508. Cure by Seller of Improper Tender or Delivery; Replacement.

(1) Where any tender or delivery by the seller is rejected because non-conforming and the time for performance has not yet expired, the seller may seasonably notify the buyer of his intention to cure and may then within the contract time make a conforming delivery.

(2) Where the buyer rejects a non-conforming tender which the seller had reasonable grounds to believe would be acceptable with or without money allowance the seller may if he seasonably notifies the buyer have a further reasonable time to substitute a conforming tender.

§ 2-509. Risk of Loss in the Absence of Breach.

(1) Where the contract requires or authorizes the seller to ship the goods by carrier

(a) if it does not require him to deliver them at a particular destination, the risk of loss passes to the buyer when the goods are duly delivered to the carrier even though the shipment is under reservation (Section 2-505); but

(b) if it does require him to deliver them at a particular destination and the goods are there duly tendered while in the possession of the carrier, the risk of loss passes to the buyer when the goods are there duly so tendered as to enable the buyer to take delivery.

(2) Where the goods are held by a bailee to be delivered without being moved, the risk of loss passes to the buyer

(a) on his receipt of a negotiable document of title covering the goods; or

(b) on acknowledgment by the bailee of the buyer's right to possession of the goods; or

(c) after his receipt of a non-negotiable document of title or other written direction to deliver, as provided in subsection (4)(b) of Section 2-503.

(3) In any case not within subsection (1) or (2), the risk of loss passes to the buyer on his receipt of the goods if the seller is a merchant; otherwise the risk passes to the buyer on tender of delivery.

(4) The provisions of this section are subject to contrary agreement of the parties and to the provisions of this Article on sale on approval (Section 2-327) and on effect of breach on risk of loss (Section 2-510).

§ 2-510. Effect on Breach on Risk of Loss.

(1) Where a tender or delivery of goods so fails to conform to the contract as to give a right of rejection the risk of their loss remains on the seller until cure or acceptance.

(2) Where the buyer rightfully revokes acceptance he may to the extent of any deficiency in his effective insurance coverage treat the risk of loss as having rested on the seller from the beginning.

(3) Where the buyer as to conforming goods already identified to the contract for sale repudiates or is otherwise in breach before risk of their loss has passed to him, the seller may to the extent of any deficiency in his effective insurance coverage treat the risk of loss as resting on the buyer for a·commercially reasonable time.

§ 2-511. Tender of Payment by Buyer; Payment by Check.

(1) Unless otherwise agreed tender of payment is a condition to the seller's duty to tender and complete any delivery.

(2) Tender of payment is sufficient when made by any means or in any manner current in the ordinary course of business unless the seller demands payment in legal tender and gives any extension of time reasonably necessary to procure it.

(3) Subject to the provisions of this Act on the effect of an instrument on an obligation (Section 3-310), payment by check is conditional and is defeated as between the parties by dishonor of the check on due presentment.

§ 2-512. Payment by Buyer Before Inspection.

(1) Where the contract requires payment before inspection non-conformity of the goods does not excuse the buyer from so making payment unless

(a) the non-conformity appears without inspection; or

(b) despite tender of the required documents the circumstances would justify injunction against honor under the provisions of this Act (Section 5-114).

(2) Payment pursuant to subsection (1) does not constitute an acceptance of goods or impair the buyer's right to inspect or any of his remedies.

§ 2-513. **Buyer's Right to Inspection of Goods.**

(1) Unless otherwise agreed and subject to subsection (3), where goods are tendered or delivered or identified to the contract for sale, the buyer has a right before payment or acceptance to inspect them at any reasonable place and time and in any reasonable manner. When the seller is required or authorized to send the goods to the buyer, the inspection may be after their arrival.

(2) Expenses of inspection must be borne by the buyer but may be recovered from the seller if the goods do not conform and are rejected.

(3) Unless otherwise agreed and subject to the provisions of this Article on C.I.F. contracts (subsection (3) of Section 2-321), the buyer is not entitled to inspect the goods before payment of the price when the contract provides

(a) for delivery "C.O.D." or on other like terms; or
(b) for payment against documents of title, except where such payment is due only after the goods are to become available for inspection.

(4) A place or method of inspection fixed by the parties is presumed to be exclusive but unless otherwise expressly agreed it does not postpone identification or shift the place for delivery or for passing the risk of loss. If compliance becomes impossible, inspection shall be as provided in this section unless the place or method fixed was clearly intended as an indispensable condition failure of which avoids the contract.

§ 2-514. **When Documents Deliverable on Acceptance; When on Payment.**
Unless otherwise agreed documents against which a draft is drawn are to be delivered to the drawee on acceptance of the draft if it is payable more than three days after presentment; otherwise, only on payment.

§ 2-515. **Preserving Evidence of Goods in Dispute.**
In furtherance of the adjustment of any claim or dispute

(a) either party on reasonable notification to the other and for the purpose of ascertaining the facts and preserving evidence has the right to inspect, test and sample the goods including such of them as may be in the possession or control of the other; and
(b) the parties may agree to a third party inspection or survey to determine the conformity or condition of the goods and may agree that the findings shall be binding upon them in any subsequent litigation or adjustment.

Part 6 Breach, Repudiation and Excuse

§ 2-601. **Buyer's Rights on Improper Delivery.**
Subject to the provisions of this Article on breach in installment contracts (Section 2-612) and unless otherwise agreed under the sections on contractual limitations of remedy (Section 2-718 and 2-719), if the goods or the tender of delivery fail in any respect to conform to the contract, the buyer may

(a) reject the whole; or
(b) accept the whole; or
(c) accept any commercial unit or units and reject the rest.

§ 2-602. **Manner and Effect of Rightful Rejection.**

(1) Rejection of goods must be within a reasonable time after their delivery or tender. It is ineffective unless the buyer seasonably notifies the seller.

(2) Subject to the provisions of the two following sections on rejected goods (Sections 2-603 and 2-604),

(a) after rejection any exercise of ownership by the buyer with respect to any commercial unit is wrongful as against the seller; and

(b) if the buyer has before rejection taken physical possession of goods in which he does not have a security interest under the provisions of this Article (subsection (3) of Section 2-711), he is under a duty after rejection to hold them with reasonable care at the seller's disposition for a time sufficient to permit the seller to remove them; but

(c) the buyer has no further obligations with regard to goods rightfully rejected.

(3) The seller's rights with respect to goods wrongfully rejected are governed by the provisions of this Article on Seller's remedies in general (Section 2-703).

§ 2-603. **Merchant Buyer's Duties as to Rightfully Rejected Goods.**

(1) Subject to any security interest in the buyer (subsection (3) of Section 2-711), when the seller has no agent or place of business at the market of rejection a merchant buyer is under a duty after rejection of goods in his possession or control to follow any reasonable instructions received from the seller with respect to the goods and in the absence of such instructions to make reasonable efforts to sell them for the seller's account if they are perishable or threaten to decline in value speedily. Instructions are not reasonable if on demand indemnity for expenses is not forthcoming.

(2) When the buyer sells goods under subsection (1), he is entitled to reimbursement from the seller or out of the proceeds for reasonable expenses of caring for and selling them, and if the expenses include no selling commission then to such commission as is usual in the trade or if there is none to a reasonable sum not exceeding ten per cent on the gross proceeds.

(3) In complying with this section the buyer is held only to good faith and good faith conduct hereunder is neither acceptance nor conversion nor the basis of an action for damages.

§ 2-604. **Buyer's Options as to Salvage of Rightfully Rejected Goods.**
Subject to the provisions of the immediately preceding section on perishables if the seller gives no instructions within a reasonable time after notification of rejection the buyer may store the rejected goods for the seller's account or reship them to him or resell them for the seller's account with reimbursement as provided in the preceding section. Such action is not acceptance or conversion.

§ 2-605. **Waiver of Buyer's Objections by Failure to Particularize.**

(1) The buyer's failure to state in connection with rejection a particular defect which is ascertainable by reasonable inspection precludes him from relying on the unstated defect to justify rejection or to establish breach

(a) where the seller could have cured it if stated seasonably; or
(b) between merchants when the seller has after rejection made a request in writing for a full and final written statement of all defects on which the buyer proposes to rely.

(2) Payment against documents made without reservation of rights precludes recovery of the payment for defects apparent on the face of the documents.

§ 2-606. **What Constitutes Acceptance of Goods.**

(1) Acceptance of goods occurs when the buyer

(a) after a reasonable opportunity to inspect the goods signifies to the seller that the goods are conforming or that he will take or retain them in spite of their non-conformity; or

(b) fails to make an effective rejection (subsection (1) of Section 2-602), but such acceptance does not occur until the buyer has had a reasonable opportunity to inspect them; or

(c) does any act inconsistent with the seller's ownership; but if such act is wrongful as against the seller it is an acceptance only if ratified by him.

(2) Acceptance of a part of any commercial unit is acceptance of that entire unit.

§ 2-607. Effect of Acceptance; Notice of Breach; Burden of Establishing Breach After Acceptance; Notice of Claim or Litigation to Person Answerable Over.

(1) The buyer must pay at the contract rate for any goods accepted.

(2) Acceptance of goods by the buyer precludes rejection of the goods accepted and if made with knowledge of a non-conformity cannot be revoked because of it unless the acceptance was on the reasonable assumption that the non-conformity would be seasonably cured but acceptance does not of itself impair any other remedy provided by this Article for non-conformity.

(3) Where a tender has been accepted

(a) the buyer must within a reasonable time after he discovers or should have discovered any breach notify the seller of breach or be barred from any remedy; and

(b) if the claim is one for infringement or the like (subsection (3) of Section 2-312) and the buyer is sued as a result of such a breach he must so notify the seller within a reasonable time after he receives notice of the litigation or be barred from any remedy over for liability established by the litigation.

(4) The burden is on the buyer to establish any breach with respect to the goods accepted.

(5) Where the buyer is sued for breach of a warranty or other obligation for which his seller is answerable over

(a) he may give his seller written notice of the litigation. If the notice states that the seller may come in and defend and that if the seller does not do so he will be bound in any action against him by his buyer by any determination of fact common to the two litigations, then unless the seller after seasonable receipt of the notice does come in and defend he is so bound.

(b) if the claim is one for infringement or the like (subsection (3) of Section 2-312) the original seller may demand in writing that his buyer turn over to him control of the litigation including settlement or else be barred from any remedy over and if he also agrees to bear all expense and to satisfy any adverse judgment, then unless the buyer after seasonable receipt of the demand does turn over control the buyer is so barred.

(6) The provisions of subsections (3), (4) and (5) apply to any obligation of a buyer to hold the seller harmless against infringement or the like (subsection (3) of Section 2-312).

§ 2-608. Revocation of Acceptance in Whole or in Part.

(1) The buyer may revoke his acceptance of a lot or commercial unit whose non-conformity substantially impairs its value to him if he has accepted it

(a) on the reasonable assumption that its non-conformity would be cured and it has not been seasonably cured; or

(b) without discovery of such non-conformity if his acceptance was reasonably induced either by the difficulty

of discovery before acceptance or by the seller's assurances.

(2) Revocation of acceptance must occur within a reasonable time after the buyer discovers or should have discovered the ground for it and before any substantial change in condition of the goods which is not caused by their own defects. It is not effective until the buyer notifies the seller of it.

(3) A buyer who so revokes has the same rights and duties with regard to the goods involved as if he had rejected them.

§ 2-609. Right to Adequate Assurance of Performance.

(1) A contract for sale imposes an obligation on each party that the other's expectation of receiving due performance will not be impaired. When reasonable grounds for insecurity arise with respect to the performance of either party the other may in writing demand adequate assurance of due performance and until he receives such assurance may if commercially reasonable suspend any performance for which he has not already received the agreed return.

(2) Between merchants the reasonableness of grounds for insecurity and the adequacy of any assurance offered shall be determined according to commercial standards.

(3) Acceptance of any improper delivery or payment does not prejudice the aggrieved party's right to demand adequate assurance of future performance.

(4) After receipt of a justified demand failure to provide within a reasonable time not exceeding thirty days such assurance of due performance as is adequate under the circumstances of the particular case is a repudiation of the contract.

§ 2-610. Anticipatory Repudiation. When either party repudiates the contract with respect to a performance not yet due the loss of which will substantially impair the value of the contract to the other, the aggrieved party may

(a) for a commercially reasonable time await performance by the repudiating party; or

(b) resort to any remedy for breach (Section 2-703 or Section 2-711), even though he has notified the repudiating party that he would await the latter's performance and has urged retraction; and

(c) in either case suspend his own performance or proceed in accordance with the provisions of this Article on the seller's right to identify goods to the contract notwithstanding breach or to salvage unfinished goods (Section 2-704).

§ 2-611. Retraction of Anticipatory Repudiation.

(1) Until the repudiating party's next performance is due he can retract his repudiation unless the aggrieved party has since the repudiation cancelled or materially changed his position or otherwise indicated that he considers the repudiation final.

(2) Retraction may be by any method which clearly indicates to the aggrieved party that the repudiating party intends to perform, but must include any assurance justifiably demanded under the provisions of this Article (Section 2-609).

(3) Retraction reinstates the repudiating party's rights under the contract with due excuse and allowance to the aggrieved party for any delay occasioned by the repudiation.

§ 2-612. "Installment Contract"; Breach.

(1) An "installment contract" is one which requires or authorizes the delivery of goods in separate lots to be separately accepted, even though the contract contains a clause "each delivery is a separate contract" or its equivalent.

(2) The buyer may reject any installment which is non-conforming if the non-conformity substantially impairs the value of that installment and cannot be cured or if the non-conformity is a defect in the required documents; but if the non-conformity does not fall within subsection (3) and the seller gives adequate assurance of its cure the buyer must accept that installment.

(3) Whenever non-conformity or default with respect to one or more installments substantially impairs the value of the whole contract there is a breach of the whole. But the aggrieved party reinstates the contract if he accepts a non-conforming installment without seasonably notifying of cancellation or if he brings an action with respect only to past installments or demands performance as to future installments.

§ 2-613. **Casualty to Identified Goods.** Where the contract requires for its performance goods identified when the contract is made, and the goods suffer casualty without fault of either party before the risk of loss passes to the buyer, or in a proper case under a "no arrival, no sale" term (Section 2-324) then

(a) if the loss is total the contract is avoided; and
(b) if the loss is partial or the goods have so deteriorated as no longer to conform to the contract the buyer may nevertheless demand inspection and at his option either treat the contract as avoided or accept the goods with due allowance from the contract price for the deterioration or the deficiency in quantity but without further right against the seller.

§ 2-614. **Substituted Performance.**

(1) Where without fault of either party the agreed berthing, loading, or unloading facilities fail or an agreed type of carrier becomes unavailable or the agreed manner of delivery otherwise becomes commercially impracticable but a commercially reasonable substitute is available, such substitute performance must be tendered and accepted.

(2) If the agreed means or manner of payment fails because of domestic or foreign governmental regulation, the seller may withhold or stop delivery unless the buyer provides a means or manner of payment which is commercially a substantial equivalent. If delivery has already been taken, payment by the means or in the manner provided by the regulation discharges the buyer's obligation unless the regulation is discriminatory, oppressive or predatory.

§ 2-615. **Excuse by Failure of Presupposed Conditions.**
Except so far as a seller may have assumed a greater obligation and subject to the preceding section on substituted performance:

(a) Delay in delivery or non-delivery in whole or in part by a seller who complies with paragraphs (b) and (c) is not a breach of his duty under a contract for sale if performance as agreed has been made impracticable by the occurrence of a contingency the non-occurrence of which was a basic assumption on which the contract was made or by compliance in good faith with any applicable foreign or domestic governmental regulation or order whether or not it later proves to be invalid.

(b) Where the causes mentioned in paragraph (a) affect only a part of the seller's capacity to perform, he must allocate production and deliveries among his customers but may at his option include regular customers not then under contract as well as his own requirements for further manufacture. He may so allocate in any manner which is fair and reasonable.

(c) The seller must notify the buyer seasonably that there will be delay or non-delivery and, when allocation is required under paragraph (b), of the estimated quota thus made available for the buyer.

§ 2-616. **Procedure on Notice Claiming Excuse.**

(1) Where the buyer receives notification of a material or indefinite delay or an allocation justified under the preceding section he may by written notification to the seller as to any delivery concerned, and where the prospective deficiency substantially impairs the value of the whole contract under the provisions of this Article relating to breach of installment contracts (Section 2-612), then also as to the whole,

(a) terminate and thereby discharge any unexecuted portion of the contract; or
(b) modify the contract by agreeing to take his available quota in substitution.

(2) If after receipt of such notification from the seller the buyer fails so to modify the contract within a reasonable time not exceeding thirty days the contract lapses with respect to any deliveries affected.

(3) The provisions of this section may not be negated by agreement except in so far as the seller has assumed a greater obligation under the preceding section.

Part 7   Remedies

§ 2-701. **Remedies for Breach of Collateral Contracts Not Impaired.** Remedies for breach of any obligation or promise collateral or ancillary to a contract for sale are not impaired by the provisions of this Article.

§ 2-702. **Seller's Remedies on Discovery of Buyer's Insolvency.**

(1) Where the seller discovers the buyer to be insolvent he may refuse delivery except for cash including payment for all goods theretofore delivered under the contract, and stop delivery under this Article (Section 2-705).

(2) Where the seller discovers that the buyer has received goods on credit while insolvent he may reclaim the goods upon demand made within ten days after the receipt, but if misrepresentation of solvency has been made to the particular seller in writing within three months before delivery the ten day limitation does not apply. Except as provided in this subsection the seller may not base a right to reclaim goods on the buyer's fraudulent or innocent misrepresentation of solvency or of intent to pay.

(3) The seller's right to reclaim under subsection (2) is subject to the rights of a buyer in ordinary course or other good faith purchaser under this Article (Section 2-403). Successful reclamation of goods excludes all other remedies with respect to them.

    As amended in 1966.

§ 2-703. **Seller's Remedies in General.** Where the buyer wrongfully rejects or revokes acceptance of goods or fails to make a payment due on or before delivery or repudiates with respect to a part or the whole, then with respect to any goods directly affected and, if the breach is of the whole contract (Section 2-612), then also with respect to the whole undelivered balance, the aggrieved seller may

(a) withhold delivery of such goods;
(b) stop delivery by any bailee as hereafter provided (Section 2-705);

(c) proceed under the next section respecting goods still unidentified to the contract;

(d) resell and recover damages as hereafter provided (Section 2-706);

(e) recover damages for non-acceptance (Section 2-708) or in a proper case the price (Section 2-709);

(f) cancel.

§ 2-704. Seller's Right to Identify Goods to the Contract Notwithstanding Breach or to Salvage Unfinished Goods.

(1) An aggrieved seller under the preceding section may

(a) identify to the contract conforming goods not already identified if at the time he learned of the breach they are in his possession or control;

(b) treat as the subject of resale goods which have demonstrably been intended for the particular contract even though those goods are unfinished.

(2) Where the goods are unfinished an aggrieved seller may in the exercise of reasonable commercial judgment for the purposes of avoiding loss and of effective realization either complete the manufacture and wholly identify the goods to the contract or cease manufacture and resell for scrap or salvage value or proceed in any other reasonable manner.

§ 2-705. Seller's Stoppage of Delivery in Transit or Otherwise.

(1) The seller may stop delivery of goods in the possession of a carrier or other bailee when he discovers the buyer to be insolvent (Section 2-702) and may stop delivery of carload, truckload, planeload or larger shipments of express or freight when the buyer repudiates or fails to make a payment due before delivery or if for any other reason the seller has a right to withhold or reclaim the goods.

(2) As against such buyer the seller may stop delivery until

(a) receipt of the goods by the buyer; or

(b) acknowledgment to the buyer by any bailee of the goods except a carrier that the bailee holds the goods for the buyer; or

(c) such acknowledgment to the buyer by a carrier by reshipment or as warehouseman; or

(d) negotiation to the buyer of any negotiable document of title covering the goods.

(3)

(a) To stop delivery the seller must so notify as to enable the bailee by reasonable diligence to prevent delivery of the goods.

(b) After such notification the bailee must hold and deliver the goods according to the directions of the seller but the seller is liable to the bailee for any ensuing charges or damages.

(c) If a negotiable document of title has been issued for goods the bailee is not obliged to obey a notification to stop until surrender of the document.

(d) A carrier who has issued a non-negotiable bill of lading is not obliged to obey a notification to stop received from a person other than the consignor.

§ 2-706. Seller's Resale Including Contract for Resale.

(1) Under the conditions stated in Section 2-703 on seller's remedies, the seller may resell the goods concerned or the undelivered balance thereof. Where the resale is made in good faith and in a commercially reasonable manner the seller may recover the difference between the resale price and the contract price together with any incidental damages allowed under the provisions of this Article (Section 2-710), but less expenses saved in consequence of the buyer's breach.

(2) Except as otherwise provided in subsection (3) or unless otherwise agreed resale may be at public or private sale including sale by way of one or more contracts to sell or of identification to an existing contract of the seller. Sale may be as a unit or in parcels and at any time and place and on any terms but every aspect of the sale including the method, manner, time, place and terms must be commercially reasonable. The resale must be reasonably identified as referring to the broken contract, but it is not necessary that the goods be in existence or that any or all of them have been identified to the contract before the breach.

(3) Where the resale is at private sale the seller must give the buyer reasonable notification of his intention to resell.

(4) Where the resale is at public sale

(a) only identified goods can be sold except where there is a recognized market for a public sale of futures in goods of the kind; and

(b) it must be made at a usual place or market for public sale if one is reasonably available and except in the case of goods which are perishable or threaten to decline in value speedily the seller must give the buyer reasonable notice of the time and place of the resale; and

(c) if the goods are not to be within the view of those attending the sale the notification of sale must state the place where the goods are located and provide for their reasonable inspection by prospective bidders; and

(d) the seller may buy.

(5) A purchaser who buys in good faith at a resale takes the goods free of any rights of the original buyer even though the seller fails to comply with one or more of the requirements of this section.

(6) The seller is not accountable to the buyer for any profit made on any resale. A person in the position of a seller (Section 2-707) or a buyer who has rightfully rejected or justifiably revoked acceptance must account for any excess over the amount of his security interest, as hereinafter defined (subsection (3) of Section 2-711).

§ 2-707. "Person in the Position of a Seller".

(1) A "person in the position of a seller" includes as against a principal an agent who has paid or become responsible for the price of goods of his principal or anyone who otherwise holds a security interest or other right in goods similar to that of a seller.

(2) A person in the position of a seller may as provided in this Article withhold or stop delivery (Section 2-705) and resell (Section 2-706) and recover incidental damages (Section 2-710).

§ 2-708. Seller's Damages for Non-acceptance or Repudiation.

(1) Subject to subsection (2) and to the provisions of this Article with respect to proof of market price (Section 2-723), the measure of damages for non-acceptance or repudiation by the buyer is the difference between the market price at the time and place for tender and the unpaid contract price together with any incidental damages provided in this Article (Section 2-710), but less expenses saved in consequence of the buyer's breach.

(2) If the measure of damages provided in subsection (1) is inadequate to put the seller in as good a position as performance

would have done then the measure of damages is the profit (including reasonable overhead) which the seller would have made from full performance by the buyer, together with any incidental damages provided in this Article (Section 2-710), due allowance for costs reasonably incurred and due credit for payments or proceeds of resale.

§ 2-709. Action for the Price.

(1) When the buyer fails to pay the price as it becomes due the seller may recover, together with any incidental damages under the next section, the price

(a) of goods accepted or of conforming goods lost or damaged within a commercially reasonable time after risk of their loss has passed to the buyer; and

(b) of goods identified to the contract if the seller is unable after reasonable effort to resell them at a reasonable price or the circumstances reasonably indicate that such effort will be unavailing.

(2) Where the seller sues for the price he must hold for the buyer any goods which have been identified to the contract and are still in this control except that if resale becomes possible he may resell them at any time prior to the collection of the judgment. The net proceeds of any such resale must be credited to the buyer and payment of the judgment entitles him to any goods not resold.

(3) After the buyer has wrongfully rejected or revoked acceptance of the goods or has failed to make a payment due or has repudiated (Section 2-610), a seller who is held not entitled to the price under this section shall nevertheless be awarded damages for non-acceptance under the preceding section.

§ 2-710. Seller's Incidental Damages.

Incidental damages to an aggrieved seller include any commercially reasonable charges, expenses or commissions incurred in stopping delivery, in the transportation, care and custody of goods after the buyer's breach, in connection with return or resale of the goods or otherwise resulting from the breach.

§ 2-711. Buyer's Remedies in General; Buyer's Security Interest in Rejected Goods.

(1) Where the seller fails to make delivery or repudiates or the buyer rightfully rejects or justifiably revokes acceptance then with respect to any goods involved, and with respect to the whole if the breach goes to the whole contract (Section 2-612), the buyer may cancel and whether or not he has done so may in addition to recovering so much of the price as has been paid

(a) "cover" and have damages under the next section as to all the goods affected whether or not they have been identified to the contract; or

(b) recover damages for non-delivery as provided in this Article (Section 2-713).

(2) Where the seller fails to deliver or repudiates the buyer may also

(a) if the goods have been identified recover them as provided in this Article (Section 2-502); or

(b) in a proper case obtain specific performance or replevy the goods as provided in this Article (Section 2-716).

(3) On rightful rejection or justifiable revocation of acceptance a buyer has a security interest in goods in his possession or control for any payments made on their price and any expenses reasonably incurred in their inspection, receipt, transportation, care and custody and may hold such goods and resell them in like manner as an aggrieved seller (Section 2-706).

§ 2-712. "Cover"; Buyer's Procurement of Substitute Goods.

(1) After a breach within the preceding section the buyer may "cover" by making in good faith and without unreasonable delay any reasonable purchase of or contract to purchase goods in substitution for those due from the seller.

(2) The buyer may recover from the seller as damages the difference between the cost of cover and the contract price together with any incidental or consequential damages as hereinafter defined (Section 2-715), but less expenses saved in consequence of the seller's breach.

(3) Failure of the buyer to effect cover within this section does not bar him from any other remedy.

§ 2-713. Buyer's Damages for Non-delivery or Repudiation.

(1) Subject to the provisions of this Article with respect to proof of market price (Section 2-723), the measure of damages for non-delivery or repudiation by the seller is the difference between the market price at the time when the buyer learned of the breach and the contract price together with any incidental and consequential damages provided in this Article (Section 2-715), but less expenses saved in consequence of the seller's breach.

(2) Market price is to be determined as of the place for tender or, in cases of rejection after arrival or revocation of acceptance, as of the place of arrival.

§ 2-714. Buyer's Damages for Breach in Regard to Accepted Goods.

(1) Where the buyer has accepted goods and given notification (subsection (3) of Section 2-607) he may recover as damages for any non-conformity of tender the loss resulting in the ordinary course of events from the seller's breach as determined in any manner which is reasonable.

(2) The measure of damages for breach of warranty is the difference at the time and place of acceptance between the value of the goods accepted and the value they would have had if they had been as warranted, unless special circumstances show proximate damages of a different amount.

(3) In a proper case any incidental and consequential damages under the next section may also be recovered.

§ 2-715. Buyer's Incidental and Consequential Damages.

(1) Incidental damages resulting from the seller's breach include expenses reasonably incurred in inspection, receipt, transportation and care and custody of goods rightfully rejected, any commercially reasonable charges, expenses or commissions in connection with effecting cover and any other reasonable expense incident to the delay or other breach.

(2) Consequential damages resulting from the seller's breach include

(a) any loss resulting from general or particular requirements and needs of which the seller at the time of contracting had reason to know and which could not reasonably be prevented by cover or otherwise; and

(b) injury to person or property proximately resulting from any breach of warranty.

§ 2-716. Buyer's Right to Specific Performance or Replevin.

(1) Specific performance may be decreed where the goods are unique or in other proper circumstances.

(2) The decree for specific performance may include such terms and conditions as to payment of the price, damages, or other relief as the court may deem just.

(3) The buyer has a right of replevin for goods identified to the contract if after reasonable effort he is unable to effect cover for such goods or the circumstances reasonably indicate that such effort will be unavailing or if the goods have been shipped under reservation and satisfaction of the security interest in them has been made or tendered.

§ 2-717. **Deduction of Damages From the Price.** The buyer on notifying the seller of his intention to do so may deduct all or any part of the damages resulting from any breach of the contract from any part of the price still due under the same contract.

§ 2-718. **Liquidation or Limitation of Damages; Deposits.**

(1) Damages for breach by either party may be liquidated in the agreement but only at an amount which is reasonable in the light of the anticipated or actual harm caused by the breach, the difficulties of proof of loss, and the inconvenience or nonfeasibility of otherwise obtaining an adequate remedy. A term fixing unreasonably large liquidated damages is void as a penalty.
(2) Where the seller justifiably withholds delivery of goods because of the buyer's breach, the buyer is entitled to restitution of any amount by which the sum of his payments exceeds

(a) the amount to which the seller is entitled by virtue of terms liquidating the seller's damages in accordance with subsection (1), or
(b) in the absence of such terms, twenty per cent of the value of the total performance for which the buyer is obligated under the contract or $500, whichever is smaller.

(3) The buyer's right to restitution under subsection (2) is subject to offset to the extent that the seller establishes

(a) a right to recover damages under the provisions of this Article other than subsection (1), and
(b) the amount or value of any benefits received by the buyer directly or indirectly by reason of the contract.

(4) Where a seller has received payment in goods their reasonable value or the proceeds of their resale shall be treated as payments for the purposes of subsection (2); but if the seller has notice of the buyer's breach before reselling goods received in part performance, his resale is subject to the conditions laid down in this Article on resale by an aggrieved seller (Section 2-706).

§ 2-719. **Contractual Modification or Limitation of Remedy.**

(1) Subject to the provisions of subsections (2) and (3) of this section and of the preceding section on liquidation and limitation of damages,

(a) the agreement may provide for remedies in addition to or in substitution for those provided in this Article and may limit or alter the measure of damages recoverable under this Article, as by limiting the buyer's remedies to return of the goods and repayment of the price or to repair and replacement of nonconforming goods or parts; and
(b) resort to a remedy as provided is optional unless the remedy is expressly agreed to be exclusive, in which case it is the sole remedy.

(2) Where circumstances cause an exclusive or limited remedy to fail of its essential purpose, remedy may be had as provided in this Act.
(3) Consequential damages may be limited or excluded unless the limitation or exclusion is unconscionable. Limitation of consequential damages for injury to the person in the case of consumer goods is prima facie unconscionable but limitation of damages where the loss is commercial is not.

§ 2-720. **Effect of "Cancellation" or "Rescission" on Claims for Antecedent Breach.** Unless the contrary intention clearly appears, expressions of "cancellation" or "rescission" of the contract or the like shall not be construed as a renunciation or discharge of any claim in damages for an antecedent breach.

§ 2-721. **Remedies for Fraud.** Remedies for material misrepresentation or fraud include all remedies available under this Article for non-fraudulent breach. Neither rescission or a claim for rescission of the contract for sale nor rejection or return of the goods shall bar or be deemed inconsistent with a claim for damages or other remedy.

§ 2-722. **Who Can Sue Third Parties for Injury to Goods.** Where a third party so deals with goods which have been identified to a contract for sale as to cause actionable injury to a party to that contract

(a) a right of action against the third party is in either party to the contract for sale who has title to or a security interest or a special property or an insurable interest in the goods; and if the goods have been destroyed or converted a right of action is also in the party who either bore the risk of loss under the contract for sale or has since the injury assumed that risk as against the other;
(b) if at the time of the injury the party plaintiff did not bear the risk of loss as against the other party to the contract for sale and there is no arrangement between them for disposition of the recovery, his suit or settlement is, subject to his own interest, as a fiduciary for the other party to the contract;
(c) either party may with the consent of the other sue for the benefit of whom it may concern.

§ 2-723. **Proof of Market Price: Time and Place.**

(1) If an action based on anticipatory repudiation comes to trial before the time for performance with respect to some or all of the goods, any damages based on market price (Section 2-708 or Section 2-713) shall be determined according to the price of such goods prevailing at the time when the aggrieved party learned of the repudiation.
(2) If evidence of a price prevailing at the times or places described in this Article is not readily available the price prevailing within any reasonable time before or after the time described or at any other place which in commercial judgment or under usage of trade would serve as a reasonable substitute for the one described may be used, making any proper allowance for the cost of transporting the goods to or from such other place.
(3) Evidence of a relevant price prevailing at a time or place other than the one described in this Article offered by one party is not admissible unless and until he has given the other party such notice as the court finds sufficient to prevent unfair surprise.

§ 2-724. **Admissibility of Market Quotations.** Whenever the prevailing price or value of any goods regularly bought and sold in any established commodity market is in issue, reports in official publications or trade journals or in newspapers or periodicals of general circulation published as the reports of such market shall be admissible in evidence. The circumstances of the preparation of such a report may be shown to affect its weight but not its admissibility.

§ 2-725. Statute of Limitations in Contracts for Sale.

(1) An action for breach of any contract for sale must be commenced within four years after the cause of action has accrued. By the original agreement the parties may reduce the period of limitation to not less than one year but may not extend it.

(2) A cause of action accrues when the breach occurs, regardless of the aggrieved party's lack of knowledge of the breach. A breach of warranty occurs when tender of delivery is made, except that where a warranty explicitly extends to future performance of the goods and discovery of the breach must await the time of such performance the cause of action accrues when the breach is or should have been discovered.

(3) Where an action commenced within the time limited by subsection (1) is so terminated as to leave available a remedy by another action for the same breach such other action may be commenced after the expiration of the time limited and within six months after the termination of the first action unless the termination resulted from voluntary discontinuance or from dismissal for failure or neglect to prosecute.

(4) This section does not alter the law on tolling of the statute of limitations nor does it apply to causes of action which have accrued before this Act becomes effective.

ARTICLE 2A / Leases

Part 1   General Provisions

§ 2A-101.   **Short Title.**   This Article shall be known and may be cited as the Uniform Commercial Code-Leases.

§ 2A-102.   **Scope.**   This Article applies to any transaction, regardless of form, that creates a lease.

§ 2A-103.   **Definitions and Index of Definitions.**

(1)   In this Article unless the context otherwise requires:

(a) "Buyer in ordinary course of business" means a person who in good faith and without knowledge that the sale to him [or her] is in violation of the ownership rights or security interest or leasehold interest of a third party in the goods buys in ordinary course from a person in the business of selling goods of that kind but does not include a pawnbroker. "Buying" may be for cash or by exchange of other property or on secured or unsecured credit and includes receiving goods or documents of title under a pre-existing contract for sale but does not include a transfer in bulk or as security for or in total or partial satisfaction of a money debt.

(b) "Cancellation" occurs when either party puts an end to the lease contract for default by the other party.

(c) "Commercial unit" means such a unit of goods as by commercial usage is a single whole for purposes of lease and division of which materially impairs its character or value on the market or in use. A commercial unit may be a single article, as a machine, or a set of articles, as a suite of furniture or a line of machinery, or a quantity, as a gross or carload, or any other unit treated in use or in the relevant market as a single whole.

(d) "Conforming" goods or performance under a lease contract means goods or performance that are in accordance with the obligations under the lease contract.

(e) "Consumer lease" means a lease that a lessor regularly engaged in the business of leasing or selling makes to a lessee who is an individual and who takes under the lease primarily for a personal, family, or household purpose [, if

the total payments to be made under the lease contract, excluding payments for options to renew or buy, do not exceed $_____].

(f) "Fault" means wrongful act, omission, breach, or default.

(g) "Finance lease" means a lease with respect to which: (i) the lessor does not select, manufacture, or supply the goods; (ii) the lessor acquires the goods or the right to possession and use of the goods in connection with the lease; and (iii) one of the following occurs:

(A) the lessee receives a copy of the contract by which the lessor acquired the goods or the right to possession and use of the goods before signing the lease contract;

(B) the lessee's approval of the contract by which the lessor acquired the goods or the right to possession and use of the goods is a condition to effectiveness of the lease contract;

(C) the lessee, before signing the lease contract, receives an accurate and complete statement designating the promises and warranties, and any disclaimers of warranties, limitations or modifications of remedies, or liquidated damages, including those of a third party, such as the manufacturer of the goods, provided to the lessor by the person supplying the goods in connection with or as part of the contract by which the lessor acquired the goods or the right to possession and use of the goods; or

(D) if the lease is not a consumer lease, the lessor, before the lessee signs the lease contract, informs the lessee in writing (a) of the identity of the person supplying the goods to the lessor, unless the lessee has selected that person and directed the lessor to acquire the goods or the right to possession and use of the goods from that person, (b) that the lessee is entitled under this Article to the promises and warranties, including those of any third party, provided to the lessor by the person supplying the goods in connection with or as part of the contract by which the lessor acquired the goods or the right to possession and use of the goods, and (c) that the lessee may communicate with the person supplying the goods to the lessor and receive an accurate and complete statement of those promises and warranties, including any disclaimers and limitations of them or of remedies.

(h) "Goods" means all things that are movable at the time of identification to the lease contract, or are fixtures (Section 2A-309), but the term does not include money, documents, instruments, accounts, chattel paper, general intangibles, or minerals or the like, including oil and gas, before extraction. The term also includes the unborn young of animals.

(i) "Installment lease contract" means a lease contract that authorizes or requires the delivery of goods in separate lots to be separately accepted, even though the lease contract contains a clause "each delivery is a separate lease" or its equivalent.

(j) "Lease" means a transfer of the right to possession and use of goods for a term in return for consideration, but a sale, including a sale on approval or a sale or return, or retention or creation of a security interest is not a lease. Unless the context clearly indicates otherwise, the term includes a sublease.

(k) "Lease agreement" means the bargain, with respect to the lease, of the lessor and the lessee in fact as found in their language or by implication from other circumstances including course of dealing or usage of trade or course of performance as provided in this Article. Unless the context clearly indicates otherwise, the term includes a sublease agreement.

(l) "Lease contract" means the total legal obligation that results from the lease agreement as affected by this Article and any other applicable rules of law. Unless the context clearly indicates otherwise, the term includes a sublease contract.

(m) "Leasehold interest" means the interest of the lessor or the lessee under a lease contract.

(n) "Lessee" means a person who acquires the right to possession and use of goods under a lease. Unless the context clearly indicates otherwise, the term includes a sublessee.

(o) "Lessee in ordinary course of business" means a person who in good faith and without knowledge that the lease to him [or her] is in violation of the ownership rights or security interest or leasehold interest of a third party in the goods, leases in ordinary course from a person in the business of selling or leasing goods of that kind but does not include a pawnbroker. "Leasing" may be for cash or by exchange of other property or on secured or unsecured credit and includes receiving goods or documents of title under a pre-existing lease contract but does not include a transfer in bulk or as security for or in total or partial satisfaction of a money debt.

(p) "Lessor" means a person who transfers the right to possession and use of goods under a lease. Unless the context clearly indicates otherwise, the term includes a sublessor.

(q) "Lessor's residual interest" means the lessor's interest in the goods after expiration, termination, or cancellation of the lease contract.

(r) "Lien" means a charge against or interest in goods to secure payment of a debt or performance of an obligation, but the term does not include a security interest.

(s) "Lot" means a parcel or a single article that is the subject matter of a separate lease or delivery, whether or not it is sufficient to perform the lease contract.

(t) "Merchant lessee" means a lessee that is a merchant with respect to goods of the kind subject to the lease.

(u) "Present value" means the amount as of a date certain of one or more sums payable in the future, discounted to the date certain. The discount is determined by the interest rate specified by the parties if the rate was not manifestly unreasonable at the time the transaction was entered into; otherwise, the discount is determined by a commercially reasonable rate that takes into account the facts and circumstances of each case at the time the transaction was entered into.

(v) "Purchase" includes taking by sale, lease, mortgage, security interest, pledge, gift, or any other voluntary transaction creating an interest in goods.

(w) "Sublease" means a lease of goods the right to possession and use of which was acquired by the lessor as a lessee under an existing lease.

(x) "Supplier" means a person from whom a lessor buys or leases goods to be leased under a finance lease.

(y) "Supply contract" means a contract under which a lessor buys or leases goods to be leased.

(z) "Termination" occurs when either party pursuant to a power created by agreement or law puts an end to the lease contract otherwise than for default.

(2) Other definitions applying to this Article and the sections in which they appear are:

"Accessions"   Section 2A-310(1).
"Construction mortgage"   Section 2A-309(1)(d).
"Encumbrance"   Section 2A-309(1)(e).

"Fixtures"   Section 2A-309(1)(a).
"Fixture filing"   Section 2A-309(1)(b).
"Purchase money lease"   Section 2A-309(1)(c).

(3) The following definitions in other Articles apply to this Article:

"Account"   Section 9-106.
"Between merchants"   Section 2-104(3).
"Buyer"   Section 2-103(1)(a).
"Chattel paper"   Section 9-105(1)(b).
"Consumer goods"   Section 9-109(1).
"Document"   Section 9-105(1)(f).
"Entrusting"   Section 2-403(3).
"General intangibles"   Section 9-106.
"Good faith"   Section 2-103(1)(b).
"Instrument"   Section 9-105(1)(i).
"Merchant"   Section 2-104(1).
"Mortgage"   Section 9-105(1)(j).
"Pursuant to commitment".   Section 9-105(1)(k).
"Receipt".   Section 2-103(1)(c).
"Sale".   Section 2-106(1).
"Sale on approval".   Section 2-326.
"Sale or return".   Section 2-326.
"Seller".   Section 2-103(1)(d).

(4) In addition Article 1 contains general definitions and principles of construction and interpretation applicable throughout this Article.

As amended in 1990.

§ 2A-104.   **Leases Subject to Other Law.**

(1) A lease, although subject to this Article, is also subject to any applicable:

(a) certificate of title statute of this State: (list any certificate of title statutes covering automobiles, trailers, mobile homes, boats, farm tractors, and the like);
(b) certificate of title statute of another jurisdiction (Section 2A-105); or
(c) consumer protection statute of this State, or final consumer protection decision of a court of this State existing on the effective date of this Article.

(2) In case of conflict between this Article, other than Sections 2A-105, 2A-304(3), and 2A-305(3), and a statute or decision referred to in subsection (1), the statute or decision controls.

(3) Failure to comply with an applicable law has only the effect specified therein.

As amended in 1990.

§ 2A-105.   **Territorial Application of Article to Goods Covered by Certificate of Title.**   Subject to the provisions of Sections 2A-304(3) and 2A-305(3), with respect to goods covered by a certificate of title issued under a statute of this State or of another jurisdiction, compliance and the effect of compliance or non-compliance with a certificate of title statute are governed by the law (including the conflict of laws rules) of the jurisdiction issuing the certificate until the earlier of (a) surrender of the certificate, or (b) four months after the goods are removed from that jurisdiction and thereafter until a new certificate of title is issued by another jurisdiction.

§ 2A-106.   **Limitation on Power of Parties to Consumer Lease to Choose Applicable Law and Judicial Forum.**

(1) If the law chosen by the parties to a consumer lease is that of a jurisdiction other than a jurisdiction in which the lessee

resides at the time the lease agreement becomes enforceable or within 30 days thereafter or in which the goods are to be used, the choice is not enforceable.

(2) If the judicial forum chosen by the parties to a consumer lease is a forum that would not otherwise have jurisdiction over the lessee, the choice is not enforceable.

§ 2A-107. Waiver or Renunciation of Claim or Right After Default.

Any claim or right arising out of an alleged default or breach of warranty may be discharged in whole or in part without consideration by a written waiver or renunciation signed and delivered by the aggrieved party.

§ 2A-108. Unconscionability.

(1) If the court as a matter of law finds a lease contract or any clause of a lease contract to have been unconscionable at the time it was made the court may refuse to enforce the lease contract, or it may enforce the remainder of the lease contract without the unconscionable clause, or it may so limit the application of any unconscionable clause as to avoid any unconscionable result.

(2) With respect to a consumer lease, if the court as a matter of law finds that a lease contract or any clause of a lease contract has been induced by unconscionable conduct or that unconscionable conduct has occurred in the collection of a claim arising from a lease contract, the court may grant appropriate relief.

(3) Before making a finding of unconscionability under subsection (1) or (2), the court, on its own motion or that of a party, shall afford the parties a reasonable opportunity to present evidence as to the setting, purpose, and effect of the lease contract or clause thereof, or of the conduct.

(4) In an action in which the lessee claims unconscionability with respect to a consumer lease:

(a) If the court finds unconscionability under subsection (1) or (2), the court shall award reasonable attorney's fees to the lessee.

(b) If the court does not find unconscionability and the lessee claiming unconscionability has brought or maintained an action he [or she] knew to be groundless, the court shall award reasonable attorney's fees to the party against whom the claim is made.

(c) In determining attorney's fees, the amount of the recovery on behalf of the claimant under subsections (1) and (2) is not controlling.

§ 2A-109. Option to Accelerate at Will.

(1) A term providing that one party or his [or her] successor in interest may accelerate payment or performance or require collateral or additional collateral "at will" or "when he [or she] deems himself [or herself] insecure" or in words of similar import must be construed to mean that he [or she] has power to do so only if he [or she] in good faith believes that the prospect of payment or performance is impaired.

(2) With respect to a consumer lease, the burden of establishing good faith under subsection (1) is on the party who exercised the power; otherwise the burden of establishing lack of good faith is on the party against whom the power has been exercised.

Part 2   Formation and Construction of Lease Contract

§ 2A-201. Statute of Frauds.

(1) A lease contract is not enforceable by way of action or defense unless:

(a) the total payments to be made under the lease contract, excluding payments for options to renew or buy, are less than $1,000; or

(b) there is a writing, signed by the party against whom enforcement is sought or by that party's authorized agent, sufficient to indicate that a lease contract has been made between the parties and to describe the goods leased and the lease term.

(2) Any description of leased goods or of the lease term is sufficient and satisfies subsection (1)(b), whether or not it is specific, if it reasonably identifies what is described.

(3) A writing is not insufficient because it omits or incorrectly states a term agreed upon, but the lease contract is not enforceable under subsection (1)(b) beyond the lease term and the quantity of goods shown in the writing.

(4) A lease contract that does not satisfy the requirements of subsection (1), but which is valid in other respects, is enforceable:

(a) if the goods are to be specially manufactured or obtained for the lessee and are not suitable for lease or sale to others in the ordinary course of the lessor's business, and the lessor, before notice of repudiation is received and under circumstances that reasonably indicate that the goods are for the lessee, has made either a substantial beginning of their manufacture or commitments for their procurement;

(b) if the party against whom enforcement is sought admits in that party's pleading, testimony or otherwise in court that a lease contract was made, but the lease contract is not enforceable under this provision beyond the quantity of goods admitted; or

(c) with respect to goods that have been received and accepted by the lessee.

(5) The lease term under a lease contract referred to in subsection (4) is:

(a) if there is a writing signed by the party against whom enforcement is sought or by that party's authorized agent specifying the lease term, the term so specified;

(b) if the party against whom enforcement is sought admits in that party's pleading, testimony, or otherwise in court a lease term, the term so admitted; or

(c) a reasonable lease term.

§ 2A-202. Final Written Expression: Parol or Extrinsic Evidence.

Terms with respect to which the confirmatory memoranda of the parties agree or which are otherwise set forth in a writing intended by the parties as a final expression of their agreement with respect to such terms as are included therein may not be contradicted by evidence of any prior agreement or of a contemporaneous oral agreement but may be explained or supplemented:

(a) by course of dealing or usage of trade or by course of performance; and

(b) by evidence of consistent additional terms unless the court finds the writing to have been intended also as a complete and exclusive statement of the terms of the agreement.

§ 2A-203. Seals Inoperative.

The affixing of a seal to a writing evidencing a lease contract or an offer to enter into a lease contract does not render the writing a sealed instrument and the law with respect to sealed instruments does not apply to the lease contract or offer.

§ 2A-204. Formation in General.

(1) A lease contract may be made in any manner sufficient to show agreement, including conduct by both parties which recognizes the existence of a lease contract.

(2) An agreement sufficient to constitute a lease contract may be found although the moment of its making is undetermined.

(3) Although one or more terms are left open, a lease contract does not fail for indefiniteness if the parties have intended to make a lease contract and there is a reasonably certain basis for giving an appropriate remedy.

§ 2A-205. Firm Offers.
An offer by a merchant to lease goods to or from another person in a signed writing that by its terms gives assurance it will be held open is not revocable, for lack of consideration, during the time stated or, if no time is stated, for a reasonable time, but in no event may the period of irrevocability exceed 3 months. Any such term of assurance on a form supplied by the offeree must be separately signed by the offeror.

§ 2A-206. Offer and Acceptance in Formation of Lease Contract.

(1) Unless otherwise unambiguously indicated by the language or circumstances, an offer to make a lease contract must be construed as inviting acceptance in any manner and by any medium reasonable in the circumstances.

(2) If the beginning of a requested performance is a reasonable mode of acceptance, an offeror who is not notified of acceptance within a reasonable time may treat the offer as having lapsed before acceptance.

§ 2A-207. Course of Performance or Practical Construction.

(1) If a lease contract involves repeated occasions for performance by either party with knowledge of the nature of the performance and opportunity for objection to it by the other, any course of performance accepted or acquiesced in without objection is relevant to determine the meaning of the lease agreement.

(2) The express terms of a lease agreement and any course of performance, as well as any course of dealing and usage of trade, must be construed whenever reasonable as consistent with each other; but if that construction is unreasonable, express terms control course of performance, course of performance controls both course of dealing and usage of trade, and course of dealing controls usage of trade.

(3) Subject to the provisions of Section 2A-208 on modification and waiver, course of performance is relevant to show a waiver or modification of any term inconsistent with the course of performance.

§ 2A-208. Modification, Rescission and Waiver.

(1) An agreement modifying a lease contract needs no consideration to be binding.

(2) A signed lease agreement that excludes modification or rescission except by a signed writing may not be otherwise modified or rescinded, but, except as between merchants, such a requirement on a form supplied by a merchant must be separately signed by the other party.

(3) Although an attempt at modification or rescission does not satisfy the requirements of subsection (2), it may operate as a waiver.

(4) A party who has made a waiver affecting an executory portion of a lease contract may retract the waiver by reasonable notification received by the other party that strict performance will be required of any term waived, unless the retraction would be unjust in view of a material change of position in reliance on the waiver.

§ 2A-209. Lessee Under Finance Lease as Beneficiary of Supply Contract.

(1) The benefit of a supplier's promises to the lessor under the supply contract and of all warranties, whether express or implied, including those of any third party provided in connection with or as part of the supply contract, extends to the lessee to the extent of the lessee's leasehold interest under a finance lease related to the supply contract, but is subject to the terms of the warranty and of the supply contract and all defenses or claims arising therefrom.

(2) The extension of the benefit of a supplier's promises and of warranties to the lessee (Section 2A-209(1)) does not: (i) modify the rights and obligations of the parties to the supply contract, whether arising therefrom or otherwise, or (ii) impose any duty or liability under the supply contract on the lessee.

(3) Any modification or rescission of the supply contract by the supplier and the lessor is effective between the supplier and the lessee unless, before the modification or rescission, the supplier has received notice that the lessee has entered into a finance lease related to the supply contract. If the modification or rescission is effective between the supplier and the lessee, the lessor is deemed to have assumed, in addition to the obligations of the lessor to the lessee under the lease contract, promises of the supplier to the lessor and warranties that were so modified or rescinded as they existed and were available to the lessee before modification or rescission.

(4) In addition to the extension of the benefit of the supplier's promises and of warranties to the lessee under subsection (1), the lessee retains all rights that the lessee may have against the supplier which arise from an agreement between the lessee and the supplier or under other law.

As amended in 1990.

§ 2A-210. Express Warranties.

(1) Express warranties by the lessor are created as follows:

(a) Any affirmation of fact or promise made by the lessor to the lessee which relates to the goods and becomes part of the basis of the bargain creates an express warranty that the goods will conform to the affirmation or promise.

(b) Any description of the goods which is made part of the basis of the bargain creates an express warranty that the goods will conform to the description.

(c) Any sample or model that is made part of the basis of the bargain creates an express warranty that the whole of the goods will conform to the sample or model.

(2) It is not necessary to the creation of an express warranty that the lessor use formal words, such as "warrant" or "guarantee," or that the lessor have a specific intention to make a warranty, but an affirmation merely of the value of the goods or a statement purporting to be merely the lessor's opinion or commendation of the goods does not create a warranty.

§ 2A-211. Warranties Against Interference and Against Infringement; Lessee's Obligation Against Infringement.

(1) There is in a lease contract a warranty that for the lease term no person holds a claim to or interest in the goods that arose from an act or omission of the lessor, other than a claim by way of infringement or the like, which will interfere with the lessee's enjoyment of its leasehold interest.

(2) Except in a finance lease there is in a lease contract by a lessor who is a merchant regularly dealing in goods of the kind a warranty that the goods are delivered free of the rightful claim of any person by way of infringement or the like.

(3) A lessee who furnishes specifications to a lessor or a supplier shall hold the lessor and the supplier harmless against any claim by way of infringement or the like that arises out of compliance with the specifications.

§ 2A-212. Implied Warranty of Merchantability.

(1) Except in a finance lease, a warranty that the goods will be merchantable is implied in a lease contract if the lessor is a merchant with respect to goods of that kind.

(2) Goods to be merchantable must be at least such as

(a) pass without objection in the trade under the description in the lease agreement;

(b) in the case of fungible goods, are of fair average quality within the description;

(c) are fit for the ordinary purposes for which goods of that type are used;

(d) run, within the variation permitted by the lease agreement, of even kind, quality, and quantity within each unit and among all units involved;

(e) are adequately contained, packaged, and labeled as the lease agreement may require; and

(f) conform to any promises or affirmations of fact made on the container or label.

(3) Other implied warranties may arise from course of dealing or usage of trade.

§ 2A-213. Implied Warranty of Fitness for Particular Purpose.
Except in a finance lease, if the lessor at the time the lease contract is made has reason to know of any particular purpose for which the goods are required and that the lessee is relying on the lessor's skill or judgment to select or furnish suitable goods, there is in the lease contract an implied warranty that the goods will be fit for that purpose.

§ 2A-214. Exclusion or Modification of Warranties.

(1) Words or conduct relevant to the creation of an express warranty and words or conduct tending to negate or limit a warranty must be construed wherever reasonable as consistent with each other; but, subject to the provisions of Section 2A-202 on parol or extrinsic evidence, negation or limitation is inoperative to the extent that the construction is unreasonable.

(2) Subject to subsection (3), to exclude or modify the implied warranty of merchantability or any part of it the language must mention "merchantability", be by a writing, and be conspicuous. Subject to subsection (3), to exclude or modify any implied warranty of fitness the exclusion must be by a writing and be conspicuous. Language to exclude all implied warranties of fitness is sufficient if it is in writing, is conspicuous and states, for example, "There is no warranty that the goods will be fit for a particular purpose."

(3) Notwithstanding subsection (2), but subject to subsection (4),

(a) unless the circumstances indicate otherwise, all implied warranties are excluded by expressions like "as is," or "with all faults," or by other language that in common understanding calls the lessee's attention to the exclusion of warranties and makes plain that there is no implied warranty, if in writing and conspicuous;

(b) if the lessee before entering into the lease contract has examined the goods or the sample or model as fully as de-

sired or has refused to examine the goods, there is no implied warranty with regard to defects that an examination ought in the circumstances to have revealed; and

(c) an implied warranty may also be excluded or modified by course of dealing, course of performance, or usage of trade.

(4) To exclude or modify a warranty against interference or against infringement (Section 2A-211) or any part of it, the language must be specific, be by a writing, and be conspicuous, unless the circumstances, including course of performance, course of dealing, or usage of trade, give the lessee reason to know that the goods are being leased subject to a claim or interest of any person.

§ 2A-215. Cumulation and Conflict of Warranties Express or Implied.
Warranties, whether express or implied, must be construed as consistent with each other and as cumulative, but if that construction is unreasonable, the intention of the parties determines which warranty is dominant. In ascertaining that intention the following rules apply:

(a) Exact or technical specifications displace an inconsistent sample or model or general language of description.

(b) A sample from an existing bulk displaces inconsistent general language of description.

(c) Express warranties displace inconsistent implied warranties other than an implied warranty of fitness for a particular purpose.

§ 2A-216. Third-Party Beneficiaries of Express and Implied Warranties.

Alternative A A warranty to or for the benefit of a lessee under this Article, whether express or implied, extends to any natural person who is in the family or household of the lessee or who is a guest in the lessee's home if it is reasonable to expect that such person may use, consume, or be affected by the goods and who is injured in person by breach of the warranty. This section does not displace principles of law and equity that extend a warranty to or for the benefit of a lessee to other persons. The operation of this section may not be excluded, modified, or limited, but an exclusion, modification, or limitation of the warranty, including any with respect to rights and remedies, effective against the lessee is also effective against any beneficiary designated under this section.

Alternative B A warranty to or for the benefit of a lessee under this Article, whether express or implied, extends to any natural person who may reasonably be expected to use, consume, or be affected by the goods and who is injured in person by breach of the warranty. This section does not displace principles of law and equity that extend a warranty to or for the benefit of a lessee to other persons. The operation of this section may not be excluded, modified, or limited, but an exclusion, modification, or limitation of the warranty, including any with respect to rights and remedies, effective against the lessee is also effective against the beneficiary designated under this section.

Alternative C A warranty to or for the benefit of a lessee under this Article, whether express or implied, extends to any person who may reasonably be expected to use, consume, or be affected by the goods and who is injured by breach of the warranty. The operation of this section may not be excluded, modified, or limited with respect to injury to the person of an individual to whom the warranty extends, but an exclusion, modification, or limitation of the warranty, including any with respect to rights and remedies, effective against the lessee is also effective against the beneficiary designated under this section.

§ 2A-217. **Identification.** Identification of goods as goods to which a lease contract refers may be made at any time and in any manner explicitly agreed to by the parties. In the absence of explicit agreement, identification occurs:

(a) when the lease contract is made if the lease contract is for a lease of goods that are existing and identified;
(b) when the goods are shipped, marked, or otherwise designated by the lessor as goods to which the lease contract refers, if the lease contract is for a lease of goods that are not existing and identified; or
(c) when the young are conceived, if the lease contract is for a lease of unborn young of animals.

§ 2A-218. **Insurance and Proceeds.**

(1) A lessee obtains an insurable interest when existing goods are identified to the lease contract even though the goods identified are nonconforming and the lessee has an option to reject them.
(2) If a lessee has an insurable interest only by reason of the lessor's identification of the goods, the lessor, until default or insolvency or notification to the lessee that identification is final, may substitute other goods for those identified.
(3) Notwithstanding a lessee's insurable interest under subsections (1) and (2), the lessor retains an insurable interest until an option to buy has been exercised by the lessee and risk of loss has passed to the lessee.
(4) Nothing in this section impairs any insurable interest recognized under any other statute or rule of law.
(5) The parties by agreement may determine that one or more parties have an obligation to obtain and pay for insurance covering the goods and by agreement may determine the beneficiary of the proceeds of the insurance.

§ 2A-219. **Risk of Loss.**

(1) Except in the case of a finance lease, risk of loss is retained by the lessor and does not pass to the lessee. In the case of a finance lease, risk of loss passes to the lessee.
(2) Subject to the provisions of this Article on the effect of default on risk of loss (Section 2A-220), if risk of loss is to pass to the lessee and the time of passage is not stated, the following rules apply:

(a) If the lease contract requires or authorizes the goods to be shipped by carrier

(i) and it does not require delivery at a particular destination, the risk of loss passes to the lessee when the goods are duly delivered to the carrier; but
(ii) if it does require delivery at a particular destination and the goods are there duly tendered while in the possession of the carrier, the risk of loss passes to the lessee when the goods are there duly so tendered as to enable the lessee to take delivery.
(b) If the goods are held by a bailee to be delivered without being moved, the risk of loss passes to the lessee on acknowledgment by the bailee of the lessee's right to possession of the goods.
(c) In any case not within subsection (a) or (b), the risk of loss passes to the lessee on the lessee's receipt of the goods if the lessor, or, in the case of a finance lease, the supplier, is a merchant; otherwise the risk passes to the lessee on tender of delivery.

§ 2A-220. **Effect of Default on Risk of Loss.**

(1) Where risk of loss is to pass to the lessee and the time of passage is not stated:

(a) If a tender or delivery of goods so fails to conform to the lease contract as to give a right of rejection, the risk of their loss remains with the lessor, or, in the case of a finance lease, the supplier, until cure or acceptance.
(b) If the lessee rightfully revokes acceptance, he [or she], to the extent of any deficiency in his [or her] effective insurance coverage, may treat the risk of loss as having remained with the lessor from the beginning.

(2) Whether or not risk of loss is to pass to the lessee, if the lessee as to conforming goods already identified to a lease contract repudiates or is otherwise in default under the lease contract, the lessor, or, in the case of a finance lease, the supplier, to the extent of any deficiency in his [or her] effective insurance coverage may treat the risk of loss as resting on the lessee for a commercially reasonable time.

§ 2A-221. **Casualty to Identified Goods.** If a lease contract requires goods identified when the lease contract is made, and the goods suffer casualty without fault of the lessee, the lessor or the supplier before delivery, or the goods suffer casualty before risk of loss passes to the lessee pursuant to the lease agreement or Section 2A-219, then:

(a) if the loss is total, the lease contract is avoided; and
(b) if the loss is partial or the goods have so deteriorated as to no longer conform to the lease contract, the lessee may nevertheless demand inspection and at his [or her] option either treat the lease contract as avoided or, except in a finance lease that is not a consumer lease, accept the goods with due allowance from the rent payable for the balance of the lease term for the deterioration or the deficiency in quantity but without further right against the lessor.

Part 3 Effect of Lease Contract

§ 2A-301. **Enforceability of Lease Contract.** Except as otherwise provided in this Article, a lease contract is effective and enforceable according to its terms between the parties, against purchasers of the goods and against creditors of the parties.

§ 2A-302. **Title to and Possession of Goods.** Except as otherwise provided in this Article, each provision of this Article applies whether the lessor or a third party has title to the goods, and whether the lessor, the lessee, or a third party has possession of the goods, notwithstanding any statute or rule of law that possession or the absence of possession is fraudulent.

§ 2A-303. **Alienability of Party's Interest Under Lease Contract or of Lessor's Residual Interest in Goods; Delegation of Performance; Transfer of Rights.**

(1) As used in this section "creation of a security interest" includes the sale of a lease contract that is subject to Article 9, Secured Transactions, by reason of Section 9-102(1)(b).
(2) Except as provided in subsections (3) and (4), a provision in a lease agreement which (i) prohibits the voluntary or involuntary transfer, including a transfer by sale, sublease, creation or enforcement of a security interest, or attachment, levy, or other judicial process, of an interest of a party under the lease contract or of the lessor's residual interest in the goods, or (ii) makes such a transfer an event of default, gives rise to the rights and remedies provided in subsection (5), but a transfer that is prohibited or is an event of default under the lease agreement is otherwise effective.

(3) A provision in a lease agreement which (i) prohibits the creation or enforcement of a security interest in an interest of a party under the lease contract or in the lessor's residual interest in the goods, or (ii) makes such a transfer an event of default, is not enforceable unless, and then only to the extent that, there is an actual transfer by the lessee of the lessee's right of possession or use of the goods in violation of the provision or an actual delegation of a material performance of either party to the lease contract in violation of the provision. Neither the granting nor the enforcement of a security interest in (i) the lessor's interest under the lease contract or (ii) the lessor's residual interest in the goods is a transfer that materially impairs the prospect of obtaining return performance by, materially changes the duty of, or materially increases the burden or risk imposed on, the lessee within the purview of subsection (5) unless, and then only to the extent that, there is an actual delegation of a material performance of the lessor.

(4) A provision in a lease agreement which (i) prohibits a transfer of a right to damages for default with respect to the whole lease contract or of a right to payment arising out of the transferor's due performance of the transferor's entire obligation, or (ii) makes such a transfer an event of default, is not enforceable, and such a transfer is not a transfer that materially impairs the prospect of obtaining return performance by, materially changes the duty of, or materially increases the burden or risk imposed on, the other party to the lease contract within the purview of subsection (5).

(5) Subject to subsections (3) and (4):

(a) if a transfer is made which is made an event of default under a lease agreement, the party to the lease contract not making the transfer, unless that party waives the default or otherwise agrees, has the rights and remedies described in Section 2A-501(2);

(b) if paragraph (a) is not applicable and if a transfer is made that (i) is prohibited under a lease agreement or (ii) materially impairs the prospect of obtaining return performance by, materially changes the duty of, or materially increases the burden or risk imposed on, the other party to the lease contract, unless the party not making the transfer agrees at any time to the transfer in the lease contract or otherwise, then, except as limited by contract, (i) the transferor is liable to the party not making the transfer for damages caused by the transfer to the extent that the damages could not reasonably be prevented by the party not making the transfer and (ii) a court having jurisdiction may grant other appropriate relief, including cancellation of the lease contract or an injunction against the transfer.

(6) A transfer of "the lease" or of "all my rights under the lease", or a transfer in similar general terms, is a transfer of rights and, unless the language or the circumstances, as in a transfer for security, indicate the contrary, the transfer is a delegation of duties by the transferor to the transferee. Acceptance by the transferee constitutes a promise by the transferee to perform those duties. The promise is enforceable by either the transferor or the other party to the lease contract.

(7) Unless otherwise agreed by the lessor and the lessee, a delegation of performance does not relieve the transferor as against the other party of any duty to perform or of any liability for default.

(8) In a consumer lease, to prohibit the transfer of an interest of a party under the lease contract or to make a transfer an event of default, the language must be specific, by a writing, and conspicuous.

As amended in 1990.

§ 2A-304. **Subsequent Lease of Goods by Lessor.**

(1) Subject to Section 2A-303, a subsequent lessee from a lessor of goods under an existing lease contract obtains, to the extent of the leasehold interest transferred, the leasehold interest in the goods that the lessor had or had power to transfer, and except as provided in subsection (2) and Section 2A-527(4), takes subject to the existing lease contract. A lessor with voidable title has power to transfer a good leasehold interest to a good faith subsequent lessee for value, but only to the extent set forth in the preceding sentence. If goods have been delivered under a transaction of purchase, the lessor has that power even though:

(a) the lessor's transferor was deceived as to the identity of the lessor;
(b) the delivery was in exchange for a check which is later dishonored;
(c) it was agreed that the transaction was to be a "cash sale"; or
(d) the delivery was procured through fraud punishable as larcenous under the criminal law.

(2) A subsequent lessee in the ordinary course of business from a lessor who is a merchant dealing in goods of that kind to whom the goods were entrusted by the existing lessee of that lessor before the interest of the subsequent lessee became enforceable against that lessor obtains, to the extent of the leasehold interest transferred, all of that lessor's and the existing lessee's rights to the goods, and takes free of the existing lease contract.

(3) A subsequent lessee from the lessor of goods that are subject to an existing lease contract and are covered by a certificate of title issued under a statute of this State or of another jurisdiction takes no greater rights than those provided both by this section and by the certificate of title statute.

As amended in 1990.

§ 2A-305. **Sale or Sublease of Goods by Lessee.**

(1) Subject to the provisions of Section 2A-303, a buyer or sublessee from the lessee of goods under an existing lease contract obtains, to the extent of the interest transferred, the leasehold interest in the goods that the lessee had or had power to transfer, and except as provided in subsection (2) and Section 2A-511(4), takes subject to the existing lease contract. A lessee with a voidable leasehold interest has power to transfer a good leasehold interest to a good faith buyer for value or a good faith sublessee for value, but only to the extent set forth in the preceding sentence. When goods have been delivered under a transaction of lease the lessee has that power even though:

(a) the lessor was deceived as to the identity of the lessee;
(b) the delivery was in exchange for a check which is later dishonored; or
(c) the delivery was procured through fraud punishable as larcenous under the criminal law.

(2) A buyer in the ordinary course of business or a sublessee in the ordinary course of business from a lessee who is a merchant dealing in goods of that kind to whom the goods were entrusted by the lessor obtains, to the extent of the interest transferred, all of the lessor's and lessee's rights to the goods, and takes free of the existing lease contract.

(3) A buyer or sublessee from the lessee of goods that are subject to an existing lease contract and are covered by a certificate of title issued under a statute of this State or of another jurisdiction takes no greater rights than those pro-

vided both by this section and by the certificate of title statute.

§ 2A-306. **Priority of Certain Liens Arising by Operation of Law.** If a person in the ordinary course of his [or her] business furnishes services or materials with respect to goods subject to a lease contract, a lien upon those goods in the possession of that person given by statute or rule of law for those materials or services takes priority over any interest of the lessor or lessee under the lease contract or this Article unless the lien is created by statute and the statute provides otherwise or unless the lien is created by rule of law and the rule of law provides otherwise.

§ 2A-307. **Priority of Liens Arising by Attachment or Levy on, Security Interests in, and Other Claims to Goods.**

(1) Except as otherwise provided in Section 2A-306, a creditor of a lessee takes subject to the lease contract.

(2) Except as otherwise provided in subsections (3) and (4) and in Sections 2A-306 and 2A-308, a creditor of a lessor takes subject to the lease contract unless:

(a) the creditor holds a lien that attached to the goods before the lease contract became enforceable,
(b) the creditor holds a security interest in the goods and the lessee did not give value and receive delivery of the goods without knowledge of the security interest; or
(c) the creditor holds a security interest in the goods which was perfected (Section 9-303) before the lease contract became enforceable.

(3) A lessee in the ordinary course of business takes the leasehold interest free of a security interest in the goods created by the lessor even though the security interest is perfected (Section 9-303) and the lessee knows of its existence.

(4) A lessee other than a lessee in the ordinary course of business takes the leasehold interest free of a security interest to the extent that it secures future advances made after the secured party acquires knowledge of the lease or more than 45 days after the lease contract becomes enforceable, whichever first occurs, unless the future advances are made pursuant to a commitment entered into without knowledge of the lease and before the expiration of the 45-day period.

As amended in 1990.

§ 2A-308. **Special Rights of Creditors.**

(1) A creditor of a lessor in possession of goods subject to a lease contract may treat the lease contract as void if as against the creditor retention of possession by the lessor is fraudulent under any statute or rule of law, but retention of possession in good faith and current course of trade by the lessor for a commercially reasonable time after the lease contract becomes enforceable is not fraudulent.

(2) Nothing in this Article impairs the rights of creditors of a lessor if the lease contract (a) becomes enforceable, not in current course of trade but in satisfaction of or as security for a pre-existing claim for money, security, or the like, and (b) is made under circumstances which under any statute or rule of law apart from this Article would constitute the transaction a fraudulent transfer or voidable preference.

(3) A creditor of a seller may treat a sale or an identification of goods to a contract for sale as void if as against the creditor retention of possession by the seller is fraudulent under any statute or rule of law, but retention of possession of the goods pursuant to a lease contract entered into by the seller as lessee and the buyer as lessor in connection with the sale or identifi-

cation of the goods is not fraudulent if the buyer bought for value and in good faith.

§ 2A-309. **Lessor's and Lessee's Rights When Goods Become Fixtures.**

(1) In this section:

(a) goods are "fixtures" when they become so related to particular real estate that an interest in them arises under real estate law;
(b) a "fixture filing" is the filing, in the office where a mortgage on the real estate would be filed or recorded, of a financing statement covering goods that are or are to become fixtures and conforming to the requirements of Section 9-402(5);
(c) a lease is a "purchase money lease" unless the lessee has possession or use of the goods or the right to possession or use of the goods before the lease agreement is enforceable;
(d) a mortgage is a "construction mortgage" to the extent it secures an obligation incurred for the construction of an improvement on land including the acquisition cost of the land, if the recorded writing so indicates; and
(e) "encumbrance" includes real estate mortgages and other liens on real estate and all other rights in real estate that are not ownership interests.

(2) Under this Article a lease may be of goods that are fixtures or may continue in goods that become fixtures, but no lease exists under this Article of ordinary building materials incorporated into an improvement on land.

(3) This Article does not prevent creation of a lease of fixtures pursuant to real estate law.

(4) The perfected interest of a lessor of fixtures has priority over a conflicting interest of an encumbrancer or owner of the real estate if:

(a) the lease is a purchase money lease, the conflicting interest of the emcumbrancer or owner arises before the goods become fixtures, the interest of the lessor is perfected by a fixture filing before the goods become fixtures or within ten days thereafter, and the lessee has an interest of record in the real estate or is in possession of the real estate; or
(b) the interest of the lessor is perfected by a fixture filing before the interest of the encumbrancer or owner is of record, the lessor's interest has priority over any conflicting interest of a predecessor in title of the encumbrancer or owner, and the lessee has an interest of record in the real estate or is in possession of the real estate.

(5) The interest of a lessor of fixtures, whether or not perfected, has priority over the conflicting interest of an encumbrancer or owner of the real estate if:

(a) the fixtures are readily removable factory or office machines, readily removable equipment that is not primarily used or leased for use in the operation of the real estate, or readily removable replacements of domestic appliances that are goods subject to a consumer lease, and before the goods become fixtures the lease contract is enforceable; or
(b) the conflicting interest is a lien on the real estate obtained by legal or equitable proceedings after the lease contract is enforceable; or
(c) the encumbrancer or owner has consented in writing to the lease or has disclaimed an interest in the goods as fixtures; or
(d) the lessee has a right to remove the goods as against the encumbrancer or owner. If the lessee's right to remove ter-

minates, the priority of the interest of the lessor continues for a reasonable time.

(6) Notwithstanding subsection (4)(a) but otherwise subject to subsections (4) and (5), the interest of a lessor of fixtures, including the lessor's residual interest, is subordinate to the conflicting interest of an encumbrancer of the real estate under a construction mortgage recorded before the goods become fixtures if the goods become fixtures before the completion of the construction. To the extent given to refinance a construction mortgage, the conflicting interest of an encumbrancer of the real estate under a mortgage has this priority to the same extent as the encumbrancer of the real estate under the construction mortgage.

(7) In cases not within the preceding subsections, priority between the interest of a lessor of fixtures, including the lessor's residual interest, and the conflicting interest of an encumbrancer or owner of the real estate who is not the lessee is determined by the priority rules governing conflicting interests in real estate.

(8) If the interest of a lessor of fixtures, including the lessor's residual interest, has priority over all conflicting interests of all owners and encumbrancers of the real estate, the lessor or the lessee may (i) on default, expiration, termination, or cancellation of the lease agreement but subject to the agreement and this Article, or (ii) if necessary to enforce other rights and remedies of the lessor or lessee under this Article, remove the goods from the real estate, free and clear of all conflicting interests of all owners and encumbrancers of the real estate, but the lessor or lessee must reimburse any encumbrancer or owner of the real estate who is not the lessee and who has not otherwise agreed for the cost of repair of any physical injury, but not for any diminution in value of the real estate caused by the absence of the goods removed or by any necessity of replacing them. A person entitled to reimbursement may refuse permission to remove until the party seeking removal gives adequate security for the performance of this obligation.

(9) Even though the lease agreement does not create a security interest, the interest of a lessor of fixtures, including the lessor's residual interest, is perfected by filing a financing statement as a fixture filing for leased goods that are or are to become fixtures in accordance with the relevant provisions of the Article on Secured Transactions (Article 9).

As amended in 1990.

§ 2A-310. **Lessor's and Lessee's Rights When Goods Become Accessions.**

(1) Goods are "accessions" when they are installed in or affixed to other goods.
(2) The interest of a lessor or a lessee under a lease contract entered into before the goods became accessions is superior to all interests in the whole except as stated in subsection (4).
(3) The interest of a lessor or a lessee under a lease contract entered into at the time or after the goods became accessions is superior to all subsequently acquired interests in the whole except as stated in subsection (4) but is subordinate to interests in the whole existing at the time the lease contract was made unless the holders of such interests in the whole have in writing consented to the lease or disclaimed an interest in the goods as part of the whole.
(4) The interest of a lessor or a lessee under a lease contract described in subsection (2) or (3) is subordinate to the interest of

(a) a buyer in the ordinary course of business or a lessee in the ordinary course of business of any interest in the whole

acquired after the goods became accessions; or
(b) a creditor with a security interest in the whole perfected before the lease contract was made to the extent that the creditor makes subsequent advances without knowledge of the lease contract.

(5) When under subsections (2) or (3) and (4) a lessor or a lessee of accessions holds an interest that is superior to all interests in the whole, the lessor or the lessee may (a) on default, expiration, termination, or cancellation of the lease contract by the other party but subject to the provisions of the lease contract and this Article, or (b) if necessary to enforce his [or her] other rights and remedies under this Article, remove the goods from the whole, free and clear of all interests in the whole, but he [or she] must reimburse any holder of an interest in the whole who is not the lessee and who has not otherwise agreed for the cost of repair of any physical injury but not for any diminution in value of the whole caused by the absence of the goods removed or by any necessity for replacing them. A person entitled to reimbursement may refuse permission to remove until the party seeking removal gives adequate security for the performance of this obligation.

§ 2A-311. **Priority Subject to Subordination.** Nothing in this Article prevents subordination by agreement by any person entitled to priority.

As added in 1990.

Part 4 Performance of Lease Contract: Repudiated, Substituted and Excused

§ 2A-401. **Insecurity: Adequate Assurance of Performance.**

(1) A lease contract imposes an obligation on each party that the other's expectation of receiving due performance will not be impaired.
(2) If reasonable grounds for insecurity arise with respect to the performance of either party, the insecure party may demand in writing adequate assurance of due performance. Until the insecure party receives that assurance, if commercially reasonable the insecure party may suspend any performance for which he [or she] has not already received the agreed return.
(3) A repudiation of the lease contract occurs if assurance of due performance adequate under the circumstances of the particular case is not provided to the insecure party within a reasonable time, not to exceed 30 days after receipt of a demand by the other party.
(4) Between merchants, the reasonableness of grounds for insecurity and the adequacy of any assurance offered must be determined according to commercial standards.
(5) Acceptance of any nonconforming delivery or payment does not prejudice the aggrieved party's right to demand adequate assurance of future performance.

§ 2A-402. **Anticipatory Repudiation.** If either party repudiates a lease contract with respect to a performance not yet due under the lease contract, the loss of which performance will substantially impair the value of the lease contract to the other, the aggrieved party may:

(a) for a commercially reasonable time, await retraction of repudiation and performance by the repudiating party;
(b) make demand pursuant to Section 2A-401 and await assurance of future performance adequate under the circumstances of the particular case; or
(c) resort to any right or remedy upon default under the lease contract or this Article, even though the aggrieved party has notified the repudiating party that the aggrieved party would

await the repudiating party's performance and assurance and has urged retraction. In addition, whether or not the aggrieved party is pursuing one of the foregoing remedies, the aggrieved party may suspend performance or, if the aggrieved party is the lessor, proceed in accordance with the provisions of this Article on the lessor's right to identify goods to the lease contract notwithstanding default or to salvage unfinished goods (Section 2A-524).

§ 2A-403. Retraction of Anticipatory Repudiation.

(1) Until the repudiating party's next performance is due, the repudiating party can retract the repudiation unless, since the repudiation, the aggrieved party has cancelled the lease contract or materially changed the aggrieved party's position or otherwise indicated that the aggrieved party considers the repudiation final.
(2) Retraction may be by any method that clearly indicates to the aggrieved party that the repudiating party intends to perform under the lease contract and includes any assurance demanded under Section 2A-401.
(3) Retraction reinstates a repudiating party's rights under a lease contract with due excuse and allowance to the aggrieved party for any delay occasioned by the repudiation.

§ 2A-404. Substituted Performance.

(1) If without fault of the lessee, the lessor and the supplier, the agreed berthing, loading, or unloading facilities fail or the agreed type of carrier becomes unavailable or the agreed manner of delivery otherwise becomes commercially impracticable, but a commercially reasonable substitute is available, the substitute performance must be tendered and accepted.
(2) If the agreed means or manner of payment fails because of domestic or foreign governmental regulation:

(a) the lessor may withhold or stop delivery or cause the supplier to withhold or stop delivery unless the lessee provides a means or manner of payment that is commercially a substantial equivalent; and
(b) if delivery has already been taken, payment by the means or in the manner provided by the regulation discharges the lessee's obligation unless the regulation is discriminatory, oppressive, or predatory.

§ 2A-405. Excused Performance. Subject to Section 2A-404 on substituted performance, the following rules apply:

(a) Delay in delivery or nondelivery in whole or in part by a lessor or a supplier who complies with paragraphs (b) and (c) is not a default under the lease contract if performance as agreed has been made impracticable by the occurrence of a contingency the nonoccurrence of which was a basic assumption on which the lease contract was made or by compliance in good faith with any applicable foreign or domestic governmental regulation or order, whether or not the regulation or order later proves to be invalid.
(b) If the causes mentioned in paragraph (a) affect only part of the lessor's or the supplier's capacity to perform, he [or she] shall allocate production and deliveries among his [or her] customers but at his [or her] option may include regular customers not then under contract for sale or lease as well as his [or her] own requirements for further manufacture. He [or she] may so allocate in any manner that is fair and reasonable.
(c) The lessor seasonably shall notify the lessee and in the case of a finance lease the supplier seasonably shall notify the lessor and the lessee, if known, that there will be delay or nondelivery

and, if allocation is required under paragraph (b), of the estimated quota thus made available for the lessee.

§ 2A-406. Procedure on Excused Performance.

(1) If the lessee receives notification of a material or indefinite delay or an allocation justified under Section 2A-405, the lessee may by written notification to the lessor as to any goods involved, and with respect to all of the goods if under an installment lease contract the value of the whole lease contract is substantially impaired (Section 2A-510):

(a) terminate the lease contract (Section 2A-505(2)); or
(b) except in a finance lease that is not a consumer lease, modify the lease contract by accepting the available quota in substitution, with due allowance from the rent payable for the balance of the lease term for the deficiency but without further right against the lessor.

(2) If, after receipt of a notification from the lessor under Section 2A-405, the lessee fails so to modify the lease agreement within a reasonable time not exceeding 30 days, the lease contract lapses with respect to any deliveries affected.

§ 2A-407. Irrevocable Promises: Finance Leases.

(1) In the case of a finance lease that is not a consumer lease the lessee's promises under the lease contract become irrevocable and independent upon the lessee's acceptance of the goods.
(2) A promise that has become irrevocable and independent under subsection (1):

(a) is effective and enforceable between the parties, and by or against third parties including assignees of the parties; and
(b) is not subject to cancellation, termination, modification, repudiation, excuse, or substitution without the consent of the party to whom the promise runs.

(3) This section does not affect the validity under any other law of a covenant in any lease contract making the lessee's promises irrevocable and independent upon the lessee's acceptance of the goods.

As amended in 1990.

Part 5 Default

A. In General

§ 2A-501. Default: Procedure.

(1) Whether the lessor or the lessee is in default under a lease contract is determined by the lease agreement and this Article.
(2) If the lessor or the lessee is in default under the lease contract, the party seeking enforcement has rights and remedies as provided in this Article and, except as limited by this Article, as provided in the lease agreement.
(3) If the lessor or the lessee is in default under the lease contract, the party seeking enforcement may reduce the party's claim to judgment, or otherwise enforce the lease contract by self-help or any available judicial procedure or nonjudicial procedure, including administrative proceeding, arbitration, or the like, in accordance with this Article.
(4) Except as otherwise provided in Section 1-106(1) or this Article or the lease agreement, the rights and remedies referred to in subsections (2) and (3) are cumulative.
(5) If the lease agreement covers both real property and goods, the party seeking enforcement may proceed under this Part as to the goods, or under other applicable law as to both the real property and the goods in accordance with that party's rights

and remedies in respect of the real property, in which case this Part does not apply.

As amended in 1990.

§ 2A-502. **Notice After Default.** Except as otherwise provided in this Article or the lease agreement, the lessor or lessee in default under the lease contract is not entitled to notice of default or notice of enforcement from the other party to the lease agreement.

§ 2A-503. **Modification or Impairment of Rights and Remedies.**

(1) Except as otherwise provided in this Article, the lease agreement may include rights and remedies for default in addition to or in substitution for those provided in this Article and may limit or alter the measure of damages recoverable under this Article.

(2) Resort to a remedy provided under this Article or in the lease agreement is optional unless the remedy is expressly agreed to be exclusive. If circumstances cause an exclusive or limited remedy to fail of its essential purpose, or provision for an exclusive remedy is unconscionable, remedy may be had as provided in this Article.

(3) Consequential damages may be liquidated under Section 2A-504, or may otherwise be limited, altered, or excluded unless the limitation, alteration, or exclusion is unconscionable. Limitation, alteration, or exclusion of consequential damages for injury to the person in the case of consumer goods is prima facie unconscionable but limitation, alteration, or exclusion of damages where the loss is commercial is not prima facie unconscionable.

(4) Rights and remedies on default by the lessor or the lessee with respect to any obligation or promise collateral or ancillary to the lease contract are not impaired by this Article.

As amended in 1990.

§ 2A-504. **Liquidation of Damages.**

(1) Damages payable by either party for default, or any other act or omission, including indemnity for loss or diminution of anticipated tax benefits or loss or damage to lessor's residual interest, may be liquidated in the lease agreement but only at an amount or by a formula that is reasonable in light of the then anticipated harm caused by the default or other act or omission.

(2) If the lease agreement provides for liquidation of damages, and such provision does not comply with subsection (1), or such provision is an exclusive or limited remedy that circumstances cause to fail of its essential purpose, remedy may be had as provided in this Article.

(3) If the lessor justifiably withholds or stops delivery of goods because of the lessee's default or insolvency (Section 2A-525 or 2A-526), the lessee is entitled to restitution of any amount by which the sum of his [or her] payments exceeds:

    (a) the amount to which the lessor is entitled by virtue of terms liquidating the lessor's damages in accordance with subsection (1); or

    (b) in the absence of those terms, 20 percent of the then present value of the total rent the lessee was obligated to pay for the balance of the lease term, or, in the case of a consumer lease, the lesser of such amount or $500.

(4) A lessee's right to restitution under subsection (3) is subject to offset to the extent the lessor establishes:

    (a) a right to recover damages under the provisions of this Article other than subsection (1); and

    (b) the amount or value of any benefits received by the lessee directly or indirectly by reason of the lease contract.

§ 2A-505. **Cancellation and Termination and Effect of Cancellation, Termination, Rescission, or Fraud on Rights and Remedies.**

(1) On cancellation of the lease contract, all obligations that are still executory on both sides are discharged, but any right based on prior default or performance survives, and the canceling party also retains any remedy for default of the whole lease contract or any unperformed balance.

(2) On termination of the lease contract, all obligations that are still executory on both sides are discharged but any right based on prior default or performance survives.

(3) Unless the contrary intention clearly appears, expressions of "cancellation," "rescission," or the like of the lease contract may not be construed as a renunciation or discharge of any claim in damages for an antecedent default.

(4) Rights and remedies for material misrepresentation or fraud include all rights and remedies available under this Article for default.

(5) Neither rescission nor a claim for rescission of the lease contract nor rejection or return of the goods may bar or be deemed inconsistent with a claim for damages or other right or remedy.

§ 2A-506. **Statute of Limitations.**

(1) An action for default under a lease contract, including breach of warranty or indemnity, must be commenced within 4 years after the cause of action accrued. By the original lease contract the parties may reduce the period of limitation to not less than one year.

(2) A cause of action for default accrues when the act or omission on which the default or breach of warranty is based is or should have been discovered by the aggrieved party, or when the default occurs, whichever is later. A cause of action for indemnity accrues when the act or omission on which the claim for indemnity is based is or should have been discovered by the indemnified party, whichever is later.

(3) If an action commenced within the time limited by subsection (1) is so terminated as to leave available a remedy by another action for the same default or breach of warranty or indemnity, the other action may be commenced after the expiration of the time limited and within 6 months after the termination of the first action unless the termination resulted from voluntary discontinuance or from dismissal for failure or neglect to prosecute.

(4) This section does not alter the law on tolling of the statute of limitations nor does it apply to causes of action that have accrued before this Article becomes effective.

§ 2A-507. **Proof of Market Rent: Time and Place.**

(1) Damages based on market rent (Section 2A-519 or 2A-528) are determined according to the rent for the use of the goods concerned for a lease term identical to the remaining lease term of the original lease agreement and prevailing at the times specified in Sections 2A-519 and 2A-528.

(2) If evidence of rent for the use of the goods concerned for a lease term identical to the remaining lease term of the original lease agreement and prevailing at the times or places described in this Article is not readily available, the rent prevailing within any reasonable time before or after the time described or at any other place or for a different lease term which in commercial judgment or under usage of trade would serve as a reasonable substitute for the one described may be used, making any

proper allowance for the difference, including the cost of transporting the goods to or from the other place.

(3) Evidence of a relevant rent prevailing at a time or place or for a lease term other than the one described in this Article offered by one party is not admissible unless and until he [or she] has given the other party notice the court finds sufficient to prevent unfair surprise.

(4) If the prevailing rent or value of any goods regularly leased in any established market is in issue, reports in official publications or trade journals or in newspapers or periodicals of general circulation published as the reports of that market are admissible in evidence. The circumstances of the preparation of the report may be shown to affect its weight but not its admissibility.

As amended in 1990.

B. Default by Lessor

§ 2A-508.　Lessee's Remedies.

(1) If a lessor fails to deliver the goods in conformity to the lease contract (Section 2A-509) or repudiates the lease contract (Section 2A-402), or a lessee rightfully rejects the goods (Section 2A-509) or justifiably revokes acceptance of the goods (Section 2A-517), then with respect to any goods involved, and with respect to all of the goods if under an installment lease contract the value of the whole lease contract is substantially impaired (Section 2A-510), the lessor is in default under the lease contract and the lessee may:

(a) cancel the lease contract (Section 2A-505(1));
(b) recover so much of the rent and security as has been paid and is just under the circumstances;
(c) cover and recover damages as to all goods affected whether or not they have been identified to the lease contract (Sections 2A-518 and 2A-520), or recover damages for nondelivery (Sections 2A-519 and 2A-520);
(d) exercise any other rights or pursue any other remedies provided in the lease contract.

(2) If a lessor fails to deliver the goods in conformity to the lease contract or repudiates the lease contract, the lessee may also:

(a) if the goods have been identified, recover them (Section 2A-522); or
(b) in a proper case, obtain specific performance or replevy the goods (Section 2A-521).

(3) If a lessor is otherwise in default under a lease contract, the lessee may exercise the rights and pursue the remedies provided in the lease contract, which may include a right to cancel the lease, and in Section 2A-519(3).

(4) If a lessor has breached a warranty, whether express or implied, the lessee may recover damages (Section 2A-519(4)).

(5) On rightful rejection or justifiable revocation of acceptance, a lessee has a security interest in goods in the lessee's possession or control for any rent and security that has been paid and any expenses reasonably incurred in their inspection, receipt, transportation, and care and custody and may hold those goods and dispose of them in good faith and in a commercially reasonable manner, subject to Section 2A-527(5).

(6) Subject to the provisions of Section 2A-407, a lessee, on notifying the lessor of the lessee's intention to do so, may deduct all or any part of the damages resulting from any default under the lease contract from any part of the rent still due under the same lease contract.

As amended in 1990.

§ 2A-509.　Lessee's Rights on Improper Delivery; Rightful Rejection.

(1) Subject to the provisions of Section 2A-510 on default in installment lease contracts, if the goods or the tender or delivery fail in any respect to conform to the lease contract, the lessee may reject or accept the goods or accept any commercial unit or units and reject the rest of the goods.

(2) Rejection of goods is ineffective unless it is within a reasonable time after tender or delivery of the goods and the lessee seasonably notifies the lessor.

§ 2A-510.　Installment Lease Contracts: Rejection and Default.

(1) Under an installment lease contract a lessee may reject any delivery that is nonconforming if the nonconformity substantially impairs the value of that delivery and cannot be cured or the nonconformity is a defect in the required documents; but if the nonconformity does not fall within subsection (2) and the lessor or the supplier gives adequate assurance of its cure, the lessee must accept that delivery.

(2) Whenever nonconformity or default with respect to one or more deliveries substantially impairs the value of the installment lease contract as a whole there is a default with respect to the whole. But, the aggrieved party reinstates the installment lease contract as a whole if the aggrieved party accepts a nonconforming delivery without seasonably notifying of cancellation or brings an action with respect only to past deliveries or demands performance as to future deliveries.

§ 2A-511.　Merchant Lessee's Duties as to Rightfully Rejected Goods.

(1) Subject to any security interest of a lessee (Section 2A-508(5)), if a lessor or a supplier has no agent or place of business at the market of rejection, a merchant lessee, after rejection of goods in his [or her] possession or control, shall follow any reasonable instructions received from the lessor or the supplier with respect to the goods. In the absence of those instructions, a merchant lessee shall make reasonable efforts to sell, lease, or otherwise dispose of the goods for the lessor's account if they threaten to decline in value speedily. Instructions are not reasonable if on demand indemnity for expenses is not forthcoming.

(2) If a merchant lessee (subsection (1)) or any other lessee (Section 2A-512) disposes of goods, he [or she] is entitled to reimbursement either from the lessor or the supplier or out of the proceeds for reasonable expenses of caring for and disposing of the goods and, if the expenses include no disposition commission, to such commission as is usual in the trade, or if there is none, to a reasonable sum not exceeding 10 percent of the gross proceeds.

(3) In complying with this section or Section 2A-512, the lessee is held only to good faith. Good faith conduct hereunder is neither acceptance or conversion nor the basis of an action for damages.

(4) A purchaser who purchases in good faith from a lessee pursuant to this section or Section 2A-512 takes the goods free of any rights of the lessor and the supplier even though the lessee fails to comply with one or more of the requirements of this Article.

§ 2A-512.　Lessee's Duties as to Rightfully Rejected Goods.

(1) Except as otherwise provided with respect to goods that threaten to decline in value speedily (Section 2A-511) and subject to any security interest of a lessee (Section 2A-508(5)):

(a) the lessee, after rejection of goods in the lessee's possession, shall hold them with reasonable care at the lessor's or the supplier's disposition for a reasonable time after the lessee's seasonable notification of rejection;

(b) If the lessor or the supplier gives no instructions within a reasonable time after notification of rejection, the lessee may store the rejected goods for the lessor's or the supplier's account or ship them to the lessor or the supplier or dispose of them for the lessor's or the supplier's account with reimbursement in the manner provided in Section 2A-511; but

(c) the lessee has no further obligations with regard to goods rightfully rejected.

(2) Action by the lessee pursuant to subsection (1) is not acceptance or conversion.

§ 2A-513. Cure by Lessor of Improper Tender or Delivery; Replacement.

(1) If any tender or delivery by the lessor or the supplier is rejected because nonconforming and the time for performance has not yet expired, the lessor or the supplier may seasonably notify the lessee of the lessor's or the supplier's intention to cure and may then make a conforming delivery within the time provided in the lease contract.

(2) If the lessee rejects a nonconforming tender that the lessor or the supplier had reasonable grounds to believe would be acceptable with or without money allowance, the lessor or the supplier may have a further reasonable time to substitute a conforming tender if he [or she] seasonably notifies the lessee.

§ 2A-514. Waiver of Lessee's Objections.

(1) In rejecting goods, a lessee's failure to state a particular defect that is ascertainable by reasonable inspection precludes the lessee from relying on the defect to justify rejection or to establish default:

(a) if, stated seasonably, the lessor or the supplier could have cured it (Section 2A-513); or

(b) between merchants if the lessor or the supplier after rejection has made a request in writing for a full and final written statement of all defects on which the lessee proposes to rely.

(2) A lessee's failure to reserve rights when paying rent or other consideration against documents precludes recovery of the payment for defects apparent on the face of the documents.

§ 2A-515. Acceptance of Goods.

(1) Acceptance of goods occurs after the lessee has had a reasonable opportunity to inspect the goods and

(a) the lessee signifies or acts with respect to the goods in a manner that signifies to the lessor or the supplier that the goods are conforming or that the lessee will take or retain them in spite of their nonconformity; or

(b) the lessee fails to make an effective rejection of the goods (Section 2A-509(2)).

(2) Acceptance of a part of any commercial unit is acceptance of that entire unit.

§ 2A-516. Effect of Acceptance of Goods; Notice of Default; Burden of Establishing Default After Acceptance; Notice of Claim or Litigation to Person Answerable Over.

(1) A lessee must pay rent for any goods accepted in accordance with the lease contract, with due allowance for goods rightfully rejected or not delivered.

(2) A lessee's acceptance of goods precludes rejection of the goods accepted. In the case of a finance lease, if made with knowledge of a nonconformity, acceptance cannot be revoked because of it. In any other case, if made with knowledge of a nonconformity, acceptance cannot be revoked because of it unless the acceptance was on the reasonable assumption that the nonconformity would be seasonably cured. Acceptance does not of itself impair any other remedy provided by this Article or the lease agreement for nonconformity.

(3) If a tender has been accepted:

(a) within a reasonable time after the lessee discovers or should have discovered any default, the lessee shall notify the lessor and the supplier, if any, or be barred from any remedy against the party not notified;

(b) except in the case of a consumer lease, within a reasonable time after the lessee receives notice of litigation for infringement or the like (Section 2A-211) the lessee shall notify the lessor or be barred from any remedy over for liability established by the litigation; and

(c) the burden is on the lessee to establish any default.

(4) If a lessee is sued for breach of a warranty or other obligation for which a lessor or a supplier is answerable over the following apply:

(a) The lessee may give the lessor or the supplier, or both, written notice of the litigation. If the notice states that the person notified may come in and defend and that if the person notified does not do so that person will be bound in any action against that person by the lessee by any determination of fact common to the two litigations, then unless the person notified after seasonable receipt of the notice does come in and defend that person is so bound.

(b) The lessor or the supplier may demand in writing that the lessee turn over control of the litigation including settlement if the claim is one for infringement or the like (Section 2A-211) or else be barred from any remedy over. If the demand states that the lessor or the supplier agrees to bear all expense and to satisfy any adverse judgment, then unless the lessee after seasonable receipt of the demand does turn over control the lessee is so barred.

(5) Subsections (3) and (4) apply to any obligation of a lessee to hold the lessor or the supplier harmless against infringement or the like (Section 2A-211).

As amended in 1990.

§ 2A-517. Revocation of Acceptance of Goods.

(1) A lessee may revoke acceptance of a lot or commercial unit whose nonconformity substantially impairs its value to the lessee if the lessee has accepted it:

(a) except in the case of a finance lease, on the reasonable assumption that its nonconformity would be cured and it has not been seasonably cured; or

(b) without discovery of the nonconformity if the lessee's acceptance was reasonably induced either by the lessor's assurances or, except in the case of a finance lease, by the difficulty of discovery before acceptance.

(2) Except in the case of a finance lease that is not a consumer lease, a lessee may revoke acceptance of a lot or commercial unit if the lessor defaults under the lease contract and the default substantially impairs the value of that lot or commercial unit to the lessee.

(3) If the lease agreement so provides, the lessee may revoke acceptance of a lot or commercial unit because of other defaults by the lessor.

(4) Revocation of acceptance must occur within a reasonable time after the lessee discovers or should have discovered the ground for it and before any substantial change in condition of the goods which is not caused by the nonconformity. Revocation is not effective until the lessee notifies the lessor.

(5) A lessee who so revokes has the same rights and duties with regard to the goods involved as if the lessee had rejected them.

As amended in 1990.

§ 2A-518.   Cover; Substitute Goods.

(1) After a default by a lessor under the lease contract of the type described in Section 2A-508(1), or if agreed, after other default by the lessor, the lessee may cover by making any purchase or lease of or contract to purchase or lease goods in substitution for those due from the lessor.

(2) Except as otherwise provided with respect to damages liquidated in the lease agreement (Section 2A-504) or otherwise determined pursuant to agreement of the parties (Sections 1-102(3) and 2A-503), if a lessee's cover is by a lease agreement substantially similar to the original lease agreement and the new lease agreement is made in good faith and in a commercially reasonable manner, the lessee may recover from the lessor as damages (i) the present value, as of the date of the commencement of the term of the new lease agreement, of the rent under the new lease agreement applicable to that period of the new lease term which is comparable to the then remaining term of the original lease agreement minus the present value as of the same date of the total rent for the then remaining lease term of the original lease agreement, and (ii) any incidental or consequential damages, less expenses saved in consequence of the lessor's default.

(3) If a lessee's cover is by lease agreement that for any reason does not qualify for treatment under subsection (2), or is by purchase or otherwise, the lessee may recover from the lessor as if the lessee had elected not to cover and Section 2A-519 governs.

As amended in 1990.

§ 2A-519.   Lessee's Damages for Non-delivery, Repudiation, Default, and Breach of Warranty in Regard to Accepted Goods.

(1) Except as otherwise provided with respect to damages liquidated in the lease agreement (Section 2A-504) or otherwise determined pursuant to agreement of the parties (Sections 1-102(3) and 2A-503), if a lessee elects not to cover or a lessee elects to cover and the cover is by lease agreement that for any reason does not qualify for treatment under Section 2A-518(2), or is by purchase or otherwise, the measure of damages for nondelivery or repudiation by the lessor or for rejection or revocation of acceptance by the lessee is the present value, as of the same date of the default, of the then market rent minus the present value as of the same date of the original rent, computed for the remaining lease term of the original lease agreement, together with incidental and consequential damages, less expenses saved in consequence of the lessor's default.

(2) Market rent is to be determined as of the place for tender or, in cases of rejection after arrival or revocation of acceptance, as of the place of arrival.

(3) Except as otherwise agreed, if the lessee has accepted goods and given notification (Section 2A-516(3)), the measure of damages for nonconforming tender or delivery or other default by a lessor is the loss resulting in the ordinary course of events from the lessor's default as determined in any manner that is reasonable together with incidental and consequential damages, less expenses saved in consequence of the lessor's default.

(4) Except as otherwise agreed, the measure of damages for breach of warranty is the present value at the time and place of acceptance of the difference between the value of the use of the goods accepted and the value if they had been as warranted for the lease term, unless special circumstances show proximate damages of a different amount, together with incidental and consequential damages, less expenses saved in consequence of the lessor's default or breach of warranty.

As amended in 1990.

§ 2A-520.   Lessee's Incidental and Consequential Damages.

(1) Incidental damages resulting from a lessor's default include expenses reasonably incurred in inspection, receipt, transportation, and care and custody of goods rightfully rejected or goods the acceptance of which is justifiably revoked, any commercially reasonable charges, expenses or commissions in connection with effecting cover, and any other reasonable expense incident to the default.

(2) Consequential damages resulting from a lessor's default include:

    (a) any loss resulting from general or particular requirements and needs of which the lessor at the time of contracting had reason to know and which could not reasonably be prevented by cover or otherwise; and

    (b) injury to person or property proximately resulting from any breach of warranty.

§ 2A-521.   Lessee's Right to Specific Performance or Replevin.

(1) Specific performance may be decreed if the goods are unique or in other proper circumstances.

(2) A decree for specific performance may include any terms and conditions as to payment of the rent, damages, or other relief that the court deems just.

(3) A lessee has a right of replevin, detinue, sequestration, claim and delivery, or the like for goods identified to the lease contract if after reasonable effort the lessee is unable to effect cover for those goods or the circumstances reasonably indicate that the effort will be unavailing.

§ 2A-522.   Lessee's Right to Goods on Lessor's Insolvency.

(1) Subject to subsection (2) and even though the goods have not been shipped, a lessee who has paid a part or all of the rent and security for goods identified to a lease contract (Section 2A-217) on making and keeping good a tender of any unpaid portion of the rent and security due under the lease contract may recover the goods identified from the lessor if the lessor becomes insolvent within 10 days after receipt of the first installment of rent and security.

(2) A lessee acquires the right to recover goods identified to a lease contract only if they conform to the lease contract.

C. Default by Lessee

§ 2A-523.   Lessor's Remedies.

(1) If a lessee wrongfully rejects or revokes acceptance of goods or fails to make a payment when due or repudiates with

respect to a part or the whole, then, with respect to any goods involved, and with respect to all of the goods if under an installment lease contract the value of the whole lease contract is substantially impaired (Section 2A-510), the lessee is in default under the lease contract and the lessor may:

(a) cancel the lease contract (Section 2A-505(1));
(b) proceed respecting goods not identified to the lease contract (Section 2A-524);
(c) withhold delivery of the goods and take possession of goods previously delivered (Section 2A-525);
(d) stop delivery of the goods by any bailee (Section 2A-526);
(e) dispose of the goods and recover damages (Section 2A-527), or retain the goods and recover damages (Section 2A-528), or in a proper case recover rent (Section 2A-529);
(f) exercise any other rights or pursue any other remedies provided in the lease contract.

(2) If a lessor does not fully exercise a right or obtain a remedy to which the lessor is entitled under subsection (1), the lessor may recover the loss resulting in the ordinary course of events from the lessee's default as determined in any reasonable manner, together with incidental damages, less expenses saved in consequence of the lessee's default.

(3) If a lessee is otherwise in default under a lease contract, the lessor may exercise the rights and pursue the remedies provided in the lease contract, which may include a right to cancel the lease. In addition, unless otherwise provided in the lease contract:

(a) if the default substantially impairs the value of the lease contract to the lessor, the lessor may exercise the rights and pursue the remedies provided in subsections (1) and (2); or
(b) if the default does not substantially impair the value of the lease contract to the lessor, the lessor may recover as provided in subsection (2).

As amended in 1990.

§ 2A-524. Lessor's Right to Identify Goods to Lease Contract.

(1) After default by the lessee under the lease contract of the type described in Section 2A-523(1) or 2A-523(3)(a) or, if agreed, after other default by the lessee, the lessor may:

(a) identify to the lease contract conforming goods not already identified if at the time the lessor learned of the default they were in the lessor's or the supplier's possession or control; and
(b) dispose of goods (Section 2A-527(1)) that demonstrably have been intended for the particular lease contract even though those goods are unfinished.

(2) If the goods are unfinished, in the exercise of reasonable commercial judgment for the purposes of avoiding loss and of effective realization, an aggrieved lessor or the supplier may either complete manufacture and wholly identify the goods to the lease contract or cease manufacture and lease, sell, or otherwise dispose of the goods for scrap or salvage value or proceed in any other reasonable manner.

As amended in 1990.

§ 2A-525. Lessor's Right to Possession of Goods.

(1) If a lessor discovers the lessee to be insolvent, the lessor may refuse to deliver the goods.

(2) After a default by the lessee under the lease contract of the type described in Section 2A-523(1) or 2A-523(3)(a) or, if

agreed, after other default by the lessee, the lessor has the right to take possession of the goods. If the lease contract so provides, the lessor may require the lessee to assemble the goods and make them available to the lessor at a place to be designated by the lessor which is reasonably convenient to both parties. Without removal, the lessor may render unusable any goods employed in trade or business, and may dispose of goods on the lessee's premises (Section 2A-527).

(3) The lessor may proceed under subsection (2) without judicial process if it can be done without breach of the peace or the lessor may proceed by action.

As amended in 1990.

§ 2A-526. Lessor's Stoppage of Delivery in Transit or Otherwise.

(1) A lessor may stop delivery of goods in the possession of a carrier or other bailee if the lessor discovers the lessee to be insolvent and may stop delivery of carload, truckload, planeload, or larger shipments of express or freight if the lessee repudiates or fails to make a payment due before delivery, whether for rent, security or otherwise under the lease contract, or for any other reason the lessor has a right to withhold or take possession of the goods.

(2) In pursuing its remedies under subsection (1), the lessor may stop delivery until

(a) receipt of the goods by the lessee;
(b) acknowledgment to the lessee by any bailee of the goods, except a carrier, that the bailee holds the goods for the lessee; or
(c) such an acknowledgment to the lessee by a carrier via reshipment or as warehouseman.

(3)(a) To stop delivery, a lessor shall so notify as to enable the bailee by reasonable diligence to prevent delivery of the goods.
(b) After notification, the bailee shall hold and deliver the goods according to the directions of the lessor, but the lessor is liable to the bailee for any ensuing charges or damages.
(c) A carrier who has issued a nonnegotiable bill of lading is not obliged to obey a notification to stop received from a person other than the consignor.

§ 2A-527. Lessor's Rights to Dispose of Goods.

(1) After a default by a lessee under the lease contract of the type described in Section 2A-523(1) or 2A-523(3)(a) or after the lessor refuses to deliver or takes possession of goods (Section 2A-525 or 2A-526), or, if agreed, after other default by a lessee, the lessor may dispose of the goods concerned or the undelivered balance thereof by lease, sale, or otherwise.

(2) Except as otherwise provided with respect to damages liquidated in the lease agreement (Section 2A-504) or otherwise determined pursuant to agreement of the parties (Sections 1-102(3) and 2A-503), if the disposition is by lease agreement substantially similar to the original lease agreement and the new lease agreement is made in good faith and in a commercially reasonable manner, the lessor may recover from the lessee as damages (i) accrued and unpaid rent as of the date of the commencement of the term of the new lease agreement, (ii) the present value, as of the same date, of the total rent for the then remaining lease term of the original lease agreement minus the present value, as of the same date, of the rent under the new lease agreement applicable to that period of the new lease term which is comparable to the then remaining term of the original lease agreement, and (iii) any incidental damages

allowed under Section 2A-530, less expenses saved in consequence of the lessee's default.

(3) If the lessor's disposition is by lease agreement that for any reason does not qualify for treatment under subsection (2), or is by sale or otherwise, the lessor may recover from the lessee as if the lessor had elected not to dispose of the goods and Section 2A-528 governs.

(4) A subsequent buyer or lessee who buys or leases from the lessor in good faith for value as a result of a disposition under this section takes the goods free of the original lease contract and any rights of the original lessee even though the lessor fails to comply with one or more of the requirements of this Article.

(5) The lessor is not accountable to the lessee for any profit made on any disposition. A lessee who has rightfully rejected or justifiably revoked acceptance shall account to the lessor for any excess over the amount of the lessee's security interest (Section 2A-508(5)).

As amended in 1990.

§ 2A-528. Lessor's Damages for Non-acceptance, Failure to Pay, Repudiation, or Other Default.

(1) Except as otherwise provided with respect to damages liquidated in the lease agreement (Section 2A-504) or otherwise determined pursuant to agreement of the parties (Sections 1-102(3) and 2A-503), if a lessor elects to retain the goods and the disposition is by lessor elects to dispose of the goods and the disposition is by lease agreement that for any reason does not qualify for treatment under Section 2A-527(2), or is by sale or otherwise, the lessor may recover from the lessee as damages for a default of the type described in Section 2A-523(1) or 2A-523(3)(a), or, if agreed, for other default of the lessee, (i) accrued and unpaid rent as of the date of default if the lessee has never taken possession of the goods, or, if the lessee has taken possession of the goods, as of the date the lessor repossesses the goods or an earlier date on which the lessee makes a tender of the goods to the lessor, (ii) the present value as of the date determined under clause (i) of the total rent for the then remaining lease term of the original lease agreement minus the present value as of the same date of the market rent at the place where the goods are located computed for the same lease term, and (iii) any incidental damages allowed under Section 2A-530, less expenses saved in consequence of the lessee's default.

(2) If the measure of damages provided in subsection (1) is inadequate to put a lessor in as good a position as performance would have, the measure of damages is the present value of the profit, including reasonable overhead, the lessor would have made from full performance by the lessee, together with any incidental damages allowed under Section 2A-530, due allowance for costs reasonably incurred and due credit for payments or proceeds of disposition.

As amended in 1990.

§ 2A-529. Lessor's Action for the Rent.

(1) After default by the lessee under the lease contract of the type described in Section 2A-523(1) or 2A-523(3)(a) or, if agreed, after other default by the lessee, if the lessor complies with subsection (2), the lessor may recover from the lessee as damages:

   (a) for goods accepted by the lessee and not repossessed by or tendered to the lessor, and for conforming goods lost or damaged within a commercially reasonable time after risk of loss passes to the lessee (Section 2A-219), (i) accrued and unpaid rent as of the date of entry of judgment in favor of the lessor, (ii) the present value as of the same date of the

rent for the then remaining lease term of the lease agreement, and (iii) any incidental damages allowed under Section 2A-530, less expenses saved in consequence of the lessee's default; and

   (b) for goods identified to the lease contract if the lessor is unable after reasonable effort to dispose of them at a reasonable price or the circumstances reasonably indicate that effort will be unavailing, (i) accrued and unpaid rent as of the date of entry of judgment in favor of the lessor, (ii) the present value as of the same date of the rent for the then remaining lease term of the lease agreement, and (iii) any incidental damages allowed under Section 2A-530, less expenses saved in consequence of the lessee's default.

(2) Except as provided in subsection (3), the lessor shall hold for the lessee for the remaining lease term of the lease agreement any goods that have been identified to the lease contract and are in the lessor's control.

(3) The lessor may dispose of the goods at any time before collection of the judgment for damages obtained pursuant to subsection (1). If the disposition is before the end of the remaining lease term of the lease agreement, the lessor's recovery against the lessee for damages is governed by Section 2A-527 or Section 2A-528, and the lessor will cause an appropriate credit to be provided against a judgment for damages to the extent that the amount of the judgment exceeds the recovery available pursuant to Section 2A-527 or 2A-528.

(4) Payment of the judgment for damages obtained pursuant to subsection (1) entitles the lessee to the use and possession of the goods not then disposed of for the remaining lease term of and in accordance with the lease agreement.

(5) After default by the lessee under the lease contract of the type described in Section 2A-523(1) or Section 2A-523(3)(a) or, if agreed, after other default by the lessee, a lessor who is held not entitled to rent under this section must nevertheless be awarded damages for nonacceptance under Section 2A-527 or Section 2A-528.

As amended in 1990.

§ 2A-530. Lessor's Incidental Damages.
Incidental damages to an aggrieved lessor include any commercially reasonable charges, expenses, or commissions incurred in stopping delivery, in the transportation, care and custody of goods after the lessee's default, in connection with return or disposition of the goods, or otherwise resulting from the default.

§ 2A-531. Standing to Sue Third Parties for Injury to Goods.

(1) If a third party so deals with goods that have been identified to a lease contract as to cause actionable injury to a party to the lease contract (a) the lessor has a right of action against the third party, and (b) the lessee also has a right of action against the third party if the lessee:

   (i) has a security interest in the goods;
   (ii) has an insurable interest in the goods; or
   (iii) bears the risk of loss under the lease contract or has since the injury assumed that risk as against the lessor and the goods have been converted or destroyed.

(2) If at the time of the injury the party plaintiff did not bear the risk of loss as against the other party to the lease contract and there is no arrangement between them for disposition of the recovery, his [or her] suit or settlement, subject to his [or her] own interest, is as a fiduciary for the other party to the lease contract.

(3) Either party with the consent of the other may sue for the benefit of whom it may concern.

§ 2A-532. **Lessor's Rights to Residual Interest.** In addition to any other recovery permitted by this Article or other law, the lessor may recover from the lessee an amount that will fully compensate the lessor for any loss of or damage to the lessor's residual interest in the goods caused by the default of the lessee.

As added in 1990.

REVISED ARTICLE 3 / Negotiable Instruments

Part 1   General Provisions and Definitions

§ 3-101.   **Short Title.**   This Article may be cited as Uniform Commercial Code-Negotiable Instruments.

§ 3-102.   **Subject Matter.**

(a) This Article applies to negotiable instruments. It does not apply to money, to payment orders governed by Article 4A, or to securities governed by Article 8.

(b) If there is conflict between this Article and Article 4 or 9, Articles 4 and 9 govern.

(c) Regulations of the Board of Governors of the Federal Reserve System and operating circulars of the Federal Reserve Banks supersede any inconsistent provision of this Article to the extent of the inconsistency.

§ 3-103.   **Definitions.**

(a) In this Article:

(1) "Acceptor" means a drawee who has accepted a draft.

(2) "Drawee" means a person ordered in a draft to make payment.

(3) "Drawer" means a person who signs or is identified in a draft as a person ordering payment.

(4) "Good faith" means honesty in fact and the observance of reasonable commercial standards of fair dealing.

(5) "Maker" means a person who signs or is identified in a note as a person undertaking to pay.

(6) "Order" means a written instruction to pay money signed by the person giving the instruction. The instruction may be addressed to any person, including the person giving the instruction, or to one or more persons jointly or in the alternative but not in succession. An authorization to pay is not an order unless the person authorized to pay is also instructed to pay.

(7) "Ordinary care" in the case of a person engaged in business means observance of reasonable commercial standards, prevailing in the area in which the person is located, with respect to the business in which the person is engaged. In the case of a bank that takes an instrument for processing for collection or payment by automated means, reasonable commercial standards do not require the bank to examine the instrument if the failure to examine does not violate the bank's prescribed procedures and the bank's procedures do not vary unreasonably from general banking usage not disapproved by this Article or Article 4.

(8) "Party" means a party to an instrument.

(9) "Promise" means a written undertaking to pay money signed by the person undertaking to pay. An acknowledgment of an obligation by the obligor is not a promise unless the obligor also undertakes to pay the obligation.

(10) "Prove" with respect to a fact means to meet the burden of establishing the fact (Section 1-201(8)).

(11) "Remitter" means a person who purchases an instrument from its issuer if the instrument is payable to an identified person other than the purchaser.

(b) Other definitions applying to this Article and the sections in which they appear are:

"Acceptance"   Section 3-409
"Accommodated party"   Section 3-419
"Accommodation party"   Section 3-419
"Alteration"   Section 3-407
"Anomalous indorsement"   Section 3-205
"Blank indorsement"   Section 3-205
"Cashier's check"   Section 3-104
"Certificate of deposit"   Section 3-104
"Certified check"   Section 3-409
"Check"   Section 3-104
"Consideration"   Section 3-303
"Draft"   Section 3-104
"Holder in due course"   Section 3-302
"Incomplete instrument"   Section 3-115
"Indorsement"   Section 3-204
"Indorser"   Section 3-204
"Instrument"   Section 3-104
"Issue"   Section 3-105
"Issuer"   Section 3-105
"Negotiable instrument"   Section 3-104
"Negotiation"   Section 3-201
"Note"   Section 3-104
"Payable at a definite time"   Section 3-108
"Payable on demand"   Section 3-108
"Payable to bearer"   Section 3-109
"Payable to order"   Section 3-109
"Payment"   Section 3-602
"Person entitled to enforce"   Section 3-301
"Presentment"   Section 3-501
"Reacquisition"   Section 3-207
"Special indorsement"   Section 3-205
"Teller's check"   Section 3-104
"Transfer of instrument"   Section 3-203
"Traveler's check"   Section 3-104
"Value"   Section 3-303

(c) The following definitions in other Articles apply to this Article:

"Bank"   Section 4-105
"Banking day"   Section 4-104
"Clearing house"   Section 4-104
"Collecting bank"   Section 4-105
"Depositary bank"   Section 4-105
"Documentary draft"   Section 4-104
"Intermediary bank"   Section 4-105
"Item"   Section 4-104
"Payor bank"   Section 4-105
"Suspends payments"   Section 4-104

(d) In addition, Article 1 contains general definitions and principles of construction and interpretation applicable throughout this Article.

§ 3-104.   **Negotiable Instrument.**

(a) Except as provided in subsections (c) and (d), "negotiable instrument" means an unconditional promise or order to pay a fixed amount of money, with or without interest or other charges described in the promise or order, if it:

(1) is payable to bearer or to order at the time it is issued or first comes into possession of a holder;

(2) is payable on demand or at a definite time; and

(3) does not state any other undertaking or instruction by the person promising or ordering payment to do any act in addition to the payment of money, but the promise or order may contain (i) an undertaking or power to give, maintain, or protect collateral to secure payment, (ii) an authorization or power to the holder to confess judgment or realize on or dispose of collateral, or (iii) a waiver of the benefit of any law intended for the advantage or protection of an obligor.

(b) "Instrument" means a negotiable instrument.

(c) An order that meets all of the requirements of subsection (a), except paragraph (1), and otherwise falls within the definition of "check" in subsection (f) is a negotiable instrument and a check.

(d) A promise or order other than a check is not an instrument if, at the time it is issued or first comes into possession of a holder, it contains a conspicuous statement, however expressed, to the effect that the promise or order is not negotiable or is not an instrument governed by this Article.

(e) An instrument is a "note" if it is a promise and is a "draft" if it is an order. If an instrument falls within the definition of both "note" and "draft," a person entitled to enforce the instrument may treat it as either.

(f) "Check" means (i) a draft, other than a documentary draft, payable on demand and drawn on a bank or (ii) a cashier's check or teller's check. An instrument may be a check even though it is described on its face by another term, such as "money order."

(g) "Cashier's check" means a draft with respect to which the drawer and drawee are the same bank or branches of the same bank.

(h) "Teller's check" means a draft drawn by a bank (i) on another bank, or (ii) payable at or through a bank.

(i) "Traveler's check" means an instrument that (i) is payable on demand, (ii) is drawn on or payable at or through a bank, (iii) is designated by the term "traveler's check" or by a substantially similar term, and (iv) requires, as a condition to payment, a countersignature by a person whose specimen signature appears on the instrument.

(j) "Certificate of deposit" means an instrument containing an acknowledgment by a bank that a sum of money has been received by the bank and a promise by the bank to repay the sum of money. A certificate of deposit is a note of the bank.

§ 3-105. Issue of Instrument.

(a) "Issue" means the first delivery of an instrument by the maker or drawer, whether to a holder or nonholder, for the purpose of giving rights on the instrument to any person.

(b) An unissued instrument, or an unissued incomplete instrument that is completed, is binding on the maker or drawer, but nonissuance is a defense. An instrument that is conditionally issued or is issued for a special purpose is binding on the maker or drawer, but failure of the condition or special purpose to be fulfilled is a defense.

(c) "Issuer" applies to issued and unissued instruments and means a maker or drawer of an instrument.

§ 3-106. Unconditional Promise or Order.

(a) Except as provided in this section, for the purposes of Section 3-104(a), a promise or order is unconditional unless it states (i) an express condition to payment, (ii) that the promise or order is subject to or governed by another writing, or (iii) that rights or obligations with respect to the promise or order

are stated in another writing. A reference to another writing does not of itself make the promise or order conditional.

(b) A promise or order is not made conditional (i) by a reference to another writing for a statement of rights with respect to collateral, prepayment, or acceleration, or (ii) because payment is limited to resort to a particular fund or source.

(c) If a promise or order requires, as a condition to payment, a countersignature by a person whose specimen signature appears on the promise or order, the condition does not make the promise or order, the condition does not make the promise or order conditional for the purposes of Section 3-104(a). If the person whose specimen signature appears on an instrument fails to countersign the instrument, the failure to countersign is a defense to the obligation of the issuer, but the failure does not prevent a transferee of the instrument from becoming a holder of the instrument.

(d) If a promise or order at the time it is issued or first comes into possession of a holder contains a statement, required by applicable statutory or administrative law, to the effect that the rights of a holder or transferee are subject to claims or defenses that the issuer could assert against the original payee, the promise or order is not thereby made conditional for the purposes of Section 3-104(a); but if the promise or order is an instrument, there cannot be a holder in due course of the instrument.

§ 3-107. Instrument Payable in Foreign Money. Unless the instrument otherwise provides, an instrument that states the amount payable in foreign money may be paid in the foreign money or in an equivalent amount in dollars calculated by using the current bank-offered spot rate at the place of payment for the purchase of dollars on the day on which the instrument is paid.

§ 3-108. Payable on Demand or at Definite Time.

(a) A promise or order is "payable on demand" if it (i) states that it is payable on demand or at sight, or otherwise indicates that it is payable at the will of the holder, or (ii) does not state any time of payment.

(b) A promise or order is "payable at a definite time" if it is payable on elapse of a definite period of time after sight or acceptance or at a fixed date or dates or at a time or times readily ascertainable at the time the promise or order is issued, subject to rights of (i) prepayment, (ii) acceleration, (iii) extension at the option of the holder, or (iv) extension to a further definite time at the option of the maker or acceptor or automatically upon or after a specified act or event.

(c) If an instrument, payable at a fixed date, is also payable upon demand made before the fixed date, the instrument is payable on demand until the fixed date and, if demand for payment is not made before that date, becomes payable at a definite time on the fixed date.

§ 3-109. Payable to Bearer or to Order.

(a) A promise or order is payable to bearer if it:

(1) states that it is payable to bearer or to the order of bearer or otherwise indicates that the person in possession of the promise or order is entitled to payment;

(2) does not state a payee; or

(3) states that it is payable to or to the order of cash or otherwise indicates that it is not payable to an identified person.

(b) A promise or order that is not payable to bearer is payable to order if it is payable (i) to the order of an identified person or (ii) to an identified person or order. A promise or order that is payable to order is payable to the identified person.

(c) An instrument payable to bearer may become payable to an identified person if it is specially indorsed pursuant to Section 3-205(a). An instrument payable to an identified person may become payable to bearer if it is indorsed in blank pursuant to Section 3-205(b).

§ 3-110. **Identification of Person to Whom Instrument Is Payable.**

(a) The person to whom an instrument is initially payable is determined by the intent of the person, whether or not authorized, signing as, or in the name or behalf of, the issuer of the instrument. The instrument is payable to the person intended by the signer even if that person is identified in the instrument by a name or other identification that is not that of the intended person. If more than one person signs in the name or behalf of the issuer of an instrument and all the signers do not intend the same person as payee, the instrument is payable to any person intended by one or more of the signers.

(b) If the signature of the issuer of an instrument is made by automated means, such as a check-writing machine, the payee of the instrument is determined by the intent of the person who supplied the name or identification of the payee, whether or not authorized to do so.

(c) A person to whom an instrument is payable may be identified in any way, including by name, identifying number, office, or account number. For the purpose of determining the holder of an instrument, the following rules apply:

(1) If an instrument is payable to an account and the account is identified only by number, the instrument is payable to the person to whom the account is payable. If an instrument is payable to an account identified by number and by the name of a person, the instrument is payable to the named person, whether or not that person is the owner of the account identified by number.

(2) If an instrument is payable to:

(i) a trust, an estate, or a person described as trustee or representative of a trust or estate, the instrument is payable to the trustee, the representative, or a successor of either, whether or not the beneficiary or estate is also named;

(ii) a person described as agent or similar representative of a named or identified person, the instrument is payable to the represented person, the representative, or a successor of the representative;

(iii) a fund or organization that is not a legal entity, the instrument is payable to a representative of the members of the fund or organization; or

(iv) an office or to a person described as holding an office, the instrument is payable to the named person, the incumbent of the office, or a successor to the incumbent.

(d) If an instrument is payable to two or more persons alternatively, it is payable to any of them and may be negotiated, discharged, or enforced by any or all of them in possession of the instrument. If an instrument is payable to two or more persons not alternatively, it is payable to all of them and may be negotiated, discharged, or enforced only by all of them. If an instrument payable to two or more persons is ambiguous as to whether it is payable to the persons alternatively, the instrument is payable to the persons alternatively.

§ 3-111. **Place of Payment.** Except as otherwise provided for items in Article 4, an instrument is payable at the place of payment stated in the instrument. If no place of payment is stated, an instrument is payable at the address of the drawee or maker stated in the instrument. If no address is stated, the place of payment is the place of business of the drawee or maker. If a drawee or maker has more than one place of business, the place of payment is any place of business of the drawee or maker chosen by the person entitled to enforce the instrument. If the drawee or maker has no place of business, the place of payment is the residence of the drawee or maker.

§ 3-112. **Interest.**

(a) Unless otherwise provided in the instrument, (i) an instrument is not payable with interest, and (ii) interest on an interest-bearing instrument is payable from the date of the instrument.

(b) Interest may be stated in an instrument as a fixed or variable amount of money or it may be expressed as a fixed or variable rate or rates. The amount or rate of interest may be stated or described in the instrument in any manner and may require reference to information not contained in the instrument. If an instrument provides for interest, but the amount of interest payable cannot be ascertained from the description, interest is payable at the judgment rate in effect at the place of payment of the instrument and at the time interest first accrues.

§ 3-113. **Date of Instrument.**

(a) An instrument may be antedated or postdated. The date stated determines the time of payment if the instrument is payable at a fixed period after date. Except as provided in Section 4-401(c), an instrument payable on demand is not payable before the date of the instrument.

(b) If an instrument is undated, its date is the date of its issue or, in the case of an unissued instrument, the date it first comes into possession of a holder.

§ 3-114. **Contradictory Terms of Instrument.** If an instrument contains contradictory terms, typewritten terms prevail over printed terms, handwritten terms prevail over both, and words prevail over numbers.

§ 3-115. **Incomplete Instrument.**

(a) "Incomplete instrument" means a signed writing, whether or not issued by the signer, the contents of which show at the time of signing that it is incomplete but that the signer intended it to be completed by the addition of words or numbers.

(b) Subject to subsection (c), if an incomplete instrument is an instrument under Section 3-104, it may be enforced according to its terms if it is not completed, or according to its terms as augmented by completion. If an incomplete instrument is not an instrument under Section 3-104, but, after completion, the requirements of Section 3-104 are met, the instrument may be enforced according to its terms as augmented by completion.

(c) If words or numbers are added to an incomplete instrument without authority of the signer, there is an alteration of the incomplete instrument under Section 3-407.

(d) The burden of establishing that words or numbers were added to an incomplete instrument without authority of the signer is on the person asserting the lack of authority.

§ 3-116. **Joint and Several Liability; Contribution.**

(a) Except as otherwise provided in the instrument, two or more persons who have the same liability on an instrument as makers, drawers, acceptors, indorsers who indorse as joint payees, or anomalous indorsers are jointly and severally liable in the capacity in which they sign.

(b) Except as provided in Section 3-419(e) or by agreement of the affected parties, a party having joint and several liability who pays the instrument is entitled to receive from any party having the same joint and several liability contribution in accordance with applicable law.

(c) Discharge of one party having joint and several liability by a person entitled to enforce the instrument does not affect the right under subsection (b) of a party having the same joint and several liability to receive contribution from the party discharged.

§ 3-117.   Other Agreements Affecting Instrument.   Subject to applicable law regarding exclusion of proof of contemporaneous or previous agreements, the obligation of a party to an instrument to pay the instrument may be modified, supplemented, or nullified by a separate agreement of the obligor and a person entitled to enforce the instrument, if the instrument is issued or the obligation is incurred in reliance on the agreement or as part of the same transaction giving rise to the agreement. To the extent an obligation is modified, supplemented, or nullified by an agreement under this section, the agreement is a defense to the obligation.

§ 3-118.   Statute of Limitations.

(a) Except as provided in subsection (e), an action to enforce the obligation of a party to pay a note payable at a definite time must be commenced within six years after the due date or dates stated in the note or, if a due date is accelerated, within six years after the accelerated due date.

(b) Except as provided in subsection (d) or (e), if demand for payment is made to the maker of a note payable on demand, an action to enforce the obligation of a party to pay the note must be commenced with six years after the demand. If no demand for payment is made to the maker, an action to enforce the note is barred if neither principal nor interest on the note has been paid for a continuous period of 10 years.

(c) Except as provided in subsection (d), an action to enforce the obligation of a party to an unaccepted draft to pay the draft must be commenced within three years, after dishonor of the draft or 10 years after the date of the draft, whichever period expires first.

(d) An action to enforce the obligation of the acceptor of a certified check or the issuer of a teller's check, cashier's check, or traveler's check must be commenced within three years after demand for payment is made to the acceptor or issuer, as the case may be.

(e) An action to enforce the obligation of a party to a certificate of deposit to pay the instrument must be commenced within six years after demand for payment is made to the maker, but if the instrument states a due date and the maker is not required to pay before that date, the six-year period begins when a demand for payment is in effect and the due date has passed.

(f) An action to enforce the obligation of a party to pay an accepted draft, other than a certified check, must be commenced (i) within six years after the due date or dates stated in the draft or acceptance if the obligation of the acceptor is payable at a definite time, or (ii) within six years after the date of the acceptance if the obligation of the acceptor is payable on demand.

(g) Unless governed by other law regarding claims for indemnity or contribution, an action (i) for conversion of an instrument, for money had and received, or like action based on conversion, (ii) for breach of warranty, or (iii) to enforce an obligation, duty, or right arising under this Article and not governed by this section must be commenced within three years after the [cause of action] accrues.

§ 3-119.   Notice of Right to Defend Action.   In an action for breach of an obligation for which a third person is answerable over pursuant to this Article or Article 4, the defendant may give the third person written notice of the litigation, and the person notified may then give similar notice to any other person who is answerable over. If the notice states (i) that the person notified may come in and defend and (ii) that failure to do so will bind the person notified in an action later brought by the person giving the notice as to any determination of fact common to the two litigations, the person notified is so bound unless after seasonable receipt of the notice the person notified does come in and defend.

Part 2   Negotiation, Transfer, and Indorsement.

§ 3-201.   Negotiation.

(a) "Negotiation" means a transfer of possession, whether voluntary or involuntary, of an instrument by a person other than the issuer to a person who thereby becomes its holder.

(b) Except for negotiation by a remitter, if an instrument is payable to an identified person, negotiation requires transfer of possession of the instrument and its indorsement by the holder. If an instrument is payable to bearer, it may be negotiated by transfer of possession alone.

§ 3-202.   Negotiation Subject to Rescission.

(a) Negotiation is effective even if obtained (i) from an infant, a corporation exceeding its powers, or a person without capacity, (ii) by fraud, duress, or mistake, or (iii) in breach of duty or as part of an illegal transaction.

(b) To the extent permitted by other law, negotiation may be rescinded or may be subject to other remedies, but those remedies may not be asserted against a subsequent holder in due course or a person paying the instrument in good faith and without knowledge of facts that are a basis for rescission or other remedy.

§ 3-203.   Transfer of Instrument; Rights Acquired by Transfer.

(a) An instrument is transferred when it is delivered by a person other than its issuer for the purpose of giving to the person receiving delivery the right to enforce the instrument.

(b) Transfer of an instrument, whether or not the transfer is a negotiation, vests in the transferee any right of the transferor to enforce the instrument, including any right as a holder in due course, but the transferee cannot acquire rights of a holder in due course by a transfer, directly or indirectly, from a holder in due course if the transferee engaged in fraud or illegality affecting the instrument.

(c) Unless otherwise agreed, if an instrument is transferred for value and the transferee does not become a holder because of lack of indorsement by the transferor, the transferee has a specifically enforceable right to the unqualified indorsement of the transferor, but negotiation of the instrument does not occur until the indorsement is made.

(d) If a transferor purports to transfer less than the entire instrument, negotiation of the instrument does not occur. The transferee obtains no rights under this Article and has only the rights of a partial assignee.

§ 3-204.   Indorsement.

(a) "Indorsement" means a signature, other than that of a signer as maker, drawer, or acceptor, that alone or accompanied by other words is made on an instrument for the purpose of (i) negotiating the instrument, (ii) restricting payment of the instrument, or (iii) incurring indorser's liability on the instrument, but regardless of the intent of the signer, a signature and its accompanying words is an indorsement unless the accompanying words, terms of the instrument, place of the signature, or other circumstances unambiguously indicate that the signature was made for a purpose other than indorsement. For the purpose of determinating whether a signature is made on an instrument, a paper affixed to the instrument is a part of the instrument.

(b) "Indorser" means a person who makes an indorsement.

(c) For the purpose of determining whether the transferee of an instrument is a holder, an indorsement that transfers a security interest in the instrument is effective as an unqualified indorsement of the instrument.

(d) If an instrument is payable to a holder under a name that is not the name of the holder, indorsement may be made by the holder in the name stated in the instrument or in the holder's name or both, but signature in both names may be required by a person paying or taking the instrument for value or collection.

§ 3-205. Special Indorsement; Blank Indorsement; Anomalous Indorsement.

(a) If an indorsement is made by the holder of an instrument, whether payable to an identified person or payable to bearer, and the indorsement identifies a person to whom it makes the instrument payable, it is a "special indorsement." When specially indorsed, an instrument becomes payable to the identified person and may be negotiated only by the indorsement of that person. The principles stated in Section 3-110 apply to special indorsements.

(b) If an indorsement is made by the holder of an instrument and it is not a special indorsement, it is a "blank indorsement." When indorsed in blank, an instrument becomes payable to bearer and may be negotiated by transfer of possession alone until specially indorsed.

(c) The holder may convert a blank indorsement that consists only of a signature into a special indorsement by writing, above the signature of the indorser, words identifying the person to whom the instrument is made payable.

(d) "Anomalous indorsement" means an indorsement made by a person who is not the holder of the instrument. An anomalous indorsement does not affect the manner in which the instrument may be negotiated.

§ 3-206. Restrictive Indorsement.

(a) An indorsement limiting payment to a particular person or otherwise prohibiting further transfer or negotiation of the instrument is not effective to prevent further transfer or negotiation of the instrument.

(b) An indorsement stating a condition to the right of the indorsee to receive payment does not affect the right of the indorsee to enforce the instrument. A person paying the instrument or taking it for value or collection may disregard the condition, and the rights and liabilities of that person are not affected by whether the condition has been fulfilled.

(c) If an instrument bears an indorsement (i) described in Section 4-201(b), or (ii) in blank or to a particular bank using the words "for deposit," "for collection," or other words indicating a purpose of having the instrument collected by a bank for the indorser or for a particular account, the following rules apply:

(1) A person, other than a bank, who purchases the instrument when so indorsed converts the instrument unless the

amount paid for the instrument is received by the indorser or applied consistently with the indorsement.

(2) A depositary bank that purchases the instrument or takes it for collection when so indorsed converts the instrument unless the amount paid by the bank with respect to the instrument is received by the indorser or applied consistently with the indorsement.

(3) A payor bank that is also the depositary bank or that takes the instrument for immediate payment over the counter from a person other than a collecting bank converts the instrument unless the proceeds of the instrument are received by the indorser or applied consistently with the indorsement.

(4) Except as otherwise provided in paragraph (3), a payor bank or intermediary bank may disregard the indorsement and is not liable if the proceeds of the instrument are not received by the indorser or applied consistently with the indorsement.

(d) Except for an indorsement covered by subsection (c), if an instrument bears an indorsement using words to the effect that payment is to be made to the indorsee as agent, trustee, or other fiduciary for the benefit of the indorser or another person, the following rules apply:

(1) Unless there is notice of breach of fiduciary duty as provided in Section 3-307, a person who purchases the instrument from the indorsee or takes the instrument from the indorsee for collection or payment may pay the proceeds of payment or the value given for the instrument to the indorsee without regard to whether the indorsee violates a fiduciary duty to the indorser.

(2) A subsequent transferee of the instrument or person who pays the instrument is neither given notice nor otherwise affected by the restriction in the indorsement unless the transferee or payor knows that the fiduciary dealt with the instrument or its proceeds in breach of fiduciary duty.

(e) The presence on an instrument of an indorsement to which this section applies does not prevent a purchaser of the instrument from becoming a holder in due course of the instrument unless the purchaser is a converter under subsection (c) or has notice or knowledge of breach of fiduciary duty as stated in subsection (d).

(f) In an action to enforce the obligation of a party to pay the instrument, the obligor has a defense if payment would violate an indorsement to which this section applies and the payment is not permitted by this section.

§ 3-207. Reacquisition. Reacquisition of an instrument occurs if it is transferred to a former holder, by negotiation or otherwise. A former holder who reacquires the instrument may cancel indorsements made after the reacquirer first became a holder of the instrument. If the cancellation causes the instrument to be payable to the reacquirer or to bearer, the reacquirer may negotiate the instrument. An indorser whose indorsement is canceled is discharged, and the discharge is effective against any subsequent holder.

Part 3 Enforcement of Instruments

§ 3-301. Person Entitled to Enforce Instrument. "Person entitled to enforce" an instrument means (i) the holder of the instrument, (ii) a nonholder in possession of the instrument who has the rights of a holder, or (iii) a person not in possession of the instrument who is entitled to enforce the instrument pursuant to Section 3-309 or 3-418(d). A person may be a

person entitled to enforce the instrument even though the person is not the owner of the instrument or is in wrongful possession of the instrument.

§ 3-302. Holder in Due Course.

(a) Subject to subsection (c) and Section 3-106(d), "holder in due course" means the holder of an instrument if:

(1) the instrument when issued or negotiated to the holder does not bear such apparent evidence of forgery or alteration or is not otherwise so irregular or incomplete as to call into question its authenticity; and

(2) the holder took the instrument (i) for value, (ii) in good faith, (iii) without notice that the instrument is overdue or has been dishonored or that there is an uncured default with respect to payment of another instrument issued as part of the same series, (iv) without notice that the instrument contains an unauthorized signature or has been altered, (v) without notice of any claim to the instrument described in Section 3-306, and (vi) without notice that any party has a defense or claim in recoupment described in Section 3-305(a).

(b) Notice of discharge of a party, other than discharge in an insolvency proceeding, is not notice of a defense under subsection (a), but discharge is effective against a person who became a holder in due course with notice of the discharge. Public filing or recording of a document does not of itself constitute notice of a defense, claim in recoupment, or claim to the instrument.

(c) Except to the extent a transferor or predecessor in interest has rights as a holder in due course, a person does not acquire rights of a holder in due course of an instrument taken (i) by legal process or by purchase in an execution, bankruptcy, or creditor's sale or similar proceeding, (ii) by purchase as part of a bulk transaction not in ordinary course of business of the transferor, or (iii) as the successor in interest to an estate or other organization.

(d) If, under Section 3-303(a)(1), the promise of performance that is the consideration for an instrument has been partially performed, the holder may assert rights as a holder in due course of the instrument only to the fraction of the amount payable under the instrument equal to the value of the partial performance divided by the value of the promised performance.

(e) If (i) the person entitled to enforce an instrument has only a security interest in the instrument and (ii) the person obliged to pay the instrument has a defense, claim in recoupment, or claim to the instrument that may be asserted against the person who granted the security interest, the person entitled to enforce the instrument may assert rights as a holder in due course only to an amount payable under the instrument which, at the time of enforcement of the instrument, does not exceed the amount of the unpaid obligation secured.

(f) To be effective, notice must be received at a time and in a manner that gives a reasonable opportunity to act on it.

(g) This section is subject to any law limiting status as a holder in due course in particular classes of transactions.

§ 3-303. Value and Consideration.

(a) An instrument is issued or transferred for value if:

(1) the instrument is issued or transferred for a promise of performance, to the extent the promise has been performed;

(2) the transferee acquires a security interest or other lien in the instrument other than a lien obtained by judicial proceeding;

(3) the instrument is issued or transferred as payment of, or as security for, an antecedent claim against any person, whether or not the claim is due;

(4) the instrument is issued or transferred in exchange for a negotiable instrument; or

(5) the instrument is issued or transferred in exchange for the incurring of an irrevocable obligation to a third party by the person taking the instrument.

(b) "Consideration" means any consideration sufficient to support a simple contract. The drawer or maker of an instrument has a defense if the instrument is issued without consideration. If an instrument is issued for a promise of performance, the issuer has a defense to the extent performance of the promise is due and the promise has not been performed. If an instrument is issued for value as stated in subsection (a), the instrument is also issued for consideration.

§ 3-304. Overdue Instrument.

(a) An instrument payable on demand becomes overdue at the earliest of the following times:

(1) on the day after the day demand for payment is duly made;

(2) if the instrument is a check, 90 days after its date; or

(3) if the instrument is not a check, when the instrument has been outstanding for a period of time after its date which is unreasonably long under the circumstances of the particular case in light of the nature of the instrument and usage of the trade.

(b) With respect to an instrument payable at a definite time the following rules apply:

(1) If the principal is payable in installments and a due date has not been accelerated, the instrument becomes overdue upon default under the instrument for nonpayment of an installment, and the instrument remains overdue until the default is cured.

(2) If the principal is not payable in installments and the due date has not been accelerated, the instrument becomes overdue on the day after the due date.

(3) If a due date with respect to principal has been accelerated, the instrument becomes overdue on the day after the accelerated due date.

(c) Unless the due date of principal has been accelerated, an instrument does not become overdue if there is default in payment of interest but no default in payment of principal.

§ 3-305. Defenses and Claims in Recoupment.

(a) Except as stated in subsection (b), the right to enforce the obligation of a party to pay an instrument is subject to the following:

(1) a defense of the obligor based on (i) infancy of the obligor to the extent it is a defense to a simple contract, (ii) duress, lack of legal capacity, or illegality of the transaction which, under other law, nullifies the obligation of the obligor, (iii) fraud that induced the obligor to sign the instrument with neither knowledge nor reasonable opportunity to learn of its character or its essential terms, or (iv) discharge of the obligor in insolvency proceedings;

(2) a defense of the obligor stated in another section of this Article or a defense of the obligor that would be available if the person entitled to enforce the instrument were enforcing a right to payment under a simple contract; and

(3) a claim in recoupment of the obligor against the original payee of the instrument if the claim arose from the transaction that gave rise to the instrument; but the claim of the obligor may be asserted against a transferee of the instrument only to reduce the amount owing on the instrument at the time the action is brought.

(b) The right of a holder in due course to enforce the obligation of a party to pay the instrument is subject to defenses of the obligor stated in subsection (a)(1), but is not subject to defenses of the obligor stated in subsection (a)(2) or claims in recoupment stated in subsection (a)(3) against a person other than the holder.

(c) Except as stated in subsection (d), in an action to enforce the obligation of a party to pay the instrument, the obligor may not assert against the person entitled to enforce the instrument a defense, claim in recoupment, or claim to the instrument (Section 3-306) of another person, but the other person's claim to the instrument may be asserted by the obligor if the other person is joined in the action and personally asserts the claim against the person entitled to enforce the instrument. An obligor is not obliged to pay the instrument if the person seeking enforcement of the instrument does not have rights of a holder in due course and the obligor proves that the instrument is a lost or stolen instrument.

(d) In an action to enforce the obligation of an accommodation party to pay an instrument, the accommodation party may assert against the person entitled to enforce the instrument any defense or claim in recoupment under subsection (a) that the accommodated party could assert against the person entitled to enforce the instrument, except the defenses of discharge in insolvency proceedings, infancy, and lack of legal capacity.

§ 3-306.   **Claims to an Instrument.**   A person taking an instrument, other than a person having rights of a holder in due course, is subject to a claim of a property or possessory right in the instrument or its proceeds, including a claim to rescind a negotiation and to recover the instrument or its proceeds. A person having rights of a holder in due course takes free of the claim to the instrument.

§ 3-307.   **Notice of Breach of Fiduciary Duty.**

(a) In this section:

(1) "Fiduciary" means an agent, trustee, partner, corporate officer or director, or other representative owing a fiduciary duty with respect to an instrument.

(2) "Represented person" means the principal, beneficiary, partnership, corporation, or other person to whom the duty stated in paragraph (1) is owed.

(b) If (i) an instrument is taken from a fiduciary for payment or collection or for value, (ii) the taker has knowledge of the fiduciary status of the fiduciary, and (iii) the represented person makes a claim to the instrument or its proceeds on the basis that the transaction of the fiduciary is a breach of fiduciary duty, the following rules apply:

(1) Notice of breach of fiduciary duty by the fiduciary is notice of the claim of the represented person.

(2) In the case of an instrument payable to the represented person or the fiduciary as such, the taker has notice of the breach of fiduciary duty if the instrument is (i) taken in payment of or as security for a debt known by the taker to be the personal debt of the fiduciary, (ii) taken in a transaction known by the taker to be for the personal benefit of the fiduciary, or (iii) deposited to an account other than an account

of the fiduciary, as such, or an account of the represented person.

(3) If an instrument is issued by the represented person or the fiduciary as such, and made payable to the fiduciary personally, the taker does not have notice of the breach of fiduciary duty unless the taker knows of the breach of fiduciary duty.

(4) If an instrument is issued by the represented person or the fiduciary as such, to the taker as payee, the taker has notice of the breach of fiduciary duty if the instrument is (i) taken in payment of or as security for a debt known by the taker to be the personal debt of the fiduciary, (ii) taken in a transaction known by the taker to be for the personal benefit of the fiduciary, or (iii) deposited to an account other than an account of the fiduciary, as such, or an account of the represented person.

§ 3-308.   **Proof of Signatures and Status as Holder in Due Course.**

(a) In an action with respect to an instrument, the authenticity of, and authority to make, each signature on the instrument is admitted unless specifically denied in the pleadings. If the validity of a signature is denied in the pleadings, the burden of establishing validity is on the person claiming validity, but the signature is presumed to be authentic and authorized unless the action is to enforce the liability of the purported signer and the signer is dead or incompetent at the time of trial of the issue of validity of the signature. If an action to enforce the instrument is brought against a person as the undisclosed principal of a person who signed the instrument as a party to the instrument, the plaintiff has the burden of establishing that the defendant is liable on the instrument as a represented person under Section 3-402(a).

(b) If the validity of signatures is admitted or proved and there is compliance with subsection (a), a plaintiff producing the instrument is entitled to payment if the plaintiff proves entitlement to enforce the instrument under Section 3-301, unless the defendant proves a defense or claim in recoupment. If a defense or claim in recoupment is proved, the right to payment of the plaintiff is subject to the defense or claim, except to the extent the plaintiff proves that the plaintiff has rights of a holder in due course which are not subject to the defense or claim.

§ 3-309.   **Enforcement of Lost, Destroyed, or Stolen Instrument.**

(a) A person not in possession of an instrument is entitled to enforce the instrument if (i) the person was in possession of the instrument and entitled to enforce it when loss of possession occurred, (ii) the loss of possession was not the result of a transfer by the person or a lawful seizure, and (iii) the person cannot reasonably obtain possession of the instrument because the instrument was destroyed, its whereabouts cannot be determined, or it is in the wrongful possesion of an unknown person or a person that cannot be found or is not amenable to service of process.

(b) A person seeking enforcement of an instrument under subsection (a) must prove the terms of the instrument and the person's right to enforce the instrument. If that proof is made, Section 3-308 applies to the case as if the person seeking enforcement had produced the instrument. The court may not enter judgment in favor of the person seeking enforcement unless it finds that the person required to pay the instrument is adequately protected against loss that might occur by reason of a claim by another person to enforce the instrument. Adequate protection may be provided by any reasonable means.

§ 3-310. **Effect of Instrument on Obligation for Which Taken.**

(a) Unless otherwise agreed, if a certified check, cashier's check, or teller's check is taken for an obligation, the obligation is discharged to the same extent discharge would result if an amount of money equal to the amount of the instrument were taken in payment of the obligation. Discharge of the obligation does not affect any liability that the obligor may have as an indorser of the instrument.

(b) Unless otherwise agreed and except as provided in subsection (a), if a note or an uncertified check is taken for an obligation, the obligation is suspended to the same extent the obligation would be discharged if an amount of money equal to the amount of the instrument were taken, and the following rules apply:

(1) In the case of an uncertified check, suspension of the obligation continues until dishonor of the check or until it is paid or certified. Payment or certification of the check results in discharge of the obligation to the extent of the amount of the check.

(2) In the case of a note, suspension of the obligation continues until dishonor of the note or until it is paid. Payment of the note results in discharge of the obligation to the extent of the payment.

(3) Except as provided in paragraph (4), if the check or note is dishonored and the obligee of the obligation for which the instrument was taken is the person entitled to enforce the instrument, the obligee may enforce either the instrument or the obligation. In the case of an instrument of a third person which is negotiated to the obligee by the obligor, discharge of the obligor on the instrument also discharges the obligation.

(4) If the person entitled to enforce the instrument taken for an obligation is a person other than the obligee, the obligee may not enforce the obligation to the extent the obligation is suspended. If the obligee is the person entitled to enforce the instrument but no longer has possession of it because it was lost, stolen, or destroyed, the obligation may not be enforced to the extent of the amount payable on the instrument, and to that extent the obligee's rights against the obligor are limited to enforcement of the instrument.

(c) If an instrument other than one described in subsection (a) or (b) is taken for an obligation, the effect is (i) that stated in subsection (a) if the instrument is one on which a bank is liable as maker or acceptor, or (ii) that stated in subsection (b) in any other case.

§ 3-311. **Accord and Satisfaction by Use of Instrument.**

(a) If a person against whom a claim is asserted proves that (i) that person in good faith tendered an instrument to the claimant as full satisfaction of the claim, (ii) the amount of the claim was unliquidated or subject to a bona fide dispute, and (iii) the claimant obtained payment of the instrument, the following subsections apply.

(b) Unless subsection (c) applies, the claim is discharged if the person against whom the claim is asserted proves that the instrument or an accompanying written communication contained a conspicuous statement to the effect that the instrument was tendered as full satisfaction of the claim.

(c) Subject to subsection (d), a claim is not discharged under subsection (b) if either of the following applies:

(1) The claimant, if an organization, proves that (i) within a reasonable time before the tender, the claimant sent a conspicuous statement to the person against whom the claim is asserted that communications concerning disputed debts, including an instrument tendered as full satisfaction of a debt, are to be sent to a designated person, office, or place, and (ii) the instrument or accompanying communication was not received by that designated person, office, or place.

(2) The claimant, whether or not an organization, proves that within 90 days after payment of the instrument, the claimant tendered repayment of the amount of the instrument to the person against whom the claim is asserted. This paragraph does not apply if the claimant is an organization that sent a statement complying with paragraph (1)(i).

(d) A claim is discharged if the person against whom the claim is asserted proves that within a reasonable time before collection of the instrument was initiated, the claimant, or an agent of the claimant having direct responsibility with respect to the disputed obligation, knew that the instrument was tendered in full satisfaction of the claim.

Part 4 Liability of Parties

§ 3-401. **Signature.**

(a) A person is not liable on an instrument unless (i) the person signed the instrument, or (ii) the person is represented by an agent or representative who signed the instrument and the signature is binding on the represented person under Section 3-402.

(b) A signature may be made (i) manually or by means of a device or machine, and (ii) by the use of any name, including a trade or assumed name, or by a word, mark, or symbol executed or adopted by a person with present intention to authenticate a writing.

§ 3-402. **Signature by Representative.**

(a) If a person acting, or purporting to act, as a representative signs an instrument by signing either the name of the represented person or the name of the signer, the represented person is bound by the signature to the same extent the represented person would be bound if the signature were on a simple contract. If the represented person is bound, the signature of the representative is the "authorized signature of the represented person" and the represented person is liable on the instrument, whether or not identified in the instrument.

(b) If a representative signs the name of the representative to an instrument and the signature is an authorized signature of the represented person, the following rules apply:

(1) If the form of the signature shows unambiguously that the signature is made on behalf of the represented person who is identified in the instrument, the representative is not liable on the instrument.

(2) Subject to subsection (c), if (i) the form of the signature does not show unambiguously that the signature is made in a representative capacity or (ii) the represented person is not identified in the instrument, the representative is liable on the instrument to a holder in due course that took the instrument without notice that the representative was not intended to be liable on the instrument. With respect to any other person, the representative is liable on the instrument unless the representative proves that the original parties did not intend the representative to be liable on the instrument.

(c) If a representative signs the name of the representative as drawer of a check without indication of the representative status and the check is payable from an account of the represented person who is identified on the check, the signer is not liable on the check if the signature is an authorized signature of the represented person.

§ 3-403. Unauthorized Signature.

(a) Unless otherwise provided in this Article or Article 4, an unauthorized signature is ineffective except as the signature of the unauthorized signer in favor of a person who in good faith pays the instrument or takes it for value. An unauthorized signature may be ratified for all purposes of this Article.

(b) If the signature of more than one person is required to constitute the authorized signature of an organization, the signature of the organization is unauthorized if one of the required signatures is lacking.

(c) The civil or criminal liability of a person who makes an unauthorized signature is not affected by any provision of this Article which makes the unauthorized signature effective for the purposes of this Article.

§ 3-404. Impostors: Fictitious Payees.

(a) If an impostor, by use of the mails or otherwise, induces the issuer of an instrument to issue the instrument to the impostor, or to a person acting in concert with the impostor, by impersonating the payee of the instrument or a person authorized to act for the payee, an indorsement of the instrument by any person in the name of the payee is effective as the indorsement of the payee in favor of a person who, in good faith, pays the instrument or takes it for value or for collection.

(b) If (i) a person whose intent determines to whom an instrument is payable (Section 3-110(a) or (b)) does not intend the person identified as payee to have any interest in the instrument, or (ii) the person identified as payee of an instrument is a fictitious person, the following rules apply until the instrument is negotiated by special indorsement:

(1) Any person in possession of the instrument is its holder.

(2) An indorsement by any person in the name of the payee stated in the instrument is effective as the indorsement of the payee in favor of a person who, in good faith, pays the instrument or takes it for value or for collection.

(c) Under subsection (a) or (b), an indorsement is made in the name of a payee if (i) it is made in a name substantially similar to that of the payee or (ii) the instrument, whether or not indorsed, is deposited in a depositary bank to an account in a name substantially similar to that of the payee.

(d) With respect to an instrument to which subsection (a) or (b) applies, if a person paying the instrument or taking it for value or for collection fails to exercise ordinary care in paying or taking the instrument and that failure substantially contributes to loss resulting from payment of the instrument, the person bearing the loss may recover from the person failing to exercise ordinary care to the extent the failure to exercise ordinary care contributed to the loss.

§ 3-405. Employer's Responsibility for Fraudulent Indorsement by Employee.

(a) In this section:

(1) "Employee" includes an independent contractor and employee of an independent contractor retained by the employer.

(2) "Fraudulent indorsement" means (i) in the case of an instrument payable to the employer, a forged indorsement purporting to be that of the employer, or (ii) in the case of an instrument with respect to which the employer is the is-suer, a forged indorsement purporting to be that of the person identified as payee.

(3) "Responsibility" with respect to instruments means authority (i) to sign or indorse instruments on behalf of the employer, (ii) to process instruments received by the employer for bookkeeping purposes, for deposit to an account, or for other disposition, (iii) to prepare or process instruments for issue in the name of the employer, (iv) to supply information determining the names or addresses of payees of instruments to be issued in the name of the employer, (v) to control the disposition of instruments to be issued in the name of the employer, or (vi) to act otherwise with respect to instruments in a responsible capacity. "Responsibility" does not include authority that merely allows an employee to have access to instruments or blank or incomplete instrument forms that are being stored or transported or are part of incoming or outgoing mail, or similar access.

(b) For the purpose of determining the rights and liabilities of a person who, in good faith, pays an instrument or takes it for value or for collection, if an employer entrusted an employee with responsibility with respect to the instrument and the employee or a person acting in concert with the employee makes a fraudulent indorsement of the instrument, the indorsement is effective as the indorsement of the person to whom the instrument is payable if it is made in the name of that person. If the person paying the instrument or taking it for value or for collection fails to exercise ordinary care in paying or taking the instrument and that failure substantially contributes to loss resulting from the fraud, the person bearing the loss may recover from the person failing to exercise ordinary care to the extent the failure to exercise ordinary care contributed to the loss.

(c) Under subsection (b), an indorsement is made in the name of the person to whom an instrument is payable if (i) it is made in a name substantially similar to the name of that person or (ii) the instrument, whether or not indorsed, is deposited in a depositary bank to an account in a name substantially similar to the name of that person.

§ 3-406. Negligence Contributing to Forged Signature or Alteration of Instrument.

(a) A person whose failure to exercise ordinary care substantially contributes to an alteration of an instrument or to the making of a forged signature on an instrument is precluded from asserting the alteration or the forgery against a person who, in good faith, pays the instrument or takes it for value or for collection.

(b) Under subsection (a), if the person asserting the preclusion fails to exercise ordinary care in paying or taking the instrument and that failure substantially contributes to loss, the loss is allocated between the person precluded and the person asserting the preclusion according to the extent to which the failure of each to exercise ordinary care contributed to the loss.

(c) Under subsection (a), the burden of proving failure to exercise ordinary care is on the person asserting the preclusion. Under subsection (b), the burden of proving failure to exercise ordinary care is on the person precluded.

§ 3-407. Alteration.

(a) "Alteration" means (i) an unauthorized change in an instrument that purports to modify in any respect the obligation of a party, or (ii) an unauthorized addition of words or numbers or other change to an incomplete instrument relating to the obligation of a party.

(b) Except as provided in subsection (c), an alteration fraudulently made discharges a party whose obligation is affected by the alteration unless that party assents or is precluded from asserting the alteration. No other alteration discharges a party, and the instrument may be enforced according to its original terms.

(c) A payor bank or drawee paying a fraudulently altered instrument or a person taking it for value, in good faith and without notice of the alteration, may enforce rights with respect to the instrument (i) according to its original terms, or (ii) in the case of an incomplete instrument altered by unauthorized completion, according to its terms as completed.

§ 3-408. Drawee Not Liable on Unaccepted Draft. A check or other draft does not of itself operate as an assignment of funds in the hands of the drawee available for its payment, and the drawee is not liable on the instrument until the drawee accepts it.

§ 3-409. Acceptance of Draft; Certified Check.

(a) "Acceptance" means the drawee's signed agreement to pay a draft as presented. It must be written on the draft and may consist of the drawee's signature alone. Acceptance may be made at any time and becomes effective when notification pursuant to instructions is given or the accepted draft is delivered for the purpose of giving rights on the acceptance to any person.

(b) A draft may be accepted although it has not been signed by the drawer, is otherwise incomplete, is overdue, or has been dishonored.

(c) If a draft is payable at a fixed period after sight and the acceptor fails to date the acceptance, the holder may complete the acceptance by supplying a date in good faith.

(d) "Certified check" means a check accepted by the bank on which it is drawn. Acceptance may be made as stated in subsection (a) or by a writing on the check which indicates that the check is certified. The drawee of a check has no obligation to certify the check, and refusal to certify is not dishonor of the check.

§ 3-410. Acceptance Varying Draft.

(a) If the terms of a drawee's acceptance vary from the terms of the draft as presented, the holder may refuse the acceptance and treat the draft as dishonored. In that case, the drawee may cancel the acceptance.

(b) The terms of a draft are not varied by an acceptance to pay at a particular bank or place in the United States, unless the acceptance states that the draft is to be paid only at that bank or place.

(c) If the holder assents to an acceptance varying the terms of a draft, the obligation of each drawer and indorser that does not expressly assent to the acceptance is discharged.

§ 3-411. Refusal to Pay Cashier's Checks, Teller's Checks, and Certified Checks.

(a) In this section, "obligated bank" means the acceptor of a certified check or the issuer of a cashier's check or teller's check bought from the issuer.

(b) If the obligated bank wrongfully (i) refuses to pay a cashier's check or certified check, (ii) stops payment of a teller's check, or (iii) refuses to pay a dishonored teller's check, the person asserting the right to enforce the check is entitled to compensation for expenses and loss of interest resulting from the nonpayment and may recover consequential damages if the obligated bank refuses to pay after receiving notice of particular circumstances giving rise to the damages.

(c) Expenses or consequential damages under subsection (b) are not recoverable if the refusal of the obligated bank to pay occurs because (i) the bank suspends payments, (ii) the obligated bank asserts a claim or defense of the bank that it has reasonable grounds to believe is available against the person entitled to enforce the instrument, (iii) the obligated bank has a reasonable doubt whether the person demanding payment is the person entitled to enforce the instrument, or (iv) payment is prohibited by law.

§ 3-412. Obligation of Issuer of Note or Cashier's Check. The issuer of a note or cashier's check or other draft drawn on the drawer is obliged to pay the instrument (i) according to its terms at the time it was issued or, if not issued, at the time it first came into possession of a holder, or (ii) if the issuer signed an incomplete instrument, according to its terms when completed, to the extent stated in Sections 3-115 and 3-407. The obligation is owed to a person entitled to enforce the instrument or to an indorser who paid the instrument under Section 3-415.

§ 3-413. Obligation of Acceptor.

(a) The acceptor of a draft is obliged to pay the draft (i) according to its terms at the time it was accepted, even though the acceptance states that the draft is payable "as originally drawn" or equivalent terms, (ii) if the acceptance varies the terms of the draft, according to the terms of the draft as varied, or (iii) if the acceptance is of a draft that is an incomplete instrument, according to its terms when completed, to the extent stated in Sections 3-115 and 3-407. The obligation is owed to a person entitled to enforce the draft or to the drawer or an indorser who paid the draft under Section 3-414 or 3-415.

(b) If the certification of a check or other acceptance of a draft states the amount certified or accepted, the obligation of the acceptor is that amount. If (i) the certification or acceptance does not state an amount, (ii) the amount of the instrument is subsequently raised, and (iii) the instrument is then negotiated to a holder in due course, the obligation of the acceptor is the amount of the instrument at the time it was taken by the holder in due course.

§ 3-414. Obligation of Drawer.

(a) This section does not apply to cashier's checks or other drafts drawn on the drawer.

(b) If an unaccepted draft is dishonored, the drawer is obliged to pay the draft (i) according to its terms at the time it was issued or, if not issued, at the time it first came into possession of a holder, or (ii) if the drawer signed an incomplete instrument, according to its terms when completed, to the extent stated in Sections 3-115 and 3-407. The obligation is owed to a person entitled to enforce the draft or to an indorser who paid the draft under Section 3-415.

(c) If a draft is accepted by a bank, the drawer is discharged, regardless of when or by whom acceptance was obtained.

(d) If a draft is accepted and the acceptor is not a bank, the obligation of the drawer to pay the draft if the draft is dishonored by the acceptor is the same as the obligation of an indorser under Section 3-415(a) and (c).

(e) If a draft states that it is drawn "without recourse" or otherwise disclaims liability of the drawer to pay the draft, the drawer is not liable under subsection (b) to pay the draft if the draft is not a check. A disclaimer of the liability stated in subsection (b) is not effective if the draft is a check.

(f) If (i) a check is not presented for payment or given to a depositary bank for collection within 30 days after its date, (ii) the drawee suspends payments after expiration of the 30-day period without paying the check, and (iii) because of the suspension of payments, the drawer is deprived of funds maintained with the drawee to cover payment of the check, the drawer to the extent deprived of funds may discharge its obligation to pay the check by assigning to the person entitled to enforce the check the rights of the drawer against the drawee with respect to the funds.

§ 3-415. **Obligation of Indorser.**

(a) Subject to subsections (b), (c), and (d) and to Section 3-419(d), if an instrument is dishonored, an indorser is obliged to pay the amount due on the instrument (i) according to the terms of the instrument at the time it was indorsed, or (ii) if the indorser indorsed an incomplete instrument, according to its terms when completed, to the extent stated in Sections 3-115 and 3-407. The obligation of the indorser is owed to a person entitled to enforce the instrument or to a subsequent indorser who paid the instrument under this section.

(b) If an indorsement states that it is made "without recourse" or otherwise disclaims liability of the indorser, the indorser is not liable under subsection (a) to pay the instrument.

(c) If notice of dishonor of an instrument is required by Section 3-503 and notice of dishonor complying with that section is not given to an indorser, the liability of the indorser under subsection (a) is discharged.

(d) If a draft is accepted by a bank after an indorsement is made, the liability of the indorser under subsection (a) is discharged.

(e) If an indorser of a check is liable under subsection (a) and the check is not presented for payment, or given to a depositary bank for collection, within 30 days after the day the indorsement was made, the liability of the indorser under subsection (a) is discharged.

§ 3-416. **Transfer Warranties.**

(a) A person who transfers an instrument for consideration warrants to the transferee and, if the transfer is by indorsement, to any subsequent transferee that:

(1) the warrantor is a person entitled to enforce the instrument;
(2) all signatures on the instrument are authentic and authorized;
(3) the instrument has not been altered;
(4) the instrument is not subject to a defense or claim in recoupment of any party which can be asserted against the warrantor; and
(5) the warrantor has no knowledge of any insolvency proceeding commenced with respect to the maker or acceptor or, in the case of an unaccepted draft, the drawer.

(b) A person to whom the warranties under subsection (a) are made and who took the instrument in good faith may recover from the warrantor as damages for breach of warranty an amount equal to the loss suffered as a result of the breach, but not more than the amount of the instrument plus expenses and loss of interest incurred as a result of the breach.

(c) The warranties stated in subsection (a) cannot be disclaimed with respect to checks. Unless notice of a claim for breach of warranty is given to the warrantor within 30 days after the claimant has reason to know of the breach and the identity of the warrantor, the liability of the warrantor under subsection (b) is discharged to the extent of any loss caused by the delay in giving notice of the claim.

(d) A [cause of action] for breach of warranty under this section accrues when the claimant has reason to know of the breach.

§ 3-417. **Presentment Warranties.**

(a) If an unaccepted draft is presented to the drawee for payment or acceptance and the drawee pays or accepts the draft, (i) the person obtaining payment or acceptance, at the time of presentment, and (ii) a previous transferor of the draft, at the time of transfer, warrant to the drawee making payment or accepting the draft in good faith that:

(1) the warrantor is, or was, at the time the warrantor transferred the draft, a person entitled to enforce the draft or authorized to obtain payment or acceptance of the draft on behalf of a person entitled to enforce the draft;
(2) the draft has not been altered; and
(3) the warrantor has no knowledge that the signature of the drawer of the draft is unauthorized.

(b) A drawee making payment may recover from any warrantor damages for breach of warranty equal to the amount paid by the drawee less the amount the drawee received or is entitled to receive from the drawer because of the payment. In addition, the drawee is entitled to compensation for expenses and loss of interest resulting from the breach. The right of the drawee to recover damages under this subsection is not affected by any failure of the drawee to exercise ordinary care in making payment. If the drawee accepts the draft, breach of warranty is a defense to the obligation of the acceptor. If the acceptor makes payment with respect to the draft, the acceptor is entitled to recover from any warrantor for breach of warranty the amounts stated in this subsection.

(c) If a drawee asserts a claim for breach of warranty under subsection (a) based on an unauthorized indorsement of the draft or an alteration of the draft, the warrantor may defend by proving that the indorsement is effective under Section 3-404 or 3-405 or the drawer is precluded under Section 3-406 or 4-406 from asserting against the drawee the unauthorized indorsement or alteration.

(d) If (i) a dishonored draft is presented for payment to the drawer or an indorser or (ii) any other instrument is presented for payment to a party obliged to pay the instrument, and (iii) payment is received, the following rules apply:

(1) The person obtaining payment and a prior transferor of the instrument warrant to the person making payment in good faith that the warrantor is, or was, at the time the warrantor transferred the instrument, a person entitled to enforce the instrument or authorized to obtain payment on behalf of a person entitled to enforce the instrument.
(2) The person making payment may recover from any warrantor for breach of warranty an amount equal to the amount paid plus expenses and loss of interest resulting from the breach.

(e) The warranties stated in subsections (a) and (d) cannot be disclaimed with respect to checks. Unless notice of a claim for breach of warranty is given to the warrantor within 30 days after the claimant has reason to know of the breach and the identity of the warrantor, the liability of the warrantor under subsection (b) or (d) is discharged to the extent of any loss caused by the delay in giving notice of the claim.

(f) A [cause of action] for breach of warranty under this section accrues when the claimant has reason to know of the breach.

§ 3-418. Payment or Acceptance by Mistake.

(a) Except as provided in subsection (c), if the drawee of a draft pays or accepts the draft and the drawee acted on the mistaken belief that (i) payment of the draft had not been stopped pursuant to Section 4-403 or (ii) the signature of the drawer of the draft was authorized, the drawee may recover the amount of the draft from the person to whom or for whose benefit payment was made or, in the case of acceptance, may revoke the acceptance. Rights of the drawee under this subsection are not affected by failure of the drawee to exercise ordinary care in paying or accepting the draft.

(b) Except as provided in subsection (c), if an instrument has been paid or accepted by mistake and the case is not covered by subsection (a), the person paying or accepting may, to the extent permitted by the law governing mistake and restitution, (i) recover the payment from the person to whom or for whose benefit payment was made or (ii) in the case of acceptance, may revoke the acceptance.

(c) The remedies provided by subsection (a) or (b) may not be asserted against a person who took the instrument in good faith and for value or who in good faith changed position in reliance on the payment or acceptance. This subsection does not limit remedies provided by Section 3-417 or 4-407.

(d) Notwithstanding Section 4-215, if an instrument is paid or accepted by mistake and the payor or acceptor recovers payment or revokes acceptance under subsection (a) or (b), the instrument is deemed not to have been paid or accepted and is treated as dishonored, and the person from whom payment is recovered has rights as a person entitled to enforce the dishonored instrument.

§ 3-419. Instruments Signed for Accommodation.

(a) If an instrument is issued for value given for the benefit of a party to the instrument ("accommodated party") and another party to the instrument ("accommodation party") signs the instrument for the purpose of incurring liability on the instrument without being a direct beneficiary of the value given for the instrument, the instrument is signed by the accommodation party "for accommodation."

(b) An accommodation party may sign the instrument as maker, drawer, acceptor, or indorser and, subject to subsection (d), is obliged to pay the instrument in the capacity in which the accommodation party signs. The obligation of an accommodation party may be enforced notwithstanding any statute of frauds and whether or not the accommodation party receives consideration for the accommodation.

(c) A person signing an instrument is presumed to be an accommodation party and there is notice that the instrument is signed for accommodation if the signature is an anomalous indorsement or is accompanied by words indicating that the signer is acting as surety or guarantor with respect to the obligation of another party to the instrument. Except as provided in Section 3-605, the obligation of an accommodation party to pay the instrument is not affected by the fact that the person enforcing the obligation had notice when the instrument was taken by that person that the accommodation party signed the instrument for accommodation.

(d) If the signature of a party to an instrument is accompanied by words indicating unambiguously that the party is guaranteeing collection rather than payment of the obligation of another party to the instrument, the signer is obliged to pay the amount due on the instrument to a person entitled to enforce the instrument only if (i) execution of judgment against the other party has been returned unsatisfied, (ii) the other party is insolvent or in an insolvency proceeding, (iii) the other party cannot be served with process, or (iv) it is otherwise apparent that payment cannot be obtained from the other party.

(e) An accommodation party who pays the instrument is entitled to reimbursement from the accommodated party and is entitled to enforce the instrument against the accommodated party. An accommodated party who pays the instrument has no right of recourse against, and is not entitled to contribution from, an accommodation party.

§ 3-420. Conversion of Instrument.

(a) The law applicable to conversion of personal property applies to instruments. An instrument is also converted if it is taken by transfer, other than a negotiation, from a person not entitled to enforce the instrument or a bank makes or obtains payment with respect to the instrument for a person not entitled to enforce the instrument or receive payment. An action for conversion of an instrument may not be brought by (i) the issuer or acceptor of the instrument or (ii) a payee or indorsee who did not receive delivery of the instrument either directly or through delivery to an agent or a co-payee.

(b) In an action under subsection (a), the measure of liability is presumed to be the amount payable on the instrument, but recovery may not exceed the amount of the plaintiff's interest in the instrument.

(c) A representative, other than a depositary bank, who has in good faith dealt with an instrument or its proceeds on behalf of one who was not the person entitled to enforce the instrument is not liable in conversion to that person beyond the amount of any proceeds that it has not paid out.

Part 5 Dishonor

§ 3-501. Presentment.

(a) "Presentment" means a demand made by or on behalf of a person entitled to enforce an instrument (i) to pay the instrument made to the drawee or a party obliged to pay the instrument or, in the case of a note or accepted draft payable at a bank, to the bank, or (ii) to accept a draft made to the drawee.

(b) The following rules are subject to Article 4, agreement of the parties, and clearing-house rules and the like:

(1) Presentment may be made at the place of payment of the instrument and must be made at the place of payment if the instrument is payable at a bank in the United States; may be made by any commercially reasonable means, including an oral, written, or electronic communication; is effective when the demand for payment or acceptance is received by the person to whom presentment is made; and is effective if made to any one of two or more makers, acceptors, drawees, or other payors.

(2) Upon demand of the person to whom presentment is made, the person making presentment must (i) exhibit the instrument, (ii) give reasonable identification and, if presentment is made on behalf of another person, reasonable evidence of authority to do so, and (. . .) sign a receipt on the instrument for any payment made or surrender the instrument if full payment is made.

(3) Without dishonoring the instrument, the party to whom presentment is made may (i) return the instrument for lack of a necessary indorsement, or (ii) refuse payment or acceptance for failure of the presentment to comply with the terms of the instrument, an agreement of the parties, or other applicable law or rule.

(4) The party to whom presentment is made may treat presentment as occurring on the next business day after the

day of presentment if the party to whom presentment is made has established a cut-off hour not earlier than 2 p.m. for the receipt and processing of instruments presented for payment or acceptance and presentment is made after the cut-off hour.

§ 3-502. Dishonor.

(a) Dishonor of a note is governed by the following rules:

(1) If the note is payable on demand, the note is dishonored if presentment is duly made to the maker and the note is not paid on the day of presentment.
(2) If the note is not payable on demand and is payable at or through a bank or the terms of the note require presentment, the note is dishonored if presentment is duly made and the note is not paid on the day it becomes payable or the day of presentment, whichever is later.
(3) If the note is not payable on demand and paragraph (2) does not apply, the note is dishonored if it is not paid on the day it becomes payable.

(b) Dishonor of an unaccepted draft other than a documentary draft is governed by the following rules:

(1) If a check is duly presented for payment to the payor bank otherwise than for immediate payment over the counter, the check is dishonored if the payor bank makes timely return of the check or sends timely notice of dishonor or nonpayment under Section 4-301 or 4-302, or becomes accountable for the amount of the check under Section 4-302.
(2) If a draft is payable on demand and paragraph (1) does not apply, the draft is dishonored if presentment for payment is duly made to the drawee and the draft is not paid on the day of presentment.
(3) If a draft is payable on a date stated in the draft, the draft is dishonored if (i) presentment for payment is duly made to the drawee and payment is not made on the day the draft becomes payable or the day of presentment, whichever is later, or (ii) presentment for acceptance is duly made before the day the draft becomes payable and the draft is not accepted on the day of presentment.
(4) If a draft is payable on elapse of a period of time after sight or acceptance, the draft is dishonored if presentment for acceptance is duly made and the draft is not accepted on the day of presentment.

(c) Dishonor of an unaccepted documentary draft occurs according to the rules stated in subsection (b)(2), (3), and (4), except that payment or acceptance may be delayed without dishonor until no later than the close of the third business day of the drawee following the day on which payment or acceptance is required by those paragraphs.

(d) Dishonor of an accepted draft is governed by the following rules:

(1) If the draft is payable on demand, the draft is dishonored if presentment for payment is duly made to the acceptor and the draft is not paid on the day of presentment.
(2) If the draft is not payable on demand, the draft is dishonored if presentment for payment is duly made to the acceptor and payment is not made on the day it becomes payable or the day of presentment, whichever is later.

(e) In any case in which presentment is otherwise required for dishonor under this section and presentment is excused under Section 3-504, dishonor occurs without presentment if the instrument is not duly accepted or paid.

(f) If a draft is dishonored because timely acceptance of the draft was not made and the person entitled to demand acceptance consents to a late acceptance, from the time of acceptance the draft is treated as never having been dishonored.

§ 3-503. Notice of Dishonor.

(a) The obligation of an indorser stated in Section 3-415(a) and the obligation of a drawer stated in Section 3-414(d) may not be enforced unless (i) the indorser or drawer is given notice of dishonor of the instrument complying with this section or (ii) notice of dishonor is excused under Section 3-504(b).

(b) Notice of dishonor may be given by any person; may be given by any commercially reasonable means, including an oral, written, or electronic communication; and is sufficient if it reasonably identifies the instrument and indicates that the instrument has been dishonored or has not been paid or accepted. Return of an instrument given to a bank for collection is sufficient notice of dishonor.

(c) Subject to Section 3-504(c), with respect to an instrument taken for collection by a collecting bank, notice of dishonor must be given (i) by the bank before midnight of the next banking day following the banking day on which the bank receives notice of dishonor of the instrument, or (ii) by any other person within 30 days following the day on which the person receives notice of dishonor. With respect to any other instrument, notice of dishonor must be given within 30 days following the day on which dishonor occurs.

§ 3-504. Excused Presentment and Notice of Dishonor.

(a) Presentment for payment or acceptance of an instrument is excused if (i) the person entitled to present the instrument cannot with reasonable diligence make presentment, (ii) the maker or acceptor has repudiated an obligation to pay the instrument or is dead or in insolvency proceedings, (iii) by the terms of the instrument presentment is not necessary to enforce the obligation of indorsers or the drawer, (iv) the drawer or indorser whose obligation is being enforced has waived presentment or otherwise has no reason to expect or right to require that the instrument be paid or accepted, or (v) the drawer instructed the drawee not to pay or accept the draft or the drawee was not obligated to the drawer to pay the draft.

(b) Notice of dishonor is excused if (i) by the terms of the instrument notice of dishonor is not necessary to enforce the obligation of a party to pay the instrument, or (ii) the party whose obligation is being enforced waived notice of dishonor. A waiver of presentment is also a waiver of notice of dishonor.

(c) Delay in giving notice of dishonor is excused if the delay was caused by circumstances beyond the control of the person giving the notice and the person giving the notice exercised reasonable diligence after the cause of the delay ceased to operate.

§ 3-505. Evidence of Dishonor.

(a) The following are admissible as evidence and create a presumption of dishonor and of any notice of dishonor stated:

(1) a document regular in form as provided in subsection (b) which purports to be a protest;
(2) a purported stamp or writing of the drawee, payor bank, or presenting bank on or accompanying the instrument stating that acceptance or payment has been refused unless reasons for the refusal are stated and the reasons are not consistent with dishonor;
(3) a book or record of the drawee, payor bank, or collecting bank, kept in the usual course of business which shows

dishonor, even if there is no evidence of who made the entry.

(b) A protest is a certificate of dishonor made by a United States consul or vice consul, or a notary public or other person authorized to administer oaths by the law of the place where dishonor occurs. It may be made upon information satisfactory to that person. The protest must identify the instrument and certify either that presentment has been made or, if not made, the reason why it was not made, and that the instrument has been dishonored by nonacceptance or nonpayment. The protest may also certify that notice of dishonor has been given to some or all parties.

Part 6 Discharge and Payment

§ 3-601. Discharge and Effect of Discharge.

(a) The obligation of a party to pay the instrument is discharged as stated in this Article or by an act or agreement with the party which would discharge an obligation to pay money under a simple contract.

(b) Discharge of the obligation of a party is not effective against a person acquiring rights of a holder in due course of the instrument without notice of the discharge.

§ 3-602. Payment.

(a) Subject to subsection (b), an instrument is paid to the extent payment is made (i) by or on behalf of a party obliged to pay the instrument, and (ii) to a person entitled to enforce the instrument. To the extent of the payment, the obligation of the party obliged to pay the instrument is discharged even though payment is made with knowledge of a claim to the instrument under Section 3-306 by another person.

(b) The obligation of a party to pay the instrument is not discharged under subsection (a) if:

(1) a claim to the instrument under Section 3-306 is enforceable against the party receiving payment and (i) payment is made with knowledge by the payor that payment is prohibited by injunction or similar process of a court of competent jurisdiction, or (ii) in the case of an instrument other than a cashier's check, teller's check, or certified check, the party making payment accepted, from the person having a claim to the instrument, indemnity against loss resulting from refusal to pay the person entitled to enforce the instrument; or

(2) the person making payment knows that the instrument is a stolen instrument and pays a person it knows is in wrongful possession of the instrument.

§ 3-603. Tender of Payment.

(a) If tender of payment of an obligation to pay an instrument is made to a person entitled to enforce the instrument, the effect of tender is governed by principles of law applicable to tender of payment under a simple contract.

(b) If tender of payment of an obligation to pay an instrument is made to a person entitled to enforce the instrument and the tender is refused, there is discharge, to the extent of the amount of the tender, of the obligation of an indorser or accommodation party having a right of recourse with respect to the obligation to which the tender relates.

(c) If tender of payment of an amount due on an instrument is made to a person entitled to enforce the instrument, the obligation of the obligor to pay interest after the due date on the amount tendered is discharged. If presentment is required with respect to an instrument and the obligor is able and ready to pay on the due date at every place of payment stated in the instrument, the obligor is deemed to have made tender of payment on the due date to the person entitled to enforce the instrument.

§ 3-604. Discharge by Cancellation or Renunciation.

(a) A person entitled to enforce an instrument, with or without consideration, may discharge the obligation of a party to pay the instrument (i) by an intentional voluntary act, such as surrender of the instrument to the party, destruction, mutilation, or cancellation of the instrument, cancellation or striking out of the party's signature, or the addition of words to the instrument indicating discharge, or (ii) by agreeing not to sue or otherwise renouncing rights against the party by a signed writing.

(b) Cancellation or striking out of an indorsement pursuant to subsection (a) does not affect the status and rights of a party derived from the indorsement.

§ 3-605. Discharge of Indorsers and Accommodation Parties.

(a) In this section, the term "indorser" includes a drawer having the obligation described in Section 3-414(d).

(b) Discharge, under Section 3-604, of the obligation of a party to pay an instrument does not discharge the obligation of an indorser or accommodation party having a right of recourse against the discharged party.

(c) If a person entitled to enforce an instrument agrees, with or without consideration, to an extension of the due date of the obligation of a party to pay the instrument, the extension discharges an indorser or accommodation party having a right of recourse against the party whose obligation is extended to the extent the indorser or accommodation party proves that the extension caused loss to the indorser or accommodation party with respect to the right of recourse.

(d) If a person entitled to enforce an instrument agrees, with or without consideration, to a material modification of the obligation of a party other than an extension of the due date, the modification discharges the obligation of an indorser or accommodation party having a right of recourse against the person whose obligation is modified to the extent the modification causes loss to the indorser or accommodation party with respect to the right of recourse. The loss suffered by the indorser or accommodation party as a result of the modification is equal to the amount of the right of recourse unless the person enforcing the instrument proves that no loss was caused by the modification or that the loss caused by the modification was an amount less than the amount of the right of recourse.

(e) If the obligation of a party to pay an instrument is secured by an interest in collateral and a person entitled to enforce the instrument impairs the value of the interest in collateral, the obligation of an indorser or accommodation party having a right of recourse against the obligor is discharged to the extent of the impairment. The value of an interest in collateral is impaired to the extent (i) the value of the interest is reduced to an amount less than the amount of the right of recourse of the party asserting discharge, or (ii) the reduction in value of the interest causes an increase in the amount by which the amount of the right of recourse exceeds the value of the interest. The burden of proving impairment is on the party asserting discharge.

(f) If the obligation of a party is secured by an interest in collateral not provided by an accommodation party and a person entitled to enforce the instrument impairs the value of the interest in collateral, the obligation of any party who is jointly and severally liable with respect to the secured obligation is discharged to the extent the impairment causes the party asserting discharge to pay more than that party would have been obliged to pay, taking into account rights of contribution, if impairment had not occurred. If the party asserting discharge is an accommodation party not entitled to discharge under subsection (e), the party is deemed to have a right to contribution based on joint and several liability rather than a right to reimbursement. The burden of proving impairment is on the party asserting discharge.

(g) Under subsection (e) or (f), impairing value of an interest in collateral includes (i) failure to obtain or maintain perfection or recordation of the interest in collateral, (ii) release of collateral without substitution of collateral of equal value, (iii) failure to perform a duty to preserve the value of collateral owed, under Article 9 or other law, to a debtor or surety or other person secondarily liable, or (iv) failure to comply with applicable law in disposing of collateral.

(h) An accommodation party is not discharged under subsection (c), (d), or (e) unless the person entitled to enforce the instrument knows of the accommodation or has notice under Section 3-419(c) that the instrument was signed for accommodation.

(i) A party is not discharged under this section if (i) the party asserting discharge consents to the event or conduct that is the basis of the discharge, or (ii) the instrument or a separate agreement of the party provides for waiver of discharge under this section either specifically or by general language indicating that parties waive defenses based on suretyship or impairment of collateral.

The Uniform Commercial Code (UCC) was first drafted in 1952, and has been amended several times. This is its current state.

Appendix B

Solutions to Chapter Problems

Chapter 1

Problem 1.1. Milly has not violated a law. Normally, the parking lot of a shopping mall is owned by private parties and they install the signs. Private property owners cannot make law.

Problem 1.2. (c) is correct because (a) and (b) are not correct. (a) is not correct because the objective of criminal law is to punish wrong-doers. (b) is not correct because the objective of civil law is to compensate the victim, not to punish the wrong-doer.

Problem 1.3. (a) is correct. As in the state statute quoted in the chapter, English law *may* be applied in United States courts. (b) is not correct because common law was so named because it applied to *all* the king's subjects. (c) is not correct because United States courts are not *required* to apply English law. (d) is not correct because (a) is correct.

Problem 1.4. In general, administrative regulations must meet two requirements. First, they must be within the authority granted by Congress, and, second, they must be constitutional. In this case the EPA has congressional authority to adopt regulations relating to the discharge of toxic chemicals in the environment; thus, unless the regulation has a constitutional defect, it is valid. On the other hand, the EPA has no congressional authority to regulate the qualifications of airline pilots, and, therefore, such a regulation is invalid.

Problem 1.5. Farr is liable to Echo. The holding in *Able* is that a woman may use a weapon (a baseball bat) to defend herself from a substantially larger and intoxicated assailant. On the other hand, the holding in *Carr* is that a person may not use a weapon (a baseball bat) merely to win an argument over an insignificant item of personal property. The facts in *Echo v. Farr* are closest to the facts in *Carr* in that force was used to win an argument, but not for self-protection. *Stare decisis* requires consistency and therefore Farr should be liable to Echo.

Problem 1.6. There is no conflict and Lisa and Pete may marry. There is no conflict between the federal social security statute and the state marriage requirements: they focus on different issues. Because there is no conflict, supremacy is not an issue. The laws of other states do not supersede Ohio law.

Problem 1.7. (b) is correct. Judicial opinions are collected in reporters. (a) is not correct because statutes—not judicial opinions—are found in codes. (c) is not correct because the opinion is found at *volume* 116 and *page* 1737.

Chapter 2

Problem 2.1. Without a specific knowledge of the Ohio court system, there is no way to know the answer because each state chooses a name it likes for it's trial courts of general jurisdiction. In fact, Ohio uses the name Court of Common Pleas, a name taken from English legal experience. In contrast, Utah uses the name District Court, California uses the name Superior Court, and New York uses the name Supreme Court.

Problem 2.2. (c) is correct. Second level appellate courts are courts where appeals are at the discretion of the court. Discretionary appeals are allowed by the grant of a writ of certiorari. (a) is not correct because a writ of certiorari is not used in a trial court. (b) is not correct because appeals to a first level appellate court are made as a matter of right. (d) is not correct because (c) is correct.

Problem 2.3. (d) is correct. All of the three phrases apply to state court jurisdiction over nonresidents. (a), (b) and (c) all ask whether a nonresident has had sufficient contact with the forum state to satisfy due process requirements.

Problem 2.4. (b) is correct. Jurisdiction is established and then venue is established. (a) is not correct. If there is no jurisdiction (or power) over a controversy it is pointless to ask where the (nonexistent) jurisdiction will be exercised. (c) is not correct because (a) is not correct.

Problem 2.5. (d) is correct because

neither (a) nor (b) is correct. Neither (a) nor (b) is correct because appeals from a federal district court are made as a matter of right and thus a writ of certiorai is not used. Moreover, appeals from a district court located in the 9th Circuit go to the 9th Court of Appeals and not elsewhere.

Problem 2.6. (b) is correct because federal diversity jurisdiction requires (1) diversity of citizenship and (3) an amount in controversy over $50,000. Federal question jurisdiction is a separate basis for federal court jurisdiction. (a) and (c) are not correct because (b) is correct.

Chapter 3

Problem 3.1. (a) Use of a "contingent" fee is generally considered ethical. There are, however, two perspectives on this practice. One perspective is that many people cannot afford to pay for a lawyer if they must pay by the hour; thus, use of a contingent fee structure helps those who are "poorer" to obtain legal representation, which is good. The other perspective is that clients will be more willing to sue if they are not required to pay their lawyer in the event the case is unsuccessful, as is the case with contingent fees; thus, contingent fees promote litigation, which is not good.

(b) It is not ethical to sue another person without a reasonable basis for believing the claim is justified. On the other hand, sometimes the information to know accurately if a claim is justified can only be obtained through the discovery process. In such a case, filing a lawsuit is the only way to learn "clearly" if another person is at fault.

(c) Yes, Blue's denial is ethical. Although he knows that he has some degree of liability, there are at least two things he does not know. First, Blue does not know what proportion of fault is his. That is, he does not know (for example) if he is 25% at fault or 75% at fault. Second, even if he knows the degree of fault, he does not know the dollar amount in which Brown

is injured. That is, he does not know (for example) if Brown's injuries are reasonably valued at $50,000 or $250,000. Blue should not admit liability until he knows the answer to these questions.

(d) Documents 3.4 and 3.5 illustrate the mechanics of interrogatories. Interrogatories are written questions sent to other *parties* (see footnote 2); the other parties respond with written answers. In contrast, Document 3.6 illustrates the mechanics of depositions. A deposition is the oral questioning of persons under oath (including *non*-parties) (see footnote 3) in front of a court reporter who prepares a written transcript. In general, depositions are a more flexible and useful method of gathering information. However, depositions are a much more expensive process than interrogatories. The information produced by both of these methods may be used at trial.

(e) If there is any reasonable basis for a jury concluding that White has been negligent in any degree, the motion should be denied. If the only evidence presented to the court relating to the motion for summary judgment is the deposition above, there is no evidence demonstrating negligence. The only evidence is that White fenced in his horses and did not know about the construction. On this record, the motion for summary judgment may be granted.

(f) A judgment n.o.v. may be granted only if the judge is justified in saying that there is no reasonable factual basis to support the verdict of the jury. That is, the verdict must be factually unreasonable.

(g) An appellate court would be unlikely to reverse in *Doe v. Roe* because there are facts to support the verdict. One may think that the jury's interpretation of those facts is incorrect, but, unless that interpretation exceeds the bounds of reason, the verdict may not be ignored.

Chapter 4

Problem 4.1. (a) is correct. Criminal prosecution is by government, not by private parties. (b) is not correct because "double jeopardy" prohibits more than one *criminal* prosecution for a single incident. (c) is not correct because misdemeanors are lessor criminal offenses and felonies are more serious criminal offenses.

Problem 4.2. Yes, a prosecutor has sufficient evidence to prosecute. Albert has done the prohibited act, and he is presumed to intend to do that which, in fact, he did. Thus, both act and intent have been established.

Problem 4.3. (b) is correct. If a rape is said to have occurred between parties who have at other times engaged in consensual sex, the issue of wrongful intent can be particularly difficult. It can be difficult because a sexual relationship is an emotionally-charged and private relationship. The changing emotions of the parties affect the reliability of the parties statements and there are usually no witnesses to verify those statements. (a), (c) and (d) are not correct. These offenses are more likely to occur where there are witnesses present. In addition, there is not a lawful version of murder, assault or robbery like there is to a sexual relationship.

Problem 4.4. Guilty but mentally ill.

Problem 4.5. No, Milly has not been entrapped. Entrapment requires proof that the suggestion to commit a crime and the inducement to commit a crime come from the police (or their agents). If the defendant was predisposed to commit the crime there is no entrapment. In this

case, the police merely provided Milly an opportunity to commit a crime, which at the most is a suggestion that she do it. There is no claim that the police induced or persuaded Milly to steal.

Problem 4.6. *Preponderance of the evidence* is the general "burden of proof" requirement for civil cases. *Beyond a reasonable doubt* is used in criminal cases. *Beyond a shadow of a doubt* is a phrase sometimes used in churches by participants who wish to emphasize the strength of their religious beliefs.

Problem 4.7. The IV Amendment gives people the right to "be secure in their persons, houses, papers, and effects, against unreasonable searches and seizures." Arresting Sam without probable cause is unreasonable and violates the IV Amendment. The IV Amendment applies to the conduct of state and local police officers because of the "incorporation' doctrine of the XIV Amendment.

Problem 4.8. An *arraignment* takes place before a judge of a court where the criminal trial will take place. This judge may receive a plea (such as guilty or not guilty) and may sentence the defendant if he or she pleads guilty or is found guilty.

Problem 4.9. Only a judge with the power to sentence the defendant receives a plea. Because a judge at a preliminary hearing cannot sentence the defendant, there is no purpose in his receiving a plea.

Problem 4.10. So-called "Miranda"

warnings must be given before interrogation if the resulting information is to be used against the suspect at trial. On the other hand, voluntary statements without interrogation do not require a "Miranda" warning. If Nellie's statements are truly voluntary and not induced by the police, her confession can be used against her.

Chapter 5

Problem 5.1. "Double jeopardy" prevents a person from being *criminally* prosecuted twice for the same incident. The civil action against Milly is not a criminal action because she is not in jeopardy for fine or imprisonment. Thus, there has been only one criminal action against Milly.

Problem 5.2. Assault is the (1) intentional act of placing another person in (2) immediate (3) apprehension (4) for their physical safety.

Problem 5.3. (c) is correct. This is a tort of negligence, not an intentional tort. (a) is not correct because John did not intend offensive conduct against either John or Mack. (b) is not correct for the same reason (a) is not correct. Failing to look establishes an act of negligence, but not an intentional tort.

Problem 5.4. Yes, a battery has occurred. When he agrees to play basketball, Jed agrees to the physical contact and the bumps and bruises normally associated with the game. Intentionally hitting another player with a fist is outside acceptable conduct for basketball and is therefore not impliedly consented to.

Problem 5.5. No, false imprisonment has not occurred because Milly must be aware that she is confined.

Problem 5.6. Intentional infliction of emotional distress occurs when Jed's behavior becomes extreme and outrageous to a reasonable person. The facts suggest that Jed and Milly do not have a lot in common. Jed's behavior must not merely be offensive, it must be extreme and outrageous. The content of his requests, their frequency and their context must combine over a considerable period of time for a tort to occur. (Care must be taken not to confuse the tort of intentional infliction of emotional distress in violation of state tort law with "sexual harassment" in violation of federal statutes. In some contexts, sexual harassment may occur before *intentional* infliction of emotional distress occurs.)

Problem 5.7. No, Milly cannot successfully sue Jed for defamation. As a candidate for political office, Milly is a "public figure." As a public figure, Milly cannot successfully sue Jed unless what Jed said is untrue and she demonstrates that Jed acted with "actual malice." Actual malice means that Jed knew the truth of the matter or acted in open disregard of the truth. What is "hypocrisy" in a political contest is subjective, a matter of judgment in which it is difficult or impossible to know the "truth.". Persons who disagree on a debatable issue do not act with malice.

Problem 5.8. In this actual case, the facts reported were truthful and the subject of the article was a person of legitimate public interest. There was not an invasion of privacy.

Problem 5.9. This is not fraud. Price is not the only measure of the "best deal;" it may include elements of service and reliability. In addition, a certain amount of "puffery" and salesmanship is allowed.

Problem 5.10. Trespass has not occurred because the shed moving from Jed's property to Milly's property is unintentional and involuntary. It would only be trespass if the shed was defectively constructed so that it could be said that a reasonable person knew (or should have known) that adverse weather conditions could dislodge it.

Chapter 6

Problem 6.1. Liability for negligence requires proof of the following: (1) that the defendant owed a duty to the plaintiff, (2) that the defendant violated that duty, (3) that the violation of duty proximately caused a legal injury to the plaintiff, and (4) that the plaintiff suffered a legal injury.

Problem 6.2. The change in facts changes the liability of the railroad because it changes the extent of the "foreseeability" of the railroad employees. If the railroad employees see and understand that the passenger is carrying fireworks, then they can foresee that their conduct in helping the passenger may dislodge the fireworks package and cause harm to persons in the train station, including Mrs. Palsgraff.

Problem 6.3. Foreseeability *creates* duty, without which there is no negligence or liability. In contrast, the absence of foreseeability is a safety valve which *cuts off* causation which is which is not immediate and direct ("proximate").

Problem 6.4. (b) is correct. Violation of duty is negligence. If there is no duty there is no negligence. If there is no negligence there is no liability. (a) is not correct because it is not required that injuries be specifically foreseen; all that is required is that harm or injury, in general be foreseeable. (Jed is not required to foresee that Milly will suffer a broken arm, only that she may suffer injuries.) (c) is not correct because duty is not part of proximate cause.

Problem 6.5. Nothing. Under the old "contributory negligence" system, the existence of contributory negligence was an absolute bar to the recovery of claims by the person who was contributorily negligent.

Problem 6.6. Contributory negligence is *negligent* behavior by a person asserting a claim which causes harm to the person asserting the claim. In contrast, assumption of the risk is behavior *knowingly* and *intentionally* entered into which causes harm to the person asserting a claim.

Problem 6.7. *Res ipsa loquitur* is a rule of evidence, not a defense. Application of *res ipsa loquitur* in favor of a plaintiff assumes the existence of negligence and requires the defendant to disprove the existence of negligence.

Problem 6.8. The Court adopted a "unit" rule and said that the negligence of all parties contributing to an injury would be added together as a "unit." Thus, the plaintiff was 40% negligent and the defendants together as a unit were 60% at fault. To rule otherwise, said the court, would mean, under the facts of this case, that a plaintiff injured by one defendant could recover, but a plaintiff injured by several defendants could not.

Problem 6.9. Yes, foreseeability is used in a strict liability case. Foreseeability is not used to establish duty because duty (and negligence) are not part of strict liability. However, proximate cause is part of strict liability, and foreseeability is part of proximate cause.

Chapter 7

Problem 7.1. This provision gives certainty and reinforces the value of contracts in our legal society. The provision means what it says; that is, states shall not adopt laws which impair [e.g. damage or reduce] the legal requirement that parties must perform their contract obligations.

Problem 7.2. An example of a *remedy* is an award of money damages for the breach of a contract. But, suppose, for example, that the breached contract is for the sale of a rare, one-of-a-kind Van Gogh painting. In these circumstances money damages are not adequate because there is not another of this particular painting to be purchased with money. In these circumstances a court may treat the contract as imposing a *duty* to deliver the painting and order specific performance. Specific performance is an order of a court requiring a party to a contract to do something or deliver something. Thus, the contract definition contemplates contract enforcement by remedy or by performance of a duty.

Problem 7.3. This is not a contract, it is a gift. There is no consideration: Milly contributes nothing to the transaction. She does not give Jed anything of value and she does not change her legal position or otherwise suffer a detriment. All she agrees to do is receive the gift.

Problem 7.4. The distinction between unilateral and bilateral contracts is important to help in analyzing the process of offer and acceptance. Thereafter, it is not generally an important distinction.

Problem 7.5. There is not, *in fact*, any conduct by Jed (in words or otherwise) suggesting his agreement to pay Milly. However, it is only fair that Jed reimburse Milly for the taxes, so the courts will imply—as a matter of law—a fictional reimbursement agreement on between Jed (and Milly). This is called a quasi-contract.

Problem 7.6. The contract is controlled by the common law rules of contracts. The contract is for accounting *services*, not for television sets, and personal services contracts are controlled by the common law.

Problem 7.7. Common law contract rules probably apply. If we assume that the dollar value of the physician's services is greater than the dollar value of the blood, then the transaction is predominantly a transaction for services, not goods.

Chapter 8

Problem 8.1. The "assent" or agreement of the offeree is manifested by his or her performance instead of a promise.

Problem 8.2. The issue is whether the circumstances persuade a reasonable person that Millie seriously intended to form a unilateral contract (to be accepted by performance). As a matter of judgment it appears that Millie's statement is spontaneous and more a statement of scepticism than an intention to contract. Accordingly, there is no contract and Millie is not required to pay the $100 to Jed.

Problem 8.3. No, a contract was not formed. The offer required: "If anybody calls this show." Newman did not call during the show, he called after a rebroadcast of the show and by then the offer had expired by its terms. (*Newman v. Schiff*, 778 F.2d 460)

Problem 8.4. No. The exchange of time to decide in return for payment of $50 created an option. An option is a *nonrevocable* offer. Milly's option remains in effect for the period of the option and a counteroffer does not revoke it.

Problem 8.5. If Milly and Jed had earlier agreed to this procedure there would be a contract. Normally, however, silence (failure to respond) does not create a contract.

Problem 8.6. This is an implied in fact, bilateral contract. Each of the parties has indicated agreement to the transaction in which Jed receives a candy bar and agrees to pay for it.

Problem 8.7. Milly cannot accept because Jed's note is just an inquiry ("will you paint my house"?). If, indeed, Jed's note was an offer, it clearly calls for a response after which a bilateral contract could result.

Problem 8.8. If no method of communication is specified, the offeree is impliedly authorized to use the method by which the offer was communicated. Thus a safe way for Jed to respond is by sending his response through the U.S. Mail.

Problem 8.9. No, there is not a contract. Milly's acceptance was never received by Jed, as the offer required.

Problem 8.10. The dissenting judges reasoned as follows: (1) there clearly was a contract requiring Action Ads to provide medical insurance; (2) Judes has suffered medical expenses; (3) if the contract is vague about the terms of the medical insurance that should be provided, that is the fault of Action Ads, not Judes; therefore, (4) because lack of specificity is the fault of Action Ads, it is fair for the court to estimate what normal insurance coverage would have provided and award that to Judes.

Problem 8.11. The most important factor is justifiable "reliance." In the first place, Warner made estimates knowing that to do so would "induce action;" in other words, Warner knew or should have known that others would rely on their estimate and take action thereon. Second, reliance occurred; that is, "Price relied on Warner's bid."

Chapter 9

Problem 9.1. No. Quite possibly the result would have been different. The case was decided on an exception, a "loophole": unilateral mistakes are not normally rescinded, but they are if the mistake is known to the other party. In the original decision the plaintiff's (the Whitakers) knew immediately that a mistake had been made because $500,000 was such an "outrageous" amount. In contrast, $5,000 is not such an outrageous amount and it is quite possible that the court may have concluded that this amount would not communicate to the Whitakers that a mistake had been made.

Problem 9.2. No, *caveat emptor* was not successfully applied. *Caveat emptor* means "let the buyer beware," and the court was clear that such a doctrine was not consistent with enlightened views of honesty and ethics. In short, the purchaser was entitled to believe the seller and was not required to "double check" to be sure that

the seller was telling the truth.

Problem 9.3. Misrepresentation. Even with good evidence, fraud is always troublesome to prove because the mental state (the intention) of the defendant must be proved. If all the plaintiff wants is recission, it is sufficient to prove misrepresentation because proof of wrongful intent is not required.

Problem 9.4. No, the agreement cannot be rescinded on the basis of mistake. In this case there is no mistake: both parties knew they did not know the contents of the compartment. Thus, risk was part of the transaction and the contract will be enforced.

Problem 9.5. Yes, Loral was successful. Loral was forced into the terms of the second contract by the threat of Austin that it would breach the terms of the first contract. Loral could not get the goods it needed—and that Austin had already contracted to deliver—from any other source. (It would have been perfectly lawful for Austin to refuse to contract with Loral a second time, if that was where the negotiations ended. What Austin did wrong was to threaten breach of an existing contract if the new contract did not have terms to Austin's liking.)

Problem 9.6. The opinion does not tell us who ultimately won the lawsuit. Odorizzi simply won a preliminary skirmish. The trial court threw his lawsuit out of court without a trial; but, on appeal, the lawsuit was reinstated, with the right to proceed on to trial.

Chapter 10

Problem 10.1. Remember that the law does not care whether or not a contracting party *enjoys* what he or she becomes obligated to do. (For example, football star, Steve Young, may enjoy playing football). The point is whether the contracting party becomes legally obligated to do—or not do—something which was previously not their obligation. In this case, in a bargained exchange, Millie becomes legally obligated to refrain from auto repair, and that is good consideration.

Problem 10.2. Return to the example where Millie promises to give Jed an orange and Jed promises to give Millie an apple. Suppose that because Jed gave away his apple, he could not make apple juice; because he had no apple juice, he could not make apple cider; because he could not make apple cider, he did not have any to give to his boss for Christmas; because he did not give his boss apple cider for Christmas, his boss got mad and fired him; therefore, Jed gave up his job for an orange. The point is that when people make promises in the process of contracting, all kinds of intended and unintended things happen as a result. Which of these intended and unintended things should the law take into account in deciding whether there is consideration? The answer is, take into account what the parties "bargained for." And what they bargained for is an orange and an apple.

Problem 10.3. The contract would not be enforceable because the young man would not change his legal position. If, by law, he is already prohibited from drinking, using tobacco, swearing and playing cards or billiards for money, he has a pre-existing duty which does not change by virtue of the arrangement with his uncle.

Problem 10.4. The result would be the same: the contract is valid. Contracts deal with future performance, and over time the value of one or more of the performances is likely to change. This means that changing value is one of the risks of contracting. If there is no unfairness in the formation of a contract, the courts do not usually listen to arguments which simply to the value of what was exchanged. This is particularly true in the *Brads* case where the extent of Brads' services were known to be uncertain because of his health.

Problem 10.5. Yes because there is a bargained exchange of promises by which each party will do something in the future: Jed will save the girl, which is a detriment to him (he agrees to do something he is not legally obligated to do) and Millie agrees to pay the money which is a detriment to her (and a benefit to him).

Problem 10.6. The answer, of course, depends on local government law in Kentucky (in 1963). It is the law in many states that police officers retain their authority and obligations even when off-duty. If that was the law in Kentucky in 1963, the outcome would remain the same, even if the officers worked while off-duty. Even when off-duty the police officers would have a pre-existing legal duty.

Problem 10.7. "To Milly: I promise to do yard work at your home for thirty days, at the rate of $30 per day."

Problem 10.8. Contract #1: Millie will be successful. Jed has a pre-existing duty to pay $1000, and when, in a new contract, he merely promises to pay part of what he was already under a duty to pay, he does not suffer any detriment. This is an application of the pre-existing duty rule. Contract #2: Millie will not be successful. Each party gives consideration for the promise of the other: Milly promises to give up $500 and Jed promises to pay the money on June 1 instead of July 1. One may argue that a payment 30 days early is not worth $500, but that is an argument that goes only to value. Contract #3: Millie will not be successful. Each party gives consideration for the promise of the other: the amount to be paid is *un*liquidated (disputed) and when each party gives up their right to contest the amount payable, each has suffered a detriment.

Problem 10.9. It is likely that Hoffman would lose. The doctrine of promissory estoppel holds promissors responsible for the consequences of their promises. If the promises of Red Owl were not, in fact, the real cause of Hoffman selling his grocery store and bakery, then Red Owl would not be held responsible for Hoffman's losses.

Chapter 11

Problem 11.1. The answer is no, because there is no evidence that Jed that Milly intended to use the car as a "getaway" car.

Problem 11.2. Here is the answer of the court:

Metropolitan Creditors Service of Sacramento v. Soheil Sadri

19 Cal.Rpts.2d 646 (CalApp. 1 Dist. 1993)

KING, Associate Judge.

* * *

It cannot be denied that California's historical public policy against gambling has been substantially eroded. Pari-mutuel horse racing, draw poker clubs, and charitable bingo games have proliferated throughout the state. These forms of gambling are indulged by a relatively small segment of the population, but the same cannot be said of the California State Lottery, which was passed by initiative measure and has become firmly rooted in California's popular culture. Lottery tickets are now as close as the nearest convenience store, turning many Californians into regular gamblers. * * * If it was true as observed in 1961 that "Californians cannot afford to be too pious about this matter of gambling" * * * then all the more

so in 1993 would expressions of piety on the subject ring hollow. On this score, the *Crockford's Club* decision has a point.

But the court in *Crockford's Club* [a case dealing with gambling *per se* as opposed to the enforcement of gambling debts] failed to draw the critical distinction between public acceptance of gambling itself and California's deep-rooted policy against enforcement of gambling debts—that is, gambling *on credit*. While the public policy against the former has been substantially eroded, the public policy against the latter has not.

* * *

The judgment of the municipal court [refusing to enforce the debt] is affirmed.

[Although it is a difficult question—and involves issues that go beyond what is taught in this chapter—can you think of a way the gambling casino could *lawfully* enforce the debt in California? (Sending two very big and ill-tempered men to visit with Mr. Sadri doesn't count.)

The court in the *Sadri* decision noted, with remarkable candor, that the casino could sue Mr. Sadri in Nevada (which does *not* have a policy against the enforcement of gambling debt). Then, the Nevada *judgment* could be brought to

California where the California courts would be constitutionally obligated to enforce a judgment of a sister state. ("If a licensed owner of a Nevada casino wishes to recover on a check or memorandum of indebtedness given by a California resident under such circumstances, the owner will have to obtain a Nevada state court judgment * * * which will then be entitled to full faith and credit in California regardless of our public policy.")]

Problem 11.3. The answer is yes. The court in *Noble v. Ellis* was candid in saying that using the apartment would make a difference. The court stated: "Another important factor in our determination that the lease is voidable turns on the specific factual pattern of this case. Here, Noble/Odle never moved into the apartment and thus never benefitted in any way from the lease agreement. This case may be distinguished from a situation in which tenants moved into the apartment and then, upon discovering that the apartment was never registered and never received an occupancy permit, attempt to escape future rental payments as well as demand a refund on past payments. In the latter case, the tenants' remedy rests on their ability to prove a breach of

an implied warranty of habitability . . ." In short, if Noble and Odle had used the apartment, their remedy would be the difference between the value of the apartment in a lawful condition and the value of the apartment in an unlawful condition.

Problem 11.4. This is an activity sponsored by a public school district for public school students. School districts owe a duty to duty of reasonable care to students under their care. The exculpatory clause would probably be contrary to the public interest and unenforceable.

Problem 11.5. The answer is no. Only the minor has the option to disaffirm.

Problem 11.6. Minority. Using minority, Milly must only prove her age. Using mental impairment, she—or someone acting for her—must prove a lack of mental ability, which might be difficult.

Chapter 12

Problem 12.1. No. The focus of the statute of frauds is not on the tort of fraud. The objective of the original statute of frauds was to prevent false (perjured) testimony regarding oral contracts.

Problem 12.2. A contract which is *not* controlled by the statute of frauds (for example, a six-month employment contract) is said to be "without" or "outside of" the statute of frauds. On the other hand, a contract which *is* controlled by the statute of frauds (for example, a six-year employment contract) is said to be "within" the statute of frauds.

Problem 12.3. Jed is not correct. An easement is an "interest" in land and therefore the

easement agreement must be in writing to be enforced.

Problem 12.4. If the promise of the bank is interpreted as an *unconditional* promise to pay for the flooring work, then the statute of frauds does not apply. One may argue that the bank did *not* promise to pay *in the event of the failure or default of another*; rather, the only condition was the decision to continue work. Thus, if Wilson Floors agreed to continue to work, the promise to pay was *unconditional* and outside of the statute of frauds. If the promise of the bank was outside of the statute of frauds, the promise is enforceable without reference to the main purpose rule.

Problem 12.5. The contract is

enforceable. The test for long-term contracts deals with what *may* happen, not what actually *does* happen. Is the contract hypothetically performable within one year measured from the date of contract performance? The answer is yes. Measuring from the date of formation, it was *possible* for the contract to be performed within one year. The fact that it was not *actually* performed within one year is irrelevant.

Problem 12.6. Conditional or unconditional, the promise must be in writing to be enforced. The change in facts does not change the result.

Problem 12.7. In general, testimony demonstrating fraud is *not* barred by the parol evidence rule and is admissible. (Here, though, Slavinsky is caught in a tactical dilemma. If her testimony about fraud is believed, it tends to invalidate the contract, it does not tend to amend the contract. And that is her dilemma: she wants to enforce the contract after the court allows her to orally amend it; she does not want to invalidate the contract. Thus, getting her oral testimony into evidence by claiming fraud may be counter-productive.)

Chapter 13

Problem 13.1. Yes, Jed is within "privity." In fact, both Jed and Milly are within privity. "Privity" refers to the word "private," and the contract is a private relationship between Jed and Milly.

Problem 13.2. Yes, Ms. Snyder had standing. Standing is an acknowledgment that a person has rights that are at risk and may participate in litigation concerning them. In *Snyder v. Freeman*, Ms. Snyder was an intended beneficiary, thus she was entitled to sue to enforce her contract rights (as a third party creditor beneficiary).

Problem 13.3. If, indeed, the assignment of Mr. Cunningham's contract required him to play for another *team* it would not be assignable. Here, though, the contract was merely assigned to a new owner of the *same* team, thus, the nature of his performance would not change.

Problem 13.4. Using the American rule, John wins, because the first assignee owns the contract right. Using the English rule, Judy wins because she was the first to give notice without knowledge of the claims of others.

Problem 13.5. Neither assignments nor delegations can alter the reasonable expectations of the other parties to a contract. This is particularly true with respect to contracts for the performance of personal services. Thus, Jed, the butler, cannot be forced through assignment to be the butler of another party, and, Jed cannot by delegation substitute another to be a butler in his place.

Problem 13.6. With assignment and delegation, Milly remains liable if the contract is not performed properly. With novation, Mill ceases to be a contracting party and she has no liability if the contract is not performed properly.

Chapter 14

Problem 14.1. No, this is not a condition precedent. Effective when the contract was signed, Milly has agreed to receive payments over 5 years. If a bank agrees to finance the deal, that agreement (by the bank) *cuts off* Milly's obligation. (A condition precedent *starts* a performance, it does not end it.) Therefore, the bank's commitment is a condition *subsequent*, not a condition precedent.

Problem 14.2. No, this is not a condition subsequent. The condition in this question—if it is met—*commences* Milly's obligation to purchase Blackacre; thus, it is a condition precedent.

Problem 14.3. Probably not. The normal rule is that an express condition in a contract (use Reading brand pipe) must be fully performed. In the original opinion, the court did not enforce this rule for reasons "of equity and fairness." But, if the contractor intentionally breached the contract, the reasons of equity and fairness disappear, and it is likely the court would then enforce the contract as written.

Problem 14.4. This is a matter of considered opinion. It is not unlikely that the judge would conclude that loss of electrical power should have been anticipated and standby generation provided for. In that case, Wolf Trap's defense of impossibility would not be successful.

Problem 14.5. The Opera will be successful if two requirements can be met. First, that Wolf Trap knew (foreseeability) that the Opera planned to sell the t-shirts. (In a contract of this kind, it is likely that there was a contract provision giving permission for the Opera to sell t-shirts.) Second, evidence showing that a loss of $10,000 is a reasonable calculation (definiteness). (In the full opinion, it is revealed that this was a four-night engagement and that the first three nights had gone off without a problem.) If there is a history of profits, then the amount of profits is definite and not speculative. If the requirements of foreseeability and definiteness are met, then consequential damages would be allowed.

Problem 14.6. This is a matter of considered opinion. Three years is too long. How long does it take an office manager to get a new job? Six months? If that is a reasonable estimate, then six months pay would be a reasonable amount as liquidated damages.

Problem 14.7. No, the courts will not compel the performance of personal services. In the first place, making someone do something of a personal nature they oppose is a difficult thing to do, and the courts would resist it on these practical grounds. In the second place, it has been held that forcing a person into the performance of personal services violates the prohibition in Amendment XIII of the United States Constitution against "involuntary servitude."

Chapter 15

Problem 15.1 Yes, the rules have been modified. Section 1-103 includes a list of contracting principles which have *not* been modified, and consideration is not on that list.

Problem 15.2. Yes, the Sales law applies. In *Bryant v. Tri-County Electric Membership Corp.*, 844 F.Supp. 347 (1994), the court stated: "The general view holding electricity to be a "product" sensibly accounts for the fact that electricity is created, harnessed, measured, transported, bought and sold, like products generally."

Problem 15.3. Yes, she can withdraw her offer. Section 2-205 begins: "A offer by a merchant to buy or sell goods *in a signed writing* . . ." The firm offer concept applies only to *written offers* by merchants.

Problem 15.4. With respect to time, § 2-310 provides: "Unless otherwise agreed . . . payment is due at *the time and place at which the buyer is to receive the goods* even though the place of shipment is the place of delivery." With respect to payment by check, § 2-511(2) provides: "Tender of payment is sufficient when *made by any means or in any manner current in the ordinary course of business* unless the seller demands payment in legal tender and gives any extension of time reasonably necessary to procure it. Assuming payment by check is current in the ordinary course of the wholesale small appliance business, JedMart may pay by check.

Problem 15.5. The outcome probably would not change. Section 2-207(1) provides that a confirmation is *not* an acceptance if it expressly requires the other party to agree to additional terms, which in this case are the GOVERNING LAW provisions. Without that agreement, Falconer Glass should not have proceeded to perform because without an acceptance there was no contract. However, Falconer Glass proceeded to perform. Section 2-207(3) provides that "conduct by both parties which recognizes the existence of a contract is sufficient to establish a contract for sale although the writings of the parties do not otherwise establish a contract." In such a case the "contract consist[s] of those terms on which the writings of the parties agree." Absent an agreement on the GOVERNING LAW provisions, they would not be part of the contract.

Problem 15.6. The result might change. At common law, evidence was admissible to show that there was no agreement, or that further agreement was anticipated. Technically, this was not *parole* evidence because attacking the *existence* of a contract is different than attacking the *terms* of a contract. Section 2-202 does not seem to prohibit this form of evidence. Please re-read the next-to-the-last paragraph of the *Intershoe* opinion because this is the technical difference being discussed. The plaintiff (Interstate) lost on this point because the evidence was clear that the argument was about contract terms and not about contract existence. But, *if* the language in Problem 15.6 existed, then plaintiff could argue that the confirmation slip was not the final contract and introduce evidence on what that final contract was intended to include.

Problem 15.7. The answer is uncertain. Judge Wachtler said that he was offended by a purchase price which was more than twice the fair market value of the freezer. He was also offended by credit charges which exceeded by more than $100 the retail value of the freezer. Undoubtedly, he was also offended by sophisticated sellers so obviously taking advantage of unsophisticated and poor buyers. How much may sales price and credit charges exceed fair market value without offending the conscience of a judge? Although it is a judgment call, we will say that more than doubling the fair market value in a sale to an unsophisticated and poor buyer is still unconscionable.

Chapter 16

Problem 16.1. Section 2-401(1) provides that "Title to goods cannot pass under a contract for sale prior to their identification to the contract." Goods cannot be identified to the contract before they come into existence; therefore, title to the hardware would pass to the buyer on August 1, and title to the software programming would pass to the buyer on September 1.

Problem 16.2. Honeycutt would probably win. The principal evidence of Honeycutt's failure to act in good faith was his failure to receive proper title to the boat, motor and trailer. If Honeycutt received proper title, the only claim left to Lane would be that the price Honeycutt paid was so low that he was not acting in good faith. However, it is unlikely that just getting a "good deal" on a used boat, motor and trailer would destroy Honeycutt's good faith claim.

Problem 16.3. Porter would win. The owner of goods loses them if he *entrusts* them to a merchant who thereafter sells them to an innocent third party. Under the revised facts, Wertz *stole* the painting, it was not entrusted to him; thus, § 2-403(2) does not give the merchant power to transfer good title to a subsequent buyer.

Problem 16.4. It means that Jed may reject the apples if Milly's failure to give notice of shipment caused material loss or delay. Section 2-509(1)(a) provides that "the risk of loss passes to the buyer when the goods are duly delivered to the carrier." Section 2-504(c) requires Milly to promptly notify Jed of the shipment. The penalty for failure to notify is that the failure "is ground for rejection . . . if material delay or loss ensues."

Problem 16.5. Jed. The contract is a shipment contract. Quoting from *NINTH STREET EAST, LTD v. Harrison:* "The law erects a presumption in favor of construing the agreement as a "shipment" contract, as opposed to a "destination" contract." In a shipment contract,

the risk of loss is on the buyer.

Problem 16.6. The outcome would probably not change. Section 2-503(a) requires that "tender [of delivery] must be at a reasonable hour, and if it is of goods they must be kept available for the period reasonably necessary to enable the buyer to take possession." Section 2-503(b) requires that "the buyer must furnish facilities reasonably suited to the receipt of the goods." The facts of the case are that the delivery driver delivered the goods to the store and the defendant's wife would not receive them because the driver would not carry the goods inside the store. The delivery was apparently at a reasonable hour and place; therefore, tender having been properly made, the risk of loss would shift to the defendant.

Chapter 17

Problem 17.1. Mary was forced to return the stolen painting (or it's value) just as Feigen was. The two crooks, Von Maker and Wertz were liable to Feigen for selling him a painting to which he did not get good title. [§ 2-312] Likewise, Jed is liable to Mary for selling her a painting to which she did not get good title. [§ 2-312] The factual difference is that Feigen returned the painting (or its value) and could *not* get reimbursed from the crooks, who had disappeared. On the other hand, Mary returned the painting (or its value), but *was* able to get reimbursed from Jed, who was a legitimate art dealer.

Problem 17.2. Section 2-313 provides that descriptions of the goods, and affirmations of fact or promises relating to the goods must be "part of the basis of the bargain." The warranty booklet may be part of the basis of the bargain because it is in and a part of the truck, which is examined during negotiations, or, it may be referred to in the sales agreement and become part of the bargain in that manner. Under the revised facts, Harris would win unless that warranty booklet was referred to in the sales agreement.

Problem 17.3. The court used the "reasonable expectations" test. Although there is a reference to "foreign substances" in the opinion, the court quotes the following language, from Justice Taft, with approval: "the possible presence of a piece of oyster shell in or attached to an oyster is so *well known* to anyone who eats oysters that we can say as a matter of law that one who eats oysters can *reasonably anticipate* and guard against eating such a piece of shell."

Problem 17.4. No Jed will not win. Not all boat owners water ski; many fish or do other things. Waterskiing is a particular purpose and Jed did not make Milly aware that he was relying on her to select or furnish a motor for waterskiing. Thus, §2-315 does not apply.

Problem 17.5. There is an implied warranty of fitness. Under these facts, Trans-Aire has been clear that it is relying on Northern to select a suitable adhesive. [§ 2-315] This warranty has not been eliminated by the fact Trans-Aire did not examine it. Comment 8 to § 2-316(3)(b) states: "In order to bring the transaction within the scope of 'refused to examine' in paragraph (b), it is not sufficient that the goods are available for inspection. There must in addition be a demand by the seller that the buyer examine the goods fully. The seller by the demand puts the buyer on notice that he is assuming the risk of defects which the examination ought to reveal. The language 'refused to examine' in this paragraph is intended to make clear the necessity for such demand."

Chapter 18

Problem 18.1. Jed is not correct. Section 1-203 requires that *all* contracting parties act in good faith. The only difference between merchants and non-merchants is that § 2-103(1)(b) requires that merchants must also observe commercial standards of fair dealing in their trade to be in good faith.

Problem 18.2. No, Jed is not in breach of contract. Section 2-206(1)(b), which deals with offer and acceptance in the formation of a contract, provides: "a shipment of non-conforming goods does not constitute an acceptance *if the seller seasonably notifies the buyer* that the shipment is offered only as an accommodation to the buyer." Jed's actions are not a contract acceptance because he notified Milly that his shipment of nonconforming widgets was simply an accommodation—a favor.

Problem 18.3. Under these facts, the doctrine of commercial impracticability applies. Reduction in milk production by 50%, caused by disease, was unforseen and thus it was not dealt with (allocated) in the contract. Thus, Maple Farms is not required to perform as the contract requires. But, § 2-615(b) provides that where the inability to perform "affect[s] only a part of the seller's capacity to perform, he must allocate production and deliveries among his customers." Accordingly, Maple Farms must allocate 50% of the contracted amount of milk to the school district.

Problem 18.4. Ambassador's complaint is that Tai Wah is doing nothing to correct the problem with the first shipment of recorders. If that is so, then the second shipment is likely to be defective, like the first shipment was. Ambassador should inspect the second shipment, and if the recorders are defective, refuse to accept them. This puts Tai Wah in a tight place because the goods are in the US without a buyer. That means that Tai Wah may be forced to negotiate a settlement with Ambassador. On the other hand, if the second shipment is not defective, Ambassador should accept it, but offset the payment against a settlement on the first shipment.

Problem 18.5. A seller's incidental damages are described in §2-710. They include "charges, expenses or commissions" involved in stopping delivery of goods, or transporting or storing them. Thus, if the seller, in *Madsen v. Murrey & Sons Co., Inc.*, had to store the pool tables or transport them elsewhere to sell them, the costs of doing those things would be added to the seller's recoverable damages.

Problem 18.6. If Lyn-Flex chooses to accept the non-conforming goods, they should at the same time give Moulton notice of the defects as required by §2-607(3). Then, Moulton must pay the contract price, minus damages. Damages are calculated in §2-714(2) as the difference between the actual value of the molds and the value of the molds if they had conformed to the contract. Thus, for example, if it will take $4,000 to repair the molds, the actual value of the molds is $11,000, and that is the amount Lyn-Flex must pay.

Chapter 19

Problem 19.1. Neither of the plaintiffs has suffered any significant injury. In *Jordan*, one suspects that the factory worker, was not really hurt by three flies (and other foreign material); and, in *Yong Cha Hong*, it is an unpleasant fact that worms (or miscellaneous chicken parts) are edible and not harmful. Cases of this kind are often handled on a contingent fee basis in which the attorney receives a percentage of the recovery, and the hope is that the defendant will pay money to avoid publicity. If the defendant is not afraid of publicity, the attorney has a case where he or she can prove liability, but not damage; thus, the potential recovery may be small.

Problem 19.2. This case is being tried in federal court on the basis of diversity jurisdiction. Thus, the federal court must apply Maryland state law. Not being, himself, a Maryland judge, Judge Smalkin must inquire what state law is on the question at hand.

Problem 19.3. Yes, Baldban may be safely sold. If the side effect (minor liver damage) cannot be avoided, the drug may be sold with a warning of the side effect. A warning is necessary because the side effect would not otherwise be known to the consuming public. With an adequate warning, the drug is not *unreasonably* dangerous and thus not defective.

Problem 19.4. Lutz will receive $495,000. The recovery of the plaintiff is reduced by the amount of the plaintiff's responsibility, which is 45%. $900,000, reduced by 45% is $495,000. (Return to Chapter Six for a review of comparative negligence/responsibility.)

Problem 19.5. Jed receives $100,000. In this case we simply have three different reasons why Jed is entitled to the money.

Chapter 20

Problem 20.1. This is not a negotiable instrument. A negotiable instrument contains a promise or order for a sum of money. The language giving the maker the option to deliver securities and not money means that the document is not negotiable.

Problem 20.2. It is negotiable. Section 3-106 (a) provides: "Except as provided in this section, for the purposes of Section 3-104 (a), a promise or order is unconditional unless it states (i) an *express* condition to payment" (italics added). Thus, if the instrument expressly provided, "This note will not be paid *until* I receive a 1990 Cadillac from Sam," it would not be negotiable. In the present case, however, the idea that Fred would not pay the money if the Cadillac is not delivered is only *implied*, if it exists at all.

Problem 20.3. It is not negotiable. Section 3-104 (a) (3) provides that a negotiable instrument may not "state any other undertaking or instruction by the person promising or ordering payment to do any act in addition to the payment of money."

Problem 20.4. It is not negotiable. It does not contain the words of negotiability: "pay to the order of," or "pay to bearer." In addition, it is not an enforceable contract because the purpose is illegal. If it read: "I promise to pay Louis $1,000 for painting my house," it would be a contract, but not a negotiable instrument.

Problem 20.5. It is a demand instrument. Mike is entitled to the money any time he demands it. An instrument which does not state when it is payable is payable on demand.

Problem 20.6. All of the phrases, except [a] are acceptable:

[a] eliminates negotiability. Section 3-

104 (d) provides: "A promise or order other than a check is not an instrument [instrument means negotiable instrument] if . . . it contains a conspicuous statement, however expressed, to the effect that the promise or order is not negotiable or is not an instrument governed by this Article."

[b] is acceptable because it is merely an explanation of why Sam is writing; it does not express a condition. (On this point, review the answer to exercise #5—after you have answered exercise #5.)

[c] is acceptable because § 3-108 (b) provides that "A promise or order is 'payable at a definite time' if it is payable on elapse of a definite period of time after sight or acceptance."

[d] is acceptable because §3-106 (a) provides that "A reference to another writing does not of itself make the promise or order conditional." Of course, if the phrase provided "This instrument is *subject* to the cabin lease," then the note would not be negotiable.

[e] is acceptable. The authors of Article 3 provide this commentary to § 3-112: "Under Section 3-104 (a) the requirement of a 'fixed amount' applies only to principal. The amount of interest payable is that described in the instrument."

Chapter 21

Problem 21.1. This is not a draft, check, or note. It is not a negotiable instrument; it is only an acknowledgment of debt.

Problem 21.2. (d) is the correct answer because a draft is a three-party instrument signed by a drawer; (a) is not correct because a draft is signed by a drawer, not a maker; (b) is not entirely correct because drafts may be time instruments as well as demand instruments; (c) is not correct because drafts are three-party instruments.

Problem 21.3. A check is a draft which is drawn on a bank and payable on demand; thus, all checks are drafts. Not all drafts are drawn on a bank, and not all drafts are payable on demand; thus, not all drafts are checks.

Problem 21.4. It is a time draft. It has three parties: Milly is the drawer who give a command to pay; Jed is the drawee who is commanded to pay; and, Mary, Martha or Matilda

who are the payees. (For purposes of classification, no distinction is drawn between a single payee or multiple payees.) It is a time draft because it is payable after the expiration of a period of time and is not payable on demand. The instrument is not a note because it contains an order to pay and not a promise to pay, and because it has three parties instead of two parties. The instrument is not a check because it is not drawn on a bank and is not payable on demand.

Problem 21.5. A cashier's check is a check which a bank draws on itself. Document 21.7 is a cashier's check because M.R. Owens, acting for First Bank, drawn the check on the First Bank. A teller's check is a check which a bank draws on another bank. In Document 21.8, a cashier's check is converted into a teller's check by changing the instrument so that the drawer is First Bank and the drawee is Second Bank.

Chapter 22

Problem 22.1. The *simplest* way for Jed to negotiate the instrument to Sam is for Jed to hand it to Sam. Negotiation requires delivery of an instrument which is indorsed with any

signatures necessary to create a holder. The instrument is payable to "bearer," thus no signatures are necessary to create a holder.

Problem 22.2. No. The words of negotiability ('pay to the order of" or "pay to bearer") are not necessary in indorsements. The decision whether the instrument will be negotiable was made by the issuer; he or she decides whether to use the words of negotiability. Thereafter, the function of indorsements is simply to transfer the note from person to person.

Problem 22.3.

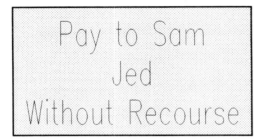

Problem 22.4. Mary can successfully present the note to Milly for payment. If Lucy had agreed to paint Jed's house, and the note was negotiated to her to pay for the paint job, then Jed can sue Lucy for breach of that contract. But, Mary can negotiate the note to the next person without inquiring to learn if the house painting agreement was performed.

Problem 22.5.

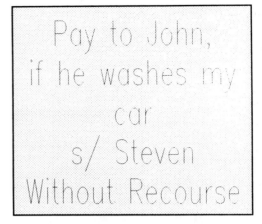

Steven directs that the note will be paid to John; the indorsement is special. The indorsement places a condition on payment of the note; the indorsement is restrictive. The indorsement is without recourse; the indorsement is qualified. The indorsement is by Steven, who is not a holder of the instrument; the indorsement is anomalous.

Chapter 23

Problem 23.1. Milly gives value when she cancels an old debt. If she had no knowledge that Jed defrauded Scott, and if she acts honestly, she is a holder in due course, and Scott must pay her. Although unusual, this is an example that a *payee* can be a holder in due course. (Scott cannot successfully assert fraud in the inducement against a holder in due course.)

Problem 23.2. Milly is not a holder in due course because she did not give value before learning of the defenses of the maker. If she had learned of the defenses after paying $500, she would be a holder in due course in the amount of $555 ($500 divided by $900 = .555 X $1,000 = $555). If she had learned of the defenses after paying the entire $900, she would be a holder in due course for $1,000.

Problem 23.3. The only form of fraud which can be successfully asserted against a holder in due course is fraud in the execution. Fraud in the execution requires proof that the maker or drawer of the negotiable instrument did not know what he or she was signing, and with reasonable diligence could not learn. In this case there is no evidence that Candace could not read the English language, and as a business person, the reasonable assumption is that she can. She simply choose not to read the document. She must pay the holder in due course. (Her recourse is to bring an action against the salesman, if he can be found.) This is not a consumer transaction because the siding is purchased for business purposes.

Problem 23.4. This is not a negotiable instrument, because the document is not payable "to the order of," or "to bearer." Because it is not a negotiable instrument, there can be no holders in due course. Milly can successfully assert his defense of fraud, and Matthew cannot successfully enforce the instrument. Of course, if the note was negotiable, Matthew would be sheltered and have the rights of a holder in due course. (Matthew knows of the fraud, but there is no evidence he was a party to it.)

Chapter 24

Problem 24.1. Sam can avoid indorser's liability. The simplest way is with a qualified indorsement, which is demonstrated with Document 22.5 in Chapter 22. The other possible way is by converting a blank indorsement into a special indorsement, without signing it, as demonstrated with Document 22.4 in Chapter 22.

Problem 24.2. Sam and Milly are both liable on the check. Mike gave notice to Sam within thirty days of date on which Mike received notice, and Sam gave notice to Milly within thirty days of the date on which Sam received notice. [See § 3-503(c)]

Problem 24.3. An indorser promises to make an instrument good to those who take it after him. Thus, Sam is liable to Mike on the indorser's liability. Milly is not liable to Sam because she did not indorse the instrument. The forger, if he can be found, is liable to Sam. Otherwise, Sam bears the loss.

Problem 24.4. ABC Banana Co. does not actually intend that the Yellow Heart Banana Co. have the money because the money is not owed since the invoice is a fake. In such a case, the indorsement is legally effective and ABC must pay on the instrument. [§ 3-404(b)]

Glossary

Glossary

abandoned property Property that an owner has discarded with the intent to relinquish his or her rights in it, or mislaid or lost property that the owner has given up any further attempts to locate

abatement If the property the testator leaves is not sufficient to satisfy all the beneficiaries named in a will and there are both general and residuary bequests, the residuary bequest is abated first (i.e., paid last).

absolute priority rule A rule that says a reorganization plan is fair and equitable to an impaired class of unsecured creditors or equity holders if no class below it receives anything in the plan.

acceptance A manifestation of assent by the offeree to the terms of the offer in a manner invited or required by the offer as measured by the objective theory of contracts. Occurs when a buyer or lessee takes any of the following actions after a reasonable opportunity to inspect the goods: The buyer or lessee either (1) signifies to the seller or lessor in words or by conduct that the goods are conforming or that the goods will be taken or retained in spite of their nonconformity, or (2) fails to effectively reject the goods within a reasonable time after their delivery or tender by the seller or lessor. Acceptance also occurs if a buyer acts inconsistently with the seller's ownership rights in the goods.

acceptance method The bankruptcy court must approve a plan of reorganization if (1) the plan is in the *best interests* of each class of claims and interests, (2) the plan is *feasible*, (3) at least one class of claims *votes* to accept the plan, and (4) each class of claims and interests is *nonimpaired*.

accession Occurs when the value of personal property increases because it is added to or improved by natural or manufactured means.

accommodation A shipment that is offered to the buyer as a replacement for the original shipment when the original shipment cannot be filled.

accommodation party A party who signs an instrument and lends his or her name (and credit) to another party to the instrument.

accord An agreement whereby the parties agree to accept something different in satisfaction of the original contract.

accord and satisfaction The settlement of a contract dispute. The *accord* is the agreement whereby parties agree to settle a contract dispute by accepting something different than provided in the original contract. *Satisfaction* is the performance of an accord.

accountant-client privilege A law enacted in approximately 20 states that says an accountant cannot be called as a witness against a client in a court action in that state; federal courts do not recognize this law.

accountant malpractice Occurs when the accountant breaches the duty of reasonable care, knowledge, skill, and judgment that he or she owes to a client when providing auditing and other accounting services to the client.

action for an accounting A formal judicial proceeding in which the court is authorized to (1) review the partnership and the partners' transactions and (2) award each partner his or her share of the partnership assets.

act of monopolizing A required act for there to be a violation of Section 2 of the Sherman Act. Possession of monopoly power without such act does not violate Section 2.

act of state doctrine States that judges of one country cannot question the validity of an act committed by another country within that other country's borders. It is based on the principle that a country has absolute authority over what transpires within its own territory.

actus reus "Guilty act"-the actual performance of the criminal act.

ademption A principle that says if a testator leaves a specific devise of property to a beneficiary, but the property is no longer in the estate when the testator dies, the beneficiary receives nothing.

adequate assurance of due performance A party to a sales or lease contract may demand an adequate assurance of performance from the other party if there is an indication that the contract will be breached by that party.

adjudged insane A person who has been adjudged insane by a proper court or administrative agency. A contract entered into by such person is *void.*

administrative agencies Agencies that the legislative and executive branches of federal and state governments establish.

administrative dissolution Involuntary dissolution of a corporation that is ordered by the secretary of state if the corporation has failed to comply with certain procedures required by law.

administrative law judge (ALJ) A judge, presiding over administrative proceedings, who decides questions of law and fact concerning the case.

Administrative Procedure Act (APA) An act that establishes certain administrative procedures that federal administrative agencies must follow in conducting their affairs.

administrative subpoena An order that directs the subject of the subpoena to disclose the requested information.

adverse action A denial or revocation of credit or a change in the credit terms offered.

adverse possession When a person who wrongfully possesses someone else's real property obtains title to that property if certain statutory requirements are met.

advertisement A general advertisement is an invitation to make an offer. A specific advertisement is an offer.

affirmative action Policy that provides that certain job preferences will be given to minority or other protected class applicants when an employer makes an employment decision.

after-acquired property Property that the debtor acquires after the security agreement is executed.

Age Discrimination in Employment Act (ADEA) of 1967 Prohibits age discrimination practices against employees who are 40 and older.

agency The principal-agent relationship; the fiduciary relationship "which results from the manifestation of consent by one person to another that the other shall act in his behalf and subject to his control, and consent by the other so to act."

agency by ratification An agency that occurs when (1) a person misrepresents him- or herself as another's agent when in fact he or she is not and (2) the purported principal ratifies the unauthorized act.

agency coupled with an interest A special type of agency relationship that is created for the agent's benefit; irrevocable by the principal.

agency law The large body of common law that governs agency; a mixture of contract law and tort law.

agency shop An establishment where an employee does not have to join the union, but must pay a fee equal to the union dues.

agent A person who has been authorized to sign a negotiable instrument on behalf of another person. The party who agrees to act on behalf of another.

agreement The manifestation by two or more persons of the substance of a contract.

aiding and abetting the commission of a crime Rendering support, assistance, or encouragement to the commission of a crime; harboring a criminal after he or she has committed a crime.

air pollution Pollution caused by factories, homes, vehicles, and the like that affects the air.

alien corporation A corporation that is incorporated in another country.

allonge A separate piece of paper attached to the instrument on which the indorsement is written.

altered check A check that has been altered without authorization that modifies the legal obligation of a party.

alternative dispute resolution (ADR) Methods of resolving disputes other than litigation.

Americans with Disabilities Act (ADA) of 1990 Imposes obligations on employers and providers of public transportation, telecommunications, and public accommodations to accommodate individuals with disabilities.

annual financial statement A statement provided to the shareholders that contains a balance sheet, an income statement, and a statement of changes in shareholder equity.

annual shareholders' meeting Meeting of the shareholders of a corporation that must be held annually by the corporation to elect directors and to vote on other matters.

answer The defendant's written response to the plaintiff's complaint that is filed with the court and served on the plaintiff.

anti-assignment clause A clause that prohibits the assignment of rights under the contract.

anticipatory breach A breach that occurs when one contracting party informs the other that he or she will not perform his or her contractual duties when due.

anticipatory repudiation The repudiation of a sales or lease contract by one of the parties prior to the date set for performance.

antideficiency statute A statute that prohibits deficiency judgments regarding certain types of mortgages, such as those on residential property.

anti-delegation clause A clause that prohibits the delegation of duties under the contract.

antidilution statutes State laws that allow persons and companies to register trademarks and service marks.

antitrust laws A series of laws enacted to limit anticompetitive behavior in almost all industries, businesses, and professions operating in the United States.

apparent agency Agency that arises when a principal creates the appearance of an agency that in actuality does not exist. Agency that arises when a franchisor creates the appearance that a franchisee is its agent when in fact an actual agency does not exist.

appeal The act of asking an appellate court to overturn a decision after the trial court's final judgment has been entered.

appellant The appealing party in an appeal. Also known as *petitioner*.

appellee The responding party in an appeal. Also known as *respondent*.

appropriate bargaining unit The group that a union seeks to represent.

approval clause A clause that permits the assignment of the contract only upon receipt of an obligor's approval.

arbitration A form of ADR in which the parties choose an impartial third party to hear and decide the dispute.

A nonjudicial method of dispute resolution whereby a neutral third party decides the case.

arbitration clause A clause in contracts that requires disputes arising out of the contract to be submitted to arbitration. A clause contained in many international contracts that stipulates that any dispute between the parties concerning the performance of the contract will be submitted to an arbitrator or arbitration panel for resolution.

area franchise The franchisor authorizes the franchisee to negotiate and sell franchises on behalf of the franchisor.

arraignment A hearing during which the accused is brought before a court and is (1) informed of the charges against him or her and (2) asked to enter a plea.

arrest warrant A document for a person's detainment based upon a showing of probable cause that the person committed the crime.

arson Willfully or maliciously burning another's building.

Article 2 (Sales) Article of the UCC that governs sale of goods.

Article 2A (Leases) Article of the UCC that governs lease of goods.

Article 3 of the UCC A code promulgated in 1952 that established rules for the creation of, transfer of, enforcement of, and liability on negotiable instruments. [374] Sets forth the requirements for finding a negotiable instrument, including checks.

Article 4 of the UCC Establishes the rules and principles that regulate bank deposit and collection procedures.

Article 4A of the UCC Article added to the UCC in 1989 that establishes rules regulating the creation and collection of and liability for wire transfers.

Article 7 of the UCC An article of the Uniform Commercial Code that provides a detailed statutory scheme for the creation, perfection, and foreclosure on common carriers' and warehouse operators' liens.   Article of the Uniform Commercial Code that governs documents of title.

Article 8 of the UCC The article of the UCC that governs transfer of securities.

Article 9 of the UCC An article of the Uniform Commercial Code that governs secured transactions in personal property.

articles of incorporation The basic governing documents of the corporation. These documents must be filed with the secretary of state of the state of incorporation.

articles of organization The formal document that must be filed with the secretary of state of form an LLC.

artisan's or mechanic's lien A statute that gives artisans or mechanics a lien on a client's property for nonpayment of repair bills. If the client does not pay for the work rendered, the lien can be perfected.

assault (1) The threat of immediate harm or offensive contact or (2) any action that arouses reasonable apprehension of imminent harm. Actual physical contact is unnecessary.

assignee The party to whom rights have been transferred.   The transferee in an assignment situation.

assignment The transfer of contractual rights by the obligee to another party.   The transfer of rights under a contract.   A transfer by a tenant of his or her rights under a lease to another.

assignment and delegation Transfer of both rights and duties under the contract.

assignment for the benefit of creditors An assignment that allows debtors voluntarily to assign title to their property to a trustee or an assignee for the benefit of their creditors.

assignor The obligee who transfers the right.   The transferor in an assignment situation.   The party who transfers the rights.

assumption of duties When a delegation of duties contains the term *assumption* or *I assume the duties* or other similar language, the delegatee is legally liable to the obligee for nonperformance.

assumption of the risk A defense a defendant can use against a plaintiff who knowingly and voluntarily enters into or participates in a risky activity that results in injury.   A defense in which the defendant must prove that (1) the plaintiff knew and appreciated the risk and (2) the plaintiff voluntarily assumed the risk.

attachment Seizure by the creditors of property in the debtor's possession in order to collect on a debt while their lawsuit is pending.   The creditor has an enforceable security interest against the debtor and can satisfy the debt out of the designated collateral.

attempt to commit a crime When a crime is attempted but not completed.

attestation The action of a will being witnessed by two or three objective and competent people.

attorney-client privilege A rule that says a client can tell his or her lawyer anything about the case without fear that the attorney will be called as a witness against the client.

at-will employees Employees who do not have employment contracts.

auction without reserve An auction in which the seller expressly gives up his or her right to withdraw the goods from sale and must accept the highest bid.

auction with reserve Unless expressly stated otherwise, an auction is an auction with reserve; that is, the seller retains the right to refuse the highest bid and withdraw the goods from sale.

audit The verification of a company's books and records pursuant to federal securities laws, state laws, and stock exchange rules that must be performed by an independent CPA.

authorized shares The number of shares provided for in the articles of incorporation.

automated teller machine (ATM) An EFTS at a convenient location that is connected on-line to the bank's computers; customers use ATMs to withdraw cash from bank accounts, cash checks, make deposits, and make payments owed to the bank.

automatic stay The result of the filing of a voluntary or involuntary petition; the suspension of certain actions by creditors against the debtor or the debtor's property.

backward vertical merger A vertical merger in which the customer acquires the supplier.

bailee A holder of goods who is not a seller or a buyer (e.g., a warehouse).   A holder of goods who is not a seller or a buyer (e.g., a warehouse or common carrier).

bailee's rights Depending on the type of bailment, bailees may have the right to (1) exclusive possession of the bailed property, (2) use of the bailed property, or (3) compensation for work done or services provided.

bailment A transaction where an owner transfers his or her personal property to another to be held, stored, delivered, or for some other purpose. Title to the property does not transfer.

bailment at will A bailment without a fixed term; can be terminated at any time by either party.

bailment for a fixed term A bailment that terminates at the end of the term, or sooner by mutual consent of the parties.

bailment for the sole benefit of the bailee A gratuitous bailment that benefits only the bailee. The bailee owes a *duty of great care* to protect the bailed property.

bailment for the sole benefit of the bailor A gratuitous bailment that benefits only the bailor. The bailee owes only a *duty of slight care* to protect the bailed property.

bailor The owner of property in a bailment.

bait and switch A type of deceptive advertising that occurs when a seller advertises the availability of a low-cost discounted item but then pressures the buyer into purchasing more expensive merchandise.

bank check A certified check, a cashier's check, or a traveler's check; the payment for which the bank is solely or primarily liable.

Bankruptcy Code The name given to the Bankruptcy Reform Act of 1978, as amended.

bankruptcy estate An estate created upon the commencement of a Chapter 7 proceeding that includes all of the debtor's legal and equitable interests in real, personal, tangible, and intangible property, wherever located, that exist when the petition is filed, minus exempt property.

bargained-for exchange Exchange that parties engage in that leads to an enforceable contract.

battery Unauthorized and harmful or offensive physical contact with another person. Direct physical contact is not necessary.

bearer paper Bearer paper is negotiated by *delivery*; indorsement is not necessary.

beneficiary The creditor in a deed of trust and note transaction. The person who is to receive the life insurance proceeds when the insured dies.
    A person or organization designated in the will that receives all or a portion of the testator's property at the time of the testator's death. Person for whose benefit a trust is created.

bequest A gift of personal property by will. Also known as a legacy.

Berne Convention An international copyright treaty. The United States and many other nations are signatories to this treaty.

bilateral contract A contract entered into by way of exchange of promises of the parties; a "promise for a promise."

bill of lading A document of title that is issued by a carrier when goods are received for transportation.

blank indorsement An indorsement that does not specify a particular indorsee. It creates *bearer paper*.

board of directors A panel of decision makers, the members of which are elected by the shareholders.

bona fide occupational qualification (BFOQ) Employment discrimination based on a protected class (other than race or color) is lawful if it is *job related* and a *business necessity*. This exception is narrowly interpreted by the courts.

bond A long-term debt security that is secured by some form of collateral.

branch A wholly owned extension of a corporate entity in a foreign country.

breach Failure of a party to perform an obligation in a sales or lease contract.

breach of contract If a contracting party fails to perform an absolute duty owed under a contract.

breach of the duty of care A failure to exercise care or to act as a reasonable person would act.

bribery When one person gives another person money, property, favors, or anything else of value for a favor in return. Often referred to as a payoff or "kickback."

building A structure constructed on land.

building codes State and local statutes that impose specific standards on property owners to maintain and repair leased premises.

burden of proof The plaintiff bears the burden of proving the allegations made in his complaint.

burglary Taking personal property from another's home, office, commercial, or other type of building.

business interruption insurance Insurance that a business purchases that will reimburse it for any revenues lost during a repair period.

business judgment rule A rule that says directors and officers are not liable to the corporation or its shareholders for honest mistakes of judgment.
A rule that protects the decisions of the board of directors, who act on an informed basis, in good faith, and in the honest belief that the action taken was in the best interests of the corporation and its shareholders.

business tort A tort based on common law and on statutory law that affects business.

buy-and-sell agreement An agreement that requires selling shareholders to sell their shares to the other share-holders or to the corporation at the price specified in the agreement.

buyer in the ordinary course of business A person who in good faith and without knowledge that the sale violates the ownership or security interests of a third party buys the goods in the ordinary course of business from a person in the business of selling goods of that kind. A buyer in the ordinary course of business takes the goods free of any third-party security interest in the goods.   A person who in good faith and even with knowledge of another's ownership or security interest in goods buys the goods in the ordinary course of business from person in the business of selling goods of that kind

bylaws A detailed set of rules adopted by the board of directors after the corporation is incorporated that contains provisions for managing the business and the affairs of the corporation.

C.O.D. shipment A type of shipment contract where the buyer agrees to pay the shipper cash upon the delivery of the goods.

cancellation A seller or lessor may cancel a sales or lease contract if the buyer or lessee rejects or revokes acceptance of the goods, fails to pay for the goods, or repudiates the contract in part or in whole.   A buyer or lessee may cancel a sales or lease contract if the seller or lessor fails to deliver conforming goods or repudiates the contract, or the buyer or lessee rightfully rejects the goods or justifiably revokes acceptance of the goods.

case brief A summary of each of the following items of a case:
1. Case Name, Citation, and Court
2. Key facts
3. Issue presented.
4. Holding of the court.
5. Court's reasoning.

cashier's check A check issued by a bank where the customer has paid the bank the amount of the check and a fee. The bank guarantees the payment of the check.

causation A person who commits a negligent act is not liable unless his or her act was the cause of the plaintiff's injuries. The two types of causation that must be proven are (1) *causation in fact (actual cause)* and (2) *proximate cause (legal cause)*.

causation in fact or actual cause The actual cause of negligence. A person who commits a negligent act is not liable unless causation in fact can be proven.

caveat emptor "Let the buyer beware," the traditional guideline of sales transactions.

certificate of amendment A document that keeps the certificate of limited partnership current.

certificate of deposit (CD) A two-party negotiable instrument that is a special form of note created when a depositor deposits money at a financial institution in exchange for the institution's promise to pay back the amount of the deposit plus an agreed-upon rate of interest upon the expiration of a set time period agreed upon by the parties.

certificate of filing A document that shows (1) whether any presently effective financing statement naming a particular debtor is on file, (2) the date and hour of any such filing, and (3) the names and addresses of the secured parties.

certificate of limited partnership A document that two or more persons must execute and sign that makes the limited partnership legal and binding.

certificate of partnership A document that a partnership must file with the appropriate state government agency in some states to acknowledge that the partnership exists.

certificate of registration A document permitting a foreign limited partnership to transact business in a foreign state.

certified check A type of check where a bank agrees in advance *(certifies)* to accept the check when it is presented for payment.

certified public accountant (CPA) An accountant who has met certain educational requirements, has passed the CPA examination, and has had a certain number of years of audit experience.

chain of distribution All manufacturers, distributors, wholesalers, retailers, lessors, and subcomponent manufacturers involved in a transaction.

chain-style franchise The franchisor licenses the franchisee to make and sell its products or distribute services to the public from a retail outlet serving an exclusive territory.

changing conditions defense A price discrimination defense that claims prices were lowered in response to changing conditions in the market for or the marketability of the goods.

Chapter 7 liquidation bankruptcy The most familiar form of bankruptcy; the debtor's nonexempt property is sold for cash, the cash is distributed to the creditors, and any unpaid debts are discharged.

Chapter 11 bankruptcy A bankruptcy method that allows *reorganization* of the debtor's financial affairs under the supervision of the bankruptcy court.

Chapter 13 A rehabilitation form of bankruptcy that permits the courts to supervise the debtor's plan for the payment of unpaid debts by installments.

charging order A document that the court issues against the debtor-partner's partnership interest in order to satisfy a debt.

check An order by the drawer to the drawee bank to pay a specified sum of money from the drawer's checking account to the named payee (or holder).

choice of forum clause Clause in an international contract that designates which nation's court has jurisdiction to hear a case arising out of the contract. Also known as a *forum-selection clause*.

choice of law clause Clause in an international contract that designates which nation's laws will be applied in deciding a dispute.

Civil Rights Act of 1866 An act enacted after the Civil War that says all persons "have the same right . . . to make and enforce contracts . . . as is enjoyed by white persons"; prohibits racial and national origin employment discrimination.

Clean Air Act A federal statute enacted in 1963 to assist states in dealing with air pollution.

Clean Air Act Amendments of 1990 Amendments that provide comprehensive regulation of air quality in the United States.

Clean Water Act The final version of the FWPCA.

close corporation A corporation owned by one or a few shareholders.

closely held corporation A corporation owned by one or a few shareholders.

closing The finalization of a real estate sales transaction that passes title to the property from the seller to the buyer.

closing arguments Statements made by the attorneys to the jury at the end of the trial to try to convince the jury to render a verdict for their client.

codicil A separate document that must be executed to amend a will. It must be executed with the same formalities as a will.

collateral Security against repayment of the note that lenders sometimes require; can be a car, a house, or other property. The property that is subject to the security interest.

collateral contract A promise where one person agrees to answer for the debts or duties of another person.

collecting bank The depository bank and other banks in the collection process (other than the payor bank).

collective bargaining The act of negotiating contract terms between an employer and the members of a union.

collective bargaining agreement The resulting contract from a collective bargaining procedure.

collision insurance Insurance that a car owner purchases to insure his or her car against risk of loss or damage.

"coming and going" rule A rule that says a principal is generally not liable for injuries caused by its agents and employees while they are on their way to or from work.

Commerce Clause A clause of the U.S. Constitution that grants Congress the power "to regulate commerce with foreign nations, and among the several states, and with Indian tribes." Clause of the U.S. Constitution that vests Congress with the power "to regulate commerce with foreign nations."

commercial impracticability Nonperformance that is excused if an extreme or unexpected development or expense makes it impractical for the promisor to perform.

commercial speech Speech used by businesses, such as advertising. It is subject to time, place, and manner restrictions.

commodities Grains, animals, animal products, foods, metals, and oil.

commodity exchange An exchange over which commodity futures contracts are bought and sold on an impersonal basis.

Commodity Exchange Act (CEA) A federal statute that regulates the trading of commodity futures contracts.

commodity futures contract An agreement to buy or sell a specific amount and type of commodity at some future date under standardized terms established by the CFTC.

Commodity Futures Trading Commission (CFTC) A federal administrative agency that administers and enforces the Commodity Exchange Act, as amended.

common carrier A firm (the bailee) that offers transportation services to the general public. Owes a *duty of strict liability* to the bailor.

common law Developed by judges who issued their opinions when deciding a case. The principles announced in these cases became precedent for later judges deciding similar cases.

common law lien A lien given to artisans, laborers, innkeepers, common carriers, and other service providers on personal property of customers to secure reasonable payment for services rendered.

common law of contracts Contract law developed primarily by state courts.

common stock A type of equity security that represents the *residual* value of the corporation.

common stock certificate A document that represents the common shareholder's investment in the corporation.

common stockholder A person who owns common stock.

comparative negligence A doctrine under which damages are apportioned according to fault. A doctrine that applies to strict liability actions that says a plaintiff who is contributorily negligent for his or her injuries is responsible for a proportional share of the damages.

compensatory damages An award of money intended to compensate a nonbreaching party for the loss of the bargain; they place the nonbreaching party in the same position as if the contract had been fully performed by restoring the "benefit of the bargain." Damages that are generally equal to the difference between the value of the goods as warranted and the actual value of the goods accepted at the time and place of acceptance.

competent party's duty of restitution If a minor has transferred money, property, or other valuables to the competent party before disaffirming the contract, that party must place the minor in status quo.

complaint The document the plaintiff files with the court and serves on the defendant to initiate a lawsuit.

complete performance Occurs when a party to a contract renders performance exactly as required by the contract; discharges that party's obligations under the contract.

composition agreement An agreement that a debtor and several creditors enter into; if the debtor is overextended and owes several creditors money, the creditors agree to accept payment of a sum less than the debt as full satisfaction of the debtor's debts.

Comprehensive Environmental Response, Compensation, and Liability Act (CERCLA) A federal statute enacted in 1980 and amended in 1986 that gives the federal government a mandate to deal with hazardous wastes that have been spilled, stored, or abandoned; commonly called *Superfund*.

comprehensive insurance A form of property insurance that insures an automobile from loss or damage from causes other than collision.

conciliation A form of mediation in which the parties choose an *interested* third party to act as the mediator.

concurrent condition A condition that exists when the parties to a contract must render performance simultaneously; each party's absolute duty to perform is conditioned on the other party's absolute duty to perform.

concurrent jurisdiction Jurisdiction shared by two or more courts.

condition A qualification of a promise. There are three types of conditions: *conditions precedent, conditions subsequent,* and *concurrent conditions*.

condition precedent A condition that requires the occurrence (or nonoccur-rence) of an event before a party is obligated to perform a duty under a contract.

condition precedent based on satisfaction Clause in a contract that reserves the right to a party to pay for the items or services contracted for only if they meet his or her satisfaction.

condition subsequent A condition, if it occurs or doesn't occur, that automatically excuses the performance of an existing contractual duty to perform.

condominium A common form of ownership in a multiple-dwelling building where the purchaser has title to the individual unit and owns the common areas as a tenant in common with the other condominium owners.

confirmation The bankruptcy court's approval of a plan of reorganization.

confusion Occurs if two or more persons commingle fungible goods; title is then acquired by confusion.

conglomerate merger A merger that does not fit into any other category; a merger between firms in totally unrelated businesses.

conscious parallelism If two or more firms act the same but no concerted action is shown, there is no violation of Section 1 of the Sherman Act.

consequential damages Foreseeable damages that arise from circumstances outside the contract. In order to be liable for these damages, the breaching party must know or have reason to know that the breach will cause special damages to the other party.

consideration Something of legal value given in exchange for a promise.

consignee The person to whom the bailed goods are to be delivered.

consignment An arrangement where a seller (the consignor) delivers goods to a buyer (the consignee) for sale.

consignor The person shipping the goods (the bailor).

Consolidated Omnibus Budget Rec-Conciliation Act (COBRA) Federal law that permits employees and their beneficiaries to continue their group health insurance after an employee's employment has ended.

consolidation The act of a court to combine two or more separate lawsuits into one lawsuit.   Occurs when two or more corporations combine to form an entirely new corporation.

conspicuous A requirement that warranty disclaimers be noticeable to the average person.

Constitution of the United States of America The supreme law of the United States.

constructive trust An equitable trust that is imposed by law to avoid fraud, unjust enrichment, and injustice.

consumer expectation test A test to determine merchantability based on what the average consumer would expect to find in food products.

consumer lease A lease with a value of $25,000 or less between a lessor regularly engaged in the business of leasing or selling and a lessee who leases the goods primarily for a personal, family, or household purpose.

Consumer Leasing Act (CLA) An amendment to the TILA that extends the TILA's coverage to lease terms in consumer leases.

Consumer Product Safety Act (CPSA) A federal statute that regulates potentially dangerous consumer products and created the Consumer Product Safety Commission.

Consumer Product Safety Commission (CPSC) An independent federal regulatory agency empowered to (1) adopt rules and regulations to interpret and enforce the Consumer Product Safety Act, (2) conduct research on safety, and (3) collect data regarding injuries.

consumer protection laws Federal and state statutes and regulations that promote product safety and prohibit abusive, unfair, and deceptive business practices.

contract in restraint of trade A contract that unreasonably restrains trade.

contract market A designated commodities exchange that trades in a particular commodities futures contract

contracts contrary to public policy Contracts that have a negative impact on society or interfere with the public's safety and welfare.

contributory negligence A doctrine that says a plaintiff who is partially at fault for his or her own injury cannot recover against the negligent defendant.

A defense that says a person who is injured by a defective product but has been negligent and has contributed to his or her own injuries cannot recover from the defendant.

conversion of personal property A tort that deprives a true owner of the use and enjoyment of his or her personal property by taking over such property and exercising ownership rights over it.

convertible preferred stock Stock that permits the stockholders to convert their shares into common stock.

cooling-off period Requires a union to give an employer at least 60 days' notice before a strike can commence.

cooperative A voluntary joining together of businesses that provides services to its members.   A form of legal enterprise, created pursuant to a state statute, that is owned by its members. Organized primarily for the economic benefit of its members.   A form of co-ownership of a multiple-dwelling building where a corporation owns the building and the residents own shares in the corporation.

co-ownership When two or more persons own a piece of real property. Also called *concurrent ownership*.

copyright infringement When a party copies a substantial and material part of the plaintiff's copyrighted work without permission. A copyright holder may recover damages and other remedies against the infringer.

Copyright Revision Act of 1976 Federal statute that (1) establishes the requirements for obtaining a copyright and (2) protects copyrighted works from infringement.

core proceedings Proceedings that bankruptcy judges decide that have to do with creditor claims, deciding preferences, confirming plans of reorganization, and so on.

corporate citizenship A theory of social responsibility that says a business has a responsibility to do good.

corporate seal A design containing the name of the corporation and the date of incorporation that is imprinted by the corporate secretary using a metal stamp on certain legal documents.

corporation A fictitious legal entity that (1) is created according to statutory requirements and (2) is a separate taxpaying entity for federal income tax purposes.   A fictitious legal entity that

is created according to statutory requirements.

corporations codes State statutes that regulate the formation, operation, and dissolution of corporations.

correlative rights doctrine A doctrine that says a landowner can make reasonable use of the groundwater under his or her property.

cost justification defense A defense in a Section 2(a) action that provides that a seller's price discrimination is not unlawful if the price differential is due to "differences in the cost of manufacture, sale, or delivery" of the product.

Counterfeit Access Device and Computer Fraud and Abuse Act of 1984 Makes it a federal crime to access a computer knowingly to obtain (1) restricted federal government information, (2) financial records of financial institutions, and (3) consumer reports of consumer reporting agencies.

counteroffer A response by an offeree that contains terms and conditions different from or in addition to those of the offer. A counteroffer terminates an offer.

Court of Appeals for the Federal Circuit A court of appeals in Washington, D.C., that has special appellate jurisdiction to review the decisions of the Claims Court, the Patent and Trademark Office, and the Court of International Trade.

Court of Chancery Court that granted relief based on fairness. Also called *equity court*.

covenant An unconditional promise to perform.

covenant of good faith and fair dealing Under this implied covenant, the parties to a contract not only are held to the express terms of the contract but also are required to act in "good faith" and deal fairly in all respects in obtaining the objective of the contract.

covenant of quiet enjoyment A covenant that says a landlord may not interfere with the tenant's quiet and peaceful possession, use, and enjoyment of the leased premises.

cover Right of a buyer or lessee to purchase or lease substitute goods if a seller or lessor fails to make delivery of the goods or repudiates the contract, or if the buyer or lessee rightfully rejects the goods or justifiably revokes their acceptance.

cram down method A method of confirmation of a plan of reorganization where the court forces an impaired class to participate in the plan of reorganization.

crashworthiness doctrine A doctrine that says automobile manufacturers are under a duty to design automobiles so they take into account the possibility of harm from a person's body striking something inside the automobile in the case of a car accident.

credit report Information about a person's credit history that can be secured from a credit bureau.

creditor beneficiary Original creditor who becomes a beneficiary under the debtor's new contract with another party.

creditor beneficiary contract A contract that arises in the following situation: (1) A debtor borrows money, (2) the debtor signs an agreement to pay back the money plus interest, (3) the debtor sells the item to a third party before the loan is paid off, and (4) the third party promises the debtor that he or she will pay the remainder of the loan to the creditor.

creditor-debtor relationship Created when a customer deposits money into the bank; the customer is the creditor and the bank is the debtor.

creditor The lender in a credit transaction.

creditors' committee The creditors holding the seven largest unsecured claims are usually appointed to the creditors' committee. Representatives of the committee appear at Bankruptcy Court hearings, participate in the negotiation of a plan of reorganization, assert objections to proposed plans, and so on.

crime A crime is a violation of a statute for which the government imposes a punishment.

criminal conspiracy When two or more persons enter into an agreement to commit a crime and an overt act is taken to further the crime.

criminal fraud Obtaining title to property through deception or trickery. Also known as *false pretenses* or *deceit*.

critical legal thinking The process of specifying the issue presented by a case, identifying the key facts in the case and applicable law, and then applying the law to the facts to come to a conclu-

sion that answers the issue presented.

cross-complaint Filed by the defendant against the plaintiff to seek damages or some other remedy.

crossover worker A person who does not honor a strike by either (1) choosing not to strike or (2) returning to work after joining the strikers for a time.

crown jewel A valuable asset of the target corporation's that the tender offeror particularly wants to acquire in the tender offer.

cruel and unusual punishment A clause of the Eighth Amendment that protects criminal defendants from torture or other abusive punishment.

cumulative preferred stock Stock that provides any missed dividend payments must be paid in the future to the preferred shareholders before the common shareholders can receive any dividends.

cumulative voting A shareholder can accumulate all of his or her votes and vote them all for one candidate or split them among several candidates.

cure An opportunity to repair or replace defective or nonconforming goods.

custom The second source of international law, created through consistent, recurring practices between two or more nations over a period of time that have become recognized as binding.

damages A buyer or lessee may recover damages from a seller or lessor who fails to deliver the goods or repudiates the contract; damages are measured as the difference between the contract price (or original rent) and the market price (or rent) at the time the buyer or lessee learned of the breach.

damages for accepted nonconforming goods A buyer or lessee may accept nonconforming goods and recover the damages caused by the breach from the seller or lessor or deduct the damages from any part of the purchase price or rent still due under the contract.

"danger invites rescue" doctrine Doctrine that provides that a rescuer who is injured while going to someone's rescue can sue the person who caused the dangerous situation.

debenture A long-term unsecured debt instrument that is based on the corporation's general credit standing.

debt collector An agent who collects debts for other parties.

debtor The borrower in a credit transaction.

debtor-in-possession A debtor who is left in place to operate the business during the reorganization proceeding.

debt securities Securities that establish a debtor-creditor relationship in which the corporation borrows money from the investor to whom the debt security is issued.

declaration of duties If the delegatee has not assumed the duties under a contract, the delegatee is not legally liable to the obligee for nonperformance.

decree of judicial dissolution A decree of dissolution that is granted to a partner whenever it is not reasonably practical to carry on the business in conformity with the limited partnership agreement.

deductible clause Clause in an insurance policy that provides that insurance proceeds are payable only after the insured has paid a certain amount of the loss.

deed A writing that describes a person's ownership interest in a piece of real property.

deed of trust An instrument that gives the creditor a security interest in the debtor's property that is pledged as collateral.

defamation of character False statement(s) made by one person about another. In court, the plaintiff must prove that (1) the defendant made an untrue statement of fact about the plaintiff and (2) the statement was intentionally or accidentally published to a third party.

default Failure to make scheduled payments when due, bankruptcy of the debtor, breach of the warranty of ownership as to the collateral, and other events defined by the parties to constitute default.

defect Something wrong, inadequate, or improper in manufacture, design, packaging, warning, or safety measures of a product.

defect in design A defect that occurs when a product is improperly designed.

defect in manufacture A defect that occurs when the manufacturer fails to (1) properly assemble a product, (2) properly test a product, or (3) adequately check the quality of the product.

defect in packaging A defect that occurs when a product has been placed in packaging that is insufficiently tamper-proof.

defective formation Occurs when (1) a certificate of limited partnership is not properly filed, (2) there are defects in a certificate that is filed, or (3) some other statutory requirement for the creation of a limited partnership is not met.

defendant's case Process by which the defendant (1) rebuts the plaintiff's evidence, (2) proves affirmative defenses, and (3) proves allegations made in a cross-complaint.

deferred posting rule A rule that allows banks to fix an afternoon hour of 2:00 P.M. or later as a cutoff hour for the purpose of processing items.

deficiency judgment Judgment of a court that permits a secured lender to recover other property or income from a defaulting debtor if the collateral is insufficient to repay the unpaid loan.

A judgment that allows a secured creditor to successfully bring a separate legal action to recover a deficiency from the debtor. Entitles the secured creditor to recover the amount of the judgment from the debtor's other property.

delegatee The party to whom the duty has been transferred.

delegation doctrine A doctrine that says when an administrative agency is created, it is delegated certain powers; the agency can only use those legislative, judicial, and executive powers that are delegated to it.

delegation of duties A transfer of contractual duties by the obligor to another party for performance.

delegator The obligor who transferred his or her duty.

demand instrument An instrument payable on demand.

demand note A note payable on demand.

deponent Party who gives his or her deposition.

deposition Oral testimony given by a party or witness prior to trial. The testimony is given under oath and is transcribed.

depository bank The bank where the payee or holder has an account.

derivative lawsuit A lawsuit a shareholder brings against an offending party on behalf of the corporation when the corporation fails to bring the lawsuit.

destination contract A contract that requires the seller to deliver the goods either to the buyer's place of business or to another destination specified in the sales contract. A sales contract that requires the seller to deliver the goods to the buyer's place of business or another specified destination.

devise A gift of real estate by will.

diffused surface water Water that has not yet joined a watercourse, such as runoff from rainfall or melting snow.

direct lawsuit A lawsuit that a shareholder can bring against the corporation to enforce his or her personal rights as a shareholder.

directors' and officers' liability insurance Insurance that covers certain liability and litigation costs incurred through the negligence of directors and officers while acting on behalf of the corporation.

disability insurance Insurance that provides a monthly income to an insured who is disabled and cannot work.

disaffirmance The act of a minor to rescind a contract under the infancy doctrine. Disaffirmance may be done orally, in writing, or by the minor's conduct.

discharge The termination of contract obligations. Actions or events that relieve certain parties from liability on negotiable instruments. There are three methods of discharge: (1) payment of the instrument; (2) cancellation; and (3) impairment of the right of recourse.

The termination of the legal duty of a debtor to pay debts that remain unpaid upon the completion of a bankruptcy proceeding. Creditors' claim that are not included in a Chapter 11 reorganization are discharged. A discharge is granted to a debtor in a Chapter 13 consumer debt adjustment only after all of the payments under the plan are completed by the debtor.

discharge in bankruptcy A real defense against the enforcement of a negotiable instrument; bankruptcy law is intended to relieve debtors of burdensome debts, including negotiable instruments.

disclosure statement A statement that must contain adequate information about the proposed plan of reorganization, which is supplied to the creditors and equity holders after court approval.

discovery A legal process during which both parties engage in various activities to discover facts of the case from the other party and witnesses prior to trial.

dishonored Occurs when an instrument has been presented for payment and payment has been refused.

disparate impact discrimination Occurs when an employer discriminates against an entire protected *class*. An example would be where a facially neutral employment practice or rule causes an adverse impact on a protected class.

disparate treatment discrimination Occurs when an employer discriminates against a specific *individual* because of his or her race, color, national origin, sex, or religion.

disposition of collateral If a secured creditor repossesses collateral upon a debtor's default, he or she may sell, lease, or otherwise dispose of it in a commercially reasonable manner.

disposition of goods A seller or lessor that is in possession of goods at the time the buyer or lessee breaches or repudiates the contract may in good faith resell, release, or otherwise dispose of the goods in a commercially reasonable manner and recover damages, including incidental damages, from the buyer or lessee.

dissension When an individual director opposes the action taken by the majority of the board of directors.

dissenting shareholder appraisal rights Shareholders who object to a proposed merger, share exchange, or sale or lease of all or substantially all of the property of a corporation have a right to have their shares valued by the court and receive cash payment of this value from the corporation.

dissolution "The change in the relation of the partners caused by any partner ceasing to be associated in the carrying on of the business"

distinctive A brand name that is unique and fabricated.

distribution of assets Upon the winding-up of a dissolved partnership, the assets of the partnership are distributed in the following order

1. Creditors (except partners who are creditors
2. Creditor-partners
3. Capital contributions
4. Profits

distribution of property *Nonexempt property* of the bankruptcy estate must be distributed to the debtor's secured and unsecured creditors pursuant to the *statutory priority* established by the Bankruptcy Code.

distributorship franchise The franchisor manufactures a product and licenses a retail franchisee to distribute the product to the public.

diversity of citizenship A case between (1) citizens of different states, (2) a citizen of a state and a citizen or subject of a foreign country, and (3) a citizen of a state and a foreign country where a foreign country is the plaintiff.

dividend Distribution of profits of the corporation to shareholders.

dividend preference The right to receive a fixed dividend at stipulated periods during the year (e.g., quarterly).

division of markets When competitors agree that each will serve only a designated portion of the market.

doctrine of sovereign immunity States that countries are granted immunity from suits in courts of other countries.

doctrine of strict liability in tort A tort doctrine that makes manufacturers, distributors, wholesalers, retailers, and others in the chain of distribution of a defective product liable for the damages caused by the defect *irrespective of fault*.

document of title An actual piece of paper, such as a warehouse receipt or bill of lading, that is required in some transactions of pick up and delivery.

A negotiable instrument developed to represent the interests of the different parties in a transaction that uses storage or transportation between the parties.

domestic corporation A corporation in the state in which it was formed.

domestic limited partnership A limited partnership in the state in which it was formed.

donee A person who receives a gift.

donee beneficiary The third party on whom the benefit is to be conferred.

donee beneficiary contract A contract entered into with the intent to confer a benefit or gift on an intended third party.

donor A person who gives a gift.

double indemnity clause A clause that stipulates that the insurer will pay double the amount of the policy if death is caused by accident.

double jeopardy clause A clause of the Fifth Amendment that protects persons from being tried twice for the same crime.

draft A three-party instrument that is an unconditional written order by one party that orders the second party to pay money to a third party.

Dram Shop Act Statute that makes taverns and bartenders liable for injuries caused to or by patrons who are served too much alcohol.

drawee of a check The financial institution where the drawer has his or her account.

drawee of a draft The party who must pay the money stated in the draft. Also called the *acceptor* of a draft.

drawer of a check The checking account holder and writer of the check.

drawer of a draft The party who writes the order for a draft.

drawer's negligence The drawer is liable if his or her negligence led to his or her forged signature or the alteration of a check. The payor bank is not liable in such circumstances.

Drug Amendment to the FDCA An amendment enacted in 1962 that gives the FDA broad powers to license new drugs in the United States.

dual-purpose mission An errand or other act that a principal requests of an agent while the agent is on his or her own personal business.

due diligence defense A defense to a Section 11 action that, if proven, makes the defendant not liable.

duress Occurs where one party threatens to do a wrongful act unless the other party enters into a contract.

duty not to willfully or wantonly injure The duty an owner owes a trespasser to prevent intentional injury or harm to the trespasser when the trespasser is on his or her premises.

duty of accountability A duty that an agent owes to maintain an accurate accounting of all transactions undertaken on the principal's behalf.

duty of care The obligation we all owe each other not to cause any unreasonable harm or risk of harm.   The obligation partners owe to use the same level of care and skill that a reasonable person in the same position would use in the same circumstances. A breach of the duty of care is *negligence*.   A duty that corporate directors and officers have to use care and diligence when acting on behalf of the corporation.

duty of compensation A duty that a principal owes to pay an agreed-upon amount to the agent either upon the completion of the agency or at some other mutually agreeable time.

duty of loyalty A duty an agent owes the principal not to act adversely to the interests of the principal.   A duty that a partner owes not to act adversely to the interests of the partnership.   A duty that directors and officers have not to act adversely to the interests of the corporation and to subordinate their personal interests to those of the corporation and its shareholders.

duty of notification An agent's duty to notify the principal of information he or she learns from a third party or other source that is important to the principal.

duty of obedience A duty that agents have to obey the lawful instructions of the principal during the performance of the agency.   A duty that partners must adhere to the provisions of the partnership agreement and the decisions of the partnership.   A duty that directors and officers of a corporation have to act within the authority conferred upon them by the state corporation statute, the articles of incorporation, the corporate bylaws, and the resolutions adopted by the board of directors.

duty of ordinary care The duty an owner owes an invitee or a licensee to prevent injury or harm when the invitee or licensee steps on the owner's premises.

Collecting banks are required to exercise ordinary care in presenting and sending checks for collection.

duty of performance An agent's duty to a principal that includes (1) performing the lawful duties expressed in the contract and (2) meeting the standards of reasonable care, skill, and diligence implicit in all contracts.

duty of reasonable care The duty that a reasonable bailee in like circumstances would owe to protect the bailed property.

duty of reimbursement A duty that a principal owes to repay money to the agent if the agent spent his or her own money during the agency on the principal's behalf.

duty of slight care A duty not to be grossly negligent in caring for something in one's possession.

duty of utmost care A duty of care that goes beyond ordinary care that says common carriers and innkeepers have a responsibility to provide security to their passengers or guests.   A duty of care that goes beyond ordinary care.

duty to cooperate A duty that a principal owes to cooperate with and assist the agent in the performance of the agent's duties and the accomplishment of the agency.

duty to indemnify A duty that a principal owes to protect the agent for losses the agent suffered during the agency because of the principal's misconduct.

duty to inform A duty a partner owes to inform his or her copartners of all information he or she possesses that is relevant to the affairs of the partnership.

duty to provide safe working conditions A duty that a principal owes to provide safe premises, equipment, and other working conditions; also includes inspection by the principal.

easement A right to use someone else's land without owning or leasing it.   A given or required right to make limited use of someone else's land without owning or leasing it.

easement appurtenant A situation created when the owner of one piece of land is given an easement over an adjacent piece of land.

easement in gross An easement that authorizes a person who does not own adjacent land the right to use another's land.

economic duress Occurs when one party to a contract refuses to perform his or her contractual duties unless the

other party pays an increased price, enters into a second contract with the threatening party, or undertakes a similar action.

Electronic Funds Transfer Act Makes it a federal crime to use, furnish, sell, or transport a counterfeit, stolen, lost, or fraudulently obtained ATM card, code number, or other device used to conduct electronic funds transfers.

electronic fund transfer systems (EFTS) Electronic payment and collection systems that are facilitated by computers and other electronic technology.

elements of a bailment The following three elements are necessary to create a bailment: (1) personal property, (2) delivery of possession, and (3) a bailment agreement.

elements of price discrimination To prove a violation of Section 2(a), the following elements must be shown: (1) The defendant sold commodities of like grade and quality, (2) to two or more purchasers at different prices at approximately the same time, and (3) the plaintiff suffered injury because of the price discrimination.

emancipation When a minor voluntarily leaves home and lives apart from his or her parents.

embezzlement The fraudulent conversion of property by a person to whom that property was entrusted.

eminent domain Power of the government to acquire private property for public purposes.

Employee Retirement Income Security Act (ERISA) A federal act designed to prevent fraud and other abuses associated with private pension funds.

employer–employee relationship A relationship that results when an employer hires an employee to perform some form of physical service.

employer lockout Act of the employer to prevent employees from entering the work premises when the employer reasonably anticipates a strike.

employment relationships (1) Employer-employee, (2) principal-agent, and (3) principal-independent contractor.

Endangered Species Act A federal statute enacted in 1973 that protects "endangered" and "threatened" species of animals.

endorsement An addition to an insurance policy that modifies it.

engagement A formal entrance into a contract between a client and an accountant.

entity theory A theory that holds that partnerships are separate legal entities that can hold title to personal and real property, transact business in the partnership name, sue in the partnership name, and the like.

enumerated powers Certain powers delegated to the federal government by the states.

environmental impact statement (EIS) A document that must be prepared for all proposed legislation or major federal action that significantly affects the quality of the human environment.

Environmental Protection Agency (EPA) An administrative agency created by Congress in 1970 to coordinate the implementation and enforcement of the federal environmental protection laws.

Equal Access to Justice Act An act that was enacted to protect persons from harassment by federal administrative agencies.

Equal Credit Opportunity Act (ECOA) A federal statute that prohibits discrimination in the extension of credit based on sex, marital status, race, color, national origin, religion, age, or receipt of income from public assistance programs.

equal dignity rule A rule that says that agents' contracts to sell property covered by the Statute of Frauds must be in writing to be enforceable.

Equal Employment Opportunity Commission (EEOC) The federal administrative agency responsible for enforcing most federal antidiscrimination laws.

equal opportunity in employment The right of all employees and job applicants (1) to be treated without discrimination and (2) to be able to sue employers if they are discriminated against.

Equal Pay Act of 1963 Protects both sexes from pay discrimination based on sex; extends to jobs that require equal skill, equal effort, equal responsibility, and similar working conditions.

Equal Protection Clause A clause that provides that a state cannot "deny to any person within its jurisdiction the equal protection of the laws."

equitable remedies Remedies that may be awarded by a judge where there has been a breach of contract and either (1) the legal remedy is not adequate or (2) to prevent unjust enrichment.

equity A doctrine that permits judges to make decisions based on fairness, equality, moral rights, and natural law.

equity securities Representation of ownership rights to the corporation. Also called *stocks*.

escheats If a person dies intestate (without a will) and has no surviving relatives, the deceased's property goes to the state.

Establishment Clause A clause to the First Amendment that prohibits the government from either establishing a state religion or promoting one religion over another.

estate Ownership rights in real property; the bundle of legal rights that the owner has to possess, use, and enjoy the property.

estate pour autre vie A life estate measured in the life of a third party.

estray statutes Statutes that permit a finder of mislaid or lost property to clear title to the property if (1) the finder reports the found property to the appropriate government agency and turns over possession of the property to this agency; (2) either the finder or the government agency posts notices and publishes advertisements describing the lost property; and (3) a specified amount of time has passed without the rightful owner's reclaiming the property.

ethical fundamentalism When a person looks to an outside source for ethical rules or commands.

ethical relativism A moral theory that holds that individuals must decide what is ethical based on their own feelings as to what is right or wrong.

ethics A set of moral principles or values that governs the conduct of an individual or a group.

European Community (Common Market) Comprises many countries of Western Europe; created to promote peace and security plus economic, social, and cultural development.

European Court of Justice The judicial branch of the European Community

located in Luxembourg. It has jurisdiction to enforce European Community law.

exclusion Part of an insurance policy that says what it will *not* cover under certain circumstances.

exclusionary rule A rule that says evidence obtained from an unreasonable search and seizure can generally be prohibited from introduction at a trial or administrative proceeding against the person searched.

exclusive agency contract A contract a principal and an agent enter into that says the principal cannot employ any agent other than the exclusive agent.

exclusive jurisdiction Jurisdiction held by only one court.

exculpatory clause A contractual provision that relieves one (or both) parties to the contract from tort liability for ordinary negligence.

executed contract A contract that has been fully performed on both sides; a completed contract.

execution Postjudgment seizure and sale of the debtor's property to satisfy a creditor's judgment against the debtor.

executive branch The part of the government that consists of the President and Vice President.

executive order An order issued by a member of the executive branch of the government.

executive powers Powers that administrative agencies are granted, such as the investigation and prosecution of possible violations of statutes, administrative rules, and administrative orders.

executory contract A contract that has not been fully performed by either or both sides.   A contract that has not been fully performed. With court approval, executory contracts may be rejected by a debtor in bankruptcy.

exempt property Property that may be retained by the debtor pursuant to federal or state law; debtor's property that does not become part of the bankruptcy estate.

exporter The selling firm in a cross-border transaction.

express agency An agency that occurs when a principal and an agent expressly agree to enter into an agency agreement with each other.

express contract An agreement that is expressed in written or oral words.

express partnership General partnership created by words, either verbal or written.

express powers Powers given to a corporation by (1) the U.S. Constitution, (2) state constitutions, (3) federal statutes, (4) state statutes, (5) articles of incorporation, (6) bylaws, and (7) resolutions of the board of directors.

express trust A trust created voluntarily by the settlor.

express warranty A warranty that is created when a seller or lessor makes an affirmation that the goods he or she is selling or leasing meet certain standards of quality, description, performance, or condition.

extortion Threat to expose something about another person unless that other person gives money or property. Often referred to as "blackmail."

extradition Sending a person back to a country for criminal prosecution.

extreme duress Extreme duress, but not ordinary duress, is a real defense against enforcement of a negotiable instrument.

failure to warn A defect that occurs when a manufacturer does not place a warning on the packaging of products that could cause injury if the danger is unknown.

Fair Credit and Charge Card Disclosure Act of 1988 An amendment to the TILA that requires disclosure of certain credit terms on credit- and charge-card solicitations and applications.

Fair Credit Billing Act (FCBA) An amendment to the TILA that regulates credit billing.

Fair Credit Reporting Act (FCRA) An amendment to the TILA that protects customers who are subjects of a credit report by setting out guidelines for credit bureaus.

Fair Debt Collection Practices Act (FDCPA) An act enacted in 1977 that protects consumer-debtors from abusive, deceptive, and unfair practices used by debt collectors.

Fair Labor Standards Act (FLSA) A federal act enacted in 1938 to protect workers; prohibits child labor and establishes minimum wage and overtime pay requirements.

Fair Packaging and Labeling Act A federal statute that requires the labels on consumer goods to identify the product; the manufacturer, processor, or packager of the product and its address; the net quantity of the contents of the package; and the quantity of each serving.

fair price rule A rule that says any increase in price paid for shares tendered must be offered to all shareholders, even those who have previously tendered their shares.

fair use doctrine A doctrine that permits certain limited use of a copyright by someone other than the copyright holder without the permission of the copyright holder.

false imprisonment The intentional confinement or restraint of another person without authority or justification and without that person's consent.

Farm Credit Administration An independent agency that oversees the Farm Credit System.

Farm Home Administration (FmHA) A USDA agency established to provide for the credit needs of farmers and ranchers who could not find credit elsewhere at reasonable rates and terms.

federal administrative agencies Administrative agencies that are part of the executive or legislative branch of government.

Federal Crop Insurance Corporation (FCIC) A body that offers crop insurance directly to farmers and reinsures insurance provided by private insurers.

Federal Insurance Contributions Act (FICA) A federal act that says employees and employers must make contributions into the Social Security fund.

federalism The U.S. form of government; the federal government and the 50 state governments share powers.

Federal Patent Statute of 1952 Federal statute that establishes the requirements for obtaining a patent and protects patented inventions from infringement.

federal question A case arising under the U.S. Constitution, treaties, or federal statutes and regulations.

Federal Reserve System A system of 12 regional Federal Reserve banks that assist banks in the collection of checks.

Federal Trade Commission (FTC) Federal government agency empowered to enforce federal franchising rules.

[706] Federal administrative agency empowered to enforce the Federal Trade Commission Act and other federal consumer protection statutes.

Federal Unemployment Tax Act (FUTA) A federal act that requires employers to pay unemployment taxes; unemployment compensation is paid to workers who are temporarily unemployed.

Federal Water Pollution Control Act (FWPCA) A federal statute enacted in 1948 that regulates water pollution.

fee simple absolute A type of ownership of real property that grants the owner the fullest bundle of legal rights that a person can hold in real property.

fee simple defeasible A type of ownership of real property that grants the owner all the incidents of a fee simple absolute except that it may be taken away if a specified condition occurs or does not occur.

felony The most serious type of crime; inherently evil crime. Most crimes against the person and some business-related crimes are felonies.

fictitious payee rule A rule that says the drawer or maker is liable on a forged or unauthorized indorsement of a fictitious payee.

fidelity insurance Insurance that an employer purchases to protect him- or herself against the dishonesty and defalcation of employees.

fiduciary duty Duty of loyalty, honesty, integrity, trust, and confidence owed by directors and officers to their corporate employers. The duty the directors of a corporation owe to act carefully and honestly when acting on behalf of the corporation.

final order rule A rule that says the decision of an administrative agency must be final before judicial review can be sought.

final prospectus A final version of the prospectus that must be delivered by the issuer to the investor prior to or at the time of confirming a sale or sending a security to a purchaser.

final settlement Occurs when the payor bank (1) pays the check in cash, (2) settles for the check without having a right to revoke the settlement, or (3) fails to dishonor the check within certain statutory time periods.

finance lease A three-party transaction consisting of the lessor, the lessee, and the supplier.

financing statement A document filed by a secured creditor with the appropriate government office that constructively notifies the world of his or her security interest in personal property.

fixed amount A requirement of a negotiable instrument that ensures that the value of the instrument can be determined with certainty.

fixed amount of money A negotiable instrument must contain a promise or order to pay a fixed amount of money.

fixtures Personal property that is permanently affixed to the real property, such as built-in cabinets in a house.

Goods that are affixed to real estate so as to become part thereof.

floating lien A security interest in property that was not in the possession of the debtor when the security agreement was executed; this includes *after-acquired property*, *sale proceeds*, and *future advances*.

Food and Drug Administration (FDA) Federal administrative agency that administers and enforces the federal Food, Drug, and Cosmetic Act (FDCA) and other federal consumer protection laws.

Food, Drug, and Cosmetic Act (FDCA) A federal statute enacted in 1938 that provides the basis for the regulation of much of the testing, manufacture, distribution, and sale of foods, drugs, cosmetics, and medicinal products.

Food Security Act of 1985 An act that says a buyer of farm products in the ordinary course of business receives the products free of any UCC security interest, even if the buyer knows of the security interest.

foreclosure Legal procedure by which a secured creditor causes the judicial sale of the secured real estate to pay a defaulted loan.

foreign corporation A corporation in any state or jurisdiction other than the one in which it was formed.

foreign distributor A local firm in a foreign country that takes title to goods and resells at a profit (or loss).

foreign limited partnership A limited partnership in all other states than the one in which it was formed.

Foreign Sovereign Immunities Act Exclusively governs suits against foreign nations that are brought in federal or state courts in the United States; codifies the principle of *qualified* or *restricted immunity*.

foreign substance test A test to determine merchantability based on foreign objects that are found in food.

foreseeability standard A rule that an accountant is liable for negligence to third parties who are *foreseeable users* of the client's financial statements. Provides the broadest standard for holding accountants liable to third parties for negligence.

forged indorsement The forged signature of a payee or holder on a negotiable instrument.   The forged signature of the payee or other holder.

forged instrument A check with a forged drawer's signature on it.

forgery Fraudulently making or altering a written document that affects the legal liability of another person.   A real defense against the enforcement of a negotiable instrument; the unauthorized signature of a maker, drawer, or indorser.

formal contract A contract that requires a special form or method of creation.

forum-selection clause Contract provision that designates a certain court to hear any dispute concerning nonperformance of the contract.

forward vertical merger A vertical merger in which the supplier acquires the customer.

four legals Four notices or actions that prevent the payment of a check if they are received by the payor bank before it has finished its process of posting the check for payment.

Fourteenth Amendment Amendment that was added to the U.S. Constitution in 1868. It contains the Due Process, Equal Protection, and Privileges and Immunities clauses.

franchise The owner of a trademark, a trade secret, a patent, or a product licenses another party to sell products or services under the franchisor's name.
     Established when one party licenses another party to use the franchisor's trade name, trademarks, commercial symbols, patents, copyrights, and other property in the distribution and selling of goods and services.

franchise agreement An agreement that the franchisor and the franchisee enter into that sets forth the terms and conditions of the franchise.

franchisee The party who is licensed by the franchisor in a franchise situation.

franchising A form of business in which the franchisee pays the franchisor for a license to use trademarks, formulas, and so on.

franchisor The party who does the licensing in a franchise situation.

fraud by concealment Occurs when one party takes specific action to conceal a material fact from another party.

fraud in the inception Occurs if a person is deceived as to the nature of his or her act and does not know what he or she is signing.   A real defense against the enforcement of a negotiable instrument; a person has been deceived into signing a negotiable instrument thinking that it is something else.

fraud in the inducement Occurs when the party knows what he or she is signing, but has been fraudulently induced to enter into the contract.   A personal defense against the enforcement of a negotiable instrument; a wrongdoer makes a false statement to another person to lead that person to enter into a contract with the wrongdoer.

fraudulent transfer Occurs when (1) a debtor transfers property to a third person within one year before the filing of a petition in bankruptcy, and (2) the transfer is made by the debtor with an intent to hinder, delay, or defraud creditors.

Freedom of Information Act An act that was enacted to give the public access to documents in the possession of federal administrative agencies. There are many exceptions to disclosure.

freedom of speech The right to engage in oral, written, and symbolic speech protected by the First Amendment.

Free Exercise Clause A clause to the First Amendment that prohibits the government from interfering with the free exercise of religion in the United States.

freehold estate An estate where the owner has a present possessory interest in the real property.

fresh start The goal of federal bankruptcy law–to discharge the debtor from burdensome debts and allow him or her to begin again.

frolic and detour When an agent does something during the course of his or her employment to further his or her own interests rather than the principal's.

frustration of purpose A doctrine that excuses the performance of contractual obligation if (1) the object or benefit of a contract is made worthless to a promisor, (2) both parties knew what the purpose was, and (3) the act that frustrated the purpose was unforeseeable.

FTC franchise rule A rule set out by the FTC that requires franchisors to make full presale disclosures to prospective franchisees.

fully disclosed agency An agency that results if the third party entering into the contract knows (1) that the agent is acting as an agent for a principal and (2) the actual identity of the principal.

future advances Personal property of the debtor that is designated as collateral for future loans from a line of credit.

future goods Goods not yet in existence (ungrown crops, unborn stock animals).

future interest The interest that the grantor retains for him- or herself or a third party.

gambling statutes Statutes that make certain forms of gambling illegal.

gap-filling rule A rule that says an open term can be "read into" a contract.

garnishment A postjudgment remedy that is directed against property of the debtor that is in the possession of third persons.

general duty A duty that an employer has to provide a work environment "free from recognized hazards that are causing or are likely to cause death or serious physical harm to his employees."

general gift Gift that does not identify the specific property from which the gift is to be made.

general-jurisdiction trial court A court that hears cases of a general nature that are not within the jurisdiction of limited-jurisdiction trial courts. Testimony and evidence at trial are recorded and stored for future reference.

generally accepted accounting principles (GAAPs) Standards for the preparation and presentation of financial statements.

generally accepted auditing standards (GAASs) Standards for the methods and procedures that must be used to conduct audits.

generally known dangers A defense that acknowledges that certain products are inherently dangerous and are known to the general population to be so.

general partners Partners in a limited partnership who invest capital, manage the business, and are personally liable for partnership debts.

general partnership A voluntary association of two or more persons for the carrying on of a business as co-owners for profit.   An association of two or more persons to carry on as co-owners of a business for profit

general principles of law The third source of international law, consisting of principles of law recognized by civilized nations. These are principles of law that are common to the national law of the parties to the dispute.

general-purpose clause A clause often included in the articles of incorporation that authorizes the corporation to engage in any activity permitted corporations by law.

generic name A term for a mark that has become a common term for a product line or type of service and therefore has lost its trademark protection.

genuineness of assent The requirement that a party's assent to a contract be genuine.

gift A voluntary transfer of title to property without payment of consideration by the donee. To be a valid gift, the following three elements must be shown: (1) *donative intent*, (2) *delivery*, and (3) *acceptance*.   A transfer of property from one person to another without exchange of money.

gift *causa mortis* A gift that is made in contemplation of death.

gift promise An unenforceable promise because it lacks consideration.

good faith Honesty in fact in the conduct or transaction concerned. This is a subjective test.

good faith purchaser for value A person to whom good title can be transferred from a person with voidable title. The real owner cannot reclaim goods from a good faith purchaser for value.

good faith subsequent lessee A person to whom a lease interest can be transferred from a person with voidable title. The real owner cannot reclaim the goods from the subsequent lessee until the lease expires.

goods Tangible things that are movable at the time of their identification to the contract.

Good Samaritan law Statute that relieves medical professionals from liability for ordinary negligence when they stop and render aid to victims in emergency situations.

good title Title that is free from any encumbrances or other defects that are not disclosed but would affect the value of the property.

government contractor defense A defense that says a contractor who was provided specifications by the government is not liable for any defect in the product that occurs as a result of those specifications.

Government in the Sunshine Act An act that was enacted to open certain federal administrative agency meetings to the public.

grace period A period of time after the actual expiration date of a payment but during which the insured can still pay an overdue premium without penalty.

grantee The party to whom an interest in real property is transferred.

grantor The party who transfers an ownership interest in real property.

greenmail The purchase by a target corporation of its stock from an actual or perceived tender offeror at a premium.

ground water Water found underground in pools or streams.

group boycott When two or more competitors at one level of distribution agree not to deal with others at another level of distribution.

group insurance plan An insurance plan that is sold to all the members of a single group, often all the employees of one employer.

guaranteeing collection A form of accommodation where the accommoda-

tion indorser guarantees *collection* of a negotiable instrument; the accommodation indorser is *secondarily liable* on the instrument.

guaranteeing payment A form of accommodation where the accommodation party guarantees *payment* of a negotiable instrument; the accommodation party is *primarily liable* on the instrument.

guarantor The person who agrees to pay the debt if the primary debtor does not.

guaranty arrangement An arrangement where a third party promises to be *secondarily liable* for the payment of another's debt.

guaranty contract The contract between the guarantor and the original creditor.

guest statute Statute that provides that if a driver of a vehicle voluntarily and without compensation gives a ride to another person, the driver is not liable to the passenger for injuries caused by the driver's ordinary negligence.

hardship discharge A discharge granted if (1) the debtor fails to complete the payments due to unforeseeable circumstances, (2) the unsecured creditors have been paid as much as they would have been paid in a Chapter 7 liquidation proceeding, and (3) it is not practical to modify the plan.

Hart-Scott-Rodino Antitrust Improvement Act Requires certain firms to notify the FTC and the Justice Department in advance of a proposed merger. Unless the government challenges the proposed merger within 30 days, the merger may proceed.

hazardous waste Solid waste that may cause or significantly contribute to an increase in mortality or serious illness, or pose a hazard to human health or the environment if improperly managed.

health insurance Purchased to help cover the costs of medical treatment, surgery, or hospital care.

hedge To try to avoid or lessen loss by making a counterbalancing investment.

heir The receiver of property under intestacy statutes.

holder What the transferee becomes if a negotiable instrument has been transferred by *negotiation*.   A person who is in possession of a negotiable instrument that is drawn, issued, or indorsed to him or his order, or to bearer, or in blank.

holder in due course (HDC) A holder who takes a negotiable instrument for value, in good faith, and without notice that it is defective or is overdue.   A holder of a negotiable instrument who takes an instrument free of all claims and personal defenses but not real defenses.

holographic will Will that is entirely handwritten and signed by the testator.

homeowners policy A comprehensive insurance policy that includes coverage for the risks covered by a fire insurance policy as well as personal liability insurance.

honor Payment of a drawer's properly drawn check by the drawee bank.

horizontal merger A merger between two or more companies that compete in the same business and geographical market.

horizontal restraint of trade A restraint of trade that occurs when two or more competitors at the *same level of distribution* enter into a contract, combination, or conspiracy to restrain trade.

hung jury A jury that cannot come to a unanimous decision about the defendant's guilt. The government may choose to retry the case.

hybrid doctrine A combination of riparian and prior appropriation doctrines in water laws.

identification of goods Distinguishing the goods named in the contract from the seller's or lessor's other goods.

illegal consideration A promise to refrain from doing an illegal act. Such a promise will not support a contract.

illusory promise A contract into which parties enter, but one or both of the parties can choose not to perform their contractual obligations. Thus the contract lacks consideration.

Immigration Reform and Control Act of 1986 (IRCA) A federal statute that makes it unlawful for employers to hire illegal immigrants.

immunity from prosecution The government agrees not to use any evidence given by a person granted immunity against that person.

impairment of right of recourse Certain parties (holders, indorsers, accommodation parties) are discharged from liability on an instrument if the holder (1) releases an obligor from liability or (2) surrenders collateral without the consent of the parties who would benefit by it.

implied agency An agency that occurs when a principal and an agent do not expressly create an agency, but it is inferred from the conduct of the parties.

implied exemptions Exemptions from antitrust laws that are implied by the federal courts.

implied-in-fact condition A condition that can be implied from the circumstances surrounding a contract and the parties' conduct.

implied-in-fact contract A contract where agreement between parties has been inferred from their conduct. A contract where agreement between parties has been inferred because of their conduct.

implied partnership General partnership implied from the conduct of the parties.

implied powers Powers beyond express powers that allow a corporation to accomplish its corporate purpose.

implied term A term in a contract that can reasonably be supplied by the courts.

implied trust A trust that is implied by law or from the conduct of the parties.

implied warranties The law *implies* certain warranties on transferors of negotiable instruments. There are two types of implied warranties: transfer and presentment.

implied warranty of authority An agent who enters into a contract on behalf of another party impliedly warrants that he or she has the authority to do so.

implied warranty of fitness for human consumption A warranty that applies to food or drink consumed on or off the premises of restaurants, grocery stores, fast-food outlets, and vending machines.

implied warranty of habitability A warranty that provides that the leased premises must be fit, safe, and suitable for ordinary residential use.

implied warranty of merchantability Unless properly disclosed, a warranty that is implied that sold or leased goods are fit for the ordinary purpose for which they are sold or leased, and other assurances.

importer The buying firm in a cross-border business transaction.

impossibility of performance Nonperformance that is excused if the contract becomes impossible to perform; must be *objective* impossibility, not subjective.

imposter A person who impersonates a payee and induces a maker or drawer to issue an instrument in the payee's name and to give it to the imposter.

imposter rule A rule that says if an imposter forges the indorsement of the named payee, the drawer or maker is liable on the instrument and bears the loss.

incidental authority Implied power that an agent has where the terms of the express agency agreement do not cover the contingency that has arisen.

incidental beneficiary A party who is unintentionally benefited by other people's contract.

incidental damages When goods are resold or re-leased, incidental damages are reasonable expenses incurred in stopping delivery, transportation charges, storage charges, sales commissions, and so on.

incontestability clause A clause that prevents insurers from contesting statements made by insureds in applications for insurance after the passage of a stipulated number of years.

incorporation by reference When integration is made by express reference in one document that refers to and incorporates another document within it.

incorporation doctrine A doctrine that says that most fundamental guarantees contained in the Bill of Rights are applicable to state and local government action.

incorporator The person or persons, partnerships, or corporations that are responsible for incorporation of a corporation.

indemnification Right of a partner to be reimbursed for expenditures incurred on behalf of the partnership.

indenture agreement A contract between the corporation and the holder that contains the terms of a debt security.

independent contractor "A person who contracts with another to do something for him who is not controlled by the other nor subject to the other's right to control with respect to his physical conduct in the performance of the undertaking" [Restatement (Second) of Agency].

indictment The charge of having committed a crime (usually a felony), based on the judgment of a grand jury.

indirect price discrimination A form of price discrimination (e.g., favorable credit terms) that is less readily apparent than direct forms of price discrimination.

indorsee The person to whom a negotiable instrument is indorsed. The party to whom a check is indorsed.

indorsement The signature (and other directions) written by or on behalf of the holder somewhere on the instrument.

indorsement of a check Occurs when a payee indorses a check to another party by signing the back of the check.

indorser The person who indorses a negotiable instrument. The payee who indorses a check to another party.

infancy doctrine A doctrine that allows minors to disaffirm (cancel) most contracts they have entered into with adults.

inferior performance Occurs when a party fails to perform express or implied contractual obligations that impair or destroy the essence of the contract.

informal contract A contract that is not formal. Valid informal contracts are fully enforceable and may be sued upon if breached.

information The charge of having committed a crime (usually a misdemeanor), based on the judgment of a judge (magistrate).

injunction A court order that prohibits a person from doing a certain act.

injury The plaintiff must suffer personal injury or damage to his or her property in order to recover monetary damages for the defendant's negligence.

innkeeper The owner of a facility that provides lodging to the public for compensation (e.g., a hotel or motel).

innkeepers statutes State statutes that limit an innkeeper's common law liability. An innkeeper can avoid liability for loss caused to a guest's property if (1) a safe is provided in which the guest's valuable property may be kept and (2) the guest is notified of this fact.

innocent misrepresentation Occurs when a person makes a statement of fact that he or she honestly and reasonably believes to be true, even though it is not. Occurs when an agent makes an untrue statement that he or she honestly and reasonably believes to be true.

in pari delicto When both parties are equally at fault in an illegal contract.

in personam jurisdiction Jurisdiction over the parties to a lawsuit.

in rem jurisdiction Jurisdiction to hear a case because of jurisdiction over the property of the lawsuit.

insane, but not adjudged insane A person who is insane but has not been adjudged insane by a court or administrative agency. A contract entered into by such person is generally *voidable*. Some states hold that such a contract is void.

Insecticide, Fungicide, and Rodenticide Act A federal statute that requires pesticides, herbicides, fungicides, and rodenticides to be registered with the EPA; the EPA may deny, suspend, or cancel registration.

INS Form I-9 A form that must be filled out by all U.S. employers for each employee; states that the employer has inspected the employee's legal qualifications to work.

Inside director A member of the board of directors who is also an officer of the corporation.

insider trading When an insider makes a profit by personally purchasing shares of the corporation prior to public release of favorable information or by selling shares of the corporation prior to the public disclosure of unfavorable information.

Insider Trading Sanctions Act of 1984 A federal statute that permits the SEC to obtain a civil penalty of up to three times the illegal benefits received from insider trading.

installment contract A contract that requires or authorizes goods to be delivered and accepted in separate lots.

instrument Term that means *negotiable instrument*.

insurable interest A person who purchases insurance must have a personal interest in the insured item or person.

insurance A means for persons and businesses to protect themselves against the risk of loss.

insured The party who pays a premium to a particular insurance company for insurance coverage.

insurer The insurance company that underwrites the insurance coverage.

intangible property Rights that cannot be reduced to physical form, such as stock certificates, CDs, bonds, and copyrights.

integration The combination of several writings to form a single contract.

integration of offerings When separate offerings that might otherwise qualify for individual exemptions are combined if they are really part of one large offering.

intellectual property Objects such as inventions, writings, trademarks, and so on, which are often a business's most valuable asset.

intellectual property rights Intellectual property rights, such as patents, copyrights, trademarks, trade secrets, and trade names are very valuable business assets. Federal and state laws protect intellectual property rights from misappropriation and infringement.

intended third-party beneficiary A third party who is not in privity of contract but who has rights under the contract and can enforce the contract against the obligor.

intentional infliction of emotional distress A tort that says a person whose extreme and outrageous conduct intentionally or recklessly causes severe emotional distress to another person is liable for that emotional distress. Also known as the *tort of outrage*.

intentional interference with contractual relations A tort that arises when a third party induces a contracting party to breach the contract with another party.

intentional misrepresentation Intentionally defrauding another person out of money, property, or something else of value.   Occurs when one person consciously decides to induce another person to rely and act on a misrepresentation. Also called *fraud*. When a seller or lessor fraudulently misrepresents the quality of a product and a buyer is injured thereby. Occurs when an agent makes an untrue statement that he or she knows is not true. Also known as *fraud* or *deceit*.

intentional tort A category of torts that requires that the defendant possessed the intent to do the act that caused the plaintiff's injuries.   Occurs when a person has intentionally committed a wrong against (1) another person or his or her character, or (2) another person's property.

intermediary bank A bank in the collection process that is not the depository or payor bank.

intermediate appellate court An intermediate court that hears appeals from trial courts.

intermediate scrutiny test Test that is applied to classifications based on protected classes other than race (e.g., *sex* or *age*).

International Court of Justice The judicial branch of the United Nations that is located in The Hague, the Netherlands. Also called the *World Court*.

international law Law that governs affairs between nations and that regulates transactions between individuals and businesses of different countries.

interpretive rules Rules issued by administrative agencies that interpret existing statutory language.

interrogatories Written questions submitted by one party to another party. The questions must be answered in writing within a stipulated time.

interstate commerce Commerce that moves between states or that affects commerce between states.

intervention The act of others to join as parties to an existing lawsuit.

***inter vivos* gift** A gift made during a person's lifetime that is an irrevocable present transfer of ownership.

***inter vivos* trust** A trust that is created while the settlor is alive.

intestacy statute A state statute that specifies how a deceased's property will be distributed if he or she dies without a will or if the last will is declared void and there is no prior valid will.

intestate The state of having died without leaving a will.

intoxicated person A person who is under contractual incapacity because of ingestion of alcohol or drugs to the point of incompetence.

intrastate offering exemption An exemption from registration that permits local businesses to raise capital from local investors to be used in the local economy without the need to register with the SEC.

invasion of the right to privacy A tort that constitutes the violation of a person's right to live his or her life without being subjected to unwarranted and undesired publicity.

involuntary petition A petition filed by creditors of the debtor; alleges that the debtor is not paying his or her debts as they become due.

issued shares Shares that have been sold by the corporation.

joint and several liability Partners are *jointly and severally liable* for tort liability of the partnership. This means that the plaintiff can sue one or more of the partners separately. If successful, the plaintiff can recover the entire amount of the judgment from any or all of the defendant-partners.

joint liability Partners are *jointly liable* for contracts and debts of the partnership. This means that a plaintiff must name the partnership and all of the partners as defendants in a lawsuit.

joint tenancy A form of co-ownership that includes the right of survivorship.

joint venture A voluntary association of two or more parties (natural persons, partnerships, corporations, or other legal entities) to conduct a single or isolated project with a limited duration.

joint will A will that is executed by two or more testators.

judgment The official decision of the court.

judgment notwithstanding the verdict (j.n.o.v.) In a civil case, the judge may overturn the jury's verdict if he finds bias or jury misconduct.

judgment on the underlying debt A right granted to a secured creditor to relinquish his or her security interest in the collateral and sue a defaulting debtor to recover the amount of the underlying debt.

judicial branch The part of the government that consists of the Supreme Court and other federal courts.

judicial decision A decision about an individual lawsuit issued by federal and state courts.

judicial decisions and teachings The fourth source of international law, consisting of judicial decisions and writings of the most qualified legal scholars of the various nations involved in the dispute.

judicial decree of dissolution Order of the court that dissolves a partnership. An application or petition must be filed by a partner or an assignee of a partnership interest with the appropriate state court; the court will issue a judicial decree of dissolution if warranted by the circumstances.

judicial dissolution Occurs when a corporation is dissolved by a court proceeding instituted by shareholders, creditors, or the state. Permitted only for certain reasons.

junior appropriator The later user under the prior appropriation "first in time, first in right" concept.

jurisdiction The authority of a court to hear a case.

jurisprudence The philosophy or science of law.

jury deliberation Process by which the jury retires to the jury room and deliberates its findings.

jury instructions Instructions given by the judge to the jury that informs them of the law to be applied in the case.

Just Compensation Clause Clause in the U.S. Constitution that mandates that the government must compensate owners and lessees for property taken under the power of eminent domain.

Kantian or duty ethics A moral theory that says that people owe moral duties that are based on universal rules, such as the categorical imperative "Do unto others as you would have them do unto you."

land The most common form of real property; includes the land and buildings and other structures permanently attached to the land.

landlord The owner who transfers the leasehold.

landlord-tenant relationship A relationship created when the owner of a freehold estate (landlord) transfers a right to exclusively and temporarily possess the owner's property to another (tenant).

land pollution Pollution of the land that is generally caused by hazardous waste being disposed of in an improper manner.

land sales contract Arrangement where the owner of real property agrees to sell the property to a purchaser, who agrees to pay the purchase price to the owner-seller over an agreed-upon period of time.

land use control The collective term for the laws that regulate the possession, ownership, and use of real property.

Lanham Trademark Act An act enacted in 1946 that provides for the registration of trademarks and service marks with the federal Patent and Trademark Office in Washington, D.C.

Lanham Trademark Act (as amended) Federal statute that (1) establishes the requirements for obtaining a federal mark and (2) protects marks from infringement.

larceny Taking another's personal property other than from his or her person or building.

law "That which must be obeyed and followed by citizens subject to sanctions or legal consequences; a body of rules of action or conduct prescribed by controlling authority, and having binding legal force." (*Black's Law Dictionary*)

law court A court that developed and administered a uniform set of laws decreed by the kings and queens after William the Conqueror; legal procedure was emphasized over merits at this time.

lease The transfer of the right to use real property for a specified period of time. A transfer of the right to the possession and use of the named goods for a set term in return for certain consideration. A transfer of the right to the possession and use of the real property for a set term in return for certain consideration; the rental agreement between a landlord and a tenant.

leasehold A tenant's interest in the property.

legal insanity A state of contractual incapacity as determined by law.

legally enforceable contract If one party fails to perform as promised, the other party can use the court system to enforce the contract and recover damages or other remedy.

legislative branch The part of the government that consists of Congress (the Senate and the House of Representatives).

lessee The person who acquires the right to possession and use of goods under a lease.

lessor The person who transfers the right of possession and use of goods under the lease.

liability insurance Automobile insurance that covers damages that the insured causes to third parties.

license Grants a person the right to enter upon another's property for a specified and usually short period of time.

licensing statute Statute that requires a person or business to obtain a license from the government prior to engaging in a specified occupation or activity.

life estate An interest in the land for a person's lifetime; upon that person's death, the interest will be transferred to another party.

life insurance A form of insurance where the insurer is obligated to pay a specific sum of money upon the death of the insured.

limited-jurisdiction trial court A court that hears matters of a specialized or limited nature.

limited liability Shareholders are liable for the corporation's debts and obligations only to the extent of their capital contributions Liability that shareholders have only to the extent of their capital contribution. Shareholders are generally not personally liable for debts and obligations of the corporation.

limited liability company (LLC) A limited liability company is an unincorporated form of business. A hybrid form of business that has the attributes of both partnerships and corporations.

limited liability partnership (LLP) A type of partnership that has only limited partners. A special form of partnership where all partners are limited partners and there are no general partners.

limited partners Partners in a limited partnership who invest capital but do not participate in management and are not personally liable for partnership debts beyond their capital contributions.

limited partnership A special form of partnership that has both limited and general partners.

limited partnership agreement A document that sets forth the rights and duties of the general and limited partners; the terms and conditions regarding the operation, termination, and dissolution of the partnership; and so on.

lineal descendants Children, grandchildren, great-grandchildren, and so on of the testator.

line of commerce Includes products or services that consumers use as substitutes. If an increase in the price of one product or service leads consumers to purchase another product or service, the two products are substitutes for each other.

liquidated damages Damages that will be paid upon a breach of contract that are established in advance.

liquidation preference The right to be paid a stated dollar amount if the corporation is dissolved and liquidated.

litigation The process of bringing, maintaining, and defending a lawsuit.

long-arm statute A statute that extends a state's jurisdiction to nonresidents who were not served a summons within the state.

lost property When a property owner leaves property somewhere because of negligence, carelessness, or inadvertence.

Magnuson-Moss Warranty Act A federal statute enacted in 1975 intended to (1) prevent deceptive warranties, (2) require disclosures by warrantors who make certain written warranties, and (3) restrict the warrantor's ability to disclaim or modify certain warranties.

mailbox rule A rule that states that an acceptance is effective when it is dispatched, even if it is lost in transmission.

mail fraud The use of mail to defraud another person.

main purpose or leading object exception If the main purpose of a transaction and an oral collateral contract is to provide pecuniary benefit to the guarantor, the collateral contract does not have to be in writing to be enforced.

maker of a CD The bank (borrower).

maker of a note The party who makes the promise to pay (borrower).

malicious prosecution When a lawsuit is frivolous, the original defendant can then sue the original plaintiff. In the second lawsuit, the defendant then becomes the plaintiff and vice versa.

management Unless otherwise agreed, each partner has a right to participate in the management of the partnership and has an equal vote on partnership matters.

marine insurance Insurance that owners of vessels purchase to insure against loss or damage to the vessel and its cargo caused by perils at sea.

Marine Protection, Research, and Sanctuaries Act A federal statute enacted in 1972 that extends environmental protection to the oceans.

mark The collective name for trademarks, service marks, certification marks, and collective marks that all can be trademarked.

market extension merger A merger between two companies in similar fields whose sales do not overlap.

Market Reform Act of 1990 A federal statute that authorizes the SEC to regulate trading practices during periods of extraordinary market volatility.

material alteration A partial defense against enforcement of a negotiable instrument by an HDC. An HDC can enforce an altered instrument in the original amount for which the drawer wrote the check.

material breach A breach that occurs when a party renders inferior performance of his or her contractual duties.

material person's lien A contractor's and laborer's lien that makes the

real property to which improvements are being made become security for the payment of the services and materials for those improvements.

maximizing profits A theory of social responsibility that says a corporation owes a duty to take actions that maximize profits for shareholders.

mediation A form of ADR in which the parties choose a *neutral* third party to act as the mediator of the dispute.

Medicinal Device Amendment to the FDCA An amendment enacted in 1976 that gives the FDA authority to regulate medicinal devices and equipment.

meeting of the creditors A meeting of the creditors in a bankruptcy case that must occur not less than 10 days nor more than 30 days after the court grants an order for relief.

meeting the competition defense A defense provided in Section 2(b) that says a seller may lawfully engage in price discrimination to meet a competitor's price.

members The owners of an LLC.

mens rea "Evil intent"—the possession of the requisite state of mind to commit a prohibited act.

Merchant Court The separate set of courts established to administer the "law of merchants."

merchant protection statutes Statutes that allow merchants to stop, detain, and investigate suspected shoplifters without being held liable for false imprisonment if (1) there are reasonable grounds for the suspicion, (2) suspects are detained for only a reasonable time, and (3) investigations are conducted in a reasonable manner.

merger Occurs when one corporation is absorbed into another corporation and ceases to exist.

merger clause A clause in a contract that stipulates that it is a complete integration and the exclusive expression of the parties' agreement. Parol evidence may not be introduced to explain, alter, contradict, or add to the terms of the contract.

midnight deadline The midnight of the next banking day following the banking day on which the bank received the on them check for collection.

minimum wage Employers must pay a statutorily mandated minimum wage to nonexempt employees. The current minimum wage is $5.15 per hour.

minor A person who has not reached the age of majority.

minor breach A breach that occurs when a party renders substantial performance of his or her contractual duties.

minor's duty of restoration As a general rule a minor is obligated only to return the goods or property he or she has received from the adult in the condition it is in at the time of disaffirmance.

mirror image rule States that in order for there to be an acceptance, the offeree must accept the terms as stated in the offer.

misdemeanor A less serious crime; not inherently evil but prohibited by society. Many crimes against property are misdemeanors.

mislaid property When an owner voluntarily places property somewhere and then inadvertently forgets it.

misrepresentation An assertion that is made that is not in accord with the facts.

misuse A defense that relieves a seller of product liability if the user *abnormally* misused the product. Products must be designed to protect against *foreseeable* misuse.

mitigation A nonbreaching party is under a legal duty to avoid or reduce damages caused by a breach of contract.

mixed sale A sale that involves the provision of a service and a good in the same transaction.

mobile sources Sources of air pollution such as automobiles, trucks, buses, motorcycles, and airplanes.

Model Business Corporation Act (MBCA) A model act drafted in 1950 that was intended to provide a uniform law for regulation of corporations.

monetary damages An award of money.

money A "medium of exchange authorized or adopted by a domestic or foreign government"

monopoly power The power to control prices or exclude competition measured by the market share the defendant possesses in the relevant market.

moral minimum A theory of social responsibility that says a corporation's duty is to make a profit while avoiding harm to others.

mortgage An interest in real property given to a lender as security for the repayment of a loan. A collateral arrangement where a property owner borrows money from a creditor who uses a deed as collateral for repayment of the loan.

mortgagee The creditor in a mortgage transaction.

mortgagor The owner-debtor in a mortgage transaction.

motion for judgment on the pleadings Motion that alleges that if all the facts presented in the pleadings are taken as true, the party making the motion would win the lawsuit when the proper law is applied to these asserted facts.

motion for summary judgment Motion that asserts that there are no factual disputes to be decided by the jury; if so, the judge can apply the proper law to the undisputed facts and decide the case without a jury. These motions are supported by affidavits, documents, and deposition testimony.

motivation test A test to determine the liability of the principal; if the agent's motivation in committing the intentional tort is to promote the principal's business, then the principal is liable for any injury caused by the tort.

multinational enterprise A firm that operates internationally.

mutual benefit bailment A bailment for the mutual benefit of the bailor and bailee. The bailee owes a *duty of reasonable care* to protect the bailed property.

mutual mistake of fact A mistake made by both parties concerning a material fact that is important to the subject matter of the contract.

mutual mistake of value A mistake that occurs if both parties know the object of the contract, but are mistaken as to its value.

mutual wills Occur where two or more testators execute separate wills that leave their property to each other on the condition that the survivor leave the remaining property on his or her death as agreed by the testators.

national ambient air quality standards (NAAQS) Standards for certain pollutants set by the EPA that protect (1) human beings (primary) and (2) vegetation, matter, climate, visibility, and economic values (secondary).

national courts The courts of individual nations.

National Environmental Policy Act (NEPA) A federal statute enacted in 1969 that mandates that the federal government consider the adverse impact a federal government action would have on the environment before the action is implemented.

National Labor Relations Board (NLRB) A federal administrative agency that oversees union elections, prevents employers and unions from engaging in illegal and unfair labor practices, and enforces and interprets certain federal labor laws.

necessaries of life A minor must pay the reasonable value of food, clothing, shelter, medical care, and other items considered necessary to the maintenance of life.

negligence A tort related to defective products where the defendant has breached a duty of due care and caused harm to the plaintiff. Failure of a corporate director or officer to exercise the duty of care while conducting the corporation's business.

negligence per se Tort where the violation of a statute or ordinance constitutes the breach of the duty of care.

negligent infliction of emotional distress A tort that permits a person to recover for emotional distress caused by the defendant's negligent conduct.

negotiable instrument A special form of contract that satisfies the requirements established by Article 3 of the UCC. Also called *commercial paper*.

negotiation Transfer of a negotiable instrument by a person other than the issuer to a person who thereby becomes a *holder*.

New York standard fire insurance form A standard fire insurance policy that protects the homeowner from loss caused by fire, lightning, smoke, and water damage.

1976 Tax Reform Act An act that imposes criminal liability on accoun-

tants and others who prepare federal tax returns if they (1) willfully understate a client's tax liability, (2) negligently understate the tax liability, or (3) wrongfully indorse a client's tax refund check.

Noerr **doctrine** Two or more persons may petition the executive, legislative, or judicial branch of the government or administrative agencies to enact laws or take other action without violating the antitrust laws.

no evidence of forgery, alterations, or irregularity requirement A holder cannot become an HDC to an instrument that is apparently forged or altered or is otherwise so irregular or incomplete as to call into question its authenticity.

Noise Control Act A federal statute enacted in 1972 that authorizes the EPA to establish noise standards for products sold in the United States.

noise pollution Unwanted sound from planes, manufacturing plants, motor vehicles, construction equipment, stereos, and the like.

nonattainment areas Regions that do not meet air quality standards.

noncompete clause An agreement whereby a person agrees not to engage in a specified business or occupation within a designated geographical area for a specified period of time following the sale.

nonconforming uses Uses and buildings that already exist in the zoned area that are permitted to continue even though they do not fit within new zoning ordinances.

noncupative will Oral will that is made before a witness during the testator's last illness.

nonfreehold estate An estate in which the tenant has a right to possession of the property but not title to the property.

nonnegotiable contract Fails to meet the requirements of a negotiable instrument and, therefore, is not subject to the provisions of UCC Article 3.

nonpossessory interest When a person holds an interest in another person's property without actually owning any part of the property.

nonprice vertical restraints Restraints of trade that are unlawful under Section 1 of the Sherman Act if their anticompetitive effects outweigh their pro-competitive effects.

nonprofit corporation A corporation that is formed to operate charitable institutions, colleges, universities, and other not-for-profit entities.

nonrecourse loan A type of loan that, if it is defaulted on, the USDA has no other choice but to take the commodities securing the loan.

nonrestrictive indorsement An indorsement that has no instructions or conditions attached to the payment of the funds.

note An instrument that evidences the borrower's debt to the lender. A debt security with a maturity of five years or less.

novation An agreement that substitutes a new party for one of the original contracting parties and relieves the exiting party of liability on the contract.

Nuclear Regulatory Commission (NRC) Federal agency that licenses the construction and opening of commercial nuclear power plants.

Nuclear Waste Policy Act of 1982 A federal statute that says the federal government must select and develop a permanent site for the disposal of nuclear waste.

objective theory of contracts A theory that says the intent to contract is judged by the reasonable person standard and not by the subjective intent of the parties.

obscene speech Speech that (1) appeals to the prurient interest, (2) depicts sexual conduct in a patently offensive way, and (3) lacks serious literary, artistic, political, or scientific value.

obsolete information Information that is no longer accurate because of time or circumstances.

Occupational Safety and Health Act A federal act enacted in 1970 that promotes safety in the workplace.

Occupational Safety and Health Administration (OSHA) A federal administrative agency that administers and enforces the Occupational Safety and Health Act.

offensive speech Speech that is offensive to many members of society. It is subject to time, place, and manner restrictions.

offer "The manifestation of willingness to enter into a bargain, so made as to justify another person in understanding that his assent to that bargain is invited and will conclude it."

offeree The party to whom an offer to enter into a contract is made. The party to whom an offer has been made.

offeror The party who makes an offer to enter into a contract. The party who makes an offer.

officers Employees of the corporation who are appointed by the board of directors to manage the day-to-day operations of the corporation.

Older Workers Benefit Protection Act (OWBPA) Prohibits age discrimination in employee benefits.

one year rule An executory contract that cannot be performed by its own terms within one year of its formation must be in writing.

"on them" item A check presented for payment by the payee or holder where the depository bank and the payor bank are not the *same* bank.

"on us" item A check that is presented for payment where the depository bank is also the payor bank. That is, the drawer and payee or holder have accounts at the same bank.

opening statements Statements made by the attorneys to the jury in which they summarize the factual and legal issues of the case.

option contract A contract on a futures contract that is also traded on commodities exchanges; for a fee, a purchaser can buy the right to buy and sell a futures contract within a set period of time.

option-to-cancel clause A clause inserted in many business contracts that allows one or both of the parties to cancel the contract.

order Decision issued by an administrative law judge.

order for relief The filing of a voluntary petition, an unchallenged involuntary petition, or a grant of an order after a trial of a challenged involuntary petition.

order paper Order paper is negotiated by (1) *delivery* and (2) *indorsement*.

order to pay A drawer's unconditional order for a drawee to pay a payee.

ordinances Laws enacted by local government bodies such as cities and municipalities, counties, school districts, and water districts.

ordinary bailments (1) Bailments for the sole benefit of the bailor, (2) bailments for the sole benefit of the bailee, and (3) bailments for the mutual benefit of the bailor and bailee.

organizational meeting A meeting that must be held by the initial directors of the corporation after the articles of incorporation are filed.

original tenor The original amount for which the drawer wrote the check.

outside director A member of the board of directors who is not an officer of the corporation.

outstanding shares Shares of stock that are in shareholder hands.

overdraft The amount of money a drawer owes a bank after it has paid a check despite insufficient funds in the drawer's account.

overtime pay An employer cannot require employees to work more than 40 hours per week unless they are paid one-and-a-half times their regular pay for each hour worked in excess of 40 hours.

pac-man tender offer Occurs when a corporation that is the target of a tender offer makes a *reverse tender offer* for the stock of the tender offeror.

palming off Unfair competition that occurs when a company tries to pass off one of its products as that of a rival.

parol evidence Any oral or written words outside the four corners of the written contract.

parol evidence rule A rule that says if a written contract is a complete and final statement of the parties' agreement, any prior or contemporaneous oral or written statements that alter, contradict, or are in addition to the terms of the written contract are inadmissible in court regarding a dispute over the contract. There are several exceptions to this rule.

partially disclosed agency An agency that occurs if the agent discloses his or her agency status but does not reveal the principal's identity and the third party does not know the principal's identity from another source.

participating preferred stock Stock that allows the stockholder to participate in the profits of the corporation along with the common stockholders.

partnership agreement A written partnership agreement that the partners sign. Also called *articles of partnership*.

partnership at will A partnership with no fixed duration.

partnership by estoppel When a person who is not a partner either makes a representation or consents to a partner's representation that he or she is a partner.

partnership capital Money and property contributed by partners for the permanent use of the partnership.

partnership for a term A partnership with a fixed duration.

partnership property Property that is originally brought into the partnership on account of the partnership and property that is subsequently acquired by purchase or otherwise on account of the partnership or with partnership funds.

partner's interest A partner's share of profits and surplus of the partnership.

part performance An equitable doctrine that allows the court to order an oral contract for the sale of land or transfer of another interest in real property to be specifically performed if it has been partially performed and performance is necessary to avoid injustice.

past consideration A prior act or performance. Past consideration (e.g., prior acts) will not support a new contract. New consideration must be given.

patent infringement Unauthorized use of another's patent. A patent holder may recover damages and other remedies against a patent infringer.

payable on demand or at a definite time requirement A negotiable instrument must be payable either *on demand* or *at a definite time*.

payee of a CD The depositor (lender).

payee of a check The party to whom the check is written.

payee of a draft The party who receives the money from a draft.

payee of a note The party to whom the promise to pay is made (lender).

payor bank The bank where the drawer has a checking account and on which the check is drawn.

penal codes A collection of criminal statutes.

per capita A distribution of the estate that makes each grandchild and great-grandchild of the deceased inherit equally with the children of the deceased.

perfection by possession of the collateral If a secured creditor has physical possession of the collateral, no financing statement has to be filed; the creditor's possession is sufficient to put other potential creditors on notice of his or her secured interest in the property.

perfection of a security interest Establishes the right of a secured creditor against other creditors who claim an interest in the collateral.

perfect tender rule A rule that says if the goods or tender of a delivery fails in any respect to conform to the contract, the buyer may opt to (1) reject the whole shipment, (2) accept the whole shipment, or (3) reject part and accept part of the shipment.

periodic tenancy A tenancy created when a lease specifies intervals at which payments are due but does not specify how long the lease is for.

permanency requirement A requirement of negotiable instruments that says they must be in a permanent state, such as written on ordinary paper.

permanent trustee A legal representative of the bankruptcy debtor's estate, usually an accountant or a lawyer; elected at the first meeting of the creditors.

per se rule A rule that is applicable to those restraints of trade considered inherently anticompetitive. Once this determination is made, the court will not permit any defenses or justifications to save it.

personal articles floater An addition to the homeowners policy that covers specific valuable items.

personal defense A defense that can be raised against enforcement of a negotiable instrument by an ordinary holder but not against an HDC.

personal property Property that consists of tangible property such as automobiles, furniture, and jewelry as well as intangible property such as securities, patents, and copyrights. Property that consists of goods (such as automobiles, furniture, and jewelry), securities, patents, copyrights, instruments,

chattel paper, documents of title, and accounts

personal satisfaction test Subjective test that applies to contracts involving personal taste and comfort.

per stirpes A distribution of the estate that makes grandchildren and great-grandchildren of the deceased inherit by representation of their parent.

petition A document filed with the bankruptcy court that sets the bankruptcy proceedings into motion.

petitioner The party appealing the decision of an administrative agency.

petition for certiorari A petition asking the Supreme Court to hear one's case.

physical or mental examination A court may order another party to submit to a physical or mental examination prior to trial.

picketing The action of strikers walking in front of the employer's premises carrying signs announcing their strike.

piercing the corporate veil A doctrine that says if a shareholder dominates a corporation and uses it for improper purposes, a court of equity can disregard the corporate entity and hold the shareholder personally liable for the corporation's debts and obligations.

plaintiff The party who files the complaint.

plaintiff's case Process by which the plaintiff introduces evidence to prove the allegations contained in his complaint.

plan of reorganization A plan that sets forth a proposed new capital structure for the debtor to have when it emerges from reorganization bankruptcy. The debtor has the exclusive right to file the first plan of reorganization; any party of interest may file a plan thereafter.

plant life and vegetation Real property that is growing in or on the surface of the land.

plea bargain When the accused admits to a lesser crime than charged. In return, the government agrees to impose a lesser sentence than might have been obtained had the case gone to trial.

pleadings The paperwork that is filed with the court to initiate and respond to a lawsuit.

point-of-sale (POS) terminal A terminal at a merchant's checkout counter that is connected on-line to the bank's computers; a debit card or credit card can be used to make purchases at POS terminals.

point sources Sources of water pollution such as paper mills, manufacturing plants, electric utility plants, and sewage plants.

police power The power of states to regulate private and business activity within their borders.

policy The insurance contract.

portability requirement A requirement of negotiable instruments that says they must be able to be easily transported between areas.

possession A lease grants the tenant *exclusive possession* of the leased premises for the term of the lease or until the tenant defaults on the obligations under the lease.

possessory lien Lien obtained by a bailee on bailed property for the compensation owed by the bailor to the bailee.

Postal Reorganization Act An act that makes the mailing of unsolicited merchandise an unfair trade practice.

posteffective period The period of time that begins when the registration statement becomes effective and runs until the issuer either sells all of the offered securities or withdraws them from sale.

potential competition theory A theory that reasons that the real or implied threat of increased competition keeps businesses more competitive. A merger that would eliminate this perception can be enjoined under Section 7.

potential reciprocity theory A theory that says if Company A, which supplies materials to Company B, merges with Company C (which in turn gets its supplies from Company B), the newly merged company can coerce Company B into dealing exclusively with it.

power of attorney An express agency agreement that is often used to give an agent the power to sign legal documents on behalf of the principal.

precedent A rule of law established in a court decision. Lower courts must follow the precedent established by higher courts.

preemption doctrine The concept that federal law takes precedent over state or local law.

preemptive rights Rights that give existing shareholders the option of subscribing to new shares being issued in proportion to their current ownership interest.

preexisting duty A promise lacks consideration if a person promises to perform an act or do something he or she is already under an obligation to do.

preferential lien Occurs when (1) a debtor gives an unsecured creditor a secured interest in property within 90 days before the filing of a petition in bankruptcy, (2) the transfer is made for a pre-existing debt, and (3) the creditor would receive more because of this lien than it would as an unsecured creditor.

preferential transfer Occurs when (1) a debtor transfers property to a creditor within 90 days before the filing of a petition in bankruptcy, (2) the transfer is made for a preexisting debt, and (3) the creditor would receive more from the transfer than it would from Chapter 7 liquidation.

preferential transfer to an insider A transfer of property by an insolvent debtor to an "insider" within one year before the filing of a petition in bankruptcy.

preferred stock A type of equity security that is given certain preferences and rights over common stock.

preferred stock certificate A document that represents a shareholder's investment in preferred stock in the corporation.

preferred stockholder A person who owns preferred stock.

prefiling period A period of time that begins when the issuer first contemplates issuing the securities and ends when the registration statement is filed. The issuer may not *condition* the market during this period.

Pregnancy Discrimination Act Amendment to Title VII that forbids employment discrimination because of "pregnancy, childbirth, or related medical conditions."

premises liability The liability of landlords and tenants to persons injured on their premises.

premium The money paid to the insurance company.

presentment A demand for acceptance or payment of an instrument made upon the maker, the acceptor, the drawee, or other payor by or on behalf of the holder.

presentment across the counter When a depositor physically presents the check for payment at the payor bank instead of depositing an on them check for collection.

presentment warranties Any person who presents a draft or check for payment or acceptance makes the following three presentment warranties to a drawee or acceptor who pays or accepts the instrument in good faith: (1) The presenter has good title to the instrument or is authorized to obtain payment or acceptance of the person who has good title; (2) the instrument has not been materially altered; and (3) the presenter has no knowledge that the signature of the maker or drawer is unauthorized.

presentment warranty Each prior transferor warrants that the check has not been altered.

pretrial hearing A hearing before the trial in order to facilitate the settlement of a case. Also called a *settlement conference.*

pretrial motion A motion a party can make to try to dispose of all or part of a lawsuit prior to trial.

price discrimination Charging different prices to different customers for the same product without any justification.

price-fixing Occurs where competitors in the same line of business agree to set the price of the goods or services they sell; raising, depressing, fixing, pegging, or stabilizing the price of a commodity or service.

primary liability Absolute liability to pay a negotiable instrument, subject to certain *real* defenses.

principal A person who authorizes an agent to sign a negotiable instrument on his or her behalf. The party who employs another person to act on his or her behalf.

principal-agent relationship An employer hires an employee and gives that employee authority to act and enter into contracts on his or her behalf.

principal-independent contractor relationship A relationship that results when a person or business that is not an employee is employed by a principal to perform a certain task on his behalf.

principle of comity Courtesies between countries based on respect, goodwill, and civility rather than law.

prior appropriation A doctrine that says the first user has priority over later users.

priority The order in which conflicting claims of creditors in the same collateral are solved.

Privacy Act An act stipulating that federal administrative agencies can maintain only information about an individual that is relevant and necessary to accomplish a legitimate agency purpose.

private corporation A corporation formed to conduct privately owned business.

private nuisance A nuisance that affects or disturbs one or a few people.

private placement exemption An exemption from registration that permits issuers to raise capital from an unlimited number of accredited investors and no more than 35 nonaccredited investors without having to register the offering with the SEC.

Private Securities Litigation Reform Act of 1995 Provides a safe harbor from liability for companies that make forward-looking statements that are accompanied by meaningful cautionary statements of risk factors.

Privileges and Immunities Clause A Clause that prohibits states from enacting laws that unduly discriminate in favor of their residents.

privity of contract The state of two specified parties being in contract.

probability of a substantial lessening of competition If there is a probability that a merger will substantially lessen competition or create a monopoly, the court may prevent the merger under Section 7 of the Clayton Act.

probate court A specialized state court that supervises the administration and settlement of an estate.

procedural due process Due process that requires the respondent to be given (1) proper and timely notice of the allegations or charges against him or her and (2) an opportunity to present evidence on the matter.

processing plant franchise The franchisor provides a secret formula or process to the franchisee, and the franchisee manufactures the product and distributes it to retail dealers.

process of certification The accepting bank writes or stamps the word *certified* on the ordinary check of an account holder and sets aside funds from that account to pay the check.

product disparagement False statements about a competitor's products, services, property, or business reputation.

production of documents Request by one party to another party to produce all documents relevant to the case prior to trial.

products liability The liability of manufacturers, sellers, and others for the injuries caused by defective products.

professional corporation A corporation formed by lawyers, doctors, or other professionals.

professional malpractice The liability of a professional who breaches his or her duty of ordinary care.

profit Grants a person the right to remove something from another's real property.

profit corporation A corporation created to conduct a business for profit that can distribute profits to shareholders in the form of dividends.

promise to pay A maker's (borrower's) unconditional and affirmative undertaking to repay a debt to a payee (lender).

promissory estoppel An equitable doctrine that prevents the withdrawl of an offer/promise by an offeror/promisor if it will adversely affect an offeree/promisee who has adjusted his or her position in justifiable reliance on the offer/promise.   An equitable doctrine that permits enforcement of oral contracts that should have been in writing. It is applied to avoid injustice.

promissory note A two-party negotiable instrument that is an unconditional written promise by one party to pay money to another party.

promoter A person or persons who organize and start the corporation, negotiate and enter into contracts in advance of its formation, find the initial investors to finance the corporation, and so forth.

promoters' contracts A collective term for such things as leases, sales contracts, contracts to purchase property, and employment contracts entered into by promoters on behalf of the proposed corporation prior to its actual incorporation.

proof of claim A document required to be filed by unsecured creditors that states the amount of their claim against the debtor.

proper dispatch An acceptance must be properly addressed, packaged, and posted to fall within the mailbox rule.

pro rata rule A rule that says shares must be purchased on a pro rata basis if too many shares are tendered.

prospectus A written disclosure document that must be submitted to the SEC along with the registration statement and given to prospective purchasers of the securities.

provisional credit Occurs when a collecting bank gives credit to a check in the collection process prior to its final settlement. Provisional credits may be reversed if the check does not "clear."

proximate cause or legal cause A point along a chain of events caused by a negligent party after which this party is no longer legally responsible for the consequences of his or her actions.

proxy card The written document that a shareholder signs authorizing another person to vote his or her shares at the shareholders' meetings in the event of the shareholder's absence.   A written document signed by a shareholder that authorizes another person to vote the shareholder's shares.

proxy contest When opposing factions of shareholders and managers solicit proxies from other shareholders, the side that receives the greatest number of votes wins the proxy contest.

proxy statement A document that fully describes (1) the matter for which the proxy is being solicited, (2) who is soliciting the proxy, and (3) any other pertinent information.

public corporation A corporation that has many shareholders and whose securities are traded on national stock exchanges.   A corporation formed to meet a specific governmental or political purpose.

publicly held corporation A corporation that has many shareholders and whose securities are often traded on national stock exchanges.

public nuisance A nuisance that affects or disturbs the public in general.

public policy exception An exception to the employment at-will doctrine that states an employee cannot be discharged if such discharge violates the public policy of the jurisdiction.

public use doctrine A doctrine that says a patent may not be granted if the invention was used by the public for more than one year prior to the filing of the patent application.

punitive damages Damages that are awarded to punish the defendant, to deter the defendant from similar conduct in the future, and to set an example for others.

purchase money security interest An interest a creditor automatically obtains when he or she extends credit to a *consumer* to purchase consumer goods.

purchasing property The most common method of acquiring title to personal property.

qualified individual with a disability A person who (1) has a physical or mental impairment that substantially limits one or more of his or her major life activities, (2) has a record of such impairment, or (3) is regarded as having such impairment.

qualified indorsement An indorsement that includes the notation "without recourse" or similar language that disclaims liability of the indorser.

qualified indorser An indorser who signs a *qualified indorsement* to an instrument.

quasi in rem jurisdiction Jurisdiction allowed a plaintiff who obtains a judgment in one state to try to collect the judgment by attaching property of the defendant located in another state.

quasi- or implied-in-law contract An equitable doctrine whereby a court may award monetary damages to a plaintiff for providing work or services to a defendant even though no actual contract existed. The doctrine is intended to prevent unjust enrichment and unjust detriment.

quiet title action An action brought by a party seeking an order of the court declaring who has title to disputed prop-

erty. The court "quiets title" by its decision.

quorum The required number of shares that must be represented in person or by proxy to hold a shareholders' meeting. The RMBCA establishes a majority of outstanding shares as a quorum.   The number of directors necessary to hold a board of directors' meeting or transact business of the board.

Racketeer Influenced and Corrupt Organizations Act (RICO) Federal statute that authorizes civil lawsuits against defendants for engaging in a pattern of racketeering activities.   An act that provides for both criminal and civil penalties for "racketeering."   A federal statute that provides for both criminal and civil penalties.   An act that provides for both criminal and civil penalties for securities fraud.

radiation pollution Emissions from radioactive wastes that can cause injury and death to humans and other life and can cause severe damage to the environment.

ratification The act of a minor after the minor has reached the age of majority by which he or she accepts a contract entered into when he or she was a minor.

rational basis test Test that is applied to classifications not involving a suspect or protected class.

Rawls's social contract A moral theory that says each person is presumed to have entered into a social contract with all others in society to obey moral rules that are necessary for people to live in peace and harmony.

real defense A defense that can be raised against both holders and HDCs.

real property The land itself as well as buildings, trees, soil, minerals, timber, plants, crops, and other things permanently affixed to the land.

reasonable person test Objective test that applies to commercial contracts and contracts involving mechanical fitness.

receiving stolen property A person (1) knowingly receives stolen property and (2) intends to deprive the rightful owner of that property.

reclamation The right of a seller or lessor to demand the return of goods

from the buyer or lessee under specified situations.

record date A date specified in the corporate bylaws that determines whether a shareholder may vote at a shareholders' meeting.   A date that determines whether a shareholder receives payment of a declared dividend.

recording statute A state statute that requires the mortgage or deed of trust to be recorded in the county recorder's office of the county in which the real property is located.

recovery of damages A seller or lessor may recover damages measured as the difference between the contract price (or rent) and the market price (or rent) at the time and place the goods were to be delivered, plus incidental damages, from a buyer or lessee who repudiates the contract or wrongfully rejects tendered goods.

recovery of goods from an insolvent seller or lessor A buyer or lessee who has wholly or partially paid for goods before they are received may recover the goods from a seller or lessor who becomes insolvent within 10 days after receiving the first payment; the buyer or lessee must tender the remaining purchase price or rent due under the contract. Also known as *capture*.

recovery of the purchase price or rent A seller or lessor may recover the contracted-for purchase price or rent from the buyer or lessee if the buyer or lessee (1) fails to pay for accepted goods, (2) breaches the contract and the seller or lessor cannot dispose of the goods, or if (3) the goods are damaged or lost after the risk of loss passes to the buyer or lessee.

redeemable preferred stock Stock that permits the corporation to buy back the preferred stock at some future date.

red light doctrine A doctrine that says a holder cannot qualify as an HDC if he or she has notice of an unauthorized signature or an alteration of the instrument, or any adverse claim against or defense to its payment.

reformation An equitable doctrine that permits the court to rewrite a contract to express the parties' true intentions.

registered agent A person or corporation that is empowered to accept service of process on behalf of the corporation.

registration statement Document that an issuer of securities files with the SEC that contains required information about the issuer, the securities to be issued, and other relevant information.

regular meeting A meeting held by the board of directors at the time and place established in the bylaws.

Regulation A A regulation that permits the issuer to sell securities pursuant to a simplified registration process.

Regulation Z An amendment to the TILA that sets forth detailed rules for compliance with the TILA.

regulatory statute A licensing statute enacted to protect the public.

Rehabilitation Act of 1973 Prohibits discrimination against handicapped persons by an employer who receives federal contracts or assistance.

rejection Express words or conduct by the offeree that rejects an offer. Rejection terminates the offer.

rejection of nonconforming goods If the goods or the seller's or lessor's tender of delivery fails to conform to the contract, the buyer or lessee may (1) reject the whole, (2) accept the whole, or (3) accept any commercial unit and reject the rest.

relevant geographical market A relevant market that is defined as the area in which the defendant and its competitors sell the product or service.

relevant product or service market A relevant market that includes substitute products or services that are reasonably interchangeable with the defendant's products or services.

relief from stay May be granted in situations involving depreciating assets where the secured property is not adequately protected during the bankruptcy proceeding; asked for by a secured creditor.

religious discrimination Discrimination against a person solely because of his or her religion or religious practices.

remainder If the right of possession returns to a third party upon the expiration of a limited or contingent estate.

rent The amount that the tenant has agreed to pay the landlord for the leased premises.

reparation proceedings Proceedings held to solve disputes between private parties.

replacement cost insurance Insurance that pays the cost to replace the damaged or destroyed property up to the policy limits.

replacement worker A worker who is hired either on a temporary or on a permanent basis to take the place of a striking worker.

replevin An action by a buyer or lessor to recover scarce goods wrongfully withheld by a seller or lessor.

reply Filed by the original plaintiff to answer the defendant's cross-complaint.

repossession A right granted to a secured creditor to take possession of the collateral upon default by the debtor.

resale price maintenance A per se violation of Section 1 of the Sherman Act; occurs when a party at one level of distribution enters into an agreement with a party at another level to adhere to a price schedule that either sets or stabilizes prices.

rescission An action to rescind (undo) the contract. Rescission is available if there has been a material breach of contract, fraud, duress, undue influence, or mistake.

reserved rights doctrine A doctrine that says the rights on federal and Native American lands have priority dating from the date of the grant or reservation.

residence contents broad form Insurance that renters purchase to cover loss or damage to their possessions.

residuary gift Gift of the estate left after the debts, taxes, and specific and general gifts have been paid.

res ipsa loquitur Tort where the presumption of negligence arises because (1) the defendant was in exclusive control of the situation and (2) the plaintiff would not have suffered injury but for someone's negligence. The burden switches to the defendant(s) to prove they were not negligent.

Resource Conservation and Recovery Act (RCRA) A federal statute that authorizes the EPA to regulate facilities that generate, treat, store, transport, and dispose of hazardous wastes.

respondeat superior A rule that says an employer is liable for the tortious conduct of its employees or agents while they are acting within the scope of its authority.

Restatement of the Law of Contracts A compilation of model contract law principles drafted by legal scholars. The Restatement is not law.

restitution Returning of goods or property received from the other party in order to rescind a contract; if the actual goods or property is not available, a cash equivalent must be made.

restricted securities Securities that were issued for investment purposes pursuant to the intrastate, private placement, or small offering exemption.

restrictive covenant A private agreement between landowners that restricts the use of their land.

restrictive indorsement An indorsement that contains some sort of instruction from the indorser.

resulting trust A trust that is created by the conduct of the parties.

revenue raising statute A licensing statute with the primary purpose of raising revenue for the government.

reverse discrimination Discrimination against a group that is usually thought of as a majority.

reversion A right of possession that returns to the grantor after the expiration of a limited or contingent estate.

Revised Article 3 A comprehensive revising of the UCC law of negotiable instruments, which was released in 1990, that reflects modern commercial practices.   A revision of Article 3 promulgated in 1990.

Revised Model Business Corporation Act (RMBCA) A revision of the MBCA in 1984 that arranged the provisions of the act more logically, revised the language to be more consistent, and made substantial changes in the provisions.

Revised Uniform Limited Partnership Act (RULPA) A 1976 revision of the ULPA that provides a more modern comprehensive law for the formation, operation, and dissolution of limited partnerships.

revocation Withdrawal of an offer by the offeror terminates the offer. Termination of a will.

reward To collect a reward, the offeree must (1) have knowledge of the reward offer prior to completing the requested act and (2) perform the requested act.

right of first refusal agreement An agreement that requires the selling shareholder to offer his or her shares for sale to the other parties to the agreement before selling them to anyone else.

right of inspection A right that shareholders have to inspect the books and records of the corporation.

right of redemption A right that says the mortgagor has the right to redeem real property after default and before foreclosure. Requires the mortgagor to pay the full amount of the debt incurred by the mortgagee because of the mortgagor's default.   A right granted to a defaulting debtor or other secured creditor to recover the collateral from a secured creditor before he or she contracts to dispose of it or exercises his or her right to retain the collateral. Requires the redeeming party to pay the full amount of the debt and expenses caused by the debtor's default.

right of subrogation The right that says the surety or guarantor acquires all of the creditor's rights against the debtor when a surety or guarantor pays a debt owed to a creditor by a debtor.

right of survivorship Rule that states that a deceased partner's right in specific partnership property vests with the remaining partners upon his or her death.

right to know provision A provision in Superfund that requires businesses to (1) disclose the presence of certain listed chemicals to the community, (2) annually disclose emissions of chemical substances released into the environment, and (3) immediately notify the government of spills, accidents, and other emergencies involving hazardous substances.

riparian doctrine A doctrine that gives riparians the right to make *reasonable use* of the body of water they border, provided it does not interfere with reasonable uses by other riparians.

riparians Landowners who own property on waterways.

River and Harbor Act A federal statute enacted in 1886 that established a permit system for the discharge of refuse, wastes, and sewage into U.S. navigable waterways.

robbery Taking personal property from another person by use of fear or force.

Robinson-Patman Act Section 2 of the Clayton Act is commonly referred to by this name.

Rule 10b-5 A rule adopted by the SEC to clarify the reach of Section 10(b) against deceptive and fraudulent activities in the purchase and sale of securities.

rule of reason A rule that holds that only unreasonable restraints of trade violate Section 1 of the Sherman Act. The court must examine the pro- and anti-competitive effects of the challenged restraint.

rules and regulations Adopted by administrative agencies to interpret the statutes that they are authorized to enforce.

Sabbath law A law that prohibits or limits the carrying-on of certain secular activities on Sundays.

Safe Drinking Water Act A federal statute enacted in 1974 and amended in 1986 that authorizes the EPA to establish national primary drinking water standards.

sale The passing of title from a seller to a buyer for a price. Also called a *conveyance.*

sale on approval A type of sale in which there is no actual sale unless and until the buyer accepts the goods.

sale or return A contract that says the seller delivers goods to a buyer with the understanding that the buyer may return them if they are not used or resold within a stated or reasonable period of time.

sale proceeds The resulting assets from the sale, exchange, or disposal of collateral subject to a security agreement.

sales agent A local employee of a foreign employer who may enter into contracts on the employer's behalf.

sales representative A local employee of a foreign employer who solicits and takes orders but does not have authority to bind the employer contractually.

satisfaction The performance of an accord.

scienter Means intentional conduct. Scienter is required for there to be a vio-

lation of Section 10(b) and Rule 10b-5.

search warrant A warrant issued by a court that authorizes the police to search a designated place for specified contraband, articles, items, or documents. The search warrant must be based on probable cause.

secondary boycott picketing A type of picketing where unions try to bring pressure against an employer by picketing his or her suppliers or customers.

secondary liability Liability on a negotiable instrument that is imposed on a party only when the party primarily liable on the instrument defaults and fails to pay the instrument when due.

"secondary meaning" When an ordinary term has become a brand name.

Section 1 of the Sherman Act Prohibits *contracts, combinations, and conspiracies* in restraint of trade. [856] Prohibits tying arrangements involving goods, services, intangible property, and real property.

Section 10(b) A provision of the Securities Exchange Act of 1934 that prohibits the use of manipulative and deceptive devices in the purchase or sale of securities in contravention of the rules and regulations prescribed by the SEC. [691] A section of the Securities Exchange Act of 1934 that prohibits any manipulative or deceptive practice in connection with the purchase or sale of any security.

Section 11 A provision of the Securities Act of 1933 that imposes civil liability on persons who intentionally defraud investors by making misrepresentations or omissions of material facts in the registration statement or who are negligent for not discovering the fraud.

Section 11(a) A section of the Securities Act of 1933 that imposes civil liability on accountants and others for (1) making misstatements or omissions of material facts in a registration statement or (2) failing to find such misstatements or omissions.

Section 12 A provision of the Securities Act of 1933 that imposes civil liability on any person who violates the provisions of Section 5 of the act.

Section 14(a) Provision of the Securities Exchange Act of 1934 that gives the SEC the authority to regulate the solicitation of proxies.

Section 14(e) A provision of the Williams Act that prohibits fraudulent, deceptive, and manipulative practices in connection with a tender offer.

Section 16(a) A section of the Securities Exchange Act of 1934 that defines any person who is an executive officer, a director, or a 10 percent shareholder of an equity security of a reporting company as a *statutory insider* for Section 16 purposes.

Section 16(b) A section of the Securities Exchange Act of 1934 that requires that any profits made by a statutory insider on transactions involving *short-swing profits* belong to the corporation.

Section 18(a) A section of the Securities Exchange Act of 1934 that imposes civil liability on any person who makes false or misleading statements in any application, report, or document filed with the SEC.

Section 2 of the Sherman Act Prohibits the act of monopolization and attempts or conspiracies to monopolize trade.

Section 2(a) of the Robinson-Patman Act Prohibits direct and indirect price discrimination by sellers of a commodity of a like grade and quality where the effect of such discrimination may be to substantially lessen competition or to tend to create a monopoly in any line of commerce.

Section 2(b) of the Robinson-Patman Act A defense that provides that a seller may lawfully engage in price discrimination to meet a competitor's price.

Section 2(c) of the Robinson-Patman Act Prohibits the payment of brokerage fees and other compensation by the seller to a buyer except for actual services rendered.

Section 2(d) of the Robinson-Patman Act Prohibits payments by sellers to buyers for advertising, promotional, or other services unless such payments are available to other buyers on proportionately equivalent terms.

Section 2(e) of the Robinson-Patman Act Requires sellers to provide promotional and other services to all buyers in a nondiscriminatory way and on proportionately equal terms.

Section 2(f) of the Robinson-Patman Act Makes it illegal for a buyer to knowingly induce or receive a discriminatory price prohibited by Section 2(a).

Section 24 A provision of the Securities Act of 1933 that imposes criminal liability on any person who willfully violates the 1933 act or the rules or regulations adopted thereunder. A section of the Securities Act of 1933 that makes it a criminal offense for any person to (1) willfully make any untrue statement of material fact in a registration statement filed with the SEC, (2) omit any material fact necessary to ensure that the statements made in the registration statement are not misleading, or (3) willfully violate any other provision of the Securities Act of 1933 or rule or regulation adopted thereunder.

Section 3 of the Clayton Act Prohibits tying arrangements involving sales and leases of goods.

Section 32 A provision of the Securities Exchange Act of 1934 that imposes criminal liability on any person who willfully violates the 1934 act or the rules or regulations adopted thereunder.

Section 32(a) A section of the Securities Exchange Act of 1934 that makes it a criminal offense for any person willfully and knowingly to make or cause to be made any false or misleading statement in any application, report, or other document required to be filed with the SEC pursuant to the Securities Exchange Act of 1934 or any rule or regulation adopted thereunder.

Section 4b of the CEA A provision of the Commodity Exchange Act that prohibits fraudulent conduct in connection with any order or contract of sale of any commodity for future delivery.

Section 5 of the Federal Trade Commission Act Prohibits unfair methods of competition and unfair and deceptive acts or practices.

Section 5 of the FTC Act Prohibits *unfair and deceptive practices*.

Section 552 of the Restatement (Second) of Torts A rule that an accountant is liable only for negligence to third parties who are *members of a limited class of intended users* of the client's financial statements. Provides a broader standard for holding accountants liable to third parties for negligence than the *Ultramares* doctrine.

Section 7 of the Clayton Act This section, as amended, provides that it is unlawful for a person or business to acquire the stock or assets of another "where in any line of commerce or in any activity affecting commerce in any section of the country, the effect of such acquisition may be substantially to lessen competition, or to tend to create a monopoly."

Section 7 of the NLRA A law that gives employees the right to join together and form a union.

Section 8(a) of the NLRA A law that makes it an *unfair labor practice* for an employer to interfere with, coerce, or restrain employees from exercising their statutory right to form and join unions.

Section 8(b) of the NLRA A law that prohibits unions from engaging in unfair labor practices that interfere with a union election.

section of the country A division of the country that is based on the relevant geographical market; the geographical area that will feel the direct and immediate effects of the merger.

secured credit Credit that requires security (collateral) to secure payment of the loan.

secured transaction A transaction that is created when a creditor makes a loan to a debtor in exchange for the debtor's pledge of personal property as security.

Securities Act of 1933 A federal statute that primarily regulates the issuance of securities by corporations, partnerships, associations, and individuals.

Securities and Exchange Commission (SEC) Federal administrative agency that is empowered to administer federal securities laws. The SEC can adopt rules and regulations to interpret and implement federal securities laws.

Securities Enforcement Remedies and Penny Stock Reform Act of 1990 A federal statute that gives the SEC greater enforcement powers and increases and expands the remedies available for securities violations.

Securities Exchange Act of 1934 A federal statute that primarily regulates the trading in securities.

security (1) An interest or instrument that is common stock, preferred stock, a bond, a debenture, or a warrant; (2) an interest or instrument that is expressly mentioned in securities acts; and (3) an investment contract.

security agreement The agreement between the debtor and the secured party that creates or provides for a security interest.

self-dealing If the directors or officers engage in purchasing, selling, or leasing of property with the corporation, the contract must be fair to the corporation; otherwise, it is voidable by the corporation. The contract or transaction is enforceable if it has been fully disclosed and approved.

Self-Employment Contributions Act A federal act that says self-employed persons must pay Social Security taxes equal to the combined employer-employee amount.

self-incrimination The Fifth Amendment states that no person shall be compelled in any criminal case to be a witness against him- or herself.

senior appropriator The earlier user under the prior appropriation "first in time, first in right" concept.

service mark A mark that distinguishes the services of the holder from those of its competitors.

service of process A summons is served on the defendant to obtain personal jurisdiction over him.

settlement of the estate The process of a deceased's property being collected, debts and taxes being paid, and the remainder of the estate being distributed.

settlor or trustor Person who creates a trust.

sex discrimination Discrimination against a person solely because of his or her gender.

sexual harassment Lewd remarks, touching, intimidation, posting pinups, and other verbal or physical conduct of a sexual nature that occur on the job.

share exchange When one corporation acquires all the shares of another corporation while both corporations retain their separate legal existence.

shareholder voting agreements Agreement between two or more shareholders agreeing on how they will vote their shares.

shipment contract A contract that requires the seller to ship the goods to the buyer via a common carrier.

The buyer bears the risk of loss during transportation. A sales contract that requires the seller to send the goods to the buyer, but not to a specifically named destination.

short-form merger A merger between a parent corporation and a subsidiary corporation that does not require the vote of the shareholders of either corporation or the board of directors of the subsidiary corporation.

sight draft A draft payable on sight. Also called a *demand draft*.

signature Any name, word, or mark used in lieu of a written signature; any symbol that is (1) handwritten, typed, printed, stamped, or made in almost any other manner and (2) executed or adopted by a party to authenticate a writing.

signature liability A person cannot be held contractually liable on a negotiable instrument unless his or her signature appears on the instrument. Also called *contract liability*.

signature requirement A negotiable instrument must be signed by the drawer or maker. Any symbol executed or adopted by a party with a present intent to authenticate a writing qualifies as his or her signature.

signer A person signing an instrument who acts in the capacity of (1) a maker of notes and certificates of deposit, (2) a drawer of drafts and checks, (3) a drawee who certifies or accepts checks and drafts, (4) an indorser who indorses an instrument, (5) an agent who signs on behalf of others, or (6) an accommodation party.

small business bankruptcy Section 217 of the Bankruptcy Reform Act of 1994 provides an expedited procedure for Chapter 11 bankruptcy filed by small businesses with less than $2 million of debt.

small claims court A court that hears civil cases involving small dollar amounts.

small offering exemption For the sale of securities not exceeding $1 million during a 12-month period.

social host liability Rule that provides that social hosts are liable for injuries caused by guests who become intoxicated at a social function. States vary as to whether they have this rule in effect.

social responsibility Duty owed by businesses to act socially responsible in

producing and selling goods and services.

Social Security Federal system that provides limited retirement and death benefits to covered employees and their dependents.

sole proprietorship A noncorporate business that is owned by one person.

A form of business where the owner is actually the business; the business is not a separate legal entity.

sources of international law Those things that international tribunals rely on in settling international disputes.

special bailees Include common carriers, warehouse companies, and innkeepers.

special federal courts Federal courts that hear matters of specialized or limited jurisdiction.

special indorsement An indorsement that contains the signature of the indorser and specifies the person (indorsee) to whom the indorser intends the instrument to be payable. Creates *order paper*.

special meeting A meeting convened by the board of directors to discuss new shares, merger proposals, hostile takeover attempts, and so forth.

special shareholders' meetings Meetings of shareholders that may be called to consider and vote on important or emergency issues, such as a proposed merger or amending the articles of incorporation.

specific duty An OSHA standard that addresses a safety problem of a specific duty nature (e.g., requirement for a safety guard on a particular type of equipment).

specific gift Gift of a specifically named piece of property.

specific performance A remedy that orders the breaching party to perform the acts promised in the contract; usually awarded in cases where the subject matter is unique, such as in contracts involving land, heirlooms, paintings, and the like. A decree of the court that orders a seller or lessor to perform his or her obligations under the contract; usually occurs when the goods in question are unique, such as art or antiques.

stakeholder interest A theory of social responsibility that says a corporation must consider the effects its actions have on persons other than its stockholders.

stale check A check that has been outstanding for more than six months.

standing to sue The plaintiff must have some stake in the outcome of the lawsuit.

stare decisis Latin: "to stand by the decision." Adherence to precedent.

state action exemptions Business activities that are mandated by state law are exempt from federal antitrust laws.

state administrative agencies Administrative agencies that states create to enforce and interpret state law.

state antitakeover statutes Statutes enacted by state legislatures that protect corporations incorporated in or doing business in the state from hostile takeovers.

statement of assignment A document that is filed when a secured party assigns all or part of his or her rights under a financing statement.

statement of policy A statement issued by administrative agencies announcing a proposed course of action that an agency intends to follow in the future.

state supreme court The highest court in a state court system; it hears appeals from intermediate state courts and certain trial courts.

stationary sources Sources of air pollution such as industrial plants, oil refineries, and public utilities.

statute Written law enacted by the legislative branch of the federal and state governments that establishes certain courses of conduct that must be adhered to by covered parties.

Statute of Frauds State statute that requires certain types of contracts to be in writing.

statute of limitation A statute that requires an injured person to bring an action within a certain number of years from the time that he or she was injured by the defective product.

statute of limitations Statute that establishes the time period during which a lawsuit must be brought; if the lawsuit is not brought within this period, the injured party loses the right to sue.

statute of repose A statute that limits the seller's liability to a certain number of years from the date when the product was first sold.

Statute of Wills A state statute that establishes the requirements for making a valid will.

statutory exemptions Exemptions from antitrust laws that are expressly provided in statutes enacted by Congress.

statutory lien A lien that codifies by statute a service provider's common law lien.

stock dividend Additional shares of stock paid as a dividend.

stock option A nontransferable right to purchase shares of the corporation from the corporation at a stated price for a specified period of time.

stock warrant A stock option that is evidenced by a certificate. Warrants can be transferable or nontransferable.

stop-payment order An order by a drawer of a check to the payor bank not to pay or certify a check.

stopping delivery of goods in transit A seller or lessor may stop delivery of goods in transit if he or she learns of the buyer's or lessee's insolvency or the buyer or lessee repudiates the contract, fails to make payment when due, or gives the seller or lessor some other right to withhold the goods.

straight voting Each shareholder votes the number of shares he or she owns on candidates for each of the positions open.

strict liability Liability without fault.

strict or absolute liability Standard for imposing criminal liability without a finding of *mens rea* (intent).

strict scrutiny test Test that is applied to classifications based on *race*.

strike A cessation of work by union members in order to obtain economic benefits.

subfranchisor An area franchisee.

subject matter jurisdiction Jurisdiction over the subject matter of a lawsuit.

sublease When a tenant transfers only some of his or her rights under the lease.

sublessee The new tenant in a sublease situation.

sublessor The original tenant in a sublease situation.

subrogation If an insurance company pays a claim to an insured for liability or property damage caused by a third party, the insurer succeeds to the right of the insured to recover from the third party.

subsidiary A separate corporation established in a foreign country, usually wholly or majority owned by the parent corporation.

substantial performance Performance by a contracting party that deviates only slightly from complete performance.

substantive due process Due process that requires that the statute or rule that the respondent is charged with violating be clearly stated.

substantive rules Government regulation that has the force of law and must be adhered to by covered persons and businesses.

subsurface rights Rights to the earth located beneath the surface of the land.

summons A court order directing the defendant to appear in court and answer the complaint.

superseding event A defendant is not liable for injuries caused by a superseding or intervening event for which he or she is not responsible.

supervening event An alteration or modification of a product by a party in the chain of distribution that absolves all prior sellers from strict liability.

supervening illegality The enactment of a statute or regulation or court decision that makes the object of an offer illegal. This terminates the offer.

supramajority voting requirement A requirement that a greater than majority of shares constitutes a quorum or the vote of the shareholders.

Supremacy Clause A clause of the U.S. Constitution that establishes that the federal Constitution, treaties, federal laws, and federal regulations are the supreme law of the land.

surety arrangement An arrangement where a third party promises to be *primarily liable* with the borrower for the payment of the borrower's debt.

syndicate A group of individuals who join together to finance a project or transaction.

taking for value requirement A holder must *give value* for the negotiable instrument to qualify as an HDC.

taking in good faith requirement A holder must take the instrument in *good faith* to qualify as an HDC.

taking possession A method of acquiring ownership of unowned personal property.

taking without notice of defect requirement A person cannot qualify as an HDC if he or she has notice that the instrument is defective in certain ways.

tangible property All real property, and physically defined personal property such as goods, animals, and minerals.

target corporation The corporation that is proposed to be acquired in a tender offer situation.

target prices Prices established by the USDA for specific farm products. The USDA pays a *deficiency payment* to farmers if the average market price for a specific product falls below the target price.

tax sale A method of transferring property ownership that involves a lien on property for unpaid property taxes. If the lien remains unpaid after a certain amount of time, a tax sale is held to satisfy the lien.

tenancy at sufferance A tenancy created when a tenant retains possession of property after the expiration of another tenancy or a life estate without the owner's consent.

tenancy at will A lease that may be terminated at any time by either party.

tenancy by the entirety A form of co-ownership of real property that can be used only by married couples.

tenancy for years A tenancy created when the landlord and the tenant agree on a specific duration for the lease.

tenancy in common A form of co-ownership where the interest of a surviving tenant in common passes to the deceased tenant's estate and not to the co-tenants.

tenant The party to whom the leasehold is transferred.

tender of delivery The obligation of the seller to transfer and deliver goods to the buyer in accordance with the sales contract.

tender offer An offer that an acquirer makes directly to a target corporation's shareholders in an effort to acquire the target corporation.

tender offeror The party that makes a tender offer.

tender of performance Tender is an unconditional and absolute offer by a contracting party to perform his or her obligations under the contract.

termination The ending of a corporation that occurs only after the winding-up of the corporation's affairs, the liquidation of its assets, and the distribution of the proceeds to the claimants.

termination by acts of the parties An agency may be terminated by the following acts of the parties: (1) mutual agreement, (2) lapse of time, (3) purpose achieved, or (4) occurrence of a specified event.

termination by operation of law An agency is terminated by operation of law if there is (1) death of the principal or the agent, (2) insanity of the principal or the agent, (3) bankruptcy of the principal, (4) impossibility of performance, (5) change in circumstances, or (6) war between the principal's and the agent's countries.

termination statement A document filed by the secured party that ends a secured interest because the debt has been paid.

testamentary trust A trust created by will; the trust comes into existence when the settlor dies.

testator The person who makes a will.

thermal pollution Heated water or material discharged into waterways that upsets the ecological balance and decreases the oxygen content.

through bill of lading A bill of lading that provides that connecting carriers may be used to transport the goods to their destination.

time draft A draft payable at a designated future date.

time instrument An instrument payable (1) at a fixed date, (2) on or before a stated date, (3) at a fixed period after sight, or (4) at a time readily ascertainable when the promise or order is issued. An instrument that specifies a definite date for payment of the instrument.

time note A note payable at a specific time.

tippee The person who receives material nonpublic information from a tipper.

tipper A person who discloses material nonpublic information to another person.

title Legal, tangible evidence of ownership of goods.

title insurance Insurance that owners of real property purchase to insure that they have clear title to the property.

Title I of the Landrum-Griffin Act Referred to as labor's "bill of rights"; it gives each union member equal rights and privileges to nominate candidates for union office, vote in elections, and participate in membership meetings.

Title VII of the Civil Rights Act of 1964 (Fair Employment Practices Act) Intended to eliminate job discrimination based on five protected classes: *race, color, religion, sex,* or *national origin.*

tort A wrong. There are three categories: (1) intentional torts, (2) unintentional torts (negligence), and (3) strict liability.

tort of misappropriation of the right to publicity An attempt by another person to appropriate a living person's name or identity for commercial purposes.

toxic air pollutants Air pollutants that cause serious illness or death to humans.

toxic substances Chemicals used for agricultural, industrial, and mining uses that cause injury to humans, birds, animals, fish, and vegetation.

Toxic Substances Control Act A federal statute enacted in 1976 that requires manufacturers and processors to test new chemicals to determine their effect on human health and the environment before the EPA will allow them to be marketed.

trade acceptance A sight draft that arises when credit is extended (by a seller to a buyer) with the sale of goods. The seller is both the drawer and the payee, and the buyer is the drawee.

trademark A distinctive mark, symbol, name, word, motto, or device that identifies the goods of a particular business.

trademark infringement Unauthorized use of another's mark. The holder may recover damages and other remedies from the infringer.

trademarks and service marks A distinctive mark, symbol, name, word, motto, or device that identifies the goods or services of a particular franchisor.

trade secret A product formula, pattern, design, compilation of data, customer list, or other business secret.

trade secrets Ideas that make a franchise successful, but that do not qualify for trademark, patent, or copyright protection.

transfer Any passage of an instrument other than its issuance and presentment for payment.

transfer warranties Any of the following five implied warranties: (1) The transferor has good title to the instrument or is authorized to obtain payment or acceptance on behalf of one who does have good title; (2) all signatures are genuine or authorized; (3) the instrument has not been materially altered; (4) no defenses of any party are good against the transferor; and (5) the transferor has no knowledge of any insolvency proceeding against the maker, acceptor, or drawer of an unaccepted instrument. Each prior transferor warrants that he or she has good title to the check and that all signatures on the check are authentic and authorized.

traveler's check A form of check sold by banks and other issuers. They are issued without a named payee. The purchaser fills in the payee's name when he or she uses the check to purchase goods or services.

treasury shares Shares of stock repurchased by the company itself.

treaties and conventions The first source of international law, consisting of agreements or contracts between two or more nations that are formally signed by an authorized representative and ratified by the supreme power of each nation.

treaty A compact made between two or more nations.

Treaty Clause Clause of the U.S. Constitution that states the President "shall have the power . . . to make treaties, provided two-thirds of the senators present concur."

treble damages Civil damages three times actual damages may be awarded

to persons whose business or property is injured by a RICO violation.

trespass to land A tort that interferes with an owner's right to exclusive possession of land.

trespass to personal property A tort that occurs whenever one person injures another person's personal property or interferes with that person's enjoyment of his or her personal property.

trial briefs Documents submitted by the parties' attorneys to the judge that contain legal support for their side of the case.

trier of fact The jury in a jury trial; the judge where there is not a jury trial.

trust Established when a person (trustor) transfers title to property to another person (trustee) to be managed for the benefit of specifically named persons (beneficiaries). A legal arrangement established when one person transfers title to property to another person to be held and used for the benefit of a third person.

trust corpus The property held in trust.

trustee The holder of legal title of the real property in a deed of trust and note transaction. Person who holds legal title to the trust corpus and manages the trust for the benefit of the beneficiary or beneficiaries.

trustor The owner-debtor in a deed of trust and note transaction.

Truth-in-Lending Act (TILA) A federal statute that requires creditors to make certain disclosures to debtors in consumer transactions.

tying arrangement A restraint of trade where a seller refuses to sell one product or service to a customer unless the customer agrees to purchase a second product or service from the seller.

UCC Statute of Frauds A rule that requires all contracts for the sale of goods costing $500 or more and lease contracts involving payments of $1,000 or more to be in writing.

UCC statute of limitations A rule that provides that an action for breach of any written or oral sales or lease contract must commence within four years after the cause of action accrues. The parties may agree to reduce the limitations period to one year. [330] The UCC provides for a four-year statute of limi-

tations for breach of warranty actions. The parties may agree to reduce this period to not less than one year.

***Ultramares* doctrine** A rule that an accountant is liable only for negligence to third parties who are in *privity of contract* or a *privity-like relationship* with the accountant. Provides the narrowest standard for holding accountants liable to third parties for negligence.

***ultra vires* act** An act by a corporation that is beyond its express or implied powers.

umbrella policy An insurance policy that extends the limits of an insured's liability coverage; pays only after the basic policy limits have been exceeded.

unauthorized signature A signature made by a purported agent without authority from the purported principal.

unconditional Promises to pay and orders to pay must be unconditional in order for them to be negotiable.

unconditional promise or order to pay requirement A negotiable instrument must contain either an *unconditional promise to pay* (note or CD) or an *unconditional order to pay* (draft or check).

unconscionability A doctrine under which courts may deny enforcement of unfair or oppressive contracts.

unconscionable disclaimer A disclaimer that is so oppressive or manifestly unfair that it will not be enforced by the court.

undisclosed agency An agency that occurs when the third party is unaware of either (1) the existence of an agency or (2) the principal's identity.

undue influence Occurs where one person takes advantage of another person's mental, emotional, or physical weakness and unduly persuades that person to enter into a contract; the persuasion by the wrongdoer must overcome the free will of the innocent party.

Occurs where one person takes advantage of another person's mental, emotional, or physical weakness and unduly persuades that person to make a will; the persuasion by the wrongdoer must overcome the free will of the testator.

unenforceable contract A contract where the essential elements to create a valid contract are met, but there is some legal defense to the enforcement of the contract.

unfair advantage theory A theory that holds that a merger may not give the acquiring firm an unfair advantage over its competitors in finance, marketing, or expertise.

unfair competition Competition that violates the law.

Uniform Commercial Code Comprehensive statutory scheme that includes laws that cover aspects of commercial transactions.

Uniform Consumer Credit Code (UCCC) A code proposed by the National Conference of Commissioners on Uniform State Laws that establishes uniform rules to regulate the entire spectrum of consumer credit.

Uniform Franchise Offering Circular (UFOC) A uniform disclosure document that requires the franchisor to make specific presale disclosures to prospective franchisees.

Uniform Gift to Minors Act and Revised Uniform Gift to Minors Act Acts that establish procedures for adults to make gifts of money and securities to minors.

Uniform Negotiable Instruments Law (NIL) The predecessor of the UCC developed by the National Conference of Commissioners of Uniform Laws; used from 1886 until 1952.

Uniform Partnership Act (UPA) Model act that codifies partnership law. Most states have adopted the UPA in whole or in part.

Uniform Probate Code (UPC) A model law promulgated to establish uniform rules for the creation of wills, the administration of estates, and the resolution of conflicts in settling estates.

Uniform Securities Act An act that has been adopted by many states; drafted to coordinate state securities laws with federal securities laws.

Uniform Simultaneous Death Act An act that provides that if people who would inherit property from each other die simultaneously, each person's property is distributed as though he or she survived.

unilateral contract A contract in which the offeror's offer can be accepted only by the performance of an act by the offeree; a "promise for an act."

unilateral mistake When only one party is mistaken about a material fact regarding the subject matter of the contract.

unilateral refusal to deal A unilateral choice by one party not to deal with another party. This does not violate Section 1 of the Sherman Act because there is no concerted action.

uninsured motorist coverage Automobile insurance that provides coverage to the driver and passengers who are injured by an uninsured motorist or hit-and-run driver.

unintentional tort or negligence A doctrine that says a person is liable for harm that is the foreseeable consequence of his or her actions.

union shop An establishment where an employee must join the union within a certain number of days after being hired.

United Nations An international organization created by a multilateral treaty in 1945.

United States Department of Agriculture (USDA) Created by Congress in 1862 to administer the country's farm-oriented programs.

unlawful detainer action Legal process that a landlord must complete to evict a holdover tenant.

unprotected speech Speech that is not protected by the First Amendment and may be forbidden by the government.

unqualified indorsement An indorsement whereby the indorser promises to pay the holder or any subsequent indorser the amount of the instrument if the maker, drawer, or acceptor defaults on it.

unqualified indorser An indorser who signs an *unqualified indorsement* to an instrument.

unreasonable search and seizure Any search and seizure by the government that violates the Fourth Amendment.

unsecured credit Credit that does not require any security (collateral) to protect the payment of the debt.

U.S. Constitution The fundamental law of the United States of America. It was ratified by the states in 1788.

U.S. courts of appeals The federal court system's intermediate appellate courts.

U.S. Department of Agriculture A federal agency empowered to inspect and grade meat and poultry consumed by humans.

U.S. district courts The federal court system's trial courts of general jurisdiction.

U.S. Supreme Court The highest court in the land. It is located in Washington, D.C.

usurp an opportunity When an agent appropriates an opportunity for him- or herself by failing to let the principal know about it.

usurping a corporate opportunity A director or officer steals a corporate opportunity for him- or herself.

usury law A law that sets an upper limit on the interest rate that can be charged on certain types of loans.

utilitarianism A moral theory that dictates that people must choose the action or follow the rule that provides the greatest good to society.

valid contract A contract that meets all of the essential elements to establish a contract; a contract that is enforceable by at least one of the parties.

variance An exception that permits a type of building or use in an area that would not otherwise be allowed by a zoning ordinance.

venue A concept that requires lawsuits to be heard by the court with jurisdiction that is nearest the location in which the incident occurred or where the parties reside.

verdict Decision reached by the jury.

vertical merger A merger that integrates the operations of a supplier and a customer.

vertical restraint of trade A restraint of trade that occurs when two or more parties on *different levels of distribution* enter into a contract, combination, or conspiracy to restrain trade.

violation A crime that is neither a felony nor a misdemeanor that is usually punishable by a fine.

voidable contract A contract where one or both parties have the option to avoid their contractual obligations. If a contract is avoided, both parties are released from their contractual obligations.

voidable title Title that a purchaser has if the goods were obtained by (1) fraud, (2) a check that is later dishonored, or (3) impersonating another person.

void contract A contract that has no legal effect; a nullity.

void title A thief acquires no title to the goods he or she steals, nor does the buyer or lessee of stolen goods.

voir dire Process whereby prospective jurors are asked questions by the judge and attorneys to determine if they would be biased in their decision.

voluntary dissolution A corporation that has begun business or issued shares can be dissolved upon recommendation of the board of directors and a majority vote of the shares entitled to vote.

voluntary petition A petition filed by the debtor; states that the debtor has debts.

voting trust The shareholders transfer their stock certificates to a trustee who is empowered to vote the shares.

waiting period A period of time that begins when the registration statement is filed with the SEC and continues until the registration statement is declared effective. Only certain activities are permissible during the waiting period.

warehouse company A bailee engaged in the business of storing property for compensation. Owes a *duty of reasonable care* to protect the bailed property.

warehouse receipt A written document issued by a person who is engaged in the business of storing goods for hire.

warranties of quality Seller's or lessor's assurance to buyer or lessee that the goods meet certain standards of quality. Warranties may be expressed or implied.

warranty A buyer's or lessee's assurance that the goods meet certain standards.   A representation of the insured that is expressly incorporated in the insurance contract.

warranty against infringements A seller or lessor who is a merchant who regularly deals in goods of the kind sold or leased automatically warrants that the goods are delivered free of any third-party patent, trademark, or copyright claim.

warranty against interference The lessor warrants that no person holds a claim or interest in the goods that arose from an act or omission of the lessor that will interfere with the lessee's enjoyment of his or her leasehold interest.

warranty disclaimer Statements that negate express and implied warranties.

warranty of fitness for a particular purpose A warranty that arises where a seller or lessor warrants that the goods will meet the buyer's or lessee's expressed needs.

warranty of good title Sellers warrant that they have valid title to the goods they are selling and that the transfer of title is rightful.

warranty of no security interests Sellers of goods warrant that the goods they sell are delivered free from any third-party security interests, liens, or encumbrances that are unknown to the buyer.

waste Occurs when a tenant causes substantial and permanent damage to the leased premises that decreases the value of the property and the landlord's reversionary interest in it.

water law A complex body of laws that regulates all water usage.

water pollution Pollution of lakes, rivers, oceans, and other bodies of water.

wetlands Areas that are inundated or saturated by surface water or ground water that support vegetation typically adapted for life in such conditions.

"white-collar crimes" Crimes usually involving cunning and deceit rather than physical force.

will A declaration of how a person wants his or her property distributed upon death.

will or inheritance A way to acquire title to property that is a result of another's death.   If a person dies with a will, his or .ier property is distributed to the beneficiaries as designated in the will. If a person dies without a will, his or her property is distributed to the heirs as stipulated in the state's intestate statute.

Williams Act An amendment to the Securities Exchange Act of 1934 made in 1968 that specifically regulates all tender offers.

winding-up Process of liquidating the partnership's assets and distributing the proceeds to satisfy claims against the partnership.

winding-up and liquidation The process by which a dissolved corporation's assets are collected, liquidated, and distributed to creditors, shareholders, and other claimants.

wire fraud The use of telephone or telegraph to defraud another person.

withholding delivery The act of the seller or lessor purposefully refusing to deliver goods to the buyer or lessee upon breach of the sales or lease contract by the buyer or lessee or the insolvency of the buyer or lessee.

work product immunity A state statute that says an accountant's work papers cannot be used in a court action in that state; federal courts do not recognize this statute.

work-related test A test to determine the liability of a principal; if an agent commits an intentional tort within a work-related time or space, the principal is liable for any injury caused by the agent's intentional tort.

workers' compensation acts Acts that compensate workers and their families if workers are injured in connection with their jobs.

writ of certiorari An official notice that the Supreme Court will review one's case.

written order A stop-payment order that is good for six months after the date it is written.

wrongful discharge The discharge of an employee in violation of a statute, an employment contract, or public policy, or tortiously. As a result, the employee can recover damages and other remedies.

wrongful dishonor Occurs when there are sufficient funds in a drawer's account to pay a properly payable check, but the bank does not pay the check.

wrongful dissolution When a partner withdraws from a partnership without having the right to do so at that time.

wrongful eviction A violation of the covenant of quiet enjoyment. Also called unlawful eviction.

wrongful termination The termination of an agency contract in violation of the terms of the agency contract. The nonbreaching party may recover damages from the breaching party. Termination of a franchise without just cause.

zoning commission A local administrative body that formulates zoning ordinances, conducts public hearings, and makes recommendations to the city council.

zoning ordinances Local laws that are adopted by municipalities and local governments to regulate land use within their boundaries. Zoning ordinances are adopted and enforced to protect the health, safety, morals, and general welfare of the community.

Index

Index